Dr KATE COOPER and Dr JEREMY GREGORY are both Senior Lecturers in the History of Christianity at the University of Manchester.

42

ELITE AND POPULAR RELIGION

ELITE AND POPULAR RELIGION

PAPERS READ AT
THE 2004 SUMMER MEETING AND
THE 2005 WINTER MEETING OF
THE ECCLESIASTICAL HISTORY SOCIETY

EDITED BY

KATE COOPER

AND

JEREMY GREGORY

PUBLISHED FOR
THE ECCLESIASTICAL HISTORY SOCIETY
BY
THE BOYDELL PRESS
2006

First published 2006

A publication of the Ecclesiastical History Society
in association with The Boydell Press
an imprint of Boydell & Brewer Ltd
PO Box 9, Woodbridge, Suffolk IP12 3DF, UK
and of Boydell & Brewer Inc.
668 Mt Hope Avenue, Rochester, NY 14620, USA
website: www.boydellandbrewer.com

ISBN 0 9546809 2 8

ISSN 0424–2084

A CiP catalogue record for this book is available
from the British Library

BR
141
. 584
vol 42

Details of previous volumes are available from Boydell & Brewer Ltd

This book is printed on acid-free paper

Typeset by Pru Harrison, Hacheston, Suffolk
Printed in Great Britain by
Biddles Ltd, King's Lynn, Norfolk

CONTENTS

IN MEMORY OF
WILLIAM H. C. FREND

PREFACE

'Elite and Popular Religion' was the theme chosen by Professor Eamon Duffy for his Presidency of the Ecclesiastical History Society in 2004–5, and, as he emphasised in his Call for Papers, the focus would be on the inter-relationship between elite and popular. As he no doubt hoped, the theme indeed proved to be a popular one, and the present volume comprises seven of the main papers delivered at the EHS summer conference held at the University of Liverpool in 2004, and at the January meeting in 2005, as well as a selection of the communications offered at the summer meeting. We are grateful to the members of the Society who lent their time and expertise to the peer review of submissions and to the authors for their responses to queries and requests for revision.

The Society wishes to thank the University of Liverpool, and especially the staff at Derby and Rathbone Halls for their co-operation at the summer conference. Thanks are also due to Dr David Wykes and his colleagues at Dr Williams's Library, London for accommodating the January meeting.

As for the previous two volumes, we want to thank Dr Barbara Crostini for her hard work in copy-editing this volume. Her dedication, care, and commitment have been hugely appreciated not only by us, but also by our authors. We are again very grateful to both the Society and to the University of Manchester for funding Barbara's editorial fellowship for the last three years, and wish her well for the future. We would also like to thank Hannah Williams for providing invaluable additional administrative support.

* * *

While the editing of this volume was in progress, we were saddened to hear of the death of Professor W. H. C. Frend. Professor Frend was one of the founder members of the Society, a past President, and a keen supporter of our activities. We were privileged to include his contribution to the summer conference of 2003 in *Studies in Church History* 41, which was published just after he died. He will be greatly missed.

Kate Cooper
Jeremy Gregory

CONTRIBUTORS

Eamon DUFFY (*President*)
  Professor of the History of Christianity, Magdalene College,
  University of Cambridge

David BAGCHI
  Lecturer in the History of Christian Thought, University of Hull

Kathryne BEEBE
  Research Student, Pembroke College, University of Oxford

Clyde BINFIELD
  Emeritus Professor, Department of History, University of
  Sheffield

Urszula BORKOWSKA OSU
  Professor of History, Catholic University of Lubin, Poland

D. A. BRADING
  Emeritus Fellow, Clare Hall, University of Cambridge

Brian CUMMINGS
  Professor of English, University of Sussex

David D'AVRAY
  Professor of History, University College London

Dermot FENLON
  The Oratory, Birmingham

Elizabeth FREEMAN
  Lecturer in Medieval European History, University of Tasmania

Sheridan GILLEY
  Emeritus Reader, Department of Theology, University of
  Durham

Colin HAYDON
  Reader in Early Modern History, University of Winchester

Andrew HOLMES
  Research Fellow, Institute of Irish Studies, Queen's University
  Belfast

W. M. JACOB
> Archdeacon of Charing Cross

Trevor JOHNSON
> Senior Lecturer in History, University of the West of England, Bristol

Ian JONES
> Research Associate, Department of Religions and Theology, University of Manchester

Sally JORDAN
> ESRC Postdoctoral Fellow, University of Reading

Linda KIRK
> Senior Lecturer in History, University of Sheffield

A. K. McHARDY
> University of Nottingham

Peter MARSHALL
> Professor of History, University of Warwick

Mary Clare MARTIN
> Senior lecturer in Education Studies, School of Education and Training, University of Greenwich

David MORGAN
> Professor of Humanities and Art History and Duesenberg Professor of Christianity and the Arts, Christ College, Valparaiso University

Éamonn Ó CARRAGÁIN
> Professor of Old and Middle English, University College, Cork

Patrick PRESTON
> Visiting Fellow in Church History, University of Chichester

William J. PURKIS
> Research Student, Emmanuel College, University of Cambridge

Catherine RIDER
> Junior Research Fellow, Christ's College, University of Cambridge

Salvador RYAN
Lecturer in Church History, St Patrick's College, Thurles, Co.
Tipperary, Ireland

Timothy C. F. STUNT
History Teacher, Wooster School, Danbury, CT, USA

R. N. SWANSON
Professor of Medieval History, University of Birmingham

Claire TAYLOR
Lecturer in History, University of Nottingham

Peter WEBSTER
Editorial Controller, British History Online, Institute of
Historical Research, University of London

John WOLFFE
Professor of Religious History, The Open University

Jamie WOOD
Research Student, Classics and Ancient History, University of
Manchester

Simon YARROW
Lecturer in Medieval History, University of Birmingham

AHR	*American Historical Review* (New York, 1895–)
BL	British Library
CChr.CM	Corpus Christianorum, continuatio medievalis (1966–)
ChH	*Church History* (New York/Chicago, 1932–)
CUL	Cambridge University Library
CYS	Canterbury and York Society (London, etc., 1907–)
Douglas, *Natural Symbols*	Mary Douglas, *Natural Symbols: Explorations in Cosmology, with a new introduction* (London, 1996 edn)
DSp	*Dictionnaire de spiritualité ascétique et mystique: doctrine et histoire* (Paris, 1968–)
Duffy, *Stripping of the Altars*	E. Duffy, *The Stripping of the Altars: Traditional Religion in England, 1400–1580* (New Haven, CT, and London, 1992)
EETS	Early English Text Society
EHR	*English Historical Review* (London, 1886–)
JEH	*Journal of Ecclesiastical History* (Cambridge, 1950–)
JMH	*Journal of Modern History* (Chicago, 1929–)
n.p.	no place (of publication)
n.s.	new series
ODNB	H. C. G. Matthew and Brian Harrison, eds, *Oxford Dictionary of National Biography*, 60 vols (Oxford, 2004)
o.s.	original series
P&P	*Past and Present: a Journal of Scientific History* (London/Oxford, 1952–)
SCH	Studies in Church History (London, Oxford and Woodbridge, 1964–)
SCH.S	Studies in Church History: Subsidia (Oxford and Woodbridge, 1978–)
STC	A. W. Pollard and G. R. Redgrave, *A Short Title Catalogue of Books Printed in England, Scotland and Ireland and of English Books Printed Abroad 1475–1640*, 3 vols (2nd edn, London, 1976–91)

INTRODUCTION

Since the Enlightenment, historians and theorists of religion have often worked with a two-tiered model of Christianity, in which the pure belief and practice of the enlightened few was perceived as constantly under pressure and in danger of corruption or distortion from the grosser religion of the multitude. This imagined polarity between the sophisticated religion of the elite and the crude religion of the people at large underlay much Enlightenment historiography, most notably Gibbon's account of the early history of Christianity, and has remained potent in such influential twentieth century works as Keith Thomas's *Religion and the Decline of Magic*. Even the future Cardinal Newman could contrast 'what has power to stir holy and refined souls' with the 'religion of the multitude' which he once described as 'ever vulgar and abnormal'. Newman, as more than one contributor to this volume shows, had in fact an acute sense of the value, even the normative value, of popular religious perceptions, but those implicit polarities and the historical condescension they encode have been recurrent and assertive ghosts, haunting the writing of religious history, in contrasts between official and unofficial religion, or those between clerical and lay, literate and illiterate, rich and poor, hierarchical and charismatic.

The 2004 conference of the Ecclesiastical History Society sought to question or at any rate to complicate these polarities by inviting exploration not of the divergence but of the interaction between elite and popular religious belief and practice. The theme, it needs to be noted, was 'Elite *and* popular religion', the two – to the extent that there are two – in tension or interaction, not one or the other in isolation. Contributors were invited to reflect on such areas as the relationship between ecclesiastical authority and popular religious practice, between orthodoxy and heterodoxy, liturgy and paraliturgy, catechesis and its assimilation, and the relation between christianity and pagan survival or revival. The theme offered scope for study of the processes and effectiveness of cultural transmission in Christian history – the relations between 'high' and 'low', 'great' or 'little' religious culture(s), in books, music, pictures and architecture – and invited exploration of the historical relationships between religion and social status.

The resulting volume ranges from the baptismal customs of Visigoth

Spain, and Christian reworking of traditional Germanic heroic values in the monumental art of Anglo-Saxon England, down to the visual culture of American Evangelicalism, or the debate about the assimilation of 'pop' and 'light swing' music in twentieth-century Anglican liturgy. What emerges again and again in these case studies, varied as they are, is the unhelpfulness of any simple bi-polar characterisation of the complexities of religious experience and religious institutions and practice. Christianity – in its concrete forms of liturgy, pilgrimage, bible and holy book, indulgences – might be experienced in simple or sophisticated ways. But simplicity or sophistication was rarely the exclusive prerogative of a single easily characterised class of Christian. Neither 'superstition' nor 'heresy' have ever been by any means confined to the poor, the uneducated, or the lay. From its very beginnings pilgrimage might be undertaken as an exercise in sophisticated contemplative experience, or more robustly as a glorified tourist trip, in which souvenirs and spiritual benefits are gathered more or less indiscriminately. But these contrasting approaches to pilgrimage might be encountered at any level of society: the poor might be recollected and devout, the rich intent on souvenir hunting, and perhaps the majority of pilgrims have been both. As Robert Swanson argues below, the history of even so central (and ultimately so contested) a practice as the cult of indulgences, displays not 'a rigid barrier between learned and lewd, clerical and lay', but a religion 'in which such distinctions tend to evaporate'.

This is perhaps more obviously true of some forms of Christianity than of others. Protestantism has characteristically mobilised such polarities for polemical purposes, manipulating concepts of degeneration and reform, corruption and renewal. These are categories which could readily be assimilated to distinctions in religious knowledge or respectability, whereas, as Sheridan Gilley has argued, the 'vulgar piety of the Victorian Catholic Church was classless'. But Protestant Christianity too has always at any rate aspired to social inclusiveness, and has sought institutions and strategies to achieve such interaction. And in its evangelical forms, as David Morgan demonstrates here, it too 'has long thrived on a fluid exchange between high and low, elite and popular'. It is therefore our hope that the essays in this volume will contribute to the liberation of the writing of religious history from tempting polarities which obscure rather than illumine.

Eamon Duffy
Magdalene College, Cambridg

ELITES AND BAPTISM:
RELIGIOUS 'STRATEGIES OF DISTINCTION' IN VISIGOTHIC SPAIN

by JAMIE WOOD

THE political connotations of godparenthood and baptismal sponsorship in creating both vertical and horizontal bonds between individuals and groups in early medieval Europe have long been recognized.[1] What follows offers a case study of sixth- and early seventh-century Visigothic Spain, asking whether the baptismal process could also serve to bring elite and popular together.[2] Elites sought to mobilize those lower down the scale than themselves in opposition to other elites at the same time as having constantly to negotiate the elite position from which they gained their authority. In sixth-century Spain the definition and redefinition of baptismal practice in church council legislation by both Catholics and Arians was an important method for achieving this dual aim of distinction and control.

* * *

While the social class of the earliest Christians is still in dispute, it is clear that from the time of Constantine onwards one of the most violent debates within Christianity was that over the use of religious authority to engage in what moderns might term 'social engineering'.[3] As Peter Brown has shown, elite and popular were by no means

---

[1] See the following articles in Rosamond McKitterick, ed., *The New Cambridge Medieval History, Vol. 2: c.700–c.900* (Cambridge, 1995): Janet L. Nelson, 'The Frankish Kingdoms, 814–898: the West', 110–41, at 128; Johannes Fried, 'The Frankish Kingdoms, 817–911: the East and Middle Kingdoms', 142–68, at 151; Julia M. H. Smith, '*Fines Imperii*: the Marches', 169–89, at 183–4; Niels Lund, 'Scandinavia, c.700–1066', 202–27, at 208; Jonathan Shephard, 'Slavs and Bulgars', 228–48, at 239; Janet L. Nelson, 'Kingship and Royal Government', 383–430, at 398, 428–9.

[2] Due to considerations of space we are unable to examine the works of the mid seventh-century bishop, Ildephonsus of Toledo. He wrote an important treatise on baptism, *De cognitione baptismi*, and another one on instruction after baptism, *De itinere deserti: San Idelfonso de Toledo. La virginidad perpetua de Santa Maria. El conocimiento del bautismo. El Camino del desierto*, ed. Vicente Blanco García and Julio Campos Ruiz (Madrid, 1971), 225–436.

[3] Peter Lampe argues that early Christianity was a lower class movement in *From Paul to Valentinus: Christians at Rome in the First Two Centuries* (London, 2003), 48–66. For those higher up the social scale see Rodney Stark, *The Rise of Christianity: a Sociologist Reconsiders History* (Princeton, NJ, 1996), 29–47.

self-consciously opposed to each other in late antiquity: they were in a kind of dialogue and consensus frequently obtained between the two.[4] Baptism and the definition of the rituals surrounding it can be considered as aiding the formation of elite-popular alliances, at the same time as allowing the ecclesiastical elite to perpetuate their dominance and manipulate the popular elements that supported them. We will test this theoretical proposition through reference to the canons of selected sixth- and seventh-century Spanish church councils.[5]

First, however, it is necessary to define what we mean by the terms 'elite' and 'popular'. As this paper focuses on the conciliar legislation, the main elite to be considered, in evidentiary terms, is the episcopacy, who constituted a majority at the councils. After their conversion to Catholicism in 589 Visigothic kings played a key role in proceedings: it was they who called the councils and ratified their *acta*. It is thus useful to see Church and State as tied into a reciprocal relationship from which each benefited. For example, bishops were given a role supervising judges in ostensibly 'secular' legislation, whereas royal officials enforced some conciliar decisions.[6] Despite these caveats, there is no doubt that it was the ecclesiastical elite that was overwhelmingly responsible for the publication of the conciliar legislation that is our concern here.

Notwithstanding the process of conciliar legislation it is vital to note that the ecclesiastical elite itself was never homogeneous.[7] There were often frictions within the elite as well as between ecclesiastical and secular elites, including the monarchy. Although this contribution focuses on the bishops, it should be noted that they were in constant contact and competition with monks, ascetics and saints. For example, in the sixth-century, St Aemilianus was forced by his bishop to become

---

[4] Peter Brown, *The Cult of the Saints. Its Rise and Function in Latin Christianity* (Chicago, IL, 1981), 32–5, 44–7, 64, 89–90.

[5] Wherever possible the councils will be consulted in the newer edition of Gonzalo Martínez Díez and Félix Rodríguez, *La colección canónica hispana*, 5 vols (Madrid, 1966–92) [hereafter: *Hispana*]. However in some cases it will be necessary to utilize *Concilios visigóticos e hispano-romanos*, ed. José Vives (Barcelona, 1963) [hereafter: Vives].

[6] Council of Narbonne (590), canon IX, Vives, 148: Jews were to pay a fine to the count, a secular official. Bishop Braulio of Zaragoza sent two letters to Recceswinth complaining about the travails involved in correcting a large *codex* the king had sent him, *Epistolario de San Braulio*, ed. Luis Terrero (Seville, 1975), XXXVIII–XLI, 150–3; P. D. King, 'King Chindasvind and the First Territorial Law-Code of the Visigothic Kingdom', in Edward James, ed., *Visigothic Spain: New Approaches* (Oxford, 1980), 148; it was probably a law code.

[7] R. Stocking, 'Visions of Community: Religious Diversity, Conciliar Authority, and Political Power in Visigothic Spain, 589–633', Ph.D. thesis, Stanford University, 1994.

a priest against his will, only to be sent back to the mountains after he gave away church property.[8] In terms of royal interaction with the ecclesiastical elite, King Sisebut (612–21) ordered the forced baptism of Jews without taking ecclesiastical advice, in spite of his supposedly close relations with Isidore of Seville.[9]

The episcopal elite itself was also given to infighting. One particular instance occurred at the second council of Seville, where disputes over the exact extent of territory controlled by the bishops of Málaga, Écija, Elvira and Cabra were resolved.[10] The authority of bishops was not only questioned by monks, ascetics and saints, who may have obscured the authority of their leaders, but by the lay elite and priests (as will be seen from the conciliar evidence). So, the elites themselves were not homogeneous; there was a considerable amount of infighting both within the 'ecclesiastical' elite and with the secular arm.

* * *

What about the popular elements? If we wanted to define the word more closely we could adopt the definition of the word *populus* in Isidore of Seville's *Etymologiae*:

> 5. The *populus* is an assembly of a human multitude, allied by the sharing of law and by agreement as if of one mind. But the *populus* differs in this respect from the plebs; because all the citizens make up the *populus*, including the higher ranks of the citizen body.
> 6. So the *populus* is the entire citizen body, while the plebs is the commons indeed. And plebs gets its name from *pluralitas* (majority), since the number of those of lower rank is greater than that of the higher ranks.[11]

Unfortunately this definition is of limited use for our purposes since it focuses on civil categories; membership of the *populus* is restricted to citizens allied in agreement under the same law. They are differentiated

---

[8] Braulio of Saragossa, *Vita Aemiliani*, 5–6, transl. in A. T. Fear, *Lives of the Visigothic Fathers* (Liverpool, 1997), 24–7.

[9] Isidore criticized Sisebut: 'At the beginning of his reign he forced the Jews into the Christian faith, indeed acting with zeal, "but not according to knowledge", for he compelled by force those who should have been called to the faith through reason', *Historia Gothorum*, 60, trans. in Kenneth Baxter Wolf, *Conquerors and Chroniclers of Early Medieval Spain* (Liverpool, 1990), 106.

[10] Vives, 163.

[11] Isidore, *Etymologiae*, IX.4.4–5, in *San Isidoro de Sevilla. Etimologías*, ed. Jose Oroz Reta and Manuel-A. Marcos Casquero, 2 vols (Madrid, 1993), I: 776.

from the more numerous commons (*plebs*). The definition pays no attention to religious matters. In religious terms we could define the *populus* as the Catholic 'faithful' as the theoretical construct of the ecclesiastical elite: they are the 'Church' in the widest sense of the word, to be protected and guided away from heresy. However, neither of these definitions gets us very far; both leave us with an undifferentiated mass. This has often led to the assumption that the mass was something on which the elite acted.

The interaction between elite and popular religion in Visigothic Spain has usually been defined in terms of opposition, the elite seeking to contain or undermine the vulgar beliefs of the people: it has been seen as an essentially concessive relationship. McKenna, writing about the survival of paganism and pagan practices in early medieval Spain, concluded that pagan practices remained longest in the countryside, and were combated through 'the education of the clergy, the exorcisms, and blessings of the Mozarabic rite, and the establishment of rural parishes and monasteries'.[12] Hillgarth saw religion as something 'presented to the people': the exorcisms developed in and particular to Spain were a response to the terrors that beset the country people.[13] In 1985 Salisbury furthered this paradigm, demonstrating how the 'Church' was able to co-opt indigenous religiosity through adaptation:

> The triumph of the universal Church in the seventh century lay not in its ability to convert villagers to official religiosity, but ultimately in its willingness to call peasants orthodox even though they persisted in their traditional beliefs.[14]

These studies are clear examples of the sorts of terminological and conceptual confusions that result from an attempt to differentiate too strictly between 'elite' and 'popular'.

The rhetoric of containment is certainly a feature of the sources. By adopting it as the dominant paradigm in our approach to the evidence, however, we are also adopting the overwhelmingly elite perspective of our evidence. For Visigothic Spain we lack the abundant hagiographical accounts we have for Merovingian Gaul, which can give us narratives of

[12] Stephen McKenna, *Paganism and Pagan Survivals in Spain up to the Fall of the Visigothic Kingdom* (Washington, D.C., 1938), 150–2.

[13] J. N. Hillgarth, 'Popular Religion in Visigothic Spain', in James, *Visigothic Spain*, 3–60, at 53–4.

[14] Joyce E. Salisbury, *Iberian Popular Religion, 600 B.C. to 700 A.D.: Celts, Romans, and Visigoths* (New York, 1985), 298–9.

particular episodes of interaction to contrast with the idealized accounts of the laws.[15] In the few instances where we do possess Visigothic-era hagiography such interaction is not difficult to see. In an important study Santiago Castellanos demonstrated how the *Vitas Sanctorum Patrum Emeritensium*, an early seventh-century hagiography from the city of Mérida, projected an atmosphere of consensus within a community we know to have been riven by conflict in the sixth-century. These conflicts and tensions operated on many levels, between: Arians and Catholics; central and local powers; members of the economic and social elite; rich and poor; and also within the Visigothic secular elite. The 'celestial happiness' provided by social unanimity was an image everyone could partake in; it was a 'product' into which all members (including the *populus*) of the Meridan church could buy.[16] Unfortunately, in the study of Visigothic Spain it is rare to have such rich narrative accounts. The present study will therefore extend this approach to the canonical sources.[17]

* * *

The law codes and church council records have their own strengths and weaknesses. There are a large number of them, they are usually well dated, they can be pinpointed to particular places, they give lists of attendees, and they often go into great detail. However, while the canons sometimes describe specific case studies in order to illuminate a particular ruling, the lack of contextual details means that we can rarely discern whether they are actually describing contemporary events or presenting a general, idealized vision of society, with little relation to objective 'reality'. As this is a study which largely focuses on the concerns, some would say paranoias, of the ecclesiastical elite, and their legal conception of how their church was to interact with other Christian congregations, and how they were to deal with their clergy and flocks, a concern with ancient pedigree, this is an issue of lesser importance, but which must nevertheless be recognized. It is certainly not claimed here that the *acta* reflect conditions anywhere other than in the minds of the signatories to these councils.[18]

---

15 Hillgarth, 'Popular Religion', 5.

16 Santiago Castellanos, 'The Significance of Social Unanimity in a Visigothic Hagiography: Keys to an Ideological Screen', *Journal of Early Christian Studies* 11 (2003), 387–419.

17 For translations of the five Visigothic-era hagiographic texts see Fear, *Lives of the Visigothic Fathers*.

18 For example, on Augustine's concern over whether the Christian message was getting

* * *

The most influential recent work on early medieval ethnicity, that of Walter Pohl, offers a way forward for understanding the comparable problem of elite and popular identities. In the introduction to the 1998 collected volume, *Strategies of Distinction: the Construction of Ethnic Communities*, Pohl argues that early medieval ethnicity 'had a double function of integration and of distinction', drawing together 'people who might differ a lot among each other, and might not be so different at all from people who do not fall into that category', at the same time as distinguishing them from other ethnically-defined communities. 'The art of distinction lay in propagating a continuum of features that made one ethnic group special without too obviously excluding groups of different origin'.[19] Ethnic identity acted to bond members of the same community to their leaders by vertical ties at the same time as separating them from members of neighbouring communities through the promotion of horizontal differences.

This paper draws on theories about 'strategies of distinction', harnessing the conciliar material to suggest methods by which the ecclesiastical elite attempted to articulate their superiority and social control over their popular followings: the use of councils to define baptismal practice and the actual performance of the baptismal process. The sources' concerns with the 'sexier' topics of heresy and peculiar examples of popular devotion divert attention away from the real issues. We would be best advised to bear this in mind when describing popular religion. It is the rites through which every member of the community theoretically had to go that concern us here, not the atypical references to heresy or 'strange' practices. For example, no-one can uncritically accept the councils' identification of active Priscillianists (adherents to a fourth-century heresy) in the Visigothic period. Although the bishops may have thought they really were dealing with Priscillianists, and some practices may have existed that could be

across to the faithful and those wishing to join the Church see Kate Cooper, 'Ventriloquism and the Miraculous: Conversion, Preaching, and the Martyr Exemplum in Late Antiquity', in Kate Cooper and Jeremy Gregory, eds, *Signs, Wonders, Miracles: Representations of Divine Power in the Life of the Church*, SCH 41 (Woodbridge, 2005), 22–45.

19 Walter Pohl, 'Introduction: Strategies of Distinction', in idem, ed., with Helmut Reimitz, *Strategies of Distinction. The Construction of Ethnic Communities, 300–800* (Leiden, 1998), 4–6. Pohl draws heavily on the theories of the sociologist Pierre Bourdieu, see, *Distinction. A Social Critique of the Judgement of Taste* (London, 1984), 466–84. Contra Pohl, Andrew Gillett, 'Introduction: Ethnicity, History, and Methodology', in idem, ed., *On Barbarian Identity. Critical Approaches to Ethnicity in the Early Middle Ages* (Turnhout, 2002), 1–18.

described as 'Priscillianist', it seems highly unlikely that there was an active Priscillianist organization in existence in this period.[20] By putting to one side such uncharacteristic references and analysing in their place the councils' attempts to define the ritual processes through which every member of the Christian community was supposed to proceed, we can come to a better understanding of how the elite interacted with those further down the religious hierarchy in Visigothic Spain.

First, though, it is necessary to establish that we can consider baptism as the sort of boundary marker, described by Pohl, intended to enforce loyalty among group members and exclusion of non-members. Social scientists ascribe boundary markers a dual role: while excluding other people, they include group members.[21] The boundaries separating ethnic communities from one another 'persist despite a flow of personnel across them'. These markers of difference are the dominant factors taken into account by the actors; however, they are not the sum of objective differences, but those that the actors themselves regard as significant.[22] Baptism, as the liturgical ritual completing entry into the church, was a vital boundary at which entry to or exclusion from the community could be signified and enforced.[23]

Baptism should not necessarily be considered as a one-off event – the immersion itself – but as a sustained process, running from the initiation of the catechumen, through the associated ceremonies and instruction to baptism itself, followed by possible later confirmation.[24] This last point is particularly important as it highlights the bishop's interest in the process; even if he was unable to perform the actual ritual itself, not only was his presence theologically necessary for the later confirmation of the rite, but it pointedly allowed him to reaffirm

---

[20] Cf. R. A. Markus, 'The Problem of "Donatism" in the Sixth Century', in *Gregorio Magno e il suo tempo*, Studia Ephemeridis 'Augustinianum' 33, 2 vols (Rome, 1991), 1: 159–66.

[21] A. P. Cohen, *The Symbolic Construction of Community* (London, 1985), 53–5, 75, 91, 102.

[22] Fredrik Barth, 'Introduction', in idem, ed., *Ethnic Groups and Boundaries. The Social Organisation of Culture Difference* (London, 1969), 9–38. Frans Theuws, 'Introduction: Rituals in Transforming Societies', in Frans Theuws and Janet L. Nelson, eds, *Rituals of Power from Late Antiquity to the Early Middle Ages* (Leiden, 2000), 1–13.

[23] Joseph H. Lynch, *Godparents and Kinship in Early Medieval Europe* (Princeton, NJ, 1986), 334.

[24] José Pijuan, *La liturgia bautismal en la España romano-visigoda* (Toledo, 1981), 35–100; J. D. C. Fisher, *Christian Initiation: Baptism in the Medieval West. A Study in the Disintegration of the Primitive Rite of Initiation* (London, 1965), 88–100; T. C. Akeley, *Christian Initiation in Spain c.300–1100* (London, 1967), 123–200; *Reallexikon für Antike und Christentum* 20 (2004), 422–96 (s.v. 'Katechese'); 497–574 (s.v. 'Katechumenat').

his status as the community's leader.[25] While offering an opportunity for communal consensus through ritual performance, baptism also reinforced existing hierarchies.[26]

It has long been recognized that ceremony and ritual were essential to the articulation of power and authority; power was performative – it had to be acted out to be most effectively demonstrated.[27] In the context of elite baptism this may be seen in the emergence of godparenthood at baptism as a method for forwarding political alliances, which through the adoption of a hierarchical parent-child relationship reinforced the predominance of 'godfather' over 'godson'.[28] What significance might the performative aspects of baptism have in the millions of baptisms where high-level power politics were not involved? Perhaps it played the same function, emphasizing and reinforcing the power of the bishop over his flock, at the point at which all were formally welcomed into the community.

There are no theoretical problems with envisaging baptism as a sign around which the community could cohere, on which they could focus their attention and identity – often in opposition to outsiders – and as a ritual expression of the pre-eminent power of the bishop over his followers. Baptism may have been one of the few occasions when the local population would meet their bishop, providing an opportunity for asserting his status. The episcopacy would thus be interested in defining and controlling the process of movement across this boundary as it both reinforced the solidarity of their own group and reaffirmed their status in relation to their followers.

The large size of some dioceses meant that the need to baptize as well as to carry out pre- and post-baptismal instruction created problems and opportunities. Maintaining contact with far-flung communities would allow the bishop to assert his authority and to ensure correct practice and belief. This was even more pressing if we accept that there was a degree of competition between Catholic and Arian bishops.[29] A

---

[25] Fisher, *Christian Initiation*, 89.

[26] Virginia Burrus, ' "In the Theatre of This Life": the Performance of Orthodoxy in Late Antiquity', in William E. Klingshirn and Mark Vessey, eds, *The Limits of Ancient Christianity. Essays on Late Antique Thought and Culture in Honour of R. A. Markus* (Ann Arbor, MI, 1999), 80–96, at 95–6.

[27] Sabine G. MacCormack, *Art and Ceremony in Late Antiquity* (Berkeley, CA, 1981), 222–66.

[28] Bernhard Jussen, *Patenschaft und Adoption im frühen Mittelalter: künstliche Verwandtschaft als soziale Praxis* (Göttingen, 1991).

[29] Jonathan P. Conant, 'Staying Roman: Vandals, Moors, and Byzantines in Late Antique

potential solution to this problem was to allow presbyters to carry out the baptismal service, but reserving the right of confirmation to bishops, ensuring their continued centrality to the process.[30] This is not to ignore the spiritual and pastoral inspirations for these developments; the episcopal imposition of hands ensured that the baptizand received the Holy Spirit.[31]

The simple fact that people were attempting to define their position on and the procedure for baptism is an indication that they considered it an important process through which, at least theoretically, everybody should go. The very act of writing about and legislating for such matters is a statement in itself, asserting the right of the ecclesiastical elite to decide under what conditions such processes were to occur, demonstrating the use of baptism for vertical differentiation between elites and their followers. Finally, the baptism ceremony reflected wider points of disagreement between Catholics and Arians; for example, the recitation of the *credo* at baptism was an opportunity for the initiate to reaffirm the basic tenets of faith, suggesting that it played a role in reinforcing horizontal differences between confessional opponents.[32]

* * *

Study of sixth-century Spanish history has largely focused on the pivotal decade of the 580s, which began with the Arian Visigothic King Leovigild's attempts to impose a compromise between Arianism and Catholicism, the religion of his Hispano-Roman subjects, and culminated in the conversion of the Visigoths to Catholicism under his son and successor, Reccared. In the early part of the decade Hermenegild, Leovigild's elder son, rebelled unsuccessfully with the support of much of the south and at some point converted to Catholicism. Despite the changing religious affiliations of the Visigothic elite, evidence that religion was an important factor in these tumultuous events has largely been seen as a construction of the sources. The importance of ethnic, political and economic factors at local, regional, and 'national' levels has been emphasized in various combinations.

North Africa, 400–700', unpublished Ph.D. thesis, Harvard University, 2004, 191–224, convincingly demonstrated that the Arian Vandals in North Africa did attempt to convert Catholics to their faith.

[30] Fisher, *Christian Initiation*, 28, 140.

[31] Ibid., 91–2.

[32] Cf. the recitation of *credo* on reconciliation of those who had been baptized into 'Arian heresy' in *Le Liber ordinum en usage dans l'église wisigothique et mozarabe d'Espagne du cinquième au onzième siècle*, ed. Marius Ferotin (Paris, 1904), xxxvii.

Examination of references to baptism in the pre-conversion conciliar legislation shows that that there was contact between Arians and Catholics, contact which the Catholic ecclesiastical hierarchy sought to limit. The reasons for the definition of baptismal practice changed in the aftermath of the conversion. Instead of separating Arians and Catholics, such definition was now intended to keep Jews and Catholics apart. At all times the episcopacy sought to reinforce their control over those further down the scale, both subordinate clergy and their flocks, by affirming their pre-eminent position in the baptismal process and stamping out any activities that may have threatened that position.[33]

In the early to mid sixth-century the Arian Visigoths gradually extended their control over the Iberian Peninsula. The mid sixth-century councils reflect the importance of baptism in this pre-conversion period, hinting that some degree of contact was occurring between the Arians and the indigenous Catholic population.[34] The council which best illustrates this point is that held at Lérida in 546.[35] Several of its canons delimit relationships between Catholics and heretics (or the rebaptized), contacts which are defined in terms of baptismal rites and status, suggesting that those defining practice at the council were aware of instances of interaction between such groups, or that they envisaged such contacts to be a distinct possibility.

Canon IX established how long those who have been rebaptized must remain penitent, repeating the guidelines of the Council of Nicaea: after a lengthy period of exclusion the penitents can share in communion and the Eucharist with the faithful under the direction of the bishop. Rebaptism was an Arian custom, not permitted by the Catholics at this time. This suggests that people had moved into Arianism and then wanted to rejoin the Catholic community, or that former Arians were attempting to join the Catholic community and expected to be rebaptized in line with the practices of their former church. The repetition of Nicaean strictures may also hint at an anti-Arian context, since this was the council at which Arianism was

---

[33] E. Thompson. 'The Conversion of the Visigoths to Catholicism', *Nottingham Medieval Studies* 4 (1960), 4–35; R. Collins, 'King Leovigild and the Conversion of the Visigoths', in idem, *Law, Culture and Regionalism in Early Medieval Spain* (Aldershot, 1992), II, 1–12.

[34] Agde (506), canon 34: Lays down the number of months a Jew who wants to convert to Catholicism must wait to be baptized, Vives, 207–08.

[35] The date may actually be 524: E. A. Thompson, *The Goths in Spain* (Oxford, 1969), 33.

first condemned. In addition to this we see an emphasis on the bishop's role as leader of his community and as its protector against heretical influences. Canon XIII stated that those Catholics who present their children for baptism into heresy were not to be admitted to the church, hinting that some Catholics may have been 'hedging their bets' by having their children baptized into Arianism, while continuing to worship as Catholics themselves. This points to a far more complex situation than the simple Goth=Arian, Hispano-Roman=Catholic equation suggests. Canon XIV prohibited Catholics from sharing meals with the rebaptized, again leading to the supposition that Catholics were indeed in close contact with Arians or former Arians who had not been reconciled to the Catholic faith properly, contact that had to be prohibited and channelled by the hierarchy. Canon IV hints at another use to which the baptismal process could be put. It reduced those involved in incestuous relationships to the status of catechumens for as long as they remained in sin; no Christian was permitted to share a meal with them.[36] Thus, it seems that a 'demotion' in baptismal status was possible for those who broke certain taboos.

While bearing in mind the previously noted dangers of adopting an overly positivistic approach to the canonical sources, the prelates at Lérida were definitely concerned with contact between Catholics and those who had been rebaptized. These anxieties were articulated through reference to the baptismal status of those at risk of contact, and were addressed through the (re)definition of the baptismal process, and sometimes through altering the baptismal status of those concerned. The rebaptized, presumably mainly former Catholics who had converted to Arianism, were excluded from normal contact with the Catholic community, except under carefully defined conditions. It also appears that some parents saw potential advantage in baptizing their children into heresy (possibly Arianism). By defining the conditions under which such contact could take place and the timescales involved, the Catholic hierarchy did not entirely close the barriers to those outside, but ensured that it was possible, under certain conditions, for people to move into their community. Such a movement was to take place on their own terms and was paralleled by strictures that made movement in the opposite direction as difficult as possible: hence the desire to end all everyday contacts. This council clearly demonstrates the dual purpose of the definition of baptismal practice: promoting the

---

[36] *Hispana*, 298, 304–06.

identity of the Catholic Christian community and enhancing episcopal authority.

* * *

The key events of the tumultuous 580s reveal the centrality of differences over baptismal practice, which was linked to other points of theological disagreement between Arians and Catholics. In 580 Leovigild held a council of Arian bishops at Toledo, described by John of Biclarum, a Catholic bishop writing in the early 590s:

> King Leovigild assembled a synod of bishops of the Arian sect in the city of Toledo and amended the ancient heresy with a new error, saying, 'Those coming from the Roman religion to our Catholic[37] faith ought not to be baptised, but ought to be cleansed only by means of the imposition of hands and the receiving of communion, and be given the "Glory to the Father through the Son in the Holy Spirit"'. By means of this seduction many of our own inclined toward the Arian doctrine out of self-interest rather than a change of heart.[38]

The removal of the need for rebaptism broke down one of the main barriers to conversion from Catholicism to Arianism. Previously the Arians had insisted on anyone wanting to join their church being rebaptized, a practice that was abhorrent to Catholics. Perhaps Leovigild recognized that the main bar to closer contact between the religions was their different rituals, which were closely tied to matters of theological disagreement between the two sides. For example, the Catholic baptism ritual included recitation of the *credo*, while the Arians recited their own *credo*. The most prominent ritual would surely have been baptism, in which every member of each church was expected to participate. Leovigild therefore softened the Arian position on rebaptism, moving it towards the Catholic practice of the imposition of hands, thereby bringing the two religious communities closer. Ritual alteration was accompanied by theological innovation: the equality of Father and Son being admitted.

Thus Gothic Arianism became Macedonianism, a fourth-century

---

[37] The Arians saw themselves as the 'catholic', i.e. the orthodox party, and those who adhered to the 'Roman' religion (i.e. Catholics) as heretics.

[38] John of Biclarum, *Chronicle*, 580, 2, trans. from Wolf, *Conquerors and Chroniclers*, 72; *Juan de Biclaro, Obispo de Gerona. Su vida y su obra*, ed. Julio Campos Ruiz (Madrid, 1960), 89–90.

heresy.[39] This heresy, named after Macedonius, bishop of Constantinople, denied the full personality and divinity of the Holy Spirit, which was seen as having been created by the Son and thus as subordinate to the Father and Son. That the majority of the Catholic ecclesiastical elite were not willing to accept any compromise short of the conversion of the Arians to the Catholic position is evidenced by the response these measures received from contemporary authors besides John of Biclarum.[40]

The Visigothic monarchy rapidly came round to the Catholic viewpoint and King Reccared, the younger brother of Hermenegild, converted in 587–589. The council celebrating the conversion, III Toledo, will now be analysed. Unsurprisingly it witnessed an aggressive affirmation of the Catholic identity of the Visigothic kingdom, and a rejection of the Arian and Macedonianist past. Importantly, the council anathematized anyone who carried out or believed in rebaptism, again suggesting that baptism was a key sticking point between Arians and Catholics.[41]

Although this council witnessed the end of baptism's role in differentiating Arians and Catholics, one of the paradigms underpinning it remained in place. Canon XIV forbade Jews from buying Christian slaves for their own use, from taking Christian wives or concubines, and from presenting children born from such unions for baptism. Restrictions that were presumably previously directed against Arians were, with royal support, thereafter directed against another outsider group, the Jews. While III Toledo witnessed the end of the use of baptism to differentiate between Christian denominations, it initiated a new trend, which was to continue well into the seventh-century. From this point onwards differentiation was frequently made – in both the royal and ecclesiastical laws – between baptized and unbaptized Jews. Baptism continued to remain important in the articulation of power relations between the bishop, his clergy and the faithful.[42]

---

[39] Thompson, *The Goths in Spain*, 85.

[40] Leander of Seville wrote two books condemning Arianism: Isidore, *De viris illustribus*, XXVIII, in *El 'De viris illustribus' de Isidoro de Sevilla*, ed. Carmen Codoñer Merino (Salamanca, 1964) [hereafter: *DVI*], 149–50. Another tract, written by Severus of Málaga, was directed against the apostate, Vincentius of Zaragoza, the only named convert to Macedonianism, *DVI*, XXX, 151. The fact that Vincentius converted suggests that some were willing to compromise.

[41] *Hispana*, 82, 61–2, 75–99.

[42] *Hispana*, 117–19: canons XI and XII legislate for penitents, emphasizing the role of the bishop in determining entry into and exclusion from the community. The *Placitum* presented to Recceswinth (649–672) by the Jews of Toledo affirms their belief in the Cath-

Canon VII of II Seville (619) forbade presbyters from instilling, by the imposition of hands, the Holy Spirit into the baptized and converts from heresies. Neither were they allowed prepare nor to anoint with baptismal chrism. These functions were specifically reserved to the bishop. Priests were not allowed to enter the baptistery, nor to anoint or sign over a child without permission in the bishop's presence.[43] This council therefore sought to re-establish episcopal primacy; the priest could not simply arrogate this responsibility to himself. The bishop's superiority was also emphasized on occasions when both priest and bishop were present. By reserving for himself the duty of reconciling people back into the fold, the bishop assumed the same role we have previously witnessed in the baptismal process – it was he who had the right to determine when and under what conditions people were to join the community. This council demonstrates that bishops were indeed worried about priests taking on some of the prerogatives traditionally reserved for the episcopacy and sought to reaffirm their rights in such areas, thereby reinforcing distinctions of rank within the community itself. Furthermore, by stating that it was the bishop's responsibility to reconcile people to the faith they also affirmed their right to determine membership of the religious community.

The desire of the episcopal elite to control their subordinates is also evident in the canons of IV Toledo (633), the last council to make repeated reference to baptism. Canon II stated that services and offices must be carried out in the same manner throughout the entire kingdom. Canon VI sought to resolve the problem of single or triple immersion at baptism: the baptizand should only be immersed once, since the triple immersion was practised by heretics. This canon should be read in the context of the bishops' desire to impose uniform practice throughout the kingdom.[44] Canon XXV reinforces this point: when presbyters for rural parishes are ordained, they receive a *libellum* from their bishop laying down correct ritual, so that they do not profane the

---

olic faith. They agree not to associate with any unbaptized Jews, *Leges Visigothorum*, XII.2.17, ed. K. Zeumer, MGH. Leges nationum Germanicarum 1 (Hannover, 1902), 425. Some bishops continued to favour Jews in the seventh century, suggesting that the episcopal elite itself was not unified, Wolfram Drews, 'Jews as Pagans? Polemical Definitions of Identity in Visigothic Spain', *Early Medieval Europe* 11.3 (2002), 189–207.

[43] Vives, 167–8.

[44] Isabel Velázquez, '*Pro patriae gentisque Gothorum statu* (4th Council of Toledo, Canon 75, A. 633)', in Hans-Werner Goetz, Jörg Jarnut and Walter Pohl, eds, *Regna and Gentes. The Relationship between Late Antique and Early Medieval Peoples and Kingdoms in the Transformation of the Roman World* (Leiden, 2003), 161–217, at 196–8.

sacraments – including baptism – through ignorance.[45] So, while still concerned to ensure the obedience of those further down the hierarchy than themselves, the bishops have taken their interest in baptism onto a new level: they are now interested in ensuring uniformity of practice throughout the realm.

* * *

The ritual process of baptism and its definition in the legislation of church councils in sixth- and early seventh-century Spain served as a 'strategy of distinction' in two senses. Firstly, in the pre-conversion period, represented by Lérida and III Toledo, the definition of correct baptismal practice, especially on the issue of rebaptism, could be used to differentiate Catholics from Arians to ensure that the orthodox faith was not tainted by heresy.[46] Additionally, as the seventh-century progressed, *baptizati iudaei* were increasingly differentiated from unbaptized Jews in both conciliar and royal legislation.

Secondly, as the liturgical process marking entry into the Catholic Church, baptism offered the opportunity for the display of the bishop's superiority over his flock and clergy. This feature was common to all of the councils examined. The act of legislating strengthened the collective identity and power of the episcopacy, distinguishing bishops from those below them in the ecclesiastical hierarchy. The entire process, from legislation to episcopal confirmation of baptism, can be understood as intimately connected with the articulation and reinforcement of episcopal primacy in the face of those further down the ecclesiastical scale, especially the mass of the faithful themselves. It should be noted, though, that this primacy was dependent on the existence of a community of the faithful in the first place. Elite and popular were, after all, bound in a reciprocal relationship, as the attempts to exclude heretics demonstrate.

University of Manchester

---

[45] *Hispana*, 183–4, 189–93, 216, 206–11: those who have fallen into heresy, have been baptized into heresy or rebaptized are excluded from entering the episcopacy.

[46] It should be noted that the four councils examined here are not the only Visigothic councils to legislate on baptismal practice.

AT ONCE ELITIST AND POPULAR: THE AUDIENCES OF THE BEWCASTLE AND RUTHWELL CROSSES

by ÉAMONN Ó CARRAGÁIN

THE Bewcastle and Ruthwell Crosses are the finest sculptured monuments to survive from early eighth-century Northumbria. For what audiences were they designed: clerics, monks or lay people? Of the two monuments, it is likely that the Bewcastle Cross is the earlier. Its designer wished to commemorate a number of benefactors of his or her community, whose names were inscribed on a panel of runic inscriptions on the west face (they are, unfortunately, now largely illegible: see figs 1 and 2). He or she was the first to introduce a number of highly significant theological ideas into Northumbrian sculpture. The Ruthwell designer, who did not set out to commemorate any individuals, expanded and developed theological ideas found in embryo on the Bewcastle Cross (figs 3 and 4). The Bewcastle and the Ruthwell Crosses, both, are best understood in terms of the theological and liturgical interests of Bede's scholarly circle, in particular of Bishop Acca of Hexham, Bede's bishop and patron; and of Bede's friend and correspondent Bishop Pehthelm of Whithorn. Hexham lies east of Bewcastle, and Whithorn west of Ruthwell: I would date Bewcastle within the episcopacy of Acca, i.e. between 709 and 731; and Ruthwell a little later, say between 732 and 740 (the year Acca died). In this period the abbot of Wearmouth-Jarrow was Hwætberht (abbot 716–c.750). Hwætberht was known as 'Eusebius' to his scholarly friends, presumably because of his interest in Eusebius of Caesarea, Constantine and the cult of the Cross. Rosemary Cramp and Richard Bailey have convincingly related the beautiful cross-slab at Jarrow to the abbacy and patronage of Hwætberht.[1] In his account of King Oswald's victory, in the sign of the Cross, at Heavenfield, Bede implies that the Cross was, for the Northumbrian aristocracy and the clerics associated with them, the primary symbol of the Christian Faith.[2] The cult of the Cross

---

[1] Rosemary Cramp, *County Durham and Northumberland*, Corpus of Anglo-Saxon Stone Sculpture 1, 2 vols (Oxford, 1984), 1: 112–13; 2: pl. 95, fig. 518, and pl. 96, figs 519–20; Richard N. Bailey, *England's Earliest Sculptors* (Toronto, 1996), 49.

[2] Bede, *Historia Ecclesiastica*, III.2, in *Venerabilis Bedae Opera Historica*, ed. Charles Plummer, 2 vols (Oxford, 1896), 1: 128.

had greatly developed within the Western Church during Bede's own adult life. About 700 AD, Pope Sergius had made the feast of the Exaltation of the Cross universal in the Western Church. Bede records in his *De temporum ratione* that Hwætberht-Eusebius had 'hastened to Rome in the time of Pope Sergius of blessed memory and stayed no little time there, learning, copying and bringing back whatever he thought necessary'.[3]

Hexham practised a powerful local variant of the cult of the Cross. Bede, writing about 730 CE, tells us that the monks there had for many years ('multo iam tempore') celebrated a Vigil at nearby Heavenfield on the anniversary of Oswald's death. Bishop Acca, Bede's own close friend and patron, developed the cult: the Hexham community had built a church at Heavenfield 'lately' ('nuper'): evidently, well after Acca became bishop in 709.[4] The devotional interest which produced the Heavenfield church is consistent with that which produced the Roman cross-slab at Jarrow. The *incipit* of the runic panel at Bewcastle refers to that cross as a 'symbol of victory' ('þis sigbecn . . .'):[5] like the Jarrow cross-slab, the Bewcastle Cross was designed as a Constantinian symbol of spiritual and political victory.

To refer to the Bewcastle monument as a 'cross' at all is, at the moment, mildly controversial. In four articles published since 1998 Professor Fred Orton of Leeds has argued that the monument was designed not as a cross, but as an obelisk; and that the Ruthwell Cross was originally designed as an obelisk, to which a cross (the upper stone) was added later.[6] But the late sixteenth- and early seventeenth-century descriptions of the Bewcastle monument by Reginald Bainbrigg, Nicholas Roscarrock, and other antiquarians in the circles of Lord William Howard and William Camden all explicitly refer to it as a cross, and Bainbrigg's description of Ruthwell explicitly calls that monument a cross. These early statements are reliable, and the

---

[3] Bede, *Historia Abbatum*, 18, in *Venerabilis Bedae Opera Historica*, ed. Plummer, 1: 383.

[4] Bede, *Historia Ecclesiastica*, III. 2, ed. Plummer, 1: 130; Bailey, *England's Earliest Sculptors*, 50.

[5] Richard Bailey and Rosemary Cramp, eds, *Cumberland, Westmorland and Lancashire North-of-the-Sands*, Corpus of Anglo-Saxon Stone Sculpture 2 (Oxford, 1988), 1: 61–3.

[6] Orton's fourth statement of this position is a good place to begin, as it contains references to his three earlier articles: Fred Orton, 'Rethinking the Ruthwell and Bewcastle Monuments: Some Deprecation of Style; Some Consideration of Form and Ideology', in George Hardin Brown and Catherine E. Karkov, eds, *Anglo-Saxon Styles* (Albany, NY, 2003), 31–67.

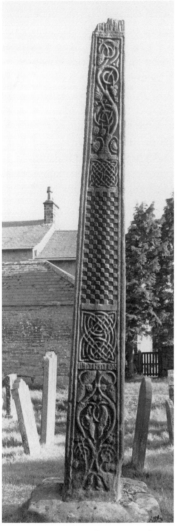

(a)

(b)

Fig. 1. The Bewcastle Cross-shaft, north and east sides:
(a) North side: panels of interlace, foliage scrolls and abstract ornament,
with spaces between panels where names were inserted (including the
surviving 'kynibur*g').
(b) East side: vine scroll, with eight surviving volutes. No inscription.
(Photos: Durham University, Corpus of Anglo-Saxon Stone Sculpture).

(a) (b)

Fig. 2. The Bewcastle Cross-shaft, south and west sides:
(a) South and west sides, showing the relationship between the sundial
(south side) and the 'Christ acclaimed by the beasts' and 'John the Baptist
acclaiming the Agnus Dei' panels (west side).
(b) The Bewcastle Cross-shaft, west side: Reading upwards: (1) the falconer;
(2) the panel of runic inscriptions; (3) Christ acclaimed by two animals and
(4) John the Baptist acclaims the Agnus Dei.
(Photos: Durham University, Corpus of Anglo-Saxon Stone Sculpture).

objections which Professor Orton raises against them are unconvincing.[7]

The iconography of the surviving Bewcastle cross-shaft is consistent with these early descriptions. On the upper half of the west face, a panel represents Christ acclaimed by two beasts. Directly above, St John the Baptist points towards the Lamb of God (fig. 2). The same sequence of panels will recur on the second broad side at Ruthwell (fig. 4). This suggests that the Ruthwell designer was familiar with the Bewcastle achievement. The Bewcastle Cross provides important evidence about the original orientation of the Ruthwell Cross. It stands where it always stood. A sundial, incorporated into one of the panels of the south side of the cross, could only function if that side faced south. Thus the figural panels on the west side of the Bewcastle Cross always faced west; to see them properly, onlookers need to face east. From early times Christians traditionally prayed facing east, oriented towards the rising sun. It is reasonable to assume that the Ruthwell Cross was originally oriented as the Bewcastle Cross still is. At Ruthwell the second broad side (with Christ acclaimed by the Beasts and the Agnus Dei) probably faced west as at Bewcastle, and consequently the first broad side (with the Annunciation) faced east.

On the west face of the Bewcastle Cross, 'Christ acclaimed by the Beasts' and the panel of runes (just below), together form the two 'inner panels' of the surviving sequence. The two 'outer' panels of the surviving sequence comprise a symbolic portrait of Christ as the Agnus Dei (above) and an aristocratic or royal portrait, the falconer (below).[8] In the central figural panel, 'Christ acclaimed by the beasts', Christ holds a scroll in his left hand; his right hand is raised in blessing. It is likely that the scroll represents the heavenly *Liber Vitae* referred to in

---

[7] See the courteous but devastating assessment of Orton's work by Richard Bailey, 'Innocent from the Great Offence', in Catherine E. Karkov and Fred Orton, eds, *Theorizing Anglo-Saxon Stone Sculpture* (Morgantown, WV, 2003), 93–103; and the discussion of Orton's treatment of the early antiquarian evidence in Éamonn Ó Carragáin, *Ritual and the Rood: Liturgical Images and the Old English Poems of the* Dream of the Rood *Tradition* (London and Toronto, 2005), 63, n. 10 (on Ruthwell); 30 and 68, n. 106 (on Bewcastle).

[8] A number of scholars have interpreted the Bewcastle falconer panel as a portrait of John the Evangelist: see the survey in Bailey and Cramp, eds, *Cumberland, Westmorland and Lancashire North-of-the-Sands*, 69–70. In recent years, scholarly consensus has swung back to a royal portrait: the decisive studies in changing the consensus were Ernst Kitzinger, 'Interlace and Icons: Form and Function in Early Insular Art', in R. Michael Spearman and John Higgitt, eds, *The Age of Migrating Ideas: Early Medieval Art in Northern Britain and Ireland* (Edinburgh and Stroud, 1993), 3–15; and Bailey, *England's Earliest Sculptors*, 66–8.

the New Testament.[9] If so, Christ's gesture of blessing presumably encompasses the scroll (the heavenly book which would be understood to contain the names of the blessed), but also the beasts who joyfully acclaim Christ, the names to be prayed for in the panel below, the falconer in the panel at the foot of this side, and any onlookers who in prayer faced east towards this side of the cross. Such onlookers would have hoped that the names of the living and dead persons, inscribed in runes on the panel just below, were inscribed in the heavenly *Liber Vitae* symbolized by the scroll which Christ blesses, and that their own names were also inscribed on it. The formal request to 'pray for their souls' could be responded to by monks and laity as well as by priests. The Bewcastle Cross implies that in that local area secular and religious social structures were interdependent and mutually supportive.

The metaphor of the heavenly *Liber Vitae* enables us to appreciate the conceptual relationship between the west side and the north and south sides of the cross-shaft: these contain a series of panels of various design (figs 1 and 2). Between each panel room was left for one further name. Some names seem to have been added, but some spaces may have been left blank. Apart from the fragment of the sacred name '[..]ssu/s' at the top of the north side, only one name is still legible, over the lowest panel of ornament on the north side: 'kynibur*g'.[10] The Bewcastle designer seems to have left space for his community to incise, or paint in, further names when appropriate. The design of the north and south sides thus enabled the community to update progressively the commemorative runic panel of the west side, which in turn refers to the heavenly *Liber Vitae* blessed by Christ in the panel just above. The east side is taken up by a magnificent vine-scroll of which eight great volutes survive. The single great uninscribed vine-scroll provides an eloquent image of the unity between Christ and the members of his body: 'I am the vine, you are the branches' (John 15:1–8).[11]

On the west side, the two visual representations of Christ were particularly appropriate to a high cross. The panel of 'Christ acclaimed by the beasts' refers to two chants sung together only at Good Friday at the ninth hour, the moment of Christ's death on the cross: the tract

---

[9] Phil. 4:3; Luke 10:20; Rev. 3:5, 5:1–10, 20:12, 21:27, 22:19; for the Old Testament background, see Dan. 7:10, 12:1.

[10] Bailey and Cramp, eds, *Cumberland, Westmorland and Lancashire North-of-the-Sands*, 62–3.

[11] On the religious significance of Anglo-Saxon vine-scroll patterns, see Bailey, *England's Earliest Sculptors*, 52–7.

'Domine audivi' taken from the Canticle of Habbakuk, which prophesied that Christ would be known 'between two living creatures' ('in medio duorum animalium'), and the tract 'Qui habitat', based on Psalm 90, which prophesied that Christ would 'tread on the lion and the dragon'. In order to refer at once to both texts, the Bewcastle designer transformed the traditional iconography of Christ's victory in Psalm 90: he or she converted the two beasts from evil to good, and reduced them to a new and significant anonymity. They are no longer lions and dragons, but simply 'duo animalia', two living creatures, who, by crossing their paws, refer to the X-shaped 'g'-rune which begins the name 'gessus kristtus', inscribed just above the panel; and, by implication, to the Greek letter 'chi', the first letter of the messianic title in Greek, 'Christos'. At Bewcastle, these converted animals take up the *orans-* or prayer-posture, raising both paws in acclamation; they acclaim Christ as the anointed one, the Messiah. As Adam was placed in paradise among the beasts on the sixth day of Creation, a Friday, so with Christ's triumph over death on Good Friday (the sixth day of Holy Week), the ancient harmony between man and animals is restored. On Good Friday, Christ, who 'did not regard equality with God as something to be exploited', reversed Adam's sin of pride. His heroic act of obedience 'to the point of death, even death on a cross' (Phil. 2:6–8) re-established the harmony of Paradise that Adam had lost.[12]

The restoration of harmony between humankind and other creatures is also implied by the falconer portrait at the foot of the west side, and by the panel in which John the Baptist points to the Lamb. By the early eighth century, that panel would have recalled a communal chant recently introduced into the Mass at the breaking of bread: 'Agnus Dei, qui tollis peccata mundi, miserere nobis' ('Lamb of God, who takes away the sins of the world, have mercy upon us'). The chant had recently been introduced by Pope Sergius, who had made the Exaltation of the Cross an official and universal feast in the Western Church. The rite of breaking the bread for Communion was always interpreted as symbolizing the breaking of Christ's body by the nails and spear on the Cross. We may thus conclude that each of the upper two panels on the Bewcastle cross-shaft symbolically represents Christ's victory on the Cross on Good Friday at the ninth hour at Jerusalem: the unique act of

---

[12] See Éamonn Ó Carragáin, 'Christ over the Beasts and the Agnus Dei: Two Multivalent Panels on the Ruthwell and Bewcastle Crosses', in Paul E. Szarmach, ed., *Sources of Anglo-Saxon Culture* (Kalamazoo, MI, 1986), 377–403.

heroic humility, through which the falconer and those whose names were commemorated on the cross might hope to have their names included in the heavenly Book of Life. The 'Christ acclaimed by two animals' and 'Agnus Dei' panels, taken in sequence, provide important evidence that the Bewcastle monument was from the beginning designed as a cross. This iconographic sequence is consistent with the opening words of the main runic inscription, which refers to the monument as 'þis sigbecn', 'this victory-standard'. Within the Roman and Constantinian tradition, the Cross was above all a symbol of victory.

The most brilliant achievement of the Bewcastle designer was to relate Christ's paschal victory on the Cross to the Christian solar cycle which commemorated his Incarnation. The sundial, on the south side of the Bewcastle cross-shaft, doubtless had practical functions.[13] But for a monastic audience, it would have recalled Psalm 18 (19), 'the heavens show forth the glory of God':

> [6]He hath set his tabernacle in the sun: and he, as a bridegroom coming out of his bride chamber,
>   Hath rejoiced as a giant to run the way.
> [7]His going out is from the end of heaven,
>   And his circuit even to the end thereof: and there is no one that can hide himself from his heat.[14]

An onlooker who proceeds around the Bewcastle Cross sunwise, from south to west, can see that the panel of foliage scroll containing the sundial is at a level which corresponds to that of the sequence of related panels, 'Christ acclaimed by two animals' and 'Agnus Dei' panels on the west side (fig. 2). These two panels not only refer to Christ's victory on the Cross at the ninth hour on Good Friday: they also refer to the sun's yearly course. In St Luke's gospel, the Angel Gabriel informed the Virgin Mary that her cousin, Elizabeth, was six months with child (Luke 1:36); the Prologue to the Gospel of St John tells us that Christ was the Light that illuminates every person that comes into the world, while John the Baptist was not the Light, but was to give testimony to

---

[13] For discussion, see Bailey and Cramp, eds, *Cumberland, Westmorland and Lancashire North-of-the-Sands*, 66.

[14] Psalm 18 (19), Douay version, which preserves the identification between Christ and the sun found in the Vulgate: '6In sole posuit tabernaculum suum; et ipse tanquam sponsus procedens de thalamo suo, Exsultavit ut gigas ad currendam viam'.

the Light (John 1:5–10). Later in the same Gospel (3:30), John the Baptist proclaims of Christ that 'he must increase, I must decrease'. It was logical for the Western Church to celebrate Christ's incarnation and nativity on the 'growing days' when the sun began to overcome the winter darkness: the Annunciation on 25 March (VIII kal. Aprilis) near the spring equinox, and the Nativity of Christ on 25 December (VIII kal. Ianuarii), near the winter solstice, a date which, in pagan Rome, had from the third century been the feast of the Unconquered Sun (*natale solis invicti*). Conversely, John the Baptist's conception and birth were celebrated on the lessening days, to proclaim that he was not the light, but that he gave testimony to the light even when the darkness seemed to overcome it: his conception was celebrated on 24 September (VIII kal. Octobris) near the Autumn equinox, and his Nativity on 24 June (VIII kal. Iulii), near the Summer solstice: a feast which counterbalanced the midwinter feast of Christmas. Thus the sequence, from Christ over the beasts to John the Baptist pointing to the Agnus Dei, refers not only to Good Friday at the ninth hour, but also to the solar cycle in which the Nativities of Christ and that of his cousin the Baptist were celebrated. The sundial on the south side prepares onlookers to appreciate the logic of juxtaposing 'Christ acclaimed by two animals' to 'John the Baptist pointing to the Agnus Dei' on the upper half of the west side of the cross-shaft (fig. 2).

The importance of seeing Christ's incarnation and his Passion in a single perspective was strengthened by the ancient Christian tradition that the first Good Friday happened on 25 March. In seventh-century Northumbria, how to calculate Easter was a major ecclesiastical problem: the Irish had one method, and the Anglo-Saxon monks had another method which they had learned from Rome. But the Northumbrians, the Irish and the Welsh all believed that Christ had died on 25 March, on the precise anniversary of the day, thirty-four years before, on which he had been conceived in the womb of the Virgin Mary. The tradition affirmed that Christ's life, from his conception in Mary's virginal womb to his triumphant death on the Cross, had the coherence and integrity of a divine plan: as Ambrosiaster had put it in the fourth century, 'the Saviour did all things at the appropriate places and times'.[15]

---

15 *Pseudo-Augustini Quaestiones Veteris et Noui Testamenti CXXVII*, ed. Alexander Souter, CSEL 50 (Vienna, 1908), Quaestio iv, p. 100: 'omnia propriis locis et temporibus gessit Salvator'. The unknown author of this treatise is referred to in modern scholarly discussion as 'Ambrosiaster'.

In the course of the seventh century, the unity and coherence of Christ's life, and in particular his virginal birth, came to be seen as issues on which the unity of the Church depended. Monotheletism, the theory that Christ did not have an independent human will, but only participated in the divine will which he shared with his Father and the Holy Spirit, threatened to split the Church. Against Monothelete byzantine emperors, Rome and the West defended the reality of Christ's human will: in effect, the reality of Christ's courage. Those who opposed Monotheletism held that Christ's human will could never be in conflict with the divine will precisely because Christ was uniquely born from the Blessed Virgin. The struggle against Monotheletism demanded that Christ's Passion be seen in the context of his Incarnation; and every educated nun, monk or cleric was aware that 25 March was the day, near the Spring equinox, on which both events had occurred. In order to affirm Christ's full humanity, as well as his divinity, a great development of Marian liturgy and devotion took place at Rome in the late seventh century.[16]

The Anglo-Saxon Church gave its official response to the Monothelete crisis on 17 September 679 at the synod of Hatfield. Theodore of Tarsus, Archbishop of Canterbury, presided; the Papal representative was John the Archcantor, the man responsible for the liturgy at St Peter's basilica in Rome which, from the time it was built in the 330s, had been the first Roman basilica to celebrate Christmas.[17] In the 670s, just before the abbot John set off with Benedict Biscop and Ceolfrid for the synod of Hatfield, St Peter's had introduced a new Mass for the feast of the Annunciation on 25 March. It is likely that the prayers of the new Mass were composed by the head of liturgy or precentor at the Basilica, John the Archcantor itself. The central idea of the new Mass was precisely that the Annunciation, which on 25 March almost always fell during Lent, should be celebrated in the context of Christ's Passion. The title of the Mass proclaimed that 25 March should be seen as 'The Annunciation of the Lord and His Passion', 'ADNUNTIATIO DOMINI ET PASSIO EIUSDEM'. Its offertory prayer stated explicitly that the congregation offered the Mass on 25

---

[16] See Michael Hurley, 'Born Incorruptibly. The Third Canon of the Lateran Council, A.D. 649', *The Heythrop Journal* 2 (1961), 216–36.

[17] See Henry Chadwick, 'Theodore, the English Church and the Monothelete Controversy', in Michael Lapidge, ed., *Archbishop Theodore: Commemorative Studies on his Life and Influence* (Cambridge, 1995), 88–95.

March 'on account of the Incarnation and likewise the Passion of our Redeemer Jesus Christ'. The collect of the Mass provides the most complex and moving statement in the Roman liturgy of the idea that Christ's birth, death and Resurrection provided a unified pattern in which humankind could share: 'Gratiam tuam quaesumus domine mentibus nostris infunde, ut qui angelo nuntiante Christi filii tui incarnationem cognouimus, per passionem eius et crucem ad resurrectionis gloriam perducamur: qui tecum...'.[18]

This prayer, the collect *Gratiam tuam*, would be used for centuries: indeed, it is still used, both in the Roman and in the Anglican liturgies (the Book of Common Prayer provides a noble translation as the collect for Lady Day, 25 March).[19] In 679 Benedict Biscop also brought back from Rome an icon of the Virgin, together with icons of the twelve apostles, to adorn the monastic church of St Peter at Wearmouth; and in the next few years, he would build next to that church a chapel dedicated to Mary.[20] Like Theodore of Tarsus, Benedict Biscop was closely in touch with the struggle against Monotheletism, and saw that Christ's virginal birth, the central rationale for the cult of the virginal Mother of God, was central to that struggle.

A generation later, in the early eighth century, the cult of the Virgin Mary was also given striking new importance at Hexham. Returning from Rome in early 705, St Wilfrid was struck down by serious illness at Meaux in Francia. St Michael the Archangel appeared to him on his sick-bed, bearing the urgent message that the Virgin Mary had obtained for him a few more years of life, so that he should fulfill a specific mission for her:

[18] *Die älteste erreichbare Gestalt des Liber Sacramentorum anni circuli der römischen Kirche (Cod. Pad. D 47, fol. 11r–100r)*, ed. L. C. Mohlberg, Liturgiegeschichtliche Quellen und Forschungen 11–12 (Münster-im-Westfalen, 1927), 29–30; transl.: 'Pour your grace into our minds, we beseech thee, O Lord: that we to whom the Incarnation of Christ your Son was made known by the message of an angel may, by his Passion and Cross, be brought to the glory of his resurrection, who with you [lives and reigns in the unity of the Holy Spirit for ever and ever, Amen]'.

[19] For an analysis of the Vatican Mass for 25 March, see Éamonn Ó Carragáin, 'Rome, Ruthwell, Vercelli: *The Dream of the Rood* and the Italian Connection', in Vittoria Dolcetti Corazza, ed., *Vercelli tra Oriente ed Occidente, tra tarda antichità e Medioevo* (Alessandria, 1999), 51–100; for the history of the 'Gratiam tuam' prayer, see idem, 'The Annunciation of the Lord and His Passion: a Liturgical Topos from St Peter's on the Vatican in *The Dream of the Rood*, Thomas Cranmer and John Donne', in Jane Roberts and Janet Nelson, eds, *Essays in Anglo-Saxon and Related Themes in Memory of Dr Lynne Grundy* (London, 2000), 339–81.

[20] Bede, *Historia Abbatum*, 6, ed. Plummer, 1: 369.

[...] you have built churches in honour of the Apostles St Peter and St Andrew; but you have built nothing in honour of St Mary, ever Virgin, who is interceding for you. You have to put this right and to dedicate a church in honour of her.[21]

Wilfrid was directed by an archangel, no less, to imitate the most up-to-date Roman devotion. Pope John VII, newly-elected in March 705, took as his motto 'servus Sanctae Mariae', 'the servant of St Mary'.[22] St Michael in effect commanded Wilfred to imitate the new pope and to take the phrase 'servus Sanctae Mariae' as the motto for the last years of his life (705–09), which spanned the short pontificate of John VII (705–07). After the vision, Wilfrid immediately enquired 'Where is Acca our priest?', and privately revealed to his chaplain the message he had received.[23] The following year (706), in a synod at the river Nidd, Wilfrid was restored to the bishopric of Hexham, the monastery of Ripon, and his Northumbrian lands.[24] At Hexham Wilfrid now built a second church, and dedicated it to the Virgin Mary. This brought Hexham closer to the liturgical spirituality of Wearmouth, where Benedict Biscop had provided a church dedicated to her a generation before. It is reasonable to assume that Wilfrid, lately come from Rome, would have provided his new church with up-to-date Roman liturgical usages. Doubtless, as a bishop often beleaguered by jurisdictional difficulties, he saw the political relevance of the papal cult of the Virgin. If, like the Pope, Wilfrid was 'servus Sanctae Mariae', this service placed clear limits on his subordination to any lesser authority, ecclesiastical or secular.[25] Just before his death in 709, in a speech which has the character of a last testament, Wilfrid stated his desire to visit Rome one last time, and 'to carry presents to the Church dedicated to St Mary the Mother of the Lord', as well as to St Paul's outside-the-walls.

Wilfrid bequeathed the monastery and bishopric of Hexham to his chaplain Acca. Acca's experience of Rome, his intimacy with Wilfrid, and his devotional interests, provide the most convincing contexts, not

---

[21] Stephen, *Life of Bishop Wilfrid*, 56: *The Life of Bishop Wilfrid by Eddius Stephanus*, ed. Bertram Colgrave (Cambridge, 1927), 122–3.

[22] See Per Jonas Nordhagen, *The Frescoes of John VII (AD 705–707) in S. Maria Antiqua in Rome* (Rome, 1968).

[23] *Life of Bishop Wilfrid*, 56, ed. Colgrave, 122–3.

[24] *Life of Bishop Wilfrid*, 60, ed. Colgrave, 128–33.

[25] On the political importance of the papal theme of service to Mary, see Eric Thunø, *Image and Relic: Mediating the Sacred in Early Medieval Rome*, Analecta Romana Instituti Danici, Supplementum 32 (Rome, 2002), 29–38.

only for the erection of the Bewcastle Cross, but also for the remarkable wealth of Marian panels on the Ruthwell Cross. As we shall see, the verse *tituli* for the two Ruthwell vine-scrolls emphasize the links between the Annunciation and the Passion, and in this way relate the solar Incarnation-cycle to the lunar Paschal-cycle. Acca, Bede's bishop and friend, was committed to two important cults: that of the Cross, centred on Heavenfield; and that of the Virgin, in which, through the message of an archangel, Hexham had lately come to imitate Wear-mouth and Rome.

Acca provides the context within which we can understand how the Ruthwell Cross expands and transforms the iconographic programme on the earlier Bewcastle Cross. The Ruthwell designer made the vine-scroll, or 'tree of life', even more central. At Bewcastle, the single great vine-scroll on the east side, an image of the blood of Christ, had been balanced against the images of Christ's Body on the west side. The Ruthwell designer now provided his cross with two matching vine-scrolls, which spread on each side from the lower to the upper stone (fig. 3). These paired vine-scrolls, by far the largest and most important icons of the Ruthwell monument, place images of Christ's blood at its very heart. At Bewcastle, the single great vine-scroll has no *titulus*; but the Ruthwell designer provided both vine-scrolls with matching *tituli*, in English verse and in runes. The vivid poem quoted in these carefully-edited *tituli* was probably composed in the aftermath of the synod of Hatfield in 679. The poem makes the cross speak, from the very heart of its experience, of its ordeal on Good Friday. It is unique in emphasizing Christ's courage when he confronts the Cross, and the dilemma of the Cross when it realizes that it must bear its Lord to his death, and so become the slayer of its Lord. It is unique in retelling the Crucifixion in terms reminiscent of the Annunciation: on 25 March Mary was troubled when the Angel Gabriel requested of her that, though she did not know man sexually, she should bear the Lord into life by the power of the Holy Spirit.[26] Since the late fourth century, theologians were agreed that she had taken a vow of perpetual virginity, which it seemed that she must now break.[27] Now, in the English poem,

---

[26] The Old English text of the Ruthwell poem is edited and discussed in Éamonn Ó Carragáin, 'The Ruthwell Crucifixion Poem in its Iconographic and Liturgical Contexts', *Peritia* 6–7 (1987–88), 1–71.

[27] Augustine, Sermon 51:18 (PL 38–9, 343); Sermon 215:2 (PL 38–9, 1073); Sermon 291:5–6 (PL 38–9, 1318–19); the theme is discussed in Kim Power, *Veiled Desire: Augustine's Writings on Women* (London, 1995), 181–2, 293.

the Cross obediently, but in startled agony, bears its Lord to his courageous death. The way in which the poem's Crucifixion narrative is
modelled on Luke's narrative of the Annunciation emphasizes not only
the similarities between the two scenes, but the tragic differences
between them. Gabriel immediately reassured Mary, resolving her
dilemma; but for the Cross, there is no reassurance, no resolution: it
must, uncomprehending, become the instrument of its Lord's death.
The English poet was unique in realizing that the Incarnation and
Passion both involved the cooperation of startled but obedient creatures, Mary at the Incarnation and the Cross at the Passion:

1   Almighty God stripped himself. When he willed to mount
    the gallows,
2   Courageous before all men,
3   [*I dared not*] bow [. . .]

5   I [lifted up] a powerful king –
6   the lord of heaven I dared not tilt:
7   men insulted the pair of us together; I was drenched with
    blood
8   poured [*from the man's side*] [. . .]

At the heart of the Ruthwell Cross, its two vine-scrolls and the vernacular *tituli*, which celebrate Christ's heroic self-giving on 25 March,
provide the unifying principle behind the rich iconographic programme of the broad sides; while the broad sides themselves set forth
the liturgical means by which the audience can enter the mystery of
Christ's heroic Passion. At the centre of the first broad side are images
of the catechumenate and baptism, the means by which Christians at
Ruthwell could enter into the paschal mystery: conversion, in the Man
born Blind; and repentance, in the Woman who was a Sinner. The
Ruthwell designer saw these images as stages in spiritual growth.
Therefore he placed them between a moving image of the Visitation,
above on the upper stone, and of the Annunciation, below, at the foot
of the slender shaft of his Cross (fig. 4 (a)). The designer saw conversion
and repentance, both of which allowed Christ to grow in the Christian
soul, as imitations of the growth of Christ within the womb of the
Virgin.[28] The Ruthwell iconography grows out of the two mysteries

---

28   See Éamonn Ó Carragáin, 'Between Annunciation and Visitation: Spiritual Birth and
the Cycles of the Sun on the Ruthwell Cross: a Response to Fred Orton', in Karkov and
Orton, eds, *Theorizing*, 131–87.

Fig. 3. The Ruthwell Cross: to right, vine-scroll with first runic verse *titulus* and, to left, part of the first broad side with (reading upwards: lower stone): healing of the man born blind; repentance of the woman who was a sinner. (Photo: Ross Trench-Jellicoe).

which took place on 25 March: the incarnation and the Passion of Christ.

The design of the second half of the Ruthwell Cross is as dynamic as that of the first half. The *titulus* for the second vine-scroll envisages the followers of Christ coming from afar, as it were in an imaginary pilgrimage, to gather at the Cross on Good Friday; the Cross, still un-comprehending, silent and overcome by sorrow, bows down to present the body of Christ to his followers. The second *titulus* reverses the themes of the first, where the dilemma of the Cross sprang from the fact that as long as Christ still lived it dared not bow, but had to stand fast:

9   Christ was on the Cross.

10   But eager ones came thither from afar,

11   the noble ones [came] together. I looked upon all that:

12   I was terribly afflicted with sorrows; I bowed [*to the hands of the men.*]

13   Wounded with arrows,

14   they laid him down limb-spent, and took their stand at the head and feet of his corpse;

15   there they looked on [*the Lord of heaven*] [. . .]

The wonderful image in which the Cross bows down to present the body of Christ to his followers occurs nowhere else in medieval art, literature or theology. But this second *titulus* ends with a moment of pause and expectation, as the followers of Christ, standing at his head and feet, contemplate Christ's dead body, emptied even of its blood. How will the narrative be completed?

Knowing that the vine-scrolls were images of the blood of Christ and of the tree of life, the Ruthwell designer had the brilliant idea of 'completing' the narrative with a powerful sequence of images of Christ's life-giving eucharistic body. As central elements in this sequence, we find developed versions of two panels we have seen at Bewcastle: Christ acclaimed by the beasts, at the top of the lower stone (here the 'X' formed by the beasts' crossed paws echoes not an X-shaped 'g'-rune, as on the Bewcastle Cross, but the similarly shaped Greek letter *chi* which begins the word 'Christus' on the upper border of the panel: 'IhS XPS'); and John the Baptist pointing to the Agnus Dei, on the upper stone (fig. 4 (b)). Below Christ acclaimed by the Beasts, the designer expanded this sequence of two images by adding a third: the earliest surviving Insular representation of the first monks, Saints Paul and Anthony, breaking bread in the desert (fig. 4 (b)). This image transformed older Roman images of the harmony between Saints Peter and Paul, the iconography of the 'concordia apostolorum'. It is best seen as the earliest surviving example of an Insular transformation of that tradition: as a 'concordia monachorum'.[29] Its form and placing at Ruthwell was inspired by a liturgical ceremony at Iona, where for over a century, since the time of St Columba, the arrival of a clerical visitor had been celebrated by a liturgical re-enactment, during the Mass, of how Saints Paul and Anthony had broken bread in the desert, when St Anthony the abbot had come to visit St Paul of Thebes in his desert hermitage.[30] At the bottom of this side of the cross-shaft, the Ruthwell designer placed the third Marian icon to survive on the monument. The Virgin bears Christ across the desert to the Holy Land, in fulfillment of the manna which had once sustained the people of Israel: a foreshadowing of the Eucharist, which sustains the Church.

Not only does the iconographic sequence of the second broad side at Ruthwell develop the sequence of two images on the upper half of the west side at Bewcastle; the two crosses have similar symbolic structures. At Bewcastle it is natural to move sunwise from the sundial on the south side, with its implication that the heavens show forth the glory of God (Psalm 18/19:1), to the panels of the upper half of the west side, which celebrate the relations between Christ and John the Baptist: the cousins whose conceptions and nativities marked into balanced quarters the yearly solar cycle. Similarly, at Ruthwell it is natural to move sunwise from the narrow sides, in which the vine-scrolls, with their runic verse *tituli*, tell of Christ's heroic victory on the Cross, to the broad sides, in which figural panels make clear the contemporary relevance of Christ's heroic humility. The first broad side shows how spiritual growth in conversion (the blind man) and repentance (the woman who was a sinner) both imitate the growth of Christ in Mary's womb (the Annunciation and Visitation). The eucharistic images of the second broad side not only complement the poem's description of how the Cross presented the body of Christ to his followers, but provide an ordered meditation in five stages on the human and symbolic ways in

[29] See Kees Veelenturf, 'Irish High Crosses and Continental Art: Shades of Iconographical Ambiguity', in Colum Hourihane, ed., *From Ireland Coming: Irish Art from the Early Christian to the Late Gothic Period and its European Context* (Princeton, NJ, 2001), 83–101.

[30] Adomnán, *Vita Columbae*, 1:44, trans. Richard Sharpe, *Adomnán of Iona: Life of St Columba* (Harmondsworth, 1991), 147, discussed by Ó Carragáin, *Ritual and the Rood*, 153–60.

which Christ was to be known: as the fulfillment of the manna (return from Egypt), in the breaking of bread (Paul and Anthony), between two living creatures (acclaimed by the beasts), as the Lamb of God (Agnus Dei), and surrounded in glory by the four Evangelists with their symbols (cross-head). Among its other achievements, the Ruthwell Cross provides a measured response to the question of how images should be used in Christian worship. It is reasonable to assume that its designer was aware, like Bede, that the Emperor Leo III had espoused iconoclasm in 726 CE, and that he had been condemned by Popes Gregory II (715–31) and Gregory III (March 731–41). In particular, Gregory III formally condemned iconoclasm and excommunicated its adherents at a synod in St Peter's on 1 November 731.[31] The Ruthwell Cross brilliantly develops the unified vision of Incarnation and Passion already found in embryo on the upper half of the west side of the Bewcastle cross-shaft: both crosses are outstanding examples of the successful inculturation of Christianity in Northumbrian society.[32]

In order to explain the theological rationale for the ways in which the Ruthwell Cross builds and expands upon the links which the Bewcastle designer had already established between Christ's Incarnation and his Passion, I have had to give an 'elitist' reading of each monument. That reading has tried to imagine the issues which an educated ecclesiastic of the circle of Bishops Pehthelm (d. 735) or Acca (d. 740) would have seen as involved, implicitly in the structure of the Bewcastle Cross, and much more explicitly in the extended programme of the Ruthwell Cross. The Ruthwell Cross is unique. Never again would any sculptured monument in the insular world be provided with such an extensive set of descriptive and ekphrastic narrative *tituli*. Never again, anywhere in Western Europe, would vine-scrolls be adorned with vernacular verse *tituli* which make clear the significance of these vine-scrolls. The Ruthwell Cross was designed in a fleeting but glorious moment, probably in the 730s, probably by a designer in touch with the circle of Bede: in particular, with Bishops Acca of Hexham to the east, and Bishop Pehthelm of Whithorn to the west. The circle included Abbot Hwætberht of Wearmouth-Jarrow and Bishop Aethilwald of

---

[31] The controversy is examined in Ó Carragáin, *Ritual and the Rood*, 257–9.

[32] For good discussions of the theory and practice of inculturation, see Anscar J. Chupungco, *Liturgical Inculturation: Sacramentals, Religiosity, and Catechesis* (Collegeville, MN, 1992), 13–31; and especially Bruno Luiselli, *La formazione della cultura europea occidentale*, Biblioteca di cultura Romanobarbarica 7 (Rome, 2003).

Fig. 4. Overall view of the iconographic programme on the broad sides of the
Ruthwell Cross, from the casts in Durham Cathedral library:
(a) First broad side (which originally faced east), reading upwards:
base, Crucifixion; shaft: (1) Annunciation; (2) Christ healing the blind man;
(3) Repentance of Mary Magdalen; (4) (upper stone) the Visitation; (5) Archer.
(b) Second broad side (which originally faced west), reading upwards: shaft:
(1) Return from Egypt; (2) Saints Paul and Anthony break bread; (3) Christ
acclaimed by two animals; (4) (upper stone) John the Baptist acclaims the
Agnus Dei; (5) St Matthew and his angel.
(Photos: Durham University, Corpus of Anglo-Saxon Stone Sculpture).

Lindisfarne (AD 721–40). The Ruthwell Cross presents the most profound and coherent meditation on the unified rites of initiation to survive from early medieval Europe.

But the Ruthwell Cross was by no means simply intended for a monastic elite. All Christians made the baptismal renunciations, and all shared in the royal priesthood of Christ through baptism: therefore, the cross was profoundly relevant to the laity. The illiterate as well as monks could appreciate the universal images of its iconographic programme. Both the Bewcastle and Ruthwell crosses incorporate, as a major part of their designs, the image of the vine-scroll. Richard North has shown that the World-Tree was an important religious symbol in pre-Christian Northumbria, and has suggested that the vine-scrolls could, by local audiences, have been seen as a new version of that ancient religious symbol.[33] North's perception is consistent with that of Jennifer O'Reilly, who has emphasized that

> the form and iconography of the Ruthwell Cross, its Christology and use of the written word show the Anglo-Saxons to be a people engrafted into the universal Church and familiar with its Romanized culture but also highly creative in adapting its conventions and integrating elements from their own tradition.[34]

The Bewcastle falconer, seen within the iconographic sequence of the west side, embodies the hope that a local aristocrat, and no doubt other members of the community he led, would be incorporated within the eucharistic Body of Christ; and that his name would be found in the heavenly Book of Life. Ruthwell avoids any such reference to a local aristocracy: its universal human images, of pregnant women, of conversion and repentance, of hermits who share their bread in the desert, emphasize even more clearly that incorporation into Christ's eucharistic body was open to all men and women, not just to aristocrats. Ruthwell, even more clearly than the Bewcastle Cross, is an eschatological monument, and stands as a silent but eloquent criticism of all manmade power-structures, racial divisions and especially (with such scenes as the man blind from birth and the woman who was a sinner) of the importance of aristocratic birth. The monument was designed to attract the attention of both men and women: any woman who looked

---

[33] Richard North, *Heathen Gods in Old English Literature* (Cambridge, 1997), 287–94.
[34] J. O'Reilly, 'The Art of Authority', in Thomas Charles-Edwards, ed., *After Rome* (Oxford, 2003), 140–89, at 153.

on the Ruthwell Cross in the eighth century could not fail to be struck by the number of female images it presented: four on the first side of the monument, and at least one on the second (the base of which may possibly once have had a nativity scene, with yet another image of the Virgin Mary). Of the five surviving images of women, three are of the Virgin Mary.

The most startling way in which the Ruthwell designer transformed the visual ideas derived (directly or indirectly) from Bewcastle is the new placing of the vine-scrolls. Instead of the one great scroll, without inscription, on the east side at Bewcastle, balanced over against the images of Christ's body on the west side, the Ruthwell Cross has two matched vine-scrolls, one on each of the narrow sides, each spreading from the lower to the upper stones. The *tituli* for the vine-scrolls celebrated human courage: vital to eighth-century christology, but also available to audiences, in the eighth century and in modern times, who had (or have) no knowledge of or interest in christology. The poem's universality stems from the fact that it brought urgent christological issues into creative contact with the traditional values of the Anglo-Saxon aristocracy, to whom strength and courage were central heroic values. The verse *tituli* dramatized a startlingly new form of heroism, in which Christ the hero does not conquer or attack other men or women, but defeats the powers of darkness by pouring forth his blood for humankind, while enduring the mockery of his human enemies, and forbidding his follower the Cross from taking vengeance on these enemies. By retelling the Crucifixion in terms reminiscent of the Annunciation, the narrative presents the whole of Christ's life, from Incarnation to Crucifixion, as a single heroic act of self-giving, based on humility. Christ's humility was first manifested at the Incarnation, when, with the obedient cooperation of Mary, he 'emptied himself, taking the form of a slave, being born in human likeness, and being found in human form' (Phil. 2:7). It was supremely exemplified at the Crucifixion, when, with the obedient cooperation of another startled creature, Christ 'humbled himself and became obedient to the point of death – even death on a cross' (Phil. 2:8). The poet achieved a revolutionary synthesis: using the latest christology, he or she revalued traditional Germanic values, transforming them towards a new Christian vision of heroism. The narrative of the *tituli* is an outstanding example of the successful inculturation of christological thought. It is also an outstanding example of the Christian tradition of *sermo humilis*: like the gospels, they express central truths of the faith in simple, comprehensible and non-technical language. Their narrative is of great interest to historians of theology: it provides clear evidence that an English poet, and at least one early eighth-century Bernician community, had grasped the issues at stake in the struggle against Monotheletism, and had fully understood the kenotic christology central to the Epistle for the sixth Sunday of Lent, Philippians 2:5–11. But the modern reception of the Old English Crucifixion narrative (usually in the longer version embedded in the dream-vision frame of *The Dream of the Rood*) has shown that it can be appreciated, not only by theologians and Christian readers, but by peoples of other faiths, and with little or no knowledge of, or interest in, Christian theology. The Ruthwell narrative is a perfect example of unobtrusive yet effective catechesis. Already in the eighth century, it would no doubt have been appreciated at various levels.[35] All those at Ruthwell who heard the poem, even those who were as yet poorly instructed and who had as yet only a vague perception of Christian thought, would have seen it to be a vivid and memorable heroic narrative about a hero 'possessing all the values that attached to a *kyningc*, *hlafard*, and *dryctin*, [. . .] a terrifyingly brave warrior'.[36] Such an uneducated audience would have as yet little idea of the wider rationale which led this particular warrior to choose his own death on the gallows: to that extent the narrative might still have puzzled as well as fascinated them. They would have had, as yet, no perception of the relations between the heroic narrative and the vine-scrolls which it complements, nor of the relationships between the vine-scrolls and the iconography of the broad sides. They would probably have 'marginalized' the narrative, in the sense of thinking that it was not relevant to the vine-scrolls and to the programmes of the broad sides. But even this primitive and uneducated understanding of the vine-scroll and its *tituli* could have provided a useful foundation on which an educated nun, monk or cleric might bring them gradually to an awareness of Christ's heroic humility, and to appreciate (for example) how the second *titulus*, in which the Cross hands on Christ's body to his followers who 'beheld there the Lord of Heaven', was complemented by the eucharistic images of the second broad side (fig. 4 (b)). Even elementary readings of the Ruthwell Cross could (and still

---

[35] For a fine analysis of how Anglo-Saxon high crosses were appreciated on various levels by the original audiences, and also by modern scholars, see J. Hawkes, 'Reading Stone', in Karkov and Orton, eds, *Theorizing*, 5–20.

[36] Orton, 'Rethinking', 53.

can) lead, gradually and naturally, to a deeper appreciation of the monument's coherence. Monks or nuns, educated by regular liturgical observance, who lived their lives in the protecting shadow of the Ruthwell Cross, would naturally come, over the years, to a full appreciation of its profound unity, its theological complexity, and how the vine-scrolls, with their unique vernacular verse *tituli*, made the cross speak from the heart of its experience on Good Friday. The Ruthwell designer deftly subverted all facile dichotomies between the 'secular' and the 'sacred', or between what is 'popular' and what is 'elitist'.

University College, Cork

ELITE REFORM AND POPULAR HERESY IN c.1000: 'REVITALIZATION MOVEMENTS' AS A MODEL FOR UNDERSTANDING RELIGIOUS DISSIDENCE HISTORICALLY

by CLAIRE TAYLOR

AMONGST various features still being evaluated as characteristic of West Frankish society in c.1000 AD, one of the most striking is that into the middle of the century a range of essentially unrelated and geographically widespread sources speak of 'heresy' newly affecting the populace. But how should we interpret these apparently diverse phenomena?[1] Of the models which heresiologists explore, too often overlooked is that proposed by Janet Nelson in this very forum in 1971. Her thesis, that a 'crisis in theodicy' produced a cognitive need for new explanations which 'heresy' answered, whilst not explicitly anthropological, focused on understanding phenomena within societal wholes.[2] This explanation was challenged by the anthropologist Talal Asad, who argued that heretical activity simply indicated urban movements over which clerics were unable to extend their authority.[3]

This paper proposes an understanding of elite and popular religious forms through a re-examination of Nelson's case, reasserting its validity by arguing that her conclusions correspond to an anthropological model for understanding religious innovation proposed by Anthony Wallace in the 1950s. Wallace asserted that similar religious phenomena should be classed as 'Revitalization Movements' (hereafter: RM).[4] I suggest, first, that the reforming 'Peace of God' movement,

---

[1] The most recent overview of the sources and interpretation of popular heresy in c.1000 is in M. D. Lambert, *Medieval Heresy: Popular Movements from the Gregorian Reform to the Reformation* (3rd edn, Oxford, 2002), 32–40.

[2] J. L. Nelson, 'Society, Theodicy and the Origins of Heresy: towards a Reassessment of the Medieval Evidence', in Derek Baker, ed., *Schism, Heresy and Religious Protest*, SCH 9 (London, 1972), 65–77.

[3] T. Asad, 'Medieval Heresy: an Anthropological View', *Social History* 11 (1986), 345–62.

[4] A. F. C. Wallace, 'Revitalization Movements', *American Anthropologist* 58 (1956), 264–81, repr. in William A. Lessa and Evon Z. Vogt, eds, *Reader in Comparative Religion: an Anthropological Approach* (4th edn, New York and London, 1979), 421–9. See also Wallace's *Religion: an Anthropological View* (New York, 1966), 31–4.

initiated at the close of the tenth century, was a failed elite attempt to resolve the crisis Nelson identifies: popular responses to both perceived social crisis and elite religious forms precipitated heresy. Secondly, such manifestations of heresy may be regarded as RM. Conclusions include some methodological implications, and the suggestion that the RM model helps to reconcile some historiographical tensions. This essay is, as Nelson's was, primarily concerned with ways of regarding heresy. It is beyond its scope to discuss in detail the many accounts of 'heresy' in the eleventh-century sources.

Eleventh-Century Society, the Peace of God and Heresy

Central to the cases made by both Asad and Nelson is the understanding that the sources must be read in the context of the wider society that produced them and in which their subjects operated. What, then, are the societal features that might help us understand the nature and origins of 'heresy'? An influential orthodoxy concerning West Frankish society runs thus. Public power, embodied by the Carolingian monarchy and delegated to regional servants such as counts, collapsed along with the dynasty in the tenth century. Authority was usurped by the servants of those servants: castellans and their retinues of lawless knights. They stole the resources of the free peasantry and reduced it to serfdom, removing from it access to public courts, the right to carry arms, and access to traditional common resources, and they imposed novel taxes and fees. This all took place within a few decades, was accompanied by environmental disasters, and was perceived as both rapid and illegal.[5]

This view of political change and its social impact has been challenged and the specific significance of the decades c.1000 undermined.[6] But this revision needs to recognize that critical qualification was applied to the orthodoxy from the outset: Nelson, for example, considered society disorientating as much because of increased horizontal mobility – rural-urban migration – as because of oppressive social relations.[7] Legal and economic sources emanating from the abbeys are at

---

[5] Originating with George Duby, *La Société au XIe et XIIe siècles dans la région mâconnaise* (Paris, 1953).

[6] Dominique Barthélemy, *La Mutation de l'an mil a-t-elle eu lieu? Servage et chevalerie dans la France des Xe et XIe siècles* (Paris, 1997); F. L. Cheyette, 'George Duby's *Mâconnais* after Fifty Years: Reading it Then and Reading it Now', *JMH* 28 (2002), 291–317.

[7] Nelson, 'Society, Theodicy and the Origins of Heresy', 68–72.

the root of the interpretative problem: the monks are certainly guilty of exaggerating disorder in their own interests as bastions of legitimate authority. Yet the scholarship on heresy in *c.*1000 still tends towards the thesis of significant social disruption. The reason is surely that, in whatever manner we read the cartularies, the assertion by clerical narratives, letters, and councils of novel and widespread heresy amongst the populace is evidence *in itself* of social disturbance, however we choose to interpret 'heresy'.

The monks responded to change by identifying themselves as protectors of the *rustici* against the warrior caste and, in the context of this ideological alliance, the tenth century saw a rise in popular interest in the relics and cults of saints, centred on the abbeys hosting them, and, in 989, the calling of the first 'Peace Council' at Charroux in Poitou.[8] The Peace united the saints and clergy with both the populace and the last remnants of 'legitimate' aristocratic power. But whereas it was once asserted that its legislation and spiritual sanctions were initiated by ordinary people invoking the *clamor* of the assembled free in the only forum that now recognized it,[9] the most convincing scholarship sees the Peace as an opportunity for churchmen and princes to extend authority over the peasantry as well as over the warriors: the crowd was no longer recorded as in attendance at councils by *c.*1030, and was no less in bondage on monastic estates than on those of secular lords.[10]

Current historiography thus tends towards the following model for understanding heresy in *c.*1000: 'heresy' – for it was not really doctrinal – was social protest against a crisis affecting the majority of the population, disillusioned with elite solutions. The sources note a preoccupation with heretical claims to live a simple, peaceful, egalitarian and communal life, and historians consider this a conscious imitation of the first Christians in a reaction against ecclesiastical wealth and novel assertions of sacramental authority. The heretics were accordingly defamed in mischievous discourses attributing to them the Manichaean misnomer. In addition bishops and monks, quarrelling over their respective authority and liberties, also accused each other, accounting

---

[8] *Sacrorum conciliorum: nova et amplissima collectio*, ed. J. D. Mansi, 54 vols in 59 (Graz, 1960–1), 29: 89–90.

[9] L. C. Mackinney, 'The People and Public Opinion in the Eleventh-Century Peace Movement', *Speculum* 5 (1930), 181–206.

[10] Most importantly in Thomas Head and Richard Landes, eds, *The Peace of God: Social Violence and Religious Response in France around the Year 1000* (Ithaca, NY and London, 1992) and R. I. Moore, *The First European Revolution, c.970–1215* (Oxford, 2000), 102–5.

for 'heresy' even amongst clergy. In other words, churchmen sought ideological weapons against 'heretics' who laid the blame for social evils at their door.[11] A more marginal model, undergoing an attempt at its rehabiliation, identifies genuine dualism and deviant cosmology that is not the fancy of clerics. It asserts the influence of Bogomilism, a Balkan form of dualism shunning the created world, the heresy being deliberately introduced to the West.[12] Both interpretations owe a good deal to the study of the historical societies in question rather than just of the form and features of 'heresy'.

Anthropological Approaches to History and Heresy

The social sciences heavily influence historical approaches. By and large, we have absorbed the implications of their debates on epistemology and come out relatively unscathed in comparison to the anthropological discipline. Perhaps because we are further removed from the object of our study, we can evaluate the way societies have identified or constructed and then persecuted 'the Other', for example, without concluding that we are in fact writing about ourselves![13] Furthermore, whilst constructing 'images of the World . . . representative of different epochs and different cultural traditions', as Aaron Gurevich put it,[14] we also observe similarities and make generalizations about human experience and activity in its historical context, including that of societal change. Context, be it power, environment, ideology, or culture, explains why sometimes past societies look similar, even familiar, but sometimes very unlike each other and our own. Human

[11] R. I. Moore, *The Origins of European Dissent* (2nd edn, Oxford, 1985), 23–45; G. Lobrichon, 'The Chiaroscuro of Heresy: Early Eleventh-Century Aquitaine as Seen from Auxerre', in Head and Landes, eds, *Peace of God*, 80–103. Relevant sources are the 'Letter of Héribert', in Lobrichon, 'The Chiaroscuro', 85–6, and *Ademari Cabannensis Chronichon*, ed. P. Bourgain *et al.*, CChr.CM 129 (1999), 170, 180.

[12] M. Frassetto, 'The Sermons of Adémar of Chabannes and the Letter of Héribert. New Sources Concerning the Origins of Medieval Heresy', *Revue Bénédictine* 109 (1999), 324–40; Claire Taylor, 'The Letter of Héribert of Périgord as a Source for Dualist Heresy in the Society of Early Eleventh-Century Aquitaine', *JMH* 26 (2000), 313–49.

[13] Amongst accounts useful to historians are Paul Rabinow's 'Representations Are Social Facts: Modernity and Post-Modernity in Anthropology', in idem, *Essays on the Anthropology of Reason* (Princeton, NJ, 1996), 28–58, and Anna Green and Kathleen Troup, 'Anthropology and Ethnohistorians', in eaedem, eds, *The Houses of History: a Critical Reader in Twentieth-Century History and Theory* (Manchester, 1999), 172–81.

[14] Aaron Gurevich, 'Historical Anthropology and the Science of History', in idem, *Historical Anthropology of the Middle Ages* (Chicago, IL, and Cambridge, 1992), 3–20, 4.

needs are in some ways unchanging, but are conceptualized, expressed and fulfilled in very different ways depending on context.

But the adoption of anthropological approaches by historians is not unproblematic. Philippe Buc has reintroduced uncertainties concerning our supposed assumption of academic and cultural distance from medieval subject matter and the neutrality of imposing social-scientific categories upon societies engaging in complex and integrated forms of behaviour. He warns against accepting textual examples of 'ritual' as representations of actual events.[15] Indeed, the historian faces a problem not encountered by all anthropologists: the object of our enquiry is not the study of human activity, but of texts purporting to tell us about it.[16] A possible application of this scepticism in heresiology concerns 'evidence' in the sources of diabolic rituals performed by 'heretics'. Buc would have us ask what the accusations really signify. But historians of heresy have never believed the sources in this respect. Far from being *misled* by sociologists into accepting the surface meaning of such reports, the best model for understanding authorial intent – the construction of a deviant 'otherness' – owes a good deal to the observations of social scientists.[17] Thus, as Nelson put it in 1980, heresy is 'now being studied in the context of a whole range of environmental influences including the social, economic, political and psychological as well as the intellectual'.[18] Furthermore, if the historian can attempt to debunk 'ritual' as a social-scientific anachronism, the anthropologist – Talal Asad in fact – can question the validity of separating activity in the historically-constructed sphere of 'religion' from other forms of human activity.[19] Alexandra Walsham observes of Buc's stance that '(i)f we may not utilize any model which is rooted in the discourses upon which we necessarily rely to recover the past then surely we are left

---

[15] Philippe Buc, *The Dangers of Ritual: between Early Medieval Texts and Social Scientific Theory* (Princeton, NJ, and Oxford, 2001), esp. 1–12.

[16] Of the enormous body of literature addressing this problem, important recent approaches in the context of heresy can be found in Caterina Bruschi and Peter Biller, eds, *Texts and the Repression of Medieval Heresy* (York, 2003).

[17] See, for example, R. I. Moore, *The Formation of a Persecuting Society: Power and Deviance in Western Europe, 950–1250* (Oxford, 1987) and Dominique Iogna-Prat, *Order and Exclusion: Cluny and Christendom Face Heresy, Judaism, and Islam, 1000–1150*, trans. G. R. Edwards (Ithaca, NY, and London, 2002).

[18] J. Nelson, 'Religion in "Histoire Total": Some Recent Work on Medieval Heresy and Popular Religion', *Religion* 10 (1980), 60–85, 60.

[19] Talal Asad, 'The Construction of Religion as an Anthropological Category', in idem, *Genealogies of Religion: Discipline and Reasons of Power in Christianity and Islam* (Baltimore, MD, 1993 [1982]), 27–54.

without any heuristic tools at all'.[20] It is clear to historians that they should bring to their approach an understanding that human activity in the past can be interpreted using anthropological tools only within the context of critical engagement with both historical societies in a diachronic sense and the historiographical legacy of their interpretation.

Thus the scholarship addresses phenomena such as popular heresy via the study of society as 'an inclusive system of human relationships and organisation within which religion constitutes a major component'.[21] If ritual and belief preserve social cohesion,[22] popular heresy may represent the assertion of a new basis for social cohesion. For Nelson, Carolingian ritual and belief accounted for suffering adequately, enabling social and psychological stability in which members of the clerical elite were society's 'ritual specialists'. But religious dissidence can arise when 'individuals are exposed to new types of social experience for which their religion offers no meaningful patterning'.[23] The mismatch between how the ritual specialists portrayed the world in c.1000 and what was actually experienced led to an ideational search for cognitively satisfying forms.

But to Asad, 'heretics' were *themselves* social change, not a response to it. They 'did not seek a fitting cosmology for a new society. . . . They sought . . . to create new forms of social life.'[24] The Church, unable to extend its stabilizing influence over new movements, identified them as in Error, in opposition to the Truth. As Asad puts it elsewhere,

(t)he medieval Church did not attempt to establish absolute uniformity of practice; on the contrary, its authoritative discourse was always concerned to specify differences, gradations, exceptions. What it sought was the subjection of all practice to a unified authority, to a single authentic source that could tell truth from falsehood.[25]

Heresy is therefore something the elite conceptualizes as not lying

---

[20] Review of *Dangers of Ritual*, *P&P* 180 (2003), 277–87, 285; see also the review by Janet Nelson in *Speculum* 78 (2003), 847–51.
[21] Nelson, 'Society, Theodicy and the Origins of Heresy', 65.
[22] Emile Durkheim, *The Elementary Forms of Religious Life*, trans. Joseph Ward Swain (2nd edn, Glencoe, 1965), esp. 262–3, 465–70.
[23] Nelson, 'Society, Theodicy and the Origins of Heresy', 70, 72.
[24] Asad, 'Medieval Heresy', 360.
[25] Asad, 'The Construction of Religion', 30.

within society and being 'safe', but as being *outside* and 'dangerous', which danger 'is a form of inimical power'.[26]

Asad's view that heresy is a social product and is not arrived at through cognitive processes resonates well with interpretations associated with the dominant school of thought on heresy in *c.*1000 noted above. Nelson's is one that might appeal to those suspecting dualist influence – although she in no sense allies herself with this interpretation – in which heresy arises out of a cognitive need to answer a doctrinal *and* social question: *unde malum* (whence evil)?[27] I shall suggest that the two positions are not mutually exclusive.

Revitalization Movements and Heresy

The concept of the RM was first outlined by Wallace in 1956. He asserted common traits in many movements that sought to transform the spiritual and material life. Social scientists have used labels such as 'nativistic movements', 'cargo cults', and 'messianic communities' for movements he considered as having some 'genotypical structures independent of local cultural differences'.[28] They emerge where individuals consciously perceive their lives to have been transformed in a manner detrimental to their interests and are experiencing transformational stress. Wallace did not understate differences between these movements, and accounted for these in terms of differing historical circumstances. Neither is the RM model in any sense a deterministic or predictive one. As such it has much to offer historians in identifying how a past movement arose, what determined the choice and timing of its forms, and why it progressed or failed to progress.

Three examples of indigenous North American RM illustrate Wallace's model. Two, addressed in Wallace's own work, concern the Iroquois of New York State. In the fifteenth century, Hiawatha's communion with the god Dekanawidah enabled him to transform his own degenerate life and unite five warring Iroquois tribes into a mutually protective League at the Great Council at Onodaga by undermining the traditional Iroquois supernatural elite and the tradition of

---

[26] Mary Douglas, *Purity and Danger: an Analysis of Concepts of Pollution and Taboo* (London, 1966); Asad, 'Medieval Heresy', 346.

[27] For discussion of schools influencing Nelson's and Asad's types of interpretations, see Alan Barnard, *History and Theory in Anthropology* (Cambridge, 2000), esp. 61–79, 120–38.

[28] Wallace, 'Revitalization', 268.

blood feuding, substituting for these a 'Condolence Ritual'.[29] The resultant thriving society floundered again following American Independence until it acted upon the visions of a Seneca chief, Handsome Lake, embracing a revivalist and ascetic culture.[30] The ethnographer Alice Beck Kehoe identified a third RM in the nineteenth-century Ghost Dance of the Paiute, founded by Jack Wilson in the context of cultural annihilation through confrontations with Europeans. In an ecstatic vision, ancestors, eternally young and happy in a promised land full of game, instructed Wilson in the new ritual which, if performed in the right way and at the right times, would hasten a unity of the living with the ancestors, undermining Christian doctrine concerning the path to salvation.[31]

This article is not the first attempt to apply Wallace's model to an understanding of eleventh-century Christendom. Around the time that Nelson and Asad were considering heresy, Vladimir G. Marinich identified popular *volkhu* uprisings by Kievans as RM. The imposition of Christianity on their pagan culture, following the conversion of Prince Vladimir in 988 AD, led to disorder especially where it coincided with other stress-inducing hardship such as famine. Uprisings were led by shamans, experiencing prophetic visions which legitimized a diverse pagan culture that had been the chief victim of Vladimir's new, deliberately unifying, religious administration. The characteristics of these uprisings, as in the North American cases, were expressed in indigenous forms which, like their targets, were constructions of a historically specific context.[32]

RM share certain key elements. They conceptualize a relationship with the *divine* in a new way, and adherents seek consciously to re-order the *world*, or at least human society. Significantly, they do not usually originate within religious authority, with Nelson's 'ritual specialists', who correspond to Wallace's 'ecclesiastical cult institutions': professionals supported economically by the laity and claiming authority over it 'in areas of behaviour . . . extending beyond ritual itself'.[33] Instead, they tend to emerge within the ranks of the laity and

---

[29] A. F. C. Wallace, *The Death and Rebirth of the Seneca* (New York, 1970), 97–8.

[30] Wallace, *Religion*, 31–4, and *Death*, 239–337.

[31] Alice Beck Kehoe, *The Ghost Dance: Ethnohistory and Revitalization* (Fort Worth, TX, 1989).

[32] Vladimir G. Marinich, 'Revitalization Movements in Kievan Russia', *Journal for the Scientific Study of Religion* 15 (1976), 61–8.

[33] Wallace, *Religion*, 87–8.

are a 'conscious, organized effort . . . to construct a more satisfying culture'.[34] Wallace's understanding of societies that produce RM accords well with Nelson's account of that which gave rise to heretical movements in c.1000. He says

> . . . religion at times is unable to patch up the dissonant cognitions of members of societies structurally riven by internal strain. . . . Reformative religious movements often occur in disorganised societies; these new religions, far from being conservative, are often radically destructive of existing institutions, aiming to resolve conflict not by manipulation of the self but by manipulation of the real world.[35]

Typically RM involve five stages: the Steady State, the Period of Individual Stress, the Period of Cultural Distortion, the Period of Revitalization, and the New Steady State. The first is like Nelson's Carolingian era in which there is a relative balance between perceived suffering and the ability of the ritual specialists to account for it, rendering it tolerable.[36] But in stage two, stress-reducing mechanisms cannot ameliorate the effects of phenomena such as increasing political or social subjection, climatic failure, economic distress or epidemic. Stage three is typified by 'anxiety over the loss of a meaningful way of life' and changed behaviour patterns in an attempt to adapt and regain control. However, 'piecemeal cultural substitution will multiply situations of mutual conflict and misunderstanding'.[37] This corresponds well to Nelson's identification of a process whereby theodicy is resolved 'in terms of a heavy reinvestment of religious capital in received religious belief and practice', clergy manipulating 'recognised symbols' in attempting to 'restore equilibrium' between humans and the supernatural.[38] Such was surely the impetus behind the Peace of God.

Where such efforts fail, a 'Period of Revitalization' may begin, typically with a distinct starting point. Adémar of Chabannes's linkage of the tragic death of pilgrims crushed at Saint-Martial to the appearance of heresy in Aquitaine, noted by Richard Landes, may suggest such a

---

[34] Ibid., 30.

[35] Ibid.

[36] But see Nelson's more recent words of warning about overestimating the stability of the Carolingian era in her review of Head and Landes, eds, *Peace of God*, in *Speculum* 69 (1994), 163–9.

[37] Wallace, 'Revitalization', 263–75, 270.

[38] Nelson, 'Society, Theodicy and the Origins of Heresy', 69–70, 72.

rupture.[39] The rupture is often marked by a dream or vision like those experienced by Jack Wilson, Hiawatha and Handsome Lake. An obvious medieval analogy is the peasant Leutard in the diocese of Châlons whose mental universe was transformed in *c.*1000 through a dream and who, like the North Americans, reformed his own life before spreading the message.[40] Expressed in the revealed message are 'longings for the establishment of an ideal state of stable and satisfying human and supernatural relations'.[41] Heretics in Périgord wanted property to be owned communally, and accounts such as that in the diocese of Arras speak of new rituals to be enacted in order that, as Wallace would understand it, harmony be restored between the human and divine worlds.[42]

If the visionary founder is heeded, they typically attract two types of follower: those first initiates who remain very close to the originator, and a second level of adherents attracted by them. The immediate circle may also experience visions, as were offered to converts to the heresy discovered in 1022 at Orléans.[43] Central to the effectiveness of such movements is the deliberate, widespread diffusion of the message by this inner circle. Modes of organization within RM are thus not organic or fluid, and this makes sense in essentially non-literate, oral cultures: it is the authority of those closest to the founder that preserves the message intact, not the permanence of written words. Kehoe and Melburn Thurman note proselytizing activity connecting the Ghost Dance with the Shawnee 'Prophet Dance' through a woman very close to the Shawnee movement's founder.[44] Certain key Italian figures were considered by Adémar of Chabannes and Bishop Gerard of Arras to have imported heresy to Orléans and Arras-Cambrai.

At the heart of the message is always the reconfiguration or rejection of the traditional religious elite and the rituals and symbols dominating stages one to three. Here we might consider heretical scorn visited upon

[39] See Richard Landes, *Relics, Apocalypse and the Deceits of History: Ademar of Chabannes, 989–1034* (Cambridge, MA, and London, 1995), 175–6 and 199–203.

[40] Rodulfus Glaber, *The Five Books of the Histories*, ed. J. France and N. Bulst (Oxford, 1989), 89–91.

[41] Wallace, 'Revitalization', 270.

[42] The 'Letter of Héribert' and *Acta Synodi Atrebatensis in Manicheos*, PL 142, 1269–1312.

[43] Paul of Chartres, *Gesta Synodi Aurelianensis*, in M. Bouquet *et al.*, *Recueil des historiens des Gaules et de la France*, 24 vols (Paris, 1738–1904), 2: 536–9.

[44] Kehoe, *Ghost Dance*, 8, 99; M. D. Thurman, 'The Shawnee Prophet's Movement and the Origins of the Prophet Dance', *Current Anthropology* 25 (1984), 530–1.

churches in Périgord and on a saint's cult in the Bazadais.[45] A new cosmology is offered and new rituals reflect this mental shift, producing new solidarities. There are good examples of both in sources for heresy in Périgord and at Orléans as well as in the North American adoption of new forms of political authority, conflict resolution and social activity. In each American case collective renewal and purity of action was central, just as it was to several of the heretical communities described in early eleventh-century Europe.

There are five sub-stages to the 'Period of Revitalization' and the early eleventh-century movements can all be seen as being destroyed in the final stage, 'Adaptation', where Wallace notes many historical movements to have failed. Here, the revolutionary organization encounters resistance from a powerful social faction. In successful movements, the message is toned down, political accommodation sought, or force used to impose change. None of these options was open in the eleventh century to people already voiceless politically and literally disarmed. In Wallace's terms, they failed because of two factors: the relative realism of their doctrines – they could not, realistically, be taken up by the elite – and the vehemence with which the elite sought to marginalize them.[46] Thus eleventh-century RM collapsed or were destroyed.

Conclusion

The significance of failed attempts by a religious elite to maintain the Steady State on its own terms is that religious vibrancy may become the prerogative of lower social strata. What emerges are religious forms resonating with both Wallace's generalized model of RM and Nelson's account of a cognitively satisfying resolution to the crisis in theodicy. Here both Wallace and Nelson are describing a functionalist process. But we do not need to reject Asad's interpretation of what took place in *c.*1000. What made sense cognitively to individuals was surely influenced by, though not a slave to, what was structurally embedded. Revitalizing forms in *c.*1000 reflect the traditional Christian tension between the Spiritual and the Material, as Good and Evil, a tension already expressed within Carolingian society but which also lay at the heart of influences that *could* have been picked up from foreign or past

---

[45] *The Book of Sainte Foy*, ed. and trans. P. Sheingorn (Philadelphia, PA, 1995), 212–13.
[46] Wallace, 'Revitalization', 270–5.

movements. So heresy in c.1000 reflects a combination of choice and impulse. Whether 'heretics' were therefore social reformers, Christian primitivists, Bogomil-inspired, or even neo-Platonists, they were engaging with the Purity/Danger tension at the heart of Christian revivalist morality. The elite, called to account but failing in its public duty of protection, was rejected, in Nelson's terms, and redrew the line, in Asad's, placing the 'heretic' beyond society. To some extent, therefore, RM correspond to a variety of sociological models and resolve tensions that led a frustrated Nelson to remark that 'human beings (are the) subjects not the objects of history'.[47]

In addition, the RM model can be employed wherever we stand on the social context for heresy: it is *perception* of change for the worse that is significant to RM, not a demonstrable pattern or time-scale for change. But the model is not so flexible and all-encompassing that it can describe *any* radical religious movement, rendering it useless to the historian. RM operate primarily in the popular sphere, so do not describe most early Christian heresies. Neither does the model apply to Waldensianism, Lollardy or Catharism, which did not require a radically altered social life for the *entire* community they addressed. RM must reshape elite-derived cosmology, and as such cannot describe most non-conformists or the orthodox religious doctrines of social movements arising in the English Civil War. It is the combination of cosmological innovation *and* social transformation that limits the set of movements which the model describes.

Finally, if the model usefully describes aspects of what occurred in c.1000, is it helpful in studying heresy further? Certain phenomena seem common to RM and so it seems useful to explore generalizations in explaining why. But it follows that what is less common or even unique to individual RM is best explained in a historicized sense. Consider two examples. We should probably look for purely historical explanations for clerical assertions that many eleventh-century heretics rejected private property and shared everything they had. Communalism is not a feature of all RM, but is an influence locatable within cultural specificities. In the eleventh century, perhaps Apostolic values or those of earlier monastic movements were being imitated (RM often revisit values of eras when 'things were better'). Alternatively, was the concept imported by others already practising it, for example prosely-

---

[47] Nelson, 'Society, Theodicy and the Origins of Heresy', 67–8.

tizing Bogomils? The eighteenth-century Iroquois were influenced to adopt the same ideal by Quaker missionaries.[48] A combination seems perfectly plausible. Conversely, common to most RM are revivalist phenomena such as extreme asceticism, visions, and repetitious or strenuous ritual. They may sensibly be understood as psychologically empowering responses to the sorts of social stresses and failed elite processes producing RM. Yet the actual forms and content of these phenomena vary greatly and surely derive from either what is already known or what can be learned. They *must* be studied in this latter context, but we *may* also learn much from considering them as reoccurring forms of human activity. This is the sort of linkage historians are sometimes unwilling to accept. But many of the questions we are used to addressing in an eleventh-century context might be explored with new eyes if we consider that they are also applicable to other popular movements and historical settings.

University of Nottingham

---

[48] Wallace, *Death and Rebirth*, 264.

ELITE AND POPULAR PERCEPTIONS OF *IMITATIO CHRISTI* IN TWELFTH-CENTURY CRUSADE SPIRITUALITY*

by WILLIAM J. PURKIS

FROM the time of the proclamation of the First Crusade in 1095 to at least the first decade of the twelfth century,[1] there was an apparently universal understanding amongst the people of Christendom that those who joined the pilgrimage-in-arms that set out to liberate Jerusalem and the Holy Land should be regarded as imitators of Christ. This was remarkable, for the imitation of Christ was understood by contemporaries to be the paramount ideal of spiritual perfection and, before 1095, only attainable by a total withdrawal from the world and a commitment to a monastic way of life.[2] Yet with Pope Urban II's Clermont sermon, the spirituality that was previously the preserve of those *milites Christi* who fought spiritual battles in the cloister was now also available to those who fought for Christ in the world.[3] As the biographer of one prominent first crusader famously put it, before the proclamation of the crusade, his subject was 'uncertain whether to follow in the footsteps of the Gospel or the world. But after the call to arms in the service of Christ, the twofold reason for fighting inflamed him beyond belief.'[4]

The idea that the crusaders were following Christ's example was

* I am grateful to the Arts and Humanities Research Board for supporting the research that led to this paper.

[1] For the purposes of this paper, my analysis of the sources for the First Crusade does not go further than the first generation of histories, most of which were written before 1110.

[2] On the idea of *imitatio Christi*, see in particular Ernest J. Tinsley, *The Imitation of God in Christ: an Essay on the Biblical Basis of Christian Spirituality* (London, 1960); Giles Constable, 'The Ideal of the Imitation of Christ', in idem, *Three Studies in Medieval Religious and Social Thought* (Cambridge, 1995), 143–248.

[3] For the preaching of the First Crusade, see especially H. E. J. Cowdrey, 'Pope Urban II's Preaching of the First Crusade', *History* 55 (1970), 177–88, repr. in idem, *Popes, Monks and Crusaders* (London, 1984), XVI; Jonathan Riley-Smith, *The First Crusade and the Idea of Crusading* (London, 1986), 13–30; Penny J. Cole, *The Preaching of the Crusades to the Holy Land, 1095–1270* (Cambridge, MA, 1991), 1–36.

[4] Ralph of Caen, 'Gesta Tancredi', *Recueil des Historiens des Croisades: Historiens Occidentaux*, ed. Académie des Inscriptions et Belles-Lettres, 5 vols (Paris, 1844–95) [hereafter: *RHC Oc.*], 3: 587–716, 606.

recorded across the sources, from eyewitness narratives such as the *Gesta Francorum* (whose anonymous author was probably a cleric)[5] to the grander monastic histories of men such as Robert of Rheims and Baldric of Bourgueil,[6] and from diplomatic sources such as charters[7] to the letters the crusaders wrote themselves whilst on the march.[8] The presence of *imitatio Christi* ideology can be most readily identified through the association of the crusader's undertaking with certain passages from the New Testament. In particular, the act of taking the cross – the outward mark of the individual's commitment to the crusade – appears to have been viewed as a tangible way to fulfil Christ's instruction that 'If anyone would come after me, he must deny himself and take up his cross and follow me' (Matt. 16:24).[9]

By travelling to the Holy Land as armed pilgrims, the crusaders were seen to be following Christ in both a literal and an analogical sense. Describing the completion of his journey to the Holy Sepulchre after Jerusalem had been successfully recovered, Fulcher of Chartres wrote that

> With this visit . . . our protracted task was finished. When we gazed upon the much longed-for Holy of Holies we were filled with immense joy. Oh how often we recalled to mind the prophecy of David which said, *We shall worship in the place where His feet have stood* (Ps. 131:7).[10]

But whilst the fulfilment of the itineraries and traditions of the Jerusalem pilgrimage served to reinforce the association between the crusaders and Christ's life on earth, it was as crusaders – as distinct from peaceful pilgrims – that these individuals were truly understood to be imitators of Christ. This distinction is important, for the men that left

---

[5] *Gesta Francorum et aliorum Hierosolimitanorum*, ed. and trans. Rosalind Hill (London, 1962), 1. On the authorship of this text, see Colin Morris, 'The *Gesta Francorum* as Narrative History', *Reading Medieval Studies* 19 (1993), 55–71.

[6] Robert of Rheims, 'Historia Iherosolimitana', *RHC Oc.*, 3: 717–882, 729–30; Baldric of Bourgueil, 'Historia Jerosolimitana', *RHC Oc.*, 4: 1–111, 16.

[7] See Jonathan Riley-Smith, *The First Crusaders, 1095–1131* (Cambridge, 1997), 62–3.

[8] *Die Kreuzzugsbriefe aus den Jahren 1088–1100*, ed. Heinrich Hagenmeyer (Innsbruck, 1901), 164.

[9] See Giles Constable, 'Jerusalem and the Sign of the Cross (with particular reference to the cross of pilgrimage and crusading in the twelfth century)', in Lee I. Levine, ed., *Jerusalem: its Sanctity and Centrality to Judaism, Christianity, and Islam* (New York, 1999), 371–81.

[10] Fulcher of Chartres, *Historia Hierosolymitana (1095–1127)*, ed. Heinrich Hagenmeyer (Heidelberg, 1913), 331–2; translation from Frances Rita Ryan, *A History of the Expedition to Jerusalem (1095–1127)* (Knoxville, TN, 1969), 131–2.

Europe in 1096 were by no means the first to undertake a penitential pilgrimage to the East.[11] They were, however, the first to undertake what Guibert of Nogent referred to as a 'new pilgrimage',[12] an expedition that required its participants to engage in warfare as part of their devotional exercise. By taking the cross, the crusader was believed to be showing his willingness not only to fight for Christ, but also to be martyred in battle if necessary, just as Christ had sacrificed his life for mankind.[13] In a letter to the West composed in 1098 to encourage recruitment for the crusade, the Greek patriarch of Jerusalem made the following exhortation: 'Come, therefore, we pray, to fight in the army of the Lord in the same place in which the Lord fought, in which Christ suffered for us, leaving you an example that you should follow in his footsteps.'[14] This motif was used by a number of commentators, but it is in Raymond of Aguilers's account of the crusade that the most striking expression of the idea can be found. Raymond described how Christ himself had appeared in a vision during the siege of Antioch in 1098 and, depicted as suffering on the cross, announced that he had ranked the crusaders into 'five orders', each of which was likened to one of the five wounds he had suffered during his Passion. The first of these orders were those crusaders whom he believed to be his closest followers:

> The first order is not afraid of spears, or swords, or any other kind of torment. This order is like me. For I came to Jerusalem, not stopping to think about swords and lances, clubs and sticks, and lastly the cross. They die for me as I died for them. And I am in them, and they are in me.[15]

At the turn of the twelfth century, therefore, there appears to have been unanimous agreement over how the *imitatio Christi* ideal was associated with crusading. Yet by the time of the Second Crusade

---

11 For Jerusalem pilgrimage before the First Crusade, see Riley-Smith, *First Crusaders*, 23–39.

12 Guibert of Nogent, *Dei gesta per Francos et cinq autres textes*, ed. Robert B. C. Huygens, CChr.CM 127a (1996), 136.

13 See Jonathan Riley-Smith, 'Death on the First Crusade', in David W. Loades, ed., *The End of Strife* (Edinburgh, 1984), 14–31; H. E. J. Cowdrey, 'Martyrdom and the First Crusade', in Peter W. Edbury, ed., *Crusade and Settlement: Papers Read at the First Conference of the Society for the Study of the Crusades and the Latin East and Presented to R. C. Smail* (Cardiff, 1985), 46–56; Shmuel Shepkaru, 'To Die for God: Martyrs' Heaven in Hebrew and Latin Crusade Narratives', *Speculum* 77 (2002), 311–41.

14 *Die Kreuzzugsbriefe*, 148.

15 *Le 'Liber' de Raymond d'Aguilers*, ed. John H. and Laurita L. Hill (Paris, 1969), 113–14.

(1145–9) a clear discrepancy had emerged between the language of crusade preaching and commonly held understandings of crusade ideology. It is therefore in the 1140s that a separation between 'elite' and 'popular' ideas about this aspect of crusade spirituality can first be identified.

In the context of the Second Crusade, to consider the attitudes of the elite is, for the most part, to consider the official preaching of the expedition by Pope Eugenius III and Abbot Bernard of Clairvaux. In this respect, the historian benefits from the fact that in order to co-ordinate the multidirectional expedition that these two men evidently had in mind[16] the preaching of the crusade relied to a great extent on the dissemination of carefully constructed crusade letters.[17] The first of these was Eugenius's *Quantum praedecessores*, the earliest surviving papal crusade encyclical and, subsequently, a template for crusade appeals at least as far as the 1180s.[18] Given the importance with which this document should therefore be held, it is remarkable that there is no suggestion within its lines that the crusader might be regarded as an imitator of Christ. Even though Eugenius acknowledged the precedents for his crusade appeal and signalled the importance of the deeds of his predecessors – especially Urban II – he totally disregarded one of the ideas that had been fundamental to the preaching of 1095. There is only one mention in *Quantum praedecessores* of the practice of the crusader taking the cross, but no connection is drawn between this custom and the Gospel passages that Urban II was reported to have cited in his Clermont sermon. Indeed, Eugenius was clearly aware of the need to provide his audience with *exempla* from which they could draw inspiration and he called, primarily, for them to recollect and live up to the achievements of their ancestors, the first crusaders who had seen to the liberation of the Holy Land.[19]

When one goes on to consider the crusade letters of Bernard of

---

[16] See Giles Constable, 'The Second Crusade as Seen by Contemporaries', *Traditio* 9 (1953), 213–79.
[17] See especially Jean Leclercq, 'L'Encyclique de S. Bernard en faveur de la croisade', *Revue Bénédictine* 81 (1971), 282–308, and 82 (1972), 312; Jean Leclercq, 'Pour l'Histoire de l'encyclique de S. Bernard sur la croisade', *Etudes de civilisation médiévale, IXe–XIIe siècles: Mélanges Edmond-René Labande* (Poitiers, 1974), 479–90.
[18] Eugenius III, 'Quantum praedecessores', ed. Paul Rassow, 'Der Text der Kreuzzugsbulle Eugens III. vom. 1. März 1146', *Neues Archiv* 45 (1924), 300–5. Note that the text used here is the version of 1 March 1146, which contained minor changes to the version of December 1145.
[19] Ibid., 303.

Clairvaux it becomes apparent that the absence of *imitatio Christi* ideology within *Quantum praedecessores* was no oversight.[20] In concordance with the pope's letter, Bernard's preaching made no reference to the Gospel passages that would portray the crusaders as fulfilling Christ's scriptural injunction to 'take up their crosses', stressing instead that the cross symbolized God's offer to his people of a unique opportunity for salvation:

> Take up [*suscipere*] the sign of the cross and you will obtain indulgence in equal part for all the sins which you have confessed with a contrite heart. If the cloth itself is bought, it is of little value; if it is worn with devotion on the shoulder, it is without doubt worth the kingdom of God. They do well, therefore, those who have taken up this heavenly sign; and they also do well . . . [those] who hurry to take hold of [*apprehendere*] what will be, for them, their salvation.[21]

It could of course be argued that the ideal of *imitatio Christi* was so embedded within crusading thought that an explicit statement or Gospel citation was not required. This seems unlikely. Many historians have commented on the precision with which these crusade letters were crafted,[22] and given the potential strength of the idea that the crusader could be perceived as following Christ's example it does not follow that a reference to the *imitatio Christi* tradition was simply meant to be inferred. Indeed, when the texts are analysed closely, Bernard's attempts to redefine crusading ideology become more apparent. The Latin verb Bernard used most frequently to describe the adoption of the sign of the cross was *suscipere*, but this was not a term that appeared in the Vulgate to express the idea of taking the cross to follow Christ; in Matthew 10:38 it is rendered as *accipere*, Matthew 16:24, Mark 8:34 and Luke 9:23 as *tollere*, and Luke 14:27 as *baiulare*. Bernard's usage of *suscipere* therefore seems to have been both innovative and deliberate.

It seems clear enough that in their preaching of the Second Crusade neither Bernard nor Eugenius – who was, of course, a former pupil of the abbot of Clairvaux – wished to renew the link between crusading

---

20 Bernard of Clairvaux, 'Epistolae', in *Sancti Bernardi Opera*, ed. Jean Leclercq, Henri Rochais and C. H. Talbot, 8 vols (Rome, 1957–77), esp. Ep. 363 (to the Archbishops of Eastern France and Bavaria), 8: 311–17, and Ep. 458 (to Duke Wladislaus and the people of Bohemia), 8: 434–7.

21 Ibid., 315.

22 See, for example, Jonathan Riley-Smith, *The Crusades: a History*, 2nd edition (London, 2005), 121–2.

and the ideal of the imitation of Christ.[23] But when one broadens the line of enquiry to other sources for the expedition, it becomes apparent that although the 'elite' – for which we should probably read 'Cistercians' – might not view crusading as a Christo-mimetic exercise, the idea of taking the cross to follow Christ was certainly to the fore of the 'popular' mind. An obvious example of the perpetuation of *imitatio Christi* spirituality is provided by Odo of Deuil, whose account of Louis VII's campaign began thus: 'In the year of the Incarnation of the Word 1146, the illustrious king of the Franks and duke of the Aquitanians . . . in order to be worthy of Christ, undertook to follow him by bearing [*baiulare*] his cross'.[24] Furthermore, as Odo neared the conclusion of his narrative, he also drew an analogy between the sacrifice made by those crusaders who had died and that which Christ had made on the cross: 'For lords to die so that their servants might live would have been an incident calling for lamentation, had not the Lord of all given an example thereof.'[25] Odo was not the only one of his contemporaries to view the piety of those who took part in the Second Crusade in the same Christo-mimetic terms that had been applied to first crusaders. For example, in a letter referring to the Second Crusade addressed to King Louis, the author – possibly the duke of Bohemia – described 'the whole army that wishes to walk in the way of Christ'.[26] Similarly, in a sermon delivered to persuade a contingent of crusaders to assist in the siege of Lisbon, the bishop of Porto was reported to have praised the crusaders for their willingness '[to exchange] all their honours and dignities for a blessed pilgrimage in order to obtain from God an eternal reward. The alluring affection of wives, the tender kisses of infants . . . all these they have left behind to follow Christ'.[27] And even such a senior churchman as Peter the Venerable, the abbot of Cluny,

---

[23] In this respect, I disagree with Cole, *Preaching of the Crusades*, 59–60, who argued that, for Bernard, crusading was associated with 'suffering and self-sacrifice in imitation of Christ', and Yael Katzir, 'The Second Crusade and the Redefinition of *Ecclesia*, *Christianitas* and Papal Coercive Power', in Michael Gervers, ed., *The Second Crusade and the Cistercians* (New York, 1992), 9, who argued that crusaders 'undertook the obligation to imitate Christ' in response to Bernard's preaching.

[24] Odo of Deuil, *De profectione Ludovici VII in orientem*, ed. and trans. Virginia G. Berry (New York, 1948), 6–7.

[25] Ibid., 118–19.

[26] Elisabeth Pellegrin, 'Membra disiecta Floriacensia', *Bibliothèque de l'Ecole des Chartes* 117 (1959), 5–56, 22.

[27] *De expugnatione Lyxbonensi*, ed. and trans. Charles Wendell David, with a foreword and bibliography by Jonathan Phillips (New York, 2001), 70–3.

wrote to King Louis in 1146 to express his support for those about to set out on crusade, asking

> For what honours, what riches, what pleasures, what home or parents can hold them back? And yet, leaving everything, they have chosen to follow their Christ, to toil for him, to fight for him, to die for him and to live for him.[28]

Whilst it is somewhat unsatisfactory to categorize Peter the Venerable amongst the 'popular' rather than with the 'elite', the distance between his writings on the spirituality of second crusaders and that of the Cistercians highlights the fact that there were at least two separate understandings of crusade ideology in the mid-twelfth century. The 'popular' understanding, as represented by individuals such as Odo of Deuil, the anonymous author of the *Conquest of Lisbon*, and Peter the Venerable, was the more conservative, and maintained the symbolic association between the crusader's cross and that which Christ had borne to Calvary. The more advanced or 'elite' understanding was reserved for the Cistercians, who believed that the cross was the *signum vitae*, a symbol of the spiritual reward that God was offering his people through participation in the crusade; as Bernard put it,

> [God] puts himself into a position of necessity, or feigns to do so, so that he can give back rewards to those fighting for him: forgiveness of sins [*indulgentia delictorum*] and eternal glory. Therefore I call blessed this generation that can take hold of a time of such indulgence, to be alive in a jubilee year that is pleasing to the Lord. The blessing is spread throughout the whole world, and everyone is flocking to this sign of life.[29]

The emphasis in Bernard's preaching was therefore not on what the crusader might attain through any self-sanctifying action, but on how God would reward the crusader with the indulgence for seizing the opportunity for salvation that had been presented to him.

The explanation for the discrepancy between the elite and popular perceptions of crusade spirituality is, I believe, twofold. The first aspect – the continued association in the popular mind of crusading with the ideology of *imitatio Christi* – requires little elucidation. I have already

---

28 *The Letters of Peter the Venerable*, ed. Giles Constable, 2 vols (Cambridge, MA, 1967), 1: 328.

29 Bernard of Clairvaux, 'Epistolae', 8: 314.

described above how potent the ideal of the imitation of Christ could be, and it is testimony to the ingenuity of Urban II's preaching that the badge of the crusader continued to be so loaded with the symbolism of *imitatio Christi* fifty years after he had delivered his Clermont sermon.[30] (Indeed, given their repeated efforts to draw a connection between the First and Second Crusades, the preaching of Eugenius and Bernard may well have inadvertently continued this association by triggering the memory of First Crusade spirituality.) In addition, despite the diversification of crusading warfare into other theatres such as Iberia and the Baltic, the ongoing connection between the crusade and the Jerusalem pilgrimage only served to preserve the idea that the crusader was an imitator of Christ. Such was the cachet of the idea of fighting in the land where Christ himself had fought (as the patriarch of Jerusalem had put it in 1098),[31] it often proved difficult to recruit crusaders for other campaigns. In Spain, for example, a distinctive feature of crusade preaching was the idea that those fighting in the peninsula might liberate an alternative route to the Holy Sepulchre, via Andalusia and North Africa.[32]

The Holy Land was to remain at the heart of crusading ideology throughout the movement's history so it is perhaps unsurprising that the ideological advancements proposed by Bernard and Eugenius in the 1140s were misapprehended. The question still remains, however, why the Cistercians themselves should have preached the spirituality of crusading in different terms to those that Urban II was reported to have used in 1095. I have already referred to Bernard of Clairvaux's developed theology of the crusade indulgence;[33] it is also evident that he was convinced that the ideal of *imitatio Christi* could only be pursued by those who had renounced the secular world for the monastic life,[34] and in this respect, the crusade – a temporary form of religious devotion designed for lay participation – could never be satisfactory.[35] It must

---

[30] Colin Morris, 'Propaganda for War: the Dissemination of the Crusading Ideal in the Twelfth Century', in W. J. Sheils, ed., *The Church and War*, SCH 20 (Oxford, 1983), 79–101, 84, argued that 'Urban ... must be credited with the invention of one of the most successful instances of the "logo" in history'.

[31] See above, n. 14.

[32] See, for example, *Historia Compostellana*, ed. Emma Falque Rey, CChr.CM 70 (1988), 379.

[33] See also Riley-Smith, *The Crusades*, 124, 133–4.

[34] See, for example, his description of the crusader who chose to fulfil his vow by joining the Cistercian order: 'Epistolae', 8: 437.

[35] Bernard's attitude towards crusading monks is also revealing: see 'Epistolae', 8:

therefore be acknowledged that Bernard took a more uncompromising line to that of writers such as Guibert of Nogent, who had thought that the First Crusade was a 'new way of earning salvation', and thus offered an alternative to entry into a professed religious life.[36]

Although Guibert and Bernard were only separated by a matter of decades, their differences were no doubt partly a result of the religious environments in which they were writing. When Urban II addressed the Council of Clermont in 1095 he was preaching during a period of radical reform, contemporary with the popularity of the eremitical movement, the rise of the canons regular, and the foundation of the Cistercian order itself.[37] Against this background of profound change it is not hard to see how his message of taking the cross to fight for Christ and the Holy Land might be accepted as but one of many ways to follow Christ's example.[38] By 1145, however, these upheavals had begun to stabilize and the religious landscape had been transformed. New forms of religious observance, each with a distinctive role to play, had proliferated, and one of the most innovative foundations to have been made during this period was the Order of the Temple. In the wake of the successful recovery of Jerusalem in 1099, the new settlements of the Latin East had required a permanent body of men to provide protection for pilgrims and to defend the Holy Land from its enemies, and the Temple, the first military order, was established for this purpose in 1120. There is overwhelming evidence to indicate that the way of life of the Templars, which combined devotional warfare with the discipline of the monastic cloister, was presented by supporters as a manifestation of the ideal of *imitatio Christi*, and it is surely no coincidence that their leading apologist was Bernard of Clairvaux. It would seem that, for the elite, it was the Templars who were the real inheritors of the Christo-mimetic spirituality of the first crusaders.

The Primitive Rule of the Templars, confirmed at the Council of Troyes in 1129, demonstrates the application of many ideas that had

---

511–12. See also Andrew Jotischky, *The Perfection of Solitude: Hermits and Monks in the Crusader States* (University Park, PA, 1995), 1–16.

[36] Guibert of Nogent, *Dei gesta*, 87.

[37] Jean Leclercq, François Vandenbroucke and Louis Bouyer, *The Spirituality of the Middle Ages* (London, 1968), 130, suggested that 'The same spirit lay behind this new kind of *peregrinatio* . . . as that which had brought about the monastic crisis and the advent of the wandering hermits'. See also Giles Constable, *The Reformation of the Twelfth Century* (Cambridge, 1996), *passim*.

[38] For the First Crusade as 'a military monastery on the move', see Riley-Smith, *First Crusade*, 2, 26–7, 113–14, 118–19, 150–2, 154–5.

also been synonymous with the First Crusade. Particular attention was paid to the relevance to the Templars of Christ's words, recorded in the Gospel of John, 'Greater love has no-one than this, that he lay down his life for his friends' (John 15:13). This ideal was most clearly stated in the Rule in a clause in which a brother was required to swear that '*I will take the cup of salvation*, that is by my death, I will imitate [*imitabor*] the death of my Lord, because just as Christ laid down his life for me, thus I am ready to lay down my life for my brothers.'[39] The citation from John was to become central to the ideology of the Templars and appeared in the texts of papal privileges such as *Omne datum optimum* (1138) and *Milites Templi* (1144). Moreover, this latter bull, issued by Pope Celestine II in 1144 only weeks before his death, made direct reference to the passage from Matthew that Pope Urban was reported to have referred to in 1095 and that Pope Eugenius would omit from *Quantum praedecessores* in 1145/6: 'The Knights of the Temple of Jerusalem, new Maccabees during this time of grace, refusing worldly desires and abandoning personal possessions, have taken up [*tollere*] Christ's cross and followed him.'[40]

There is not time here to give full consideration to the many references to the imitation of Christ within the early sources for the Order of the Temple. However, by way of conclusion, I would like to illustrate briefly how Bernard of Clairvaux himself associated this ideal with the way of life of the Templars. In a passage from his *De laude novae militiae* (composed at some point between 1129 and 1136) which once again described the willingness of the Templar to sacrifice his life for others, Bernard asked the rhetorical question, 'Why should he fear to live or fear to die when for him to live is Christ [*vivere Christus est*] and to die is gain?'[41] This citation from Philippians 1:21 is of great interest, for Bernard would return to use the verse in his crusade preaching of 1146. But in those letters Bernard adapted the phrase to the following: 'Now, O mighty soldiers, O men of war, you can fight without danger, where to conquer is glory and to die is gain.'[42] The exclusive application to the Templars of the phrase *vivere Christus est*

[39] *Die ursprüngliche Templerregel*, ed. G. Schnürer (Freiburg, 1903), 136. Citation from Ps. 116:13.

[40] *Papsturkunden für Templer und Johanniter*, ed. Rudolf Hiestand, 2 vols (Göttingen, 1972–84), 1: 215.

[41] Bernard of Clairvaux, 'Liber ad milites Templi de laude novae militiae', in *Sancti Bernardi Opera*, 3: 214.

[42] Bernard of Clairvaux, 'Epistolae', 8: 315, 436.

suggests that whilst Bernard undoubtedly viewed the crusade as a way for the pious layman to secure spiritual rewards, he believed the Temple to be the only suitable vocation for those who wished to carry out acts of sacred violence and fulfil a desire to follow Christ. The fact that Bernard's subtle use of Scripture was beyond the comprehension of the majority of his contemporaries only serves to illustrate what wide gaps could exist between elite and popular religious beliefs.

Emmanuel College, Cambridge

NARRATIVE, AUDIENCE AND THE NEGOTIATION OF COMMUNITY IN TWELFTH-CENTURY ENGLISH MIRACLE COLLECTIONS

by SIMON YARROW

THE institutional emphasis on distinctions between the elite and the ordinary faithful is a feature of a number of religions. Such distinctions permit rich and diverse forms of exchange across the lines they demarcate, not simply reducible to economic models of explanation, but subject to symbolic and cultural negotiation. These exchanges fostered social ideals, implicit understandings and modes of behaviour that helped to make hierarchy in complex societies appear cohesive, normative and consensual.[1] But a danger exists in confusing the normative value of these exchanges as represented in writing with the material and ideological effects towards which they worked. In the absence of popular religious thoughts and feelings, which Christopher Brooke rightly reminds us 'have left little memorial for posterity',[2] we are left with the discursive claims made in historical sources on behalf of elite and popular distinctions. My aim in this paper is to explore the implications of this for the study of the cult of the saints in twelfth-century England. I will argue that in such interpretive conditions, any discussion of these matters in terms of elite and popular religion risks losing sight of the discursive function of these texts and of the wider understandings and negotiations that lie behind them.

The Two-Tier Model and the Cult of Saints

No discussion of the history of elite and popular religion in connection with the cult of the saints is possible without mention of Peter Brown. Brown was the first to identify in the work of Hume a 'two-tier' under-standing of the history of religious belief and practice that has distorted modern historiography on the subject. Hume's model epitomized the

---

[1] I would like to thank Bob Moore, Elaine Fulton, Dmitri Van Den Bersselaar, Bob Sack and Kate Cooper for reading and suggesting improvements to this article. Its remaining errors are all my own.

[2] *Europe in the Central Middle Ages, 962–1154* (London, 1964, 2nd edn, 1987), 422.

demystifying values of the climate of Enlightenment to which he belonged.[3] He depicted a refined and rational Christian church periodically dragged down by the conservative and superstitious mentality of its vulgar majority. He cast the religious elite as moral arbiters of true religion, and the people as corruptive of it. Gibbon echoed this idea in his use of late antique saints' cults as evidence of the dilution of the simple and pure truths of the Early Church by recently converted pagans.[4]

Brown's knowledge of Augustine and his anthropological and psychoanalytical insights led him, in his book *The Cult of the Saints*, famously to upset this consensus. He argued for the cult of saints, not as 'a dialogue between two parties, the few and the many', but 'as part of a greater whole – the lurching forward of an increasing proportion of late antique society toward radically new forms of reverence, shown to new objects in new places, orchestrated by new leaders . . .'.[5] Within this new model of a 'greater whole', Brown retained many of the asymmetries implied in the two-tier model. He simply reversed their polarity. The 'lurching forward' was 'orchestrated' by late antique bishops, a religious elite who employed the cult of the saints to christianize the rustic country folk of their dioceses.

Brown's critique reinstated much of the historical dynamism represented by the late antique cult of the saints. Some historians however, in recent retrospective assessments of Brown's achievement, have noticed his tendency to assume too smooth a fit between the language of miracle narratives and the reality outside the text.[6] Philip Rousseau has called for a renewed concentration on the function of the text rather than the shrine or the saint,[7] whilst Paul Hayward has seen in Anglo-Saxon hagiography an element of over-optimism in its authors not fully taken account of by the classic Brownian model.[8] Relic cults

---

[3] Peter Brown, *The Cult of the Saints. Its Rise and Function in Latin Christianity* (Chicago, IL, 1981), 17.

[4] Ibid., 15.

[5] Ibid., 21–2.

[6] An important collection of articles assessing Brown's contribution is James Howard-Johnston and Paul Antony Hayward, eds, *The Cult of Saints in Late Antiquity and the Middle Ages* (Oxford, 1999). For the proceedings of another retrospective conference on the work of Peter Brown held in the USA, see S. Elm, 'Introduction', *Journal of Early Christian Studies* 6.3 (1998), 343–51 and the other articles in that issue.

[7] Philip Rousseau, 'Ascetics as Mediators and as Teachers', in Howard-Johnston and Hayward, eds, *Cult of Saints in Late Antiquity and the Early Middle Ages*, 45.

[8] Ibid., 140–2. An example of Brown's refinements of his early ideas in response to these

have evolved then in the historiography from being evidence of pagan survival to examples of elite schemes of christianization, to a stage of asking whether they were popular at all, or rather, at least of asking how we might more accurately discern the grounds upon which claims to popularity can be made on their behalf. This brings us to a position somewhere between Brown's functional approach to the sources and a more discursive reading of them as narratives appealing to a redemptive hegemony.[9]

Miracles as Calls to Belief

Brown's understanding of relic cults powerfully echoes the concerns of the Church Fathers about religious elitism, authority and pastoral duty in the early medieval church. Conrad Leyser has compared their varying articulations of the perceived relationship between the ordinary faithful of the Church and its ascetic virtuosi. Augustine offered one of the most balanced and compelling versions of this relationship. In Leyser's words he 'had a specific pastoral goal in the fifth century; to establish the absolute equality of all the faithful in the sight of God'.[10] Augustine's support for the cult of St Stephen was an illustration of this ideal put into practice. He saw monastic communities, not as theatres of elite spiritual competition, but as nodes of charitable exchange, integral to the wider operation of charity among the Christian faithful. There was to be no question of monks, saints or churchmen leaving the majority behind.[11] Their achievements as martyrs, confessors and ascetics were to be open to all as exemplars. Their posthumous miracles offered compelling evidence of God's authority and of the truth of the Resurrection, and thus the unity of the Christian Church.[12]

Gregory the Great spoke of the New Testament miracles as proof before pagan audiences of the truth of the Christian faith. He writes in

---

reassessments is 'Enjoying the Saints in the Late Antiquity', *Early Medieval Europe* 9.1 (2000), 1–24.

[9] My perspective here is something akin to that argued for by Patrick Geary, at 'the threefold intersection of genre, total textual production and historical circumstance', in 'Saints, Scholars and Society: the Elusive Goal', in idem, *Living with the Dead in the Middle Ages* (Ithaca, NY, and London, 1994), 9–29, 23.

[10] Conrad Leyser, *Authority and Asceticism from Augustine to Gregory the Great* (Oxford, 2000), 8.

[11] A seemingly strong possibility in the sensibilities of men like John Cassian and the 'Lérinian school' of asceticism: see ibid., 33–8.

[12] Peter Brown, *Augustine of Hippo. A Biography* (London, 1967), 418.

his *Homilies on the Gospels*: 'miracles were associated with holy preachers so that virtue displayed might give credence to their words'.[13] Miracles were frequently associated with preaching in *gesta martyrum* literature of the fifth and sixth centuries.[14] Gregory also saw miracles as challenging existing believers to become better Christians.[15] In his *Dialogues* Gregory developed this rhetoric of religious authority, framed in terms of its appeal to the idea of the universal Church, to a literate clerical audience and to the lay audiences to whom these clerics ministered. The purpose, according to McCready, was 'to deepen the faith of those who were already baptized Christians'.[16] These ideas informed Bede's understanding of the subject,[17] and through the literary monuments of all three, they shaped monastic perceptions of the cult of saints in twelfth-century England.

Twelfth-Century English Miracle Collections

The century and a half after the Norman Conquest was a boom time for the production of miracle collections in England. These collections were chiefly the product of Benedictine monasteries, often the great reform houses of the tenth century and cathedral communities attached to diocesan centres. Communities of regular canons and new foundations also found relics in the traditional religious locations that constituted their new surroundings as useful tools for pastoral engagement with wider lay communities.[18] Despite their diverse contexts and contents miracle stories follow a familiar narrative pattern. Along with their biblical precursors, the miracle stories recorded by the early

[13] In *Homiliae in Evangelia*, 1.4. 2–3, PL 76, 1090, cited by W. McCready, *Signs of Sanctity: Miracles in the Thought of Gregory the Great* (Toronto, 1989), 35, n. 13.

[14] See Kate Cooper, 'Ventriloquism and the Miraculous: Conversion, Preaching, and the Martyr Exemplum in Late Antiquity', in Kate Cooper and Jeremy Gregory, eds, *Signs, Wonders, Miracles: Representations of Divine Power in the Life of the Church*, SCH 41 (Woodbridge, 2005), 22–45. I want to thank the author for letting me see her article on this subject in advance of its publication.

[15] McCready, *Signs of Sanctity*, 61–4.

[16] Ibid., 57.

[17] For Bede's understanding of miracles as serving didactic needs, see B. Colgrave, 'Bede's Miracles Stories', in A. H. Thompson, ed., *Bede, his Life, Times and Writings* (Oxford, 1935), 210–29, and Benedicta Ward, 'Miracles and History: Bede's Miracles Stories', in G. Bonner, ed., *Famuli Christi* (London, 1976), 70–92.

[18] P. Hayward, 'The *Miracula inventionis beate Mylburge virginis* Attributed to "the Lord Ato, Cardinal Bishop of Ostia" ', *EHR* 114 (1999), 543–73, for a young antiquarian of Much Wenlock, whose discovery of the relics of St Milburga won the approval of the newly arrived Cluniac monks.

church, and particularly by Augustine, Gregory of Tours, Gregory the Great and Bede, provided the conventions, the structure and the language with which twelfth-century monastic observers described the miracles they saw at the tombs of their saints. The bare structure of healing miracles, the kind of miracle most common to the genre, was as follows: individuals whose sickness or failings were identified came into contact with the enshrined or portable relics of a saint, publicly experienced some form of healing or judgement, the story of which, after due processes of authentication, encouraged much rejoicing and recounting. This narrative format was a powerful elite template for accommodating and ordering diverse lay religious experiences. Its stages can be discussed in detail.

First, an illness is identified. Prior Philip, author of the miracles of St Frideswide, ascribed to Mabel from Sibford the inspiration for her own cure as from the Bible. Mabel suffered from gynaecological problems as a result of childbirth. In the autumn, bent double, bleeding and in great pain, Mabel visited the church of St Frideswide in Oxford where, on the saint's feast day, a procession of the feretory was to take place. Philip explains that the woman's faith was strengthened by the idea that she might be able to touch the feretory as it passed by the crowds and thus be healed. She did so 'like the woman of whom it can be read in the gospel that she was healed of a flow of blood when Jesus touched the hem of her robe.'[19] Bad weather disrupted the procession but the woman entered the church and was eventually cured at the saint's tomb. This example illustrates the biblical precedents the elite kept in mind when thinking about their depictions of sickness and suffering in the context of tomb-centred healing. Attention to the vivid details of sickness heightened the dramatic spectacle of the anticipated miracle.

To this detailed observation of physical ailments is added a second descriptive layer of ritual, gesture, and the performance of sickness in the liminal space normally located around the tomb. The sick and the suffering gained the attention of the saint through their petitions and prayers. Miracle collectors talk about the lengthy displays of devotion and prayer, pleading and invocations for help made by the sufferer.[20] Acts of humiliation and spiritual preparation preceded and accompa-

---

[19] Prior Philip of St Frideswide's, *The Miracles of St Frideswide*, ed. J. Van Hacke *et al.* (Brussels, 1853), *ActaSS*, October viii, cols 568–89, at 576.

[20] Phrases frequently employed include *deplorans, invocans, deprecans, maxima cum devotione pernoctans, in oratione cum maxima devotione et fidei constantia persisteret.*

nied such devotion. Indeed these acts were what made prayers effective. To approach a tomb in a condition of sin was inadvisable; numerous narratives talk of the individual confessing their sins to a priest before approaching the tomb. Others performed voluntary acts of penance and asceticism. Miracle collectors provided an exposition of these gestures and disciplines in their narratives. A London woman abstained from meat and fish in preparation for her visit to the tomb of St Frideswide. In doing so, Prior Philip explained, she 'showed with exterior works her interior devotion'.[21] Tears and groans were another important element of this repertoire of gestures. They symbolized, at least to the monastic sensibilities of their writers, a spiritual desire, a profound humility and awe of Christ's sacrifice on behalf of the sinful.[22]

The theme of these ritual gestures as exterior evidence of inward spiritual conditions recurs frequently in miracle collections. The famous freelance hagiographer, Goscelin of St Bertin, in his proem to the Life of St Aethelthryth of Ely and in some examples of his miracles, returns to this theme. A young woman, whose hand adhered to the handle of a stake used in order to work on a Sunday, presented a spectacle of her sin to onlookers. Goscelin glosses on this cautionary tale by warning 'Therefore let them . . . pay attention to this punishment and realise that without doubt he will be afflicted still more severely in his soul, even if now he may not be smitten with vengeance in his body.'[23]

Sin betrays itself in these kinds of stories through miraculously imposed afflictions. By these rhetorical means is suffering translated from the world of physical symptoms to a world of morality, free will and sin. Numerous stories recount the failure of doctors to treat physical symptoms with physical remedies. Goscelin for example, describes the behaviour of a paralysed woman who turned from doctors to St Aethelthryth: 'The voice of her inner groaning rings out, tears drench her face, the entire day is spent in prayer.'[24] The parents of a young man without speech employed these familiar performative conventions on his behalf at the tomb in Ely: 'With great contriteness of heart . . . Tears stream down their faces, prayers are heaped upon prayers. Faith within,

21 *Miracles of St Frideswide*, 578.
22 J. Leclercq, *The Love of Learning and the Desire for God*, trans. C. Misrahi (Fordham, NY, 1961), 63.
23 Goscelin of Saint Bertin, *The Hagiography of the Female Saints of Ely,* ed. and trans. R. C. Love (Oxford, 2004), 121.
24 Ibid., 111.

on the exterior their voice cries out for the hand of mercy to be extended.'[25] In his petitionary prayer at the end of his collection of the miracles of St Modwenna, Geoffrey, abbot of Burton, asked not for protection against illness but for the forgiveness of his sins and salvation.

A third feature in the narration of miracles was that of authentication. To convey and verify the dramatic disruption from the laws of nature that constituted a miracle, authors followed strict conventions of authentication in the exposition of their stories. Not all those who experienced miracles at a shrine had their experiences recorded for posterity. Reginald of Durham extravagantly noted that in one evening at the tomb of Godric, sixty people of both sexes were cured 'but because they had no known witnesses with them, they are not noted down here'.[26] Occasionally judgement of the claims some pilgrims made to having been cured was suspended until a witness from their home community could be consulted.

Miracle Stories as the Rhetoric of Redemption

The discursive shape of these stories is easy to discern. They drew momentum from the accumulation of a series of binary oppositions between interior and exterior, sin and redemption, the fragmented body and the whole body, medical healing and spiritual healing, the individual and the community.[27] Ultimately they emphasized not the difference between elite and popular religion but between belief and unbelief. The world evoked in these narratives is tidy and symmetrical, a moral economy of redemption in which good Christians have their devotion rewarded and bad ones get what is coming to them. When it behaved itself, as it typically did in these narratives, the laity formed a useful 'chorus' before which to stage the petitions, appeals, illnesses and anxieties brought by faithful souls for consideration by a saint. A blind man received his sight at the shrine of St Modwenna in Burton and 'with great joy, the abbot, his monks and the people praised God's

---

[25] Ibid., 113–15.

[26] *Libellus de Vita et Miracula S. Godrici, Heremitae, de Finchale*, ed. J. Stevenson, Surtees Society 20 (London, 1847), 426.

[27] For a stimulating discussion of the power of such binaries when ascribed to the ritual of the eucharist, see Miri Rubin, *Corpus Christi: the Eucharist in Late Medieval Culture* (Cambridge, 1991), 1–11.

power'.[28] When the iron band of a penitent broke in the church, 'the abbot, the people and the monks' were 'rejoicing and exultant to share such a patron'.[29] Again, when the translation of St Modwenna's relics is described, the 'monks, clerics and people' took part in the vigil and procession of the relics.[30] Philip, prior of St Frideswide's, Oxford, frequently used the phrases *populi stupentibus, plebs fidelis, omnium qui tunc aderant* for the crowds of joyful laity who witnessed miracles in the church.[31]

This rhetoric of social cohesion and harmony was held in creative tension with the Augustinian notion that miracles only occurred in societies that were poor of faith. It celebrated the tangible rewards afforded to those whose faith provided an example for others. It did so by co-opting them into performing a repertoire of gestures and ascetic acts – tears, prayers, fasts, confession, vigils and charity – that imitated and *ipso facto* affirmed the grounds upon which the religious claimed their particular authority. This virtuous cascade of exemplary behaviour, from the saints to their religious custodians to the faith of their lay pilgrims was glossed by Arcoid, a canon of St Paul's, in an echo of Augustine, as follows: 'Erkenwald revived the age of the early church before the eyes of all men, and indeed, by the profusion of wonders he performed, he passed judgement on us as unbelievers.'[32] The socially unifying and hierarchical imperative, to which this rhetoric appeals, is clear: miraculous *signa* are a divine response to poor faith, and failure to read these *signa* calls into question your membership of the Christian faithful.

Rhetoric, Reception, and Dissenting Voices

Measuring how far these monastic constructions of cultic practice and meaning corresponded to a 'popular' understanding of the miraculous is a difficult and often overlooked task.[33] The temptation is to read them as straightforward ethnography. But as we have seen, they are

---

[28] Geoffrey of Burton, *Life and Miracles of St Modwenna* (Oxford, 2002), 189.

[29] Ibid., 191.

[30] Ibid., 187.

[31] *The Miracles of St Frideswide*, 571 and 579.

[32] Arcoid, *Miracula Sancti Erkenwaldi*, in E. G. Whatley, *The Saint of London: the Life and Miracles of St Erkenwald* (Binhampton, NY, 1989), 135.

[33] Susan Reynolds's comment that 'The mentality of the sources and the degree to which it was shared by the whole of society also need more critical consideration', in 'Social Mentalities and the Case for Medieval Scepticism', *TRHS*, ser. 6, 1 (1991), 21–41, at 29, and

more artful than that.[34] In the space remaining I want to make some suggestions about the reception and transmission of such stories and about the possibilities for tracing irregularities in these narratives to external circumstances. The anthropologist Michael Gilsenan has drawn attention to how miracle stories circulated as part of a vernacular practice of story telling in modern Islamic society:

> every time the anthropologist sits down in a café and hears these narratives in the company of others who are far more than merely an audience but are really, participants, he, too, is an active participant. He, too is an actor in the drama, because the miracle is performed each time it is retold . . . It does not therefore matter, whether or not such and such happened or what the original miracle was, and if he goes looking for it, he will be chasing himself up a blind alley. There are endless versions of 'the same' miracle. Miracles are made every day in cafés and conversations, and it is there that they are created, reproduced and transformed.[35]

Can we make such claims for a vernacular practice of miracle story telling among the English laity? Certainly, the appeal these narratives made to a populist notion of 'we, the faithful' should surely encourage us to think, in Gilsenan's terms, about the wider social mechanisms by which their content was collected and disseminated. Goscelin of St Bertin provides a clue to the intended audiences for these stories, and one means by which they were to be transmitted:

> We ought also vigilantly to place them in the closet of our heart by attention to frequent reading, nor however, contain them only within our own walls but also to proclaim them far and wide to the praise and glory of the Godhead.[36]

It seems that monks, through repetitive reading, were meant to commit these stories to memory and recite them to wider audiences. The occa-

---

the article in full seems to me the rare case of a historian challenging scholarly assumptions about popular religious credulity.

[34] Of course ethnography is now generally understood to be more artful than previously thought, see James Clifford, 'On Ethnographic Allegory', in idem and George E. Marcus, eds, *Writing Culture: the Poetics and Politics of Ethnography* (London, 1986), 98–121.

[35] M. Gilsenan, *Recognizing Islam: Religion and Society in the Modern Middle East* (London, 1982, repr. 2000), 75.

[36] *The Hagiography of the Female Saints of Ely*, 99. The comment echoes Gregory the Great's appeal to the combined audience of clerics and laity intended for his *Dialogues*, see above n. 16.

sional use of vernacular words in some of the descriptive passages in these stories points to processes of exchange and negotiation between literate and oral cultures in their written construction.[37] The testimony authors used sheds a little more light on these stages of authorization of the miraculous. Those regarded as credible witnesses included people of good moral conduct, men of age and simple faith, and women, whose importance in the family and particularly as mothers is repeatedly emphasized in these sources.[38] A survey of the 'social settings' in which, according to these narratives, miracle storytelling occurred, might reflect more of the 'approved' agents and audiences for this populist genre and the networks fostered through them.

That some miracle collections were composed for use as material for sermons or readings for feast days testifies to some of the official circumstances in which these stories were retold. The occasional retention by monasteries of individuals willing to retell their own miracle experiences takes us further towards the informal setting of a vernacular tradition, though again perhaps in circumstances more controlled than those described by Gilsenan.[39] Miracle collectors seem particularly keen to record high status interest in the miracles performed by their saintly patrons. Geoffrey, abbot of Burton, noted that Queen Matilda, wife of Henry I, 'loved to hear about the miracles of the saints'.[40] The miracles of the saints as an interesting dinner table subject for high status laity is suggested again in a miracle of St Thomas. John of Roxburgh was saved by St Thomas from drowning in the Tweed when his horse pitched him into the river from a bridge. News of the miracle reached the court of King William of Scotland who was travelling

[37] One of the miracles of St Godric refers to an illness 'quod infirmitatis "Kinkehost" vocant Angli', see *Libellus de Vita et Miracula S. Godrici*, 373.

[38] For a discussion of the relationship of gender and testimony in miracle narratives see E. M. C. Van Houts, 'Orality in Norman Hagiography of the 11th and 12th Centuries: the Value of Female Testimonies', in eadem, *History and Family in England and the Continent, 1000–1200* (Aldershot, 1999), XV, 1–13, and K. Quirk, 'Men, Women and Miracles in Normandy, 1050–1150', in Elisabeth Van Houts, ed., *Medieval Memories, Men, Women and the Past, 700–1300* (London, 2001), 53–71.

[39] And see *The Miracles of St Frideswide*, 574, for Emmelina of Edington, whose suicide bid and subsequent loss of mind were thwarted by the joint intervention of the Virgin Mary and the region's own virgin saint, Frideswide. Emmelina remained with the community of canons at Oxford as a serving woman. She retold her story, among other visitors, to the bishop of Norwich. Marcus Bull has commented on the role of these people as 'something qualitatively distinct – a source for a miracle story', in *The Miracles of Our Lady of Rocamadour* (Woodbridge, 1999), 35.

[40] Geoffrey of Burton, *Life and Miracles of St Modwenna* (Oxford, 2002), 203–5.

through the neighbourhood. The king sent the bishop of Glasgow and his archdeacon to bring back a full account. William of Canterbury reassures us that John 'told the bishop the story just as it is written here, and he told us the same one a little later'.[41] A record of high status secular approval for such stories did little harm in enhancing a particular saint's reputation. Conversely, the socially conservative messages that these stories contained might well have been of particular reassurance to these groups. A more detailed exploration of these social contexts of reception and transmission, and of who collects miracles and who gets to transmit and 'reauthorize' them in these records, will be an important part of differentiating their social appeal.[42] From this initial inquiry, it seems that miracle stories were 'populist', were consumed by different audiences in different contexts, and often addressed social groupings that crossed elite and popular boundaries.

Another way of assessing the 'external' value of these miracle narratives is to read them closely as examples of discursive practice and to pay attention to the kinds of circumstances in which their own logic is stretched or tested. For example, Alice, the daughter of an Essex clerk, arrived at the abbey of Reading with her hand paralysed and stuck to her side, the victim of sleeping out in the sun. She was healed by the hand of St James and became laundry woman to the monks. The story should end here if it were to fit the structural conventions of miracle stories. But its author notes bitterly that Alice 'was seduced and abducted by a certain smith' and left the abbey to be his wife.[43] What is noteworthy here is the lack of any divine punishment for Alice's opportunist act of social climbing at the expense of the monks.

There are frequent references to awkward people in the narratives who behave with indifference or hostility to a particular relic cult. In fact these people, who fail to show due devotion, feign illness, or go against the interests of the saint's custodian community, are a regular feature in miracle stories, categorized as unbelievers and victims of

---

[41] *Materials for the History of Thomas Becket*, ed. R. C. Robertson and C. R. Sheppard, 7 vols (London, 1875–85), 2: ch. 41, 296–8. See Symeon of Durham, *Capitula de miraculis et translationibus S. Cuthberti*, in *Symeonis monachi opera omnia*, ed. T. Arnold, 2 vols (London, 1879–85), 2: 343, for the record of another miracle retold at court.

[42] I aim to explore this more fully in a future article.

[43] R. Kemp, 'The Miracles of the Hand of St James', *Berkshire Archaeological Journal* 65 (1970), 1–19, at 10. For the similar story of Emmelina, that more smoothly fits the narrative template, see above n. 38.

saintly punishment beatings.[44] Whether such punishments actually took place of course has little importance to the discursive function of these stories. They aim to marginalize such behaviour as part of the construction of unbelief, and in doing so they obscure its specific social character. Occasionally, with the aid of alternative sources, or through a degree of sociological speculation, we can cautiously reconstruct the general contexts of a particular dissenting response outside the discourse. A remarkable miracle story, written by Arcoid, prior of St Paul's, London, documents one such awkward customer in a way that departs from the normal conventions for this type of miracle story by attributing the following lengthy speech to him:

> You clerics have so much time on your hands that you neglect your own business and meddle with what doesn't concern you. You people, honestly, you are free to keep every day as a holiday, and you get to grow soft with idleness and to eat other peoples' food. You can sing without care both day and night, for no necessity compels you to work. Your life should be thought of as more a game or a stage play than a real occupation. If someone would feed me every day for free, and clothe me, damn me if I wouldn't strain myself for him, no matter if he wanted me to sing high or low.
> Whenever we manage to make enough money from our work for food and a bit more to drink, then we spend our feast day having a good time dancing and shouting. If you were to take an interest in our type of enjoyment you would come to think very poorly of your own solemnities and clamourings. For one thing, the jobs we work at are useful, and for another, we do them with cheerful voices, and for the sake of happiness. But you clerics with your everlasting useless dirges, you despise the life we lead, and because our type of work is not like yours, you proudly condemn it. And then you bring in some Erkenwald or other to defend your idleness, and by this authority you try to deprive me of what sustains my life. Will Erkenwald feed me if I lose my income on his account? I would be a laughing stock if I gave up my job and expected to be fed by your patron. So go on then, and keep your festivals and your old songs and your Erkenwald to yourselves, and leave off envying us, drones that you are, and let us get on with the

---

[44] See Susan Reynolds, 'Social Mentalities', 29–30, for her discussion of these scoffers as valuable evidence of scepticism.

work that strong men have to do. Whoever could persuade me to busy myself with your religion and to neglect my work, could also persuade me that I can live without eating.[45]

This rhetorical concession to the notion of religious elites as parasites is out of place when read in terms of conventional discursive forms of these narratives. It suggests the author was attempting to deal with issues topical in London of the 1140s.[46] It is interesting for its secular interpretation of what a feast day was for, and for the apparent obscurity, to at least some London folk, of Erkenwald's name. The narrative goes on to acknowledge those of the laity whose inclination was to sympathize with the dead man's argument. Others, who regarded the punishment as wholly fitting for his impiety and arrogance, provided the moral with which the author could rescue the narrative for hagiographical consumption. He tripped over a skull and died when his head hit a stone on the ground.

* * *

In this article I have aimed to explore the usefulness to historians of the two-tier model of elite and popular religion. From the evidence of miracle narratives written in twelfth-century England, I am convinced that the model is too simple to sustain a differentiated and accurate picture of the social networks articulated by relic cults. I have reviewed the uses of this model by Peter Brown and tried to suggest ways in which his approach can be modified with reference to discourse analysis. The miracle narratives I have studied worked within a populist rhetoric of conversion and redemption long established by the Church Fathers. The power of this rhetoric was encoded in the distinctions made between believers and unbelievers rather than elite and popular sections of society. A brief glance at the currency of these stories and a look at the shape of occasional distortions that occur in the narratives suggest that wider vernacular and socially differentiated understandings of the miraculous existed than have been hitherto acknowledged.

University of Birmingham

---

[45] Whatley, *The Saint of London*, 113.
[46] Other narratives in this collection hint at a background level of apathy for the cult among a section of the London people; for example, see ibid., 133–5.

ELITE AND POPULAR SUPERSTITIONS IN THE *EXEMPLA* OF STEPHEN OF BOURBON

by CATHERINE RIDER

'When I was preaching against sorcery and hearing confessions . . .'.[1]

WITH these words, the thirteenth-century Dominican friar Stephen of Bourbon recalled how in a village in the Auvergne he had found a group of women venerating a dog as a saint. He then went on to describe how he had preached against the cult and persuaded the local lord to demolish the dog's woodland shrine. Thanks to a detailed study by Jean-Claude Schmitt,[2] this encounter between educated friar and unorthodox peasants has become a famous example of interaction between elite and popular religion in the Middle Ages. But it is only one of many such encounters that Stephen describes under the heading of 'Superstitio', or Superstition. Part of the interest of these tales for the modern reader is that they provide a window on to some of the unorthodox religious practices of the Middle Ages. Even more interesting, however, is the way in which Stephen links these practices to a clear but flexible idea of the relationship between elite and popular religion.

In this paper I will argue that Stephen's preaching activities led him to construct a model of elite and popular religion that reflected his experiences. Superstition was part of that model, generally a characteristic of popular rather than elite religion, but Stephen recognized that there was no fixed dichotomy between elite and popular religion. Instead they are two ends of a spectrum, in which different people can be more or less 'elite' or 'popular'. Moreover, a person who is 'popular' in some contexts may be 'elite' in others. Nor does the divide between elite and popular always match the distinction between clergy and laity.

---

[1] 'Cum ego predicarem contra sortilegia et confessiones audirem . . .': Stephen of Bourbon, ed. A. Lecoy de la Marche, *Anecdotes historiques, légendes et apologues tirés du recueil inédit d'Etienne de Bourbon* (Paris, 1877), 325.

[2] Jean-Claude Schmitt, *The Holy Greyhound: Guinefort, Healer of Children since the Thirteenth Century*, trans. Martin Thom (Cambridge, 1983).

Stephen's attitude to superstition thus shows clearly how 'elite' and 'popular' are not fixed categories, but vary according to the observer's interests, and according to the circumstances that he is describing.

* * *

Historians of medieval religion have become very interested in questions about elite and popular religion over the last few decades. One model suggested by Jacques Le Goff and his followers (including Schmitt) is of popular or lay religion as distinct from, but in constant dialogue with, elite or clerical religion. But other historians have questioned how far social categories like 'elite' can be applied to religious beliefs.[3] Questions also remain about whether it is legitimate to distinguish popular religion from the elite variety at all, and about who the 'people' who practise popular religion are. Some historians emphasize that Christians of all social levels shared many religious beliefs and practices,[4] while others insist that there were real differences between the religious experiences of clergy and laity.[5] A careful examination of Stephen of Bourbon's attitude to superstition can thus tell us how one medieval cleric approached similar issues in the light of his own experience.

There are several reasons why it is worth focusing on Stephen particularly. First, his preaching activities were part of a wider drive from the late twelfth century onwards to educate the laity about Christianity.[6] This pastoral movement received official endorsement at the Fourth Lateran Council of 1215, which ruled that all Christians had to go to confession at least once a year and encouraged bishops to educate their clergy and promote preaching in their dioceses. It is impossible to tell how far the provisions of the Council were followed to the letter, but there is evidence that with the help of the friars, annual confession did become the norm, at least in some areas.[7] These increased levels of pastoral activity would have affected the relationship between popular

---

[3] For two recent surveys of the debate see Carl Watkins, ' "Folklore" and "Popular Religion" in Britain during the Middle Ages', *Folklore* 115 (2004), 140–50, at 141–2, and Peter Biller, 'Popular Religion in the Central and Later Middle Ages', in Michael Bentley, ed., *Companion to Historiography* (London and New York, 1997), 221–46.

[4] For example Duffy, *Stripping of the Altars*, 2.

[5] For example Rosalind and Christopher Brooke, *Popular Religion in the Middle Ages: Western Europe 1000–1300* (London, 1984), 12.

[6] On this movement, see Colin Morris, *The Papal Monarchy* (Oxford, 1989), 489–504.

[7] Alexander Murray, 'Piety and Impiety in Thirteenth-Century Italy', in G. J. Cuming and Derek Baker, eds, *Popular Belief and Practice*, SCH 8 (London, 1972), 83–106, 94.

religion and the religion of the clerical elite, and Stephen was in a position to observe this first-hand.

Secondly, although many historians have examined the literature of the pastoral movement for information about popular religion,[8] Stephen has not been much studied in this context, apart from Schmitt's work on the cult of the dog-saint Guinefort. Stephen was born in around 1180 and studied at the University of Paris, where he joined the Dominican order. After finishing his studies, he moved to the Dominican convent at Lyons, and from this base he travelled widely in south-east France, preaching and hearing confessions. Before he died in 1262, Stephen began to record his experiences in a collection of *exempla*, short stories that preachers could use to liven up their sermons and make moral points in a concrete way.[9] A large number of *exemplum*-collections were produced in the thirteenth century,[10] but Stephen's is particularly interesting because it contains a great deal of information about the religious beliefs and practices of ordinary people.

Thirdly, Stephen was influential. His *exempla* were copied into other collections and are found very widely. A word must be said about Stephen's original text, however. Many of his *exempla* were printed by A. Lecoy de la Marche in 1877, but this was not a critical edition and parts of Stephen's text were omitted. Jacques Berlioz and Jean-Luc Eichenlaub are preparing a critical edition but so far only the prologue and part one have been published.[11] Most of the time I have relied on Lecoy de la Marche's text, and the references throughout this paper refer to the page numbers of his work unless otherwise specified. However, I have also checked the printed text against one of the complete manuscripts listed by Berlioz and Eichenlaub, Oxford, Bodleian Library, MS Oriel College 68. This manuscript contains long general discussions of superstition and a number of *exempla* taken from earlier sources which are not found in the printed text.

---

[8] For example Murray, 'Piety and Impiety', 83–106, and idem, 'Religion among the Poor in Thirteenth-Century France: the Testimony of Humbert de Romans', *Traditio* 30 (1974), 285–324; Aron Gurevich, *Medieval Popular Culture: Problems of Belief and Perception* (Cambridge, 1988), 6–8.

[9] Schmitt, *Holy Greyhound*, 11–13.

[10] Claude Bremond, Jacques Le Goff and Jean-Claude Schmitt, *L'Exemplum*, Typologie des Sources du Moyen Age Occidental 40 (Turnhout, 1982), 58.

[11] *Tractatus de Diversis Materiis Predicabilibus*, ed. Jacques Berlioz and Jean-Luc Eichenlaub, CChr.CM 124 (Turnhout, 2002).

Superstitio *and Superstition*

Before turning to what Stephen's exempla tell us about the relationship between elite and popular religion, it will be useful to examine what he means by 'superstitio'. Theological writing from St Augustine onwards associated 'superstitio' with false belief, paganism and magic, and also with Christian practices that were believed to be superfluous, or added on, to true religion. Stephen's younger contemporary Thomas Aquinas was very specific, defining 'superstitio' as either worshipping beings other than God, or worshipping God in an inappropriate way.[12] Stephen, however, quotes St Augustine and then lists the practices he has in mind: 'the vain cult of divinations, incantations, sorceries, diverse demonic mockeries'.[13] As this list suggests, the exempla that follow describe a wide range of unorthodox practices including the belief in omens, divination, love magic, magic to cure sterility, secret night-time meetings where people venerate a black dog, the cult of St Guinefort, and the misuse of the host for magical purposes. Several stories also concern the 'bonae res', supernatural female beings who were believed to fly around at night and enter houses, bringing prosperity. The common feature of all these exempla is that they concern attempts to obtain material results by supernatural means that Stephen sees as illegitimate; or they concern beings and beliefs that were not part of official Christian doctrine.

Stephen also stressed that all superstitions were deceptions, perpetrated either by demons (who wished to draw people away from God), or by magicians who claimed falsely to have supernatural powers. This idea that superstition is basically fraudulent is found in much earlier medieval writing on the subject,[14] and it had two important effects on how clerical writers such as Stephen perceived those who engaged in superstitious practices. If superstition was a demonic deception then, first, most of the blame could be placed not on the superstitious person, but on the demons who had deceived him or her.[15] Secondly, it became

---

[12] Dieter Harmening, *Superstitio: Überlieferungs- und theoriegeschichtliche Untersuchungen zur kirchlich-theologischen Aberglaubensliteratur des Mittelalters* (Berlin, 1979), 33–41.

[13] 'De supersticione vani cultus divinacionum, incantacionum, sortilegiorum, ludificacionum demonum diversarum': Stephen, ed. Lecoy de la Marche, 314; Oxford, Bodleian Library, MS Oriel College 68, fol. 221v.

[14] Norman Cohn, *Europe's Inner Demons: the Demonization of Christians in Medieval Christendom* (3rd edn, London, 1993), 173.

[15] Valerie Flint, *The Rise of Magic in Early Medieval Europe* (Oxford, 1993), 156.

easy for the friars and priests for whom Stephen was writing to exclude themselves from the ranks of the superstitious because their role was to expose these frauds. Thus Stephen claimed that demons seduced the 'stupid' (stultorum), and described how the king of Castile 'laughed at' (irridens) a group of his knights who believed in omens.[16] Like the king, Stephen's audience could feel safe in the knowledge that they would not have fallen for such crude falsehoods.

Superstitious People

However, Stephen stressed that his readers, the elite who were not expected to believe in superstition, were very much in the minority. The demons, he says, seduce an 'infinite' number of people.[17] His stories also indicate that superstitious people could be found at all social levels. He opens with a story about an astronomer (astronomus) who tried to deceive a king,[18] followed by four stories about omens featuring an old woman, a countryman, a Spanish scholar, and a group of Castilian knights who are rebuked by their king for taking a flight of crows as an omen that the day's battle against the Saracens will go badly.[19] Although the king in the first story eventually saw through the astrono-mer's deception, the other believers in omens are all made ridiculous by their beliefs. Thus the knights are mocked by their king, the scholar and the countryman are both prevented from leaving their lodgings because a prankster sneezes outside the door every morning, and the old woman makes the tragic mistake of refusing to confess her sins on her deathbed because she believes that an omen says she will recover.

From omens, Stephen moves on to diviners (divinae), women who practise divination and provide magical cures and love magic. Like the believers in omens, they appear at a variety of social levels. One false diviner was a 'poor old woman' (pauper vetula) who tried to deceive a peasant (rusticus);[20] but another had servants and a manor with at least two houses. The size of her estate meant that she could overhear her servants talking to visitors in one house and then, while the servants took the guests on a detour, she could hurry to the other house and

---

16 Stephen, ed. Lecoy de la Marche, 314–15.
17 '[Q]uorum infinitus est numerus': Stephen, ed. Lecoy de la Marche, 314.
18 MS Oriel 68, fol. 222v.
19 Stephen, ed. Lecoy de la Marche, 314–15.
20 Ibid., 316.

greet the visitors with apparently uncanny knowledge of who they were and why they had come.[21]

Although *divinae* are always women, Stephen also mentions men who engage in similar activities, such as St Cyprian, who performed love magic before his conversion to Christianity.[22] He also gives some more recent examples. In one, a man masqueraded as St James and deceived a householder by pretending to know secret information about him, which he had really learned from the servants.[23] Stephen also remembers how one of his fellow students at Paris consulted a male magician ('malefici', 'magus') when his law books were stolen.[24] The magician invoked demons and made a boy look into a sword-blade to see the face of the thief, but the demons caused mischief by implicating the wrong person. Stephen was not alone in reporting this form of divination: John of Salisbury, in the twelfth century, described how when he was a child, his tutor encouraged him and another boy to look into their fingernails for images.[25] John's story suggests that clerics could be involved in this form of superstition, but Stephen himself does not suggest that the magicians he mentions were clerics.

In some cases Stephen does not record the social status of his superstitious characters. Twice he tells of women who approached diviners for help in conceiving a child, or for love magic, but he does not say who these women are.[26] In two other stories, women accuse their neighbours of holding secret meetings at which they called on Lucifer or ate in the presence of a black dog,[27] but again Stephen does not mention their social status, except to say that one of the women had previously been captured for certain crimes. The word he uses for crimes, 'maleficiis', can mean harmful magic or non-magical crimes; either way it does not suggest high social status. On the other hand, some anecdotes specifically concern lower-class people. One 'divina' caters for the villagers in a certain parish;[28] a peasant (rusticus) sees supernatural riders at night,[29] and another is deceived into thinking

[21] Ibid., 315–16.
[22] MS Oriel 68, fol. 225r.
[23] Stephen, ed. Lecoy de la Marche, 316–17.
[24] Ibid., 317–18.
[25] Richard Kieckhefer, *Magic in the Middle Ages* (Cambridge, 1989), 151.
[26] Stephen, ed. Lecoy de la Marche, 318–19.
[27] Ibid., 322–3.
[28] Ibid., 319.
[29] Ibid., 321.

that the 'bonae res' have entered his house.[30] The women who appeal to St Guinefort are also described as peasants. Thus although anyone at any social level could be superstitious, most of Stephen's stories concern those furthest from the social elite: country people, villagers and peasants, the social groups most likely to lack education and fall for the deceptions that Stephen describes.

Medieval churchmen often associated a second social group with ignorance and improper religion: women. They, too, feature prominently in Stephen's picture of superstition. Some women act as diviners, and others hold a range of unorthodox beliefs, such as the notion that they can fly around at night with the 'bonae res'. Other women again accuse their neighbours of holding secret sacrilegious meetings. Not all superstitions were exclusively female, however. St Cyprian did love magic, and men might claim to find stolen goods or know hidden information, just like the female diviners. Male peasants also claimed to have seen supernatural riders flying at night and believed in the 'bonae res'. In the latter case, it was the peasant's wife who was sceptical, but she was overruled by her gullible husband.

On the other hand, Stephen presents some superstitions as gender-specific. Apart from the historical example of St Cyprian, the superstitions concerning love, fertility and young children are all associated with women. Thus one woman is convinced that one of her female neighbours is a 'striga',[31] a murderous supernatural creature who has killed two of her children and will come for the third, although the killer turns out to be a demon in disguise.[32] Women are also prominent in the cult of St Guinefort, and call on him when they believe that their children have been snatched by the fairies.[33] Flying at night also seems to be a female occupation. Men might see the supernatural riders, but they did not claim to fly with them in Stephen's stories, although by the early modern period, records do appear of men who claimed to fly at night with the mysterious 'night people'.[34]

Stephen's picture of the people who engaged in superstition was influenced at several points by other ecclesiastical discussions of the subject. He knew the most famous text on night flights, the ninth-

---

[30] Ibid., 324.
[31] On 'strigae', see Cohn, *Europe's Inner Demons*, 162–6.
[32] Stephen, ed. Lecoy de la Marche, 319–21.
[33] Ibid., 325–8.
[34] Wolfgang Behringer, *Shaman of Oberstdorf: Chonrad Stoeckhlin and the Phantoms of the Night*, trans. Erik Midelfort (Charlottesville, VA, 1998), 23.

century 'Canon Episcopi' much studied by historians of early modern witchcraft,[35] and quotes sections of it. Some of Stephen's *exempla* were also borrowed from earlier sources, such as St Cyprian's love magic and a story about a woman who tried to steal the host at mass in order to use it for magic. Like Stephen, these sources and many other earlier ecclesiastical works associated superstition with ignorance, stupidity and peasants.[36] They also often (but not always) associated love and reproductive magic, and flying at night, with women.[37] Stephen's association of superstition with peasants and women is thus coloured by his reading, but the fact that he also includes many of his own anecdotes suggests that he believed that his own observations were consistent with what he had read.

So, how 'popular' does Stephen think that superstition is? It is certainly popular in the sense of being frequently found, seducing 'infinite' numbers of people. It is also popular in the sense that it can be found at many social levels: Stephen's stories feature knights and wealthy women as well as peasants. Only one social group is conspicuously absent: the clergy, with the exception of the student at Paris and two monks who see demons in the woods one night.[38] Thus although Stephen never discusses whether any particular social group is more prone to superstition than any other, his *exempla* do imply a distinction between a non-superstitious clerical elite, and a superstitious lay populace. However, Stephen's laity were not monolithic. Peasants appear more often than other social groups, women more than men, and elderly women most of all.

This sliding scale of superstition meant that although the distinction between clergy and laity often corresponded with that between elite and popular, it did not have to do so. Many people could be members of either the non-superstitious elite or the superstitious populace depending on the circumstances. Knights or wealthy women might be superstitious, but on another occasion a local lord helped Stephen to stamp out the cult of St Guinefort. Laypeople did sometimes see superstition for the deception it was: a neighbour, presumably a layman, exposed the man who pretended to be St James, and two women who visited a diviner were horrified when they realized that her magic

---

[35] Cohn, *Europe's Inner Demons*, 167–72.
[36] Harmening, *Superstitio*, 278–9.
[37] Flint, *Rise*, 233–5, 124.
[38] MS Oriel 68, fol. 225v.

involved demons. However, if Stephen is unwilling to generalize about the laity, his picture of the clergy is more uniform. Although the student at Paris lapsed into superstition, he is exceptional. I would argue that Stephen was reluctant to present clerics as superstitious because he believed that the clergy had a distinct pastoral role, and it is this that I will examine in the final section of this paper.

The Role of the Clergy

The fact that Stephen nowhere describes a superstitious person as a 'cleric' is especially interesting because here he differs from some other thirteenth-century *exemplum*-collections. For example, Caesarius of Heisterbach, a Cistercian monk writing between 1219 and 1223, includes several stories about clerics ('clerici') who engage in necromancy, calling up demons with incantations and magic circles. According to Caesarius, students could also learn necromancy from masters in Toledo,[39] much as they learned theology, law and medicine in the schools of Paris, Bologna and Salerno. These stories of clerical magicians probably had some basis in reality. In the twelfth and thirteenth centuries, a number of magical texts were translated from Arabic into Latin, some of which included explicit references to demons. These texts were circulating at the University of Paris by the mid thirteenth century, where several writers claimed to have seen them.[40] Because they were written in Latin and required knowledge of astrology and sometimes the liturgy, these texts were probably used by clerics,[41] and were not necessarily typical of popular magical practices. Stephen's story of the student who consulted a magician in Paris shows that he knew that the educated could become involved with magical practitioners. But, unlike John of Salisbury, he does not specify that the magicians in his story are clerics.

It seems that Stephen did not regard clerical necromancy as relevant in a work which was designed to teach friars how to preach to the laity. Instead, his stories stress the dangers of unorthodoxy in popular religion, and the crucial role of the educated preacher in stamping this out.

[39] Caesarius of Heisterbach, *Dialogue on Miracles*, trans. H. von E. Scott and C. C. Swinton Bland, vol. 1 (London, 1929), 42–3, 315–20.
[40] David Pingree, 'The Diffusion of Arabic Magical Texts in Western Europe', in *La Diffusione delle Scienze Islamiche nel Medio Evo Europeo* (Rome, 1987), 79–82.
[41] Kieckhefer, *Magic*, 155.

Time after time, the clerics in Stephen's stories persuade the laity that they are wrong to be so superstitious. In one story, a priest persuaded his parishioners not to consult a diviner, by faking an illness and thereby proving her diagnosis wrong.[42] Another parish priest demonstrated to an old woman that she did not really walk through walls with the 'bonae res' by locking her in the church, beating her and challenging her to escape if she could.[43] When a Breton woman accused her neighbour of being a 'striga' and killing her two children, the local bishop proved that a demon was in fact responsible. Stephen himself was consulted in the two cases where women accused their neighbours of attending diabolical gatherings, and each time he interviewed both the accuser and the accused and declared the accusations to be false. Stephen, too, tried to stamp out the cult of St Guinefort. On this occasion, he was specifically engaged in preaching against 'sorcery'. Stephen's pastoral mission thus provides the key to his distancing of the non-superstitious clerical elite from the superstitious laity.

Conclusion

This paper has been a very brief survey of Stephen's thoughts on elite and popular superstitions. It would be interesting to compare his treatment with a wider range of *exemplum*-collectors to assess how much of his presentation is unique. It would also be interesting to look at his view of other unorthodox religious beliefs, notably heresy, which has its own section in Stephen's text.[44] The patterns that emerge from Stephen's *exempla* on superstition are not absolutely clear-cut. He makes no explicit statements about which groups of people are most likely to be superstitious, and his *exempla* only suggest general trends. However, two related points emerge. First, any layperson of any social status can potentially be either elite or non-elite, depending on the circumstances. Stephen does not emphasize class or gender distinctions when discussing superstitious people as a whole; the word he uses is 'stupid'. But, according to his stories, clerics were much less likely to fall into this category than were peasants and women.

---

[42] Stephen, ed. Lecoy de la Marche, 319.
[43] Ibid., 324.
[44] On some of these see Jacques Berlioz, ' "Les Erreurs de cette doctrine pervertie . . .". Les croyances des cathares selon le dominicain et inquisiteur Etienne de Bourbon', *Hérésis* 32 (2000), 53–67.

Secondly, Stephen's presentation of superstition is closely linked to his own interest in pastoral care. Although anyone *could* be superstitious, superstition for Stephen is predominantly a lay sin and linked to a lack of education. Thus the clerics in Stephen's stories fall easily into the role of an elite whose role is to investigate reports of superstitious behaviour and expose the errors that they find. However, this presentation of a non-superstitious clergy does not tell the whole story, as Caesarius of Heisterbach's stories of clerical necromancy show. Stephen's *exempla* thus show some of the ways in which one churchman's own interests and experiences led him to define 'elite' and 'popular' religion in a certain way. They also show how flexible these categories can be, prompting historians to look more closely at how elite writers define 'popular religion', why, and in what circumstances.

University of Cambridge

SUPERIOR SPIRITUALITY *VERSUS* POPULAR PIETY IN LATE-MEDIEVAL ENGLAND

by A. K. McHARDY

When K. B. McFarlane wrote his biography of John Wycliffe he was surprised to find that the hero who emerged was not Wycliffe himself but his implacable opponent, William Courtenay, the archbishop of Canterbury from 1381 to 1396. 'Justice has never been done to Courtenay's high qualities, above all to the skill and magnanimity with which he led his order through the crisis that now threatened it', he wrote admiringly, adding by way of explanation that, 'Since the reformation his has been the unpopular side.'[1] The impression McFarlane gave is that there were two ecclesiastical camps in late fourteenth-century England: heretical and orthodox. The fabric of English church life was fractured then, for ever, by the beliefs and work of Wycliffe and his adherents; was not McFarlane's biography entitled *John Wycliffe and the Beginnings of English Nonconformity*? Yet McFarlane's assessment of heresy was that this was far from being a monolithic movement; indeed, in a private letter he wrote, 'Wycliffe was merely an extremist in a widespread reform movement.'[2]

The purpose of this paper is to argue that the orthodox Church during Wycliffe's time was similarly far from united. Quite apart from the distinctions which reflected social divisions,[3] orthodoxy was diverse, and even, I would argue, fragmented; and perhaps the sharpest and most acrimonious divisions were between those who regarded themselves as the officer corps of the Church militant, and the less acute, the misguided even, who formed the 'other ranks'. The material

---

[1] K. B. McFarlane, *John Wycliffe and the Beginnings of English Nonconformity* (London, 1952), 71.

[2] To Karl Leyser, 24 July 1945: privately printed in K. B. McFarlane, *Letters to Friends 1940–1966* (Oxford, 1997), 40.

[3] Cathedral fraternities were recruiting royal and aristocratic members at this time. At Lincoln the earl of Nottingham was admitted in 1385, and the following year the king and queen, and the earl of Derby were admitted on the same day: Lincolnshire Archives Office [hereafter: LAO], D&C A/2/27, fols 8 and 13. Dr Helen Phillips draws my attention to the social snobbery of religious observance to be found in Chaucer's 'Canterbury Tales', for example in the Miller's Tale and Reeve's Tale.

will be drawn from Wycliffe's own diocese, the huge see of Lincoln, during the second half of the fourteenth century.

* * *

The best known of this evidence for diversity arose as a result of a political episode, the so-called 'Norwich Crusade' of 1383. After discussion in parliament a crusade against the Clementist count of Flanders was preferred over a crusade against the similarly schismatic king of Castile. A crusade had the advantage of being funded not by taxation (which made the government unpopular) but by the donations of the faithful. The resulting popular enthusiasm surprised the ecclesiastical establishment, and it prompted Henry Knighton's famously scathing reflection:

> This bishop [Henry Despenser of Norwich] had collected a huge and incredible sum of money . . . especially from ladies and from other women; for it is said that a single lady contributed £100. And some gave more than they could afford, it is believed, so that they could gain the resulting benefits of absolution both for themselves and their loved-ones. And so the secret treasure of the realm which was in the hands of women was exposed. And the men behaved in just the same way, both rich and poor, according to the value of their goods, and beyond, so that both their deceased friends and they themselves should be absolved. For they would not be absolved unless they contributed according to their ability and resources. . . . For that bishop had amazing indulgences, with absolution from pain and guilt for that crusade, granted to him by Pope Urban VI, by whose authority he absolved both the dead and the living, if their contribution was sufficient, through himself and his agents. For it was said that some of those agents asserted that, at their command, angels would descend from heaven, and would snatch the souls languishing in purgatory away from their tortures and instantly conduct them to the heavens.[4]

As a canon of Leicester Abbey Knighton's political loyalties were to John of Gaunt, whose scheme for a Castilian crusade had not received parliamentary, hence national, backing. It is also clear that Knighton had a poor opinion of women. Even so, his comments on the funding of this expedition surely indicated a level of scepticism about the efficacy

---

[4] *Knighton's Chronicle 1337–1396*, ed. and trans. G. H. Martin (Oxford, 1995), 324; my own translation.

of indulgences, and certainly about the methods used to sell them; as a canon regular, his own critical superiority to the credulous laity, of whatever rank, is implied.

Also superior in attitude to this campaign was Thomas Walsingham of St Albans Abbey whose comments on the crusade are less well-known; but *his* scorn was not for gullible laymen, but for unscrupulous clergy. 'Many who found the peace of the cloister displeasing, sought, either through [the bishop], or someone else, licence from the abbot, which he was not able to refuse, to cross over to military matters and the clash of arms'. Walsingham saw Urban VI's desperate financial position as the root of this abuse, and continued,

> many, both those of the secular habit and those professed in a rule, because they keenly wanted to escape from under the yoke of obedience to a superior, sent money to Rome where they knew that everything was corrupt, asking that they be designated as papal chaplains, so that by this agreement they would be absolved from obedience to prelates.[5]

Walsingham's sense of superiority was over those clerics, both seculars, but more especially regulars, who were unable to persevere in their chosen way of life.

Our next example was a man who not only progressed from being a secular cleric to becoming a regular, but whose spiritual journey took him from the popular – or perhaps even prosaic – to the highest level of measurable spirituality. This was Adam Horsley, a clerk in the royal administration.[6] King's clerks do not usually enjoy a high reputation for their inner life, for not only were they non-resident, but they were often considerable pluralists, and made money on the side from such business practices as money-lending. Adam Horsley seems at first sight to conform only too well to that pattern. Indeed, when those assessing the clergy of Lincolnshire, Leicestershire and Rutland[7] for the clerical poll tax of 1377 came to list the rector of St John the Baptist Church, Stam-

---

[5] *Gesta abbatum monasterii Sancti Albani*, ed. Henry Thomas Riley, RS 28, 3 vols (London, 1867–9), 2: 416–17.

[6] Much of what follows is based on Joy M. Russell-Smith, 'Walter Hilton and a Tract in Defence of the Veneration of Images', *Dominican Studies* 7 (1954), 180–214. I wish to record my gratitude to the late Miss Russell-Smith for her help and kindness, given many years ago, on the subject of Adam Horsley.

[7] Technically, the archdeaconries of Lincoln, Stow, Leicester, and the deanery of Rutland.

ford, they distinguished him in a unique way. 'Adam the rector', they said, 'is non resident.'[8] Adam Horsley was an exchequer clerk, and had been for several years, for he was presented by the crown to St John's, Stamford, in June 1369.[9] Evidently he had no intention of serving his cure in person, for on 30 September of the same year letters dimissory were granted to 'Adam Horsley, clerk', to be advanced to all orders, both minor and sacred, by any catholic bishop,[10] and during the following winter and spring Horsley was ordained acolyte, deacon and priest by the bishop of London. On the last two occasions he was in distinguished company since other ordinands at the same ceremonies included two *magistri* from Queen's College, Oxford, Nicholas Hereford and John Trevisa.[11] In October 1375 he was appointed Controller of the Great (or Pipe) Roll of the Exchequer, an office he held until 15 January 1382, on which day he was appointed foreign apposer at the Exchequer.[12] He continued to be paid for that office until Hilary quarter 1385.[13]

Meanwhile, however, Horsley was considering a change of career, and he had also come into contact with Walter Hilton, a Cambridge-educated canon lawyer who himself passed from legal practice to a hermit's life, and who ended his days a canon in the Augustinian priory at Thurgaton, Nottinghamshire. During the 1380s Hilton acted as an 'agony uncle' to Adam Horsley, among others,[14] and Horsley was the recipient of a letter of Hilton's, 'The Usefulness and Superiorities (or Excellences) of Religion' (*De utilitate et prerogativis religionis*).[15] This was designed to strengthen his resolve to enter an order, specifically the Carthusian order, a resolve which had apparently been tested by Wycliffe's attacks on the religious life. Commenting upon the

8   *Clerical Poll-Taxes of the Diocese of Lincoln 1377–1381*, ed. A. K. McHardy, Lincoln Record Society 81 (Lincoln, 1992), no. 164.
9   26 June: *Calendar of Patent Rolls 1367–70* [hereafter: Cal. Pat. Rolls], 280.
10   LAO, Register 12 (John Buckingham, Memoranda), fol. 79v.
11   Acolyte, 22 Dec. 1369, deacon 30 March, priest 13 April 1370, *Registrum Simonis de Sudbiria*, ed. R. C. Fowler, CYS 14 and 38, 2 vols (London, 1927 and 1938), 2: 73, 80, 82.
12   Apposers were auditors of the sheriffs' accounts. The post was not abolished until 1833.
13   J. C. Sainty, *Officers of the Exchequer*, List and Index Society, Special Series 18 (London, 1983), 73 and 81. For occasions when Horsley acted with exchequer colleagues, for example, as executor, see *Calendar of Close Rolls 1381–5*, 605, 621, 626.
14   A. B. Emden, *Biographical Register of the University of Cambridge to 1500* (Cambridge, 1963), 305–6. There is, of course, a large bibliography on the author of *The Scale of Perfection*. Miss Russell-Smith did not complete her projected edition of Walter Hilton's letters.
15   *Walter Hilton's Latin Writings*, ed. John P. H. Clark and Cheryl Taylor, Analecta Cartusiana 124, 2 vols (Salzburg, 1987), 1: 119–72.

sentence[16] that entry into religion removes every spiritual stain, Hilton wrote:

> He believes it who wants to. I acknowledge that I similarly believe the words of the church (speaking) on this, which never errs. I pin my faith to these words. Perhaps a heretic might scoff, but I am not ashamed of such simplicity.

He concluded by asking,

> So what are you worried about? What are you afraid of? The foundation is secure, without stain of error or heresy or divine transgression, because religion is founded upon the rock which is Christ; it will not fall, therefore it will not fail. . . . If poisonous winds should blow, namely doctrines and dogmas of the heretics verbally attacking it, religion will not fall but it will stand secure because it is founded upon the firm rock of Christ.[17]

Horsley did indeed become a regular. By March 1385 he had resigned his rectory, and he left crown employment at the same time. Whether he immediately joined the Carthusians is not so clear, though. To examine the possibility that Horsley's path to the Carthusian order was not a direct one, we must both consider his place of origin, and examine the evidence of his namesake. The place-name Horsley occurs in five counties, from Gloucestershire to Northumberland, but in 1370 when 'divers officers of the exchequer' were sent to all the counties of England to affeer amercements, Adam Horsley was sent into Gloucestershire.[18] It was common exchequer practice to send clerks to their area of origin to collect money, and though this is not conclusive evidence, the presence of another man with the same unusual name in

---

16 Spiritual maxim, F. L. Cross and E. A. Livingston, eds, *The Oxford Dictionary of the Christian Church* (Oxford, 1997), 1482.

17 'Credat qui velit, ego fateor me similiter credere verbis ecclesie hoc dicentis, que neminem fallit. Hiis verbis fidem adhibeo. Forsan ridere hereticus, sed hanc simplicitatem non erubesco. . . . Cur ergo trepidas? Quid times? Fundamentum securum est absque labe erroris vel heresis vel divine transgressionis, quia supra petram, id est Christum, fundata est religio; non cadet, ideo non deficiet . . . si flaverint venti pestiferi, doctrine scilicet et dogmata hereticorum illam verbis impugnancium, non ruet religio, set stabit secura quia fundata est supra firmam petram Christum': *Hilton's Latin Writings*, 1: 170–1, lines 887–94 (my translation).

18 Expenses were paid on Tuesday 4 Dec.: *Issue Roll of Thomas de Brantingham, Bishop of Exeter, Lord High Treasurer of England, A.D. 1370*, ed. Frederick Devon (London, 1835), 402, 404–5.

Gloucestershire supports the likelihood that the exchequer clerk with high spiritual aspirations was a Gloucestershire man. The 'other Adam Horsley' was a canon of St Augustine's Abbey, Bristol. Ordained priest by Bishop Trillek of Hereford in June 1351,[19] on three occasions from January 1370 to January 1395 Adam Horsley, a canon of the house, was nominated to act as the abbot's attorney in Ireland.[20] When Archbishop Courtenay made a visitation of the abbey in October 1384 he evidently found conditions unsatisfactory, for the following year he wrote to complain that the canons had departed from their regulation white habit, and had taken to wearing items of black and brown clothing, while in the spring of 1386 he suspended Brother Adam Horsley, canon of Bristol, from administering the goods of the house. Though undated, Courtenay's letter was probably written in May 1386, and required a report by midsummer.[21] (In singling out Horsley the archbishop was perhaps too harsh, for the house had been in financial disarray since 1366, and was not to recover during the abbacy of Henry de Shalyngford *alias* Blebury, 1365–88.)[22]

In the same year that Adam Horsley, canon of Bristol, was being castigated by the archbishop of Canterbury, the prior of Beauvale, Nottinghamshire, was granted permission by the chapter-general of the Carthusians within the Roman obedience to admit to the order Adam clerk of the king of England ('Dominum Adam clericum Regis Angliae'). Dr Sargent, who discovered this reference, commented that

> It is unusual that a clerk already, presumably in major orders, would have to be given permission to join the order. Normally, this would be required only if the candidate had already been professed in another order (particularly the Cistercians and mendicants), or if he could not obtain release from his own bishop.[23]

---

[19] *Registrum Johannis de Trillek, Episcopi Herefordensis*, ed. J. H. Parry, CYS 8, 2 vols (London, 1912), 2: 562 and 564.

[20] 22 Jan. 1370 for 3 years, *Cal. Pat. Rolls 1367–70*, 342; 12 May 1378, for 3 years, *Cal. Pat. Rolls 1377–81*, 202; 30 Jan. 1395 for 2 years, *Cal. Pat. Rolls 1391–96*, 531.

[21] Printed from Reg. Courtenay (Canterbury) in Joseph Henry Dahmus, *The Metropolitan Visitations of William Courteney Archbishop of Canterbury 1381–1396* (Urbana, IL, 1950), 144, 146–7.

[22] *Victoria History of the County of Gloucester, vol. 2*, ed. William Page (London, 1907–), 77–8; David M. Smith & Vera C. M. London, *The Heads of Religious Houses: England and Wales, II: 1216–1377* (Cambridge, 2001), 348.

[23] Michael G. Sargent, *James Grenehalgh as Textual Critic*, Analecta Cartusiana 85, 2 vols (Salzburg, 1984), 2: 580–1.

We can only speculate on the reasons which took the case of Adam Horsley, for it can be no other, to a general meeting of the order. He was not prominent enough in royal service for his departure to have been obstructed by the crown, yet his bishop, while he was a rector in Stamford, was a notable patron of the Carthusian order and would surely have welcomed a conversion to this Rule. The possibility may be raised that Adam Horsley either entered the Augustinian order briefly, or that he was confused with his namesake (and probably kinsman) who was a professed Augustine canon of Bristol.

By whatever route he travelled, Adam Horsley, in or after 1386, became a canon in the Carthusian house which lay closest to Walter Hilton's eventual destination, for Beauvale was some twenty-five miles from Thurgaton Priory. By joining the most austere religious order Adam Horsley had identified himself as a person of serious spirituality. But he went further; the colophons of some manuscripts of Hilton's letter describe Horsley as having lived 'laudabiliter' as a Carthusian, and this accolade is given only after rigorous procedures, and only extremely rarely.[24] No one, it seems, scaled the spiritual heights more successfully than did the absent rector of St John Baptist, Stamford, and his career shows the gulf which could exist between the theological avant-garde and the provincial parishioners in the later fourteenth century.

* * * *

Since Adam Horsley's zeal for spiritual improvement did not prompt him to exercise his rectorial duties in person, the work of parish priest at St John Baptist, Stamford, would have been done by Thomas the parochial chaplain, who was listed in the 1377 tax assessment, and perhaps by another chaplain called Raymond, who was also in the parish at that time. William the celebrant, another cleric also named in the tax list, was probably fulfilling the will of a pious testator by saying a specified number of Masses.[25] Their Christian names are all we know of such men as these, but they provided the pastoral care of the Church in late-medieval England, and in this parish formed the link between the highly-educated, high-thinking rector and the lives of his flock. We cannot even be sure that Thomas and Raymond had any personal links with Adam Horsley, since it is possible that they were appointed by a previous rector.

---

24 Russell-Smith, 'Walter Hilton and a Tract', 181, n. 4.
25 *Poll-Taxes of Lincoln*, ed. McHardy, no. 164.

Horsley's final enthusiasm for the Carthusian order was shared by the man who was bishop of Lincoln during the later fourteenth century. John Buckingham (bishop 1363–98) founded a cell in both the London and Coventry charterhouses, and he was a visitor to (in August 1386) and benefactor of Hull charterhouse.[26] During the 1380s and early 1390s the bishop of Lincoln himself was wrestling with piety problems on two fronts. On the one hand, from 1382 until 1394 John Buckingham, Wycliffe's long-serving diocesan, was pursuing a series of individuals whose advanced and shocking ideas would qualify them as Lollards;[27] disapproval of the veneration of images, and a 'downgrading' of the importance of the Mass in spiritual life were two important features of their belief. On the other hand, however, he was taking action against popular practices which went in the other direction, beyond orthodoxy and into superstition.[28] One case (in 1386) concerned the veneration being accorded to a wayside cross known as 'Jurdan Cros', in Rippingale. This parish was on the edge of the fenland area of south Lincolnshire, and crosses were sometimes set up to mark or strengthen ill-defined boundaries in such places.[29] In September 1386 Buckingham ordered two local rectors (Master John Bottlesham of Ingoldsby and Thomas Boston of Folkingham) to cite before a session of his court of audience sitting at Sleaford 'the rectors, chaplains and all minister of Rippingale church to appear to give evidence about the miracles that are supposed to have taken place at the cross'.[30] Another cause of the bishop's dismay was a practice at Nettleham, a parish just outside Lincoln, and indeed the site of an episcopal manor house. At Easter, during the communion celebration, the parishioners brought to church, and caused the priest to bless, bacon and eggs (the latter hardboiled and shelled) that were then distributed to every house

---

26 'John Buckingham', *ODNB*.

27 A. K. McHardy, 'Bishop Buckingham and the Lollards of Lincoln Diocese', in Derek Baker, ed., *Schism, Heresy and Religious Protest*, SCH 9 (1972), 131–45.

28 For what follows see Dorothy M. Owen, 'Bacon and Eggs: Bishop Buckingham and Superstition in Lincolnshire', in G. J. Cuming and Derek Baker, eds, *Popular Belief and Practice*, SCH 8 (1972), 139–42.

29 Rose Mitchell and David Crook, 'The Pinchbeck Fen Map: a Fifteenth-Century Map of the Lincolnshire Fenland', *Imago Mundi* 5 (1999), 24–50, esp. 43.

30 The session was to be held before Master John Botsham and/or Master John Bannebury on the first juridical date after the feast of St Michael in Monte Tumba, 17 October, LAO, Register 12 (John Buckingham Memoranda), fol. 349v. Rippingale rectory was divided into two portions, one worth two thirds, and other, one.

in the parish, a practice which Buckingham tried to prevent at Easter 1397.[31]

It may be that the presence of Lollardy within his diocese made Buckingham particularly sensitive to manifestations of undisciplined enthusiasm. His objection to miracles being performed at a wayside cross was not shared by, for example, Thomas Walsingham who, under the year 1389, reported that 'events which could with good reason be said to be miraculous and believable' took place at a certain cross erected in the high road near Wymondham Priory, Norfolk, events which were designed by divine providence to 'strengthen those of godly faith, and to discomfit the heretics'.[32] Nor were the bishop's objections to the devotions at the Rippingale cross shared by the papacy. Buckingham's court must have found against the parishioners, but it was they who had the final word; in January 1391 papal licence was granted to the rector of two-thirds of the living to build a chapel where the cross was, and to have mass and other divine offices celebrated there. The reason given was that the cross, said to be a hundred years old, was a place where miracles occurred, and to which 'great multitudes with offerings resort from the said diocese [of Lincoln] and from other parts of England'.[33] The bishop, faced with university-inspired heresy on one hand and popular, if not actually pagan practices on the other, must have felt like a man trying to ride two unruly horses at once.

* * *

This paper began with the premise that division of the English Church into two parts, heretical and orthodox, during the age of John Wycliffe was too simplistic, and failed to take account of the diversity of orthodox belief and practice. Not all divisions were between the elite and the popular, for geographical divisions, reflected in different liturgies (the Uses of Sarum and York) and veneration of local saints, were surely also important. There was also the great gap in experience and outlook between those who worshipped in a church with music, which in this period was becoming increasingly elaborate, and the great majority for whom the liturgy was entirely spoken; this is an area where

---

[31] Ibid., fol. 450. His prohibition of this practice was dated 16 March 1397; Easter day was 22 April.

[32] Thomas Walsingham, *The St Albans Chronicle, I: 1376–1394*, ed. J. Taylor, W. Childs, and L. Watkiss (Oxford, 2003), 882–3. Wymondham Priory was a cell of St Albans.

[33] *Calendar of Papal Registers: Papal Letters, IV (1362–1404)*, 368.

the mere historian fears to tread, but it was an important, and growing division between one kind of ecclesiastical aristocracy and the common experience.[34] The examples examined here have shown how many were the divisions among the orthodox, and that the Church cannot have presented a united front to heresy since it was itself so fragmented into men and women, clergy and laity, regular and secular, measured authority and undisciplined enthusiasm, even divided between English honesty and the corruption of the foreign papacy. Among heretics too there was, of course, an intellectual gulf between the academic Wycliffites and the populist Lollards. The fragmented and diverse nature of the English Church in the later fourteenth century would surely have permitted *anyone* to say with sincerity: 'I am spiritual, you are devout, he is superstitious.'

University of Nottingham

[34] The work of the historian Clive Burgess is important here, and that by the musicologists Roger Bowers, Magnus William and David Skinner. A forthcoming volume on colleges in the later Middle Ages, edited by Clive Burgess and Martin Heale, will shed more light on this development.

KNIGHTS, COOKS, MONKS AND TOURISTS: ELITE AND POPULAR EXPERIENCE OF THE LATE-MEDIEVAL JERUSALEM PILGRIMAGE

by KATHRYNE BEEBE

T HE Church of the Holy Sepulchre in the late Middle Ages was the centre of a range of pilgrimage activity in which elite and popular beliefs and practices overlapped and complicated each other in exciting ways. The Jerusalem pilgrimage, in the fourteenth and fifteenth centuries in particular, abounded in multiple levels of 'elite' and 'popular' experience. Through the pilgrimage writings of a fifteenth-century Dominican pilgrim named Felix Fabri, this paper will explore two specific levels: the distinction between noble and lower-class experiences of the Jerusalem pilgrimage (both physical and spiritual), and the distinction between spiritually 'elite' and 'popular' conceptions of pilgrimage itself – that uneasy balance between the spiritually-sophisticated, contemplative experience of pilgrimage promoted by St Jerome and the more 'popular' interest in traditional 'tourist' activities, such as gathering indulgences or stocking up on holy souvenirs and relics to take home.[1] However, as we will see, even these tourist acts were grounded in the orthodox spirituality of late-medieval piety, and the elite and popular experiences of pilgrimage, whether social or spiritual, were not so distinct as they may first appear.

While this paper will focus on elite and popular aspects of late-medieval pilgrimage, fifteenth-century pilgrims were by no means alone in their desire to experience first-hand the places made holy by contact with the divine, nor in their wish to capture that experience in written pilgrimage accounts.[2] Many early pilgrimage reports, especially

---

[1] Publications useful to the study of medieval pilgrimage include Colin Morris and Peter Roberts, eds, *Pilgrimage: the English Experience from Becket to Bunyan* (Cambridge, 2002); J. Stopford, ed., *Pilgrimage Explored* (York, 1999); and several by Diana Webb including *Pilgrims and Pilgrimage in the Medieval West* (London, 1999) and *Medieval European Pilgrimage, c.700–c.1500* (Basingstoke, 2002). The standard reference work remains Jonathan Sumption's *Pilgrimage: an Image of Mediaeval Religion* (London, 1975, repr. 2002).

[2] Useful assessments and studies of early Jerusalem pilgrimage can be found in the collection of essays edited by Robert Ousterhout, *The Blessings of Pilgrimage* (Urbana, IL, 1990). Georgia Frank explores early-Christian pilgrimage not only to holy places but also to

those written in the fourth century by Egeria,[3] Jerome,[4] the anonymous 'Piacenza'[5] and 'Bordeaux'[6] pilgrims, as well as those of later ages, including Theoderich's *Guide to the Holy Land* (*c.*1173)[7] and the *c.*1280 *Description of the Holy Land* by Burchard of Mt Sion,[8] could be explored fruitfully for their revelations about the elite and popular spiritual aspects of early Christian pilgrimage, as well as the way the opportunities of pilgrimage varied between the social elite and less 'noble' travellers. However, the relative ease of travel in the later Middle Ages encouraged the highly organized, 'package tour' character of the fifteenth-century Jerusalem pilgrimage and fostered a significant increase in the sheer volume of pilgrims – and pilgrim writers. The numerous accounts left by late-medieval pilgrims, with their wealth of detail and personal observations, provide an especially useful entrée into the exploration of the intricate relationship between popular and elite aspects of Holy Land pilgrimage.

Noble and Lower-Class Experiences of the Pilgrimage

The problems of determining exactly the class of pilgrim making the long overland or sea journey to the Holy Land in the later Middle Ages are immediately complicated by the challenge that most historians face:

holy persons in *The Memory of the Eyes: Pilgrims to Living Saints in Christian Late Antiquity* (Berkeley, CA, 2000). More general studies of fourth-century pilgrimage include P. W. L. Walker, *Holy City, Holy Places?: Christian Attitudes to Jerusalem and the Holy Land in the Fourth Century* (Oxford, 1990); E. D. Hunt, *Holy Land Pilgrimage in the Later Roman Empire AD 312–460* (Oxford 1982); and Blake Leyerle, 'Landscape as Cartography in Early Christian Pilgrim Narratives', *Journal of the American Academy of Religion* 40 (1996), 119–43. A useful collection of later pilgrimage accounts is John Wilkinson, *Jerusalem Pilgrimage, 1099–1185* (London, 1988).

[3] Egeria, *Itinerarium Egeriae*, in *Itineraria et alia geographica*, ed. P. Geyer and O. Cuntz, CCh.SL 175–6 (Turnhout, 1965) [hereafter: Geyer and Cuntz (1965)], 35–103, transl. into English by John Wilkinson, *Egeria's Travels to the Holy Land* (rev. edn, Jerusalem, 1981).

[4] Jerome, *Epistulae* (esp. *Ep.* 46, 58, and 108), ed. H. Wace and P. Schaff, *St. Jerome: Letters and Select Works*, Select Library of the Nicene and Post-Nicene Fathers, 2nd ser. (Oxford, 1893; repr. 1989), 6: 60–5, 119–23, 195–212 respectively.

[5] Piacenza Pilgrim, *Pseudo-Antonini Placentini itinerarium*, in Geyer and Cuntz (1965), 127–74, transl. John Wilkinson, *Jerusalem Pilgrims before the Crusades* (Warminster, 1977), 79–89.

[6] Bordeaux Pilgrim, *Itinerarium Burdigalense*, in Geyer and Cuntz (1965), 1–34, transl. (in extracts) by Wilkinson, *Egeria's Travels*, 153–63.

[7] Theoderich, *Guide to the Holy Land*, ed. Ronald Musto, transl. Aubrey Stewart (2nd edn, New York, 1986).

[8] Burchard of Mt Sion, *Description of the Holy Land*, transl. Aubrey Stewart (London, 1896).

the rich tend to leave written records; the poor usually do not. Our main sources of information about pilgrimage, be they guidebooks, indulgence lists, or narrative accounts, were generally written by the educated elite, for the educated elite. However, sometimes we do get glimpses of a greater pilgrim population through these narratives, and it is in one of these in particular – the *Evagatorium*, or 'Wanderings', of Brother Felix Fabri – that we can begin to see the complicated social layers that influenced pilgrim experience in the Holy Land.

Called the 'Proust of the genre',[9] Felix Fabri wrote a detailed account of his two trips to the Holy Land in 1480 and 1483–4. Felix provides a good example of the pilgrim, who, though not-quite elite himself, nevertheless moved in high noble circles. He financed both his Jerusalem pilgrimages by attaching himself as chaplain to the household of local nobles: the governor of Upper Bavaria in 1480, and in 1483–4 as chaplain to four knights of some of his region's most noble families.

In doing so, Fabri surmounted the biggest obstacle to non-noble pilgrims, the sheer cost of the journey. The knight Santo Brasca, who happened to be on Felix Fabri's first pilgrimage in 1480, advised that the pilgrim bring with him two bags – one full of patience, the other of money. Brasca plainly states he was writing for the upper-class pilgrim, one 'who loves his life and is accustomed to live delicately at home'.[10] While in port, Brasca advises the pilgrim to 'not count what he has paid the captain, because this is a voyage on which the purse must not be kept shut'.[11] Pilgrims were also not limited to the official pilgrim galleys – for a greater expense, they could also charter a private 'sailing' ship or travel disguised to avoid paying the tariffs required by the Sultan, which were less for merchants, sailors, and servants.[12] Yet, these financial challenges were not insurmountable for the less well-off. Brasca reassures his readers that poor men might also undertake the voyage for a reduced price on a self-catering option.[13]

Concessions were also occasionally made for friars and other reli-

---

[9] Donald Howard, *Writers and Pilgrims* (Berkeley, CA, 1980), 38. Fabri is most accessible to readers of English in *Felix Fabri, circa 1480–1483 [Wanderings in the Holy Land]*, transl. Aubrey Stewart, 1 vol. in 2 (London, 1892–3) [hereafter: Fabri, *Wanderings*], or in Hilda Prescott's *Jerusalem Journey: Pilgrimage to the Holy Land in the Fifteenth Century* (London, 1954) and *Once to Sinai: the Further Pilgrimage of Friar Felix Fabri* (London, 1957).

[10] Santo Brasca, *Viaggio in Terrasanta*, quoted in *Canon Pietro Casola's Pilgrimage to Jerusalem . . . 1494*, transl. M. M. Newett (Manchester, 1907), 11.

[11] Ibid., 12.

[12] Ibid., 95.

[13] Ibid., 12–13.

gious. Francesco Suriano,[14] a Franciscan brother of a noble Venetian family himself, reports that Franciscans going solely out of devotion were charged fifteen or twenty ducats, while space was made on pilgrim galleys for friars on 'official business' in a special package deal – the first two friars rode free, and any additional friars were only ten ducats each.[15] On merchant galleys and private charted ships, however, Suriano says that all friars were carried without charge 'for the love of God'.[16]

At the same time, the wealthy also facilitated the journeys of poorer pilgrims, either by bringing them along as servants, by making provisions in their wills to send paupers to make the pilgrimage on their behalf, or through charitable donations. Margery Kempe, the Norfolk mystic who made the trip in 1414–15, almost certainly financed her long sojourn through the generous gifts of supporters such as Philip Repingdon, Bishop of Lincoln, who gave her 'twenty-six schelyngys and eight pence to byen hyr clothyg wyth and for to prey for hym' in Jerusalem.[17] Felix Fabri's 'spiritual' pilgrimage instruction manual, *Die Sionpilger* – a book of devotional exercises intended for those who could not go physically to the Holy Land – suggests that a worldly pilgrim, who is himself each day on 'mental' pilgrimage, might sponsor a poor pilgrim to do a 'real' day's journey for him.[18] Fabri himself received aid from both the Dominican provincial of his district and the prior of his convent in Ulm, in addition to the funds given him as chaplain to the son of the governor of Upper Bavaria.[19]

Practices such as begging and acting as 'professional pilgrims' ensured that rich and poor rubbed elbows (and bumped heads) throughout the long Jerusalem pilgrimage. Fabri's own 1483–4 pilgrimage group included the four noble lords who acted as his patrons; their attendants; a count; the dean of Mainz Cathedral (later archbishop and 'author' of a pilgrimage guide in his own right); a printer and engraver described by Fabri as an 'armour-bearer and servant' to the count;[20] several lesser knights; several priests; a few

---

[14] Suriano, a Franciscan from a noble Venetian family, was secretary to the Prior of Mount Sion in 1483 and served as Prior in 1493 and 1512. See ibid., 384–5, n. 76.

[15] Ibid., 95.

[16] Ibid.

[17] Ibid.

[18] Felix Fabri, *Felix Fabri, Die Sionpilger*, ed. Wieland Carls (Berlin, 1999), 81.

[19] Fabri, *Wanderings*, 1: 6.

[20] Ibid., 2: 104.

Minorite friars; and one Conrade, a 'barber, lute-player, cook and manciple'.[21]

Yet for all the material differences of quality of life (for every Pietro Casola eating from gold and silver dishes with his galley captain, there is a middle-class William Wey complaining about the ship's 'stynkyng water'),[22] those typical distinctions of class were found everywhere in medieval society at the time, not just on pilgrimage. Despite the different standards of luxury available during the tip, noble and lower-class pilgrims still saw the same churches, visited the same places in the Holy Land, and heard the same stories from the Franciscan guides in the Holy Sepulchre, no matter what differences in amenities they managed to procure along the way.

The spiritual opportunities of the pilgrimage were open to all despite their class, and in the end, the most profound difference that class seems to have made to individual physical experience of the Jerusalem pilgrimage was concentrated in one specific aspect of the journey – the knighting at the Holy Sepulchre.

A knighthood of the Holy Sepulchre signalled exclusivity and power. It granted a singular prestige in an age when knighthood had became devalued due to the plethora of new orders created by sovereigns eager to collect the higher taxes that such knighthoods entailed. Only in Jerusalem could pilgrims be dubbed knights of the Holy Sepulchre, and according to the rules, only noble pilgrims could be knighted. The knighthood was in place by at least 1418, when the Seignior Nompar de Caumant records that he had a hospitallier from Rhodes knight him in the Holy Sepulchre.[23] The knighthood of the Holy Sepulchre eventually required four degrees of nobility in the candidate's ancestry,[24] and was recognized world-wide – unlike, says Fabri, other knighthoods, whose members were 'not recognized as knights by others, but are laughed at, and called lady-knights, and pussy-cat knights'.[25] After the dubbing ceremony, a nobleman could hang his arms in the Sepulchre, and in the 1480s, newly-dubbed knights could stop off in Rhodes on the return journey to enroll their names in a book and receive a certificate to take home. By 1494, Pietro Casola reports

---

[21] Ibid.

[22] See: *The Itineraries of William Wey*, ed. B. Bandinel, Roxburghe Club 75 (London, 1857), 67.

[23] Sumption, *Pilgrimage*, 266.

[24] Fabri, *Wanderings*, 1: 608.

[25] Ibid., 617.

that he helped prepare the certificates of authentication right there in the Holy Land.[26] The knighthood required no specific obligations or duties beyond the customary pious offering made to the Franciscans of Mt Sion and a vague pledge to defend the Church, the pope, and to 'stir up the minds of all men' to help the captive plight of the Holy Land.[27] The prestige of this knighthood counted as a strong motivation for nobles to make the Jerusalem pilgrimage, as we see in the case of Fabri's first pilgrimage in 1480, when the governor of Upper Bavaria sent his son, George, to Jerusalem specifically 'to receive knighthood there'.[28]

However, the nobility were not the only ones attracted to the knighthood. During Fabri's second pilgrimage, a fist-fight broke out in the Holy Sepulchre when it turned out that a pilgrim, 'of too low estate to bear the dignity of knighthood',[29] jumped in at the end of the queue of nobles and had himself dubbed a knight, too. Certain other knights and barons objected; the interloper's friends defended him, and it took the father guardian of Mt Sion to step in and calm down the 'serious riot'. He ruled that the pilgrim was 'in no wise' a knight and stripped him of his knighthood.[30] As we can see, certain pilgrims used these pilgrimages to better their social class, even by subterfuge. But while this episode emphasizes the pilgrimage's perceived ability to improve a traveller's social prestige, it does not change the fact that the knighting ceremony in the Holy Sepulchre seems to have been primarily a secular affair, with primarily secular motives and benefits. The main *spiritual* reasons for the Jerusalem pilgrimage – indulgences, devotion, prayer, and other spiritual benefits, as well as the holy sites visited – remained open to all, no matter what the class.

Popular and Elite Spiritual Pilgrimage Practices

In this second part of this essay, we will see that the spiritual aspects of the pilgrimage were also divided along elite and popular lines – lines drawn not only by modern scholars, but also by Fabri himself. When looking at pilgrimage from this angle, the distinction becomes not necessarily one between social class, but between levels of education

---

[26] *Canon Pietro Casola's Pilgrimage*, 265.
[27] Fabri, *Wanderings*, 1: 608.
[28] Ibid., 6.
[29] Ibid., 2: 623.
[30] Ibid., 624.

and spiritual understanding – between 'high' and 'low' concepts of theology and the 'elite' and 'popular' spiritual activities that comprised the Jerusalem pilgrimage.

Felix Fabri made this distinction between levels of understanding the meaning of the pilgrimage both in his discussion of the motivations of why one went on pilgrimage, and in his description of pilgrims' tourist activities. 'Worldly noble people', he wrote in *Die Sionpilger*, 'come to the Holy Grave to become knights', but 'spiritual people come therefore to the holy places that they might learn God's grace . . . and raise themselves in prayer to contemplate God'.[31] In the the *Evagatorium*, Fabri worries that his brothers in Ulm would think he did not possess a sufficiently 'elite', that is *spiritual*, desire for making a second pilgrimage, suspecting him 'to be light-minded and impatient of the quiet of the cloister . . . or guilty of the sin of idle curiosity, or moved by frivolity'.[32]

Frivolous desire for novelty and travel, instead of a serious spiritual longing to encounter the Divine, was seen as a failing of worldly pilgrims, but even the very practice of pilgrimage contained within itself a conflict of purpose. Certain strands of Christian thought theorized that since God was omnipresent, pilgrimage to an actual physical spot was not necessary and could even be a lazy substitute for a much more difficult interior journey. We see this tension in Saint Jerome, who writes of Paula's deep emotional response to the site of Christ's birth, describing her almost mystical vision of Christ in the manger.[33] Yet in a letter to Paulinus of Nola, Jerome also cautions against limiting the Divine to one specific place: 'What is praiseworthy is not to have been at Jerusalem but to have lived a good life while there'.[34]

Fabri is acutely aware of Jerome's criticism of pilgrimage without proper inner devotion. He asserts that the very stones in the courtyard of the Holy Sepulchre seemed to 'breathe forth' holiness, yet also argues that

> Good and simple Christians believe that if they were at the places where the Lord Jesus wrought the work of our redemption, they would derive much devotion from them; but I say to these men of a truth that *meditation about these places, and listening to descriptions of*

---

them, is more efficacious than the actual seeing and kissing of them. Unless a pilgrim hath before his eyes some living example of devotion, the place helps him little in the matter of true holiness.[35]

Yet Fabri is also the same man who fills his pockets with pebbles from holy places and who, while condemning those nobles who carve their coats of arms in the Holy Sepulchre and chip off bits of stone to take home with them, nevertheless keeps as a relic a bit of chipped stone from the Holy Sepulchre that he inherited from a dying pilgrim on his first voyage.

Relic collecting is the activity most commonly associated with 'tourist' or 'popular' behaviour, even by contemporary medieval pilgrim writers. Whether rich or poor, noble or ordinary, all pilgrims engaged in relic collecting. Fabri remarks that noblemen, in particular, had a mania for collecting relics of the Holy Innocents – a risky business, since it was said that Saracens made fake Holy Innocents from the bodies of un-baptized babies 'to delude the unwary and cheat them out of their money'.[36] Pilgrims collected relics such as these in part because of a popular belief that they possessed magical healing properties. Fabri reports that the pilgrims took pebbles and clay from the field from which Adam was made since they were said to prevent a traveller from suffering fatigue, stumbling, falling, or harm. The trained Dominican in Fabri knows better than to credit outright these relics with what might appear to be such 'magical' qualities: 'Whether this be true anyone can prove who pleases; I took no pains to notice', he remarks. Then, in a bit of fence-sitting, adds, 'but I suffered neither from fatigue nor falls'.[37]

Yet, relic collecting also could be seen to have sophisticated spiritual roots; this 'tourist activity' could also reflect a 'higher' form of piety, and Fabri uses all his elite spiritual understanding and training to justify it. For Fabri, collecting dead babies or chipping off chunks of the Holy Sepulchre is clearly wrong, but 'the case of those who pick up pebbles at holy places, and pick up relics there without defacing the holy places, is different; for to do this is holy and pious'.[38] He makes reference to the second book of Kings, where Naaman begs Elisha to allow him to carry away stones from the Holy Land with which to build an altar. Fabri

---

[35] Fabri, *Wanderings*, 2: 60 (my italics).
[36] Ibid., 1: 567.
[37] Ibid., 2: 412–13.
[38] Ibid., 85.

then compares Naaman's Old Testament estimation of the worth of the Holy Land with the value that the physical presence of Christ, Mary, and the Apostles added to that worth. Fabri then adds that even Eastern Christians recognize the value of the Holy Land and collected pebbles of their own. Moreover, they took great pains to obtain materials made in Cologne, where the relics of their countrymen, the Three Kings, were kept. And if the Eastern Christians showed such reverence for the land in which their three kings were buried, asks Fabri, 'what wonder if we Westerns show honour to the land of the sepulchre of the Lord, the King of all kings?'[39] The line between superstition and piety often proved to be a very thin one on the Jerusalem pilgrimage.

Other typically 'tourist' activities performed both by those with 'popular' and 'elite' spiritual training involved carving one's name or coat of arms on the walls – an activity that earned its own specific prohibition in a list of 'thou shalt nots' given to the pilgrims by the Franciscan guides at the Holy Sepulchre. This rule did not have the desired effect, however, and the practice certainly crossed both social and spiritual divisions; noblemen may have secretly carved their coats of arms while pretending to kneel at a tomb in prayer, but Fabri reports that

> some simple labouring men take charcoal [as well] and write their own unknown names and the names of their rustic calling on the walls. Even some of the clergy and religious were led astray by apish folly into doing this, and befouled the walls with the ink which they had brought with them to write accounts of the holy places withal.[40]

The activity that combined the greatest range of popular and elite practice was also the greatest 'popular' draw to pilgrimage sites – that of gaining indulgences. This also drew some of the sharpest criticism, from everyone from Lollards to Martin Luther to Erasmus. Such a topic is much too big for the scope of this paper, and the popular and elite aspects of indulgence collecting have been dealt with by numerous scholars.[41] I only mention it here to say that Fabri was a whole-hearted supporter of the practice. His book of pilgrimage is filled with different crosses inserted into the text to tell the reader the exact place and

---

[39] Ibid., 214–17.
[40] Ibid., 85.
[41] See Duffy, *Stripping of the Altars*, Sumption's *Pilgrimage*, and Diana Webb's volumes mentioned above at n. 1, for a useful starting point.

amount of proffered indulgences. Moreover, in *Die Sionpilger*, he argues that his readers (or hearers) could gain even *greater* indulgences than the physical Jerusalem pilgrim, since those blessings obtained through meditation, reading and prayer were granted not by bishops and prelates, but by God himself.[42]

Eamon Duffy has shown how prayers such as the immensely 'popular' 'Fifteen Oes of St Bridget' were nevertheless spiritually sophisticated and drew on 'scriptural, patristic, and liturgical sources, as well as on the Bonaventuran tradition of affective meditation'.[43] Fabri's pilgrimage spirituality also illustrates just this kind of high and low combination. In proving the value of collecting relics, or in vividly describing a holy spot to excite the imagination of his readers, Fabri – like the 'Oes' – also draws upon scriptural, patristic and liturgical sources, and even adapts the high spiritual concepts of meditation found in Bonaventure for his *Die Sionpilger*.

As we have seen, someone as spiritually astute as Fabri was not indifferent to the more 'popular' types of piety already mentioned. Fabri's faith in these mere 'tourist' activities was founded on the belief of efficacy of offering prayers in those spots made holy by the passion of Christ, a belief he backs with sophisticated spiritual references and traditions. He writes that he hoped his prayers in the Holy Sepulchre would be granted, 'beseeching God that by virtue of that most efficacious prayer once offered at that place on the Cross'.[44]

Conclusion

In the end, the elite and popular, high and low aspects of the Jerusalem pilgrimage make it a perfect example of the way in which these differing registers or modes of religious practice interacted with and informed one another. As today, where some tourists enjoy £1,000 'Beatles pilgrimage' package tours and some shoestring backpackers scrape by on ten pounds a day, yet all visit the very same Liverpool, pilgrim galley 'package tours' offered noble and poor pilgrims transport to the very same sites, no matter what their class – but the motivations of individual pilgrims, especially where the knighthood of the Holy Sepulchre was concerned, may indeed have been affected by class

---

[42] Fabri, *Sionpilger*, 79.
[43] Duffy, *Stripping of the Altars*, 252.
[44] Fabri, *Wanderings*, 2: 623.

considerations. However, the actual spiritual experience of the Jerusalem pilgrimage did not have to do with class lines, nor necessarily even educational lines, but with varying inner devotion and interest. As Fabri shows us, clerics were just as likely to scratch their names on tombs as 'worldly' noblemen, and 'worldly' noblemen just might be secretly sporting hair shirts underneath their coats of mail.

Fabri and his narrative may be a particularly vivid illustration of the combination of popular and elite because of his calling. As a Dominican preacher, he had a responsibility both to be extremely learned and to have the ability to use that learning for the benefit of ordinary listeners. Fabri recognized this himself, for he produced two versions of his *Wanderings* – a Latin *Evagatorium* intended for his Dominican brethren and a vernacular Swabian-German *Pilgerbuch*,[45] to which he added entertaining material to capture the attention of his patrons' servants. Yet these two versions differ only in slight details – not in essentials of the narrative.

In conclusion, we can see that 'popular' religion, with its relics and indulgences and other seemingly 'simplistic' concepts of the Jerusalem pilgrimage, was not the only influence on pilgrim experience in the Holy Land, nor was it necessarily so 'popular' and unsophisticated after all. Through narratives such as Fabri's, in tales told by those who had made the journey, in the explanations and on-the-spot Franciscan tour guiding at the Holy Sepulchre, all pilgrims had access both to elite and popular conceptions of the pilgrimage. Put another way, what is commonly seen as 'popular' about the Jerusalem pilgrimage cannot, and should not, be so easily separated from the 'elite' conceptions of spirituality and pilgrimage of the time. By exploring these complications, we gain a better sense of the true nature of a journey in which each pilgrim was there (at least to some extent) to kneel, in T. S. Eliot's phrase, 'where prayer has been valid', and to take part in the redemption and grace the Crucifixion offered to all – whether knight, cook, monk or tourist.

Pembroke College, Oxford

---

[45] For the *Evagatorium*, see Konrad Haßler, *Fratris Felicis Fabri Evagatorium in Terrae Sanctae et Egypti peregrinationem*, Bibliothek des Litterarischen Vereins 2–4 (Stuttgart, 1843–9). For the *Pilgerbuch*, see *Die Pilgerfahrt des Bruders Felix Faber ins Heilige Land*, ed. Helmut Roob (Berlin, 1964), or in modern German: *In Gottes Namen fahren wir*, ed. and transl. Gerhard Sollbach (Kettwig, 1990).

CISTERCIAN NUNS IN MEDIEVAL ENGLAND: UNOFFICIAL MEETS OFFICIAL

by ELIZABETH FREEMAN

L ATE twentieth-century scholarship on the Cistercian monastic order was dominated by the distinction between elite and popular. The terminology was specific to the Cistercian debate – namely, 'ideals' versus 'reality' rather than 'elite' versus 'popular' – but the logic of a high Cistercian culture and a low Cistercian culture is one that students of any elite/popular debate will find familiar. The indispensable modern survey of Cistercian history, published in 1977, is the key promoter of this argument, with its title presenting an eloquent statement of its thesis: *The Cistercians: Ideals and Reality*.[1] Although the focus of current investigations into elite and popular religion is undoubtedly the extent to which both varieties of religion are legitimate cultural forces which influence and depend on each other,[2] the Cistercian argument was formulated in a much more hierarchical way and clearly saw the elite Cistercian life as the more legitimate of the two monastic expressions. The argument is that members of the Cistercian order exhibited a more or less ideal form of corporate religious life during the first one hundred years of the order's existence, but that after the late twelfth century the order gradually lost its purity. Two aspects of popular life infiltrated the enclosed world of the cloister: first, the grubby realities of economics;[3] and, second, interactions with women, generally meaning interactions with the increasing numbers of Cistercian nunneries.[4]

In speaking of the ideals/reality debate in the past tense, I do not claim that the influence of the debate has ended. Although this schol-

---

[1] Louis J. Lekai, *The Cistercians: Ideals and Reality* (Kent, OH, 1977). For the wide influence of the ideals/reality logic, see John R. Sommerfeldt, ed., *Cistercian Ideals and Reality* (Kalamazoo, MI, 1978).

[2] Any number of works could be cited. John Van Engen's work repays thoughtful reading; see his 'The Christian Middle Ages as an Historiographical Problem', *AHR* 91 (1986), 532–52, and 'The Future of Medieval Church History', *ChH* 71 (2002), 492–522.

[3] Strongly argued by Bennett D. Hill, *English Cistercian Monasteries and their Patrons in the Twelfth Century* (Urbana and Chicago, IL, and London, 1968), 150–5.

[4] As Lekai put it, twelfth-century Cistercian leaders feared that involvement in nuns' affairs might 'endanger the purely contemplative character of the Order': *The Cistercians*, 347.

arly tradition has been roundly criticized, tearing apart one scholarly axiom is proving easier than knowing what to put in its place.[5] It is true that important nunnery research by Brigitte Degler-Spengler has taught us to read well-known sources in new ways, by showing that Cistercian General Chapter legislative sources allegedly antagonistic to thirteenth-century nuns may in fact indicate that nuns were already integrated into the broader Cistercian order.[6] But, even so, the misconception that there were no Cistercian nuns at all until the thirteenth century dies hard.[7] Although Degler-Spengler and Constance Berman have demonstrated once and for all that women lived as Cistercian nuns in the twelfth century, the ambiguous status of the early Cistercian nuns means that it is still common to discuss Cistercian monks in one part of a scholarly study and to discuss Cistercian nuns in a separate part, thus demonstrating that Cistercian scholarship has yet to re-think the order as an integrated male and female religious institution.[8]

This ambiguous status is particularly apparent with English Cistercian nuns. As so often with women's religion in England, we can invoke that delightfully ambiguous term, 'a special case'.[9] In a nutshell, there simply were not very many English Cistercian nuns, contrasted against the hundreds of Cistercian nuns' houses elsewhere in Europe. The standard view is that between the twelfth and sixteenth centuries there were only two fully incorporated houses of English Cistercian

---

[5] For criticisms see Constance B. Bouchard, 'Cistercian Ideals versus Reality: 1134 Reconsidered', *Cîteaux: Commmentarii Cistercienses* 39 (1988), 217–31, and Constance H. Berman's *The Cistercian Evolution: the Invention of a Religious Order in Twelfth-Century Europe* (Philadelphia, PA, 2000), 39–45, and 'Were There Twelfth-Century Cistercian Nuns?', *ChH* 68 (1999), 824–64.

[6] Brigitte Degler-Spengler, 'The Incorporation of Cistercian Nuns into the Order in the Twelfth and Thirteenth Century', in John A. Nichols and Lillian Thomas Shank, eds, *Hidden Springs* (Kalamazoo, MI, 1995), 85–134.

[7] For the (now-challenged) idea that early Cistercian nuns were opposed by the wider Cistercian order, see Sally Thompson, 'The Problem of the Cistercian Nuns in the Twelfth and Early Thirteenth Centuries', in Derek Baker, ed., *Medieval Women*, SCH.S 1 (Oxford, 1978), 227–52.

[8] Even the outstanding book by David H. Williams still confines nuns to a separate chapter at the end (*The Cistercians in the Early Middle Ages* [Leominster, 1998]), thus following the same approach as Lekai's *The Cistercians*.

[9] The term has a rich heritage in studies of medieval women's religion; e.g. Brenda Bolton, 'Thirteenth-Century Religious Women: Further Reflections on the Low Countries "Special Case"', in Juliette Dor, Lesley Johnson, and Jocelyn Wogan-Browne, eds, *New Trends in Feminine Spirituality: the Holy Women of Liège and their Impact* (Turnhout, 1999), 129–57.

nuns, that is abbeys, with twenty-five unofficial priory communities which claimed Cistercian identity but were not accepted as such.[10] On one level, this bipartite classification is not in dispute. It is true that the convents of Tarrant in Dorset and Marham in Norfolk do appear in different kinds of sources compared with the other twenty-five houses. The Tarrant and Marham sources have a certain official-ness to them and thereby beguile us into accepting that these two were the only English nunneries whose inhabitants interacted with the Cistercian world and, indeed, were the only English nunneries accepted by the Cistercian world.

But, even though I do not dispute that Tarrant and Marham were official Cistercian nunneries, this should not blind us to the stories of the unofficial Cistercian houses. This is where current understandings of the mutual dependency of elite and popular are so helpful. As Van Engen has put it, even when ecclesiastical authorities (i.e. elites) seem to be determining religious ideology and practice, they nonetheless depend for their very authority on those who have no authority.[11] In other words, the identities of official organizations are formed more than we might think by exterior influences, and we can learn much about the self-appointed centres of religious culture when we examine those groups allocated to the periphery. In the case of the English Cistercians, this means that nunneries on the margins of the institution necessarily still contribute to the history of the institutional centre of the order and so must be studied not only in their own right but also for the insights they can bring into an understanding of the Cistercian order at its widest.

Modern terminology on English nuns shows the strong pull of the ideals/reality logic, in which there is a hierarchy of form that a monastery should aspire to. Tarrant and Marham have been credited as the only two 'fully' Cistercian abbeys.[12] The remaining twenty-five communities have been referred to, variously, as: peculiar Cistercian nuns; so-called Cistercians; Cistercians of a special kind; or simply as 'Cistercians' in quotation marks.[13] First, these terms diminish the unof-

---

[10] The figures come from David Knowles and R. Neville Hadcock, *Medieval Religious Houses: England and Wales* (London, 1971) [hereafter: *MRHEW*], 271–7, which in turn come from Eileen Power, *Medieval English Nunneries c.1275 to 1535* (Cambridge, 1922), 685–92.

[11] Van Engen, 'The Future of Medieval Church History', 516–17.

[12] Coburn V. Graves, 'Stixwould in the Market-Place', in John A. Nichols and Lillian Thomas Shank, eds, *Distant Echoes* (Kalamazoo, MI, 1984), 213–35, 213.

[13] *MRHEW*, 271; Sally Thompson, *Women Religious: the Founding of English Nunneries*

ficial nunneries by defining them more by the qualities they lack than by the qualities they possess. Second, the terms assume that a so-called Cistercian nunnery in the twelfth century was the same as a so-called Cistercian nunnery in the thirteenth century, and so on. But such changelessness over time is extremely unlikely. This relates not just to the internal activities of the nuns themselves, but also to how other groups conceived of the houses – English Cistercian abbots, royalty, bishops, papacy, and the Cistercian General Chapter in France.

Tarrant and Marham provide good examples of the differing ways in which medieval nunneries might or might not become involved in official Cistercian affairs, and also of the different groups that were prepared to recognize nunneries as Cistercian. Tarrant in Salisbury diocese and Marham in Norwich are the only English nunneries accepted by all scholars to have been Cistercian. These were the only two houses for which the General Chapter took responsibility, as evidenced by notices of incorporation and supervision in the annual statutes from Cîteaux. Tarrant appeared in the statutes in the 1240s and 1250s, and Marham in the 1250s.[14] In the latter case it was specifically stated that the house 'sought incorporation into our order'. So in Burgundy in the mid-thirteenth century these two houses were recorded for all time in the official documentation of the Cistercian order.

This is a modest basis on which to base a claim for Cistercian affiliation, although this is indeed the evidence generally presented in order to claim the official status of these two houses. There is in fact further medieval evidence that the two houses were seen as legitimate Cistercian nunneries (seen as such by Cistercian monks, that is). Here I refer to lists of Cistercian monasteries, often added as reference guides at the back of Cistercian cartularies or in compilations of Cistercian customs and statute proceedings. From such lists we can learn that somewhere in Europe (probably in France) in the late thirteenth century a Cistercian considered England to have two 'abbeys of nuns, daughters of Cîteaux', namely Tarrant in the diocese of Salisbury and

---

after the Norman Conquest (Oxford, 1991), 98; Coburn V. Graves, 'English Cistercian Nuns in Lincolnshire', *Speculum* 54 (1979), 492–9, 493; Sharon K. Elkins, *Holy Women of Twelfth-Century England* (Chapel Hill, NC, and London, 1988), 84–8.

[14] Joseph M. Canivez, ed., *Statuta Capitulorum Generalium Ordinis Cisterciensis*, 8 vols (Louvain, 1933–41) [hereafter: *Statuta*], on Tarrant, 2: 271 (ann. 1243, no. 62) and 2: 434 (ann. 1257, no. 50); on Marham, 2: 355 (ann. 1250, no. 43) and 2: 363 (ann. 1251, no. 26).

Marham in the diocese of Norwich.[15] We learn that the same belief in two English nunneries was also held by a German Cistercian monk at Altenberg abbey in the late fifteenth or sixteenth century.[16] Finally, we learn that at Newenham Cistercian abbey in Exeter diocese, in the second half of the fourteenth century, just one Cistercian nunnery was considered to belong to the 'Abbeys of the Cistercian order in England, Wales, and Scotland', and this was Tarrant.[17]

Modern scholars who produce lists of Cistercian houses are therefore in good company – this list-making was a preoccupation among medieval Cistercians also. What we learn from all this can never be comprehensive (Newenham included only the relatively nearby Tarrant in its list, the house with which it had already enjoyed a good century of pastoral interactions, but it omitted Marham), but what it can show is that when we look at certain 'official' kinds of sources we gain a certain 'official' image of the Cistercian order, one which gives quite a restricted picture of English Cistercian nuns. Another kind of list – of Cistercian houses and their tax payments – reveals that in the late thirteenth century the Cistercian monks at Beaulieu in Winchester diocese considered that the only Cistercian nunneries (in this case in Canterbury province) were Tarrant and Marham.[18] Thus, if we look for the official we find the official, which clearly takes us to Tarrant and Marham.

But this is not to say that the unofficial monastery had no history in relation to the overall monastic order. Sometimes this history was recognized and recorded by people outside the institution. In the 1270s,

---

15 Oxford, Keble College, MS 36, fol. 9r. In 1859 Thomas Phillipps bought the manuscript from Guglielmo Libri, the infamous pillager of French libraries, hence possibly suggesting a French origin.

16 Düsseldorf, Universitäts- und Landesbibliothek, MS C 32, fols 263v–267v, at fol. 267r. The listing of female Cistercian houses is printed in Franz Winter, *Die Cistercienser des nordöstlichen Deutschlands*, Part 3: *Von 1300 bis zur Reformation* (Gotha, 1871), 175–83, and *s.v.* 'Cîteaux (Abbaye)' in *Dictionnaire d'histoire et de géographie ecclésiastiques* (Paris, 1953), 12: cols 852–74, 860–2. On the manuscript, see Hans Mosler, *Die Cistercienserabtei Altenberg* (Berlin, 1965), 45, and 'Kurzinventar der Handschriften der Universitäts- und Landesbibliothek Düsseldorf', <http://www.manuscripta-mediaevalia.de/hs/kataloge-online.htm> (consulted 13 December 2004).

17 Oxford, Bodleian Library, MS Top. Devon d. 5, fol. 120v. This manuscript contains Newenham Abbey's cartulary, *c.*1347, with later additions (such as the abbey listing) towards its end.

18 London, BL, MS Addit. 70510, fol. 166r. This manuscript contains Beaulieu Abbey's cartulary. At the end are random texts, including a 1270s list of houses owing payment to Edward I.

at the same time as the internal Cistercian tax listing reported only Tarrant and Marham as female houses in Canterbury province, in Lincoln diocese (which was also in Canterbury province) seven female religious houses were being recognized as Cistercian by Henry III, by the bishop of Lincoln, and by the Cistercian abbot of Kirkstall, although not, famously, by the abbot of Cîteaux.[19]

If we jump ahead to the fifteenth century, there is a burst of evidence referring to female houses as Cistercian. In the mid-fifteenth century English bishops quite regularly referred to certain female communities as Cistercian houses.[20] Mortuary rolls also referred to female houses as 'of the Cistercian order', which is particularly important evidence if we take it that mortuary rolls provide an insight into how the given community saw themselves and wished to represent themselves, rather than how others saw them.[21] Houses which in earlier centuries were referred to as Benedictine, or which even in the same century were named Benedictine, now advertised themselves as 'of the Cistercian order'. This could mean many things – that differences between monastic orders were so minimal that religious personnel or scribes did not really know which order a house belonged to and could get confused, or, equally, that differences were minimal and that it was in a certain community's interests to claim membership of the

[19] Studies of this event include Graves, 'English Cistercian Nuns in Lincolnshire', and Linda Rasmussen, 'Order, Order! Determining Order in Medieval English Nunneries', in Linda Rasmussen *et al.*, eds, *Our Medieval Heritage: Essays in Honour of John Tillotson for his 60th Birthday* (Cardiff, 2002), 30–49, 33–7. Another nunnery in Lincoln diocese, St Michael's Stamford, pursued the same claim independently, and won additional support from Edward I and the archbishop of York; London, The National Archives (TNA), Public Record Office (PRO), E 326/11356.

[20] Multiple references appear in *Visitations of Religious Houses in the Diocese of Lincoln, Injunctions and Other Documents from the Registers of Richard Flemyng and William Gray Bishops of Lincoln, A.D. 1420–1436*, ed. A. Hamilton Thompson, 3 vols (London, 1969 [1919]) – e.g. Catesby, Heynings, Legbourne, Nun Cotham, St Michael's Stamford, and Stixwould nunneries.

[21] Three rolls from Durham are relevant. On the roll of Bishop Walter Skirlaw (d. 1405–6), Nun Cotham was identified as Cistercian. On the joint roll of Priors William of Ebchester (d. 1456) and John Burnby (d. 1464), Baysdale, Catesby, Handale, Keldholme, Legbourne, Marham, Nun Appleton, Nun Cotham, Sinningthwaite, St Michael's Stamford, Stixwould, Swine, Tarrant, and Wykeham were all identified as Cistercian, while Farewell, Neasham, and St Bartholomew's Newcastle all appear as 'of the order of St Bernard'. On the roll of Prior Robert Ebchester (d. 1488), Greenfield, Handale, Keldholme, Legbourne, Nun Cotham, Rosedale, Sinningthwaite, St Michael's Stamford, Swine, and Tarrant are identified as Cistercian, while Stixwould appears as 'of the order of St Bernard'. The rolls are printed in *The Obituary Roll of William Ebchester and John Burnby, Priors of Durham*, ed. James Raine (Durham, London, and Edinburgh, 1856).

Cistercians at this time. Notarial documents can also help here, as we find, in the early sixteenth century, female communities arranging for notaries to copy out key papal bulls which specify Cistercian freedoms from tithes and episcopal supervision of elections.[22] I would not reject either of these possibilities – either confusion regarding the differences between orders, or self-interest leading certain communities to claim Cistercian affiliation in return for the hope of Cistercian privileges.

However, all of this makes more sense if we simultaneously entertain a third possibility, namely that the Cistercian abbots themselves had been undertaking an active recovery of female houses in the fifteenth century. It is all very well to employ notaries to copy out documents alluding to one's Cistercian status, but the very fact that female communities would think of doing this, and would think they might get away with this, leads us to suspect there must have been some pre-existing relationship between these nunneries and the Cistercian order. And this takes us back to the official Cistercian sources – General Chapter statutes, and letters sent from the English visitors general to Cîteaux. For it is in the second half of the fifteenth century and into the early sixteenth century that the English nuns reappear in these official sources, recorded specifically at the initiative of the abbots.[23]

One late-medieval abbot who made a concerted attempt to bring English nuns into the Cistercian fold was the influential Marmaduke Huby, abbot of Fountains between 1495 and 1526.[24] In July 1523 there was an exchange of letters between Huby and one of Henry VIII's border barons.[25] At this point Huby had been a monk for sixty years,

22 In 1510 Elizabeth Nawton, the prioress of Neasham nunnery in Durham diocese, employed a notary to copy Lucius III's papal bull from 1184/85 on Cistercian freedom from episcopal interference, the 'Monastice sinceritas'; Northallerton, North Yorkshire County Record Office, ZRL 5/18. My thanks to Eddie Jones for supplying a transcript. Similarly, as part of a lengthy but sporadic history of asserting Cistercian status, in 1528 the nunnery of St Michael's Stamford employed a notary to copy Honorius III's 1220s bull which granted the Cistercians exemption from tithe payments; London, TNA, PRO, E 326/10568.

23 *Statuta* entries appear in 1491, 1520, and 1533. Letters appear in *Letters from the English Abbots to the Chapter at Cîteaux 1442–1521*, ed. C. H. Talbot (London, 1967), and below.

24 On Huby, see Derek Baker, 'Old Wine in New Bottles: Attitudes to Reform in Fifteenth-Century England', in Derek Baker, ed., *Renaissance and Renewal in Christian History*, SCH 14 (Oxford, 1977), 193–211, and C. H. Talbot, 'Marmaduke Huby Abbot of Fountains (1495–1526)', *Analecta Sacri Ordinis Cisterciensis* 20 (1964), 165–84.

25 London, BL, MS Addit. 24965. Four letters are relevant: Thomas Dacre's letter to Marmaduke Huby, 10 July 1523 (fols 166v–167r); Huby's letter to Dacre, 18 July (fol. 26r); Dacre's letter to William Clifton, vicar-general of Durham, 21 July (fol. 172v); and William Blithman's letter to Dacre, 26 July (fol. 28r). The 18 July letter is published in *Memorials of the Abbey of St. Mary of Fountains, Vol. I*, ed. John R. Walbran (Durham, London, and Edin-

with over twenty of these as one of the joint commissioners of all the English Cistercian houses. The person who began the correspondence was Thomas, third Lord Dacre of the North, warden-general of the Anglo-Scottish marches. In 1523 he had Anglo-Scottish hostilities on his mind, but nonetheless Dacre took the time to write a letter informing Huby of a problem with the election of the prioress at St Bartholomew's nunnery in Newcastle. As abbot of the Fountains mother-house, Huby was ultimately responsible for all abbots in his related daughter-houses, and one of these abbots (the abbot of Newminster) had elected a new prioress named Agnes Lawson, as though he held jurisdiction over the nunnery. But Dacre maintains that this is out of order: he has researched the matter in the episcopal registers and in fact the bishop of Durham has authority to officiate at such an election. There are many precedents for this, Dacre says, and his lord cardinal (unnamed, but Wolsey) has already sent his representative along to annul the election. Dacre wants to know what Huby is going to do about this problem initiated by his presumptuous charge.

Huby writes back an odd letter. It is effectively a history lesson on Cistercian nuns. Huby says that the Cistercian monastic order was founded in France about four hundred years ago, then it was quickly brought into England and Wales where, within a hundred years, there were eighty-two 'monasteries' of monks and sixty-four 'places and monasteries' of nuns. From the outset, Huby says, the English and Welsh Cistercians, both monks and nuns, were exempt from episcopal jurisdiction. However, about two hundred years ago, the nuns began to disregard their vow of chastity, and 'by one and by other by little and little they slipped away from the obedience of our religion'.[26] Now they have fallen into the jurisdiction of the bishops, a situation which Huby believes to be both a financial inconvenience to the nuns and an affront to the Cistercian order.

Huby's main argument is that the legitimate place of Cistercians was one of freedom from episcopal control. Coming from Huby, this argument is not surprising. Over his career Huby had been unrelenting in his arguments for Cistercian independence from episcopal influence. Towards the end of his commissioner's career he had stood firm against university-educated Cistercians who wanted to appeal to outside

burgh, 1863), 239–42. My thanks to Nigel Ramsay for introducing me to this correspondence.

26 *Memorials of the Abbey of St. Mary of Fountains*, ed. Walban, 240.

authorities – patrons, secular courts, potentially also bishops – to settle disputes. Huby thought this would be the thin end of the wedge leading to external bodies dominating Cistercian affairs. Equally, in the late 1480s Huby had written urgently to Cîteaux in response to the papal bull *Quanta in Dei ecclesia*, in which Innocent VIII authorized the archbishop of Canterbury to visit and reform religious houses such as the Cistercians, notwithstanding their traditional exemptions. Huby believed such archiepiscopal powers would be 'the ruin of the order'.[27] So it is somehow fitting that the last letter we know Huby to have written in his life was an argument in favour of Cistercian independence from bishops' interference.

However, even Huby admits to a problem. Something is certainly different about Cistercian nuns in England (he quickly loses interest in Wales) compared to their sisters on the continent. In France, Flanders, Picardy, and Germany the nuns remain subject to Cistercian father-abbots, but this is not so in England. Huby posits that the relationship of Cistercian nuns to abbots is less formalized in England than in continental Europe, which suggests that modern scholars invoking the 'special case' argument may well be correct, correct in this point at least. Possibly Huby is suggesting that there are nuns in England who follow the Cistercian *ordo* (the way of life) but are not part of the other *Ordo* (the institutional structure or *Ordo Cisterciensis*), with all its formal links, where a given male house formally and officially oversees a given female house.[28] Huby certainly preferred nunneries to be official rather than unofficial (he proudly writes that he has brought three southern nunneries back from the bishops to the authority of father-abbots, and his earlier letters as commissioner refer to female houses that he was actively bringing [back?] into the Cistercian community[29]), but nonetheless he recognized the valid place of the unofficial houses in the Cistercian order.

Huby goes on to say more, but it should be clear already that he was prepared to see Cistercian nuns in places modern scholars have not

27 Talbot, *Letters From the English Abbots*, no. 50.

28 On the distinction between the Cistercian *ordo* and *Ordo*, see Michael Casey, 'Bernard and the Crisis at Morimond. Did the Order Exist in 1124?', *Cistercian Studies Quarterly* 38 (2003), 119–75.

29 See Huby's involvement with Cook Hill priory in the 1490s; Talbot, *Letters from the English Abbots*, nos 66, 77; *Statuta*, 6: 22 (ann. 1491, no. 49). The nuns of Pinley also appear in Cistercian correspondence in the early 1500s; possibly Huby had a hand in overseeing this community also.

looked. Although I have been unable to locate Huby's sources for his figure of sixty-four nunneries, undoubtedly the very well-read Huby had a solid reason for choosing this number. That is, Huby knew something about the history of medieval Cistercian nuns that we today do not, and his tantalizingly broad understanding of what it meant to be a Cistercian and his desire to reclaim English nunneries for the Cistercian order should encourage us that there is still more female Cistercian history to uncover. Importantly, when it came to defending the Cistercians' key privilege of episcopal exemption, Huby was prepared to use the unofficial houses as examples. In other words, when defending one of the defining characteristics of the Cistercian order, Huby seemed to realize something that commentators on elite and popular religion have since stressed and something that adherents of the ideals/reality division for so long ignored, namely, that communities on the margins of an institution play an intrinsic role in the official history of that institution.[30]

University of Tasmania

[30] This research was supported by the Australian Research Council.

THE MOST TRAVERSED BRIDGE:
A RECONSIDERATION OF ELITE AND POPULAR RELIGION IN LATE MEDIEVAL IRELAND*

by SALVADOR RYAN

RECENT years have witnessed the study of late medieval religion change and develop almost beyond recognition. In particular, the phenomenon of 'popular' or 'traditional' religion has increasingly been placed under the microscope. A succession of studies has questioned the view that an unbridgeable chasm existed between the religious sensibilities of the privileged echelons of society (the higher clergy and members of the nobility) and those of the lower social orders.[1] The apparent sea-change in our understanding of how many expressions of belief and devotion were shared across a wide social spectrum has led, however, to more questions than answers. Indeed, the most pressing of these surely concerns the terms 'popular'

* I wish to acknowledge the support of the Irish Research Council for the Humanities and Social Sciences in providing me with a Post-Doctoral Research Fellowship during the tenure of which this article was completed.

[1] Natalie Zemon Davis, 'Some Tasks and Themes in the Study of Popular Religion', in Charles Trinkaus and Heiko Oberman, eds, *The Pursuit of Holiness in Late Medieval and Renaissance Religion* (Leiden, 1974), 307–36; Peter Burke, *Popular Culture in Early Modern Europe* (New York, 1978); Willem Frijhoff, 'Official and Popular Religion in Christianity', in Pieter Hendrick Vrijhof and Jacques Waardenburg, eds, *Official and Popular Religion: Analysis of a Theme for Religious Studies* (The Hague, 1979), 71–117; André Vauchez, *La Spiritualité du Moyen Âge occidental* (Paris, 1975); idem, *The Laity in the Middle Ages: Religious Beliefs and Devotional Practices* (Notre Dame, IN, 1993); Raoul Manselli, *La Religion populaire au Moyen Âge: problèmes de méthode et d'histoire* (Montreal, 1975); Trevor Johnson, 'The Recatholicisation of the Upper Palatinate, 1621–circa 1700', unpublished Ph.D. thesis, University of Cambridge, 1991; Duffy, *Stripping of the Altars*; Marc Forster, *The Counter-Reformation in the Villages: Religion and Reform in the Bishopric of Speyer, 1560–1720* (Ithaca, NY, 1992); idem, *Catholic Revival in the Age of the Baroque: Religious Identity in Southwest Germany 1550–1750* (Cambridge, 2001); Aron Gurevich, *Medieval Popular Culture: Problems of Belief and Perception* (Cambridge, 1995); R. W. Scribner, 'Is a History of Popular Culture Possible?', *History of European Ideas* 10 (1989), 175–91; idem, 'Introduction', in R. W. Scribner and Trevor Johnson, eds, *Popular Religion in Germany and Central Europe, 1400–1800* (New York, 1996); Christopher Marsh, *Popular Religion in Sixteenth-Century England: Holding their Peace* (New York, 1998); Salvador Ryan, 'Popular Religion in Gaelic Ireland, 1445–1645', unpublished Ph.D. thesis, 2 vols, National University of Ireland Maynooth, 2002; Willem Frijhoff, 'Epilogue', in Willem Frijhoff, *Embodied Belief: Ten Essays on Religious Culture in Dutch History*, ed. Joris van Eijnatten and Fred Van Lieburg (Hilversum, 2002), 275–89; Carl Watkins, ' "Folklore" and "Popular Religion" in Britain during the Middle Ages', *Folklore* 115 (2004), 140–50.

and 'elite' themselves and whether these categories have become all but obsolete. This paper re-examines these terms and their usefulness in the light of current scholarship, arguing that although an identifiable body of religious ideas routinely crossed social and cultural boundaries in the medieval period, it nevertheless used a variety of vehicles in order to do so. The distinction between 'popular' and 'elite' religion, then, can be found not so much at the level of cargo but in its mode of transport.

Defining Popular and Elite Religion

The two-tier model has been described in various ways in the past. The distinction was couched in terms of institutional as opposed to non-institutional religion, official versus non-official religion, learned as against unlearned religion, orthodoxy versus heresy and indeed religion itself as opposed to superstition or even magic. In more recent times, this two-tier model has been exposed as inadequate and misleading. Peter Burke has gone some way towards allowing the educated strata of society participation in the popular piety of the unlearned in his delineation of 'great' and 'little' cultures. While the 'great' culture of the elites remains a foreign territory to the majority of the population, both the 'little' and 'great' cultures can be accessed by the higher orders of society, giving the lie to the idea that the nobleman could not be pious in a 'popular' sort of way.[2] However, the problem with Burke's view is that it allows for no filtering of religious ideas from the top down. In effect, it presents an elite world of religion that is essentially watertight. It implies, for instance, that higher clergy, who were spiritually nourished out of an elite tradition, brought nothing of that tradition with them when preaching to mixed audiences, promulgating new devotions or making significant inroads in scholarship. It is, in essence, akin to claiming that the influence of Aquinas's eucharistic theology on Mass-going lower social orders in the late medieval period was negligible. Martin Ingram speaks of a 'cultural consensus', uniting all levels, while Eamon Duffy, recognizing the shared and inherited character of religious belief, chooses to replace the term 'popular religion' with 'traditional religion', indicating a degree of religious homogeneity across the social divide.[3] However, even the term 'traditional', as

---

[2] Burke, *Popular Culture*, 28.
[3] Martin Ingram, 'Ridings, Rough Music and the Reform of Popular Culture', *P&P* 105 (1984), 79–113, at 105; Duffy, *Stripping of the Altars*, 4–5.

admitted by Duffy, has its problems. Although, its root meaning has the sense of something 'handed down' or 'passed along', in modern parlance 'traditional' is suggestive of what is native to a particular country or region, as in 'traditional music and dance' or 'traditional cuisine', often over a long period of time. Since much of what constituted late medieval religion was not, in fact, native to any particular region, and, furthermore, did not always have a long history, this term appears almost as problematic as the one it was supposed to replace.

Recently, I have tentatively suggested an alternative approach to this problem which, although presenting its own difficulties, may nevertheless offer a way forward.[4] This involves a re-engagement with the older term 'popular religion' at the level of its root meaning – 'belonging to the people'. It postulates that religious belief involves a personal engagement with a body of doctrine received from a teaching authority (in the case of the late medieval period and for the purposes of this paper, the Catholic Church). This engagement elicits a response in both faith and praxis. The most important articles of faith, as found in the formula *Credo in unum Deum*, are confessed and adhered to by large numbers of people but not always in identical fashion. Theology, being the rendering of an account or rationale of God, works at a number of different levels. Failure to appreciate this results in a superficial analysis of the history of religious belief, regardless of period or location. First, it works at a very general level, whereby an account of God is provided within the ambit of the deposit of faith as received in Revelation. This account of God, while retaining its orthodoxy, becomes increasingly nuanced when it is examined at the level of individual cultures, societies and ethnic groupings. Indeed, even at the level of the individual, a theological response to Christian doctrine is required. In essence, the whole Christian Church – in its regional, cultural, ethnic and individual constituents – is called to provide an answer both collectively and personally to the question Christ posed in the gospels: 'Who do you say I am?' (Matt. 16:15.) The response to this question is shaped not only by the official doctrine that is received from the teaching Church or that which is filtered through the shades of a given culture or society, but also from within the margins of personal lived experience. Thus Voltaire's (1694–1778) famous remark that 'If God created us in His image, we have more than returned the compliment' operates

---

4 Salvador Ryan, 'The Most Contentious of Terms: towards a New Understanding of Late Medieval Popular Religion', *Irish Theological Quarterly* 68 (2003), 281–90.

both at macrocosmic and microcosmic levels. If one begins from this understanding, 'popular religion' comprises the engagement of both individuals and groups with a set of doctrines, leading to a variety of responses. These responses may, in certain cases, be skewed and uncertain, lacking intellectual finesse; at other times they might be deeply insightful or even spiritually moving. Historical studies have shown to great effect that deviations from theological orthodoxy were not always the preserve of the peasant nor, indeed, theological understanding the sole possession of the learned nobleman.[5]

This definition of 'popular religion', however, is not without its problems. If, in fact, all who engage with and respond to a body of doctrine practise 'popular religion', regardless of intellectual or social status, one wonders whether there is room for a separate category entitled 'elite religion'. If, as indicated by Burke, the 'great tradition' could participate in the religious culture of the 'little tradition' and in turn, as suggested above, the little tradition had access, via a variety of media, to the 'great tradition', how, then, can scholars continue to speak of 'elite religion'? It appears that, as noted by Ingram, something of a cultural consensus can be identified in the late medieval period that spanned a variety of social orders. More particularly, a distinctive and identifiable religious culture pervaded Western Europe in the Middle Ages that was largely shared across the divide. Its central tenets are found in myriad examples at all levels, indicative of the effective transmission of religious ideas. What distinguishes elite religion from popular religion (although the elites necessarily participated in popular religion too) is not its content, but its forms or, as noted metaphorically above, the vehicles it used rather than the cargo it carried. While a wealthy and learned individual might have personal access to the latest devotional fad in manuscript or book form, his unlearned counterpart could encounter similar material by means of a sermon heard, an iconographic depiction viewed or, perhaps, a text discussed by a more literate friend. Indeed, the local existence of a religious text might bind a wide range of people together in common awareness of the nub of its contents, as noted by Brian Stock, even if the levels of access to the text itself varied.[6] What follows below is a concise examination of how this may have worked in practice, using the model of late medieval Ireland.

---

[5] See Ryan, 'The Most Contentious of Terms', 287–90.
[6] Brian Stock, *Listening for the Text: on the Uses of the Past* (Baltimore, PA, 1997), 23, 36, 140–58.

The particular cargo in question comprises two texts: one detailing how one should confess one's sins and the second explaining the benefits to be accrued from attending Mass.

Bridging the Devotional Divide in Late Medieval Gaelic Ireland

The Fourth Lateran Council decree *Omnis utriusque sexus* (1215) enjoined upon all believers who had attained the age of reason to confess their sins and receive communion yearly under pain of excommunication.[7] While historians have rarely praised fifteenth-century Ireland for the vibrancy of its ecclesiastical life,[8] there were, nevertheless, many groups of religious that adopted spiritual revival as their primary objective. The most important of these were the mendicant orders that participated in what became known as the Observant reform, a movement which advocated a return to the ideals of their founders and a strict observation of the Rule. The fifteenth century witnessed a rapid expansion in the number of Observant houses, particularly in Gaelic areas in the north west of the country.[9] On the whole, among the mendicant orders, ninety new friaries were established between 1400 and 1508.[10] One of the consequences of reform was a greater emphasis on the development of the spirituality of the laity. From the mid fifteenth century onwards, the Irish Franciscan province encouraged the establishment of the secular Third Order, which catered for those who wished to lead more sacramentalized lives. Franciscan tertiaries observed the seven canonical hours and were expected to attend Mass daily in addition to confessing and receiving the Eucharist three times a year. Illiterate lay members were also welcomed, being required to recite twelve *Pater Nosters* and *Glorias* at Matins (seven for the other hours) in addition to a *Credo* and Psalm 50.[11] Proximity to a

---

7   Nicholas Tentler, *Sin and Confession on the Eve of the Reformation* (Princeton, NJ, 1977), 21–2.

8   Canice Mooney, *The Church in Gaelic Ireland, 13th to 15th Centuries* (Dublin, 1969); John Bossy, 'The Counter-Reformation and the People of Catholic Ireland, 1596–1641', in T. Desmond Williams, ed., *Historical Studies* 8 (1971), 155–69, at 171; John Watt, *The Church in Medieval Ireland* (Dublin, 1972); Patrick J. Corish, *The Irish Catholic Experience: a Historical Survey* (Dublin, 1985); Peter O'Dwyer, *Towards a History of Irish Spirituality* (Dublin, 1995), 132.

9   Colmán Ó Clabaigh, *The Franciscans in Ireland, 1400–1534: from Reform to Reformation* (Dublin, 2002), 58–79.

10   O'Dwyer, *Irish Spirituality*, 135.

11   Ó Clabaigh, *Franciscans in Ireland*, 84–7.

Franciscan house was a practical requisite, in order to facilitate attendance at the liturgy.

The activities of the Franciscan Order provide a useful example of
the manner in which religious ideas circulated between different
groups within Gaelic Ireland. Firstly, Irish Franciscans were regularly
exposed to the latest European ideas, through attendance at triennial
continental chapters and as a result of frequent visitations to Irish foundations by foreign commissaries. The surviving late fifteenth- and early
sixteenth-century catalogue of the Franciscan friary of Youghal,
County Cork, demonstrates that the friars could boast of possessing
some of the most important and recent continental theological and
devotional works. One of these, the *Confessionale-Defecerunt* of
Antoninus of Florence (1389–1459) is documented as having a particularly wide influence. A list of sixteen conditions for a good confession,
found in this work, proved exceptionally popular. Two fifteenth-
century Irish Franciscan manuscripts from houses in Cork and Clare
contain this list, which suggests that it was used widely as a practical
tool for instructing penitents.[12] The recommendations included
simplicity, humility and honesty, deep contrition and a confidence that
the confessed sins would be forgiven. Most importantly, perhaps, the
penitent was advised to confess at least three times a year. This last
recommendation suggests that this text embraced lay tertiary members
of the order for whom this was a requirement. Apart from the text's
obvious relevance as a tool in preaching, it was also to prove popular in
non-clerical circles. A composite collection of prayers and legends in
the *Leabhar Chlainne Suibhne* (Book of the MacSweenys), commissioned
for Donegal noblewoman Máire, wife of Eoghan Ruadh Mac Suibhne
Fanad in 1513, contains the same list. Furthermore, we know, from an
obit later inserted into the manuscript, that the contents of Máire's
collection closely matched her own devotional practices. She may first
have heard of the 'sixteen conditions' from Donegal Franciscans and
then chose to have the list included in the book that was compiled for
her use.[13] Elsewhere, a number of bardic religious poems, composed
mainly by laymen, contain references to many of the recommendations
listed in the 'sixteen conditions'.[14] However, these references are diffuse

---

[12] Georges Dottin, 'Notice du manuscrit irlandais de la bibliothèque de Rennes', *Revue
Celtique* 15 (1894), 79–91; Ó Clabaigh, *Franciscans in Ireland*, 122–3.
[13] Ryan, 'Popular Religion', 1: 328.
[14] See 'Confession of Sins', ed. Lambert McKenna, in *The Irish Monthly*, Yearly Volume
(1922), 28–31; idem, *Aithdioghluim Dána: a Miscellany of Irish Bardic Poetry*, 2 vols (Dublin,

and varied and not explicitly identified as belonging to the formula itself. It appears likely that these poets, or indeed their patrons, may have heard these recommendations preached in sermons, remembered some of them, and later had them included in their penitential works. It was not uncommon for poets to admit to partially remembering a story heard in church, which they later attempt to reconstruct with varying degrees of success in verse. Here, the division between content and form, which may distinguish popular and elite religion, becomes relevant. While, in this instance, the content of the message conveyed remains roughly equivalent, it has come loose from its original packaging: indeed, Antoninus of Florence's formula of 'sixteen conditions', as found in manuscript copies, disappears completely in bardic verse.

It was important that the message contained in the 'sixteen conditions' formula reached a wide audience. If all believers were expected to confess and receive the Eucharist yearly, it was imperative that they be properly instructed on how correctly to fulfil their duty. For lay tertiary members of the Franciscan order, the need was even more pressing. As noted above, not all tertiaries were literate and accommodation was made for the non-literate by allowing them to recite basic prayers in fulfilment of the canonical hours requirement. Similarly, it is unlikely that the non-literate were ignorant of the 'sixteen conditions' simply because they could not read the text. In fact, the evidence of a member of the Paris province who was visitator to Ireland, suggests that the pastoral care offered by the mendicant orders, of which the recommendations for confession formed a part, spanned all social orders, stating that among the 'wild Irish' the Observants are feared, obeyed and adored 'not only by the peasants but by the lords who hold them in such reverence as to endure from them blows from a stick'.[15] The Franciscan order made continuous efforts to ensure that the teachings and devotions they promulgated reached the widest audiences possible. This can be observed in the example of the *Imago pietatis* or 'Image of Pity', displaying Christ as the Man of Sorrows surrounded by the instruments of the passion and bearing his five wounds, which appeared in woodcuts across Europe, England and Ireland in the four-

1939–40), I: poems 50, v.23; 69, v.16; 64, v.40; 77, v.39; 84, v.2; 94, v.32; idem, *Philip Bocht Ó hUiginn* (Dublin, 1931), poem 25, v.3. For bardic verse and the spread of religious ideas see Salvador Ryan, 'A Slighted Source: Rehabilitating Irish Bardic Religious Poetry in Historical Discourse', *Cambrian Medieval Celtic Studies* 48 (2004), 75–101.

15   Ó Clabaigh, *Franciscans in Ireland*, 78.

teenth and fifteenth centuries.[16] This image offered many thousands of years of pardon to devotees who prayed the required set of prayers before it. The fact that the obligatory prayers were comprised simply of five *Pater Nosters*, five *Aves* and a *Credo*, no more than the minimum requirement for lay Catholics who wished to avail themselves of the sacraments according to the Sarum Use, demonstrates that this devotion was made accessible to the many rather than the few.[17] The 'Image of Pity' was linked to the Five Wounds devotion and served as a visual aid for wealthy and not-so-wealthy owners of books of hours right across Europe, who gazed at the image when reciting a wide selection of Five Wounds prayers, which varied greatly in their complexity.[18] Its wide appeal is attested by the variety of prayers that could legitimately be recited before it. At the execution of three Irish Catholics in 1581 a Protestant minister reports that one of the men said to the others 'Let us say pater nosters 5, 5 aves and 5 credes in remembrance of the 5 wounds of Christ', illustrating that, in times of crisis, perhaps the simplest approach was deemed to be the best.[19]

A second notable devotional boundary-crosser was the *merita missae* or 'benefits of the Mass' formula. This list of favours to be accrued by attending Mass and, more specifically, seeing the eucharistic host, quickly spread in manuscript form across Europe from the thirteenth century onwards. Invariably attributed to some well-respected Church Father such as Ambrose or Augustine, its stamp of orthodoxy was assured.[20] These benefits were certainly preached by the higher clergy for in 1375 Bishop Brinton of Exeter instructed his congregation that after seeing God's body no desire for food would be felt (in an Irish version of the list, this benefit alternatively promises the avoidance of indigestion!), oaths would be forgiven, eyesight would not fade, one would not suffer sudden death, nor indeed would one age at all during that time and finally, one's every step would be guarded by angels.[21]

[16] For an Irish example see Fergus O'Farrell, 'Our Lord's Pity in Ennis Friary', *North Munster Antiquarian Journal* 22 (1980), 33–7.
[17] The Sarum Use was commonly employed in late medieval Ireland. See E. C. Whitaker, *Documents of the Baptismal Liturgy* (London, 1970), 237.
[18] For a discussion of the Five Wounds devotion in Ireland see Salvador Ryan, 'Reign of Blood: Aspects of Devotion to the Wounds of Christ in Late Medieval Gaelic Ireland', in Joost Augusteijn and Mary Ann Lyons, eds, *Irish History: a Research Yearbook* (Dublin, 2002), 137–49.
[19] M. V. Ronan, *The Irish Martyrs of the Penal Laws* (London, 1935), 51.
[20] Ryan, 'Popular Religion', 1: 359.
[21] Miri Rubin, *Corpus Christi: the Eucharist in Late Medieval Culture* (Cambridge, 1992), 63.

This list was not solely designed for the use of prelates such as Brinton. Indeed the *Doctrinal of Sapyence*, a French pastoral manual for 'symple prestes that understande not the scriptures [. . .] to lerne and teche to theyre paryshens', translated in 1489 by Caxton, contained the list, which was obviously deemed suitable fare also for the congregations of 'simple priests'.[22] In Ireland, a list of fourteen *merita missae* is found in the fifteenth-century Gaelic devotional collection entitled *Liber Flavus Fergusiorum* and also in Máire Ní Mháille's 1513 religious compilation, alluded to above, illustrating its popularity with the Gaelic nobility.[23] It is conceivable that these benefits were widely preached in Gaelic Ireland as, once again, part of the list's content appears elsewhere, divided from the unit. One promise listed in the *Liber Flavus Fergusiorum* – that every step taken on the way to Mass is enumerated in anticipation of a heavenly reward – is cited as early as the thirteenth-century bardic poetry of Giolla Brighde Mac Con Midhe.[24] Another benefit listed in the same collection – that whatever sins one commits between masses will be forgiven – seems to have had wide appeal if we are to believe a report on the Irish filed by Lord Justice Wallop in June 1582: 'And hearing Mass on Sunday or Holyday they think all the week after they may do what heinous offence soever and it is dispensed withal'.[25] Perhaps the numerous benefits attributed to seeing the host at Mass directly prompted the well-documented behaviour of those who rushed from church to church just to be present for the elevation of the host.[26] Indeed, the preamble to the Irish text of the benefits found in both *Liber Flavus Fergusiorum* and *Leabhar Chlainne Suibhne* suggests a desire to make known that the reception of the benefits was conditional upon attendance at the entire eucharistic liturgy, '*ó tosach co deiredh*' ('from beginning to end'), in an effort to dissuade devotees from avariciously snatching as many elevations as possible in order to amass a quick spiritual fortune.[27] Furthermore, the promise that one's business would prosper may have prompted some, such as the Irish woman who stole a host to increase the price of her wine, as recounted in the

---

22 Duffy, *Stripping of the Altars*, 56, 100.
23 Gearóid Mac Niocaill, 'Disiecta membra', *Éigse* 8 (1955–7), 74–7, at 74.
24 N. J. A. Williams, *The Poems of Giolla Brighde Mac Con Midhe* (Dublin, 1980), poem 21, v.37.
25 *State Papers concerning the Irish Church in the Time of Queen Elizabeth*, ed. W. Maziere Brady (London, 1868), 59.
26 R. N. Swanson, *Religion and Devotion in Europe, c.1215–c.1515* (Cambridge, 1995), 182.
27 Mac Niocaill, 'Disiecta membra', 74.

thirteenth-century *Liber exemplorum*, to take matters into their own hands.[28]

It is difficult to categorize a list such as the *merita missae* as belonging exclusively to any particular social grouping. While wealthy Gaelic noblewomen such as Máire Ní Mháille had direct access to the list, others were more than likely aware of its general thrust from oral transmission or indeed as part of a formal sermon delivered in church. The same applies to the 'sixteen conditions', which likewise escaped its original form to circulate with ease across the social and ecclesiastical divide. Devotional lists such as these travelled widely, demonstrating that the bridge between high theology and low praxis, just as that between elite religion and its popular counterpart, was a real one in the late medieval period and one that cannot be ignored in future research: indeed it was the most traversed bridge.

St. Patrick's College
Thurles,
Co. Tipperary,
IRELAND

---

[28] Ryan, 'The Most Contentious of Terms', 287.

PRAYER AND PARTICIPATION IN
LATE MEDIEVAL ENGLAND

by R. N. SWANSON

AT some point in the 1520s the printer Richard Pynson ran off a poster to spread information about an indulgence.[1] The sheet has a poor survival rate: what appears to be the unique extant copy exists as printer's waste used for book-binding, and is now badly damaged. Nevertheless, the bit which matters for present purposes is almost intact. It notes that Cardinal Wolsey had offered a pardon of ten years and ten Lents to all who recited a specific psalm and set of prayers 'for the most noble and prosperous estate of our soverayne lorde king Henry the .viii. the quene and the pryncesse', which could be gained once each day. In addition, all the other bishops of the realm had offered forty days of pardon to everyone who recited five Our Fathers, five Hail Marys, and a Creed for the same intent. (How often that indulgence could be gained is unclear: it may have been secured at each recitation.) The Latin prayers specified to gain Wolsey's pardon were printed on the bottom half of the sheet, but more than half of that text is now lost.

The conditions surrounding this indulgence seem to epitomize a supposed division in the practices of late medieval English spirituality, between an educated readership which could take advantage of Wolsey's pardon by reciting the texts (possibly displayed on a wall, or mounted on hand-held tablets), and an audience which, having had the indulgence explained to them by those who could read, would then recite the memorized triad of traditional prayers – the Our Father, Ave, and Creed. However, such a separation was by no means rigid. Those on the 'learned' side of the divide could also gain the more general pardon; indeed Pynson's poster clearly states that those who 'say the

---

[1] Bryn Mawr, PA, Bryn Mawr College Library, Special Collections (gift of Howard Lehman Goodhart), bound into 878 P7 AC. I am grateful to Marianne Hansen for providing images, and other assistance. The sheet is listed in A. W. Pollard and G. R. Redgrave (rev. W. A. Jackson, F. S. Ferguson and K. F. Pantzer), *A Short-Title Catalogue of Books Printed in England, Scotland, and Ireland, and of English Books Printed Abroad (1475–1640)*, 3 vols (2nd edn, London, 1976–91), no. 14077c.146. The section of text considered in this paragraph is reproduced in the appendix below.

sayde psalme with the suffrages, as oft as they say' the Paternosters, Aves, and Creed with the required intention 'shal[l have a]nd enioye all the foresayd pardon'.

The levels of accessibility within this pardon exemplify a clearly identifiable aspect of medieval religious practice: an ostensible division which creates an impression of exclusion and elitism, yet at the same time accommodates and includes. The advanced latinity required for the Wolsey pardon (and, perhaps, the additional labour of working through what may have been a lengthy process of recitation) gains a fairly hefty pardon; the more basic recitations, from memory, by rote, earn a lesser reward. Yet, at the same time, the prayers all work to the same end: to the benefit of Henry VIII, Catherine of Aragon, and their daughter Mary. This suggests an awareness of differences in people's potential participation in and contribution to the totality of catholic religious practice, but a recognition that everyone could make a contribution, and a determination to ensure that everyone could play a part if they so wished, and share in the rewards. (For it is also important that all recipients of the indulgence shared a common goal of personal salvation and a speedy transit through Purgatory: only that concern made the offer of indulgence worth making.) The acceptance of such variation is, perhaps, another manifestation of the attitude expressed in the twelfth-century maxim of 'diversity without adversity', a further demonstration of the range of discourse communities which combined in the overarching community of the catholic church.[2]

If that view is correct, then attitudes to such diversity without adversity are worth investigating in more detail. While historical analyses of religious practice can too easily adopt an interpretative approach which seeks to cleave catholicism by imposing divisions (of elite and popular, learned and lewd, lay and clerical), it can be argued that the imperatives and shared goals and aspirations of pre-Reformation catholicism meant that awareness of difference in fact encouraged processes of accommodation, and arrangements to ensure that participation was as extensive as possible. The discussion here is anchored in evidence of practices in England; but identical attitudes and imperatives certainly operated overseas.[3] The discussion is also, necessarily, brief.

---

[2] It can thus be integrated into the issues considered in R. N. Swanson, 'Unity and Diversity, Rhetoric and Reality: Modelling "the Church"', *Journal of Religious History* 20 (1996), 156–74.

[3] See, e.g., the indulgence issued collectively by a group of cardinals for devotions before the image of the Veronica in Linköping cathedral in 1412: the literate were to say the

* * *

Basic to this approach is the foundational status of the traditional three prayers within medieval catholicism. The Our Father, the Hail Mary, and Creed should have been firmly inculcated into all Christians as part of their basic religious training, in a sense as default prayers, standard devotional settings which could be enhanced if desired, but which certainly did not have to be. Their core standing was annually affirmed by their integration into the confessional process: everyone was annually tested on their knowledge of the texts – albeit in Latin rather than English.[4] As core prayers, they were both ubiquitous and useful, serving a wide variety of purposes, including imposition as a penance.[5] The constant repetition of demands for recitation of single or multiple Aves, Our Fathers, and Creeds serves only to emphasize their status as the basic prayers of the medieval Church. People were encouraged to go beyond them if they could, but the triad remained the foundational devotional units. Thus, in the *Lay Folks' Mass Book*, they are woven into the counterpoint between the priestly and popular liturgies.[6] They were the lowest common factor of medieval religion: everyone was expected to know them, regardless of status and education.[7] Public display of their significance, and ubiquity, is attested in the fashions for prayer beads in the late medieval period: rosaries could be high status artefacts,

---

prayer '*Salva sancta facies*'; for the 'layci illiterati' an Our Father and Ave would suffice: Alexander Seibold, *Sammelindulgenzen: Ablaßurkunden des Spätmittelalters und der Frühneuzeit*, Archiv für Diplomatik Schriftgeschichte, Siegel- und Wappenkunde: Beiheft 8 (Cologne, Weimar and Vienna, 2001), 282. Compare the devotion to the Veronica in an English primer (see n. 19 below).

[4] *John Mirk's Instructions for Parish Priests, Edited from MS Cotton Claudius A II and Six Other Manuscripts, with Introduction, Notes and Glossary*, ed. Gillis Kristensson, Lund Studies in English 49 (Lund, 1974), 115.

[5] *The Register of John Waltham, Bishop of Salisbury, 1388–1395*, ed. T. C. B. Timmins, CYS 80 (1994), nos 1119, 1146; R. H. Helmholz, *The Oxford History of the Laws of England, volume I: the Canon Law and Ecclesiastical Jurisdiction from 597 to the 1640s* (Oxford, 2004), 622, n. 108 (this a demand for five Paters, five Aves, and a Creed – a package itself almost a standard unit, regularly mentioned in devotions before indulgenced images).

[6] *The Lay Folks' Mass Book*, ed. T. F. Simmons, EETS, o.s. 71 (1879), 2–60, *passim*.

[7] See, for instance, the stipulation of daily recitations of Our Father and Ave (together with more complex orations) in the prayers required of pupils at the school associated with the Greyndoore chantry at Newland, Glos.: *Registrum Thome Spofford, episcopi Herefordensis, A.D. MCCCCXXII–MCCCCXLVIII*, ed. A. T. Bannister, CYS 23 (1919), 282. They are also included in prayers stipulated for the fellows and scholars in the early statutes of Corpus Christi College, Oxford: *Statutes of the Colleges of Oxford*, 3 vols (London, 1853), 2: Statutes of Corpus Christi College, 45 [separately paginated].

but were by no means exclusively so, as the outbreak of the Western Rising in 1549 attests.[8]

The normality, the ordinariness, of such prayers appears in the vignette of Joan Clyfland of Norwich in the 1420s, following her customary routine on entering a church and saying five Paternosters in honour of Christ, and five Aves in honour of the Virgin.[9] It also appears more provocatively in the case of William Colyn of South Creake, who in 1415 received a penance from his parish priest to say five Paters and five Aves before the pietà in his parish church. William, however, 'asserted and said ... that it would be more meritorious for him to say the said five pater nosters and aves before God in the sacrament of the altar', and so he did. The twist here is that 'for that reason he was reputed a Lollard'.[10]

The ubiquity of these three prayers allowed them to become almost a currency of spirituality, to be cashed in by anyone capable of reciting them. This is particularly noticeable in relation to indulgences, which were regularly offered for such devotions. In 1490, for instance, Bishop Alcock of Ely, having recently consecrated and dedicated the bells and altars at Gamlingay, offered forty days of pardon to all who knelt at the sound of the bells and said fifteen Paternosters and fifteen Aves for the good estate of whole church, the bishop as consecrator, the king and queen, and for the souls of all the dead. To increase his personal benefit, he added a further forty days for anyone saying an additional five Aves with the added clause, 'Gode have mercy of John, busshop of Ely, that halawde the altares ande bellys aforeseyde'.[11] Similar clusters of Our Fathers and Hail Marys (requiring fewer recitations) appear in other devotional contexts elsewhere in Alcock's register, being likewise rewarded with indulgences.[12]

Nevertheless, there were other prayers besides these three: late medieval primers are full of them. Often they are in Latin; always the fact of their being written – or printed – encourages a sense of their being in a

---

8 Christine Peters, *Patterns of Piety: Women, Gender and Religion in Late Medieval and Reformation England* (Cambridge, 2003), 57–9 (Peters emphasizes a gendering in types of beads, but that is another issue beyond present concerns); B. L. Beer, *Rebellion and Riot: Popular Disorder in England during the Reign of Edward VI* (n.p. [Kent, OH], 1982), 55–6.

9 *Heresy Trials in the Diocese of Norwich, 1428–31*, ed. Norman P. Tanner, Camden Society, 4th ser., 20 (London, 1977), 44.

10 Ibid., 89–90.

11 CUL, EDR G/1/6, 54–5.

12 Ibid., 55, 72–4.

different category from the usual three, and therefore presented to different recipients. Often the triad appears as well, a complementary positioning which may raise questions about the status of the more complex prayers. Eamon Duffy has concluded that

> The prescription of Paters and Aves after every Latin devotion in a primer ... is a strong indication that the readership envisaged was expected to have at best only a partial comprehension of the Latin 'holy wordes', and consequently to be in need of supplementing their recitation with prayers which they could be expected to understand.[13]

This is not a statement to challenge; but it may be one to refine, for Paters and Aves are also found prescribed at the end of prayers in English, and in those instances it is unlikely that they are added as a bonus to negate incomprehension. They thus appear added at the end of every line in some versions of a prayer to be recited over indulgenced beads; while the saying of five Our Fathers and five Aves at the end of another English devotion earned six hundred days of pardon.[14] In both cases – as is also the case with many of the Latin prayers – the Ave and Pater count as free-standing units, but units whose recitation actually enhances the accompanying prayer. In any event, both prayers (and the Creed, when required) were to be recited in Latin, not English: despite the seeming proliferation of English versions (either as free-standing units, or embedded in longer texts), their knowledge and understanding in the vernacular was not officially encouraged, and was indeed sometimes taken as a sign of heretical inclinations.[15]

* * *

Precisely because the basic prayers were basic, supposedly universally known, they do not attract attention. Yet their function merits more thought. They were foundational, a starting point for future devotional development. They were also the prayers which could be demanded to ensure the widest scale of participation in any devotional endeavour. It

---

[13] Duffy, *Stripping of the Altars*, 219.

[14] BL, MS Harley 4012, fol. 109r–v: these 600 days were in addition to the 100 years earned by reciting the English text without the additional prayers.

[15] G. H. Russell, 'Vernacular Instruction of the Laity in the Later Middle Ages in England: Some Texts and Notes', *Journal of Religious History* 2 (1962), 98–119; *Lollards of Coventry, 1486–1522*, ed. Shannon McSheffrey and Norman Tanner, Camden Society Publications, 5th ser., 23 (Cambridge, 2003), 72–3.

would, of course, be wrong to deny gradations in spiritual activity, sometimes explicit, which encourage differentiations and distinctions in analyses. Characteristic here is the distinction between learned and lewd brought out in the certificate recording the activities of the gild of St Katherine at Norwich in 1389. When the fraternity commemorated the dead, the learned were to say *placebo* and *dirige*, while the unlearned recited twenty Our Fathers and as many Aves.[16] Yet while there is here an assertion of distinction, there is also an assertion of comparability, of equivalence, perhaps equipotence. Such sentiments also appear elsewhere. While literate hermits were expected to say Aves and Our Fathers as adjuncts to the canonical hours, those who were illiterate said multiple repetitions to substitute for the more complex texts.[17] The conditions attached to one of the pardons offered at Syon abbey made allowance for similar substitution, requiring the saying of a Pater and Ave, 'or what othir devoute praier it be'.[18] More explicit is a statement with regard to the indulgence associated with devotion to the Veronica. The prayer '*Salve sancta facies*' was to be said before the image, being rewarded with 10,000 days of indulgence. However, in one instance the pardon seems to be divorced from the prayer, to reward devotion to the image rather than the use of the specific Latin text. One of the last of the traditional Sarum primers, printed at Paris in 1534, carries a note which clearly extends the pardon's availability, stipulating that 'they that kan not say this prayer, lette them say v. Paternoster, v. Ave, and v. Credo in deum'.[19]

* * *

The extension of the indulgence associated with the devotion to the Veronica attests the utility of the basic prayers as a means of inclusion and extension: their recitation was integrative, not divisive. This was no accident, but appears characteristic of a recognition by the ecclesiastical authorities that the prayers, as basic devotional units, offered a way to ensure extensive opportunities for Christians of every status and standing to participate in the life of the Church at all levels. It applied even in areas where division, exclusiveness, and selectivity might appear most essential, such as warfare and crusades. Yet even here the prayers

---

[16] *English Gilds*, ed. T. Smith, L. T. Smith and L. Brentano, EETS, o.s. 40 (1870), 20.

[17] V. Davis, 'The Rule of Saint Paul, the First Hermit, in Late Medieval England', in W. J. Sheils, ed., *Monks, Hermits and the Ascetic Tradition*, SCH 22 (Oxford, 1985), 203–14, 210–11.

[18] Oxford, Bodleian Library, MS Ashm. 750, fol. 140r–v.

[19] *Hore beatissime virginis Marie . . .* (Paris, 1534), fol. 73v. Cf. n. 3 above.

served a purpose, allowing wide-spread involvement and participation, without requiring everyone to go off to fight. Indeed, in such ventures the aim was often to harness the power of prayer as much as that of the sword. In the Scottish campaign of 1333, for instance, indulgences were offered to those invoking divine aid for Edward III. People who joined a Friday procession were rewarded with forty days of indulgence. Clergy who were unable to join the processions, but recited the penitential psalms with other prayers on Wednesdays and Fridays, gained twenty days. Laypeople likewise unable to process were encouraged to say fifty Our Fathers and Aves, to secure fifteen days of pardon.[20] Graded rewards also appeared in the pardons to support the anti-Hussite crusade of 1427,[21] but here added refinements suggest greater distinctions. Those fasting and praying to secure the crusaders' victory were offered sixty days of pardon, but the prayers had to be suitable. For the 'indocti seu illiterati' it would suffice to say ten Paternosters and ten Aves. Greater demands were made of the 'docti vero et litterati', who had to say the seven penitential psalms with a litany and collects, and other prayers 'ad id congruentibus'.[22] However, there were suggestions of leniency: for those whose condition did not allow such strenuous praying (or fasting) the obligations could be converted into other pious acts. This, again, suggests a concern for inclusion and integration, to allow participation in the crusading activity for as many as possible.

That process clearly resulted from a clerical decision to extend benefits widely by deliberately adopting the lowest common factor. Some signs of integration, of participation through prayer, offer a different perspective, which may amount to non-clerical appropriation of clerical formulae, thereby integrating them into a lay liturgical round. How far, if at all, such appropriation was actively encouraged is unclear, although one prayer which does seem to have escaped from the chancel into the wider world is the general bidding prayer, usually recited by the priest at mass to incite the laity to pray for a broad spectrum of concerns affecting the Churches militant and dormant. Broadly similar versions of the same prayer survive from across late medieval England;[23]

[20] *Chartulary of Winchester Cathedral*, ed. A. W. Goodman (Winchester, 1927), no. 170.

[21] Oxford, Bodleian Library, MS Tanner 165, fol. 91r–v.

[22] Ibid., fol. 94v.

[23] E. Calvert, 'Extracts from a Fifteenth Century MS', *Transactions of the Shropshire Archaeological and Natural History Society*, 2nd ser., 6 (1894), 99–106, 104–6; Simmons, *Lay Folks' Mass Book*, 64–80; *Death and Memory in Medieval Exeter*, ed. David Lepine and Nicholas Orme, Devon and Cornwall Record Society, n.s. 47 (Exeter, 2003), 337–9.

its repetition in the vernacular would have drummed it into generations of memory. That gave it mobility: a version had by 1389 been
integrated into the liturgy of at least one local fraternity, and thereby
moved into a guildhall.[24] More intriguingly, the prayer seems also to
have been used by Margery Kempe to structure some of her personal
devotions: her recorded list of intentions has striking affinities with the
list of intentions recorded in the bidding prayer, including the various
ranks within the Church, secular rulers, infidels, heretics and sinners,
the sick, and the souls in Purgatory.[25]

* * *

The evidence of the prayers, the encouragement of participation in religious activity through prayer and the evidence for the reality of that
participation and integration reveal not a distinction between elite and
popular religion, with a rigid barrier between learned and lewd or clerical and lay, but a religion in which such distinctions tend to evaporate.
Of course it is possible – and easy – to assert distinctions, especially on
the basis of literacy, and some of them would certainly have been valid.
Yet their overall reality may be questioned. Distinctions between the
'literate' and the 'illiterate' may in fact be fundamentally flawed
precisely because they focus so much on reading and textuality. The
very repetitiveness of medieval religious practice demands the integration of another factor, which is all too easily ignored: memory. Because
prayer texts appear in books, it is assumed that they were only accessed
through books; but this cannot always have been the case. Yet why
should the ability to recite the *De profundis* reflect anything more than a
good memory, be more valid as an indication of literacy than repeating
the 'neck verse' to avoid hanging in cases of benefit of clergy (if a single
specified verse actually existed for that purpose)?[26] Many prayers must
have been consigned to memory, repeated from the mind rather than
the page. This vastly increases the potential for their acquisition, and for
their recitation. The prayers to be said for the royal family to earn
Wolsey's indulgence of the 1520s are listed on the broadsheet, but some
of the (fragmentary) wording suggests an appeal to memory for parts of

---

[24] *English Gilds*, ed. Smith, Smith, and Brentano, 22–3; see also 110–12, 114–15.
[25] *The Book of Margery Kempe*, ed. S. B. Meech and H. E. Allen, EETS, o.s. 212 (1940),
250–1.
[26] For the neck verse see *The Reports of Sir John Spelman*, ed. J. H. Baker, Selden Society
Publications 93–4 (London, 1976–7), 2: 329.

the recitations.[27] More firmly memorized must have been some of the prayers which earned indulgences when said in churchyards for the souls buried there: it is quite incongruous to expect them to have been looked up and read out on every occasion.[28]

There is a final point to be made. Even if the distinctions which can be imposed on medieval religious practice were distinctive – which is a separate issue – their significance may be overstated, by making the religious context within which they operated too mundane, too terrestrial. In the process of dissection it is all too easy to overlook a basic fact about medieval catholicism: whether one distinguishes between rich and poor, learned or lewd, clerical or lay, elite or popular, what ultimately mattered was not earthly experience, but celestial bliss. All hoped they were going to the same destination. It is certainly valid, and necessary, to clarify how the religion was lived out by the different social groups, and the different societies, who collectively called themselves Christians; but these distinctions and differentiations were merely functional, rarely fundamental. The experience of the journey may have differed greatly for each individual *viator*, the routes and modes of access reflecting personal capacities, capabilities, and situations; but they were all heading (they hoped) in the same direction, towards the same goal. The journey had to be collaborative, fuelled by the imperatives and demands of *caritas*. That, in the end, was what was really important.

University of Birmingham

---

[27] See above, n. 1. The damage to this part of the sheet prevents full reconstruction. There was at least one full Latin prayer; a 'Gloria patri et filio' points to at least a doxology to be recited from memory.

[28] The prayer 'Avete omnes anime fideles' (with variant wordings) occurs in both manuscript and printed primers, rewarded with indulgences: CUL, MS Ee.1.14, fol. 136r–v; *Hore beatissime virginis Marie*, fol. 144r. For another churchyard prayer, ibid., fol. 152r–v.

APPENDIX

The English text of Pynson's broadsheet indulgence rewarding prayers for Henry VIII, Catherine of Aragon, and Princess Mary.[29]

The most reuerende father in go[d lorde] Thomas cardynall of yorke, legate de later of the see apostolyk, P[rim]at & chaunceller of Englande, of his goodnes & charyte hath gyuen & g[raun]ted to all that say this psalme with the suffrages here after folowynge for the most noble & prosperous estate of our souerayne lorde kyng Henry the .viii. the queen & the pryncesse, for euery day that they do say the same .x. yeres & .x. lentes of pardon.

Also the moost reuerende father in god lorde wylliam, archbysshope of Caunterbury, legate of the see apostolique & primat of all England, hath gyuen and graunted to all persones that say .v. Pater nosters .v. Aues and a Crede .xl. dayes of pardon.

Also the right reuerende father in god lorde Cuthbert, bysshope of [Lo]ndon hath semblably gyuen and graunted .xl. dayes of pardon.

A[lso] my lorde of wynchester hath gyuen and graunted .xl. dayes of pardon.

Also my lorde of Lyncolne hath gyuen and graunted .xl. dayes of pardon. And in like wyse al other bysshopes of the realme, eche by hym[sel]fe hath gyuven and graunted .xl. dayes of pardon.

And they tha[t]hat say the sayde psalme with the suffrages, as oft as they say .v. [Pater n]osters .v. Aues, and a Crede for the moost noble & prosperous [estate of] our souerayne lorde the kyng, the queen, and the pryncesse, shal[l haue a]nd enioye all the foresayd pardon with goddes blessing and th[eirs.]

God saue the kynge.

---

[29] See above, n. 1. The original spelling is retained, but an ampersand replaces Pynson's sign for 'and'. Abbreviations are silently extended. Material in square brackets reconstructs lost text. Paragraphing replaces paraph marks. Punctuation has been modernized.

ELITE AND POPULAR RELIGION: THE BOOK OF HOURS AND LAY PIETY IN THE LATER MIDDLE AGES

by EAMON DUFFY

THE very phrase 'elite and popular religion' is laden with potentially misleading polarities. In talking about elite religion or popular religion, are we contrasting notions of orthodoxy with heterodoxy or superstition, or the religion of the clergy with the religion of the laity, or the religion of the rich with the religion of the poor, or the religion of the polite and educated with the religion of the unwashed and unlettered, or the religion of the thinking individual over against the religion of the undifferentiated multitude, or the disciplined and liturgically-based official religion of the institutional Church with something more charismatic, less structured – or some permutation of any of the above?

I suggested the theme of this conference not to endorse these contrasts and polarities, but in the hope that our proceedings might help subvert them. I don't doubt that such contrasts can be useful aids to analysis, and they have underlain work which has had far-reaching impact on the practice of religious history, like Keith Thomas's *Religion and the Decline of Magic*. I confess that I instinctively distrust them as interpretative keys to the religious energies of the past, however, because they often seem to me to darken rather than illuminate the complexities of religious practice, partly because I myself was formed in a religious ethos, that of small-town Catholic Ireland in the 1950s, to which most of these contrasts manifestly did not apply in any straightforward sense. In that world the dragooned and catechized clerical religion of the Tridentine Church, mediated through the Irish nineteenth-century devotional revolution and the teaching of modern religious orders like the De La Salle and Christian brothers, the Marists and the Mercy nuns, flourished alongside and was practised by the same people who embraced an older and less easily regimented piety of pilgrimage and patron, holy well and sacred thorn-bush, and educated schoolmasters recited the rosary like the farm-labourers they knelt beside at Mass. That formation, and the grounding it gave one in the concrete practicalities of religious practice, has no doubt imposed its own blinkers, but it has also been a priceless resource to me in my own work as a historian of religion, a perpetual and salutary corrective to paper theory.[1]

One might epitomize the alleged polarities I have sketched (and wish to question) in a convenient shorthand, as the contrast between the religion of the bead and the religion of the book, with whatever gulf that implies between a religion of uninformed mechanical repetition and a religion which is text-based, discursive, rational, verbalized. We therefore need to remind ourselves that this contrast was to all intents and purposes invented a mere five centuries ago by rootless humanists like Erasmus, and seized on by the sixteenth-century protestant reformers for polemical purposes. In reality, for much of Christian history the exponents of the religion of the book and those of the religion of the bead have been, if not always identical, then at least overlapping constituencies.

In this paper I want to explore some aspects of that overlap by considering the Book of Hours, a religious artefact which was probably invented in England in the second quarter of the thirteenth century, and which at first sight seems to epitomize the polarities I have been discussing at almost every level. On closer examination, however, I believe it can be seen to subvert or at any rate to soften them. The Book of Hours straddles all the divides I have touched on. It was a book designed for lay people seeking to imitate clerical prayer, it was a book designed originally for the aristocratic and wealthy, which moved decisively down-market and became in the end a book equally available to minor country gentry and strong farmers, to city shopkeepers and merchants, and indeed, with the invention of print, affordable by anyone capable of reading at all.[2]

---

[1] In the preface to the 1996 re-issue of Mary Douglas's anthropological classic, *Natural Symbols*, she similarly describes how as a student she came to question the prevailing academic orthodoxies of Durkheimian analysis of the place of fear, emotion and ecstasy in religious ritual, by reflecting on the banal practicalities of her own experience of ritual as a Catholic schoolgirl participant in the Corpus Christi processions of 1940s Highgate and Hampstead. Here were none of the spontaneous outbursts, the ecstatic chanting, the dancing, which her University textbooks told her were intrinsic aspects of ritual behaviour. Instead, she recalled ritual occasions dominated by concern about order and precedence, whether the Embroidery Gild walked ahead of the Boy Scouts and behind the friends of St Vincent De Paul, where the tea would be served, who had the box of matches? The catholic rituals she knew had no 'rolling in the aisles or spontaneous witnessing in the Spirit', and were decisively 'not conducive to the arousing of emotion which Durkheim seemed to think was the function of ritual: something was wrong, either with Durkheim or the religion': Mary Douglas, *Natural Symbols: Explorations in Cosmology* (London, 1996), xv.

[2] General introductions to the medieval Book of Hours, mostly however focusing on

It is a book whose official contents were precisely that – official – derived directly from the liturgy, and consisting essentially of Latin psalms, hymns and authorized suffrages arranged round the hours of the monastic day. From its very beginnings, however, it also contained vernacular and Latin prayers much more directly reflective of lay concerns and aspirations. These prayers proliferated in the later Middle Ages, appealing equally to the average parishioner and the exalted aristocrat, and, with their attendant indulgences and miraculous promises, would become one of the major selling points of printed Books of Hours. As we shall see, they ensured that the prayer regimes inculcated by the use of the Book of Hours, which are often considered bookish, elitist and rarified, were in fact firmly rooted in the world of popular devotion and popular belief, and not always so very far removed from what we might be tempted to call magic. At every level then, the Book of Hours is a bridging text, holding together rather than polarizing the conventions of lay and clerical piety, the belief systems and devotional practices of educated and ignorant, rich and poor, orthodox and marginal.[3]

In England the Book of Hours emerged as part of the great extension of religious provision for lay people associated with the Fourth Lateran Council and the popular Christianity of the friars. The likely social provenance of the earliest surviving English Book of Hours is suggestive here. It was produced in Oxford c.1240 by William de Brailes, a commercial scribe working in the warren of stationers shops round the Church of St Mary the Virgin. To judge by the decorative scheme, the book was commissioned by a woman, whose name may have been Susannah, and whose family were probably parishioners and benefactors of the parish church of St Lawrence, North Hinksey.[4] Susannah herself was almost certainly a client of the Dominicans, with spiritual advisers in the Oxford house: vernacular (French) prayers to the Virgin were added to fill up some blank pages at the back of the book at the

the more lavish examples, in Christopher de Hamel, *A History of Illuminated Manuscripts* (2nd edn, London, 1994), 168–99; Roger S. Wieck, *The Book of Hours in Medieval Art and Life* (London, 1988); idem, *Painted Prayers: the Book of Hours in Medieval and Renaissance Art* (New York, 1997); Janet Backhouse, *Books of Hours* (London, 1985); John Harthan, *Books of Hours and their Owners* (London, 1977).

3 For this dimension of the contents of Books of Hours, cf. Duffy, *Stripping of the Altars*, 266–98.

4 Claire Donovan, *The de Brailes Hours: Shaping the Book of Hours in Thirteenth-Century Oxford* (London, 1991).

same time as the main commission began with a reminder to say an Our Father, and a Hail Mary for three named Dominicans – Richard of Newark, Richard of Westey and Bartholomew of Grimston, for all friars, Preachers and for her confessors.[5] Incidentally, this injunction to the book owner to repeat Our Fathers and Hail Maries for these Dominicans is an example of that overlap I indicated between the religion of the bead and of the book, and would be often replicated throughout the history of the Book of Hours. Two centuries on, the most famous illustration in Mary of Burgundy's lavish Book of Hours carefully locates the use of the book within a devotional regime which included, with no apparent sense of hierarchy, the recitation of the rosary, the use of devotional images, the recitation of the liturgical office and the cultivation of extended devotional meditation on the passion.[6] Preaching at the funeral of Joan, Lady Cobham in 1344, John Sheppey, bishop of Rochester, reported the mixed nature of her prayer-regime, liturgical, devotional, and rote-repetitious, with her Book of Hours at its centre: 'on no day would she willingly come down from her chamber or speak with any stranger, until she had said matins and the Hours of Our Lady, the Seven Psalms and the Litany, almost every day'; then at Mass, 'when the priest was silent', she said some private prayers in French (no doubt from texts in her book) and some Paternosters and Hail Maries.[7]

According to one recent reckoning from the century after 1240 only about a dozen Books of Hours survive for England: interestingly, most of those which date from the thirteenth century can be associated with women, no fewer than six out of eight contain what appear to be portraits of their female owners and several suggest a connection between their owners and the religious orders, especially the friars.[8] They were of course expensive, and took time to establish themselves widely in lay regard. The accidents of survival make attempts at statistical precision illusory in this context, but fewer than three dozen in all

[5] The prayers are reproduced in Donovan, *The de Brailes Hours*, 126.

[6] Reproduced in facsimile in *The Hours of Mary of Burgundy: Codex Vindobonensis 1857 Vienna, Österreichische Nationalbibliothek*, ed. Eric Inglis (London, 1995), fol. 14v: this illustration of Mary of Burgundy at prayer was one of the points of departure for the important essay on prayer and the Book of Hours by John Bossy, 'Prayers', *Transactions of the Royal Historical Society*, 6th ser., 1 (1991), 137–48.

[7] Katheryn A. Smith, *Art, Identity and Devotion in Fourteenth-Century England: Three Women and their Books of Hours* (London and Toronto, 2003), 1–2.

[8] See discussions of thirteenth-century Books of Hours for women in Donovan, *The de Brailes Hours*, 183–200; Smith, *Art, Identity and Devotion*, 11–47.

survive for England before the end of the fourteenth century. From the early fifteenth century onwards, however, they were being effectively mass produced for the English market, as for the rest of north-western Europe, and they become an increasingly common devotional accessory, superseding the Psalters which till then had been the most popular prayer-book for literate lay people.

From the beginning, Books of Hours were lavishly decorated with elaborate borders, initials and miniatures. If they were expressions of the religion of the word, and of a newly awakened lay appetite for religious instruction and a more active and personalized devotional regime, they were also very much part of the religion of the image, and the pictures were at least as important to their users as the texts they accompanied.[9] Once again, the very format of these books invites us to resist simplistic polarities.

But the presence of pictures, textual illumination and marginal decoration made such books enormously costly, and to begin with they certainly were the preserve of royalty and aristocracy, or the wealthiest urban elite. Indeed, the cost was often not so much a drawback of such books, as part of their point, and their decorative schemes were often designed to draw attention to wealth and dynastic alliances as much as religious preferences. Here indeed was a manifestation of social elitism.[10] Lavish manuscript Books of Hours would go on being produced into the sixteenth century: nevertheless, they also moved inexorably and decisively down-market. This, it should be noticed, is a development that predates print, for already by the early fifteenth century Books of Hours were being mass-produced in dozens of stationers shops across Europe, but especially in France and the Netherlands.[11] So, before and after print, the Book of Hours was everywhere in the late Middle Ages. In the late fourteenth century the French poet Eustache Deschamps satirized this appetite, which he thought was specially strong in women, for the last word in devotional display:

[9] Smith, *Art, Identity and Devotion*, 152–248.

[10] Ibid., 20–8.

[11] Nicholas Rogers, 'Patrons and Purchasers: Evidence for the Original Owners of Books Produced in the Low Countries for the English Market', in Bert Cardon, Jan Van der Stock and Dominique Vanwijnsberghe, eds, *'Als Ich Can': Liber Amicorum in Memory of Professor Dr Maurits Smeyers*, 2 vols (Leuven, 2002), 2: 1165–81, summarizing part of Rogers's invaluable unpublished M. Litt. thesis, 'Books of Hours Produced in the Low Countries for the English Market', University of Cambridge, 1984.

Get me an Hours of the Virgin,
Matched to my high degree,
The finest the craftsmen can manage
As graceful and gorgeous as me:
Paint it with gold and with azure
With gold clasps to fasten it down,
So the people will gasp when I use it,
'That's the prettiest prayer-book in town'.[12]

By the early fifteenth century the Book of Hours had become much more widely accessible, and wealthy bourgeois women felt naked if they too did not possess an example of this most chic of devotional fashion accessories. Its social cachet sprang from its iconic function: wherever we turn in representations of later medieval and renaissance lay prayer, the Book of Hours is present, for example, in Memling's well-known Donne Triptych, painted in 1478, depicting Sir John Donne and his wife in prayer before the Virgin and child. Elizabeth Donne, née Hastings, was the sister of that Sir William for whom the Hastings Hours was made. Her rapt state of prayer is symbolised here by her own Book of Hours.[13]

Books of Hours were, from the start, intensely personal objects, carried about in a sleeve or at the belt, passed from hand to hand, like the fifteenth-century London merchant who bequeathed 'my primer with gilt clasps whereupon I am wont to say my service' or the London waxchandler Roger Elmsley who in 1434 left to a favourite godchild 'a prymmer to serve God with'. In 1395 the Hampshire widow, Lady Alice West, who had taken a vow of chastity after her husband's death, bequeathed to her son Thomas 'a peyre Matyns bookis and a peire bedes, and a rynge with which I was yspousyd to God, whiich were my lordes his fadres'.[14] Notice there once again the convergence of the religion of the book and the bead. But in any case, that cluster of religious

---

[12] I paraphrase Deschamps's lines, quoted more literally in *The Hours of Mary of Burgundy*, ed. Inglis, 60–1.

[13] Reproduced in Richard Marks and Paul Williamson, eds, *Gothic: Art for England 1400–1547* (London, 2003), catalogue no. 213; Lorne Campbell, ed., *The Fifteenth-Century Netherlandish Schools*, National Gallery Catalogues (London and New Haven, CT, 1998), 377. Similar (later) examples from the reign of Henry VIII reproduced as Marks and Williamson, eds, *Gothic*, catalogue no. 276 and pl. 49 (Knyvett altarpiece); catalogue no. 135 (Withypool altarpiece).

[14] Frederick J. Furnivall, ed., *The Fifty Earliest English Wills in the Court of Probate, London, A.D. 1387–1439: with a Priest's of 1454*, EETS 78 (London, 1882) 5, 102.

and domestic sanctities is entirely characteristic of the devotional world of which the Book of Hours was the principle token, and this process of transmission within families and kinship groups might go on for generations and even centuries.

But books were also passed on outside families. Many devout people had more than one Book of Hours, and in addition to passing them on to children or god-children, they might be given or bequeathed to friends, chaplains, or servants. A printed Book of Hours published in 1528 and now in the Pierpoint Morgan Library in New York nicely epitomizes this sort of transmission history: given by Catherine of Aragon to a lady-in-waiting, it had then moved on through that recipient's family: an inscription on the fly-leaf records that

> Thys boke was good queen Katrins boke and she gave yt to Mrs Coke hir woman and she gave yt to Katryne Ogle hyr dawghter and she gave yt to Robert Ogle her husband and the sayd Roger wyll that at my deth she shall have the sayd boke ageyn and non other to have yt.[15]

Roger Ogle, evidently an opponent of the Henrician reformation, was clearly concerned to keep this devotional relic of 'Good Queen Katherine' in the family, but books often did gravitate outside the families for which they were made, and in the process more often than not moved down-market, not least because the very dynastic additions – portraits, coats of arms and obit entries – which at first made them emblems and expression of elite religion, combined now to lower their value, and constituted a problem for new users. There is in the Bodleian a once handsome but long since battered and disbound late fourteenth-century Book of Hours produced in an Oxford stationers for the Wyllylie family, minor Shropshire gentry from the Much Wenlock area. The book passed by marriage from the Wyllylies into the Parlour family, hereditary foresters of Morfe: obits for members of both tribes were entered into the calendar. By the later fifteenth century, however, the Parlours had evidently fallen on hard times, either financially or genetically, for the book moved out of the family altogether, and was acquired, probably by purchase, by another Shropshire household, the Wegges. They or whoever sold the book to them carefully dealt with the removable traces of the earlier history of the book by pumicing out

---

15 New York, Pierpoint Morgan Library, PML 1034 (STC 15959), final flyleaf, recto.

of the vellum all the Wyllylie and Parlour obits, which can now only be read under ultra-violet light. The new owners were still gentry, but not nearly so grand as the Wyllelies, as is evidenced by their willingness to buy a century-old prayer-book second-hand rather than commissioning a new book of their own. They started afresh, however, entering their own series of obits at the turn of the fifteenth and sixteenth centuries. An Egge daughter married into the Corbets early in the sixteenth century, and another married a Ward. The book, still in use and by now into its second set of covers, moved on in the female line, and therefore in the course of the later sixteenth century accumulated Egge, Corbert and Ward obits and birthday entries, until at length the family, until then Catholic, evidently conformed to the new religion, and new entries ceased altogether.[16] In the same way, a handsome manuscript Book of Hours produced *c.*1450 for Ann, daughter of Richard duke of York, and duchess of Exeter, and now in Sidney Sussex College library, had by the mid-Tudor period fetched up in a middle-class household in Ipswich, where its flyleaves and blanks were being used as a copy-book to instruct young Edmond Church in handwriting and good manners.[17] We catch a glimpse of the economic realities behind this sort of social descent in the note inside a Book of Hours made originally for Edward Plantagenet, and now at Ushaw College, Durham, which records that an early sixteenth-century owner, Edward Ashton of Chadderton, had picked it up second-hand for three shillings, well within the buying-power of even a modest yeoman or city merchant or shop-keeper.[18]

But there was no need for merchants, shopkeepers or country gentry to resort to the second-hand-book sellers to acquire a Book of Hours. From the end of the fourteenth century the stationers' shops of the Low Countries and Northern France were catering for a mass market, producing manuscript books on vellum with a largely plain or lightly decorated text, and where such full-page illustrations as were provided were bulk-bought in sets by the stationers from hack artists, and tipped into the volumes to dress them up. Nearly two hundred of such assembly-line books for England survive, and a large proportion of their known owners were, as Nicholas Rogers, the leading authority on

---

[16] Oxford, Bodleian Library, MS Don.d.206, *passim*: information from Professor John Barron, who is preparing a study of the book for the Bodleian Record.

[17] Sidney Sussex MS 37, fols 154v–156.

[18] Ushaw College MS 43, fol. 136.

these books, has observed, 'middling merchants and local gentry, people with social pretensions who would be attracted by something which looked more expensive than it really was'.[19]

All this ensured that in the course of the fifteenth century the Book of Hours and the religion it represented ceased to be the monopoly of aristocracy and the upper gentry, and became an integral part of the religious experience of the urban and rural 'middling sort': the King's Lynn housewife and small-time brewer Margery Kempe owned a Book of Hours, and they are a common bequest in the wills of merchants and better-off shop-keepers. But the decisive democratizing of the Book of Hours came at the end of the fifteenth century, with the arrival of print. Books of Hours became, in terms of numbers of editions, quite simply and without any rival the chief product of the new technology.

The character and content of the printed Book of Hours is too large a topic for a single essay. Here I want to focus on the way in which these printed books mediated between elite and popular book culture, and religion. Many of the early printed Books of Hours were themselves sumptuous objects, printed on vellum and designed to mimic manuscript. In 1494 Wynken de Worde produced his first printed Hour, containing a lavish selection of the devotions which had become regular additions to manuscript books over the course of the previous century and a half. In terms of decoration and illustration, de Worde's edition was not particularly sophisticated or lavish. It was, however, produced, as its colophon states, at the request of the Queen Mother, Lady Margaret Beaufort; it was printed on vellum, and in several of the surviving copies the floral borders have been hand-coloured: unsurprisingly, the provenance of the surviving copies is largely aristocratic.[20] Continental publishers produced even more lavish books, making better use of the new technology, and exploiting more effectively the fact that the impression of sumptuousness could now be achieved at a much lesser cost. Indeed, print made possible cheap Books of Hours which were incomparably more beautiful than all but the most lavish manuscript books, capable of rivalling some of the great aristocratic commissions of the high Middle Ages. So by the sixteenth century every prosperous shopkeeper who aspired to devotional gentility could have their own splendid Book of Hours at, relatively speaking, bargain

---

[19] Rogers, 'Books of Hours Produced in the Low Countries', 48.
[20] This is the case with one of the two CUL copies, Inc.5.J.1.2, a copy owned both by the earl of Surrey and Sir William Parr.

prices, and with a degree of iconographic complexity and sophistication which till the advent of print had been available only to the most aristocratic of book-owners.[21]

The printed Books of Hours for the English market form a fascinating and underexplored area of study. I have space here to emphasize just a few points. The content of all printed Books of Hours, considered simply as a collection of texts, was broadly similar – you got the same basic range of prayers whatever price you paid, and it was common for publishers to produce up- and down-market versions of the same basic sequence of texts, with cruder or more refined illustrations according to price.[22] The objects themselves, considered as artefacts, were fantastically varied, ranging from magnificently bound and decorated books on vellum, often hand coloured, which must in some instances have cost just as much as one of the cheaper manuscript books, down to tiny and mostly unornamented texts printed on rough paper which can only have cost a few pence. That variety overlaying a standardized set of contents meant that rich and poor inhabited distinct but interpenetrating devotional worlds. We can best get a sense of this interplay between variety and similarity by looking at some printed Books of Hours across the price range. At the aristocratic end, there are examples from one of the best of the Parisian printers for England, Simon Vostre and Philip Pigouchet, who produced sumptuous and highly elaborate books, often on vellum, with a dense iconographic programme derived from and elaborating on the manuscript traditions of the fifteenth century. One of his most beautiful books, produced in 1520 for the English market, combined Gothic decorative features with the most spectacular Renaissance full-page biblical scenes at the start of each of the hours.[23] Other books were plainer, moving away from the manuscript tradition towards books conceived of not as a single decorated page, but as made of movable type. Wynken de Worde produced books of this more modern kind: characteristically, in one handsome

---

[21] Examples of cheap, mass-produced manuscript illustrations from fifteenth-century books for the English market in Alain Arnould and Jean-Michel Massing, eds, *Splendours of Flanders* (Cambridge, 1993), catalogue nos 32, 33, 39. Representative pages from mass-produced printed Books of Hours in Marks and Williamson, eds, *Gothic*, catalogue nos 224–6, and in Duffy, *Stripping of the Altars*, pl. 88–97.

[22] Cf. STC 15973, a small octavo Latin Book of Hours printed by Regnault in 1531, with STC 15970, half the size, containing identical text, and the same sequence of illustrations, but simpler and cruder in execution.

[23] STC 15926.

Book of Hours published in 1519 he illustrated the text by using block-prints from other publications. A suffrage to St Anne, for example, is illustrated with a picture apparently derived from a charter or indulgence printed for the Gild of St Anne at Lincoln, signalling, in this handsome book, a direct link to the popular religious world of the gild, the indulgence and the local pilgrimage.[24] In the same book the popular set of prayers known as the 'Oes of St Brigid', a regular item in Books of Hours, is prefaced by a block originally cut for use in devotional publications, including free-standing editions of the 'Oes', issuing from Syon Abbey itself, a link in the other direction to one of the major power-houses of devotional writing in early Tudor England.[25]

* * *

I want to turn now to a brief consideration of the content and use of the Book of Hours, to see how they impact on our problematic polarities between elite and popular religion. The Book of Hours was, of course, a *book*, and reading involves both literacy on the part of the user, and a degree of attention to the text which involves focusing down on it. So historians have convinced themselves that the appearance of prayer-books for lay people must have signalled a retreat on the part of the users from the communal religion of their neighbours. And this raises the question of whether or not the Book of Hours is a cause, or at any rate a signal, of the growth of individualism. Some serious historians of religion have tended to think so. Colin Richmond has associated the popularity of the Book of Hours with other manifestations of privatization in religion, such as the private pew and the domestic chapel. By private pews he has in mind elaborate structures like the Harling or Spring chapels, in the churches of East Harling, Norfolk, or Lavenham in Suffolk. Built inside the parish church yet not altogether part of it, such pews constituted, Richmond considers, private enclaves within which the gentry could get on with the practice of an elite religion increasingly remote from the public religion of the parishioners at large, who were essentially outsiders to this private and propertied religion. In there, he argues,

---

24 STC 15922, fol. lxi (illustration).
25 Ibid., fol. cxxiii. The blockprint of St Brigid, used also in the Bridgetine treatise, *The Dietary of Ghostly Helth* in the following year, 1520, is reproduced in Duffy, *Stripping of the Altars*, pl. 61.

they were, so to speak, getting their heads down, turning their eyes from the distractions posed by their fellow worshippers, [and] at the same time talking them off the priest and his movements and gestures. Such folk, in becoming isolated from their neighbours, were also insulating themselves against communal religion, possibly even religion per se, for how can you be religious on your own?[26]

And indeed, in the illustration from her Book of Hours to which allusion has already been made, Mary of Burgundy appears to be very much in retreat, in her own room, jewelry and clothing scattered before her, her lap-dog on her lap. Her portrait serves as frontispiece to a devotion on the joys of the Virgin Mary which was supposedly revealed to Thomas Becket in a vision of the Virgin. Using this prayer seems to transport Mary herself into a visionary setting, which we see through the window – into a public church where she and her attendants kneel before the Virgin and Child, larger than life. The picture shows us the user of the Book of Hours in the first place as a solitary, therefore, in line with the Dominical instruction on prayer in Matthew 6:6, 'tu autem cum orabis intra in cubiculum tuum, et cluso ostio tuo ora Patrem tuum in abscondito'.[27]

It is perfectly clear that the use of Books of Hours by lay people in the late Middle Ages is indeed an aspect of the promotion of lay interiority, the personalizing of religion which had been one of the aims of pastoral strategy and spiritual direction since at least the time of the reform papacy, and which is such a feature of the late medieval devotional landscape – the world of Margery Kempe. The Books of Hours offered lay people a share in what was essentially a monastic form of piety. The interiority of that piety is classically articulated in the opening lines of Anselm's *Proslogion*: 'Eia nunc, homuncio, fuge paululum occupationes tuas...':

Come now, little man, turn aside for a while from your daily employment, escape for a moment from the weight of your thoughts. Put aside your weighty cares, let your burdensome distractions wait, free yourself awhile for God and rest awhile in

<hr>

[26]   Colin Richmond, 'Religion and the Fifteenth-Century Gentleman', in Barrie Dobson, ed., *The Church, Politics and Patronage in the Fifteenth Century* (Gloucester, 1984), 199.

[27]   'But thou, when thou shalt pray, enter into thy chamber and, having shut the door, pray to thy Father in secret.'

him. Enter the inner chamber of your soul, shut out everything
except God and that which can help you in seeking him, and when
you have shut the door, seek him.[28]

This is the medieval Church's idealized situation for prayer and meditation, but Richmond and other historians paradoxically insist that its
attainment represented a threat, in the form of an exclusive alternative,
to the *official* religion of the community, in particular to the community of the parish, a wedge between elite and popular religious practice.[29]

This contention seems to me to rest on a simple misunderstanding
of what the personalization of religion involves. The late medieval
Church measured its success not on how far it could *prevent* people
interiorizing their religion, but how far it actually succeeded in helping
them to do just that. And interiority is by no means to be equated with
individualism. People prayed their Book of Hours often, perhaps
usually, alone, and indeed fifteenth-century and early Tudor devotional and conduct books often recommended the recitation of Matins
or Vespers in one's closet, which, as noted above, was Lady Cobham's
practice. But it was almost as common for people to recite their hours
in public rooms, as a dozen Tudor portraits make clear, and as we
glimpse in George Cavendish's well-known anecdote about Thomas
Cromwell, consumed with self-pity on hearing on All Saints' day, 1529,
of the fall of his patron Wolsey, tearfully reciting the Matins of our
Lady from his Book of Hours in the window seat of the Great Chamber
of the palace at Esher, 'which had been since' Cavendish observed drily
– he was writing during Cromwell's later ascendancy –, 'a very strange
sight'.[30] Moreover, the arrival of printed Books of Hours opened up
new possibilities for communal recital. Most gentry and many bourgeois households would have held more than one copy of the Book of
Hours, but communal recitation would have been hindered by the fact
that no two books were identical, and finding one's way around them
was anyway not always a quick business. Printed books, by contrast,
were uniform, had tables of contents and indices, and regularly adver-

---

[28] *St Anselm's Proslogion: with a Reply on behalf of the Fool*, ed. M. J. Charlesworth (Oxford, 1965), 110.

[29] The case for the divisive nature of lay interiority is argued for most insistently by Jonathan Hughes, *The Religious Life of Richard III: Piety and Prayer in the North of England* (Stroud, 1997), 104–53.

[30] Neville Williams, *The Cardinal and the Secretary* (London, 1975), 152.

tised themselves as easy to navigate oneself around – 'set out along without any searching'.[31] Moreover, since they were cheap, a single household could own multiple copies. The Holbein drawing of the household of St Thomas More in the late 1520s is one of the most famous images of a Renaissance family.[32] The picture, in which almost everyone is holding a book, has been variously interpreted, not least as a Humanist household in which the written and printed word held pride of place. It has not been much noticed, however, that everyone is holding the same book: they have set aside books of different thicknesses and size, which lie on floor and window-ledge. The identical book in every hand is a prayer-book, in fact the Book of Hours, as is plain from the fact that Dame Alice, More's wife, is kneeling at her prayer desk. Through Holbein's eyes, we are privileged flies on the wall at a London bourgeois household's family prayers, and the More family are about to start a communal recitation of Our Lady's Matins.

But it was equally common to recite one's Matins in church. Margery Kempe tells us how a falling wedge of stone from the roof of her parish church dashed her Book of Hours from her hands and concussed her as she was reciting her Matins one morning,[33] and an Italian tourist in England in the 1490s noted that literate townspeople liked to go with a companion to church and recite their Hours 'verse by verse, in a low voice, after the manner of churchmen'.[34] '*After the manner of churchmen*'. That, of course, was one of the essential features of the Book of Hours. It offered lay people a suitably slimmed down and simplified share in the Church's official cycle of daily prayer, and so it was not so much a rival to the religion of the official Church as an aspect of it, cementing the lay devotee more closely to the institution by encouraging him or her to participate in its formal worship. The lay person who recited these prayers was thereby being equipped to understand and appropriate words which they routinely heard recited by clergy and ministers in the public liturgy. What sense does it make, I wonder, to talk of idiosyncrasy and individualism, when we are

---

[31] See, for example, the title-page of STC 15973, published by Francis Regnault in 1531 (reproduced in Duffy, *Stripping of the Altars*, pl. 93).

[32] Reproduced in Oskar Batschmann and Pascal Griener, *Hans Holbein* (London, 1997), 160 (illustration).

[33] S. B. Meech and H. E. Allen, *The Book of Margery Kempe*, EETS o.s. 212 (London, 1940), 212, 221.

[34] *A Relation . . . of the Island of England . . .*, ed. Charlotte Augusta Sneyd, Camden Society o.s. 37 (London, 1847) 23.

confronted by the spectacle of hundreds and indeed thousands of lay people reciting more or less identical prayers, day in and day out, often in their parish churches, surrounded by the neighbours they are supposedly distancing by this very act, some at least of whom are similarly engaged in reciting the same words at the same time? And we need to remind oursleves here, as we have seen, that the prayers of these books were not merely used privately: major sections of them were regularly recited collectively as part of the public worship of the whole community, or of some of its constituent subgroupings, such as the gilds. The key item in the Books of Hours here was the office for the Dead, that is, Vespers, Matins and Lauds of the Dead, or 'Dirige' as it was known from the opening word of the opening antiphon of Matins. This service was an invariable and popular feature of Books of Hours, and unlike the Little Hours of the Virgin, which formed the first part of all such books, it was neither simplified or abbreviated, but included the full text of the Church's official prayers for the dead. The inclusion of obit notices in the calendar of such books was a reminder to the user to recite this office on the appropriate anniversary. But the office was also one of the most familiar parts of the Church's formal liturgy, publicly recited as part of every funeral, and often subsequently on weekly, monthly and yearly commemorations: gilds usually required their members to attend these recitations for deceased brethren, and literate lay people were encouraged or expected to join in. In almost all illustrated Books of Hours, the Dirige is preceded by a picture of this part of the funeral liturgy being celebrated by clergy often accompanied by lay people.[35]

And certainly the proud owners and users of Books of Hours did not conceive themselves to be separating from their neighbours, or the public worship of the parish. The wealthy Devon clothier John Greneway and his wife Joan kneel in the porch of the parish church of St Peter at Tiverton with their Books of Hours before them. They placed those self-images with books not in the isolation of their private chantry chapel, but prominently above the south door, a key spot where marriages and the first part of baptism were celebrated, inside the splendid porch they built for their neighbours' comfort and convenience against the wind and damp of Exe valley winters. It would simply not be possible to find a more communal context in which to

---

[35] See the examples collected in Anne F. Sutton and Livia Visser-Fuchs, *The Hours of Richard III* (Stroud, 1990), figs 12–19 and pl. 2.

depict the use of a Book of Hours. A number of early sixteenth-century Easter Sepulchres portray the donors reading from Books of Hours before the risen Christ or the Trinity. The Easter Sepulchre was the focus of the parish community's most intense corporate adoration of the sacrament in Holy Week, and once again, the use of the Book of Hours in such a context hardly indicates devotional isolation.[36]

A late fifteenth-century prayer added to the flyleaf of a Book of Hours now in Lambeth Palace Library suggests that its owner while praying at Mass understood perfectly well the communal nature of the mystery being enacted before his eyes:

> Most mercyfull Lord I beseche thee heartely off thy mercy and grace and forgyfnes of my synnes and thow wyll make me partner of the effects and graces of thy moste lessyd bodye and blode the whyche be mynysterd her in thys blessed masse also I beseche thee to mak me partener of all masys that ys seyd thys daye in thys churche and in all holly churchys. I beseche tthee heartely to make me a pertener of all suffragys of holly church and of all good dedys they whychge be done off all crysten men. Jesu, Jhesu, Jhesu mercy ....[37]

* * *

What light does all this throw on some of the wider questions about the relationship between elite and popular religion in the later Middle Ages? As we have seen, Professor Colin Richmond has suggested that the Book of Hours was an instrument or at any rate a symptom of a regrettable privatizing of religion, the retreat of landowners and urban elites from their neighbours, and the creation of a private sphere of religiosity which distanced them from the wider community and laid the ground for the reformation. Much more emphatically, Dr Jonathan Hughes has maintained that the most significant thing about the spread of the Book of Hours was the 'challenge' it posed 'to institutional, parish-orientated religion': the use of these books

> reinforced individuality, emphasizing the close relationship that exists between the worshipper and God, who provides a source of

---

[36] Examples include the Gounter monument at Racton, the Ernley Monument at West Wittering, and the Sackville monument at Westhampnett, all in Sussex: the Sackville monument is illustrated in Duffy, *Stripping of the Altars*, pl. 9.

[37] Lambeth Palace Library MS 459, fol. 1r.

strength against the hostility of neighbours, the frustrations of dealing with people.[38]

Both Richmond and Hughes were developing hints in a remarkable paper published by Professor John Bossy in 1991, in which, among many fertile suggestions, a distinction is made between two main types of medieval prayers: social prayers, which were 'mainly something to do with one's relation to one's neighbour', and whose archetype is the Our Father; and devotional prayers 'more directly to do with one's relation to God or other objects of religion', whose archetype is the Hail Mary. Bossy considered that most of the prayers of the Books of Hours were social prayers, but often negatively so, many of them revealing a preoccupation with the pray-er's safety, and in particular, with their deliverance from their earthly enemies. These concerns were rooted of course in the fact that the fundamental core of the Books of Hours was the Psalter, and the Psalms, he thought, were mainly concerned in this way with deliverance from distress and tribulation. The Books of Hours were therefore, in Bossy's words, '*me* prayer books, full of *me* prayers'. At the end of his paper he has a savage aside on 'the dense smog of self-centredness, malice and sanctified whingeing which comes off the prayer-books'.[39]

Despite the vehemence of that phrase, Bossy's paper is a subtle and nuanced one, and he was not straight-forwardly *attacking* the voice of late medieval prayer, which he argued was balanced and controlled by an essentially healthy liturgical piety, focused on the Elevation in the Mass. Nevertheless, indeed for that very reason, his paper sets up a tension between the private piety of the Books of Hours, which, despite their 'social' concerns, he considers to have been individualistic and self-centred, on the one hand, and on the other hand, the pluralistic but socially unifying piety surrounding the Elevation in the mass, which he sees as altogether more robustly social. Richmond endorses this charge that the late medieval users of Books of Hours did indeed whinge when they prayed: he had in mind this sort of thing, from the prayer-book of George, earl of Shrewsbury, *c.*1500:

> Most dere lorde and savyour swete jesu I beseche they moost curteys goodnes and benygne favour to be to me moost wretched creature favourable lorde protectour keper and defender and in all

---

[38] Hughes, *Religious Life of Richard III*, 123.

[39] Bossy, 'Prayers', 137–48.

necessytees and nedes be to my shelde and protectyon ayenst al myne enemyes bodely and goostly. Mercyfull Jesu I have none other truste hope ne succour but in the allonely my dere lorde swete Jhesus the whyche of thy infynite goodness madeest me of nought lyke unto thy moost excellent ymage.

And so on. Richmond offers what is to my mind what is for him an uncharacteristically reductionist socio-political explanation of the tone of this prayer, speculating that this cringeing tone might have had political overtones: 'Could the mode', he asked, 'be a particularly upper class one: the English nobility behaving towards their Lord as they wished others to behave towards them?'[40]

There is no space to deal with these issues fully here, but this, I think, simply won't do: we are dealing here with a matter of rhetorical register which is by no means new in the later Middle Ages, and which is certainly not the special preserve of aristocracy. The elaborate penitential deference of these English prayers reproduces pretty closely the equally 'cringeing' tone of many of the Latin devotions which lay people found in their books, such as the famous prayer 'O Bone Jesu', and which had been a staple of devotion for centuries, with exemplars in writers like St Anselm.

* * *

And that brings us squarely to the actual prayers of the Book of Hours, which so far we have barely considered. It was called a Book of Hours, of course, because it contained a standardized selection of psalms, antiphons, hymns and prayers, arranged for recitation in honour of Mary at each of the eight monastic divisions or hours of the day. As the book evolved, to these 'hours' of the Virgin were added the office for the dead or 'Dirige' (Matins, Lauds and Prime of the dead), the short Hours of the Cross, which in books for the English market were usually inserted between the Hours of the Virgin, the long Psalm 119 called the Commendations, the seven penitential psalms and fifteen gradual psalms, the litany of the saints, and a series of individual 'suffrages' or short prayers to saints, especially to the Virgin Mary. By the fifteenth

---

[40] Colin Richmond, 'Margins and Marginality: English Devotion in the Later Middle Ages', in Nicholas Rogers, ed., *England in the Fifteenth Century: Proceedings of the 1992 Harlaxton Symposium* (Stamford, 1994), 242–52. The quoted prayer is from Bodleian Library, Gough Liturgical MS 7, fol. 81v, a prayer-book (not a Book of Hours) compiled for George, earl of Shrewsbury, *c.*1500.

century this core had been augmented by additional devotions to the Trinity, the Wounds, the Passion and the Holy Face of Jesus, and prayers to the Virgin such as the 'Obsecro Te', and the 'O Intemerata', the 'Stabat Mater', or the Marian hymn against the plague 'Stella Coeli extirpavit'. Many also included eucharistic devotions like the 'Anima Christi', designed to be used at Mass, and almost all contained the shortened versions of the psalter known respectively as St Bernard's verses (seven verses only) or, even more commonly, the much more extended St Jerome's Psalter.[41]

By the late fifteenth century, however, Books of Hours were liable to be expanded further with prayers, devotions, holy pictures encountered in the burgeoning devotional ethos of late medieval England and copied, glued or stitched into standard books. The devotional character of this cumulative evolution of the Book of Hours should give us pause before we associate its use with the growth of individualism and a retreat from public religion. The devotional temperature of the four-teenth and fifteenth century was admittedly rising steadily, as late medieval Christianity went through the religious equivalent of global warming, inspired in part by the preaching and devotional regime of the Franciscans, and partly by a growing hunger for religious variety and intensity on the part of lay men and women with time, leisure, literacy, and, not least, money on their hands. But if we are to judge from the evidence of Books of Hours, the result was not a move towards mysticism and interiority, it seems to me, but the growth of an ever more obviously *instrumental* approach to prayer. The people who copied extra prayers into their books were interested in what in the *Stripping of the Altars* I called 'Charms, Pardons and Promises': they wanted prayers which carried indulgences, or legends guaranteeing spiritual or material benefits, especially protection against life's troubles and the terrors of death.[42] Thus, while many new texts were added to the standard devotions included in Books of Hours, the additions are characterized not by a reclusive interiority, but by a robust interest in measurable results. Late medieval people collected prayers much as we collect recipes, and for rather similar reasons.

The additional material, found in hundreds of surviving books, is very varied, but beneath the variety there is a consistency of tone and preoccupation which links aristocratic and plebeian religious aspira-

---

41 Routine contents analysed in Wieck, *Painted Prayers*, *passim*.
42 Duffy, *Stripping of the Altars*, 266–98.

tions. Rather than attempt a bogus synthesis or statistical analysis, I will attempt to provide a sense of the general character of the process of devotional accretion I am describing here by considering a single book. I offer as an example CUL Ii.6.2, a cheapish manuscript Book of Hours produced for the English market in Bruges around 1400 or a little earlier, which makes it one of the first surviving examples of the wave of mass-produced works for an expanding literate class imported into England. It is brightly illustrated, but the pictures are of poor quality, of a type mass-produced in sets by hack artists, and bought in job lots by the stationer, to be bound into production-line manuscripts like this one as required, in order to dress them up.

This process left many blank pages in each Book of Hours, and successive owners of this particular book added their own material on the blanks. The book has obits in the calendar for residents of Badingham and Hevingham in Suffolk. By the early sixteenth century the book had passed into the hands of the Roberts family of Middlesex. The Roberts had been prosperous people in Willesden and Neasden since the thirteenth century, latterly acting as bailiffs for the Dean and Chapter of St Paul's. In the course of the fifteenth and sixteenth centuries the family steadily amassed land, both freehold and rented, so that by Elizabeth's reign they would be among the most substantial landowners in Middlesex: much of this land had been church property, so I suppose we should include the Roberts among the hard-faced men who did well out of the Reformation.[43] There is not the slightest hint in their book, however, that they were protestants. Their manuscript additions to the book, some of them signed or in the same hand as Roberts family entries, offer a good cross-section of the sort of material with which late medieval people made their own voice heard in their Books of Hours. They include the following: a table to calculate the conjunctions of the moon, Latin rhymes on the life of the Virgin, and the passion of Christ, a short spell in English to quench flames if your house should happen to catch fire, a rhyme royal stanza on the merits of the mass, and a seven line Latin rhyme about the Virgin.[44] Turning the page, there is a coat of arms, with quarterings of Norfolk families from Tilney and Thorp. Opposite has been written a long devotional instruction on the need to prepare against sudden death by constantly renewed acts of contrition

---

[43] On the Roberts family, see D. K. Bolton in *The Victoria County History of Middlesex*, ed. T. F. T. Baker, 12 vols (Oxford, 1911–1982), 7: 216–17, 238.

[44] CUL Ii.6.2, fol. 1 recto-verso.

and resolutions of amendment, and by undertaking to make a sacramental confession at the first opportunity 'accordyng to the commandments of all holy church', accompanied by alms and good deeds.[45] On subsequent pages there has been added a Latin prayer to St Dorothy and a Latin rubric on the benefits of keeping an image of the saint in your house (Dorothy is a Roberts family name), a prayer 'for women to conceyve a childe', a version of the Charlemagne prayer, which was a charm based on the names of Jesus, attributed here to Joseph of Arimathea, prayers to St Cornelius, St John the Baptist, St George, St Erasmus, St Frideswide, and again to St Dorothy, a prayer to the Virgin as Empress of hell for help at the hour of death, a prayer in English to Jesus and Mary for forgiveness of sins, beginning 'O my sovereign Lord Jesu', a prayer to St Michael attributed to Richard of Chichester, a list of the times of births of five of Thomas Roberts' twenty-four children, a short scheme of meditation, in Latin, on sin and the brevity of life, a Latin prayer against the pestilence and an injunction to say the 'Stella Coeli extirpavit' plague hymn at the Elevation, two versions of the very common Elevation prayer, for use at mass – 'O Jhesu Lorde, welcom thu be, / in forme of brede as Y the se, / Jhesu for they holy name, / schelde me thys day fro soro and shame . . .' –, a slightly expanded version of the Latin prayer to the blessed sacrament, 'Anima Christi', the Latin collect 'Adesto Domine supplicationibus nostris', which asks for God's guidance and protection in all the changes and chances of life (it was often included in printed Books of Hours, to be recited 'for travellers'), an extraordinary Latin charm using the sign of the cross, the titles of Jesus and an anecdote about the Apostle Peter to banish the plague: this was followed by another charm with an English rubric which explained that the Hail Mary had to be said kneeling one hundred times a day for ten days, holding an alms for the poor in your hand; you then kissed the money and gave it to a poor man or woman in honour of the Annunciation, and then 'without doubt ye shall have that thynge ye pray for lawfully with Goddes grace'. This rubric, incidentally, was signed in 1553 by Edmund Roberts, who left his signature in half a dozen other places in the book, with the remark that he had 'used well this prayer'. The manuscript additions conclude with a characteristic Tudor moralizing rhyme, urging the reader 'Joy in God whose grace is beste / Obeye thy prince and live in awe / Helpe the poor to lyve in rest / And never synne against the lawe'.

---

45 Ibid., fol. 3.

It will be evident from these additions to the Roberts family book that much generalization about the drift towards interiority and individualism in late medieval lay piety needs to be carefully qualified. In particular, the role of the Book of Hours in the widening gap between elite and popular piety which some historians have discerned seems to me questionable. We are not dealing here with the amateur mystics or men and women in flight from the world. The added prayers in CUL Ii.6.2 range from devotions to name saints to prayers to be said at the Elevation of the host at Mass, they include elaborate penitential prayers to be used as a temporary substitute for the sacrament of penance, and also several prayers which are in fact charms, designed to fend off evil or procure material good. The prayers as a whole are churchly, sacramental, attentive to the saints, concerned with meritorious acts of charity: they are highly supernatural, but in no sense otherworldy. There are prayers here to stop your house burning down or to help a woman to conceive a baby, and it is quite clear that some of these prayers were thought of as instrumental rather than merely supplicatory: done properly, they are guaranteed to work. Yet these are not the prayers of ignorance. They were written into a book made for and used by wealthy and influential men and women: Thomas Roberts, who died in 1543, and whose surviving children are all listed in the book,[46] was clerk of the Peace and coroner of Middlesex, a man of weight and education. The prayers come from a repertoire of such things which was appreciated at the very top of the social ladder: one of the additional prayers used by the Roberts family, the English invocation to Jesus and Mary, 'O my sovereign Lord Jesus', was a favourite addition in Books of Hours, and is also found, for example, in the sumptuous Talbot Hours, now in the Fitzwilliam Museum in Cambridge.[47] Far from being a symptom of and instrument for upperclass devotional exclusivity and isolation, in the late medieval Book of Hours, elite and popular religion converge.

University of Cambridge

---

[46] Ibid., fol. 33.
[47] Ibid., fol. 23v: Fitzwilliam Museum MS 40–1950, fols 132–135.

POPULAR AND ELITE RELIGION:
FEASTDAYS AND PREACHING

by DAVID D'AVRAY

Problems with the Categories

IN rejecting the distinction between elite and popular religion, Eamon Duffy's presidential address echoes a much earlier contribution to Studies in Church History. Arnaldo Momigliano found the dichotomy misleading where Christian historians of Late Antiquity were concerned, as Dermot Fenlon points out later in this volume, showing that the other historians too were thinking along the same lines.[1] In the present volume Professor Duffy makes a similar point with great force for a different time and place, late medieval England. Here and in his *Stripping of the Altars* the liturgy has a key role in his argument. He observes that Books of Hours or Primers are a form of the monastic office. Taking his thought further on lines he clearly intends, one could argue that the psychology of prayer is similar in the two cases and similar to the rosary also. In all three cases thoughts need not be about the words, for the focus of the prayer may be different, but the words work as a mantra to shut out distractions and create a devout frame of mind.

Liturgy as a Common Religious Culture

Stripping of the Altars elucidates the 'seasons and signs' of the liturgical year and the ways in which they structured the religious feelings of the whole community, clerical and lay.[2] Once again this line of thought can be extended. The general point is almost self-evident but so central as to be worth articulating before proceeding along more specific lines of investigation: most of the main trends in late medieval devotion reflect the patterns and emphases of the liturgical year, as established from even before the medieval period. The illiterate layman or woman who did not perhaps hear much preaching or receive much verbal instruc-

---

[1] See in this volume Dermot Fenlon, 'Elite and Popular Religion: the Case of Newman', 372–82.
[2] Duffy, *Stripping of the Altars*, Part I, A, 1.

162

tion of any kind might nevertheless have an awareness of the general meaning of those great feasts where labour stopped and rituals were conducted in church, especially since the church was probably the most impressive building to which most people had access and the liturgical services the most solemn and grandiose collective rituals. This collective awareness, growing over centuries, helps account for certain emphases that go beyond applications of obvious Christian themes. For information about feasts that covers the whole medieval period one must still rely on Hauck's classic *Church History of Germany*, so the following remarks apply to the German *Sprachraum* only, but they may well hold good for western Europe generally. According to Hauck the following feasts were on a par with Sunday in the Carolingian period: Christmas, St Stephen, John the Evangelist, the Holy Innocents, the Octave of Christmas, Epiphany and its Octave, the Purification of the Virgin, Easter Week, the Rogation Days, the Ascension, Whitsun,[3] John the Baptist, Peter and Paul, Martin and Andrew.[4] This suggests some obvious but central causal connections: the devotions to Christ's humanity would have been shaped by the feast of Christmas (as well as by the rituals from Good Friday to Easter); the preoccupation with penance and self-mortification[5] would be shaped by Lent; the Purification of the Virgin will have fuelled devotion to the Virgin and, by the time of Burchard of Worms's *Decretum*, the Assumption and the Nativity of the Virgin are also included as feasts.[6] The canon from which this comes got into the hugely influential *Decretum* of Gratian.[7]

Liturgy and Popular Devotion to Martyrs

Martyr's feasts too are prominent among Carolingian holidays of obligation: in addition to martyrs who are also apostles, about whom more

[3] Hauck seems to have slipped into an enumeration of major feasts, even if they fall on a Sunday, despite his initial statement that this moderate number of feasts 'den Sonntagen stand ... gleich': Albert Hauck, *Kirchengeschichte Deutschlands*, 2 (5th edn, Leipzig, 1935): 289.

[4] Ibid.

[5] That medieval people imitated Christ by giving things up is a basic building block in the argument of Caroline Walker-Bynum, *Holy Feast and Holy Fast. The Religious Significance of Food to Medieval Women* (Berkeley, CA, 1987).

[6] PL 140, col. 640. The canon has been traced back to Haito of Basel's Capitulary, ch. 8: see Hartmut Hoffmann and Rudolf Pokorny, *Das Dekret des Bischofs Burchard von Worms. Textstufen – Frühe Verbreitung – Vorlagen*, MGH, Hilfsmittel 12 (Munich, 1991), 184. For Burchard's canon law collection see R. W. Southern, *Scholastic Humanism and the Unification of Europe*, i: *Foundations* (Oxford, 1994), 244–6 (giving further references).

[7] Gratian, *Decretum*, PARS III D. 3 de cons. c. 1: *Corpus iuris canonici*, ed. E. Friedberg, 2 vols (repr. Graz, 1955), 1: col. 1353.

below, we have St Stephen, the Holy Innocents, and John the Baptist. In Burchard's list, and so Gratian's too, St Laurence is added.

This may help explain a popular obsession with martyrdom that goes far beyond what the institutional Church intended to encourage. The idea of martyrdom was indeed central to Christianity in this as in many periods. It was bound up with the whole idea of the sacrifice of Christ and the imitation of his passion. The Church wanted the laity to internalize such ideas: but I have in mind something less firmly grounded in the rationality of the religion and more likely to derive from misunderstanding. The extreme version of this was the cult of the holy dog, St Guinefort. A study by Jean-Claude Schmitt[8] has made this well-known. The dog had saved a baby, but appeared at first sight to have harmed it. The dog was killed, then its innocence was recognized and it was treated as a saint. This is an extreme case of a more general tendency to worship people who had been put to death when innocent. The historian of this phenomenon is André Vauchez.[9] Among the examples he gives are Margaret of Roskilde, killed by her husband; Redegonde of Wellenberg, eaten by wolves; and Nantvin, a German pilgrim unjustly accused of pederasty by the peasants of Wolfrats-hausen and burned alive.[10] As these cases show, the popular penchant for the cult of martyrs transcended particular types, such as the cult of political 'martyrs' (like Simon de Montfort) in England, or of children supposedly killed by Jews. These species of the genre require particular explanations which need not detain us here. The larger problem is to explain the general phenomenon. Vauchez make it clear that church authorities tended to oppose this type of cult in its grass-roots form.[11]

This popular preoccupation with martyrdom is a different case from the others just touched on because there is a real divergence here between popular and elite (or at least official) religion. Actually this is a case where the discredited distinction works not badly, in a subsidiary role, as it sometimes can when used with care and discrimination. Martyrs like these had no chance of official canonization. That tended to keep popular canonization outside the mainstream of medieval

---

8 *Le Saint lévrier. Guinefort, guérisseur d'enfants depuis le XIIIe siècle* (Paris, 1979).

9 *La Sainteté en Occident aux derniers siècles du Moyen Age d'après les procès de canonisation et les documents hagiographiques*, Bibliothèque des Écoles Françaises d'Athènes et de Rome 241 (Rome, 1981), 174–203.

10 Ibid., 174–6.

11 Ibid., 174. Vauchez distinguishes this grass-roots form from the cult of the martyred or suffering leader, analysed at 187–203.

religion. Experience and vivid feelings alone are a little directionless without conceptual and verbal articulation.

Another Pair of Categories

To recapitulate the argument so far: the distinction between elite and popular religion is not a good general framework for medieval religious history, because so much of medieval religion transcended the distinction; still the distinction may continue to play an important if more marginal role when it comes to phenomena like popular canonization of people who died by violence.

One could leave it at that, keeping the distinction but relegating it to the borders of religious history. Yet there is more to be said about categories. When categories are much discussed it is usually because something in the past has not yet been properly broken down into its elements for purposes of further interpretation. Historians propose concepts that do not quite fit what they are trying to describe, others point out the shortcomings and propose that the concepts be abandoned altogether, but the real answer may be to try again to build a conceptual schema that comes closer to labelling the different parts of the phenomena being studied. Precise and purpose-built concepts are needed if we are to analyse out the elements in the messy amalgam of past realities.

Abstract and Concrete Religious Thought

Into the central place from which the 'elite-popular' distinction has been ejected I suggest we move instead a distinction between abstract and concrete religious thought. By that I mean something close to what Newman expressed by the terms 'notional' and 'real'. With notional or abstract religious thought the signs in the mind are predominantly verbal. With 'real' religious thought the mental signs are more concrete. They may be visual images, emotional memories, memories of concrete decisions taken one way or other, memories of experiences undergone, etc.

A good deal of religious thinking is easily classifiable in one or the other category. Scholastic theology is one of the great cultural creations, but most of it tends to fall on the abstract side of the spectrum. This is not simply because it is so intellectual. The attempts to popularize schemas of virtues and vices in the later Middle Ages also tend towards the abstract side except when backed up by *exempla* or analogies (which is a reminder that our dichotomy is a tool for analysing composites rather than neat either/or classification). Calvin's *Institutes* or at least large parts of the work tend towards the 'notional'. (Again a proviso: a text might be abstract or notional as read by one person and concrete and vivid as read by another, because of experience supplied by the reader. Even so it could be replied that the concrete sentiment is not primarily generated by the text.) If Mark Pattison was right about mainstream preaching from the Restoration to the mid-eighteenth century, its demonstrations of the Gospels' veracity also tended towards abstraction.[12] The abstract and notional, note, can be found at the popular level. Catechisms tend to that side of the spectrum unless some article is transformed by experience or perhaps an image into concrete thought.

On the other hand, the emotional preaching and hymns of the early Methodists would certainly tend towards the concrete; so do processions and prayers before crucifixes; so too the conversion experiences of evangelical Christians or visits to the confessional by Catholics. Abstention from work and even play turned Puritan respect for the Old Testament into a lived experience. Liturgy and services tend to make religious thinking concrete.

The distinction slides easily into another one with which it only partly overlaps: the dichotomy between intellectual and emotional religion. The elision should be resisted because concrete religious thought is a broader category than emotional religion. Rituals make thinking concrete and 'real' even if they are emotionally quite dry. The fact that they are actions rather than just words and that they create a real likeness of what they are trying to represent makes them concrete.

The Combination of Abstract and Concrete

Religious thought should not necessarily be segregated into one category or another. It can happen but need not. The categories are ideal types, tools for analysis of a complex reality. One point of distinguishing them is that it makes one notice what a difference it makes when they are combined, as they often are. I have suggested that concrete religious thought tends to be directionless on its own. For maximal causal impact,

---

12 Mark Pattison, 'Tendencies of Religious Thought in England, 1688–1750', in idem, *Essays and Reviews* (12th edn, London, 1865), 306–98.

an experience, image or remembered emotion needs to crystallize around a conviction that can in some way be verbalized. Conversely, on the other hand the verbalized conviction on its own will tend to be a relatively weak causal force compared with the conviction embodied in concrete thought. Concrete thought cannot be identified with emotional religion but it certainly tends to carry a stronger emotional charge and to have more of an impact on others because of that. These are generalizations of the sort that it would be futile to try to demonstrate deductively or inductively. They are really an appeal to common sense and the experience of historians: suggestions which seem evident once formulated, but which still help to clarify analysis.

Application to the History of Feastdays and Preaching

The following interpretative schema may therefore be suggested for the specific theme of this paper. Holidays of obligation made religious thought concrete because they had a practical effect on everybody's life, not least on the lives of the laity because they would get off work. In the early middle ages, the laity may have only been aware that apostles, martyrs, the Virgin etc. were of great significance, without being able to articulate why. From the twelfth century on preachers began to give coherent verbal explanations. Insofar as the verbal explanation by preachers reinforced the impact of a holiday of obligation, and conversely, the experience of the holiday was shaped by preaching, we have major themes in the history of later medieval religious sentiment (both popular and elite). Until the high Middle Ages most people had the experience of feasts with accompanying emotions, perhaps powerful, but probably ill-defined and lacking a coherent formulation of the doctrines they went with. Once the doctrines were given form through preaching there were reservoirs of lived liturgical experience to draw on.

This could happen when the holiday had existed for centuries and the preaching was added. Or again a feast might become a holiday in the last medieval centuries with preaching being added accordingly. This general schema may now be illustrated with examples.

The Apostolic Life

In the central Middle Ages and after, the ideal of the apostolic life had a tremendous appeal for large numbers of religiously minded men and women, orthodox and heretical alike.[13] Herbert Grundmann presents the apostolic life movement as growing out of the Gregorian reform, though it rapidly turned against the institutional church.[14] This explanation works well up to a point. As early as the Synod of Rome in 1059 under Nicholas II we find the apostolic life, understood as life in community, proposed as an ideal to and for the clergy: 'And we ask and advise, that they aim with intensity at the apostolic life, that is, the common one'.[15] The adjective 'apostolic' then took on a life of its own, rather as the adjective 'equal' has done in recent centuries. Evidently, the apostles did not only live a life in community. They preached, and they were poor.

The papacy may have fostered these aspects of the ideal even a century before Innocent III. According to a life of Bernard of Tiron, Paschal II gave him

> the following office, namely, that he should preach to the peoples, hear confessions, give penances, baptize, go around [different] regions, and carry out with care all the functions which a public preacher should do. And after he had given him the task of representing (*vicem*) the apostolate, he was unwilling that a vicar of the apostles, whom he was sending to preach without money, should lack sustenance, and he advised him to accept the food of the body from those whom[16] he was refreshing with the word of salvation.[17]

---

[13] H. Grundmann, *Religiöse Bewegungen im Mittelalter. Untersuchungen über die geschichtlichen Zusammenhänge zwischen der Ketzerei, den Bettelorden und der religiösen Frauenbewegung im 12. und 13. Jahrhundert und über die geschichtlichen Grundlagen der deutschen Mystik* (Hildesheim, 1961). Note also the classic essay by M.-D. Chenu, 'Monks, Canons and Laymen in Search of the Apostolic Life', in idem, *Nature, Man, and Society in the Twelfth Century. Essays on New Theological Perspectives in the Latin West*, selected, edited and trans. by J. Taylor and L. K. Little (Chicago, IL, 1968; repr. Phoenix, AR, 1979), 202–38.

[14] Grundmann, *Religiöse Bewegungen*, 13–18, notably at 14: 'Die durch die Reformbewegung erweckten Geister begannen zu fragen, ob die kirchliche Ordinierung des Priesters die einzige und ausreichende Berechtigung zur Vollziehung des christlichen Heilswerkes sei; ob nur die Kirche berufen und dazu eingesetzt sei, allein durch die von ihr bestellten Vertreter den göttlichen Heilsplan, den die Evangelien und die Apostel verkündet hatten, zu verwirklichen; ob nicht jeder einzelne Christ durch die Gebote der Evangelien und das Beispiel der Apostel aufgerufen sei, sein Leben unmittelbar nach den evangelischen und apostolischen Normen auszurichten; und ob andererseits derjenige ein echter Priester sein könne, der zwar von der Kirche dazu ordiniert is, aber nicht lebt, wie das Evangelium es verlangt und wie die Apostel lebten'.

[15] Duane V. Lapsanski, *Perfectio evangelica. Eine begriffsgeschichtliche Untersuchung im frühfranziskanischen Schrifttum*, Veroffentlichungen des Grabmann-Institutes zur Erforschung der Mittelalterlichen Theologie und Philosophie n.F. 22 (München, 1974), 2.

[16] The Latin has 'quod' here: emend to 'quos'?   [17] Lapsanski, *Perfectio*, 16, n. 64.

Papal advocacy of the apostolic ideal helps explain its success. Is the explanation adequate? Ultimately this is a matter of opinion, but I am sceptical. Not everything that was advocated by the papacy aroused such deep enthusiasm.

Is the solution to be found in social and economic history,[18] say in the 'rise of the money economy', occurring in approximately the same period? There are clearly important links here, especially so far as the 'apostolic poverty' aspect of the ideal was concerned.[19] That can hardly be the whole story, however, for the apostolic ideal cannot be reduced to poverty; it is also worth noting that the industrial revolution did not produce a corresponding emphasis on poverty in the religious movements that accompanied it. Neither the 'apostolic life' in general nor 'apostolic poverty' in particular are automatic features of Christian revivals generally, certainly not with that degree of specificity and force.

Could it be instead that the popes were leaning on a door already ajar with hinges well oiled by centuries of liturgical preparation? The model would then be this. The liturgical calendar rams home the idea that the apostles were holy, but the implications of that were unclear because the apostolic ideal could not be articulated verbally by most people. The Gregorian reform gave an articulate verbal form to the ideal which was then taken out of the hands of the official Church and carried in many directions on a wave of enthusiasm. Concepts met an existing liturgical practice and they reinforced one another.

In the list of Carolingian holidays of obligation compiled by Hauck, several apostles were included: John the Evangelist, Peter and Paul, and Andrew. In the following period the liturgical progress of the apostles is

---

[18]   This kind of explanation has been around a long time, as Grundmann's implicit attack on it reminds us: 'Seit dem Ende des 19. Jahrhunderts sind zwar manche Versuche unternommen worden, die religiösen Bewegungen des Mittelalters als einen geschichtlichen Gesamtvorgang zu begreifen. Aber dabei stand das Interesse für die sozial- und wirtschaftsgeschichtliche Bedeutung jener Bewegungen so stark im Vordergrund, daß man ihren religiösen Sinn und Gehalt geradezu verkannte und umdeutete in eine zeitbedingte Verschleierung der eigentlichen, sozialen Motive und Ziele. Hätten es diese Versuche nicht bei einer neuen "Auffassung" des historischen Verlaufs in großen Zügen bewenden lassen, hätten sie es unternommen, diese "Auffassung" an der Deutung der Überlieferung und der Erklärung der geschichtlichen Vorgänge im Einzelnen zu erproben, so hätte sich die Meinung, die religiösen Bewegungen des Mittelalters seien im Grunde soziale oder gar "proletarische" Bewegungen, von selbst berichtigen müssen' (*Religiöse Bewegungen*, 8).

[19]   Lester K. Little, *Religious Poverty and the Profit Economy in Medieval Europe* (London, 1978).

striking. At the Synod of Erfurt in 932 the feasts of the apostles have a prominent place. Chapter I orders

> That henceforth the feasts of the twelve apostles should be solemnized with the greatest veneration . . . . For we cannot doubt that those whom we know to be of higher merit in heaven should also be worshipped by us through the distinction of greater honour.[20]

This council was an important event, summoned by King Henry I of Germany and held in his presence.[21] Chapter II begins as follows: 'In accordance with the canons, we wish that secular pleas should in no way take place on Sundays or other feast days . . .'.[22] In view of the previous chapter, feasts of the apostles must be included in the reference to 'feast days'.

In England, Ethelred's Code of 1008 (14.1) declared that '. . . at the festival of every Apostle there is to be fasting and festivity, except that we enjoin no fast for the festival of St. Philip and St. James, because of the Easter festival'.[23] Ethelred's legislation was not necessarily enforced, but it must have come to the notice of many, and the clergy could well have made it a reality at grass roots level.

The progress of the feasts of the apostles on continental Europe was not uninterrupted. The Bavarian synod of Dingolfing includes among top-ranking feasts only Philip and James (1 May), Peter and Paul (29 June) and Andrew (30 Nov.); the other apostles seem to have been wrapped up with Peter and Paul and celebrated on the same day.[24] Even this implies and would have implied to contemporaries a significant emphasis on apostolic sanctity. When we turn to Burchard of Worms's popular canon law collection, moreover, all the apostles are in the top rank. Book 2 ch. 77 of his Canon Law collections lays it down 'That priests should announce to their flocks which days should be observed as feasts throughout the year'. Among them are 'the twelve apostles,

---

[20] *Die Konzilien Deutschlands und Reichsitaliens 916–1001, Teil 1: 916–960*, ed. Ernst-Dieter Hehl, MGH Concilia vi, 1 (Hannover, 1987), 107.

[21] Ibid., 97; cf. Andreas Amiet, 'Die liturgische Gesetzgebung der deutschen Reichskirche in der Zeit der sächsischen Kaiser, 922–1023', *Zeitschrift für schweizerische Kirchengeschichte* 70 (1976), 1–106 and 209–307, at 36.

[22] *Die Konzilien*, ed. Hehl, 108.

[23] *English Historical Documents* I, c. 500–1042, ed. D. Whitelock (London, 1955), 407, no. 44.

[24] Amiet, 'Die liturgische Gesetzgebung', 60, 61–2; note however that Amiet also affirms that: 'Johannes der Evangelist wird nicht namentlich genannt, ist jedoch in den drei Tagen nach Weihnachten eingeschlossen' (60).

especially however saints Peter and Paul, who illuminated the world with their preaching'.[25] As noted above, the decree from which this comes got into Gratian's *Decretum*, thus achieving maximum authority and publicity.

In the meantime, the ideal of the 'apostolic life' was being spread by example and word: holy men are described in the language of the apostolic life.[26] The concept was protean but pervasive.[27] People understood it differently, but each person or group to its own satisfaction. Everyone knew that 'apostolic' was good. In time, the preaching of the friars, a true mass medium,[28] was a powerful added voice capable of presenting the ideal in a coherent verbal form.[29] The liturgical calendar would have prepared a whole society for the various verbal articulations of the ideal. In the light of these considerations the enthusiasm and force of the apostolic life movement ceases to be puzzling.

We may now turn to two late medieval themes, the ideal of the holy intellectual woman, and devotion to the papal office. In both cases the observations relate mainly to the German *Sprachraum*, for which the preliminary work has already been done, but the pattern probably holds good for Latin Europe as a whole.

Katherine of Alexandria

With the apostolic life idea the liturgical calendar came before extensive verbal articulation of the ideal. The next two cases to be considered are different. In both of them, the liturgy and preaching are closer to

---

[25] PL 140, col. 640; see above, n. 6.

[26] The language has been traced by Grundmann, *Religiöse Bewegungen*, 40, n. 57.

[27] Of the religious movement of the time Grundmann writes: 'Es gibt "Schlagworte" und "Leitmotive" dieser Bewegung, die zwar jeweils verschieden vestanden, interpretiert und angewandt wurden, aber eben dadurch erkennen lassen, um welche Fragen es bei diesen religiösen Auseinandersetzungen ging. Das Gemeinsame und das Verschiedene ist gerade an der jeweiligen Verwendung und Deutung solcher "Schlagworter" deutlich zu beobachten. Besonders aufschlußreich ist dafür der Leitgedanke des "apostolischen Lebens", der allenthalben im 12. Jahrhundert lebendig wirksam war, aber auf sehr verschiedene Weise verwirklicht wurde' (ibid., 504).

[28] D. L. d'Avray, *Medieval Marriage Sermons. Mass Communication in a Culture without Print* (Oxford, 2001), 15–30, and idem, *Medieval Marriage and its Meaning. Symbolism and Society* (Oxford, 2005), ch. 1.

[29] D. L. d'Avray, *The Preaching of the Friars. Sermons Diffused from Paris before 1300* (Oxford, 1985), section I.iii on *The Apostolic Life*, esp. 44–52. This analyses an example of preaching on the Apostolic Life, from the model sermon collection of the thirteenth-century Dominican Pierre de Reims.

being in step. In both cases, a saint is 'promoted' liturgically in the later Middle Ages, and we are able to see the way the meaning of the saint was articulated in medieval preaching. The focus will be on the idea of the papal office as represented by St Peter, and the ideas of female intellectuality and of the mystical marriage with Christ as represented by St Katherine of Alexandria.

The history of Katherine's feastday and of sermons for it are an excellent source for perceptions of female excellence. So far as the feastday is concerned one must continue to work mainly from the lists in Hauck's classic *Kirchengeschichte Deutschlands*, while noting the need for a European-wide survey. Hauck's list of holidays of obligation for the Carolingian period, quoted above, does not specify any female saints at all apart from the Virgin Mary, a special case.[30] The list in Burchard of Worms's early eleventh-century *Decretum*, which was incorporated into Gratian's synthesis, does not include any women at all (not counting feasts of the Virgin).[31] By the beginning of fourteenth century Katherine of Alexandria and Mary Magdalen had entered the elite group in some places at least.[32] They were not quite the only ones to make it in the Middle Ages.[33] Even so, a holiday of obligation for a woman had rarity value. Messages about female sanctity would stand out more. It is the more interesting to know what was said about Katherine in sermons for this feast. Here I will concentrate on one theme only: her dialectical skill.[34]

Katherine did not merely profess her faith and suffer. She first refuted the elite orators of the pagan empire. I have discussed some of

---

[30]   See above, n. 3.

[31]   See above, n. 6. Because there were diocesan feasts and feasts for the dedication of individual churches, it is possible that there were some local holidays of obligation for women.

[32]   D'Avray, 'Katherine of Alexandria and Mass Communication in Germany: Woman as Intellectual', in Nicole Bériou, D. L. d'Avray *et al.*, eds, *Modern Questions about Medieval Sermons. Essays on Marriage, Death, History and Sanctity* (Spoleto, 1994), 401–8, at 403, n. 8 (for both women). Hauck notes that 'Die Feier des Katherinentags wurde in "Eichst." [Eichstatt?] erst 1354 eingeführt' (Hauck, *Kirchengeschichte*, 5.1: 373, n. 1). On Mary Magdalen see the excellent study by Katherine Jansen, *The Making of the Magdalen. Preaching and Popular Devotion in the Later Middle Ages* (Princeton, NJ, 2000).

[33]   Hauck notes that St Elizabeth's feast was promoted to the top category in Würzburg from 1407 (ibid.).

[34]   Katherine deserves a full study along the lines of Jansen, *Making of the Magdalen*. For England there is already Katherine J. Lewis, *The Cult of St Katherine of Alexandria in Late Medieval England* (Woodbridge, 2000).

the evidence for this elsewhere.[35] Here one more piece may be added from one of the most popular model sermon collections, the so called *Sleep securely* (*Dormi secure*) by Johannes de Verdena, which survives in at least sixteen editions between 1488 and the end of 1500.[36] It will be remembered that a sermon in any copy of any edition could have been used again and again for different congregations and that when a model sermon is preached even on one occasion the message gets to many people. This means that ideas in model sermon collections would on the whole have had a far wider diffusion than ideas in almost any other genre of early printed book, so that they are one of the most important sources for the history of late medieval religion:

> So therefore we read that the emperor, seeing that she spoke with such prudence, and that she called Christ the true son of God, and asserted that idols were demons, and that he could not match her wisdom, secretly wrote to tell all the grammarians and rhetoricians to hurry to the praetorium at Alexandria, to receive immense rewards if they conquered the virgin speaker by putting their case. Therefore fifty orators who excelled all the men in the world in all wisdom and knowledge were brought from different provinces. When they asked why they had been called from such remote parts, Caesar replied: We have among us a girl of incomparable sense and prudence who confutes all the wise men, and asserts that our gods are demons. If you get the better of her you will return home with great honour. Then one replied indignantly: What a great plan of the emperor, when he summons so many wise men from remote parts of the world to take on one girl, when one of our little hangers on could very easily defeat her. And they said: Let the girl be brought before us, so that she may be convinced of her temerity and admit that she has never seen wise men before. But when the virgin learned of the struggle that she was about to face, she commended herself entirely to the Lord. And behold, an angel of the Lord came to her side and urged her to stand firm, affirming that not only could she not be conquered by them, but that in addition she would convert them and send them towards the crown of martyrdom. [. . .] Therefore, when the orators said that it

35 D'Avray, 'Katherine', 404–7.
36 For a list see Ruth Horie, '*Ecclesia Deo dedicata*. Church and Soul in Late Medieval Dedication Sermons', Ph.D. thesis, University College London, 1988, 265–7.

was impossible for God to become man, or to suffer, the virgin then showed that this was predicted even by the gentiles. For the Sibyl said: Happy is that God who hung from the high cross; again she said that Christ had died and risen again from the dead. For out of the humility of human nature he was able to die and out of his divinity to rise from the dead. And thus she brought them all to silence, and they were made altogether speechless. Then the emperor full of great indignation asked them how they could allow themselves to be so disgracefully defeated by a girl on her own.[37]

The fact that a female saint's intellectual capacities and ability in debate are such a prominent theme is a significant fact in the history of medieval attitudes to women. This side of Katherine would have been reinforced by art too, as the 'Katherine disputes with the philosophers' motif has been found to be one of the most common of the images associated with her, both in Germany and generally.[38] Probably however the fact of feast in place of work would make more impression on the average person even than pictures.

[37] *Sermones dormi securi* (Paris, 1503 edn: British Library call number C.125.b.18), Sermon lxvi, unfoliated: 'Unde legitur consequenter quod imperator, videns quod ita prudenter loquebatur, et quod Christum verum dei filium dixit, et ydola demonia asseruit, et eius sapientie obviare non potuit, mandavit occulte per litteras ut omnes grammatici et rethores ad pretorium Alexandrie festinarent, immensa munera recepturi si concionatricem virginem suis assertionibus superarent. Adducti sunt igitur de diversis provinciis quinquaginta oratores qui omnes homines in mundo in omni sapientia et scientia excellabant (*sic*). Quibus interrogantibus cur tam a remotis partibus vocati essent, Cesar respondit: Est apud nos puella sensu et prudentia incomparabilis, que omnes sapientes confutat, et deos nostros demones affirmat, quam si superaveris cum magno honore ad [a *edn.*] propria redibitis. Tunc unus indignatus respondit: O magnum imperatoris consilium qui ad unius puelle conflictum tot sapientes mundi de remotis partibus advocavit, cum unus ex nostris clientulis eam poterat levissime confutare. Et dixerunt: Adducatur coram nobis puella ut sua temeritate convicta numquam se sapientes vidisse agnoscat. Sed cum virgo certamen quod sibi imminebat didicisset, totam se Domino commendabat. Et ecce angelus Domini astitit ei et ut constanter staret ammonuit, asserens quod non solum ab illis vinci non posset, sed insuper illos conversos ad palmam martyrii destinaret. . . . Cum ergo oratores deum fieri hominem, aut pati impossibile dicerent, tunc virgo hoc etiam a gentilibus esse predictum ostendit. Nam Sybilla dixit: Felix ille deus ligno qui pendet ab alto; item dixit Christum passum et resurrexisse a mortuis. Nam ex humilitate humane nature mori potuit et ex divinitate resurgere. Et sic fecit [fectit *edn.*] omnes obmutescere et muti penitus effecti sunt. Tunc imperator nimio fervore repletus increpare eos cepit: Cur ab [ad *edn.*] una puella tam turpiter se vinci permitterent?'.

[38] Bruce A. Beatie, 'St. Katharine of Alexandria in Medieval German Illustrative Cycles: a Problem beyond Genre', in H. Heinen and Ingeborg Henderson, eds, *Genres in Medieval German Literature*, Goeppinger Arbeiten zur Germanistik 439 (Goeppingen, 1986), 140–56, Appendix I, 155.

The sermon does not just say that Katherine refuted the pagan intellectuals but also gives an idea of her line of argument. We have an objection about the absurdity of God suffering, and an answer in terms of Christ's two natures, with Sibylline authority thrown in. Here the listeners are being drawn to the abstract side of the spectrum of religious thought. We find the same thing in sermons about papal authority.

Devotion to the Papacy

It was noted above that the feast of Sts Peter and Paul was one of those treated like a Sunday from Carolingian times. Interestingly, though, St Peter was liturgically 'promoted' in the late Middle Ages. In much of Germany and England he acquired two top-level feasts, in addition to the feast of Sts Peter and Paul.[39] (For the rest of Europe the topic has not been investigated to my knowledge.) By the end of the Middle Ages it would seem that, apart from the special case of the Virgin Mary, no other saint was brought home so emphatically to the laity by the liturgy. The question is whether this liturgical emphasis on St Peter was used to bring home points about the papacy. Liturgical history needs the history of preaching and vice versa to get the sense of the impact of ideas.

One cannot assume *a priori* that sermons on St Peter would propagate devotion to the papal office. There were other things one could do with a sermon about him, and in fact a study of thirteenth-century sermons suggests that the papacy was not a central theme of sermons for the saint at that period:

> . . . many preachers, and not the least important of them, seem to be more concerned to draw attention to the faults of the pope and the bishops, grouped together under the generic word 'prelati', than to underline the continuity of apostolic tradition across the centuries under the powerful impetus of the Spirit.[40]

---

[39] D. L. d'Avray, 'Papal Authority and Religious Sentiment in the Late Middle Ages', in Diana Wood, ed., *The Church and Sovereignty c.590–1918. Essays in Honour of Michael Wilks*, SCH.S 9 (Oxford, 1991), 393–408, at 406, following Hauck, *Kirchengeschichte*, 5.1: 372–3. For England, see C. R. Cheney, 'Rules for the Observance of Feast-Days in Medieval England', *Bulletin of the Institute of Historical Research* [now *Historical Research*] 34 (1961), 117–47, at 136–44 and 147.

[40] J. G. Bougerol, 'La Papauté dans les sermons médiévaux français et italiens', in Christopher Ryan, ed., *The Religious Roles of the Papacy: Ideals and Realities 1150–1300*, Pontif-

More research on the thirteenth century is needed, but I think it likely that it will confirm this impression.

All the more interesting that at the end of the Middle Ages, when the liturgical profile of the prince of the apostles had been raised so much higher, sermons enjoying a wide diffusion should emphasize the connection between him and his successors the popes, using preaching as propaganda for the papacy. It should be said immediately that this propaganda was not commissioned. The sermons studied are in incunable collections of models produced without papal intervention. There was no equivalent in late medieval Europe to the Books of Homilies issued under Edward VI and Elizabeth I. Synods did produce pastoral materials for priests but they were a different genre from liturgical sermons. I have used incunables because the number of editions gives a fair assurance that they were influential, when combined with the fact that they were intended for feasts that were holidays of obligation.[41] The three sermon collections to which reference is made each survive in multiple editions: Meffret in seven,[42] Michael Lochmayr in four,[43] and Leonardus de Utino in sixteen.[44]

The aspect of these sermons that should be foregrounded in the context of this lecture is their argumentative character. They reason from authorities, canon law and scripture or the two in combination. This brings them closer to the 'abstract' end of our spectrum. We need to keep in mind that the abstract argumentation was embedded in the experience of a liturgy for the laity on a holiday from work.

Meffret uses familiar authorities from the New Testament as evidence of Peter's authority, notably John 21:15–17 and the 'Thou art Peter' passage from Matthew 16. He says that these powers are evident in Peter's successors, the popes. Other prelates have great powers and dignities – examples are listed. These however are derived from papal authority and the pope can take them away. That the pope can do that is 'proved' from two canon law authorities, both from Gratian's *Decretum*. This combination of scripture and canon law is characteristic

ical Institute of Mediaeval Studies, Papers in Mediaeval Studies 8 (Toronto, 1989), 247–75, at 249.

[41] In what follows, I select and represent less rebarbatively data first published in d'Avray, 'Papacy and Religious Sentiment', where passages paraphrased here are quoted in Latin and translated, with canon law citations identified.

[42] Horie, 'Ecclesia Deo Dedicata', 273–6.

[43] Ibid., 272–3.

[44] Ibid., 268–72.

of the sub-genre of pro-papal preaching. The pope's superiority to the emperor is demonstrated by arguments from ritual. The emperor prostrates himself to be crowned by the pope. The emperor should hold the pope's stirrup when he mounts his horse. Secular law is mentioned as evidence for the last point. Throughout this passage Gratian argues rather than simply asserting.[45]

In Michael Lochmayr we find similar sorts of reasoning. Peter was given plenitude of jurisdiction. It is the same with his successors the popes, whereas other prelates have only a partial power which derives from the pope. He gives canon law authority. Lochmayr then argues from ritual: the pope has the right to use the pallium every day, whereas other prelates can use it only at certain times and places. That point too is demonstrated with a canon law citation. Then the range of papal powers is listed: for instance the power to make authoritative declarations on divine and natural law.[46] From Leonardus de Utino, he of the seventeen editions, we may take a more reflective discussion of the religious hierarchy in the Old Testament and after Christ. He summarizes two decrees from Gratian's *Decretum* giving arguments for papal authority. From the first he argues that the distinction between supreme pontiffs and lesser priests goes back to the time of Moses, who made Aaron the supreme pontiff and his sons lesser priests. However the New Testament marks a decisive stage. Christ made the seventy-two disciples lesser priests, the twelve apostles greater priests, and Peter the supreme pontiff, giving him the keys of the kingdom of heaven and praying that his faith might not fail. The next canon law authority is used to emphasize that St Peter's power did not derive from the apostles but from Christ. On the contrary, Peter had power over the other apostles. The same structure was passed on to his successors (the popes) and theirs (the other bishops).[47]

These familiar legitimations of papal authority need to be placed in their historical context. By the time the collections including these model sermons were printed the papacy had emerged from crises that had shaken its authority: the Schism and Conciliarism. Leonardus de Utino's argument that the pope did not derive his authority from the bishops should perhaps be seen as an implicit answer to Conciliarist ideas. Indeed, all the passages discussed could be interpreted as a reac-

[45] D'Avray, 'Papacy and Religious Sentiment', 399–401.
[46] Ibid., 401–2.
[47] Ibid., 402–4.

tion against those who played down papal authority. This unsolicited late medieval propaganda for the papacy has not I think been sufficiently noticed. How effective was it? To measure the efficacy of propaganda is never easy even when one has voting patterns and opinion polls to go on, let alone for the later Middle Ages. Still, if the general considerations developed earlier in this lecture have anything in them, the effect of the propaganda may have been considerable. Not only did these incunable model sermons enjoy a wide diffusion. The situations in which they were preached combined with their contents to produce the mixture of concrete and abstract thought which, it was suggested, is an especially powerful force on the mind. Conceptual reasoning and textual authorities supporting papal power would have been presented to congregations in a setting conducive to fixing them in the mind: a break in routine to make a special occasion, a day free from work.

Conclusion

In tune with the presidential address at this year's conference, I have played down the usefulness of the dichotomy in the title of this volume, for western medieval religious history at least, though I have argued that it can be helpful every now and again. It may have been trying to do the work better done by a related distinction: between religious thought which is more verbal and abstract, on the one hand, and, on the other, religious thought which is more concrete, say by being embodied in action and ritual (there being many different sorts of concrete religious thought). Distinguishing only in order to unite, it was argued that when the two types of thinking are combined they are more powerful than either alone as a force in religious history. This helps explain the power of the apostolic life ideal, where centuries of preparation by the liturgical calendar were – so runs the hypothesis – activated by verbal and conceptual popularizations of the idea from the time of the Gregorian reform. The same schema was then applied to two other themes in religious history: Katherine of Alexandria as an embodiment of female sanctity, and the idea of the papacy at the end of the Middle Ages. It was argued that in these cases liturgical facts on the ground, the experience of holidays of obligation, affecting the calendar and the pattern of life, came together with preaching that would have reached large numbers of people and structured attitudes verbally and conceptually, fostering among other things the idea of a woman who could defend her faith with arguments, and of the papal office as legitimated by evidence. The cases are not quite symmetrical. In one, a woman saint is shown arguing; in the other, the preacher gives argument and evidence for papal authority. Still, both knit devout feelings together with rationality and make an appeal to verbal reasoning. Preaching can be found anywhere on the spectrum of concrete and abstract thought, and I have not done justice to the vivid and concrete elements in preaching for these feasts, but the point was to show that both verbal and abstract elements went into the compound and strengthened it.

Finally, these excursions into the history of holiday preaching show priests and people working together. A holiday of obligation meant a special liturgy for the priest and more work, and for the laity it meant a break from normal work to focus the mind on the saint of the day: but for both there was a change in the pattern of life. With sermons, the priest preached and the laity listened, on and off, but the message would tend to bridge the gap between their cultures. As a general rule, furthermore, the sermons preached by priests or religious to the laity are similar to the sermons they preached to each other.[48] All in all, at least so far as the Middle Ages are concerned, the history of liturgy and the history of preaching are among the worst fields in which to use systematically the phrase 'elite and popular religion'.

University College London

---

[48] This is one of the central arguments of d'Avray, *The Preaching of the Friars*.

FROM ROYAL PRAYER BOOKS
TO COMMON PRAYERS:
RELIGIOUS PRACTICES IN LATE MEDIEVAL
AND EARLY MODERN POLAND

by URSZULA BORKOWSKA OSU

THE Union between Poland and Lithuania, whose foundations were laid in 1386 with the baptism of Jagiello, the pagan grand duke of Lithuania, and his marriage to Queen Jadwiga (Hedwig), daughter of the last king of Poland, marked the beginning of a systematic Christianization to which the pagan Lithuanians offered remarkably little resistance.[1] Recent research on religious practice under the ruling Jagiellonian dynasty in Poland and Lithuania (1386–1572) shows that royal piety was often designed to elicit participation at a popular level, cementing both the diffusion of Christian involvement across the newly unified kingdom, and in turn the role of the royal family at its centre. Surviving royal accounts and prayer books can offer a privileged insight into the personal religion of the monarchs and their relatives. These accounts, although only partially extant, constitute an objective source by which religious practices may be understood. Created for bureaucratic reasons, to keep order in the Treasurer's Chancery, rather than to present the king as pious, they detail expenses for masses and other *opera pia* of the king and his family, recording the rhythm of royal religious practices – for the day, the week and the whole liturgical year. The accounts also provide evidence of sacramental practices and royal almsgiving.[2] Pious literature composed at the behest of the Jagiellons, combined with extant pedagogical treatises and didactic sermons delivered in the presence of the

---

[1] Jerzy Kłoczowski, *A History of Polish Christianity* (Cambridge, 2000), 50–65.

[2] Jerzy Semkowski, *Akta Skarbowe Rzeczypospolitej w Archiwum Akt Dawnych w Warszawie. Przewodnik po zespolach. I. Akta Skarbowe Rzeczypospolitej.* [Financial Records of the Commonwealth in Old Records Archives in Warsaw. A Guide Book. I. Financial Accounts of the Commonwealth (Warsaw, 1975); Urszula Borkowska, 'Rachunki królewskie jako źródło poznania praktyk religijnych Jagiellonów' [Royal Account Books as the Source for Religious Practices of the Jagiellons], in Urszula Borkowska, ed., *Peregrinatio ad veritatem. Studies dedicated to Alexandre Witkowska* (Lublin, 2004), 47–64.

monarch, is particularly valuable in admitting us into the world of royal Christian education.[3]

Contemporary opinions of royal piety, drawn from numerous funeral speeches, were delivered on the occasion of the death of any royal family member.[4] Similar opinions were repeated in the historiographical works of the fifteenth- and sixteenth-century chroniclers. The Jagiellons' grants of charters and privileges to various churches provide valuable information about their activity as pious founders while the introductory statements of these documents or *arengae* frequently explain the motivation underlying particular foundations.[5]

Jagiellonian religious practices are most clearly revealed in eleven royal prayer books, a few surviving from the many once in royal possession. Four are fifteenth-century, while the remaining *libelli precum* date to the first half of the sixteenth century. (*Habent sua fata libelli* – four of these are to be found in Great Britain, four in Germany, one in Milan, and only two in Poland). The variety of texts of the prayer books that survive strongly suggests a personal interest by their owners in the choice of content and iconography.[6]

Oldest of all the volumes is the mysterious work known as *Vladislav of Warna's Prayer Book*, including prayers with special formulae related to the practices of crystallomancy.[7] The second volume is the *orationale* created in Bohemia for Vladislav II Jagiellon (1456–1516), king of Bohemia and Hungary,[8] while the third is a fragment of the prayer

---

[3] Eadem, 'Edukecje Jagiellonois' [Education of the Jagiellons], *Roczniki Historyczne* 71 (2005), 99–119; 'Edukacja i mecenat artystyczny Władysława Jagiellończyka, króla Czech i Węgier' [The Education and Artistic Patronage of Wladislaw Jagiellon, King of Bohemia and Hungary], in Henryk Gmiterek, ed., *Polacy w Czechach, Czesi w Polsce. X–XVIII wiek* [Poles in Bohemia and Bohemians in Poland. Tenth to Eighteenth Centuries] (Lublin, 2004), 193–209.

[4] Eadem, 'The Funeral Ceremonies of the Polish Kings from the Fourteenth to the Eighteenth Centuries', *JEH* 36 (1985), 513–33.

[5] Eadem, 'The Jagiellonians as Founders of Ecclesiastical Institutions in the Grand Duchy of Lithuania and Poland', in D. Popp and R. Suckale ed., *Die Jagiellonien. Kunst und Kultur einer europäischen Dynastie an der Wende zur Neuzeit* (Nürnberg 2002), 123–30.

[6] Eadem, *Królewskie modlitewniki. Studium z kultury religijnej epoki Jagiellonów (XV i początek XVI wieku* [The Royal Prayer Books. A Study of the Religious Culture of the Jagiellonian Period (Fifteenth and Early Sixteenth Centuries)] 2nd edn (Lublin, 1999).

[7] Oxford, Bodleian Library, MS 15 857. L. Bernacki, R. Ganszyniec and W. Podlacha, eds, *Modlitewnik Władysława Warneńczyka w zbiorach Biblioteki Bodlejańskiej* [Vladislav of Warna's Prayer Book] (Lwów, 1928).

[8] Kraków, Jagiellonian Library, MS 4289, described in Zofia Ameisenowa, *Rękopisy i pierwodruki iluminowane Biblioteki Jagiellońskiej* [Illuminated Manuscripts and Old Printed Books in the Jagiellonian Library] (Wroclaw, 1958).

book belonging to Alexander Jagiellon (1461–1506; reigned 1501–6).[9] The group of fifteenth-century texts includes the so-called *Book of Hours of Wilanów*, the prayer of Italian origin used by Queen Bona Sforza (1494–1557).[10] Another two prayer books, those for Sigismund I (1464–1548; reigned 1507–48) and Queen Bona were composed in the sixteenth century in the workshop of the talented painter, Stanislaus Samostrzelnik.[11] He was involved in the creation of a further three prayer books, possibly used as royal gifts for state officers of the highest rank, two going to the Crown Chancellor, Christopher Szydłowiecki (1464–1532),[12] and a third, written in Polish, to the Lithuanian Chancellor, Olbracht Gasztołd (d. 1539).[13] One with a special purpose is the prayer book – also in Polish – made for Princess Hedwig (1513–73), the eldest daughter of Sigismund I, and used as an aid for confession.[14]

* * *

What can be said of Jagiellonian piety from the religious contents of the prayer books? Their daily prayer most obviously expressed their feelings and attitudes towards the supernatural world and earthly circumstances. They offered the image of God as Ruler, the cult of the Holy Cross, combined with sorrowful overtones of their devotion,

[9] London, BL, MS add. 38603, described in Kazimierz Dobrowolski, *Ustęp z dziejów polskiej kultury umysłowej w drugiej połowie XV wieku* [An Example of Polish Intellectual Culture at the End of the Fifteenth Century] (Kraków, 1928).

[10] Warsaw, Royal Castle Library, unnumbered manuscript. Illuminations published by Stanisław Tomkiewicz, 'Modlitewnik Królowej Bony w Wilanowie' [Queen's Bona Prayer Book in Wilanów], *Prace Komisji Historii Sztuki* 5 (1930–34), 30–44.

[11] London, BL, MS add. 15 281, and Oxford, Bodleian Library, MS Douce 40, described in Z. Ameisenowa, *Cztery rękopisy iluminowane z lat 1524–1538 w zbiorach obcych* [Four Illuminated Manuscripts in Foreign Collections] (Kraków, 1967); Barbara Miodońska, *Miniatury Stanisława Samostrzelnika* [Stanislaus Samostrzelnik's Miniatures] (Warsaw, 1983), 47–72.

[12] One of his two prayer books, divided into three parts, is kept in Milan. The text divided into two is in the Biblioteca Trivulziana as Cod. 459 and 460. The miniatures are in the Biblioteca Ambrosiana, MS F 277 Inf.; see Ameisenowa, *Four Manuscripts*, 18 ff. The second prayer book: *Orationes beati Basilii Magni et Johanni Chrisostomi accesu ad sanctissimam eucharistiam* belongs to the collections of Wawel Royal Castle in Kraków (without number). U. Borkowska, 'Odzyskany modlitewnik Krzysztofa Szydłowieckiego' [Christopher Szydłowiecki's Prayer Book Regained], in J. A. Spież and Z. Wielgosz, eds, *Benedyktyńska praca. Studia historyczne ofiarowane O. Pawłowi Sczanieckiemu w 80 rocznicę urodzin* (Krakow, 1997), 212–24.

[13] Munich, Bayerisches Nationalmuseum, MS 3663. Miodońska, *Miniatury Stanisława Samostrzelnika*, 73–7.

[14] Erlangen, University Library, MS 1798: *Zabytek języka polskiego z początku wieku XVI w zbiorach Biblioteki Uniwersytetu w Erlangen* [Monument of Polish Language from the beginning of the sixteenth century in the Collection of Erlangen University], ed. L. Malinowski (Krakow, 1898).

intense Marian piety, and an awareness of a profound relationship with the patrons of the Polish Kingdom, especially with St Stanislaus. The prayer books provide a particular insight into those eschatological and existentialist fears so typical of the epoch. The books mirror the ever-growing interest in death and care for deceased family members.[15]

These prayer books fulfilled many functions for their owners, being used daily at Mass, in preparation for the sacrament of penitence, providing prayers after confession, as well as morning and evening prayer. In the *orationale* which belonged to Sigismund I, we find notes by himself and his wife Bona concerning the birth of their children. Bona even added medical recipes, her favourite adagio and events which she deemed worth remembering. Unfortunately, other surviving prayer books have generally lost their first and last pages, and so we can not know if they ever bore similar traces.[16]

In the extant Jagiellonian prayer books there are portraits of their patrons kneeling and praying before the icons of Christ and the Mother of God. Their names are there too: set down in texts of prayers entreating God to forgive their sins, and in praise of Him. They prayed for themselves and for others, living and dead. Apart from repeated prayers to God for help in his reign, Sigismund I adds a special prayer for his own Kingdom. Finally, these prayer books were a testimony of orthodoxy, showing awareness of the grave threat to the Catholic faith in the first half of the sixteenth century.[17]

Some of the manuscripts, outstandingly ornamental in form, must be classified as luxury books, although their contents are identical to what is found in cheaper manuscripts and printed prayer books, such as those increasingly popular from the fifteenth century onwards. These included the *Hours of Blessed Virgin Mary*, the *Hortulus animae* (published repeatedly in the Polish translation from 1514 as *The Soul's Paradise*), or *Antidotarius animae* (the latter not well-known in Poland). The similarity lies in the fact that all these prayer books contain the so-called 'effective' prayers. They express the same belief in the wondrous power of the host in the Mass, the value of the mysterious names of God, and of the sign of the Cross repeated many times during prayer. Numerous prayers are related to the promises of the astronomical years of indulgence. Both types of *libelli precum* contain sets of *Pater* and *Ave*; these

---

[15] Borkowska, *The Royal Prayer Books*, 183–255.
[16] Ibid., 97–9, 263–9.
[17] Ibid., 255–63.

were prayers taught to every child in each parish school throughout the kingdom. Recent research reveals a high density of Polish schools, matching those of England and France, and an increase in the number of well-qualified teachers in such schools.[18] Male children were taught to read and write in Latin, using the texts of psalms and hymns, and to sing in choir to enliven the Sunday Mass liturgy. During those Masses the people received religious instruction through sermons in the vernacular, and recited basic prayers, truths of the faith and morality.[19]

Royal accounts offer certain incidental insights into the activities of Polish schools, making very often mention of *pueri recordantes*, pupils rushing into the king's path as he travelled across the vast Jagiellonian state. Children were present at the king's arrival in villages and towns, and they enlivened by their singing the celebration of Mass and Vespers in which the king participated. Their songs and hymns were related to the particular moment of the liturgical year. Hence, they could sing the Lent hymn of *Patris Sapientia*, the Advent antiphons such as *O Sapientia* and the hymn *Verbum caro factum est* – all texts one can find in the royal prayer books. The boy singers came to the king with texts and notes (*cum carminibus in carte, cum cedulis*), in order to be given alms, testifying to the high quality of their education both in song and in Latin.[20]

As we may infer from the same royal accounts, the daily rhythm of royal religious practices began with Mass, wherever the court happened to stay. On Sundays and other holidays the king joined in public religious ceremonies with his subjects. Aware that the sight of the monarch praying with his subjects was exemplary to the average citizen, he used prayer books, participated in singing, heard a sermon, and made a Mass offering appropriate to his royal position.[21]

As to the frequency of receiving the two sacraments, penitence and

---

[18] Eugeniusz Wiśniowski, 'The Parochial School System in Poland towards the Close of the Middle Ages', *Acta Poloniae Historica* 27 (1973), 29–44.

[19] Izabela Skierska, *Obowiązek mszalny w sredniowiecznej Polsce* [Die Messepflicht im mittelalterlichen Polen] (Warsaw, 2003), 198–211.

[20] U. Borkowska, 'Królewskie miłosierdzie' [Royal Charity], in Danuta Gawinowa, ed., *Kultura sredniowieczna i staropolska. Studia ofiarowane Aleksandrowi Gieysztorowi w pięćdziesieciolecie pracy naukowej* [Studies dedicated to Aleksander Gieysztor] (Warsaw, 1991), 683–94.

[21] U. Borkowska, 'Codzienny i odświętny ceremoniał religijny na dworze Jagiellonów' [Ordinary and Festive Religious Ceremonial at the Court of the Jagiellons], in M. Markiewicz and R. Skowron, eds, *Theatrum ceremoniale na dworze książąt i królów polskich* [Theatrum ceremoniale at the Courts of Kings and Princes in Poland in the Late Middle Ages] (Krakow, 1999), 61–85, 78–9.

Eucharist, Vladislav Jagiello, for example, influenced by Queen Jadwiga, confessed and received Communion at Easter, Pentecost, the Assumption of the Blessed Virgin Mary and at Christmas, probably the occasions on which Jadwiga herself also participated. After her death, Jagiello confined himself to taking the Eucharist during Easter and Christmas.[22] From the accounts, we know that the other Jagiellons did the same.

* * *

Other royal religious ceremonies were related to the cycle of the liturgical year, confirming, for example, the attendance of the king and his family in the Advent Mass (*Rorate coelis*) celebrated just before dawn. For such a celebration to take place special papal permission was required, for which the Polish kings had to apply. On Christmas day the Jagiellons attended two or three Masses. Similarly to the Christmas day also on Epiphany the king used to give the Mass offering in gold coins which symbolized his royal dignity.[23]

Lent was the time of more intense almsgiving and fasting. Vladislav Jagiello fasted every day during the whole of Lent, and he attended Mass to hear a sermon.[24] Indeed, Lent was a period of intense catechetical instruction for the Court.

The accounts provide details of religious practices during Holy Week. Holy Wednesday was the day when the king used to grant abundant alms (Jan Olbracht, and then Sigismund I devoted 100 florins to that end) to the patients of Holy Spirit Hospital, the largest in Kraków. The entries in the accounts may lead us to the conclusion that on that day the king, accompanied by his court, used to visit the sick and attended the penitentiary prayers in the hospital church. The papal bulls issued for the Canons of the Holy Spirit were accompanied with special indulgences, thanks to which on Holy Wednesday the church was visited by enormous crowds of Krakow's faithful.[25]

The royal family attended liturgical celebrations on Holy Thursday, Friday and Saturday. Thursday was traditionally devoted to the office of the *mandatum*. Vladislav Jagiello and his son Casimir Jagiellon not only

---

[22] Joannis Dlugossii, *Annales seu Cronicae incliti Regni Poloniae, liber XI et XII*, ed. M. Kowalczyk (Krakow, 2001), 125.

[23] Borkowska, 'Ordinary and Festive Religious Ceremonial', 75–6.

[24] *Codex epistolaris saeculi XV*, ed. A. Lewicki, A. Sokołowski and J. Szujski, 3 vols (Krakow, 1876–94), 2: 328.

[25] Borkowska, 'Ordinary and Festive Religious Ceremonial', 77–8.

participated in this liturgical ceremony in the church but also repeated it in the Castle rooms every year. Kneeling before twelve poor men, they kissed their feet, serving them at table in person, giving each one 12 *groszes*, and providing new clothing. This custom, described by a fifteenth-century chronicler, seems to be well-established at the Polish Court, in a fashion parallel to other European monarchies.[26]

On Holy Friday Vladislav Jagiello

> From the very first light of the dawn up until the last shade of the night . . . barefoot and in penitential clothes, with his face covered in a hood, visited all churches, where he prayed for a long time on his knees, crying over the torment and the death of the Saviour, giving many alms to the poor.[27]

The later records of other Jagiellons bear out the kings' *deambulatio ecclesiae* on Holy Fridays, and their gifts of large sums of money for alms. On that day the king visited the churches accompanied by crowds of his own subjects.[28] The penitents used to wander from church to church, among them members of religious organizations and guilds, bearing crosses and singing the Litany of the Saints and penitential psalms. Crowds of beggars gathered in all the churches, hoping for alms.[29]

The king also had a chance to pray with his people while taking part in processions organized on various holidays. As the accounts tell us, when the king stayed in Kraków, he often used to participate in this form of collective supplication.[30] Among the numerous processions of the liturgical year, the Eucharistic processions were the most celebrated. This tradition originated in the fourteenth century, when the liturgical calendars of the particular dioceses in Poland were enriched by the feast of Corpus Christi.

Vladislav Jagiello initiated the tradition of a procession on 15 July for the feast of the Sending out of the Apostles. His contribution to the

---

26 Ibid., 79. A. Chevalier de Gottal, *Les Fêtes et les arts à la court de Brabant à l'aube du XVe siècle* (Frankfurt, 1996), 173.

27 *Codex epistolaris saeculi XV*, 2: 328.

28 Royal Accounts (John Olbracht and Alexander: Warsaw, Old Records Archive, MS 25, fols 17–18; MS 27, fol. 68; MS 31, fol. 71; Prince Sigismund Jagiellon's *deambulatio* on Good Friday in Buda in Hungary (MS 29, fols 78 and 162v, 281, 378), in Silesia (MS 33, fols 75 and 184). From 1518 his accounts many times note a sum of 100 florins which on Good Friday king Sigismund got from his Treasurer to distribute among the poor.

29 *Kronika mieszczanina krakowskiego z lat 1575–1595* [Chronicle of a Cracow Burgher from 1575–1595], ed. Henryk Barycz (Krakow, 1930), 147.

30 Borkowska, 'Ordinary and Festive Religious Ceremonial', 81–3.

liturgy was to add the first Polish national holiday, commemorating the victory in 1410 over the Teutonic Order on the fields of Grunwald. Year after year, the procession started from Wawel Cathedral, accompanied by appropriate solemn antiphons and songs – probably in Polish – and the king joined in, if he was in Kraków at the time. The participants beseeched God for peace and protection against their enemies. The ceremonial *Te Deum laudamus*, sung at the tomb of St Stanislaus on the way back from the procession, on the very spot where Jagiello left the banners seized from the Teutonic knights as an offering, marked the conclusion of the celebrations.[31]

* * *

It seems that with the reign of the first Jagiellons, the pilgrimage movement began to increase. From the fifteenth century onwards, pilgrimages were undertaken to sites which gradually became the national *loca sacra*. Amongst these were the Bald Mountain, with a Benedictine monastery housing the relics of the Holy Cross; Clair Mountain in Częstochowa with the icon of the Virgin Mary; or the Poznań Carmelite church founded by Jagiello, where Three Miraculous Hosts were worshipped. The custom of undertaking pilgrimage to sacred places, initiated by the founder of the dynasty, thus became a fixed and distinctive feature of the religious life of all the descendant Jagiellons.[32]

They participated in pilgrimages from Wawel Cathedral to the church at Skałka, related to the May and September festivals of St Stanislaus. They often undertook such pilgrimages in honour of this patron saint of Poland, that took place on each Friday. In this way they continually repeated the rite of the penitential pilgrimage, which became the inherent element of the coronation ceremony of the Polish kings from the fifteenth century.[33] This was not only meant as an act of expiation for the killing of the bishop of Kraków by King Bolesław the Bold in the eleventh century, but it also signalled that the Kingdom was

---

[31] T. Lalik, 'O patriotycznym święcie Rozesłania Apostołów w Małopolscy w XV w.' [Patriotic Feast of the Sending out of the Apostles], *Studia Źródłoznawcze* 26 (1981), 25–32.

[32] U. Borkowska, *Polskie pielgrzymki Jagiellonów* [Polish Pilgrimages of the Jagiellons], in H. Manikowska and H. Zaremska, eds, *Peregrinationes. Pielgrzymki w kulturze dawnej Europy* [Pilgrimages in European Culture] (Warsaw, 1995), 185–203.

[33] Eadem, 'Theatrum Ceremoniale at the Polish Court as a System of Social and Political Communication', in Anna Adamska and Marco Mostert, eds, *The Development of Literate Mentalities in East Central Europe*, Utrecht Studies in Medieval Literacy 9 (Turnhout, 2003), 432–52, 9.

placed under the patronage of St Stanislaus, whose tomb in Wawel Cathedral became a veritable *ara patriae*.[34]

* * *

As one may infer from the outline of the religious practices presented above, the monarchs did not only come into 'physical' contact with their subjects, with whom they shared pilgrimages, processions and celebrations of Mass, daily or on festive occasions. The Jagiellons also participated in the community of religious rites, attitudes and behaviour, initiating popular cults and liturgical traditions. They accepted the whole content of the common liturgy, prayer texts and songs, in which was intermixed the authentically Christian with some almost magical view of life. This led to the considerable degree of consolidation of the community of the faithful, regardless of social status.

There is no denying that the presence of numerous chaplains, preachers and confessors, well-educated and chosen according to their high moral standards, ensured to the royal environment the rhythm of regular practices of piety and on-going religious education. In this sense the royal milieu may be considered the elite. But taking into consideration the co-existence of both learned and almost magical piety in the texts of the prayer books, based on the efficacy of word or deed, it seems that, in the study of religious culture, it is extremely difficult to set the borderline between that which is elitist and that which is of popular character.

Catholic University of Lublin, Poland

---

[34] Michał Rożek, '*Ara Patriae*: Dzieje grobu św. Stanisława w katedrze na Wawelu' [Ara Patriae: the History of St Stanislaus's Tomb in Wawel Cathedral], *Analecta Cracoviensia* 11 (1979), 433–60.

POETS, PEASANTS, AND PAMPHLETS:
WHO WROTE AND WHO READ
REFORMATION *FLUGSCHRIFTEN*?

by DAVID BAGCHI

IN the early 1520s, there appeared from the press of Michael
Buchführer in Erfurt a pamphlet entitled *A Dialogue or Conversation
between a Father and a Son concerning the Teachings of Martin Luther and
Other Matters of the Christian Faith*.[1] It was an unremarkable publication,
a typical Reformation *Flugschrift* in almost every respect: it was quarto
size, sixteen pages long, unbound, with a woodcut illustration on the
title page depicting the main events described in the pamphlet. The
dialogue is between a student home from the university of Wittenberg
and his peasant father: the son converts his father to Luther's cause, and
his mother consigns to the flames the family's prized letter of indulgence. The pamphlet is anonymous.

In her book on German lay pamphleteers, Miriam Usher Chrisman
attempted to categorize the social class of the pamphlet's author from
internal evidence. She did not challenge Otto Clemen's suggestion that
the author was a peasant with some education;[2] in fact, she agreed that
the author 'comes from a popular milieu and speaks for the lower
ranks'.[3] But she explains that, as her classification scheme had no category of 'peasant' in which to place this author, she ranked him instead
in the lowest of the five social categories she had, alongside artisans,
middling burghers, and popular poets.

---

[1] *Ein Dialogus oder Gesprech zwischen einem Vater und Sohn die Lehre Martini Luthers und
sonst andere Sachen des christlichen Glaubens belangend* (Erfurt: Michael Buchführer, n.d.
[*c*.1523]). Microform reproduction in Hans-Joachim Köhler *et al.*, *Flugschriften des frühen 16.
Jahrhunderts* (Zug: Interdokumentation A.G., 1978–88). Modern editions in *Flugschriften aus
den ersten Jahren der Reformation*, ed. Otto Clemen, 4 vols (Leipzig, 1907–11, repr. Nieuwkoop,
1967), 1: 21–52, and *Die Reformation in zeitgenössischen Dialog*, ed. Werner Lenk (Berlin, 1968),
153–67. English translation in Carl S. Meyer, 'A Dialog or Conversation Between a Father
and His Son About Martin Luther's Doctrine (1523)', in Carl S. Meyer, ed., *Luther for an
Ecumenical Age. Essays in Commemoration of the 450th Anniversary of the Reformation* (St Louis,
MI, 1967), 82–107.

[2] *Flugschriften*, ed. Clemen, 1: 21.

[3] Miriam Usher Chrisman, *Conflicting Visions of Reform. German Lay Propaganda
Pamphlets, 1519–1530* (Atlantic Highlands, NJ, 1996), 234.

What is interesting in relation to the theme of this volume is Chrisman's assumption that peasants could not have been involved in so elite an activity as writing pamphlets: she had not created a category for any writer below the rank of skilled worker. In this assumption, she was merely reflecting the still current consensus that Reformation *Flugschriften* purporting to be by manual labourers, or in which the name of the author was omitted altogether, were in fact the work of clever humanists (the *poetae* of our title). It was a literary confidence trick designed to indicate, to other members of the literate elite, an enormous groundswell of popular support for the Reformation. Modern scholarship is agreed that it was poets, and not peasants, who wrote and read the pamphlets.

In this paper I want briefly to review the process by which *Flugschriften* have ceased to be seen in scholarly literature as popular artefacts and have been re-classified as elite. I wish to demonstrate that, though the current consensus has come about for the best of reasons, it is based nonetheless on a questionable assumption, driven by ideology, about the impermeability of the categories of 'elite' and 'popular'. More importantly, it runs counter to the available evidence.

For centuries, Reformation pamphlets were excluded from serious scholarly attention because of their cheap and shoddy appearance, their lack of literary merit, and their unglamorous preoccupation with the concerns of the poor and the common: *die armen Leute* and *der gemeine Mann*. Then, in 1930, Gottfried Blochwitz indicated how useful they might be for mainstream historical and theological scholarship.[4] Blochwitz regarded the pamphlets as reliable indicators of the extent to which Luther's message had spread through all levels of society, even the lowest. The timing of this article was unfortunate: over the next decade and more, Nazi ideology would promote the ideal of 'the common [German] man', and this was reflected in a general scholarly interest at the time in *volkisch* lore and movements.[5] Reformation pamphlets became object-lessons in the successful propagandizing of a populace, and were hailed, quite literally, as weapons in a propaganda war. Arnold Berger edited two selections of pamphlets in the early

[4] Gottfried Blochwitz, 'Die antirömischen deutschen Flugschriften der frühen Reformationszeit (bis 1522) in ihrer religiös-sittlichen Eigenart', *Archiv für Reformationsgeschichte* 27 (1930), 145–254.

[5] For a summary of this trend, with suggestions for further reading, see R. W. Scribner, 'Ritual and Popular Religion in Catholic Germany at the Time of the Reformation', in idem, *Popular Culture and Popular Movements in Reformation Germany* (London, 1987), 17.

'thirties with uncompromisingly militaristic titles: *Stormtroopers of the Reformation* and *Satirical Field Artillery against the Reformation*.[6] Perhaps because of the enthusiasm with which pamphlet studies were prosecuted during the Third Reich, the immediate post-war years saw a decline of interest in them. Not until the 1970s did interest fully revive, and in German-language scholarship at least it was informed by a quite different ideological framework. Now pamphlet studies were influenced by the neo-Marxism of the Frankfurt School, and in particular by Habermas's concept of *bürgerliche Öffentlichkeit*, the idea that what we call 'public opinion' is in fact no more than an internal bourgeois dialogue.[7] These studies were followed in the late 1970s and 80s by the work of Hans-Joachim Köhler and his pamphlet research unit based at Tübingen, who subjected very large samples of pamphlets to an array of approaches, including communication theory and propaganda analysis,[8] and opinion research.[9] More recently, as we have seen, the American scholar Miriam Usher Chrisman undertook an analysis of pamphlets by German lay writers which differentiated them by social class and emphasized the way in which their opposing messages – the 'conflicting visions of reform' of Chrisman's title – were influenced by class difference.

It is quite understandable that post-war pamphlet scholarship deliberately moved away from the assumptions and conclusions that dominated the scholarship of the Nazi period. The idea of taking propaganda at face-value, and of presenting Luther as the literary leader of the people (*Volksführer*), whose message was heard and repeated at all levels of society, seems extremely suspect in retrospect.[10] The Marxian

---

[6] *Die Sturmtruppen der Reformation: Ausgewählte Flugschriften der Jahre, 1520–25*, ed. Arnold E. Berger (Leipzig, 1931), and idem, *Satirische Feldzüge wider der Reformation: Thomas Murner, Daniel von Soest* (Leipzig, 1933).

[7] See especially Bernd Balzer, *Bürgerliche Reformationspropaganda: Die Flugschriften des Hans Sachs in den Jahren 1523–25* (Stuttgart, 1973) and J. Schütte, *'Schympf red': Frühformen bürgerliche Agitation in Thomas Murners 'Grossen Lutherischen Narren' (1522)*, Germanistische Abhandlungen 41 (Stuttgart, 1973).

[8] For an overview, see Hans-Joachim Köhler, 'Die Flugschriften der frühen Neuzeit. Ein Überblick', in Werner Arnold, Wolfgang Dittrich and Bernhard Zeller, eds, *Die Erforschung der Buch- und Bibliotheksgeschichte in Deutschland* (Wiesbaden, 1987).

[9] Hans-Joachim Köhler, 'Erste Schritte zu einem Meinungsprofil der frühen Reformationszeit', in Volker Press and Dieter Stievermann, eds, *Martin Luther. Probleme seiner Zeit* (Stuttgart, 1986), 244–81.

[10] Note A. Centgraf's timely Berlin dissertation of 1940, entitled 'Martin Luther als Publizist. Geist und Form seiner Volksführung'. It is cited by Hella Tompert in 'Die Flugschrift als Medium religiöser Publizistik. Aspekte der gegenwärtigen Forschung', in Josef

approaches that followed the Second World War offered a valuable corrective. But it could be argued that they so emphasize class conflict as to exclude the possibility of any community of interest or activity. This is why Köhler and Chrisman and others take it as axiomatic that no-one below the rank of artisan could have written pamphlets.[11] But it is an axiom inspired as much by ideology as the axioms it replaced.

Is it then possible that manual labourers such as peasants could have *read* pamphlets?[12] The problem here is of course the very low rates of literacy in Germany in the early sixteenth century (between five and ten per cent).[13] Of course, the illiterate were not prevented from accessing the content of pamphlets in indirect ways. Reading aloud was still more common than silent reading, and it appears to have been common practice for a literate member of the community to read the contents of a pamphlet out aloud for sake of the unlettered.[14] Many pamphlets were particularly suited to such treatment, either because they were themselves the texts or summaries of sermons,[15] or else because the diction and rhythm adopted was that of spoken German, as was especially the case with Eberlin von Günzburg's works.[16] It was even said

Nolte, Hella Tompert, and Christoph Windhorst, eds, *Kontinuität und Umbruch. Theologie und Frömmigkeit in Flugschriften und Kleinliteratur an der Wende vom 15. zum 16. Jahrhundert*, Spätmittelalter und Frühe Neuzeit 2 (Stuttgart, 1978), 211–21, 218, as an example of a study influenced by Nazi ideology.

[11] See, for example, Hans-Joachim Köhler, ' "Der Bauer wird witzig": Der Bauer in den Flugschriften der Reformationszeit', in Peter Blickle, ed., *Zugänge zur Bäuerlichen Reformation* (Zurich, 1987), 196–8; Chrisman, *Conflicting Visions*, 7; Peter Matheson, *The Rhetoric of the Reformation* (Edinburgh, 1998), 84. It should, however, be noted that Matheson also distances himself from this orthodoxy, referring to 'an articulate and crusading minority, *which may or may not* be speaking for a wider constituency' (ibid., 27–8, emphasis mine).

[12] It should of course be acknowledged that terms such as 'Bauer' and 'gemeine Mann' had no fixed meaning. A peasant in Saxony might enjoy considerable independence, and even the opportunity to amass some wealth, while a peasant in south-western Germany might be in effect a serf. Equally, 'gemeine Mann' was an unspecific term for the lower classes in general. See Peter Blickle, *Gemeindereformation: Die Menschen des 16. Jahrhundert auf dem Weg zum Heil* (Munich, 1985), trans. by Thomas Dunlap as *Communal Reformation: the Quest for Salvation in Sixteenth-Century Germany* (Atlantic Highlands, NJ, 1992), and Robert Lutz, *Wer war der gemeine Mann? Der dritte Stand in der Krise des Spätmittelalters* (Munich, 1979). In my view, the imprecision of these terms makes it even more difficult to assume that no such person could have written pamphlets.

[13] Köhler, 'Überblick', 338.

[14] See R. W. Scribner, 'Flugblatt und Analphabetentum. Wie kam der gemeine Mann zu reformatorischen Ideen?', in Hans-Joachim Köhler, ed., *Flugschriften als Massenmedium der Reformationszeit* (Stuttgart, 1981), 65–76.

[15] For sermon summaries, see Bernd Moeller, 'Was wurde in der Frühzeit der Reformation in den deutschen Städten gepredigt?', *Archiv für Reformationsgeschichte* 75 (1984), 176–93.

[16] See Monika Rössing-Hager, 'Wie stark findet der nichtlesekundige Rezipient

that the availability of pamphlets meant that better sermons could be heard in taverns than in churches.[17] Rather than compartmentalize the Reformation pamphlet as a literary product of and for a literate elite, we should think instead of the 'hybridization' of media, whereby print (both word and image) and other visual and oral forms worked together in a completely integrated manner to convey Reformation propaganda.[18] The contents of pamphlets might be summarized in short ditties by the colporteurs who sold them, or they might be communicated through woodcut illustrations accompanying the text, as was the case with *A Dialogue Between a Father and a Son*. As the late Bob Scribner showed, the message embodied in the Reformation pamphlet was conveyed by more means than literacy alone.[19]

However, there is evidence of literacy in the strict sense in unlikely places. One would hardly expect the harsh conditions endured by the silver and copper miners of the Austrian Tyrol to be conducive to reading. But we find that, by the middle of the sixteenth-century, the miners of Kitzbühel owned a wide selection of theological books and pamphlets, in Latin as well as in German, including many of the works of Luther, of Johann Eck, the Catholic controversialist, and of Hans Sachs, the cobbler-poet and pamphleteer.[20] This evidence suggests that we are not entitled to deny to any social group the possibility that they could read pamphlets, and indeed might invest relatively heavily in them. The reading of pamphlets was not an exclusively elite activity.[21]

Berücksichtigung in der Flugschriften?', in H.-J. Köhler, ed., *Flugschriften als Massenmedium*, 77–137. See also R. W. Scribner, 'Oral Culture and the Transmission of Reformation Ideas', in Helga Robinson-Hammerstein, ed., *The Transmission of Ideas in the Lutheran Reformation* (Blackrock, 1989), 83–104.

[17] Heinrich von Kettenbach, *Ein Sermon zu der löblichen Statt Ulm zu seynem Valete*, in *Flugschriften*, ed. Clemen, 2: 107.

[18] R. W. Scribner, *For the Sake of Simple Folk. Popular Propaganda for the German Reformation* (2nd rev. edn, Oxford, 1994), xv. The concept of hybridization is borrowed from Marshall McLuhan.

[19] Scribner, *For the Sake of Simple Folk, passim*.

[20] See John L. Flood, 'Subversion in the Alps: Books and Readers in the Austrian Counter-Reformation', *The Library*, 6th ser., 12 (1990), 185–211. Flood's findings are summarized in idem, 'Le Livre dans le monde germanique à l'époque de la Réforme', in Jean-François Gilmont, ed., *La Réforme et le livre. L'Europe de l'imprimé (1517–v.1570)* (Paris, 1990), 29–104, at 94–5.

[21] Mark U. Edwards, Jr. has argued that the very large number of pamphlets produced in the early 1520s – some six million copies for a total population of only twelve million, or twenty copies for each literate person – suggests that we have seriously underestimated the extent of literacy in the Holy Roman Empire. See his *Printing, Propaganda and Martin Luther* (Berkeley and Los Angeles, CA, 1994), 39. Köhler ('Überblick', 337) puts the estimate of the

But could peasants *write* pamphlets? Again, it seems at first sight inherently unlikely. Apart from the skill of writing and composition involved, there was the question of finding printers willing to handle their work. But it was not impossible, as the grievances of the peasants published at the time of the Peasants' War show. In publishing them, the peasants were undoubtedly helped by educated sympathizers. The most famous set, *The Twelve Articles of the Peasants*, published in Memmingen in 1525, was drawn up by Sebastian Lotzer, a journeyman furrier and lay preacher, with the help of the preacher of Memmingen, Christoph Schappeler.[22] Even if we allow for the refraction of what we might call the genuine peasant voice through these scribes, it is unlikely that this voice was seriously distorted. Had the Twelve Articles not fairly represented the demands and aspirations of large numbers of peasants, they would not have been adopted by so many local peasant communities, being reprinted in no fewer than fifteen cities. Peasants had no trouble in gaining access to presses, given favourable circumstances.

So in principle there was nothing preventing peasants from writing and publishing pamphlets. But did they? An important objection is the generally high level of education that the alleged peasant writers demonstrate. Hans-Joachim Köhler used the presence of references to the classics, to the Fathers and schoolmen, or to Canon Law, as a test for detecting elite writers posing as peasants.[23] Chrisman gives the example of a dialogue, purportedly by a peasant, in which one protagonist refers to Thomas Aquinas and the fact that in later life he renounced his own writings and hailed the Bible as the only source of truth.[24] At first sight, the objection seems to be decisive. But on closer inspection these references are not as impressive as they seem. The Fathers and others are merely name-checked, not quoted, nor are the titles of specific works mentioned. It would not require any specialist knowledge to compile a short list of names. Such lists were already in the public domain: Luther himself had been citing proof-texts from the Fathers, schoolmen, and

total number of pamphlets sold between 1518 and 1530 at ten million. To make the same point slightly differently, I would suggest that the readier availability of worthwhile reading material was itself an incentive to greater literacy: the pamphlets created a market, as well as catering for one.

22 For details, see Tom Scott and Bob Scribner, eds, *The German Peasants' War* (Atlantic Highlands, NJ, 1991).

23 Köhler, ' "Der Bauer wird witzig" ', 11.

24 Chrisman, *Conflicting Visions*, 7.

Canon Law against papal primacy, for instance, since 1519. And one would not have had to have undergone years of training in scholastic theology to learn of Thomas Aquinas's breakdown: it was the sort of edifying story one might easily pick up from attentive listening to sermons. In short, the learning displayed in these pamphlets is derivative, and is fully compatible with a lack of formal education. If Chrisman and Köhler are right, we have to assume that clever writers engaged in a subterfuge in which they passed themselves off as unlearned, but were not quite clever enough to remove all the tell-tale traces of learning from what were otherwise careful fictions. In the absence of other evidence, the alternative explanation is much more plausible: that unlearned writers garnished their work with references to authorities they had heard of but not read to give their own arguments more weight.

It is not my intention in this paper to suggest that all Reformation pamphleteers were the people they purported to be: we are dealing with propaganda, after all. My task has been the much more limited one of questioning the *a priori* assumption that certain pamphleteers could *not* have been who they said they were. This assumption itself rests on another assumption, that our categories of 'elite' and 'popular' represent impenetrable boundaries. The evidence, for instance of the book-owning miners, points to a much more complex and fluid relationship between the two categories. And this fluidity should not really surprise us. The Church and academia had always provided a means by which the talented sons of manual workers could, under certain circumstances, move from a 'popular' to an 'elite' milieu within their own lifetimes. The expansion of German universities in the fifteenth and sixteenth centuries multiplied these opportunities. Peasants could and did become poets, and in doing so straddled two worlds, having strong natural sympathies for their families and first-hand knowledge of the problems they faced, but in addition having the ability, when the occasion arose, of expressing their concern in public. (Perhaps one reason for the vehement denunciation, by evangelicals and Catholics alike, of Luther's perceived betrayal of the peasants in 1525, was because they were in many cases 'sons of the soil' themselves.)

This takes us back to the anonymous pamphlet with which we began. The situation it describes, of a student returning home to his peasant family and burning to share his new-found convictions with unsuspecting relatives, is one that would have been familiar to those who made the transition between milieux, and who embraced evangelical teachings (as many did: more than 40% of the first Reformation preachers were from rural poor, urban poor, or artisan families).[25] Whoever wrote the pamphlet, and however idealized the dialogue, it represents one of many occasions in the early-modern period when the elite and the popular overlapped.

University of Hull

---

[25] R. W. Scribner, 'Practice and Principle in the German Towns: Preachers and People', in Peter Newman Brooks, ed., *Reformation Principle and Practice. Essays Presented to Arthur Geoffrey Dickens* (London, 1980), 97–117, at Table 4. One of Scribner's preachers fits the pattern exactly. Bartholomeus Rieseberg was an agricultural labourer until, at the age of seventeen, he sought an education. Attaching himself to a succession of tutors and schools he eventually enrolled at the university of Wittenberg in 1518. He became a convinced Lutheran, and eventually returned to his own village as its pastor (Scribner, 'Practice and Principle', 106).

SOME ITALIAN VERNACULAR RELIGIOUS BOOKS, THEIR AUTHORS AND THEIR READERS, 1543–8

by PATRICK PRESTON

W HAT might count as elite religion and popular religion within the restricted sphere of literate culture? The answer here is in terms of the production and reception of religious texts. Who wrote them and who read them, and with what kinds of assumptions and attitudes? Here I discuss the following questions: do the categories 'elite' and 'popular' divide up the field without remainder? Are 'elite' and 'popular' necessarily at odds? If 'elite' and 'popular' are not necessarily at odds, are they sometimes so?

To answer these questions, I consider three books and how they relate to elite and popular religion: Pietro Aretino's *Vita di Tomaso*, first published in 1543; the *Beneficio di Cristo crocefisso*, also first published, anonymously, in 1543; and Catarino's *Discorso contro la dottrina e le profetie di Fra Girolamo Savonarola*, published in 1548. These sources have been chosen because they were published within five years of each other, they are interestingly different, and they are written in different genres. I consider them here in chronological order.

* * *

The first edition of Aretino's *Vita di Tomaso*[1] appeared in 1543. Aretino was born the son of a cobbler in 1492, in Arezzo.[2] What education he had was on informal lines. Though he was excluded from the social and intellectual elite by the circumstances of his origin and upbringing, he rose to eminence first by the assistance of patrons – Agostino Chigi, Popes Leo X and Clement VII, and Federico Gonzaga, Marquis of Mantua[3] – and then, after taking up permanent residence in Venice, by his own efforts. In spite of his lack of formal education, he had considerable literary ability, and was able to make his living by the use of his pen: he wrote plays, poems, letters, pornography and religious works

---

[1] The edition used here is in *Le Vite dei Santi. Santa Caterina Vergine, San Tommaso d'Aquino 1540–1543*, ed. F. Santin (Rome, 1977) [hereafter: 'Vita'].
[2] P. Larivaille, *Pietro Aretino fra Rinascimento e Manierismo* (Rome, 1980), 19.
[3] For details of Aretino's career before his arrival in Venice, see Larivaille, *Pietro Aretino*, 18–74.

with equal facility and no qualms of conscience. Aretino's career as a versatile professional writer makes it difficult to describe his works, including his religious works, as either high culture (into which he had never been initiated) or low culture (from which he had long since escaped). Aretino, so to speak, had standing but not status.

Between 1534 and 1543, he wrote seven religious books, most of them republished several times.[4] The *Vita di Tomaso* is the last of them. It is a Life of St Thomas Aquinas dedicated to the Marchese del Vasto, allegedly a distant relative of the great Dominican, and draws on the various lives and legends of the saint[5] to provide the scaffolding for Aretino's elaboration of the story. It is difficult to identify Aretino's intended audience. Though it was in his professional interest to maximize the number of his readers, he has chosen a subject – a great philosopher and theologian – that *prima facie* would deter all but a few specialists. A hagiographical solution to this problem is possible: to ignore the philosophy and theology and concentrate on a life of great piety, devotion and humility, illuminated by good works and consummated by miracles. A work written in this way might have appealed more broadly, for instance to nuns on the one hand, and literate artisans and businessmen on the other. However, proposing to identify Aretino's intended audience in this way runs into difficulties. The main difficulty is not that Aretino offends decency by including a graphic account of the temptation of Aquinas by a beautiful prostitute[6] (and so makes the *Vita* unsuitable for the consecrated), nor that he treats difficult theological questions, such as the relationship between God's foreknowledge and human freedom[7] (and so deters the layman), but that his style, frequently very elaborate, and larded with references to the visual arts, is an obstacle to the unsophisticated reader. Only detailed

---

4   *Passione* (6 editions); *Salmi* (9 editions); *Umanità di Cristo* (9 editions); *Genesi* (7 editions); *Vita di Maria* (5 editions); *Vita di Caterina* (5 editions); *Vita di Tomaso* (1 edition). In addition, in 1551, *Genesi*, *Umanità* and *Salmi* were published together in one volume; and in 1552 *Vita di Maria*, *Vita di Caterina* and *Vita di Tomaso* were also published together in one volume.

5   See 'Vita', 9, for the details.

6   'Vita', 237–9. The seventh of the rules that precede the Roman Index of 1564 explicitly condemns obscenity in books (*Index Librorum Prohibitorum* (Lyons, 1564), 22). The sentiment against everything that could conceivably titillate can be seen in the very adverse reaction in 1541 to the nude figures in Michelangelo's *Last Judgement*. See R. de Maio, *Michelangelo e la Controriforma* (Bari, 1978), 22.

7   'Vita', 268–9. Other similarly knotty problems that occur in the 'Vita' are, 'Why were Adam and Eve told to go forth and multiply before the Fall' (254–5), and 'Why was God perfectly perfect?' (255–7).

quotation could do justice to the exuberance of this style, with its complicated rhetorical tissue of conceit, hyperbole,[8] circumlocution and elegant variation, and its fondness for long lists of grammatically parallel locutions. Here is a typical example of the long list. Aretino puts it into the mouth of Aquinas's elder brother when he is trying to make the saint abandon his vocation as a Dominican:

> I would say that it is no marvel if the malice of the friars uses terms appropriate to their misdeed, because they are so perfidious in their hatreds, so criminal in their deeds, so proud in their lordship, so arrogant in giving judgment, so cruel in their opinions, so efficacious in their deceits, so insolent in their intrigues, so importunate in their demands, so unbridled in their desires, so inept in their habits, and so bestial in their behaviour that apart from the sacrament, I cannot see in them anything good.[9]

This style has been plausibly described as Mannerist.[10] Since Mannerism was an elaborate and esoteric style that flourished in courts, Aretino may well have aimed his *Vita di Tomaso* at an audience of courtiers, that is to say at a social, not an intellectual elite. The fact that the *Vita di Tomaso* in terms of the number of editions to which it ran was the least popular of all Aretino's religious works[11] suggests that the uptake in court circles was limited. There are therefore at least three good reasons for claiming that the *Vita* cannot be classified by applying to it the distinction between elite religion and popular religion: it does not originate in the context of either elite or popular religion for its author as a *poligrafo*,[12] i.e. an intellectual *avant la lettre*, stood outside both; it does not appear to have been favoured by the social elite at which it was probably aimed; and even if it had been, it is not clear that the religion of a social elite can, without more ado, be properly described as elite religion. Here then, we have a religious book that resists classification on 'either/or' lines, because it is neither. This is the answer then to the first of my questions above: 'elite' and 'popular' do not divide up the field without remainder.

---

[8] See, for instance, 'Vita', 308, where four lines after 'the faith of the faithfully faithful' occurs 'humility most humbly humble'.

[9] 'Vita', 227.

[10] See Larivaille, *Pietro Aretino*, 9.

[11] See above, n. 4.

[12] For an elucidation of this term, see P. F. Grendler, *Critics of the Italian World 1530–1560. Anton Francesco Doni, Nicolo Franco e Ortensio Lando* (Madison, WI, 1969), 10–14, 65–9.

* * *

We are fairly well informed about the origin of the *Beneficio di Cristo*,[13] though each of the four editions of this work was published anonymously.[14] The first draft was the work of the Benedictine monk Benedetto Fontanini da Mantova.[15] He had made his profession in 1511 at San Benedetto Po, a house distinguished in the first half of the sixteenth century for its learning. After over twenty years as a monk in Mantua and Venice, he was posted to Sicily in 1537. He wrote the first draft in Sicily, perhaps in 1540–1,[16] drawing on his experience in Mantua and Venice, and on his knowledge of the work of Valdes in Naples. It was reworked by Marcantonio Flaminio, who polished the style and fortified the argument against the kind of objections that it was feared the Dominican zealot and anti-Lutheran polemicist Catarino might make against it.[17] According to Professor Thomas Mayer,[18] others might also have had a hand in the finished work, Valdes perhaps, but more probably Cardinals Pole and Contarini. There can be little difficulty therefore in describing this religious book as originating in the world of elite religion, whether the criterion of elite religion is social, political or intellectual. The scholarly Dom Benedetto was by no means the only one from a distinguished academic background. Contarini had been educated at the University of Padua, Valdes at the University of Alcala, and Pole at the Universities of Oxford and Padua. The social and political standing of the two princes of the Church was even more impressive. Contarini was a Venetian nobleman and diplomat; Pole was a relative of Henry VIII. Both had been members of the Reform Commission appointed by Paul III in 1536. Later Contarini was papal legate at the Regensburg Colloquy, and Pole had the same status at the Council of Trent. Marcantonio Flaminio, a distinguished humanist poet, some time secretary of Baldassare Castiglione, was offered but refused the post of Secretary of the Council of Trent.[19] But

---

13 *Trattato utilissimo del beneficio di Christo crocifisso, verso i Christiani* (Venice, 1543) [hereafter: *Beneficio di Cristo*]. I have used the English translation of this work by Ruth Prelowski in J. A. Tedeschi, *Italian Reformation Studies in Honor of Laelius Socinus* (Florence, 1965).

14 Ibid., 95.

15 The details were divulged by Pietro Carnesecchi at a hearing before the Inquisition Tribunal. See S. Caponetto, *La Riforma Protestante nell'Italia del Cinquecento* (Turin, 1992), 89.

16 Ibid., 91.

17 T. Mayer, *Reginald Pole, Prince and Prophet* (Cambridge, 2000), 121.

18 Ibid., 120–1.

19 Flaminio refused the office, and it was thereupon offered to Angelo Massarelli, who accepted it.

the *Beneficio di Cristo* must have circulated well outside the elite sphere in which it had been conceived, for according to Peter Paul Vergerio, it sold 40,000 copies. This number is probably exaggerated,[20] but there is no doubt that the sales were enormous. The names of some of the people who read it are known. They include Cardinals Morone and Badia, the Abbot Gregorio Cortese, and Bishop Cristoforo Madruzzo. They can all with propriety be described as representative of elite religion. Mostly however we do not know who read it but the suspicion must be that many readers came from the ranks of those newly literate groups of artisans, schoolmasters and merchants to whom Silvana Seidel Menchi has attributed much importance in her discussion of evangelical religion in Italy in the 1540s.[21] Such groups lacked the attributes of the elite group – political and social eminence, and much more importantly here, formal education. Without sustained formal education a sophisticated critical attitude to religious texts is impossible: what you see is what you get, and without initiation into the academic disciplines, you do not see much.

Nevertheless, readers who were literate but not educated in a wider sense were able to grasp part of a message that originated in elite circles because of the nature of the message and the way in which it was transmitted. Though Luther is never mentioned, the message of the *Beneficio di Cristo* is for the most part the Lutheran doctrine of salvation by faith alone, but it is communicated simply and directly in about 30,000 words and deals very briefly with Original Sin, the written Law, justification and predestination. In one sense therefore it is a work of theology, but it is neither academic nor technical. It is above all optimistic and practical. We are told that we may confidently expect that the justice of Christ will be able to justify everyone. We are told how to recover the image of God, and four remedies are prescribed against lack of confidence. It is a classic of Christian spirituality with a very wide range of appeal. It transcends the polarities with which the distinction between elite and popular religion threatens us. But it has to be admitted that at the same time it deeply divided the ranks of the social, political and intellectual elite within the Church by its sins of commission and omission: on the one hand its endorsement of the most conspicuous of all Lutheran doctrines; and on the other by making no

---

[20] Caponetto, *Riforma Protestante*, 95.

[21] S. Seidel Menchi, 'Italy', in B. Scribner *et al.*, eds, *The Reformation in National Context* (Cambridge, 1994), 189–92.

mention of the institutional Church. The relationship between Christ and the sinner in the *Beneficio* is in all but a very tenuous sense unmediated.[22] It is not therefore surprising that this extraordinary work first appeared on the Roman Index of Prohibited Books in 1559, nor that in due course the Inquisition hunted it almost to extinction.

Because it appealed to readers from very different backgrounds with very different intellectual aptitudes who read it in different ways, the *Beneficio di Cristo* bridges the gap between elite religion and popular religion, and since it can therefore be both elite and popular at the same time, we have the answer to the second of the questions raised at the beginning of this article: these two categories are not essentially at odds.

* * *

But though they are not essentially at odds, can they sometimes be so? Catarino's *Discorso contra la dottrina e le Profetie di Fra Girolamo Savonarola* (1548)[23] shows that they can. Here again we are well informed about the author and about the circumstances in which this work originated. The author was certainly an elitist. He was born in Siena in 1484 of good family, some of the members of which from time to time held office in the city government. His sister was the abbess of a Dominican convent in the city. He was educated first as a humanist and then at the University of Siena as a lawyer. He graduated in 1502 and was immediately appointed to teach civil law in the University. Under the posthumous influence of Savonarola, he entered the Dominican Order at San Marco in Florence in 1517. In 1527, he was prior of the Sienese Dominican priory of Santo Spirito. He was a prolific author. His output included one work of humanist historiography, four legal works and over thirty works of theology. He was a papal theologian at the Council of Trent, bishop of Minori from 1546, archbishop of Conza in 1551 and would have been made a cardinal had he not died on the way to Rome to receive that honour in 1552. We know that Catharinus was an elitist: it is easy to document his objection to Luther's appeal to the laity against the Church,[24] his opposition to translation of the Bible into the

---

[22] The sinner, not the Church, is the Bride of Christ. Two sacraments are however mentioned: Eucharist and Baptism.

[23] *Contro la Dottrina e le profezie di Fra Girolamo Savonarola* (Venice, 1548).

[24] Ambrosius Catharinus Politus, *Speculum Haereticorum* (Cracow, 1540), 15r (as this edition is not paginated, the reference has been given counting the title page as 1r).

vernacular,[25] and his contempt for the involvement of women and artisans in theological debates.[26] The laity should learn all that it needs to know about the faith from the pulpit.[27] We also know much about the circumstances in which *Contro la dottrina e le profezie di Fra Girolamo Savonarola* was written, for the author begins his work with sketching them out for us. One reason for writing this book is his desire to admit that his early enthusiasm for Savonarola was a mistake. He had already recanted in brief in the *Claves Duae* (1543).[28] Now he does so at length. But there is more to it than the mere desire to set the record straight. Savonarolism is not dead. Having precipitated a crisis in 1498 and a disaster in 1527–30, it again threatens trouble. Fra Girolamo has become the object of a cult, not only in Florence but also at the Minerva in Rome:

> if they so presumptuously wish to consider him a saint, they should at least not adore him as many of them as I know for certain did and still have not stopped doing. They have either pictures or statues of him with letters that say 'Prophet and martyr'. Again there are others who keep ashes or other things of him and they venerate them as holy relics against the decrees of the popes.[29]

This, says Catarino, is contrary to the canons, which have made the recognition of saints the right of the pope. Worse, it is a flagrant challenge to the judgement of the Church, which had condemned and punished Savonarola. But Savonarola, we understand, is held up to be not only a saint, but also a prophet and martyr. To make this man a martyr, Catarino argues, would be to say that he was right on a matter of the faith and that the Church was wrong.[30] For Catarino, this is totally unacceptable, and his tactic in the remainder of the *Discorso* is

---

[25] Ambrosius Catharinus Politus, 'Quaestio an expediat scripturas in maternas linguas transferri', in *Enarrationes in quinque priora capita libri Geneseos* (Rome, 1551–2).

[26] Ibid., col. 336.

[27] Ibid., col. 337.

[28] Ambrosius Catharinus Politus, *Claves Duae ad aperiendas intelligendasve scripturas sacras* (Lyons, 1543), 136.

[29] Catharinus, *Dottrina e profetie*, 18r.

[30] Catarino was well aware of the tendency of some members of the Dominican Order to suppose that on some issues the Church could be wrong, since it was one of the issues that cropped up in the controversy over the Immaculate Conception of the Virgin in Siena 1527–30. See P. Giacinto Bosco, 'Intorno a un carteggio inedito di Ambrogio Caterino' , *Memorie Domenicane* 67 (1950), 157.

therefore to discredit Savonarola so thoroughly as to make the cult of him preposterous.

If there were no more to it than this, the *Discorso* would merely be a work that aimed to scotch a development within the world of elite religion: it would pit one Dominican against others. But if that were the case, it would be impossible to explain why this work is written in Italian, and not in Latin. A Dominican audience would be sure to know Latin. The use of the vernacular is here an unmistakeable symptom of the desire to reach a wider audience. The fact is that Savonarolism since 1494 had always had a following outside the Dominican Order, which continued long after the debacle of 1530, as the case of the proletarian *Capi rossi* shows.[31] Where in the great crisis of 1494 Savonarola and the learned convent of San Marco had endorsed the apocalyptic millenarianism endemic in Florentine popular culture,[32] his incorrigible followers in the Dominican Order were now involved in promoting on their own initiative a dangerous[33] cult of their hero as saint and martyr, on which elite religion and popular religion could again coalesce.

In Catarino's *Discorso* therefore elite and popular religion are related in a complex fashion. His diatribe shows well enough not only the popularist potential of the unofficial cult of Savonarola with its paraphernalia of ashes and relics, but also his total opposition to it: the elitist condemns not only a popular initiative that he despises, but even his fellow Dominicans who have aided and abetted it. But his objection to it is principled, for he condemns a flagrant challenge to the authority and the prerogatives of the papacy.

[31] See L. Polizzotto, *The Elect Nation. The Savonarolan Movement in Florence 1494–1545* (Oxford, 1994), 344–5, 437.

[32] See D. Weinstein, *Savonarola and Florence. Prophecy and Patriotism in the Renaissance* (Princeton, NJ, 1970), especially ch. 1, 27–66, which stresses the contribution of the Fraticelli and the Ciompi to the evolution of this myth.

[33] How dangerous it was can be seen from the reaction of Paul IV, when the Jesuit Laynez censured some extracts from the works of Savonarola in full consistory. The pope reacted in anger. Almost shouting, he said, 'This is Martin Luther, this is pestiferous doctrine. What are you doing, Monsignori, what are you waiting for . . . This must be stopped. Get rid of it. Do you not see how this man is fighting against the Holy See?' In his vexation, the pope then stood up in great indignation and stamped his feet on the floor. 'Even if he is dead, he and all the other heretics must be subjected to this See, because Christ wished all the world to obey it'. In fact the Jesuit attack on Savonarola's teaching had been prompted by Catarino's *Discorso*. See P. Simoncelli, 'Momenti e figure del savonarolismo romano', *Critica Storica* 11, n.s. 1 (1974), 57.

* * *

Oversimplification, it is said, is the occupational disease of philosophers.[34] In using the elite/popular distinction in discussions of religion historians are susceptible to the same disease. The three examples considered above have been assembled to suggest the variety of relationships between elite and popular religion that might be found even in a very brief period in a very restricted area.

University of Chichester

---

[34] J. L. Austin, *Philosophical Papers* (2nd edn, Oxford, 1970), 252.

'EVERYONE SHOULD BE LIKE THE PEOPLE': ELITE AND POPULAR RELIGION AND THE COUNTER REFORMATION

by TREVOR JOHNSON

IT is now over two decades since a cluster of studies by Natalie Zemon Davis, Bob Scribner, Marc Venard, Roger Chartier, Richard Trexler, William Christian, Carlo Ginzburg and others significantly modified our ways of thinking about religion in early modern Europe and in particular about the relationship between 'elite' and 'popular' religion, or as many had conceived it, between religion as preached and religion as practised.[1] It had been simpler when writers who thought about such things had drawn neat boundaries between elite and popular and regarded communication between them as an exclusively one-way, top-down, process. They had also tended to regard the popular aspect of the polarity as qualitatively inferior to its elite corollary, depicting it variously as instrumental, functional, un-spiritual, somatic, irrational, unreflective, mechanical, amoral, magical or superstitious, or indeed as all of these things together, as if 'the people', a group generally defined in class terms as the socially subordinate, exhibited a vast collective unconscious. Additionally, much ethnography had taken such a divide as axiomatic, the German *Volkskunde* tradition, for example, often positing a process of transmission or 'sinking' of cultural forms from the elite down to the popular level.[2] Such assumptions, which moreover uncritically reflected a notion of 'religion' which is restricted to a formal doctrinal corpus, defined and authenticated by the very body charged with its maintenance, were damaged by the historical revolution of the 1970s and 1980s and will

---

[1] Landmark discussions of these developments include: Natalie Zemon Davis, 'From "Popular Religion" to Religious Cultures', in Steven Ozment, ed., *Reformation Europe: a Guide to Research* (St Louis, LA, 1982), 321–41; R. W. Scribner, 'Interpreting Religion in Early Modern Europe', *European Studies Review* 13 (1983), 89–105; Craig Harline, 'Official Religion – Popular Religion in Recent Historiography of the Catholic Reformation', *Archiv für Reformationsgeschichte* 81 (1990), 239–62.

[2] Robert W. Scribner, 'Volksglaube und Volksfrömmigkeit. Begriffe und Historiographie', in Hansgeorg Molitor and Heribert Smolinsky, eds, *Volksfrömmigkeit in der Frühen Neuzeit* (Münster, 1994), 121–38.

not do for most scholars now, despite having informed a number of still influential historical schemata.[3] Indeed it has become axiomatic in scholarship on early modern religion to abandon such a rigid polarity in favour of more refined constructs and cultural models.

This shift has arisen first from a desire to move away from value-laden traditionalism (an aim which in many instances began with a conscious privileging of the 'popular' and the marginal) and secondly from a dissatisfaction with the lack of precision inherent in the older elite/popular dichotomy, given the inability of its exponents to agree as to the basis on which the two groups allegedly exhibiting distinct religious cultures have been defined, whether socially, intellectually, professionally, or by some other criterion. Admittedly, there have been attempts to compose new, more meaningful, polarities. In his influential 1981 discussion of the pilgrimage culture of early modern Castile, for example, William Christian rejected the reification of elite and popular religion and pointed to homogeneity across social and educational divides, but advocated an alternative model of 'local' versus 'universal' religion. This has had the value of adding an important spatial dimension to the debate, but one might argue that it comes at the possible cost of glossing over significant differences of experience among the various groups which together comprised 'local' society.[4]

More helpful therefore has been the notion of a cultural field within which individuals and social groups interact, or, to translate into specifically religious terms, a 'sacred system' in which participants appropriate beliefs and rites. This model has the merit of preserving an appreciation of the complexities of cultural differentiation (of which local-universal represents just one axis) and allows such analytical categories as gender, age and class to be employed. It has enabled some scholars, especially of the pre-Reformation Church, to emphasize the homogeneity of Catholic devotion, with the liturgy as the unifying heart of the cultural field and with a focus on the 'ordinary' rather than

[3] To cite perhaps the two best known works: Jean Delumeau, *Le Catholicisme entre Luther et Voltaire* (Paris, 1971); Keith Thomas, *Religion and the Decline of Magic: Studies in Popular Beliefs in Sixteenth- and Seventeenth-Century England* (London, 1971).

[4] 'All evidence indicates that the kind of local religion described was shared by most of the people of Madrid and Toledo (and, for that matter, of Seville, Barcelona and Florence) and was as characteristic of the royal family as it was of unlettered peasants. One is therefore led to question the idea of "popular religion", as distinct from some other kind': William Christian, *Local Religion in Sixteenth-Century Spain* (Princeton, 1981), 8. See also Simon Ditchfield, ' "In Search of Local Knowledge": Rewriting Early Modern Italian Religious History', *Cristianesimo nella storia* 19 (1998), 255–96.

the 'sensational' aspects of religion.[5] Others have preferred to empha-size diversity and the manifold ways in which individuals and groups could fish religious language and ritual from a common pool to suit their own needs. The notion of a shared 'sacred system' provides the conceptual framework for one of the most successful studies on this theme in English for Counter-Reformation Europe, David Gentilcore's marvellous evocation of the religious culture of Southern Apulia. Here, we find a bewildering variety of modes of accessing the sacred, some of them drifting in and out of official ecclesiastical approval or censure, with, for most of the population, convenience, cost and (above all) perceived efficacy, not dogmatic loyalty or treason, constituting the overriding criteria. In this system, we learn, even the Devil could play a positive role, viewed by many Apulians less as the embodiment of ulti-mate evil than as a cunning trickster who could, on occasion, prove useful to have on one's side when other sources of preternatural power failed.[6]

Nonetheless, it is possible to argue that the retention of a loosely-defined elite/popular distinction can have some analytical value, as a marker or reminder of tensions within any sacred system. This could be the fundamental tension, as Salvador Ryan has described it, between the magisterium's articulation of doctrine and the personal (or 'popular') response to doctrine, by rich and poor, educated and illiterate alike.[7] But it can also be conceived as a shorthand expression for the impact on religious practice of broader tensions around competing sources of authority and generated by the practices of power, whether political, intellectual or cultural. This is not to affirm the inevitability of hege-mony or to deny the agency of the subordinate. Indeed the notion of negotiation, used impressively by Gentilcore (as in negotiation between centre and periphery), suggests that 'elites' had to bargain and therefore to partially surrender, to adapt and to accommodate 'popular' initiatives in order to make headway. Use of the word 'negotiation', however, can seem a rather weak way of accounting for the reality of power at its most coercive, as experienced by victims of the Holy Office and other tribunals. Moreover, the Counter Reformation was in part defined by

---

5   Duffy, *Stripping of the Altars*. On 'ordinary' versus 'sensational', see Harline, 'Official Religion – Popular Religion', 252, n. 83.

6   David Gentilcore, *From Bishop to Witch. The System of the Sacred in Early Modern Terra d'Otranto* (Manchester, 1992).

7   Salvador Ryan, ' "The Most Contentious of Terms": Towards a New Understanding of Late Medieval "Popular Religion" ', *Irish Theological Quarterly* 68 (2003), 281–90.

systematic and protracted campaigns, supported by new mechanisms and methods, on behalf of ecclesiastical as well as political authorities to 'reform' their contemporaries' religion (and 'reform' implies a sense of distance between the religion of the reformer and that to be reformed, at least in the former's eyes, as well as a desire to bridge the gap). Finally, as Bob Scribner pointed out in justification of the use of the term 'popular religion', the period in question used its own system of conceptual polarities, of binary opposites, which pitted learned against unlearned, poor against rich, the subordinate against the powerful and Carnival against Lent. Sometimes 'contrariety' was just a rhetorical trope, but it could be argued nonetheless that language, by clustering varied concepts into polarities, could, in contingent circumstances, actually serve to create realities of domination and subordination, the most egregious example being the stereotype of diabolical witchcraft.[8] The following pages offer some reflections on how this claim might work for some aspects of belief and practice across Catholic Europe in the one hundred and fifty years or so after the Council of Trent.

* * *

An obvious point of departure is provided by the period's official definitions, for it was in these, especially in the Reformation century, that we can chart the systematic distinctions drawn by religious professionals which approximate to the later elite/popular construct, in which a widening breach between religion as preached and that as practised was rhetorically created. The increasing tendency to apply the negative category of 'superstition' to widespread aspects of the cosmology and practice of the laity, especially the peasantry, was as marked a feature of the Counter Reformation as it was of magisterial Protestantism.[9] Whilst Trent itself did not pronounce, the hundreds of works of Catholic moral theology published throughout Europe in the wake of the Council tended to posit a clear demarcation between religion and 'superstition' and deployed neat taxonomies, often in the context of catechetical explanation of the First Commandment. Although couched in the terms and structures earlier advanced by

8 Bob Scribner, 'Introduction', in Bob Scribner and Trevor Johnson, eds, *Popular Religion in Germany and Central Europe, 1400–1800* (Basingstoke, 1996), 1–15. On early modern dual classification, Stuart Clark, *Thinking with Demons. The Idea of Witchcraft in Early Modern Europe* (Oxford, 1997).

9 For a recent discussion of this theme, Helen Parish and William G. Naphy, eds, *Religion and Superstition in Reformation Europe* (Manchester, 2002), 'Introduction', 1–22.

Aquinas, each instance revealed local inflections and, often, the urgencies of the reformist agenda. For the Pamplona Thomist, Francisco Larraga, for example, 'superstition' could be a sin of omission or commission, the latter comprising vices of excess or defect (termed 'irreligion'). Five types of superstition (idolatry, diabolical divination, vain observance, magic and *maleficium*) are further divided into sub-types. The potentially wide-reaching category of 'vain observance' is defined as the employment of useless and or inappropriate means, whether the desired end be the prevention of evil or the achievement of good. Turning ethnographer to find empirical data, Larraga cites and condemns the local practice of keeping eggs laid on Good Friday as fire extinguishers; cures by *ensalmos* (charms), 'as old women are accustomed to use'; or avoidance of any gathering of thirteen 'for fear that one of the company will die that year'. Vain observance can be accompanied by an explicit or implicit pact with the Devil, the latter pact being either heretical (if it negates an article of faith) or not. Vain observance is a mortal sin *ex genere suo*, but when the pact is not explicit, the sin may be (and usually is) venial, bearing in mind a person's simplicity, ignorance, or doubts.[10]

Ignorance and simplicity, indeed, were generally recognized as mitigation in such treatises. Implied was an awareness of a fundamental social and cultural divide between those with access to education and those (the illiterate peasantry was surely held in view here) who did not. However, whether those who employed these terms conceived of the religion of the 'simple folk' as deficient *in toto* is questionable. How the shortcomings of ignorance were to be overcome nonetheless perplexed many minds. The solution of Trent was a more professionalized and confident clergy which could in turn better indoctrinate its flock. For the more exemplary pastors, no social group was beyond enjoyment of a purified yet rich devotional life; however this did not imply dull uniformity, but rather rich diversity. For François de Sales, 'devotion must be differently exercised by the gentleman, the artisan, the servant, or the prince, by the widow, the maid or the wife; and not only that, but the practice of devotion must be accommodated to the strength, the activities and the duties of each'.[11]

---

[10] Francisco Santos y Grosin, *Promptuario de la theologia moral, compuesto primeramente por el P. M. Fr. Francisco Larraga, del Sagrado Orden de Predicatores, despues reformado, y corregido . . .* (Madrid, 1780), 422–4.

[11] François de Sales, *Introduction a la Vie Devote*, Part I, Chapter 3, in *Les Oeuvres de Sainct*

But there was coercion too. A feature of the period is that where theologians led in the construction of complex classifications of unorthodox belief and practice, secular magistrates soon followed. Duke Maximilian I of Bavaria's mandate *Against Superstition, Magic, Witchcraft and other Punishable Diabolical Arts* of 1611, one of the most comprehensive pieces of legislation of its kind, required twenty-one folios to itemize the practices it was condemning, plus a further twelve folios to list the penalties. As an example ('one of a thousand', it claimed), the mandate reproduced a 'blessing' (*Segen*), or curative charm, for sick cattle:

> Ob das sey, dass die heilig Junckfraw
> Maria das Kindt Jesum gebar,
> So kumme disem Their das blatt ab,
> In Namen Gottes Vatters, Sohns und heiligen Geists.[12]

And the mandate glossed it:

> Here there is not only vain observance (*vanitas*), in that the most holy Incarnation of Christ, which occurred for the salvation of the human race, is applied to help an unreasoning animal, but also blasphemy in that this non-rhyming charm questions whether Mary bore Jesus.[13]

However, neat cataloguing and the insistence by post-Tridentine Church and proto-absolutist State alike on a sharper demarcation between licit and illicit approaches to the sacred belied the blurred nature of this boundary, which even Maximilian's mandate recognized when it went on to affirm that the Devil often appears as an angel of light. The frontier was especially difficult to patrol given the Church's own trumpeting of the miraculous, and its emphasis on sacramentals (protective rituals and blessed objects which were widely, if unofficially, viewed as automatically efficacious), its highlighting of the importance of special times and special places where and when the sacred might be better accessed, or its recommendation of the repetition of devotions a set number of times. The quotidian use of sacra-

---

François de Sales, *Evesque et Prince de Geneve, Instituteur des Religieuses de la Visitation de Sancte Marie*, Vol. I (Paris, 1669), cols 4–5.

[12] Wolfgang Behringer, *Mit dem Feuer vom Leben zum Tod: Hexengesetzgebung in Bayern* (Munich, 1988), 174: 'If the Blessed Virgin Mary bore the Child Jesus, lift the sickness from this animal, in the name of God, the Father, the Son and the Holy Spirit' (my translation).

[13] Ibid.

mentals could easily have a whiff of vain observance about it, as indeed Protestants had not been slow in pointing out. Behind their original diffusion may have lain a certain strategy of substitution: an attempt to replace unofficial objects and rituals with canonical ones. Yet when the latter so closely resembled the former, it is hard to see how in practice these conceptual boundaries could have been strictly maintained. Rather one suspects that, at least for a long period, new measures were simply adopted alongside the old and that confusion reigned under the mitigating cover of 'ignorance' and 'simplicity'. As apotropaic and counter-magical resources, orthodox sacramentals fitted seamlessly into a culture which had as its daily accoutrements a variety of protective talismans, amulets, herbs, medals, printed prayers, charms and images. The ambiguous divide between canonical and non-canonical is indicated by the frequent suspicion of *superstitio* which surrounded even ecclesiastically-endorsed blessings in the eyes of some divines. In seventeenth-century Germany a number of theologians attacked as 'superstitious' the 'Zachary-Blessing', a plague-prophylactic usually abbreviated to a series of letters, even though it had been invoked during the Council of Trent and had been expressly confirmed by Gregory XIII. Similarly the 'Benedict-Penny' was repeatedly banned by German bishops, even whilst being simultaneously promoted by the Benedictine order.[14]

Despite anxieties, the cult of sacramentals, which had flourished before Trent, did not stop with the Council. Far from it: many old blessing formulae were maintained (if some were criticized) and new ones were constantly created, not displacing the old but adding to the pool. Indeed a kind of arms-race intensified, as counter-magical benedictions developed to keep pace with what Martin del Rio and other demonologists warned was an escalating threat from witchcraft and Protestant scepticism. Alongside Tolentino-Bread, one now had access to new Jesuit sacramentals like Ignatius-Water and Xavier-Water. Clearly in a Catholic context such canonical blessings could not be considered 'superstitious', except in so far as the attitude of those resorting to them was based on a (non-canonical) faith in their automatic efficacy (*ex opere operato*). Yet precisely this dubious faith seems to have straddled all social classes and could be found among the most elite practitioners. It was then not formal theology, but its practical application (and the latter's rhetorical defence) which blurred the line.

---

14 M. Brauneck, *Religiöse Volkskunst* (Cologne, 1978), 296–7.

In Spain, for example, the Carmelite scapular enjoyed a resurgence in the seventeenth century when narratives of miracles attributed to it were assiduously collected and diffused by historians from both branches of the order. Fray José de Santa Teresa's six-hundred-page hagiographical companion, *Flores del Carmelo* (Madrid, 1678) reveals that high social rank or senior academic position were no barriers to an apparently simple-minded faith in the quasi-automatic efficacy of this particular talisman. In a story from 1611, a noblewoman of Salamanca obsessed by demons was kept safe by wearing the scapular. Another Salamanca tale quoted the testimony of a university professor, Fray Pedro Cornijo, who recalled being awoken one night by strange cries:

> Immediately I got up and, wearing only my nightshirt, I ran to the place where the voices were coming from. Before going downstairs I remembered that I did not have my scapular on, and felt strangely helpless, so I went straight back for it, and having put it on, went to find the source of the voices. After searching all the chambers, I could no longer hear the voices . . . the whole convent was asleep, so I went back to bed. The next day in the city I encountered the curate of San Isidro, surrounded by a crowd of people, exorcizing a possessed man. At the cries of the patient, the exorcisms of the priest and the noise of the bystanders, I went to have a look at the demoniac, who noticed me, smiled and said: 'I led the father a merry dance last night with my moaning. I tell you, if he had come out without his scapular, the joke would have been on him. You have it to thank for that'.[15]

The Carmelite scapular, of course, had a soteriological function as well as a protective one, since the so-called Sabbatine Bull promised speedy liberation from Purgatory for anyone dying wearing it. As Christine Göttler's study of the art of Purgatory in Antwerp and Bologna makes clear, this was an important part of the Discalced Carmelites' pitch for patronage and support. Rival orders offered similar lifelines, such as the Franciscan cord or the Dominican rosary. Following the crisis in the early sixteenth century, a revival of interest in indulgences was accelerated by Gregory XIII's generosity with the treasury of merits, which by extending the role of the privileged altar at which a single Mass could gain a plenary indulgence, shook up the post-Reformation pardon

15 Fray José de Santa Teresa, *Flores del Carmelo. Vidas de los Santos de Nuestra Señora del Carmen, que reza su religion, assi en comun, como en particulares conventos* (Madrid, 1678), 351.

system.[16] Not all concerns of the common people were therefore this-worldly: salvation, compassion towards the dead and fear of the pains of Purgatory figured powerfully in the shared religious imagination. If popular religion was not without soteriological interest, neither was it dominated by a cult of materialistic petitionary prayer to the preclusion of a moral economy. John Bossy has shown how before the Counter Reformation this centred on the Mass and the sacraments and customs which cemented relations between kith and kin, family, household, neighbourhood and community, and served to mitigate the social ills of feud and enmity. If the post-Tridentine focus on clericalism and obsession with the narrowing of religious activity into parochial structures had here a negative result, as Bossy argues, this did not imply the destruction of a popular moral economy, but may well have opened up a divide between a parochially based *dévot* piety and a continuing extra-parochial religious culture.[17]

* * *

Given the principle of intercession, much of the sacred system centred on the figures of saints, who seem to have dominated the Catholic world's cultural field, almost to the eclipse of Christ, as mediators of sacred power. Engagement with the saints, therefore, exposed shared values, but also differentiation, and again underlines the difficulty of predicating fixed cultural boundaries. If the Tridentine Church tried to foster other ways of looking at saints, including extolling them as exemplars of heroic holiness and fashionable piety, and if hagiography was gradually brought into line with new universal standards emanating from Rome (the 'curial positivism' identified by Simon Ditchfield), then the miracle-working power of saintly intercession was certainly no less enthusiastically promoted or received.[18]

New cults sometimes struck a particularly common touch, as if to extend socially the gallery of role models. Perhaps the least known of the five figures canonized in 1622 was San Isidoro Labrador, the medi-

---

16 Christine Göttler, *Die Kunst des Fegefeuers nach der Reformation. Kirchliche Schenkungen, Ablaß und Almosen in Antwerpen und Bologna um 1600* (Mainz, 1996), and, for a similar emphasis, Pierroberto Scaramella, *Le Madonne del Purgatorio. Iconografia e religione in Campania tra Rinascimento e Controriforma* (Genoa, 1991).

17 John Bossy, 'The Counter-Reformation and the People of Catholic Europe', *P&P* 47 (1970), 51–70.

18 Simon Ditchfield, *Liturgy, Sanctity and History in Tridentine Italy: Pietro Maria Campi and the Preservation of the Particular* (Cambridge, 1995); idem, 'Sanctity in Early Modern Italy', *JEH* 47 (1996), 98–112.

eval Spanish farmer, who may well seem insignificant compared with Ignatius Loyola, Francis Xavier, Philip Neri and Teresa of Ávila, but whose elevation to the altar nonetheless raised the profile of the laity in general and the Spanish peasantry in particular.[19] But in this regard even clerics could somehow be taken as representatives of a popular constituency. One could interpret as reaching out to the unlearned the cult of latter-day holy fools, such as the Italian Capuchin, Giuseppe da Copertino (1603–63).[20] Among those enjoying an unofficial cult was the Carmelite friar, Francisco del Niño Jesús (1547–1604), one of several Spanish mendicants of the period made famous for their ignorance, candour and artless simplicity through books, images and drama, in Francisco's case as the unlikely hero of Lope de Vega's comedy, *El Rustico del Cielo* ('Heaven's Rustic'). When the friar was called upon to exorcize a female demoniac, a contemporary biographer recorded, even the Devil cried 'now here comes this idiot to persecute me!'[21]

Even when not themselves directly 'of the people', the most emblematic Counter-Reformation saints might enjoy a cultic diffusion which could sometimes take surprising forms, suggesting perhaps both the 'popular' appropriation of an official cult and a large common ground of expectation and approach. The twin canvases of the miracles of Loyola and Xavier painted by Rubens for the Antwerp Jesuit Church in 1616 show the former exorcizing the demon-possessed and the latter healing plague victims and apparently resuscitating the dead. It has been suggested that possession and plague were here metaphors for heresy, while dispossession and miraculous healing were allegories of the triumph of the Church over her satanically-inspired enemies.[22] However miracle (as well as anxiety around the Devil's assaults against vulnerable individuals) was salient in the dissemination of the cult of these and other Jesuit saints in a way that was not reducible to metaphor. Loyola in life had not exorcized, yet he was posthumously often connected with the expulsion of demons, an association made as early as Ribadeneira's 1572 biography of Ignatius and which had become a *topos* even before his canonization. In Germany, moreover, he became

---

[19] Giovanni Papa, *Le cause di canonizzazione nel primo periodo della Congregazione dei Riti (1588–1634)* (Vatican City, 2001), 260.

[20] Gentilcore, *From Bishop to Witch*, 165–7.

[21] José de Jesús Maria, *Historia de la vida y virtudes de fray Francisco del Niño Jesús* (Madrid, 1670), 39.

[22] Christine M. Boeckl, 'Plague Imagery as Metaphor for Heresy in Rubens' *The Miracles of Saint Francis Xavier*', *The Sixteenth Century Journal* 27 (1996), 979–95.

an *allgemeiner Nothelfer*, an all-purpose patron for all manner of needs and emergencies, although his relics were particularly used to facilitate child-birth. However unexpected, these aspects of the Loyola-cult were so officially sanctioned as to merit artistic representation in the public spaces of Jesuit churches, whilst miracle, as well as heroic virtue, appeared in the various other media propagandizing Jesuit saints, including theatre, poetry and music.[23]

The variegated nature of cult can be seen in the twin example of two saints with Central European associations canonized in the eighteenth century, John Nepomuk and Fidelis of Sigmaringen. The cult of Nepomuk, a fourteenth-century Czech martyr who had died rather than break the seal of the confessional, touched different groups in special ways. For the clergy he was a patron of the sacrament of penance and of the priestly dignity, in particular that of the higher clergy (he was almost universally depicted in the choir dress of an eighteenth-century canon). For the Austrian Habsburg and Bavarian Wittelsbach houses he was a dynastic patron. Taking their cue from his watery death, for people who worked on rivers or needed to cross over them he was a highly regarded protector, as the many bridges in Central Europe and South Germany bearing Baroque statues of him attest. Finally all, dynasts and river folk alike, could carry 'Nepomuk-Tongues', small protective amulets in the shape of the organ which had maintained a brave silence and which had become an icon and talisman in its own right. Nepomuk's biographer, the Czech Jesuit Bohuslav Balbín, unsurprisingly stressed the saint's stoicism, but also had much to say on his posthumous miracles and the lively cult that had arisen around his relics in Prague, of which the centrepiece was his uncorrupted tongue.[24] The history of the cult of the Capuchin martyr, Fidelis of Sigmaringen (1578–1622), slain by heretics during the Thirty Years War and subject of a recent study by Matthias Ilg,[25] similarly shows an appeal to particular social or occupational groups and institutions, in this case the Capuchin order, the local Austrian authorities and the Catholic soldiers

---

[23] On Jesuit songs set to popular melodies, see Dietz-Rüdiger Moser, *Verkündigung durch Volksgesang. Studien zur Liedpropaganda und -katechese der Gegenreformation* (Berlin, 1981).

[24] Bohuslav Balbín, *Vita S. Joannis Nepomuceni sigilli sacramentalis Protomartyris* (Augsburg, 1730).

[25] Matthias Ilg, 'Der Kult des Kapuzinermärtyrers Fidelis von Sigmaringen als Ausdruck katholischer Kriegserfahrungen im Dreißigjährigen Krieg', in Matthias Asche and Anton Schindling, eds, *Das Strafgericht Gottes. Kriegserfahrungen und Religion im Heiligen Römischen Reich Deutscher Nation im Zeitalter des Dreißigjährigen Krieges* (Münster, 2002), 291–439.

who were the friar's earliest devotees and among whom his violent wartime death continued to have particular resonance.

Ambiguities and tensions within a shared sacred system did not only appear in the case of new saints, but were present even in the cults of the very oldest, as is evident from the 'war' between St Paul and St John in that much-contested outpost of Christianity, the island of Malta. Carmel Cassar's intriguing study of social memory in early modern Malta suggests that whilst this was partly defined and manipulated by social and political elite, its tropes were often of populist origin. Central to the construction and maintenance of historical memory was the issue of whether Malta had preserved its Christianity unbroken through the centuries and whether such continuity could be traced back to St Paul's shipwreck on the island in AD 60. Arguing in favour of Pauline foundation and Christian continuity, the Maltese Jesuit, Gerolamo Manduca (1574–1643), drew on the evidence of text and epigraphy but he also investigated popular oral tradition, communicated, as he put it, 'by the very old, according to tradition, who themselves have no concept of time'. Gian Francesco Abela, a seventeenth-century writer who closely followed Manduca, believed that the tattooed crosses sported by many of his contemporaries were a relic of an era when such symbols were needed to distinguish Christians from the heathen. Such research helped to revive the cult of St Paul (centred on the grotto at Rabat where the apostle had allegedly lived for three months) and demonstrated that the Maltese did not owe their Catholic fervour to the new power on the island, the Knights of St John, who were strongly advocating the cult of their own saintly patron. Travellers reported the allegedly miraculous properties of the limestone from the grotto and throughout Italy wandering 'Pauliani' would sell 'Maltese earth' for its curative properties, especially against snake-bite.[26]

The use of oral tradition and the observation of popular custom by Manduca and Abela shows that elite interest in the religion of the people was not always simply reformist, but could have a scientific quality, as is also evident in the investigations undertaken by the German Jesuit polymath, Athanasius Kircher, into the *Tarantella*, the Southern Neapolitan popular ritual dance said to cure the bite of the

---

[26]   Carmel Cassar, *Society, Culture and Identity in Early Modern Malta* (Msida, Malta, 2000), 199–219.

tarantula.[27] More generally, the study of Counter-Reformation sanctity can reveal the internal dynamism of a shared religious culture, and the sometimes contradictory priorities, needs and solutions of different regions and social groups. If the grand story is one of the growing importance of central institutions, such as the Congregation of Rites, in defining sanctity, monitoring cults and seeking to distinguish between valid and invalid observance, then the study of reception shows how such distinctions could easily become blurred.

* * *

Much of the encounter between elite and popular cult was place- or space-bound. The Counter Reformation inherited topographies of sacrality, above all in wonder-working shrines of the saints which attracted vows and pilgrims. To these it added new sites and new forms of sacred space, such as the 'deserts' created by the Discalced Carmelites in Spain, Portugal and Italy from the late sixteenth century, or the great Calvaries, those reproductions of the *via dolorosa* and the scene of the passion, of which perhaps the best known prototype was the *Sacro Monte* at Varallo in Piedmont, where pilgrims (including Carlo Borromeo) processed through dozens of chapels featuring life-size terracotta tableaux of scenes from Sacred History.[28] Such Calvaries seem to have been especially in vogue in Poland, where at least five major sites were established during the Counter Reformation.[29] Replicas of the *Scala Santa* proliferated in the Holy Roman Empire and Central Europe, as did those of the Virgin's *Sancta Casa* at Loreto.[30]

Such new schemes had in common a programmatic quality and a sense of managed and controlled devotion and were accompanied by an increase in clerically organized and directed pilgrimage. This same stress on the management of piety can be seen in the transformation of existing sites of sacrality, the shrines of the relics and images of the

---

27 Ingrid D. Rowland, *The Ecstatic Journey: Athanasius Kircher in Baroque Rome* (Chicago, IL, 2000), 84.

28 On the deserts, Benoit Marie de la Sainte-Croix, *Les Saints Déserts des Carmes Déchaussés* (Paris, 1927). The classic description of Varallo is Samuel Butler, *Ex Voto* (London, 1888).

29 Jerzy Kloczowski, *A History of Polish Christianity* (Cambridge, 2000), 158.

30 For the most recent work on *Scala Sancta* reproductions, with a focus on the Czech lands, see Martin Elbel, 'Budování poutního místa: Svaté schody pri františkánském klášere v Olomouci', *Folia Historica Bohemica* 20 (2002), 215–39, which charts how the richly-indulgenced *Scala Sancta* erected by the Franciscans of Olomouc in the early eighteenth century was initially opposed by other religious orders but received popular support, especially after a *via dolorosa* was added to it.

saints which were the supreme examples of the localization of the sacred, of the attempt to fix its power in a place. Often ancient and of obscure origin, their Counter-Reformation history manifests both continuity and change, as may be observed in the Marian shrine of Scherpenheuvel in the Spanish Netherlands.[31] Before the Reformation pilgrims had sought cures from a small wooden carving of the Virgin resting in the branches of an isolated oak tree on top of the 'Sharp Hill' near Zichem. An original legend told of a shepherd's discovery of the figure and of its strange refusal to leave its tree. The statue disappeared when the region came under Calvinist control in the 1580s, but was replaced when the Spanish reoccupied the area and fresh miracles were enthusiastically reported by the garrison and its Jesuit chaplains. The local clergy organized formal processions and had a small wooden chapel built by the tree, the town councils of Brussels and Antwerp made donations and the Habsburg rulers of the Spanish Netherlands, Albrecht and Isabella, credited the Madonna with the triumph of Spanish arms at Ostend. The fame of the shrine rose still further when witnesses testified to having seen the statue weep blood, taken as the Virgin's sorrow at the sins of the Netherlanders. However, at this point, the diocesan authorities, alarmed by reports that pilgrims were taking away leaves, branches and bark for home-cures, intervened decisively and had the tree chopped down. The image was transferred to a new stone chapel equipped with four confessional-boxes. Torn from 'popular' grasp in high-handed fashion, the wood from the felled oak was used to make rosary beads and a number of Marian statues, modelled on the original, some of which in turn wrought miracles. A cure attributed to a splinter of the Sharp-Hill oak administered to the daughter of Francesco Gonzaga, imperial ambassador to the Holy See, gained another high-born devotee to the shrine and facilitated Paul V's concession of a plenary indulgence for its pilgrims. More clergy were appointed to organize the cult, manage the pilgrims, lead processions and offer the sacraments. Finally, under patronage of the Archdukes, a grand new basilica was constructed, surrounded by a square and ancillary buildings and cordoned off from the surrounding countryside by a bastioned *trace*, creating a veritable fortress of the Faith and a national shrine for the Spanish Netherlands.

The history of Scherpenheuvel illustrates a common Counter-

---

[31] For the following, Luc Duerloo and Marc Wingens, *Scherpenheuvel. Het Jeruzalem van de Lage Landen* (Leuven, 2002).

Reformation phenomenon of 'elite' appropriation of a 'popular' shrine, symbolized by the felling of the oak and the re-modelling of the site's sacred topography. In this instance, clerical control of the pilgrimage, imposed through the discipline of procession and confessional, was accompanied by its politicization into a tool of triumphalist reassertion of Habsburg authority. The dismissive ecclesiastical approach to the lay cult of the tree and the desire to efface it and transfer the focus of devotion unambiguously to the Virgin herself suggest a hardening of difference between religious cultures. Yet cheap later-seventeenth-century illustrations of Scherpenheuvel preserved the memory of the shrine's rustic origins, whilst recording its physical transformation. Apparently ordered and homogenized processional forms could mask differentiation and even here the pilgrimage did not entirely lose the raucous and festal character generally associated with such rituals.[32]

* * *

Perhaps the most dramatic episodes of encounter between an elite world of urban sophistication and disciplined post-Tridentine spirituality on the one hand, and what to many divines was the *terra incognita* of peasant religious culture on the other, were the rural missions undertaken by Jesuits and other religious on an increasingly systematic basis from the late sixteenth century, campaigns analysed with great insight by Louis Châtellier.[33] The aim of the missions, when teams of religious would visit a parish for a week or more, was to address the problems of ignorance and simplicity which allegedly hindered acceptance of the Faith, to provoke conversion of hearts, to reform manners and to introduce or consolidate new devotions. In a spirit less of scientific description than of a vainglorious desire to ape, at least rhetorically, their counterparts overseas, these missionaries commonly spoke of the European rural world as 'Our Indies'.[34] In the field, it is easy to

[32] Isidoro Moreno Navarro, a student of the rituals surrounding sacred images in modern Spain, has described communal festivals as constituting important 'signs of identification' for the community as a whole which celebrates them, but also as representing 'rituals of division' when regarded from within that community: Isidoro Moreno Navarro, 'Niveles de significación de los iconos religiosos y rituales de reproducción de identidad en Andalucía', in Pierre Cordoba and Jean-Pierre Etienvre, eds, *La fiesta, la ceremonia, el rito* (Granada, 1990), 91–103, at 95.

[33] Louis Châtellier, *The Religion of the Poor. Rural Missions in Europe and the Formation of Modern Catholicism, c.1500–1800* (Cambridge, 1997).

[34] Piotr Skarga, architect of the Jesuit mission in Poland, commented that there was no need to go to the exotic and remote Indies to find pagans and infidels to missionize, since 'Lithuania is a veritable India': Harro Höpfl, *Jesuit Political Thought. The Society of Jesus and the*

regard the blood-curdling sermons on death and Hell and the lavishly mounted penitential exercises which formed the centrepieces of such missions as emblematic of the Counter Reformation's disciplinary tendencies: as an adjunct to the tentacles of diocesan power, an extension of the confessional and a catechetical crammer. The Jesuits took it as axiomatic that leaders (such as themselves) led and the mass of the *rudi et imperiti* followed.[35] Yet to focus on the missions in terms purely of discipline risks a distortion, while more dubious still would be an assertion that the missionaries swallowed their own rhetoric and really saw their subjects as akin to pagans in need of Christianization, or that they genuinely believed that the European peasantry possessed a separate religious culture, or had no religion at all.

Nonetheless, condescension was a hallmark of the missionary approach and can be seen in the strategic manipulation of the emotions of the rural congregations. Above all, rhetorically provoked weeping was taken as indicating the successful assimilation of a reformist message and tears became the recognized lubricant of Counter-Reformation devotion. Juan Bautista Escardó (1581–1652), a renowned Jesuit preacher from Mallorca, gave advice on the tropes and gestures which the missionary could use to 'break down' his congregation:

> At the end of a sermon on death, some preachers like to take hold of a human skull. For the performance to work well, they first prepare their listeners with an *apparatus* [a short preface] and with a *coloquio*, as is done when using a sacred image; and later when they show it to the congregation, they use the figure of the *demonstración* [act of showing something and pointing to it so that the listeners can see it; and saying 'look'], and then the preacher puts various questions to it and makes it reply to the preacher and also talk to the congregation. And the questions asked by the preacher, to which he responds himself, relate first to his [the deceased's] body and then to his soul, asking what has become of the beauty of his face, what has become of his hair, his eyes, his ears and his tongue, what was his particular judgement and what sentence did the Supreme Judge give him? After the questions, they tell him to preach to the congregation and . . . describe the pains that he is

---

State, c.1540–1630 (Cambridge, 2004), 12; Henry Kamen notes that the same metaphor was applied by Spanish Jesuits to Asturias and Galicia in the sixteenth century: *The Phoenix and the Flame. Catalonia and the Counter Reformation* (New Haven, CT, 1993), 85.
[35] Höpfl, *Jesuit Political Thought*, 70.

suffering in hell and how much he regrets that he will have to endure them for ever. And then the preacher will say: 'Brothers, what this dead person has said he has not said on his own behalf, because he doesn't need to since now there is no escape for him. Rather, he has preached for our benefit. So, how can we profit from his sermon?'[36]

Escardó was clear that the impact of employing such special effects as skulls and crucifixes in a sermon depended on the fervour, talent and common sense of the preacher.[37] Not everyone, not even every Jesuit, had the knack. The seventeenth-century Polish cavalier, Jan Chryzostom Pasek, recorded in his laconic memoirs the bungled attempt of one Jesuit military chaplain to exhort his troops:

Father Dabrowski goes riding round and preaching to the other regiments, weeping more than talking, for such was his weakness that although not a bad preacher, each time he began to talk he broke down and wept, not finishing his sermons, and making people laugh.[38]

That the missionaries consciously altered their style and methods to suit their audience, adapting themselves 'to the people's capabilities', was no less a hallmark of their endeavours.[39] In the Jesuit missions in Germany, as elsewhere, this involved a sweetening of the disciplinary message by encouragement of local cultures of the miraculous, including endorsement of village pilgrimage shrines and the enthusiastic distribution of the above-mentioned Jesuit sacramentals, Ignatius-Water and Xavier-Water. During a mission in the Eiffel in 1736, for example, the Ignatius-Water which had been blessed by the missionaries was sprinkled by the peasants on their fields to exterminate a plague of caterpillars.[40]

---

[36] Félix Herrero Salgado, *La oratoria sagrada en los siglos XVI y XVII*, Vol. III (Madrid, 2001), 3: 404.

[37] Ibid., 3: 400.

[38] Catherine S. Leach, *Memoirs of the Polish Baroque. The Writings of Jan Chryzostom Pasek, a Squire of the Commonwealth of Poland and Lithuania* (Berkeley and Los Angeles, CA, and London, 1976), 15.

[39] David Gentilcore, ' "Adapt Yourselves to the People's Capabilities": Missionary Strategies, Methods and Impact in the Kingdom of Naples, 1600–1800', *JEH* 45 (1994), 269–94.

[40] Trevor Johnson, 'Blood, Tears and Xavier-Water: Jesuit Missionaries and Popular Religion in the Eighteenth-Century Upper Palatinate', in Scribner and Johnson, eds, *Popular Religion*, 183–202.

Although the missionaries took the positive results of such strategies (in the shape of more numerous and enthusiastic audiences) as vindication of their approach, their internal correspondence reveals a thirst for the miraculous as insatiable as that of any peasant. Indeed, rather than necessarily indicating distinct and antithetical sensibilities, the missions may be more usefully seen as revealing a shared religious culture. Moreover, even the macabre and blood-curdling penitential rituals may, from the villager's perspective if not the missionary's, have had something of a carnivalesque quality about them, overwhelming or subverting the superficial message of moral reform. Not that the result was always and everywhere a satisfying harmony, for the missions could leave heightened and debilitating fears in their wake. In August 1718 the priest of Zusmarshausen expressed relief that since the recent Jesuit mission his parishioners had kept 'from all grave sins'. However, he wrote:

> One thing concerns me greatly: many people who attended the sermons, people who I know have lived pure lives for twenty years, have been frightfully plagued, almost to despair, by the wickedness of the Devil and the sorcerers. They have terrible pains in their limbs, they cannot sleep or eat. As a result the Devil spreads calumnies and mockeries against the mission. By means of relics and blessings I have brought some amelioration.[41]

* * *

By the middle of the eighteenth century, 'Enlightenment' critique presented new challenges to elite and popular faith alike. Whilst the Spanish cleric, Benito Feijoo (1676–1764), lambasted the 'superstitions' of the *vulgo* in his works, ecclesiastical and secular authorities across Catholic Europe were busily suppressing pilgrimages and other manifestations of popular devotion, from motives of public order as much as from disdain for a deficient religious culture.[42] The religious orders too suffered from extensive sequestration and the Society of Jesus was suppressed. The two centuries of Counter Reformation which preceded

[41] Bernhard Duhr, 'Die kurpfälzischen und kurbayerischen Volkmissionen im 18. Jahrhundert', *Historisch-politische Blätter für das katholische Deutschland* 170 (1922), 510–26, 565–80, 637–55, here at 572–3.

[42] On the transformation of elite attitudes to pilgrimage, see Rebekka Habermas, *Wallfahrt und Aufruhr. Zur Geschichte des Wunderglaubens in der frühen Neuzeit* (Frankfurt, 1991).

the 'Enlightenment' enjoyed perhaps a less antagonistic relationship between the religious cultures of the Catholic world, reformist drives notwithstanding. In analysing these developments, the shortcomings of a historical model of religious change based on a single sharp polarity between elite and popular have already been pointed out. Clearly, we must be wary of rigid taxonomies that ascribe to such shorthand devices a fixed ontological reality. In so far as they can be discerned at all, the patterns of interaction are too complex for that, whilst it is only as 'relation', in the dynamic of encounter, confrontation, mutual misunderstanding, power struggle and tension, as well as in sharing, that such an analytical category can make any sense. Nonetheless, keeping in view some sort of distinction, however crudely defined, reminds us that the experience of religion is always embodied, and thus embedded, in differentiated situations, where many variables influence religious experience and practice. With an eye to what Bob Scribner called the 'situational dialectic', the relational approach offers ways into a richer understanding of the many processes within what is tradition-ally (and equally crudely) termed the Counter Reformation.[43] For a long time the movement was symbolized by a few key events such as the Council of Trent, the reign of Philip II, or the foundation of the Society of Jesus. Now, however, a particular, tangled relationship between elite and popular religiosity is also seen a defining character-istic. Recent research has suggested that far from imposing a uniformity of faith and practice and achieving a victory for narrow discipline and regulation, the movement's outcome was to foster diversity, within an overarching canopy of shared fundamental assumptions. Chief of these was a universal faith in the immanence of the divine, of the possibility at any moment of supernatural eruption into the earthly world. This was shared by all social groups and all sections of the church, but, because it was so integral to traditional popular practice, became over time to be especially associated with it. Perhaps a lament at the loss of a shared culture was at the back of the mind of a late-eighteenth-century biographer of the French missioner, Grignion de Montfort, when he pondered: 'would it not be desirable that as regards devotions, everyone should be like the people?'[44]

University of the West of England, Bristol

---

[43] Bob Scribner, 'Introduction', in Scribner and Johnson, eds, *Popular Religion*, 1–15.
[44] Châtellier, *The Religion of the Poor*, 182–3.

MARTIN MARPRELATE AND THE POPULAR VOICE*

by BRIAN CUMMINGS

THE curious career of 'Martin Marprelate, gentleman' is one of the most notorious and at the same time elusive episodes in the history of English puritanism, inspiring endless if largely futile speculation into the identity of its author.[1] Part literary canard, part political scandal, part detective story, for around a calendar year between October 1588 and September 1589, Martin and his associates kept one step ahead of the pursuivants and produced seven scurrilous tracts aimed at the ecclesiastical hierarchy. Adding spice to the story, their main targets, John Whitgift, archbishop of Canterbury, and John Aylmer, bishop of London, were also the officers empowered by the Star Chamber in 1586 both to examine religious dissidents and to supervise the press.[2] To keep up his cottage industry of satire and vilification, Marprelate moved his printing press from county to county (from Surrey to Northamptonshire to Warwickshire to Lancashire), from private dwelling to private dwelling, and turned the failure of his pursuers into further occasion for ridicule, insult, and his own popular triumph over adversity. Like a will o' the wisp, he could disappear into the bushes and then emerge in a printed book whenever he wanted. Even after the main part of the operation was broken up and the typeface destroyed, he managed to get out one final tractlet as a last snook at the authorities. And then, whereas the printmen were examined and tortured, and Whitgift went after the more serious elements of the presbyterian cause with relentless violence, Martin himself escaped entirely.[3] Possibly one or other of the men arrested, and in one or two

---

* I am very grateful to the Leverhulme Trust for the award of a Research Fellowship which enabled the writing of this piece; and also to Patrick Collinson and Alexandra Walsham for reading a draft with their customary erudition and wit.

[1] With nice humour, the *ODNB* has accorded to Marprelate (along with select other non-existent persons such as John Bull) his own entry (by Joseph Black, 36: 746–7). For the latest scholarship on the question of authorship, see also the entries in *ODNB* for John Penry (by Claire Cross, 43: 617–19) and Job Throckmorton (by Patrick Collinson, 54: 690–2).

[2] Cyndia Susan Clegg, *Press Censorship in Elizabethan England* (Cambridge, 1997), 58.

[3] A warrant for the torture of three individuals involved in the printing of the tracts was issued at Bridewell on 24 August 1589. See John H. Langbein, *Torture and the Law of Proof* (Chicago, IL, and London, 1977), 112–13.

cases executed, was Martin, but if so he was never identified as Martin and never confessed to the writing.[4] Marprelate remained ever the maverick. Thus began his second career, in afterlife, as historians both literary and ecclesiastical combed the records hundreds of years later to establish his identity. Once the Shakespearean industry got hold of him the inevitable farce ensued: not only known radicals like John Udall, John Penry and Job Throckmorton were placed in the conspiracy, but all the usual Elizabethan suspects, the earl of Oxford and even (on the wilder edges of fantasy) the Bard himself.

Such speculation has had the effect of obscuring the significance (whether literary or religious) of the seven scandalous tracts themselves, and of the plethora of written replies including ones probably by John Lyly, Thomas Nashe, and Gabriel Harvey.[5] Among the many issues raised by the tracts is a classic example of the problem of popular culture. Vulgar, even rollicking in style, Marprelate was denounced as the very opposite of a 'gentleman', yet his only known haunts were country houses, and his publication in private presses announced clearly private means. The copious depositions in the Marprelate examinations now preserved among the Harleian and Lansdowne papers at the British Library and the Ellesmere papers at the Huntington Library reveal plenty of ready money to finance Martin's operation. His first *Epistle* was produced from the secondary residence in East Molesey (near Kingston-upon-Thames) of an affluent widow, Mrs Crane, who ran what Patrick Collinson (with a Martinist wit of his own) has

---

[4] The examination of those found to be involved in the printing of the Marprelate tracts went on for longer than the controversy itself. Among those examined were Martin's patrons Sir Richard Knightley and John Hales, one of his printers, John Hodgkins, the book-binder Henry Sharpe, and several other associates. Robert Waldegrave the printer was released without indictment, as was Job Throckmorton, nowadays the main candidate as at least one of the 'Martins'. John Udall later died in prison while on charges unrelated to Marprelate. John Penry, who was identified as Martin by Thomas Nashe and others but who specifically and repeatedly denied the identification, was hanged in May 1593 for seditious writing, but not for the authorship of the Marprelate tracts. The transcriptions of various interrogatories and depositions in the Marprelate case made by Thomas Baker in 1716 (London, BL, MS Harley 7028 to 7050) are printed in Edward Arber, *An Introductory Sketch to the Martin Marprelate Controversy 1588–1590* (London, 1895), 81–104. Arber also reprints the Brief of the Attorney General, Sir John Puckering, 121–36.

[5] The treatises and anonymous replies are listed in STC 17453–17465. Also in Peter Milward, *Religious Controversies of the Elizabethan Age: a Survey of Printed Sources* (London, 1978), nos 318–20, 322, 327–9. The various forms of reply and counter-reply are listed in ibid., nos 321, 323–6, 330–33, 334–38, 339–40, 341–5, and more ancillary post-ripostes and re-visitations in nos 346–59.

described as a 'puritan salon' in London.[6] Martin then moved to the homes of a friend in the minor gentry, Sir Richard Knightley, and of one of his relatives, John Hales, a comfortable Coventry businessman. Martin's social conundrums do not end there. If he mixed in goodly, godly company, he splattered his writings with low jokes and the occasional mild blasphemy. In the words of Dover Wilson, the Shakespeare scholar, he was 'a puritan who had been born a stage clown, [and] a disciple both of Calvin and of Dick Tarleton'.[7]

At the same time, his louche, loud manners emerged from the same literary stable as housed highly learned, puritan divines. Similar social and theological ambiguities surround his other associates. Robert Waldegrave, the main printer involved, was heavily implicated in heterodox theological production, but he was a serious printer who later went on to gain King James's royal privilege in Edinburgh. In Scotland, one of his books was Sir Philip Sidney's impeccably gentrified *Countess of Pembroke's Arcadia* and another, curiously enough, an edition of poems by the Jesuit martyr Robert Southwell.[8] Into any rigid class-based mould, Martin simply will not fit. Caught between the gentry and the peasantry, chapel and marketplace, town and shires, and high and low Church, the Marprelate tracts are an eminently appropriate place to discuss the many strange misappropriations involved in elite and popular religion.

If Martin himself, whoever he was, mixed in very different and sometimes dodgy company, there is also the vexed question, from the point of view of elite and popular religion, of his readership. Who were the readers of Marprelate? The natural corollary of his low jokes seems to be low readers. The form of the pamphlets themselves suggests cheap print.[9] One of them, the third in order of production, is a one-page broadsheet.[10] With cheap print, apparently, come cheap and plentiful

---

[6] Patrick Collinson, *The Elizabethan Puritan Movement* (London, 1967), 393.

[7] J. Dover Wilson, 'The Marprelate Controversy', in A. W. Ward and A. R. Waller, eds, *The Cambridge History of English Literature, Vol. 3: Renascence and Reformation* (Cambridge, 1909), 383.

[8] *Saint Peters Complaint. With Other Poems* (Edinburgh: Robert Waldegrave, [1599]), STC 22960.

[9] The phrase 'cheap print' comes of course from Tessa Watt, *Cheap Print and Popular Piety, 1550–1640* (Cambridge, 1993). The fullest recent account of the Marprelate tracts in relation to contemporary pamphleteering is in Joad Raymond, *Pamphlets and Pamphleteering in Early Modern Britain* (Cambridge, 2003), 27–52.

[10] *Certaine Minerall/ and Metaphisicall Schoolpoints/ to be defended by the reuerende Bishops/ and the rest of my cleargie masters of the Conuocation house/ against both the vniuersities/ and al the reformed*

readers. Joseph Black, on the basis of the depositions, has estimated print runs of between 700 and 1000 copies.[11] Witnesses recalled paying prices between 6d and 9d, although in one case – perhaps for the broadsheet – only 2d. Humfrey Newman, a cobbler nicknamed 'Brownbread', charged with the distribution of the books published in Coventry, assiduously peddled them through the county and down to London.[12] They were sold from homes and under the counter in shops: however small in number or however stealthily read, they appeared to be everywhere.

Such at least was the fear of the authorities. During the first wave of examinations after the initial discoveries of Martin's mode of production, it was said in one deposition that the earl of Hertford, 'aboutt Easter last', was shown:

> a litle packett of writings or bookes, wch when ye Earle had seene, he willed the servante to tell his brother from him, that he liked not that course: addinge, that as they shoote at Bishoppes now, so will they doe at the Nobilitie also, if they be suffered.[13]

A radicalized plebeian readership rallying to the cause of separatist puritanism was one of the reasons expressed by Whitgift for feeling that the tracts represented a new and especially unruly form of puritan danger.[14] That the earl of Hertford was one of the readers of the tracts, however, suggests other routes of reception, not so easily classifiable. Parts of the tracts are aimed at theologically sophisticated readers, other parts seem expressly designed to offend them. In any case, jokes, while socially highly specific in their meaning, are notoriously difficult to pin down to one social audience. It is just possible, given the admittedly outlandish speculation that Lord Burghley had a sense of humour, that some of the passages quoted with such outrage by Whitgift in his frequent letters on the subject brought forth a little smirk of recognition from the old fox himself. Burghley characteristically swung both ways, playing the part (with whatever honesty) of lordly friend to Penry

---

Churches in Christendome. Wherin is layd open/ the very Quintessence of all Catercorner diuinitie ([Coventry: Robert Waldegrave, 1589]).

11 *ODNB*, 36: 747.

12 'Sir John Puckering's Brief against Humfrey Newman', in Arber, *Introductory Sketch to the Marprelate Controversy*, 131 (from London, BL, MS Harley 7042).

13 'Breife instructions touchinge the Printer and place of Printinge the .3. first bookes of Martin and ye Minerall Conclusions, all beinge printed in a Dutch letter', London, BL, MS Lansdowne 61, fol. 68r.

14 Whitgift to Lord Burghley, 24 August 1589, London, BL, MS Lansdowne 61, fol. 5v.

up to the day before his hanging.[15] The extent to which Marprelate entertained those whom he overtly attacked, and subverted those whom he overtly supported, is one of the many intriguing questions of literary effect which the tracts raise.

The Marprelate phenomenon thus confirms the insight, which goes back to the pioneering studies of pre-modern popular culture by Anton Gurevich, Natalie Zemon Davis and Peter Burke, that popular forms are often preserved through several intervening levels of acculturation.[16] Indeed, in many cases, as with many genres of medieval popular dance and song, the only surviving examples may occur in aristocratic or clerical sources.[17] In these circumstances any presumed divisions between 'popular' and 'elite', or 'simple' and 'learned', or 'high' and 'low', become difficult to maintain. In this essay my effort is to see how methods of understanding a so-called 'popular' literary culture – and the problems involved with them – may be applied to the interpretation of religious culture. The Marprelate case is an exceptionally fruitful example to take, as interesting and complicated an affair in bibliographical and stylistic terms as it is in terms of religious controversy and politics. However, the historiography of the Marprelate case also shows that the mutual infiltration of literary and religious history is still very much in its infancy.

It is immediately obvious that the Marprelate tracts have a divided audience, that they occupy a space between different audiences. Yet, as Peter Lake has recently argued in *The Antichrist's Lewd Hat*, Martin's audience is not only socially mixed, it is also constructed, one might say manufactured. Martin self-consciously addresses his audience through his work, and in the process summons an audience into being of his own making, effectively inventing his own audience. Lake argues that this is part of the political aim of the tracts: 'to construct and then invoke a body of "public", "godly" opinion in order to force the regime's hand'.[18] This makes the task of positioning Martin in relation

---

[15] Albert Peel, ed., *The Notebook of John Penry 1593*, Camden Society, 3rd ser. 67 (London, 1944), 62.

[16] Aron Gurevich, *Medieval Popular Culture: Problems of Belief and Perception*, Eng. tr. (Cambridge, 1988); Natalie Zemon Davis, *Society and Culture in Early Modern France* (Stanford, CA, 1975); Peter Burke, *Popular Culture in Early Modern Europe* (London, 1978).

[17] See John Stevens, *Words and Music in the Middle Ages* (Cambridge, 1986), 162 and 175; and Ardis Butterfield, *Poetry and Music in Medieval France* (Cambridge, 2002), 125–6 and 142–4.

[18] Peter Lake, with Michael Questier, *The Antichrist's Lewd Hat: Protestants, Papists and Players in Post-Reformation England* (New Haven, CT, and London, 2002), 506.

to elite and popular religion considerably more complex. Continuing from Lake's argument, we have to take several factors into account. Firstly, that Martin's reading public is not the same thing as some general public which we might construe as being available to read it, although interpreting a reading public may teach us something about the complexities of understanding a more 'general' public. Secondly, that Martin's work, like any literary work, has an imagined and implied audience as well as a real one. The intended audience of a literary work is therefore different from the milieu from which it is produced, and its actual audience or audiences may be different again. The imagined and real audiences of a work may sometimes be coterminous, and sometimes not, within the same work. An interesting corollary of this is that an imaginary reading public may have effects on the constitution of a 'real' public, just as much as the other way around. Furthermore, all of these questions about audience and a reading public also involve questions about meaning. For the meaning of a work is a different thing from its social process of composition or reception. In addition, a work may have more than one meaning; these meanings may be intended for different audiences; and yet unintended audiences may also pick up unintended meanings.

Nobody could find the writings of Martin easy to place, and not only because its authorship was hidden and its place of printing a secret. It is part of the fiction of the writings to disorient the implied relationship between author and reader. The famously fake colophons, such as on the title-page of the first of the tracts (the *Epistle*), 'Printed oversea in Europe within two furlongs of a Bounsing Priest at the cost and charges of M Marprelate gentleman', do more than make fun of the identifications of printer and place required by the censors.[19] They disrupt the decorum of meaning, so that Martin appears to be writing from nowhere, to no one in particular, or else to anyone he chooses. From the first moment, the reader is on the back foot, guessing Martin's next move. It is no easier to predict the direction of Martin's prose once the *Epistle* proper begins. Both the mode of address, and the identity of the addressee, change at will. Overtly, the *Epistle* is presented as a formal

---

[19]   *Oh read ouer D. John Bridges, for it is a worthy worke: Or an epitome of the fyrste Booke of that right worshipfull volume written against the Puritanes . . . Compiled . . . by the reuerend and worthie Martin Marprelate . . . The Epitome is not yet published but it shall be when the Bishops are at conuenient leysure to view the same. In the meane time let them be content with this learned Epistle* ([East Moseley: R. Waldegrave, 1588]) [hereafter: *Epistle*], A1r.

challenge 'To the right puisante/ and terrible Priests', but the lampooning style of such an address places it instead with another kind of reader entirely, over the heads of the priests or behind their backs, sniggering at the stream of jokes at the expense of 'your venerable masterdomes'.[20] Such a reader can be assumed to be a puritan in sympathies, indeed of the more radical and presbyterian sort, one who will not blanch at such sentiments as: 'and to be briefe/ all the Bb. in England/ wales/ and Ireland/ are pettie popes/ & pettie Antichristes' (A3v). Sometimes Martin appears to be addressing puritan readers directly; but then he will change tack in the next sentence, referring to the puritans in the third person as if he has nothing to do with them.

Martin is not always in control of these manoeuvres. His changes of voice and position can be so volatile that the prose becomes convoluted and opaque. Yet in this very volatility it is possible to see why Dover Wilson saw Martin as a precursor of Swift's *A Tale of a Tub*.[21] Like Swift, he keeps his readers constantly on edge, in the way that sentences go on just long enough for the reader to lose grip of the point only then for it to come back with a sudden kick. Or in the way it is unclear which direction a voice is coming from, whether it is authorized as Martin's, or who Martin is when he says it. Every so often, even the most sympathetic reader, agreeing readily with the flow of argumentation, and heady with the intoxicating pleasure of finding his worst enemies laid low by incessant satire, will nonetheless perhaps pull up short at the sheer violence of Martin's conclusions. Like all the best stand-up comics, Martin has a habit of taking his audience further than it wants to go, or further than it feels it should be allowed to go, even if it might want to. There is a fine line between Martin's popularizing prophetic railing and implicit sedition, as when he exclaims to the bishops: 'Do you think that you shalbe suffred any longer/ to break the law of God/ and to tyrannize ouer his people her Maiesties subiectes?' (F1v). It is a line Martin's readers will perhaps be less ready to cross. Remarks akin to this, since it implies active redress being sought against the official religion, were indeed extracted and used in indictments during this decade.[22]

[20] Ibid., A2r. Further references in text.

[21] Dover Wilson, 'The Marprelate Controversy', 398. The comparison is made in more extended fashion by R. A. Anselment, *'Betwixt Jest and Earnest': Marprelate, Milton, Marvell, Swift and the Decorum of Religious Ridicule* (Toronto, 1979).

[22] See for instance the extracts from the writings of John Penry cited against him in his indictment for 'seditious writing' in 1593, printed in Sir Edward Coke, *Booke of Entries* (London: A. Islip, 1614), pp. 352v–353v.

Yet almost as dangerous for the reader are moments of apparent levity. One of the funniest anecdotes in the first tract concerns the priest Sir Geoffrey Jones of Warwickshire, whose habit was to resort to an alehouse in the morning. Either after one drink too many or because he owes so much money to his gambling friends, he makes an oath never to go to the alehouse again. Sir Geoffrey's unaccustomed vow of sobriety causes him great distress and physical discomfort, but Martin wryly adds, 'I thinke the tap had great quietnes and ease thereby'.[23] At this point a Chaucerian turn comes in the narrative. Sir Geoffrey satisfies both his vow and his desperate craving for a drink by coming up with the ruse that if he gets someone to carry him to the alehouse he won't break his oath. However, as with Chaucer, the narrator quickly becomes complicit in the matter under narration. Martin shows both in his style of humour and in his range of reference a familiar acquaintance with drinking houses, gaming parlours, card-tables and bowling. At least one or two of his stories appear to come from prostitutes. Not unlike Lucio in *Measure for Measure*, Martin establishes his popular credentials (showing himself to be one of the lads) while denouncing the bishops for indulging in the same. For the reader, too, comes the same danger of guilt by association. Too much pleasure at the punch line manifests too much knowledge of where the joke is coming from. Marprelate puts his readers in this kind of bind all the time, especially since the style veers so widely and so suddenly, apparently without control. As a consequence, a reader never has any assurance about the limits of tolerance involved in identifying with the matter in front of him. He cannot know when he will next be compelled to mix with the lower orders, perhaps (perish the thought) might start feeling the same things as them. Martin, meanwhile, can mix it with anybody, which is exactly what makes him so attractive and so dangerous.

What are the political implications of Martin's improvisatory style, his furious blarney and rock-and-roll puritanism? Collinson's classic account places Marprelate at a moment of crisis in the presbyterian movement in 1588, as the defeat of the Armada reduced the need for compromise, and death intervened to remove both the puritans' grandest patron Leicester (and shortly Mildmay and Walsingham, too) and their most skilful popular advocate, John Field. The Marprelate tracts are a symptom of a sense of incipient apocalypse – heralding

---

[23] *Epistle*, F2v.

either unexpected miraculous success or gloriously defiant but cata-strophic failure – and of the desperation that went with it. Collinson calls the tracts an outlet for a 'mood of angry frustration on the extremist fringe of the movement'.[24] At the same time, Collinson finds Marprelate's resort to popular comedy, what Martin himself calls his 'merie vaine', intrinsic to his political message.[25] Comedy is not mere chaff to the kernel of Calvinist theology. Richard Bancroft, at this time Whitgift's chaplain, was careful to commission comedians as well as theologians in reply, using professional wits and stage-players who were not the usual recipients of Lambeth patronage. Collinson shows how Martin's comedy is also related to the discovery of the Marprelate press, and, at least indirectly, to the downfall of the puritan movement which followed. In the penultimate tract, *Martin Senior*, in a typically extravagant comic invention, Martin provides cod instructions for the pursuivants to follow in sniffing the Martinists out. He tells them to 'go into Northampton and Warwickeshires' and 'to keepe watch and warde for Sharpe and Penry, and if they can take them, let them bring them vp'.[26] Perhaps it is hubris, perhaps it is a sign that the game was already up: *Martin Senior* was published in July 1589, and Henry Sharpe, the book-binder who first stitched Marprelate and then stitched him up, was among those examined within the next month. He was in Penry's pay, although Penry later absolved him of any blame for blabbing to the enforcers. Penry's Northampton house was raided in turn in January 1590, although the man himself kept out of harm's way until his trial and execution in 1593. In the wake of these arrests came a series of trials of presbyterians who had nothing whatsoever to do with Martin or his texts. Whether or not Martin provided the lead which betrayed them to the authorities, his writing appears in retrospect like a loose cannon, which left clearer forensic traces for Bancroft and others to follow than did the pursed lipped writings of the uptight theologians of the clan-destine presbyterian classes.

Among literary commentators, Lorna Hutson has suggested that it was Martin's style as much as his content that caused political offence: Whitgift's instinct was that satire was politically more dangerous than

24 Collinson, *Elizabethan Puritan Movement*, 391.
25 *Epistle*, E4r.
26 *The iust censure and reproofe of Martin Junior. Wherein the rash and vndiscreete headines of the foolish youth, is sharply mette with, and the boy hath his lesson taught him, I warrant you, by his reuerend and elder brother Martin Senior, sonne and heire vnto the renowmed Martin Mar-prelate the Great* ([Wolston: J. Hodgkins, 1589]), A4v. Hereafter *Martin Senior*.

high theology.[27] Cyndia Clegg, in her characteristically downbeat style, demurs, playing down the political significance of Martin's dissentient style and perhaps more justly finding, in Hutson's assumption that satire is more daring and dangerous than theology, a literary critic's careless prejudice.[28] It is Lake, a religious historian, however, who makes the greatest claims for the political significance of Martin's comedy. The Marprelate tracts constitute a distinctive intervention in what might be called the politics of style. Up to this point, the presbyterian movement had consciously represented itself in a high, learned, academic manner. This self-representation had a political meaning: the presbyterians were not political subversives, as Whitgift claimed, but part of the central protestant legacy, the long reformation of the papist past. They sought refinement of the established religion, not a further religious revolution. Martin speaks by contrast in a quite different voice. Although John Field, Thomas Norton and John Stubbes had previously orchestrated (under Burghley's and Leicester's clientage, in part) popular campaigns in a puritan cause, Martin's populist rhetoric, Lake says, comes out of the blue. In literary terms this is not quite true. Martin has his forebears in the polemical tracts and ballads of the Henrician, Marian and Edwardian reigns, in the *Plowman's Tale* and the *Pilgrim's Tale*, in some of the work of (later Bishop) John Ponet; also (in his use of dialogue) in the more serious tradition that runs in divergent paths from Thomas More right up to Martin's associate, Udall. It is tempting to find some obscure ancestry in that greatest of all English alliterated radicals, Piers Plowman himself, whose printer, Robert Crowley, at a later date visited Field and Wilcox in Newgate in 1573.[29] Lake's argument that Martin's abandonment of an elite for a popular mode of literature represents some serious form of style wars, however, merits some further commentary.

This requires a closer examination of what we might call Marprelate's popular voice. So far I have been concerned with discussing the tracts in terms of their reception, their implied and perhaps real audience. Finally, I wish to turn to the identity of Martin as author. Not, I hasten to add, in terms of who he really was: if Collinson says he does not know for certain, then I think we can safely say no one does.[30] The

---

[27] *Thomas Nashe in Context* (Oxford, 1989), 200–1.

[28] *Press Censorship*, 193.

[29] For Crowley's puritan connections, see Collinson, *Elizabethan Puritan Movement*; the visit to Newgate is described at 121.

[30] Patrick Collinson, 'Literature and the Church', in David Loewenstein and Janel Mueller, eds, *The Cambridge History of Early Modern English Literature* (Cambridge, 2002), 390.

much more interesting question of identity is that which is implicated in Martin's voice in the text. Who is Martin, there? The answer is, maybe, that Martin Marprelate himself does not know who Martin Marprelate is. He is not at all the simple demagogue that Lake is in danger of making him sound like. He chatters to himself, he swears, he rants, he makes pranks. Yet he also reads Greek, quotes freely from the Bible, is trained in logic as well as being expert in chop logic. He can do the high style as well as the low. Just as he seems to write in between different audiences, now to the bishops, now to the commons, now to the puritans, now to the gentry, so it is not true to talk in terms of Martin's style so much as his styles, his mixed modes, his double plots. Martin's prose revels in this prolix form of polyvalency, indeed comments on it self-reflexively, as when he compiles a spoof catalogue of his own collected works: 'First my Paradoxes, 2. my Dialogues, 3. my Miscelanea, 4. my Variae leciones, 5. Martins dreame, 6. Of the liues and doings of English popes, 7. my Itinerarium, or visitiations, 8. my Lambathismes'.[31]

Furthermore, there is more than one Martin. Some of this proliferation of split personalities and voices could be a cover for multiple authorship. The circumstances of production may have made more than one author necessary, and the constraints of censorship and persecution certainly made it convenient. This can be observed in the in-joke which announces the *Theses Martinianae* as the product of 'a prety stripling of his, Martin Junior'.[32] *The iust censure and reproofe*, which follows in the series, is likewise declared to be penned 'by his reuerend and elder brother Martin Senior, sonne and heire vnto the renowmed Martin Mar-prelate the Great'.[33] As if to pre-empt the debate about authorship that the tracts were destined to provoke, they ascribe to themselves a genealogy of three separate authors, yet all with the same name, on their very title pages. Yet multiple authorship is also an aspect of comic style. Martin is a split personality from the start, within the text of the *Epistle* and thereafter. He refers to himself in the first, second, and third persons, in the singular and the plural. There is a Martin in every shire and every village: he is simply 'the Metropolitane

---

Collinson argues that the issue of authorship is beside the point, and that in any case a 'syndicate' may be a better term for the texts' origin.

[31] *Epistle*, F2r.

[32] *Theses Martinianae: That is, Certaine demonstrative Conclusions . . . Published and set foorth . . . by . . . Martin Junior* ([Wolston: J. Hodgkins, 1589]), A1r. Hereafter *Martin Junior*.

[33] *Martin Senior*, A1r.

of al the Martins in England'.[34] If Martin is hanged, 'there wil 20. Martins spring in my place'.[35]

There is an appeal in this to the idea of Martin as Everyman, as the sheer embodiment of the popular voice. In the preface to the second of the tracts, the *Epitome*, this notion begins to go to his head:

> I am fauored of all estates (the puritans onely excepted.) I haue bene entertayned at the Court: Euery man talkes of my worship. Manye would gladly receiue my bookes/ if they coulde tell where to finde them.[36]

Marprelate here is a synecdoche for a kind of public that the government fears is all too real. Martin claims to be able to impersonate in himself public opinion as a whole, of any class or any part of the public spectrum. Of course this is a fiction, but it is a fiction which relates to the history of early modern religion, and especially the religion of Protestants, in interesting ways. Ever since Luther's 'priesthood of all believers', there was a means available of imagining the religious laity in terms that were separate from any particular social location. Especially to a group such as the godly puritans, this offered a way of reaching out directly to its public, bypassing the local and hierarchical networks mapped out by parishes and dioceses. Again, from Luther on, the most natural way of imagining and hence appealing to this public was via the printed book. In some contexts, the idea of a reading public could thus replace or else become identical with the religious community. The political implications of this are obvious. An appeal through readership was a way of obviating the authority of the prince or the bishop: it created a religion without walls, without boundaries.

This gives Whitgift another reason to hate Martin, as well as personal pique. This is in some ways worse than political presbyterianism, it is a kind of presbyterianism of the printed page. For Martin is a highly sensitive register of his public, and of the power and procedure of the literary act. One of the reasons why everybody else as well as he exaggerated his importance was that he knew and openly declared the power of the printed book as a cultural agent. Yet of course Martin did

---

34 *Oh read ouer D. John Bridges, for it is worthy worke: Or an epitome of the fyrste Booke of that right worshipfull volume written against the Puritanes . . . Compiled . . . by the reuerend and worthie Martin Marprelate* ([Fawsley: Robert Waldegrave, 1588]), A2r. Hereafter *Epitome*.
35 *Hay any worke for Cooper: or a briefe Pistle directed by waye of an hublication to the reuerende Bysshops* ([Coventry: Robert Waldegrave, 1589]), D3v.
36 'To all the Cleargie masters wheresoeuer', Preface to *Epitome*, A2r.

exaggerate his importance: his voice died with his press. His public was nowhere near so united as he imagined it. There is a hint of this in his comment that he is 'fauored of all estates (the puritans only excepted.)'. In the reference to the opprobrium of the puritans, sidelong though it is, we sense that Martin's popular voice is fractured within itself, divided against itself and potentially uncertain of itself. Martin is the mediator, the chameleon, who panders to his public, merges with it, identifies with it – but who also alienates, infuriates and disturbs it. It is hard to find a single puritan who does not disown Martin, at least in public. Thomas Cartwright testified to his 'great misliking and grief for so naughty and disorderly a curse as that was'.[37] Even John Penry declared that 'I dislyked many thinges in Marten for his maner, & for his matter of writing'.[38] Such disavowals are hardly straightforward either: Penry made his from prison, in the course of denying to Burghley that he was Martin, as had been claimed. Penry had every reason to dissemble, and he must have known from the evidence weighed up against him that it was well established that he had aided and abetted Martin, indeed lived in the same house, over several months. Even his disclaimer, 'I aunswer y^t my name is Iohn Penri and not Marten Marprelat' (fol. 29v) is capable of being deciphered as a Martinian irony. Job Throckmorton, in a printed defence of himself in 1594 against the accusations of Matthew Sutcliffe, adopted a similarly equivocal line: 'I am not Martin, I knewe not Martin'.[39]

Martin himself in his printed voice was a past master at avowals and disavowals of his own person. One of his most original and brilliant techniques is his capacity for ironic self-reference:

> I am not disposed to iest in this serious matter. I am called Martin Marprelat. There be many that greatly dislike of my doinges. I may haue my wants I know. For I am a man. But my course I knowe to be ordinary and lawfull.[40]

Martin's tone here in *Hay any worke for Cooper* is defensive. Yet as well as an apologia for his own work he begins in the same paragraph to offer an outline of a theory of his own satirical method:

---

[37] *A brief Apologie of Thomas Cartwright against all such slanderous accusations as it pleaseth Mr. Sutcliffe in seuerall pamphlettes most iniuriously to loade him with* (London, 1596), C2v.

[38] Penry, draft of a letter to Burghley, May (?) 1593, San Marino, CA, Huntington Library, MS Ellesmere 483, fol. 30v.

[39] *The Defence of Job Throkmorton against the Slaunders of Maister Sutcliffe*, E2.

[40] *Hay any worke for Cooper*, C4v.

I sawe the cause of Christs gouernment/ and of the Bishops Antichristian dealing to be hidden. The most part of men could not be gotten to read any thing / written in the defence of the on and against the other. I bethought mee therefore/ of a way whereby men might be drawne to do both/ perceiuing the humors of men in these times (especially of those that are in any place) to be giuen to mirth. I tooke that course. I might lawfully do it, I/ for iesting is lawful by circumstances/ euen in the greatest matters.[41]

In a way that is remarkable for a sixteenth-century English text, Martin interrupts the joking for a moment to provide a philosophical justification for his jokes. He uses arguments which are reminiscent of Latin humanist defences of comedy going back to Erasmus's *Encomium Moriae*: his folly functions as 'a couert/ wherin I would bring the truth into light' (C4v).[42] He provides, too, a social rationale: 'mirth' is an especially effective device in relation to the educated elite ('those that are in any place').

Martin's moral seriousness at this moment comes as a jolt, as another example of his juxtaposition of divergent styles. As a result, it only gradually appears out of the shadows that Martin here (for once) means what he says:

My purpose was and is to do good. I know I haue don no harme howsoeuer som may iudg Martin to mar al. They are very weake ons that so think. In that which I haue written I know vndoubtedly/ that I haue done the Lord and the state of this kingdom great seruice. Because I haue in som sort/ discouered the greatest enemies thereof.[43]

At the same time as this uncharacteristically quiet dignity, however, is a sense of the bafflement that he has caused – and his own bafflement that the misunderstanding has been quite so complete. The unusually pompous reproachfulness of Martin's assertion that he has 'done the Lord and the state of this kingdom great seruice' belies the realization that his readers have largely failed to see it that way, even those who regard themselves as on the same side of the argument. It is as if Martin is master of his public and at the same time its slave, and it is not at all

---

41 Ibid.

42 For examples of Renaissance arguments connecting comedy with theology, see M. A. Screech, *Laughter at the Foot of the Cross* (Harmondsworth, 1997).

43 Hay any worke for Cooper, C4v.

clear at points like this who is gulling whom. For there is the most extraordinary sincerity involved in Martin's artifice, and he cannot bear to see how playing the fool in a just and honest cause nonetheless endangers and enfeebles him just as it gives him his greatest power and fame. In his creation of a new popular voice, Martin himself was its first and most spectacular victim. Popular culture was the undoing as it had been the making of him.

University of Sussex

DIVINE IDEA AND 'OUR MOTHER': ELITE AND POPULAR UNDERSTANDING IN THE CULT OF OUR LADY OF GUADALUPE OF MEXICO*

by D. A. BRADING

IN 1648 the creole elite of Mexico City was enthralled to learn that in December 1531 the Virgin Mary had appeared to a poor Indian and had miraculously imprinted on his cape the likeness of herself, which was still venerated in the chapel at Tepeyac just outside the city limits. The moment was opportune, since in 1622 Archbishop Juan Pérez de la Serna had completed the construction of a new sanctuary devoted to Our Lady of Guadalupe and in 1629 the image had been brought to the cathedral in a vain attempt to lower the flood waters that engulfed the capital for four years. In effect, *Image of the Virgin Mary, Mother of God of Guadalupe* (1648) was a heartfelt response to the growth in devotion to the Mexican Virgin; and its author, Miguel Sánchez, wrote as if inspired by a particular revelation, since his only guides were oral tradition and the stimulus of other apparition narratives. A creole priest, renowned for his piety, patriotism and great learning, Sánchez appears to have modelled his account on Murillo's history of Our Lady of Pilar and her apparition at Zaragoza to St James, which is to say, to Santiago, the patron saint of Spain. When the Virgin appeared at Tepeyac to Juan Diego, she addressed the Indian in these terms:

> You should know, son, that I am the Virgin Mary, Mother of the true God. I want a house and a chapel, a church to be built for me, in which to show myself a merciful Mother to you and yours, to those devoted to me and to those who seek me in their necessities.[1]

In both these narratives, the Virgin not merely appears, but also

* This paper in part summarizes material and arguments presented in my *Mexican Phoenix. Our Lady of Guadalupe: Image and Tradition across Five Centuries* (Cambridge, 2001).

[1] Miguel Sánchez, *Imagen de la Virgen María, Madre de Dios de Guadalupe, milagrosamente aparecida en la ciudad de México. Celebrada en su historia, con la profecía del capítulo doce del Apocalipsis* (Mexico, 1648). All references are to *Testimonios históricos guadalupanos*, ed. Ernesto de la Torre Villar and Ramiro Navarro de Anda (Mexico, 1982), which provides the first complete re-edition of the original text; see here 177–81.

bequeaths an image of herself. Moreover, Sánchez noted that 'Diego' was Juan's *sobrenombre*, a term which can be taken to imply that the Indian was the Santiago of Mexico.[2]

These developments may be placed in a wider context. In *Likeness and Presence* (1994), Hans Belting asserted that the cult of holy images in Western Europe experienced a profound crisis in the sixteenth century. On the one hand, the Protestant Reformation unleashed a 'revolutionary iconoclasm', in which all representations of the saints, angels, Mary and the Holy Trinity were cleared from churches on the grounds that the devotion they attracted was a form of idolatry. On the other hand, the Renaissance introduced the primacy of aesthetic values, so that representations now expressed the quality of the artist's inspiration and talent. The Virgins painted by Raphael and Murillo thus evoked admiration for their beauty; they rarely, if ever, became the object of a particular cult. If this dual challenge of the Reformation and Renaissance did not destroy all devotion, it was because, so Belting argues, the clergy actively promoted the cult of ancient images, renovating and rebuilding their sanctuaries, and publishing accounts both of their miraculous origins and of cures performed through their influence. In effect, such images were relics from an earlier age and their renewed prominence signified a fossilization of devotion.[3]

To understand the force of Belting's argument, it should be noted that he traces the role of holy images in Christian worship from their appearance in the Eastern Church during the sixth and seventh centuries. Moreover, he observes that in both the Greek and Latin Churches a distinction emerged between images which simply represented their heavenly originals, and images which possessed a sacred power or presence and hence received a particular devotion. These cult images often came to possess their own sanctuaries and became renowned for the miraculous cures they performed. All this, of course, is a phenomenon familiar to any student of the Spanish Church. However, there is little evidence of any crisis in this devotion during the sixteenth century and Belting's implicit chronology cannot be readily applied to the Iberian Peninsula. Most of the great holy images of Spain, as distinct from the relics of Santiago at Compostella, only became the objects of widespread devotion during the fourteenth

---

[2] At this time the term *sobrenombre* could indicate an epithet, a title or a surname.
[3] Hans Belting, *Likeness and Presence: a History of the Image before the Era of Art*, trans. Edmund Japhcott (Chicago, IL, 1994), 458–9, 471–4.

century and their cult continued unabated until at least the late eighteenth century. Moreover, in Seville, for example, it was during the late sixteenth and early seventeenth centuries that the confraternities commissioned the images of Christ in his Passion and of his sorrowing Mother, which to the present day are carried through the streets of the city during Holy Week.[4] These images can certainly be esteemed as artistic masterpieces; but their purpose was to evoke intense devotion. And what of America? Where does Our Lady of Guadalupe of Mexico fit into Belting's thesis? In effect, the conquest and settlement of the New World led to the emergence of a great number of miraculous images of Christ and the Virgin Mary, which soon came to possess their own sanctuaries and at times become patrons of cities and kingdoms.

The reaction of the Universal Church when confronted with the challenge of iconoclasm, be it in the eighth or sixteenth century, was to endorse the traditional veneration of images but also to warn the faithful of the danger of idolatry. In 787, the Seventh General Church Council, the second held at Nicaea, strongly commended the veneration offered to images of Christ, the Virgin Mary, saints and angels.[5] When the Roman Church was accused of promoting idolatry by the Protestant reformers, its reaction was slow and hesitant. But in session 25 of the Council of Trent (1545–63) the tradition was re-affirmed, albeit accompanied by a strong warning against superstition and a demand that bishops regulate the cult in their diocese. The Council's decree echoed the teaching of Nicaea:

> And they must also teach that images of Christ, the virgin mother of God and the other saints should be set up and kept, particularly in churches, and that due honour and reverence is owed to them, not because some divinity or power is believed to lie in them as reason for the cult, or because anything is to be expected from them, or because confidence should be placed in images as was done by pagans of old; but because the honour showed to them is referred to the original which they represent: thus through the images which we kiss and before which we uncover our heads and go down on our knees, we give adoration to Christ and veneration

---

4   William A. Christian Jr., *Apparitions in Late Medieval and Renaissance Spain* (Princeton, NJ, 1981), 12–41; Juan Miguel González Gómez and José Roda Peña, *Imaginería processional de la Semana Santa de Sevilla* (Seville, 1992), *passim*; Susan Verdi Webster, *Art and Ritual in Golden Age Spain* (Princeton, NJ, 1998), 12–41.

5   *Decrees of the Ecumenical Councils*, ed. Norman Tanner, 2 vols (London, 1990), 1: 135–6.

to the saints whose likeness they bear. And this has been approved by the decrees of councils, especially the second council of Nicaea, against the iconoclasts.[6]

Thus the Church Fathers assembled at Trent denied any suggestion that 'some divinity or power' might reside in holy images.

The decrees and declarations of Church Councils are one thing, the life and practices of the Christian people are quite another. Within the Latin Church there existed a select number of holy images housed in sanctuaries dedicated to them, which attracted pilgrims from afar, acted as patrons of cities and provinces, and were imbued with a numinous power or presence sufficient to generate spiritual relief and even phys-ical cures among the faithful who came to pray. How were these cults justified and indeed encouraged? To start with, Catholic churchmen drew upon the teachings of the Greek Fathers and, in particular, on those theologians who had defended holy images from the onslaughts of the iconoclastic campaigns of the eighth century. Had not St John Damascene demonstrated that the Church had employed holy icons since its first years? To deny the possibility, and indeed the desirability, of representations of Jesus Christ was to deny his very humanity and hence to reject the reality of his Incarnation as true man and true God. On a philosophical plane, St John framed 'the Great Chain of Images', which descended by stages from the Trinity itself, where the Son was the image of the Father, to the most simple icon. And if the Holy Spirit was thought to dwell in the saints, it was clear that he also remained close to their tombs and images, not to mention the icons of Christ and his Mother.[7] At much the same time, St Theodore of Studios argued that an icon was like the shadow of its heavenly prototype, or, to change the metaphor, it resembled a likeness stamped on wax. In scholastic vein, he asserted that 'Christ is the prototype of his image . . . the artifi-cial image is the same as its archetype in likeness, but different in essence . . . It is not the essence of the image we venerate', which was to say, the canvas and paint, 'but the form of the prototype which is stamped on it . . . the image has one form with its prototype; therefore they have the one veneration'.[8] No matter how distant or faint, icons

[6] Ibid., 2: 774–6.

[7] For the concept of the 'Great Chain of Images', see Jaroslav Pelikan, *Imago Dei: the Byzantine Apologia for Icons* (New Haven, CT, 1990), 159–76.

[8] St Theodore the Studite, *On the Holy Icons*, trans. Catherine P. Roth (Crestwood, NY, 1981), 47, 100–10.

thus possessed something of the power and presence of their heavenly originals. In the sixteenth century the works of these two theologians were translated into Latin and published in many editions across the Catholic world, their arguments invoked to justify and promote the cult of holy images.

But there was available in the hispanic world another, albeit heterodox, justification of miraculous images. It was to be found in the *Nova Apocalypsis*, a book of revelations written by Blessed Amadeus of Portugal, Joannes Menesius da Silva (1431–82), a Franciscan visionary and reformer, who began his career as a monk in the Jeronymite monastery of Our Lady of Guadalupe.[9] In his manuscript, which circulated after his death, it was the eighth and last 'rapture' that is significant for our purpose, since he here portrayed Mary as informing the apostles that she would be 'bodily present' in her holy images until the end of the world, and that her presence would be demonstrated by the miracles she performed through them.[10] Although Amadeus's writings were condemned in Rome as heretical, in Spain, Antonio Ortiz, a Franciscan of the San Gabriel province, wrote a commentary on the *Nova Apocalypsis*, which included all or a great part of the manuscript. In 1543, St Peter of Alcántara, who succeeded Ortiz as provincial of San Gabriel, testified that the text of this translation had been considered by the cardinal archbishop of Seville, Alonso Manrique, the chief inquisitor of Spain, whose theologians found nothing in it to cause scandal.[11] In effect, the reformed branch of the Franciscans in Castile accepted and endorsed the doctrine that Mary was present in her cult images.

Most images in Spain which worked miracles were endowed with either an apostolic or a miraculous origin. Our Lady of Guadalupe, for example, had been sculpted by St Luke and thereafter sent by Pope Gregory to San Leandro, the archbishop of Seville, only then to be hidden in Extremadura following the Moorish invasion, its whereabouts finally revealed to a poor herdsman by the Virgin Mary herself.[12] The most striking of these apparition narratives took the form of twin treatises on the sanctuary of Our Lady of Pilar and the excellencies of

---

[9]   Ana Morisi-Guerra, 'The *Apocalypsis Nova*: a Plan for Reform', in Majorie Reeves, ed., *Prophetic Rome in the High Renaissance Period: Essays* (Oxford, 1992), 27–50, 129–83.

[10]   For the 'eighth rapture', see below at n. 29.

[11]   Arcángel Barrado Manzano, *San Pedro de Alcántara. Estudio documentado y crítico de su vida* (Caceres, 1995), 36–8, 183–4; Ramón Mujica Pinilla, *Angeles apócrifos en la América virreinal* (2nd edn, Lima, 1996), 55–79.

[12]   Christian, *Apparitions*, 87–94.

the city of Zaragoza, published in 1616 by Diego Murillo, a Franciscan chronicler, whose devotion was matched by his ebullient patriotism. To start with, he cited Hierocles as saying that 'the patria is a God and the first and principal parent' for its citizens, so that the obligation to serve one's country 'is so old that it starts with nature and is more compelling . . . than that which we owe to the parents who bore us'.[13] With such sentiments, it is not surprising that he celebrated the laws and institutions of both Zaragoza and the kingdom of Aragon. But he also insisted that St James, the son of Zebedee, had preached the gospel in Zaragoza and had named its first bishop. Moreover, while in the city, the Virgin Mary appeared to him, standing on a column of jasper, and said to him: 'Son Diego, I am your protector . . . build me a church in my name . . . I shall work wonderful signs, especially to help those who in their necessity come to this place'.[14] Before departing, the Virgin left a small wooden statue of herself, crowned, with the child Jesus in her arms, standing on a column, and promised St James that 'until the end of the world I shall preserve this pillar in the place where it now stands'.[15]

The theological implications of this narrative were all important. Not merely was Zaragoza signalized as a bishopric whose foundation was preceded only by the sees of Jerusalem and Antioch, it also figured as the city where 'there thus began the holy use of images so agreeable to God'.[16] Careful to note that the Council of Trent had taught that the purpose of images was to awaken devotion to their heavenly originals through lively representation, nevertheless, Murillo asserted that in Zaragoza it had been the Virgin herself who had introduced the cult of her image. Moreover, he recalled that St John Damascene had claimed that images had been venerated since the first days of the Church and insisted that 'God is accustomed to work through images, which are also books and preach silently to us and at times with greater effect than by writings'.[17] Murillo concluded on a patriotic note by affirming that Christ had 'entrusted the Church to St Peter, his Mother to St John, and Spain to St James: the three most beloved things'.[18]

---

[13] Diego Murillo, *De las excelencias de la insigne y nobilísima ciudad de Zaragoza* (Barcelona, 1616), 1–3, 8–15, 32.
[14] Diego Murillo, *Fundación milagrosa de la capilla angélica y apostólica de la Madre de Dios del Pilar* (Barcelona, 1616), 1–13, 67–9.
[15] Ibid., 258, 272–3.
[16] Ibid., 273.
[17] Ibid., 133.
[18] Ibid., 61–5.

* * *

The excitement aroused by Miguel Sánchez's *Image of the Virgin Mary* can be observed in the comment of his censor, Pedro de Rozas, an Augustinian friar, who praised Sánchez, since 116 years after the apparitions, 'he took up his pen, so that which we only knew from tradition without distinction, we now understand circumstantially and defined with authority and principle'.[19] In effect, the creole clergy were here confronted not with any simple narrative designed to stir the piety of the faithful, but instead were obliged to grapple with a dense, convoluted text, filled with citations from Scripture and the Church Fathers. From the outset, Sánchez presented himself as a disciple of St Augustine, observing that 'in matters of importance I do not know how to act or to speak other than by the hand and tongue of St Augustine'.[20] In particular, he took from the African saint the employment of typological exegesis, magnifying and interpreting the figures and scenes of his narrative by comparison and identification with figures and scenes of the Old and New Testaments. Writing in an exalted strain, as if inspired by the discovery, he invited his readers to perceive the likeness between the Virgin of Guadalupe and the Woman of chapter twelve of the Apocalypse, and indeed asserted that the Woman seen in vision by St John the Evangelist on Patmos bore the likeness of the Mexican Virgin. There was thus an identity 'in the image of heaven by prophecy and, in the image of earth, the copy by miracle'.[21] Moreover, since the Woman of the Apocalypse had been traditionally interpreted as a type or figure of both Mary and the Church, it followed that Mary's apparition in New Spain marked the foundation of the Mexican Church. It was thus the Mother of God who 'prepared, disposed and contrived her exquisite likeness in this her Mexican land, which was conquered for such a glorious purpose, won that there should appear so Mexican an image'.[22]

As usually employed in the seventeenth century, scriptural typology consisted of little more than a metaphorical comparison as, for example, when Charles V was compared to King David and Philip II to Solomon. So too, when Sánchez depicted the conquest of Mexico as a holy war in which Cortés and his companions 'enjoy the title of an

---

[19] *Testimonios históricos*, 153–5.
[20] Ibid., 259–60.
[21] Ibid., 158.
[22] Ibid., 164.

army of angels' engaged in the destruction of Satan's 'imperial monarchy with seven crowns',[23] he framed a metaphorical comparison with St Michael's role in the Apocalypse. But, in his account of the Virgin's apparitions, he modelled the narrative on the encounters of Moses with the Almighty at Horeb and on Mount Sinai and thereby converted Juan Diego into the Mexican personification of the Hebrew patriarch. Twice the Virgin despatched the Indian to inform Juan de Zumárraga, the Franciscan archbishop of Mexico, that she wished to have a chapel built at Tepeyac, and twice the bishop rebuffed him. The Virgin then instructed Juan Diego to ascend Mount Tepeyac and gather flowers and roses in his cape and present them to Zumárraga as a sign. But, when he opened his cape before the bishop, the flowers had been transfigured into a likeness of the Virgin. As can be observed, the Mexican Moses descended Mount Tepeyac carrying flowers rather than the Tablets of the Law, only then for his cape, woven from cactus fibre, to become the Mexican Ark of the Covenant, filled with the presence and likeness of Mary. Moreover, when Zumárraga placed the image in the chapel he had built at Tepeyac, that hill figured not merely as another Sinai but also as the Mexican Zion, the site of the Temple of a new Jerusalem.[24]

Although future generations were to deride Sánchez for what they took to be his Baroque conceits, in reality he composed a narrative which constituted a foundation myth of both the Mexican Church and patria. Whereas, in his *Monarchy of the Indies* (1615), Juan de Torquemada had celebrated the Franciscan spiritual conquest of New Spain, by contrast, Sánchez now attributed the conversion of the native peoples of Mexico to the direct intervention of the Mother of God.[25] In his endeavour, he wrote: 'I was moved by the patria and mine own, by companions and citizens, and by all those of this New World'.[26] In effect, Mary had become both patron and mother of the Mexican people, since 'for Mary to appear among flowers was to signalize this land as her own, not only as possession, but as her patria', with the consequence that all the citizens of the capital were thus related to Mary through her image, 'which is re-born in the city where they were

23 Ibid., 170.
24 Ibid., 183–6.
25 Juan de Torquemada, *Los veinte y un libros rituales y monarquía indiana*, ed. Miguel León-Portilla *et al.*, 7 vols (Mexico, 1975–83), 2: 9–10, 30, 326–30.
26 *Testimonios históricos*, 255–8.

born; and the patria, although a common mother, is the most beloved mother'.[27]

Towards the close of his account, Sánchez commented on Our Lady of Los Remedios, an image which had been brought over by one of the conquerors, and thereafter lost until the Virgin appeared to an Indian nobleman, don Juan, to inform him as to its whereabouts. Subsequently, the image was adopted as patron by the city council of Mexico and was so venerated for the miracles it performed that, when the seasonal rains were slow to arrive, the Virgin was carried in solemn procession from her sanctuary to the cathedral, escorted by confraternities and religious communities. As a former chaplain at the sanctuary of Los Remedios, Sánchez was familiar with the history of this miraculous image published by Luis de Cisneros in 1622. Ever adept at finding scriptural figures to define the significance of this image and its Mexican counterpart, he identified Ruth the Moabitess as a figure of Los Remedios, since she had left her country to assist her widowed mother-in-law, Noemi, in Bethlehem. By contrast, Noemi the Israelite was a figure of the Guadalupe. He declared:

> I venerate in Ruth and Noemi the two miraculous images of the Virgin Mary. In Ruth, that of Los Remedios, who came from Spain accompanying the conquerors with love of its land for its remedy, favouring them in its conquest. In Noemi, that of Guadalupe, the creole which appeared in Mexico.[28]

In 1660 there appeared a concise, readable outline of the apparitions and miracles of Our Lady of Guadalupe, explicitly extracted from Sánchez, which purged the narrative of all scriptural allusions but skilfully retained the colloquies between Juan Diego and Mary. Written by Mateo de la Cruz, a Jesuit from Puebla, and first published in that city, it was reprinted in Madrid in 1661 and thus carried news of the Mexican Virgin across the Atlantic. It was Cruz who first consulted old Church calendars and established that Mary had first appeared to Juan Diego on Saturday 9 December 1531, so that the revelation of her image to Zumárraga occurred on Tuesday 12th of that month. Equally important, he asserted that the Guadalupe image possessed all the iconographical attributes of Mary in her Immaculate Conception, a doctrine anticipated in prophecy by St John in his description of the

---

[27] Ibid., 229–33, 248–56.
[28] Ibid., 238–41, 247–9.

Woman of the Apocalypse. Cruz followed Sánchez in contrasting the origins of Los Remedios and Guadalupe, 'calling that image the conqueror and *gachupina*, because it came with the conquerors from Spain, and this the *criolla*, because it appeared miraculously in this land, where it had its origin among flowers'.[29] Moreover, he then proceeded to compare the Mexican Virgin with Our Lady of Guadalupe of Extremadura, first indicating the similarities in the apparition narratives and their devotion, only then to emphasize the radical distinction: 'that image St Luke made; this, either God painted, or the Virgin herself, or, at the very least, the angels painted'.[30] Whereas the Mexican image descended from heaven, its Spanish counterpart could thus only boast of an apostolic origin.

The exaltation that governed the clerical elite of Mexico in the years which followed the publication of Sánchez's work was further illustrated in 1661, in the first printed sermon preached in honour of the Guadalupe, where José Vidal de Figueroa, who was later to become chancellor of the cathedral chapter, invoked neo-platonic theology to argue that prior to the creation of the world, God 'first painted Mary in his mind', a dictum that he immediately applied to the Guadalupe: 'that Image which appeared is the copy of that which God thought when he chose her for his Mother'.[31] In effect, the Virgin of Tepeyac was 'a portrait image of the idea of God . . . a hidden sacrament'.[32] If this were not enough, Vidal then raised the question: if the Virgin had appeared in Mexico to promote faith in her Son, why did she not appear with the Christ-child in her arms? His answer was abstruse and audacious:

> This image is a portrait of Mary's exemplar, when God represented her as the Mother of his Son: she thus carries in her arms, not the Word made man, but the Son of God transformed into light, which is that which illumines her hands . . . Mary appears in Mexico without the God Child in her arms, but surrounded by light: the miracle is so stupendous because the mystery is so

---

[29] Mateo de la Cruz, *Relación de la milagrosa aparición de la Santa imagen de la Virgen de Guadalupe, sacado de la historia que compusó Br. Miguel Sánchez* (Puebla, 1660), repr. in *Testimonios históricos*, 279–80.

[30] Ibid., 281.

[31] José Vidal de Figueroa, *Teórica de la prodigiosa imagen de la Virgen Santa María de Guadalupe de Mexico* (Mexico, 1661), 3.

[32] Ibid., 5.

ancient, since it takes its origin in eternity, when the Son of God was light, *erat lux vera*, and he was not made man until much later.[33]

In effect, we here encounter a neo-platonic concept of creation, in which the archetypes of the world were present in the mind of God from all eternity, with reality conceived as emanations from those divine ideas.

The degree to which the theology of the Greek Fathers influenced the Mexican clergy can be observed in a sermon preached in 1733 by José de Villa Sánchez, a Dominican, who asserted that whereas the leading Marian images of Spain had been painted or sculpted by St Luke, by contrast it had been God who had sent the Guadalupe to America to convert its peoples. Moreover, God had taken his copy

> from the same beauty, from the very face of the sovereign person of Mary . . . Most Holy Mary and her Image of Guadalupe are two portraits, identical twins, drawn by the same omnipotent hand, copied from that original which God has within himself.[34]

In a bold figure, Villa Sánchez further argued that the visit of the three kings to Bethlehem, guided by a star or the Holy Spirit, signified that Christ, a winged sun, had been born to bring light to the three parts of the world represented by those kings. But Mary, in her Guadalupan image, was the star of America, albeit bathed in the sun, and hence 'for this sacred image of Guadalupe was reserved the mission of this New World'.[35] Thus, a clear antithesis was drawn between the Old and the New World, with America the particular domain of Mary, its conversion more effected by the attraction of her image than by the persuasion of the gospel.

Towards the close of his *Image of the Virgin Mary,* Miguel Sánchez declared that although Mary fought the Devil through all her images, she acted most powerfully through those miraculous images which possessed their own sanctuaries, since these churches acted as spiritual fortresses where the faithful could obtain help and protection from demonic attack. All the more reason for the people of Mexico to visit Tepeyac, where they would encounter 'a new paradise, a new Adam,

---

33 Ibid., 8–9.

34 Juan de Villa Sánchez, *Sermón de la milagrosa imagen de Nuestra Señora de Guadalupe* (Mexico, 1734), 4–10.

35 Ibid., 17–23.

Juan Diego; and a new Eve, Mary'.[36] Here was a note which was echoed
by Francisco de Florencia, the Jesuit chronicler of holy images, who in
his *Polestar of Mexico* (1688), declared that in the Guadalupe, Mary was
'reborn in her image and through her image in this flowery Christendom, in her new Nazareth and Patria of the Indies'.[37] Moreover,
Florencia cited the eighth 'rapture' of Blessed Amadeus of Portugal
both in his *Polestar of Mexico* and in his *Origin of the Two Celebrated
Sanctuaries of New Galicia* (1694), in the latter case adding examples:

> Know you my children, said the Lady, that through the grace of
> my Lord Jesus Christ I shall also be with you bodily until the end
> of the world; not in the Sacrament of the Altar, as is my Son, since
> that is neither convenient nor decent, but in my Images of brush
> (as is that of Guadalupe of Mexico) or of sculpture (as are those of
> San Juan, that of Zapopan, that of Los Remedios of Mexico and
> others) and then you shall know that I am in them, when you see
> that some miracles are made through them.[38]

In this revelation the Virgin thus announced that she was bodily
present in certain images, much in the same way that Christ was
present in the Eucharist. But since her presence was demonstrated by
the performance of miracles, obviously she was not present in all her
representations, but only in those which attracted pilgrimage and widespread devotion, and which possessed their own sanctuaries.

The doctrine of the real presence of Mary in the miraculous images
and sanctuaries was also sustained by a direct comparison with the real
presence of Christ in the sacrament of the Eucharist. In 1709, a Mexican
Jesuit, Juan de Goicoechea, preached the sermon during the consecra-
tion of the majestic new sanctuary at Tepeyac that was completed in
that year. In a familiar figure, he compared the entrance of the
Guadalupe into the new sanctuary to the entrance of the Ark of the
Covenant in the temple constructed by Solomon, saluting the Mexican

36 *Testimonios históricos*, 248–56.
37 Francisco de Florencia, *La Estrella del Norte de México* (Mexico, 1688), reprinted in
*Colección de obras y opúsculos pertenecientes a la milagrosa aparición de la bellísima imagen de Nuestra
Señora de Guadalupe, que se venera en su santuario de México*, 2 unnumbered vols (Madrid, 1785),
2: 591–604.
38 Francisco de Florencia, *Origen de los dos célebres santuarios de la Nueva Galicia, obispado de
Guadalajara en la América Septentrional* (3rd edn, Mexico, 1766), 150; on Amadeus, Florencia
cited Baltazar de Medina, *Crónica de la santa provincia de San Diego de México de religiosos
descalzos de N.S.P. Francisco de la Nueva España* (Mexico, 1682), 123, where Medina noted that
San Pedro de Alcántara had approved of the *Nova Apocalypsis*.

Virgin as 'a mystical, incorruptible ark'.[39] Marvelling at the way in which the image had survived the erosion caused by the humid, nitrous airs of Tepeyac, he further acclaimed it as 'a sacramental image and the sacrament of images'.[40] In complicated prose, he affirmed:

> The continuous miracle through which she is present in her painting, according to appearances, like Christ in the Eucharist, in which the substance of the bread is destroyed, the accidents remain without support of the substance, colours of bread and wine suspended in the air, like the colours of our Marvellous Phoenix also suspended in the air.[41]

According to this analogy, in the same way that the bread and wine were changed, through transubstantiation, into the body and blood of Christ without any change in the accidents of bread and wine, so equally and yet differently, the flowers gathered by Juan Diego had been transfigured into the image of Mary. So important was this analogy to Goicoechea that he declared that although the new sanctuary might well crumble into eventual ruin, the image of Guadalupe would remain forever, 'sacramented in a cape', since Blessed Amadeus had recorded the promise of the Virgin that her miraculous images would endure until the last days of the world.[42]

* * *

It was one thing to preach panegyrical sermons, it was quite another to arouse popular devotion or to persuade the Roman authorities to recognize the peculiar standing of the Mexican Virgin. What is clear, however, was that the creole elite of New Spain, many of whose sons became priests in this epoch, were so impressed by the religious and patriotic significance of her presence that they subscribed liberally to finance the construction of a magnificent new sanctuary at Tepeyac and an entire series of subordinate sanctuaries that were built in all the leading cities of the viceroyalty. But devotion was further strengthened at all levels of society by the publication in 1675 of *Mexico's Happiness*,

---

[39] Juan de Goicoechea, *La maravilla inmarcesible y milagro continuado de Santísima Señora Nuestra en su prodigiosa imagen de Guadalupe de México* (Mexico, 1709), 2–4. This sermon is repr. in facsimile edn in *Siete sermones guadalupanos 1709–1765*, ed. David A. Brading (Mexico, 1994), no continuous pagination.

[40] Ibid., 4–5.

[41] Ibid., 23–6.

[42] Ibid., 27–8.

in which Luis Becerra Tanco, a secular priest and university professor, provided a translation 'from the Mexican language', which was to say, Nahuatl, of the colloquies of the Virgin Mary and Juan Diego.[43] The text he drew on had been published in 1649 by Luis Laso de la Vega, the chaplain at Tepeyac, who the previous year had contributed an enthusiastic endorsement of Miguel Sánchez's revelatory work, in which he saluted that author as 'the most fortunate creole of all our nation' and confessed that: 'I and all my predecessors have been like sleeping Adams, possessing this second Eve in the paradise of their Mexican Guadalupe'.[44] What he wrote, however, was a remarkably attractive account of Mary's apparitions, from which he eliminated all the scriptural and theological references inserted by Sánchez.

If in substance, which is to say, in factual detail, the accounts provided by Sánchez and Laso de la Vega are much the same, in style and dramatic structure they differed profoundly. Whereas few peasants, let alone Indians, have ever spoken the language placed in the mouth of Juan Diego by Sánchez, by contrast in Nahuatl the Indian speaks with a simple, natural eloquence. Both texts are rhetorical; but if one relies on scriptural metaphors, the other draws on native traditions of oratory. The contrast also stems from changes in the dramatic structure. Whereas in Sánchez, Juan Diego's first two encounters with Zumárraga are described in retrospect, when the Indian recounts to the Virgin what has happened, in Laso de la Vega, Juan Diego is presented as speaking face to face with the bishop. In effect, the Nahuatl version relies on dialogue and the colloquies are skilfully developed so as to heighten the dramatic effect. At the same time, the Nahuatl use of diminutives as forms of address and the poetic characterization of person and place infuse the text with a decidedly un-European flavour.[45]

To observe how the two accounts differ, one only has to note that in Nahuatl, the Virgin addressed the Indian as 'Juanito, Juan Dieguito', and again as 'Juanito, the youngest of my children'; in response, the Indian addresses the Virgin as 'My Lady, My Child, My Queen'.

---

[43] Luis Becerra Tanco, *Felicidad de México en el principio y milagroso origin que tuvo el santuario de la Virgen María Nuestra Señora de Guadalupe extramuros: en la aparición admirable de esta soberana Señora y de su prodigiosa imagen*, ed. Antonio de Gama (2nd edn, Mexico, 1675), 11–14.

[44] *Testimonios históricos*, 263–4.

[45] See *The Story of Guadalupe. Luis Laso de la Vega's 'Huei tlamahuiçoltica' of 1649*, ed. and trans. Lisa Sousa, Stafford Poole and James Lockhart (Stanford, CA, 1998), 63–5, 69–71, 79.

Whereas in Sánchez Juan Diego hears sweet music of angelic choirs and remains enchanted prior to seeing the Virgin, in Laso de la Vega the effect of the music was such that he exclaims: 'Am I in the earthly paradise of which our ancestors, the elders, spoke? Am I perhaps in heaven?'[46] When he sees the Virgin, in the Spanish version he is simply filled with wonder at her radiant beauty, but in the Nahuatl account he sees the landscape transformed:

> And when he arrived in her presence, he was filled with the greatest wonder at how her perfect beauty surpassed all things. Like the sun her clothes radiated, as if throwing out rays, and with these rays the stones and rock on which she stood were radiant with light. The earth which surrounded her appeared resplendent like precious stones, as if bathed in the light of the rainbow. And the *mesquites* and *nopales* and other bushes which were there seemed like emeralds and their foliage was like turquoises, and their trunks and branches shone like gold.[47]

But, together with poetic enlargement, there went a strain of natural eloquence. After Juan Diego was rebuffed by Zumárraga for the first time, in Sánchez, he suggests to the Virgin that she should send someone else, a person 'to whom they give more credit'.[48] In the *Nican mopohua*, as Laso's account has come to be called, this plea was extended into a moving statement, when the Indian says:

> I dearly beseech you, I beg you, My Lady, My Queen, My Daughter, that you charge someone from among the nobles, the well-known and esteemed and honoured, to take your message, so that he will be believed. For truly I am a little man . . . I am the tail, I am a wing, I am of the little people, and you, my child, the youngest of my daughters, Lady, you send me to a place where I do not walk and where I cannot stop.[49]

Here, the rhetorical resources of Nahuatl yield an utterance of

---

46 The text is repr. in *Testimonios históricos*, 282–308; see also the variant translations in Jesús Galera Lamadrid, *Nican mopohua: breve análisis literario e histórico* (Mexico, 1991), 136–7, in which, together with the Nahuatl original, he prints in parallel columns the translations by Luis Becerra Tanco (1675), Primo Feliciano Velásquez (1926), Angel María Garibay (1978) and Mario Rojas Sánchez (1978).

47 Ibid., 140–1.

48 *Testimonios históricos*, 182.

49 Galera Lamadrid, *Nican mopohua*, 158–9.

genuine eloquence. So too, later, when Juan Diego informs the Virgin that his uncle is on the point of death, she comforts him, tells him not to be afraid, and reminds him: 'Am I not here, who am your mother? Are you not under my shadow and protection? Am I not the source of your joy? Are you not in the hollow of my mantle, in the embrace of my arms?'[50]

Once again, we can observe how pastorally effective would have been the reading of such a passage. All this pointed to the conclusion, where Laso de la Vega argued that it was through Mary's apparition and her miraculous image that idolatry had been crushed in Mexico, since although the Franciscans had begun the task of overthrowing the Devil's kingdom, it was thanks to the Virgin that the eyes of the natives were opened and they were converted.[51]

In 1736–7, both the creole elite and the Indian community of Mexico City, not to mention the ever-growing number of mestizos and mulattoes, were assaulted by a great plague that raged for several months, carrying of some 40,000 souls. When material remedies failed to quell the epidemic, the city council and the cathedral chapter both voted to elect Our Lady of Guadalupe as principal patron of the capital. The archbishop of Mexico, Juan Antonio de Vizarrón y Eguiarreta, who was then also acting as viceroy of New Spain, accepted the election and with all due ceremony proclaimed 'as principal patron of this city the sovereign Queen of the Angels, in her admirable image of the miraculous advocation of Guadalupe'.[52] Such was the enthusiasm engendered by these proceedings that city councils and diocesan chapters throughout the vast viceroyalty united to acclaim the Virgin of Tepeyac as their patron. Despite a certain degree of opposition, the result was that, in December 1746, two councillors of Mexico City and two dignitaries of its chapter entered the bedroom of the Archbishop Vizarrón y Eguiarreta, who was soon to die, and acting on behalf of 'all the venerable ecclesiastical chapters and all the most noble cities and councils of the kingdoms of New Spain and those of Guatemala, New Galicia and New Vizcay', solemnly swore to take 'Our Lady the Virgin Mary in her prodigious advocation of Guadalupe' as their 'universal and General Patron'.[53] It was the chronicler of the great plague, Cayetano de Cabrera

---

[50] Ibid., 190–1.

[51] *Testimonios históricos*, 305–7.

[52] Cayetano de Cabrera y Quintero, *Escudo de armas de México* (Mexico, 1746), 285–98.

[53] Ibid., 516–19; see also Antonio Pompa y Pompa, *El gran acontecimiento guadalupano* (Mexico, 1967); Vizarrón died on 25 January 1747.

y Quintero, who argued in *Shield of Arms of Mexico* (1746) that the election of a patron was 'the deliberate, spontaneous promise of a Christian people especially to reverence under sworn oath some canonised saint, in order to obtain his intercession before God'.[54] The premise of this affirmation was that New Spain formed a Christian commonwealth, which was jointly governed and represented by the spiritual and temporal authorities, institutions at that time dominated by American Spaniards.

All that remained was to obtain papal approbation of this election. A distinguished Jesuit, Juan Francisco López, was despatched to Rome for this purpose. By then the ground had been prepared by the decision of the Vatican, issued in 1699, to grant Our Lady of Loreto, the premier Marian image of Italy, her own feast, with particular mass and office, on 10 December, within the Octave of the Immaculate Conception. So too, in 1723, Our Lady of Pilar at Zaragoza had been granted a similar honour, with her feast day set on 12 October.[55] In the event, Benedict XIV approved of the election of Our Lady of Guadalupe as principal patron of New Spain and, in a papal bull issued on 25 May 1754, transferred the celebration of her feast to 12 December, with its own mass and office, within the Octave of the Immaculate Conception. Among the many sermons which celebrated this event, that preached by Cayetano de Torres, a professor of theology, emphasized Mexico's good fortune, since:

> The Holy Church did for the Image of Guadalupe what it is not accustomed to do for other innumerable miraculous images of the same Lady ... Without doubt the privilege of a particular Mass and Office granted to our Image of Guadalupe is a most singular favour and very difficult to obtain from the Apostolic See ... Very rare are the images which have obtained it until the present.[56]

What rendered the case extraordinary was that the Mexican Church did not possess 'original notices or authentic documents of the Miracle and Apparition'. As it was, the 'Oracle of the Vatican' had canonized the image. Whereas the identity of the Guadalupe as a representation of the

54 Ibid., 314–16, 331–3.

55 Esteban Anticoli, *Historia de la aparición de la Santísima Virgen María de Guadalupe en México*, 2 vols (Mexico, 1897), 2: 89.

56 Cayetano Antonio de Torres, *Sermón de la Santísima Virgen de Guadalupe* (Mexico, 1757), 21.

Woman of the Apocalypse had merely been a concept for preaching, now that identity was 'a solid truth'.[57]

It was left to Francisco Javier Lazcano, a leading Jesuit and professor of the theology of Súarez at the University of Mexico, to celebrate both the Mexican Virgin and Juan Diego. On 12 December 1758 he began his *Panegyrical Sermon,* preached at Tepeyac, by praising the capital as 'our imperial court, Head of Septentrional America', distinguished above all other cities by its possession of 'the Image of Mary painted by the same Lady'. Whereas in Judea Mary had given birth to 'the Image of the Eternal Father, figure of the substance of the Father', in Mexico she 'portrayed to life her incarnated Jesus in the luminous mirror of her most beautiful face'. Moreover, if Mary had appeared in the flesh in Palestine and in vision to St John on the Isle of Patmos, her apparition in Mexico 'was superior, not in the substance, but in the mode'. Although Mary had uttered the Magnificat in her visit to St Elizabeth, she comported herself as a passing 'guest and stranger', whereas 'she wished to be our compatriot, to be a native and as if born in Mexico; to be a conqueror and first settler'. After such assertions it was only to be expected that Lazcano should have pronounced that 'the painting of the Apocalypse had been the copy and our Guadalupe the original'. But he surpassed other preachers when he invited the congregation, whom he oddly identified as 'the Hispanic Moctezuma Nation', to admit that were it not for the truths of the Catholic faith, they would be on their knees worshipping Mary in her Guadalupe image as the 'supreme Goddess'. His panegyric reached an imperial conclusion when, on commenting on the papal bull confirming the *guadalupana* as patron of New Spain, Lazcano exclaimed: 'Mexico received the faith of Jesus Christ from Rome. Now Mexico has paid back Rome with the apostolate of the most tender love of Mary. The Sovereign Tiara bends the knee before the miraculous Mexican'.[58]

If Lazcano employed neo-platonic concepts to exalt the heavenly origin and character of Mary's image, he also adopted the identification of Juan Diego with Moses first advanced by Miguel Sánchez in his *Image of the Virgin Mary.* In his *Guadalupan Zodiac* (1750, repr. 1776), he framed a series of meditations, arranged by the months of the year, for

---

[57] Ibid., 32.

[58] Francisco Javier Lazcano S.J., *Sermón panegyrico al ínclito patronato de María Señora Nuestra en su milagrosísima imagen de Guadalupe sobre la universal Septentrional América* (Mexico, 1759), *passim.*

those who visited the sanctuary at Tepeyac in search of confession and communion. Here he insisted on the role of the 'Venerable Neophyte Juan Diego of the lowest *plebe* of the Indians', and compared him to Santiago, the 'Patron of the Spains', to whom all Spaniards owed devotion, adding that Mary had appeared to 'a good Christian of your name, the Venerable Juan Diego'. So too, he emphasized the presence of Mary in her sanctuary:

> I chose this place and I sanctified it eternally for my Name so that my heart shall have a dwelling and my eyes will see . . . my people will look for me in this temple, I will hear them kindly, granting them what they ask of me.[59]

But the meditations concluded with a powerful comparison between Juan Diego and Moses, in which Lazcano followed Sánchez in the application of biblical typology to the events enacted at Tepeyac and Mexico. Moreover, if scriptural figures were still often invoked as little more than ingenious metaphors, by contrast, Lazcano presented the apparition of Mary as an extension of Christian revelation and depicted Juan Diego as the personification of Moses. Had not Mary appeared to Juan Diego to send him as her ambassador to Bishop Juan de Zumárraga so as to liberate her chosen people from their enslavement?

> Who does not see in this embassy the harmonious conduct of the God of Israel wonderfully repeated, when he appeared to Moses in the bush that was pierced with ardent flames in order to liberate his people from the tyranny of Pharoah? There God spoke from within the burning bush on Mount Horeb; here Mary spoke from within the centre of the Sun, on a mount covered with thorns. There God spoke with Moses sending him as his ambassador to Pharoah; here Mary spoke with Juan Diego, also sending him as her ambassador to the illustrious bishop. Moses excused himself with God, owing to the unworthiness of his person, begging him to send somebody else in his place; and Juan Diego excused himself with Our Lady Mary owing to the meanness of his condition, begging her in the same way to send a person of some standing. God does

[59] Francisco Javier Lazcano S.J., *Guadalupano zodiaco para recibir de la escogida como el Sol María Señora Nuestra* (Mexico, 1750, repr. 1776), unpaginated: see meditation for 12 September.

not accept the excuse of Moses; Mary does not accept the excuse of Juan. Moses begs God for signs for him to be believed and Our Lord God gives them to him; Juan Diego begs for signs from Mary for him to be believed and Mary also gives them to him. God works unheard-of prodigies in the court of Pharoah through the hand of Moses; and through the hands of Juan Diego, in the Imperial Court of the West, there is revealed the delicate, never before seen, portent of Mary. And if the Church worships in the burning bush of Horeb a precious symbol of the fruitful Virgin of Our Lady Mary, we offer all and infinite thanks to Our God for having given us in the Guadalupan Image of Mary a great and beautiful miracle of the luminous bush of Horeb.[60]

Here in this extraordinary sequence, the scriptural basis of the apparition narrative first enunciated by Miguel Sánchez is clearly recreated. At the same time, the apparition of both Mary and her holy image in Mexico is defined as a decisive moment in the history of the Christian Church.

* * *

On 15 September 1810, Miguel Hidalgo y Costilla, a provincial parish priest, called out the masses of central Mexico in rebellion against Spanish domination. For their banner he gave his followers an image of Our Lady of Guadalupe and later inscribed on their flags the slogans: 'Long live religion! Long live our most holy Mother of Guadalupe! Long live Ferdinand VII! Long live America and death to bad government!' But the Indians and mestizos who joined his movement soon simplified these war-cries into 'Long live the Virgin of Guadalupe and death to the *gachupines*!', the latter term the popular name for European Spaniards.[61] Whereas in 1746 Our Lady of Guadalupe had been acclaimed as patron of the kingdom of New Spain, she was now hailed as the mother and symbol of an insurgent Mexican nation. And although, during the tragic years of the 1850s, the triumphant Liberals first stripped the clergy of their property and privileges and then separated Church and State, the shrine at Tepeyac still continued to attract pilgrims and devotion. Indeed, during the 1880s, the radical journalist, Ignacio Manuel Altamirano, visited the sanctuary, by then connected to the city centre by trams, and confessed:

---

60 Ibid., meditation for 12 October.
61 Lucas Alamán, *Historia de Méjico* (4th edn, Mexico, 1968), I: 243–5.

There are to be found all the races of the old colony, all the classes of our republic, all the castes of our democracy, all the clothes of our civilisation, all the opinions of our politics, all the varieties of vice and all the masks of virtue in Mexico . . . No-one is exceptional, no-one is distinguished: it is equality before the Virgin; it is the national idolatry.[62]

After noting how bitterly divided were the Mexicans on political issues and how profoundly stratified was their society by race and class, he observed that it was only in the sanctuary of Our Lady of Guadalupe that they put aside their differences, and concluded that: 'The day in which the Virgin of Tepeyac is not adored in this land it is certain that there shall have disappeared, not only Mexican nationality, but also the very memory of the dwellers of Mexico today'.[63]

In the early twentieth century, when Mexico was devastated by the wars of the Mexican Revolution, the peasant followers of Emiliano Zapata entered Mexico City carrying the banner of Our Lady of Guadalupe and many of these Indians from the State of Morelos visited Tepeyac, venerating the Virgin as the symbol of their struggle for justice and land. So also, when the post-revolutionary regime of the 1920s sought to limit the number of priests licensed to say mass, the bishops placed the country under an interdict and bands of rural Catholics moved into rebellion. Although the rebels were called *Cristeros*, since their war-cry was 'Long Live Christ the King', that slogan was inscribed on banners of Our Lady of Guadalupe, who was saluted as 'Our Queen and Mother'.[64] By the close of the twentieth century the new basilica that had been built at Tepeyac could barely accommodate the millions of pilgrims that now came from all parts of Mexico and the United States.

University of Cambridge

---

[62] Ignacio Manuel Altamirano, 'La fiesta de Guadalupe' (1884), repr. in *Testimonios históricos guadalupanos*, 1127–33.

[63] Ibid., 1209–10.

[64] Brading, *Mexican Phoenix*, 313–16, 336.

PIETY AND POISONING
IN RESTORATION PLYMOUTH

by PETER MARSHALL

C AN we identify a pre-eminent physical location for the encounter between elite and popular religious mentalities in seventeenth-century England? A once fashionable and almost typological identification of 'elite' with the Church, and 'popular' with the alehouse, is now qualified or rejected by many historians. But there has been growing scholarly interest in a third, less salubrious, locale: the prison. Here, throughout the century and beyond, convicted felons of usually low social status found themselves the objects of concern and attention from educated ministers, whose declared purpose was to bring them to full and public repentance for their crimes. The transcript of this process is to be found in a particular literary source: the murder pamphlet, at least 350 of which were published in England between 1573 and 1700.[1] The last two decades have witnessed a mini-explosion of murder-pamphlet studies, as historians and literary scholars alike have become aware of the potential of 'cheap print' for addressing a range of questions about the culture and politics of early modern England. The social historian James Sharpe has led the way here, in an influential article characterizing penitent declarations from the scaffold in Foucauldian terms, as internalizations of obedience to the state.[2] In a series of studies, Peter Lake has argued that the sensationalist accounts of 'true crime' which were the pamphlets' stock-in-trade also allowed space for the doctrines of providence and predestination, providing Protestant authors with an entry point into the mental world of the people.[3] Most recently, Lynn Robson has built on

[1] Lynn Robson, 'No Nine Days Wonder: Embedded Protestant Narratives in Early Modern Prose Murder Pamphlets 1573–1700', unpublished Ph.D. thesis, University of Warwick, 2003.

[2] James Sharpe, ' "Last Dying Speeches": Religion, Ideology and Public Execution in Seventeenth-Century England', *P&P* 107 (1985), 144–67.

[3] Peter Lake, 'Deeds against Nature: Cheap Print, Protestantism and Murder in Early Seventeenth-Century England', in Kevin Sharpe and Peter Lake, eds, *Culture and Politics in Early Stuart England* (Basingstoke, 1994), 257–83; idem, 'Popular Form, Puritan Content? Two Puritan Appropriations of the Murder Pamphlet from Mid-Seventeenth-Century London', in Anthony Fletcher and Peter Roberts, eds, *Religion, Culture and Society in Early*

this approach, portraying the murder pamphlet as a fundamentally Protestant form, rooted in the theologies of original sin and justification by faith, and identifying its close cousinage to devotional writings on the art of dying.[4]

This paper focuses upon a single, previously unexamined murder pamphlet, though hardly a typical one. *Hell Open'd, or, The Infernal Sin of Murther Punished* was written in 1676 by the Presbyterian minister John Quick. The declared authorship was unusual – the overwhelming majority of murder pamphlets were anonymous – as was Quick's voluminous treatment: at 96 pages it is one of the longest, if not the very longest of the entire genre. As with all such sources, we are not hearing a genuine conversation: the voices of the felons are reported, if not ventriloquized, for us by the clerical author. Nonetheless, a close reading of Quick's text reveals much about ministerial strategies for reaching the most wretched of the populace, and about the responses they might evoke. It tells us something about relations between Church and Dissent in one part of the South West, and, more generally, it helps us to take the temperature of a religious culture, which even in godly circles, is often supposed to have cooled a degree or two in the post-Restoration decades. John Sommerville has argued that the characteristic features of popular religion in the Restoration were 'a decline of confidence, a contracting sphere for God's agency, and a lowering of affective tone'.[5] A foray into the world of John Quick suggests a rather different picture.

* * *

Quick was a native of Plymouth and resident there in the spring of 1676: it was a local *cause célèbre* which prompted the writing of *Hell Open'd*. On 23 August 1675, the family of Mr William Weeks, a Plymouth dyer, were seized with 'frequent vomitings and violent purgations . . . accompanied with grievous pains and swellings in their stomacks'.[6] Weeks and his granddaughter survived, though his wife

Modern Britain (Cambridge, 1994), 313–34; *The Antichrist's Lewd Hat: Protestants, Papists and Players in Post-Reformation England* (New Haven, CT, and London, 2002), 3–183.

4 Robson, 'No Nine Days Wonder', *passim*. Other works making use of the genre include Frances Dolan, *Dangerous Familiars: Representations of Domestic Crime in England 1550–1700* (New York, 1994); Malcolm Gaskill, *Crime and Mentalities in Early Modern England* (Cambridge, 2000).

5 C. John Sommerville, *Popular Religion in Restoration England* (Gainesville, FL, 1977), 5.

6 *Hell Open'd*, 1.

Elizabeth, and daughter Mary did not. A coroner's jury concluded that they had been poisoned, and two suspects were soon arrested: Mrs Week's maid servant, an orphan named Anne Evans, and the grand-daughter's nurse, Philip[pa] Cary. Between 25 August and 22 September, Evans and Cary were held in Plymouth while the magis-trates pieced together a sorry tale from the depositions of no fewer than nineteen witnesses. Elizabeth Weeks was a hard mistress: it was reported that Evans was made to rise at four in the morning on the sabbath, and she was supposed to have said that she would run away with the mountebanks rather than endure more of her treatment. Meanwhile there had been a falling out between Cary and Mistress Weeks 'concerning the frying of pilchards'.[7] But there was more to it than this: Elizabeth had called the nurse 'whore', and said 'that she was her husband's whore'.[8] Cary secretly swore revenge, and persuaded the hapless Evans to place ratsbane (arsenic) in a dish of pottage she was preparing for the family, telling her that 'when the old woman was gone, that we should live so merry as the days were long'.[9] The girl eventually admitted doing so, though protesting she had not thought it would cause death. Cary strenuously denied any part in the affair. At the end of September, the pair were despatched to the prison at Exeter to spend six months awaiting the assizes. At the trial, Evans was found guilty of petty treason and murder, and sentenced to be burned; Cary was to hang. A petition for transportation was denied, and an attempt by Cary to claim 'benefit of belly' was dismissed after a jury of matrons found her not to be pregnant. Upon the request of Master Weeks, the judge designated Plymouth the place of execution, and a crowd vari-ously reported to be between 10 and 20,000 turned out to see the grisly event on 29 March 1676.[10]

* * *

While Quick provides his readers with a full circumstantial account of the crime, and of the 'rare spectacle' of the double execution, the real drama of his narrative is played out in the temporal and psychological space between the two events, as he and other ministers 'discoursed' with the two women, first in Exeter gaol, and again in Plymouth on the

---

7 Ibid., 3–22 (quote at p. 7).
8 Ibid., 7.
9 Ibid., 11.
10 Ibid., 22–25, 57–67.

eve of the execution. Sharpe is inclined to see clergymen engaged in this activity as 'agents of the state' and 'embodiments of the secular power'.[11] But these labels hardly apply to Quick, a dissenting minister who had been deprived of his living at nearby Brixton under the Clarendon Code.[12] Nor was Quick in any sense a hack writer specializing in this kind of sensationalist reportage, such as the chaplain or 'Ordinary' of Newgate was to become in the eighteenth century.[13] His other publications comprise a smattering of funeral sermons, a catechism, a tract condemning marriage to a deceased wife's sister, as well as a learned history of the Huguenot Church, the work for which he is chiefly remembered today.[14] Nonetheless, Quick took to the task in distinctly writerly fashion, with vocative appeals to his 'Reader', and a lively facility for scene-painting.[15] What he offers his readers is a compelling psycho-drama, a tale of two sinners – the young misguided maid, and the older, more conniving nurse. It opens with an early morning visit to Exeter gaol, and a collective address to those condemned at the recent assizes: 'You are here judged of man, and you must die; but what also if you are condemned of God, and must to Hell for ever?'[16] How did they expect to escape His dreadful wrath? The prisoners offered what they clearly thought was the right answer – by repenting – but Quick made short work of this: 'you think to put off Gods wrath with your pittiful repentance?'[17] A great and terrible God demanded satisfaction, full amends and a ransom; if they could not bring it, 'they must expect as soon as they had died, to be damned for ever'.[18] This, of course, was only phase one of a classic evangelical conversion strategy. Quick went on to offer 'a discourse made of Christ, adapted to their capacities', emphasizing that His death was the price of redemption to all penitent

---

11 Sharpe, ' "Last Dying Speeches" ', 159, 165.

12 A. G. Matthews, *Calamy Revised* (Oxford, 1934), 401–2.

13 Peter Linebaugh, 'The Ordinary of Newgate and his Account', in J. S. Cockburn, ed., *Crime in England 1550–1800* (London, 1977), 246–69.

14 Alexander Gordon, 'Quick, John (*bap.* 1636, *d.* 1706)', rev. Stephen Wright, *ODNB* at http://www.oxforddnb.com/view/article/22952 (consulted 19 August 2005); A. C. Clifford, 'Reformed Pastoral Theology under the Cross: John Quick and Claude Brousson', *Western Reformed Seminary Journal* 5 (1998), 21–35. A collection of lives of eminent nonconformist divines did not make it into print: 'Icones Sacrae Anglicanae' (MS in Dr Williams' Library, London, MS 38.34/5).

15 For example, *Hell Open'd*, 39, 85, 65–6.

16 Ibid., 26.

17 Ibid., 27–8.

18 Ibid., 28.

believers, 'and that this was now offered unto them upon these terms of confessing and abhorring their sins'.[19]

Quick was armed with a sense of vocation that was ministerial in both a pastoral and clericalist sense. He styled himself God's 'ambassador', and wrote elsewhere attacking 'sorry mechanicks' who 'take upon them to over-rule and correct their pastors'.[20] There was, he later opined, 'not a Minister of the Gospel, who doth not by vertue of his office lie under an indispensable obligation to destroy sin and save sinners'.[21] It was to be achieved in this case by using the threat of hell-fire to break the women's spirits, and bring them to an unfettered acknowledgement of their utter sinfulness; a prelude to accepting the free offer of Christ's atoning sacrifice. In a series of subsequent interviews, Evans responded by becoming, at least in Quick's representation, the model of penitence. 'She fell a trembling and weeping, and desired my help and direction'.[22] This took the form of an instruction to review her life, remembering that 'by every sin that you have been guilty of, you have crucified Christ afresh'.[23] She was to exercise herself in continual prayer, until God 'do make your hard heart wax soft within you'.[24] At first this led her to believe that she was damned, but Quick endeavoured to persuade her 'she was nearer Heaven than she was aware of'.[25] By the eve of execution she was ready to acknowledge that she would not despair of mercy, for had not the good thief found it at the last hour? As she was bound to the stake, Quick sought to comfort her, and edify the spectators, with a long extempore prayer, calling on God to remember that 'she is the purchase of thy Son's blood, Oh, let him not loose her!... 'Tis late indeed that she comes unto thee, but not too late ... Late repentance is seldom true, but yet true repentance is never too late'.[26] Quick assured Anne that God would send his angels in a fiery chariot to convey her soul to heaven, and she wept, thanking him for his labour of love on her behalf.[27]

[19] Ibid., 2–9.

[20] Ibid., 31; *The Dead Prophet yet speaking. A Funeral Sermon Preached at Plaisterers-Hall, Feb. 15. 1690* (London, 1691), 20.

[21] *A Serious Inquiry into that Weighty Case of Conscience Whether a Man may Lawfully Marry his Deceased Wife's Sister* (London, 1703), epistle.

[22] *Hell Open'd*, 41.

[23] Ibid., 41–2.

[24] Ibid., 42.

[25] Ibid., 46.

[26] Ibid., 69.

[27] Ibid., 71–3.

The nurse's tale offers a stark contrast to this satisfying, if heart-wrenching, denouement. Through several interviews with Quick, she stuck to protesting her complete innocence, placing all the blame on Evans, and accusing the judge and jury of convicting her unjustly. In the process she withstood very considerable psychological pressure from Quick and other ministers, working almost in shifts to get her to confess. Cary was variously told that she was 'one of the most bloody women, that ever came into this gaol'; 'that she was drowned over and over in blood-guiltiness'; 'that she was a brazen impudent hypocrite, thus to dissemble with God and man'; 'that in the day of Judgment, I should be a witness against her, and it would be a fearful thing, that God Almighty should tell her; did I not send minister upon minister to convert, reconcile and save thee?'; 'that she was going into a lake of fire and brimstone there to be tormented for ever and ever; and when she was in the midst of those eternal torments, she would remember that I had told her of it'.[28]

Yet Cary would not budge, and was even prepared to contradict the minister on points of faith. When he insisted that she could not get to heaven without confession, 'being a main and principal ingredient into repentance', she retorted 'that it was enough to confess to God, and why should she confess unto men?'[29] Quick hoped that she would not follow the example of her brother, a professional thief hanged the previous year, who had delayed any admission of guilt till he was about to be turned off the ladder. 'To which she rejoyned, that her brother had made a godly end, and she was sure he was now in Heaven, and did wish she might make as good an end'.[30] In the face of repeated asser-tions of her certain damnation, she wept, 'but she hoped it would not be so bad with her as I spake'.[31] The usual fallback in cases of convicts protesting their innocence was to persuade them that their sentence of death was nonetheless just, either for other capital crimes committed, or for general sinfulness.[32] But Cary would not collaborate here either, only admitting at the very end to having been a liar, swearer, and sabbath-breaker, and to once receiving stolen money from her brother. As the halter was placed around her neck, she exclaimed, 'Judge and

[28] Ibid., 45, 50, 64, 77.
[29] Ibid., 33–4.
[30] Ibid., 36.
[31] Ibid.
[32] Sharpe, ' "Last Dying Speeches" ', 155–6; Robson, 'No Nine Days Wonder', 264–5.

revenge my cause, O Lord!' At the last she was asked if she would have anyone pray for her, and pointed wordlessly to Quick. But because she would not confess her sin of murder, 'he durst not take the name of God in vain for her sake'.[33] Instead, 'Mr R. the minister conceived a pithy and pertinent prayer'.[34]

* * *

This tragic moment of refusal, with an Anglican minister stepping forward to observe the formalities, points up the distinctively nonconformist character of Quick's narrative. It is shot through with the subjectivity, interiority, and attention to the autobiographical, which N. H. Keeble has seen as characteristic of nonconformist culture.[35] Generically, it belongs to what Peter Lake has termed 'Puritan appropriations of the murder pamphlet'. This is not to say that *Hell Open'd* is a work of overt confessional propaganda.[36] The text gives no indication of Evans's or Cary's denominational allegiances, and it displays a noticeably respectful attitude towards the conformist clergy ('the reverend and learned ministers of Plymouth')[37] who co-operate with Quick and other dissenters in their ministry to the condemned. This seems to confirm the intuition of recent historians that the 'sober' nonconforming ministers often remained on good terms with Church of England clergy in the Restoration period.[38] Yet there is no mistaking the distinctively godly dynamic of Quick's conversion narrative. As Anne Evans is fastened to the stake, he is able to contain any impatience he may have felt that it was 'thought requisite that the established Order of the Church should be observed'.[39] But when two unnamed persons proceed 'to instruct her in the nature of Faith, that it was to take Christ as Lord and King, and to submit unto all his Laws, to be governed by them, and in particular to this of suffering the punishment inflicted on her for her sin' (they had clearly read their Foucault),

---

[33] *Hell Open'd*, 63, 77.

[34] Ibid., 78.

[35] N. H. Keeble, *The Literary Culture of Nonconformity* (Leicester, 1987).

[36] For evidence that murder pamphlets could fulfil this function, see Peter Lake, 'Puritanism, Arminianism and a Shropshire Axe-Murder', *Midland History* 15 (1990), 37–64; Robson, 'No Nine Days Wonder', 73.

[37] *Hell Open'd*, 37.

[38] John Spurr, *The Restoration Church of England, 1646–1689* (New Haven, CT, and London, 1991), 44–6; Jeremy Gregory, *Restoration, Reformation and Reform, 1660–1828* (Oxford, 2000), 187–91.

[39] *Hell Open'd*, 66.

Quick's patience gives out. 'Gentlemen; do not trouble her, 'tis unseasonable now to catechize her in doctrinals; she stands in need of some sovereign cordials to revive and support her drooping spirits'.[40]

An assessment of the respective strengths of nonconformist and Anglican piety in meeting the spiritual needs of the most vulnerable and wretched in English society is beyond the compass of this paper. But the ways in which the nonconformist outlook might operate in demotic mode is worth some further consideration. Let us return to our starting-point: the prison as a site of encounter between popular and elite. It was the considered view of John Bunyan that 'God sometimes visits prisons more / than lordly palaces'.[41] Quick did not appear to share this sacralizing gaze. The prison, he remarks, is 'the very suburbs of Hell . . . a seminary of all villanies, prophaneness, and impieties'.[42] On his first meeting with the condemned, Quick asks them who or what Jesus Christ was, and what He had done for them. Predictably, they could not tell. 'None that knows a gaol will conceive this a fable. Hardly any but atheists, and the most ignorant wretches in the whole county are clapt up there'.[43] Yet these were not just contemporary platitudes. Quick knew about prisons, and about Exeter gaol in particular, having been incarcerated there for three months in 1663–4 for continuing to officiate at Brixton after his ejection. In 1673 he was imprisoned again, in the Plymouth Marshalsea, after the collapse of the crown's second declaration of indulgence. Quick's prison ministry thus had deeply personal resonances. After one of his conferences with Anne Evans, he delivered a mini-sermon to the prisoners flocking about him in the court of the gaol, telling them that thirteen years before, 'I was confined unto this place, but blessed be God for no evil that I had done'. However, the experience had taught him

> to compassionate all prisoners. And the mercies (being a stranger and prisoner), I found by the good providence of my God in this house, have made me pay yearly some vows and thank-offerings to Him within these walls.[44]

It seems legitimate to propose here that Quick and his fellow casualties

---

40 Ibid., 74.
41 Cited in N. H. Keeble, *The Restoration* (Oxford, 2002), 145.
42 *Hell Open'd*, 22–3.
43 Ibid., 28.
44 Ibid., 51.

of the Anglican purge of 1662, the victims of 'Black Bartholomew', could bring to their ministry in the gaols an empathetic insight that their conforming colleagues did not.

Quick's reference to divine providence suggests another way in which the barriers of understanding might be breached, or at least punctured. The work of Alexandra Walsham has persuasively presented an interest in providential occurrences as a form of 'cultural cement' between the Protestant clergy and the people. But both she and others detect a waning interest in providentialism in elite circles after the civil wars.[45] In the Puritan murder pamphlets he has studied from the 1650s and 60s, Lake finds a spiritualized or moralized emphasis on providence, but 'no pseudo-miraculous providentialism'.[46] Yet in Quick's text, this more traditional variety is never far below the surface. He rehearses, for example, the case of a young criminal 'whose curled black locks upon the gallows instantly turned white',[47] a declaration that he would have lived so long had he obeyed his superiors. Quick's description of the Plymouth executions displays distinctly Foxean touches. Despite 'all the skill and diligence' of the executioner, he was unable to light the pyre until well after Anne had expired from strangulation.[48] The wind then shifted to blow the smoke into the face of the nurse, 'as if God had spoken to her, the smoke of my fury, and flames of my fiery vengeance are now riding upon the wings of the wind towards thee'.[49] When Cary is finally turned off the ladder, 'she went out like the snuff of a candle, leaving a stench behind her'.[50]

Alongside such portents, ghosts make several appearances in Quick's text. Anne Evans was reported to have said that she would not lie one night in the house after Mistress Weeks was buried, 'for that she was sure she would appear again as a spirit'.[51] This was an understandable fear of judgement, rather than a popular superstition to be reproved. Murderers characteristically presumed upon secrecy, and yet, Quick observed, 'how miraculously have they been detected? Dreams, appari-

---

[45] Alexandra Walsham, *Providence in Early Modern England* (Oxford, 1999), *passim* and 333–4; Keith Thomas, *Religion and the Decline of Magic* (Harmondsworth, 1973), 125–32.

[46] Lake, 'Popular Form, Puritan Content?', 331.

[47] *Hell Open'd*, 87.

[48] Ibid., 74–5.

[49] Ibid., 75.

[50] Ibid., 79.

[51] Ibid., 20.

tions, and meer circumstances have detected and convicted them'.[52] Again, this was a conviction born of experience. As a minister in rural Devon, Quick had heard, and later assembled in manuscript, various local traditions about Mrs Leakey, the mother-in-law of John Atherton, a Somerset rector, and subsequently bishop of Waterford in Ireland. She had returned from the grave to expose his incest and infanticide, and to warn him (unsuccessfully) to mend his ways: Atherton was hanged for sodomy in 1640.[53] Quick's interest in apparitions was such that he speculated whether the perplexing refusal of Cary to confess to her crime might have been due to the threatening presence of a ghost; he had heard of a similar case from a minister in Cornwall.[54]

* * *

From one perspective, the discourses in the gaols of Exeter and Plymouth seem to represent the most starkly confrontational encounter of elite and popular, involving a total asymmetry of power and resources. But from another, we can identify more complex processes at work here, in the activities (or at least the representational strategies) of a minister whose priorities were not identical with those of the state Church or the law, who shared something at least of the mental world of the prison inmates, and who knew their experience of the powerlessness of incarceration at first-hand. Nor should we forget that the genre in which he chose to express himself – the news or murder pamphlet – was itself a thoroughly hybrid cultural form. In his seminal 1985 article on 'The Godly and the Multitude in Stuart England', Eamon Duffy sought to overturn the stereotyped view that Puritan clergy were simply unremittingly hostile to the mass of the population, and suggested that many ejected nonconformist ministers in particular can be shown to have had an abiding concern for the evangelization and instruction of the poor.[55] Quick's prison ministry can be regarded as a sub-specialism of that larger project. But we should pause before lauding too much the pastoral achievement of what is, after all, a study

[52] Ibid., 89. For examples in cheap print of secret murders exposed by ghosts, see Malcolm Gaskill, 'Reporting Murder: Fiction in the Archives in Early Modern England', *Social History* 23 (1998), 14–16; Robson, 'No Nine Days Wonder', 53–4.

[53] London, BL, Sloane MS 1818, fols 178r–187v. The accounts were later printed in [Nicholas Bernard], *Some Memorials of the Life and Penitent Death of Dr John Atherton* (London, 1711), 4–14.

[54] *Hell Open'd*, 82–3.

[55] Eamon Duffy, 'The Godly and the Multitude in Stuart England', *The Seventeenth Century* 1 (1985), 31–55.

in failure. Writers of murder pamphlets typically did not dwell over-long on the unrepentant.[56] Quick was unusual in making the centre-piece of his narrative Philippa Cary's complete failure to respond to his call for conversion, something he was patently puzzled and challenged by.[57] Remarkably, Quick resisted the temptation to make the maid and the nurse into emblems of election and reprobation.[58] He refused to speculate on whether Cary was indeed damned, observing that 'God can come in, if he please, between the bridge and water, the cup and the lip.'[59] Moreover, he was clearly troubled by the nagging suspicion that she might indeed be telling the truth, making him rehearse the counter-arguments at considerable length. Dying persons were to be credited, but only if they were persons of credit. Cary was known to be of bad character: 'a man might with a wet finger, prove her guilty of foul and frequent adulteries'.[60] A truly innocent person would have been less concerned for her life, knowing she was assured of salvation. Or alternatively, her innocence 'would have ingaged her to a more curious and exact scrutiny into her life past, to have found out the true cause of Gods anger in shortning her days'.[61]

Quick's narrative, in other words, points both to the potential and the limitations of the affective 'heart-religion' which was the bedrock of nonconformist piety. It confirms what Duffy, Margaret Spufford and others have long insisted upon, that Puritanism was no respecter of social boundaries, and could evoke a heartfelt response on the lowest rungs of society.[62] But where the high-octane tactics failed, there was simply bafflement, and no adequate pastoral response.

University of Warwick

---

[56] A point made by Robson, 'No Nine Days Wonder', 60.

[57] Revealingly, when an abridgement of Quick's text was included in the compendium, *The Wonders of Free-Grace: or, A Compleat History of all the Remarkable Penitents that have been Executed at Tyburn and Elsewhere* (London, 1690), the editor decided to 'mostly touch upon the penitent' (161).

[58] For instances of this, see Lake, 'Deeds against Nature', 280–2.

[59] *Hell Open'd*, 79.

[60] Ibid., 81.

[61] Ibid., 65, 79–81.

[62] Duffy, 'Godly and the Multitude'; Margaret Spufford, 'The Importance of Religion in the Sixteenth and Seventeenth Centuries', in eadem, ed., *The World of Rural Dissenters 1520–1725* (Cambridge, 1995), 1–102.

PATERNALISM AND ROMAN CATHOLICISM:
THE ENGLISH CATHOLIC ELITE IN
THE LONG EIGHTEENTH CENTURY*

by SALLY JORDAN

THERE is a general acceptance amongst historians of English Catholicism in the Early Modern period that Catholic landlords were paternalistic towards their tenants, that they were generally in turns charitable and controlling, their behaviour invasive yet motivated by a desire for religious and social harmony within the manor. Early modern English Catholicism was certainly seigneurial, with a requirement by the landlord, as suggested by John Bossy, to pay attention to the tenants' well-being and 'also to their faith and morals'.[1] Michael Mullett echoes these sentiments with regard to late eighteenth-century Catholics who relied 'on the kind hearts of those who wore the coronets'.[2] The idea of Catholic paternalism is also endorsed by several social and economic historians, such as James M. Rosenheim, who wrote with regard to Lancashire, '[the] Roman Catholic gentry sustained closer connections with local communities than did aristocrats elsewhere'.[3] This paper will examine the issue of paternalism on Catholic estates and in the local community to show that the Catholic elite, like their non-Catholic counterparts, gave money to the poor and established schools and almshouses. The focus of this philanthropy, however, was on other Catholics. The Catholic elite were also able to help their tenants, who were usually Catholic, and tie them more closely to the estate by not rack-renting their property and by not hiding behind estate stewards. There were two main reasons for the Catholic elite to focus their efforts on their poorer brethren: without the help of the Catholic elite in providing chapels and relief, Catholicism in England would have floundered; the Catholic elite were also

* I wish to thank the Economic and Social Research Council for providing funding for this project.

[1] John Bossy, *The English Catholic Community, 1570–1850* (London, 1975), 174–5.

[2] Michael A. Mullett, *Catholics in Britain and Ireland, 1558–1829* (Basingstoke, 1998), 143.

[3] James M. Rosenheim, *The Emergence of a Ruling Order. English Landed Society 1650–1750* (London, 1998), 203.

required by the tenets of the Church to be generous to the poor in order to achieve salvation. Helping those less fortunate than themselves meant saving both their religion and their souls.

Definitions of paternalism might incorporate a wide range of issues but this paper takes the general model of 'ruling, guiding and helping'. The conscientious paternalistic landowner might be protective of his tenants and the local community, setting the regulations of the estate and punishing transgressors. His guidance might include encouraging religious and moral behaviour and he must also aid the poor and suffering and act in a way that would benefit those under his care.[4] It is the desire to help tenants and the local community which will be the main focus of this paper.

* * *

Non-Catholic landlords were generally paternalistic towards their tenants and local communities in this period; they provided money for the poor, they cared for the welfare of old and sick tenants and were willing to negotiate on rents in periods of economic instability.[5] Yet, the long eighteenth century was also a period of immense social and economic change which caused an adjustment in the nature of landlord-tenant relationships. While the traditional bond between landowner and land-occupier may not have been broken by these changes, it was certainly weakened. The development of the post of professional estate steward and a rise in commercialism distanced the landowning elite from their tenants, the fashion for a country park often led to the physical removal of tenants' houses from the view of the landowner and the industrial revolution later in the century reduced the country's economic reliance on agriculture.[6]

These changes affected all landowners, but many Catholic landowners differed from their non-Catholic counterparts in certain respects and these differences allowed the Catholic elite to become more closely tied to their estates and the people who worked their land.

[4] David Roberts, *Paternalism in Early Victorian England* (London, 1979), 4–5.

[5] G. E. Mingay, *English Landed Society in the Eighteenth Century* (London, 1963), 208, 275, 284; Kim Lawes, *Paternalism and Politics: the Revival of Paternalism in Early Nineteenth-Century Britain* (Basingstoke, 2000), 12; Paul Langford, ed., *The Eighteenth Century 1688–1815* (Oxford, 2002), 151–2, 186; W. M. Jacob, *Lay People and Religion in the Early Eighteenth Century* (Cambridge, 1996), ch. 6, 155–85.

[6] D. R. Hainsworth, *Stewards, Lords and People* (Cambridge, 1992); Mingay, *English Landed Society*, 189–201; idem, ed., *The Cambridge Agrarian History of England and Wales. Vol. 6: 1750–1850* (Cambridge, 1989), 565.

An antipathy towards professional estate stewards and lawyers ensured certain Catholic landowners would be heavily involved in estate affairs and therefore in regular contact with their tenants.[7] The desire to maintain control over the running of the estate stemmed from a suspicion, expressed by Nicholas Blundell of Little Crosby in Lancashire, that 'when concerns of Moment are left to stewards and especially to Attorneys they grow Rich, by their Masters poverty'.[8] This sentiment was echoed by the Catholic gentleman Stephen Tempest, who believed attorneys would attempt to foster discord within an estate in order to create business for others in their profession.[9] Stewards were employed by some of the Catholic elite but they tended to be tenants on the estate, granted a restricted role and firmly of the Catholic religion. Marmaduke Constable of Everingham in Yorkshire tried to ensure the honesty and credibility of his steward by employing his own chaplain to supervise his estate affairs whilst an understeward was sacked because he married a non-Catholic.[10]

Another difference between Catholic and non-Catholic landowners concerned the anti-Catholic laws. Amongst other restrictions, the penal laws denied the Catholic elite participation in national and local politics which ensured their attention would not be regularly diverted from their estates and the local community. The Catholic elite might still spend the occasional season in London or Bath, or visiting friends and relatives in Britain or on the continent, but these represented the only distractions from what was, essentially, their main and often their only source of income.[11] Many members of the Catholic elite, including the Fermors in Oxfordshire and the Throckmortons of Warwickshire, became so wary of causing bad feeling at election time that they refused to direct their tenants on how to vote.[12] Nicholas Blundell substituted

---

[7] Hainsworth, *Stewards*, 48–52.

[8] Lancashire Record Office [hereafter: LRO], DDBL/54/42, Tenants' Book, 2.

[9] [Stephen Tempest], *Religio Laici: or a Layman's Thoughts Upon his Duty to God, his Neighbour and Himself* (2nd edn, London, 1768), 42.

[10] *Constable of Everingham Estate Correspondence, 1725–43*, ed. Peter Roebuck, Yorkshire Archaeological Society Record Series 136 (York, 1974); idem, 'Absentee Landownership in the Late Seventeenth and Early Eighteenth Centuries: a Neglected Factor in English Agrarian History', *Agricultural History Review* 21 (1973), 1–17, 5.

[11] Jacobite activity might force some members of the Catholic elite to flee abroad during periods of instability but this affected a very small minority. For other reasons for absenteeism in general, see Roebuck, 'Absentee Landownership', 11–14.

[12] Sally Jordan, 'Catholic Identity, Ideology and Culture: the Thames Valley Catholic Gentry from the Restoration to the Relief Acts', unpublished Ph.D. thesis, University of Reading, 2003, 200–1.

chattel leases for freehold leases on his Lancashire estate in order to prevent local people voting, because 'the Land-Lord who sends his Tenants to vote gaines more ill will from the Person whom he votes against (which is long remembred;) then he does good will from the Person he votes for'.[13] The Catholic elite were well aware that animosity caused by elections could spell renewed hostility and perse- cution. Catholic landowners also had a higher financial burden than their non-Catholic counterparts in the shape of the double land-tax assessment and the cost of sending children abroad for education. This meant that estate returns were a high priority for the Catholic elite and that favourable arrangements for tenants did not stem from a lack of need for a high income.

It was the religious connection between Catholic landlords and those living in or near the estate that was the main difference between non-Catholic and Catholic landowners, in particular the self-imposed requirement of the latter to provide a chapel and chaplain for Catholics in the local community. This provision of a chapel meant Catholic squires were regularly inviting members of the local community into their houses for a proscribed, if no longer secret, act of worship. Not all tenants of Catholic landlords were Catholic, especially in the south of the country, but there is a general correlation between the presence of a Catholic landed family in a parish and the existence of a Catholic congregation.

Examples of the generosity of the Catholic elite to those in the local community abound, but must come with an important caveat. An ostensibly all-embracing concern for the local community was actually rooted in a narrow religious paternalism and a desire to aid local Cath- olics rather than the parish as a whole. One reason for this, aside from a general desire found in all denominations to care for those of one's own communion, was that the statutory poor relief system was intimately connected to or associated with the Church of England; the overseers of the poor were required to interact with churchwardens, the parish vestry and justices of the peace, whilst pensions were often handed out after Sunday service. It would be interesting to know whether poor Catholics were ever refused relief because of their religion, but certainly the association of the parish relief system with the Church of England may have led those outside the established Church to depend

---

13   LRO, DDBL/54/42, 7.

on the benevolence of those of their own faith.[14] In general, Catholic philanthropy was designed to benefit those of the Catholic religion. The Hales family, as lords of the manor in the mid-eighteenth century, used their management of the almshouses at Hackington in Kent to benefit local Catholics.[15] Sir Roger Martin gave money for poor Catholics in or near Melford, Suffolk, where his house, Long Melford Place, was situated.[16] The almshouses established by William Petre in the parish of Ingatestone, Essex, in the sixteenth century were intended for Catholics despite being usurped by the rector for poor Anglicans for much of the eighteenth century.[17] The school established by Catherine, the Dowager Lady Petre, in Essex was reported as being 'popish' in 1720. Among Lady Yate's various charitable foundations was an apprenticeship for two Catholic children in Chaddesley Corbett, Worcestershire, though with the allowance that Protestant children might benefit if there were no potential Catholic recipients. It is unlikely that it was ever used for Protestants and certainly in the mid-eighteenth century Sir Robert Throckmorton was continuing to place out local Catholic children.[18]

The Catholic elite also displayed an economic paternalism towards their Catholic tenants in the eighteenth century. Whilst other land-owners might attempt to raise estate income by rack-renting their land and letting existing leases fall into abeyance, many Catholic landowners continued to use copyhold and leases for lives throughout the century.[19] The Welds of Lulworth in Dorset only started converting some of the numerous copyhold properties on their estate to long leases for lives in the later eighteenth century.[20] In Northumberland, it

---

[14] Joanna Innes, 'The "Mixed Economy of Welfare" in Early Modern England: Assessments of the Options from Hale to Malthus (c.1683–1803)', in Martin Daunton, ed., *Charity, Self-Interest and Welfare in the English Past* (London, 1996), 139–80, 145; Paul Slack, *The English Poor Law, 1531–1782* (Cambridge, 1995), 20, 37.

[15] *The Speculum of Archbishop Thomas Secker*, ed. Jeremy Gregory, Church of England Record Society 2 (Woodbridge, 1995), 36.

[16] T. G. Holt, 'Long Melford and the Martin Family', *London Recusant* 8 (1978), 2–8, 3.

[17] Stewart Foster, 'The Ginge Petre Charity Almshouses, Ingatestone', *Essex Recusant* 24 (1982), 59–63, 59.

[18] Lillian Lascelles and Elizabeth Guise-Berrow, 'Churchwardens' Presentments 1644–1768', *Worcestershire Recusant* 6 (1965), 21–45, 44.

[19] Mingay, *Agrarian History*, 198–230; many landlords were converting leases to rack rents in the eighteenth century though this varied from county to county; see M. E. Turner, J. V. Beckett and B. Afton, *Agricultural Rent in England, 1690–1914* (Cambridge, 1997), 26–9.

[20] Dorset Record Office [hereafter: DRO], D/WLC/M82; *Returns of Papists 1767*, ed. E. S. Worrall, Catholic Record Society Occasional Publication, 2 vols (London, 1989), 2: 169–70.

appears the Haggerston family were granting longer leases to Catholic tenants than their Protestant counterparts, whilst, in 1767, the vicar of Ellingham believed the Haggerstons would only let land to Catholics.[21] The Blundells of Little Crosby of Lancashire, whose tenants were almost certainly all Catholic, had an estate largely composed of leases for lives; tenements were normally only rack-rented at the tenant's request. One tenant by the name of William Blundell, probably not a relation, was allowed to take a tenement on a half rack-rent because he was in debt and had no children. When he still could not manage this arrangement, he asked the lord of the manor to take it back in hand in return for an annuity.[22] This was a common arrangement on the Blundell estate for those who could not afford a fine but who were considered to be good tenants, although the tenant was not usually given a particularly good deal.

Two of the rare and short-lived examples of rack-renting on the Blundell estate suggest that tenants were paying over 20 shillings per acre on agricultural land in 1738 and 1755, compared to 5.5 shillings and 7 shillings per acre found in the national rent index for the same years.[23] Presumably, high rack-rents were used to encourage tenants to lease thereby tying them more closely to the estate. The Blundells also used an unusual form of tenant right whereby heirs of good tenants might expect favourable terms in a lease.[24] Another example of this narrowly focused economic paternalism is that of Marmaduke Constable of Everingham, Yorkshire, who, when informed that his tenant Anna Bell, who was not a Catholic, could not pay her rent, ordered his chaplain-steward, John Bede Potts, to 'quitt her of her Cottage, and all others that do not [pay their rent]'. Yet he also allowed tenants to keep half a year's rent in hand and asked Potts to 'give in Charity every halfe year five pounds to my poor Catholick Tennants att Everingham or elsewhere upon my estate'. It appears that when Constable displayed benevolent paternalism towards his tenants this would only extend to his co-religionists.[25]

---

[21] John Bossy, 'More Northumbrian Congregations', *Recusant History* 10 (1969), 11–34, 12–13.

[22] LRO, DDBL/54/42, 9. For religion of tenants, LRO, QDP/1/1–8 (papists' estates).

[23] LRO, DDBL/54/42, 133, 216–17; Turner, Beckett and Afton, *Agricultural Rent*, 314–15.

[24] Andrew Gritt, 'Aspects of Agrarian Change in South-West Lancashire, c.1650–1850', unpublished Ph.D. thesis, University of Central Lancashire, 2000, 106–21.

[25] *Constable of Everingham*, 54, 59–60.

The reasons behind the paternalism of Catholic landowners are various. Aside from the necessities of providing a place of worship to Catholics, Catholic landed families would have shared the general concerns of the English elite in wanting to maintain the social order, regulate the labour market and bring civilized behaviour to the poor. It was expected that the elite would give regular voluntary contributions to the poor outside of the statutory poor rate, regardless of religious proclivity, as long as this charity did not promote idleness.[26] A regular complaint of social commentators in the late seventeenth and early eighteenth centuries concerned the perceived and possibly erroneous 'superior charity' and voluntary giving of Catholic countries in comparison with England, whilst John Wesley bemoaned the conspicuous consumption of England and thought the rich should gain and save only to give to the poor.[27]

Various Anglican commentators in the eighteenth century saw a more sinister explanation behind the close connection between Catholic landlords and the people of the parish. In the 1730s, Bishop Potter accused Thomas Stonor of Stonor, Oxfordshire, of using charity to make Catholic converts of the local community, which Stonor denied, criticizing 'such stingy Prelates as Potter [who] will neither do charity themselves nor permit others to do it'.[28] The 1767 Returns of Papists also brought up many instances of Anglican vicars defending the fact that certain parishes were full of Roman Catholics because they were in some way dependent on a landowning Catholic family.[29] If charity and conversions to Catholicism were so closely connected then all parishes containing an elite Catholic family dispensing charity should have contained high Catholic populations. This was not the case, especially in the south of England, and although a desire to convert led to some paternalistic acts of charity, some families were unwilling to use such methods for fear of provoking their Anglican neighbours.[30]

The Catholic elite might be influenced by the advice of their peers

---

[26] Colin Jones, 'Some Recent Trends in the History of Charity', in Daunton, ed., *Charity*, 51–63, 55.

[27] Innes, 'Mixed Economy of Welfare', 154–5; Henry D. Rack, *Reasonable Enthusiast. John Wesley and the Rise of Methodism* (London, 2002), 360–7.

[28] J. A. Williams, 'Some Eighteenth-Century Conversions', *Essex Recusant* 3 (1961), 129–33, 129–30.

[29] Ibid., 129–30.

[30] Eamon Duffy, '"Poor Protestant Flies": Conversions to Catholicism in Early Eighteenth-Century England', in Derek Baker, ed., *Religious Motivation: Biographical and Sociological Problems for the Church Historian*, SCH 15 (Oxford, 1978), 289–304, 296–8.

and ecclesiastical superiors when considering their duty towards the local community and tenants: '[He who is possessed of a great landed estate] is under a strict Obligation, both as a Christian, a moral Man, and a good Citizen, of making his Dependents live comfortably and happily under his Patronage'.[31] The tenants were the estate, they provided the landlord with his income, they farmed his soil and were the link between the Lord and his lands; good tenants should therefore be highly valued:

> your Tenants justly claim a reasonable Consideration from you; it is their Due, for they are particularly embark'd in your Interest; and there is such a Kind of Connexion between you and them, as there is between you and your Estate.[32]

Catholic landlords would also find guidance from their devotional reading: whilst lay Catholic commentators emphasized the moral and social aspect of estate management, religious authors concentrated on the evil of riches and the vital issue of performing charitable acts in order to obtain salvation. A respect for the social hierarchy and pastoral care of one's inferiors was highlighted by Bishop Challoner in *The Garden of the Soul*, the most popular work of Catholic devotion of the period: 'we must have a due Care of our Children, and of others that are under our Charge, both as to their Souls and Bodies'.[33] It was well known by Catholics and non-Catholics in the Early Modern period that Roman Catholicism was a religion that relied heavily, both financially and spiritually, on such works of charity. This was highlighted by William Blundell of Little Crosby, who recorded in his notebook the possibly apocryphal comments of the Duke of Buckingham in the late seventeenth century:

> being asked by my Lady Castlemaine what religion he was of, answered that he had not faith enough to be a Presbyterian, nor good works enough to be a Papist, and therefore he was an honest old Protestant without faith or good works.[34]

Whilst this quotation might be more suggestive of thoughts on the Church of England in this period, the fact remains that good works

---

[31] Tempest, *Religio Laici*, 40.

[32] Ibid., 76.

[33] Richard Challoner, *The Garden of the Soul: or a Manual of Spiritual Exercises and Instructions for Christians, who (Living in the World) Aspire to Devotion* (Dublin, 1759), 25.

[34] *Crosby Records: a Cavalier's Notebook*, ed. T. Ellison Gibson (London, 1880), 188.

were seen to be a vital part of the Catholic faith. Anglican and dissenting voluntary charities had to play down the idea of achieving salvation by good works to avoid being labelled 'popish', whilst still emphasizing that God approved of charitable endeavours.[35]

The Catholic elite were regularly reminded by the clergy of the importance of good works. Bishop Challoner wrote in his treatise, *Think Well On't*:

> As often as we visit the sick, or those that are in prison, or reconcile together those that are at variance with one another; as often as we fast on days commanded by the church – give alms to the poor that pass by our door, &c. By these, and such like works, our small sins are daily redeemed.[36]

This was by no means the only way to salvation but it was an essential part. Elizabeth Heneage of Hainton (1734–1800), who built chapels at Newport and Cowes on the Isle of Wight and regularly provided money for the poor, was praised by Bishop Walmesley for her good works: 'Your spirit of Charity is undoubtedly beyond expression, and your reward will certainly be so too'.[37] Those who did not perform good works could expect the opposite – 'those who do not relieve the Poor, shall go into eternal Punishment, and that those who do, into Life everlasting'.[38] The Catholic elite would also be reminded by the Catholic clergy of the evils of riches and the corruptible nature of money: 'For they that will become rich, fall into Temptation, and into the Snare of the Devil, and into many unprofitable and hurtful Desires, which drown Men in destruction and Perdition'.[39] John Gother believed that every month the rich should pass on to the poor anything beyond their actual needs. This idea was later echoed by Wesley, and several modern commentators have called him a 'traditionalist Catholic' with regard to his ideas on social issues.[40]

---

[35] Innes, 'Mixed Economy of Welfare', 154–5.

[36] *The Christian's Companion Consisting of the Catechism of the London District; Think Well On't; and the Daily Companion* (2nd edn, Lisbon, 1812), 159.

[37] *Isle of Wight Registers*, transcribed with historical introductions by R.E. Scantlebury, Catholic Record Society 59 (London, 1968), 67.

[38] Tempest, *Religio Laici*, 82; for similar reminders in the nineteenth century, see Sheridan Gilley, 'English Catholic Charity and the Irish Poor in London', *Recusant History* 11 (1972), 179–95, 179–80.

[39] Challoner, *Garden of the Soul*, 32.

[40] Marion Norman, 'John Gother and the English Way of Spirituality', *Recusant History* 11 (1972), 306–19, 315; *The Journal of the Rev. John Wesley A.M.*, introduction by the Rev.

In a period when landowners in general were starting to distance themselves from their tenants, raising rack-rents later in the century and hiding behind an estate steward, the persisting paternalism of the Catholic elite is highly significant. A desire to care for the local Catholic community, who were not likely to find protection elsewhere, an intention to achieve life everlasting and to act as a good citizen, ensured the Catholic elite would continue acts of charity and benevolence to Catholics less fortunate than themselves. Instances can also be found of philanthropic Anglicans and dissenters bestowing generous amounts on their co-religionists. Examples exist of favourable leasing arrangements made by the Anglican clergy in the diocese of Canterbury, who used this method to present the Church 'as a paternalistic landlord' thereby 'building up lay support within local society'.[41] It is significant, however, that one must turn to the Anglican clergy to find a parallel with the Catholic elite.

Levels of paternalism amongst the Catholic elite towards their tenants and local community waned by the end of the eighteenth century, simply because the number of Catholics under elite protection and control fell in a period when the number of Catholic noble and gentle families had decreased dramatically, either through a failure in the male line or apostasy. Although other Catholics often inherited the estates of the disappearing families, it was impossible to maintain a high level of hands-on management on properties spread over several counties, often at a distance of several hundred miles. Urbanization and the rise in the number of non-agricultural occupations available during the industrial revolution also allowed more independent, town-based Catholic communities to spring up, especially in the north.[42] Charity, Catholicism and community were ultimately forced to make allowances for capital investment, industry and independence.

University of Reading

F. W. Macdonald (London, 1921), 219; David Hempton, *Methodism and Politics in British Society 1750–1850* (Stanford, CA, 1984), 233.

[41] Jeremy Gregory, *Restoration, Reformation and Reform, 1660–1828: Archbishops of Canterbury and their Diocese* (Oxford, 2000), 117–19.

[42] Bossy, English Catholic Community, 324–8.

RURAL RELIGION AND THE POLITENESS OF PARSONS: THE CHURCH OF ENGLAND IN SOUTH WARWICKSHIRE, C.1689–C.1820

by COLIN HAYDON

JOSEPH Arch, the agricultural trade unionist, was born in 1826 at Barford in south Warwickshire. In his autobiography, he recalled, as a boy, witnessing the Eucharist in the village church:

> First, up walked the squire to the communion rails; the farmers went up next; then up went the tradesmen, the shopkeepers, the wheelwright, and the blacksmith; and then, the very last of all, went the poor agricultural labourers . . . [N]obody else knelt with them . . . '[N]ever for me!',

vowed Arch.[1]

By contrast, a century before, the churchwarden of Barcheston, also in south Warwickshire, recorded a glowing tribute to the village's septuagenarian, infirm pastor. The rector resolutely undertook his duties, 'preaching every Sunday; catechiseing the children; and expounding som part of the catichism: and doing all other offices as becoms a faithful minister; to the great satisfaction of the parish'.[2]

Both sources are, of course, problematical or suspect: Arch's autobiography self-consciously charts the making of an agitator; churchwardens' returns may be formulaic or merely reveal leading parishioners' opinions. Nevertheless, the two quotations plainly prompt several questions. If, in the early nineteenth century, as Arch maintained, 'the Church had lost its hold . . . on the labourers in the country districts',[3] how far did this result from a growing – and avoidable – clerical elitism? Can processes of religious and cultural estrangement be accurately traced from the fragmentary and uneven sources available? If so, how valid is it to envisage a simple elite/popular divergence?

This essay considers further evidence from south Warwickshire, an

---

[1] *The Autobiography of Joseph Arch*, ed. John Gerard O'Leary (London, 1966), 25–6.

[2] Unless otherwise stated, information about specific parishes derives from Worcester, Worcestershire Record Office [hereafter: Worcestershire RO], BA 2289, Ref. 807.

[3] *Autobiography of Joseph Arch*, 25.

overwhelmingly rural locality, for the years *c.*1689–*c.*1820, and particularly for the later part of the period.

* * *

The Toleration Act of 1689 effectively ended legal coercion to attend the Church of England's services. The bishops of Worcester, whose diocese included most of south Warwickshire, therefore urged their clergy to minister yet more energetically, crafting their teaching for 'a common Audience', containing some with 'inferior Capacities', even 'the lowest Capacity'.[4] Plain, intelligible, properly prepared sermons on Christianity's essential tenets, Bishops Stillingfleet (1689–99) and Maddox (1743–59) agreed, would best effect a 'real Improvement in Piety and Virtue'.[5] Certainly the surviving manuscript sermons of William Richardson, vicar of Brailes, 1651–95, were painstakingly composed, crisply imparting Christian doctrine;[6] and Richard Jago, after preaching at Harbury in 1755, noted the need to pitch sermons appropriately.[7] Additionally, Bishops Thomas (1683–89), Stillingfleet, and Maddox all stressed the importance of catechizing;[8] and churchwardens' presentments from 1714, 1717, 1719, and 1722 reveal that this duty was discharged immensely conscientiously in the Kineton deanery in south Warwickshire.[9] Rote-learning by catechists – 'onely like Parrots' – was insufficient;[10] a basic understanding of doctrine was essential. Much attention, too, was to be paid to services and the sacraments. Maddox stated that the Church's services were to be performed 'always seriously, gravely and distinctly', and the 'holy *Sacraments . . .* administered with the utmost Reverence and Devotion', following careful preparation of the people.[11]

These bishops' advice appears appropriate for 'a common Audience'. The laity seemingly appreciated sermons: one revealing churchwardens' presentment from Wellesbourne, dated 1684, noted that no

---

[4]   Isaac Maddox, *The Charge of Isaac, Lord Bishop of Worcester* (London, [1745?]), 17, 22.

[5]   Edward Stillingfleet, *The Bishop of Worcester's Charge to the Clergy of his Diocese* (London, 1691), 15–16; Maddox, *Charge of Isaac*, 22.

[6]   Warwick, Warwickshire County Record Office [hereafter: Warwickshire CRO], DR 308/24/1–14.

[7]   Richard Jago, *The Causes of Impenitence Consider'd* (Oxford, 1755), 3.

[8]   William Thomas, *The Bishop of Worcester. His Letter to the Clergy of his Diocess* [sic] (London, 1689), *passim*; Stillingfleet, *Charge*, 17–20; Maddox, *Charge of Isaac*, 22–4.

[9]   Worcestershire RO, BA 2289, Ref. 807.

[10]   Thomas, *Bishop of Worcester*, 14.

[11]   Maddox, *Charge of Isaac*, 21.

parishioners came 'only to the preaching'. Maddox believed catechizing produced an informed 'Christian Audience'.[12] Respecting the Eucharist, the number of communicants was, certainly by the 1780s, low in the Kineton deanery,[13] but the Prayer Book's pungent warnings about unworthy reception – and not religious indifference – probably explain this.

Church attendance sometimes reveals services' popularity. The parishioners 'are generally due Comers to Church', Tysoe's church-wardens noted in 1699, and at Burmington in 1690, when the chapel needed repairs, 'the people . . . constantly . . . [met] together [for worship] in a convenient house, being the farme of . . . the Earle of Northampton'. Churchwardens' presentments between 1689 and 1730 contain remarkably few criticisms of the parish clergy; and, given that a noticeable number of churchwardens were unable to sign their names, it seems unlikely that these documents reflect just superior parishioners' views.[14] Occasionally, clergymen proved disastrous. Abraham Kent, Whitchurch's negligent rector from 1705 to 1711, loathed the parish and contemptuously described his flock as 'my Rusticks'.[15] But the paternalistic Squire Marriett effected his removal:[16] high and low had shared expectations of ministers.

The Church's hierarchical outlook seems respected by Arch's fore-bears. Church interiors – with hatchments, squires' boxes, the humble's benches – proclaimed it; and, in the 1740s, a wrangle about a pew at Whatcote reveals how 'Civil orderly People' wanted their standing formalized parochially.[17] At Brailes in the 1730s, some parishioners loathed the Welsh curate, Walter Evans, partly because they thought his origins lowly for a clergyman.[18] A 1674 presentment from Combrook gratefully acknowledged the powerful Verney family's aid for the chapel.

Church funding, building, and repairs could be sources of pride for both aristocrats and their inferiors. Gentlemen matched grants from

---

12 Ibid., 22.
13 Surveys of, and statistics for, the Worcester diocese's Kineton deanery are derived from *The State of the Bishopric of Worcester, 1782–1808*, ed. Mary Ransome, Worcestershire Historical Society n.s. 6 (Leeds, 1968), 160–88.
14 Worcestershire RO, BA 2289, Ref. 807.
15 Oxford, Bodleian Library, MS Rawl. Lett. 7, fols 176r, 180r.
16 BL, Add. MS 34740, fols 138v–9r, 140v–1r.
17 Worcestershire RO, BA 2765, Ref. 713.021, fol. 72.
18 Worcestershire RO, BA 2632, Ref. 797.6 (iii), Deposition of John King.

Queen Anne's Bounty to augment poor livings.[19] In the 1680s, Squire Parker splendidly remodelled Honington church and, in 1750, Sir Charles Mordaunt erected a new chapel at Walton Deyville. New decorations might bear the names of churchwardens who commissioned them. Gradually, too, gifts of chalices, patens, flagons, and almsdishes were received. And humbler parishioners, it seems, willingly contributed to levies for church or chapel repairs: between 1674 and 1708, when levies were collected at Honington, Stratford-upon-Avon, and Tidmington, *very* few parishioners apparently refused to pay. In 1736, a parish levy was raised to repair Wasperton church, and the local gentry gave additional sums and fittings.[20] A pleasing church gave widespread satisfaction.

* * *

During the eighteenth and early nineteenth centuries, south Warwickshire became increasingly sophisticated. Its towns prospered and developed leisure facilities for elite and polite society. Warwick, attractively and expensively rebuilt after its disastrous fire of 1694, had its races, public library, shops, pleasant inns, and a weekly newspaper.[21] Stratford-upon-Avon became a 'neat and well-built' town.[22] Leamington developed rapidly as a spa from the 1790s; soon, besides the Pump Room and baths, it boasted assembly rooms, a circulating library, reading rooms, and a picture gallery.[23] Road improvements facilitated travel – notably to the intellectual centres of Birmingham and Oxford – and the countryside developed pockets of sophistication. By the 1790s, Kenilworth and Wellesbourne had book clubs; Wellesbourne's 'consisted of the principal clergy and gentry of the place and its neighbourhood'.[24] By 1815, visitors to Edgehill could enjoy the prospect from a 'spacious and well-conducted Inn', and Halford's pleasant inn and 'delightful' bowling green attracted nearby gentry in the summer.[25] The appeal of urban refinement could affect traditional worship. It seems, for instance, that Shipston on Stour's superior services attracted

[19] London, Church of England Record Centre, K 7199, 7321, 7334, 7387.

[20] Oxford, St John's College, Archive MS 269, fols 11v–12v, 19r, 69r, 74av, 87v.

[21] William Field, *An Historical and Descriptive Account of the Town and Castle of Warwick; and of the Neighbouring Spa of Leamington* (Warwick, 1815), 48, 50, 63–4.

[22] *A Brief Account of Stratford-upon-Avon* (Stratford-upon-Avon, n.d.), 8.

[23] Field, *Account of the Town and Castle of Warwick*, 284, 326, 327.

[24] Warwickshire CRO, MI 142, Entry, 23 September 1797; William Field, *Memoirs of the Life, Writings, and Opinions of the Rev. Samuel Parr, LL.D.*, 2 vols (London, 1828), 1: 207.

[25] Field, *Account of the Town and Castle of Warwick*, 356, 363.

middle-class families from neighbouring country parishes.[26] But here, ironically if predictably, old-fashioned deference and fashionable politeness collapsed, with, by 1745, 'uneasiness and quarrells about Sittings':[27] the insecure 'middling sort' were especially sensitive regarding matters of status.

Growing civility and sociability also affected the clerics themselves. Abraham Kent and Walter Evans had sometimes roistered and drunk excessively, aping old-fashioned squires.[28] But increasingly parsons wished to appear progressive, polite, genteel.

* * *

From the mid eighteenth century, the values of livings and the clergy's status rose appreciably in south Warwickshire. There was much enclosure, and parsons could gain from tithe commutation. Between 1745 and 1782, the primary visitation of Bishop Hurd (1781–1808), the values of the Kineton deanery's parishes increased markedly, and they continued to rise thereafter. By the 1770s and 80s, clerics appeared more obviously gentlemen than hitherto. The proportion of those of genteel birth rose; so did the parsons' academic standing.[29] In the late eighteenth century, the mansions of Charlecote and Newbold Comyn passed to two clergymen, respectively the Revd John Hammond and the Revd Edward Willes. Charles Mills, MP for Warwick, 1802–26, and William Mills, MP for Coventry, 1805–12, were the sons of John Mills, rector of Barford.[30] Along with landowning gentlemen, some clergymen became turnpike trustees, and, of sixty-six Justices appointed for Warwickshire in 1831, twenty-four were clerics.[31] This ostentatious alliance with elite interests was likely to alienate the 'meaner sort'. So too was clerical involvement in politics, so much the preserve of landed society and the 'middling sort'. John Morley, curate of Hampton Lucy, 1786–1814, and vicar of Wasperton, 1791–1814, was a committed Whig, as was the vicar of Wellesbourne from 1778 to 1829, John Henry Williams, who publicly denounced the conflict with France from 1793

---

26 Colin Haydon, 'The Church in the Kineton Deanery of the Diocese of Worcester, c.1660–c.1800', in Jeremy Gregory and Jeffrey S. Chamberlain, eds, *The National Church in Local Perspective: the Church of England and the Regions, 1660–1800* (Woodbridge, 2003), 153.

27 Worcestershire RO, BA 2608, Ref. b. 807.093.

28 London, Lambeth Palace Library, Eee 10/187, *passim*; Worcestershire RO, BA 2638, Ref. 795.61; BA 2632, Ref. 797.6 (iii), *passim*.

29 Haydon, 'Kineton Deanery', 150–1.

30 *The House of Commons, 1790–1820*, ed. R. G. Thorne, 5 vols (London, 1986), 4: 590, 593.

31 10 Geo. III, c. 63; *Parliamentary Papers* 35 (1831–32), 262.

to 1802. Conservative gentlemen were irritated by Morley's and Williams's politics;[32] so also, probably, were their social inferiors, given the widespread plebeian loyalism and Francophobia of the 1790s and 1800s. Other parsons supported the Younger Pitt. The Revd Daniel Gaches, vicar of Wootton Wawen, 1766–1805, chaired the loyalist association at Henley-in-Arden, and James Davenport, vicar of Stratford-upon-Avon, 1787–1841, acted as chaplain to the town's first volunteer company.[33] But, in time, Davenport's extreme conservatism became alienating too: he was the only man in Stratford to sign a county petition against the 1832 Reform bill.[34]

* * *

Clerical culture adapted to these changes. One obvious example of this is the clergy's discarding of many supernatural beliefs. John Ward was vicar of Stratford-upon-Avon from 1662 to 1681, and was keenly interested in medicine and Restoration science. But the supernatural fascinated him too. He believed in astrology, spells worked by demons, the demonic pact, and some folk and magical remedies for sickness.[35] To some parishioners, this scholarly parson resembled a necromancer: he was 'once bluntly askt . . . what Cabalists . . . [he] had in . . . [his] Studie'.[36] Abraham Kent sometimes recalled that, when young, he had met a conjurer who offered to teach him the magical arts. He had refused; but, he maintained, 'had . . . [he] the like offer again . . . [he] would embrace it willingly'.[37] Judging by the folk-lore recorded by Victorian and later antiquaries, plebeian credence in magic persisted in eighteenth-century rural Warwickshire. There was belief in ghosts, witches, magical healing, and fairies; and in a range of superstitions concerning luck.[38] A young labourer, in 1736, considered explaining some vile conduct by claiming that he had acted when 'Bewitched Mad or Drunk'.[39] But, in 1755, after an apparition was supposedly sighted in Harbury churchyard, the vicar, Richard Jago, loftily disdained to discuss

[32] Warwickshire CRO, MI 142, Entry, 19 June 1797; Field, *Memoirs of . . . Parr*, 1: 206–7.

[33] BL, Add. MS 16931, fol. 70r; London, The National Archives [hereafter: TNA], WO 13/4573.

[34] Nicholas Fogg, *Stratford-upon-Avon* (Chichester, 1986), 135.

[35] London, Wellcome Institute for the History of Medicine [hereafter: Wellcome Institute], Western MSS 6170–74 detail Ward's many interests.

[36] Wellcome Institute, Western MS 6173, fol. 1109.

[37] Worcestershire RO, BA 2638, Ref. 795.61, #13.

[38] Haydon, 'Kineton Deanery', 169–72.

[39] Worcestershire RO, BA 2632, Ref. 797.6 (iii), Deposition of Joseph Wilkes.

the occurrence in his Sunday sermon.[40] Likewise, in 1797, some 'common People' reported seeing a ghost near Wasperton, but John Morley did not attempt to disabuse them rationally, though he viewed the claim as 'ridiculous and superstitious'.[41] Why did 'enlightened' parsons neglect to uproot these 'vulgar superstitions'? Perhaps, privately, some thought they checked infidelity's growth. More probably, most viewed them as quaint and generally harmless, playthings for ignorant minds. This was condescension in the modern, and not the contemporary, sense.

The clergy's cultural pursuits became increasingly refined. The Revd James Wilmot, Barton-on-the-Heath's rector from 1783 to 1807, was 'well known at County and Convivial Meetings',[42] and John Morley patronized drama at Stratford and enjoyed convivial dining, Sunday tea-drinking, and the *Gentleman's Magazine*.[43] John Henry Williams apparently enjoyed music and was well read; in the early 1790s, he was president of Wellesbourne's book club.[44] In his parsonage, Richard Jago, 'a man of true taste',[45] composed his 'ingenious' poems: *The Blackbirds*, *The Swallows*, and the interminable *Edge-Hill*. The Revd Edward Willes 'lived retired at his own beautiful villa . . . devoted to the improvement of his estate and to the pleasures of literature'.[46] The clerics' alignment with polite recreations seems firm, their divorce from popular culture glaring. The latter is neatly captured by the celebrated Samuel Parr's May Day fêtes at Hatton – revivals of 'a pleasant custom of olden times'.[47] 'The master of the rustic ceremonies' greeted 'with smiles and merry jests, the rosy-faced girls he met . . . archly inquiring after their absent friends and favourites'; 'pleasure brightly shone in many a rustic countenance; whilst those of higher grade seemed to throw off all reserve . . .'.[48] The class fissure appears stark in this, an educated witness's, account,[49] and it seems unlikely it was lost on the 'meaner sort'. Parr's latest biographer concluded that his sermons

[40] Jago, *Causes of Impenitence*, title page, 3.
[41] Warwickshire CRO, MI 142, Entry, 9 August 1797.
[42] *Gentleman's Magazine* 83, Part 2 (1813), 546.
[43] Warwickshire CRO, MI 142, *passim*.
[44] Ibid., Entry, 10 November 1797; Field, *Memoirs of . . . Parr*, 1: 206–7.
[45] *A Complete Edition of the Poets of Great Britain*, ed. Robert Anderson, 14 vols (London, 1792–95), 11: 678.
[46] Field, *Memoirs of . . . Parr*, 1: 205.
[47] Ibid., 2: 322.
[48] Ibid., 2: 323, 324.
[49] Field was a Unitarian minister.

'were often too academic for his rural hearers';[50] and Parr could be graceless, as on an occasion when Dr Routh of Magdalen College, Oxford, visited Hatton and attended church. '[N]ow there is only one person present who can understand what I am going to say next', Parr bluntly told the congregation.[51] The remark resembles an observation of his friend Daniel Gaches: once, when sparring over Greek with Parr, who had gained the advantage, Gaches lamented he had become 'a barbarian amidst barbarians' in his 'retired village'.[52]

South Warwickshire's rural parsons also increasingly became physically, as well as culturally, remote from their flocks. John Henry Williams thought a parson must be his congregation's 'teacher and . . . neighbour',[53] but, during the eighteenth century, clerical non-residence inexorably increased. Some country clergy chose to live in towns. James Wilmot, when curate of Kenilworth, 'resided partly at Warwick, occasionally at Oxford . . . and sometimes in London'.[54] Nathaniel Booth, vicar of Wolford, 1780–87, lived in Merton College, Oxford, and tutored there.[55] Pluralism became common. In 1754, Richard Jago obtained the vicarage of Snitterfield, worth £140 a year. With two other livings, Jago now enjoyed, his friend William Shenstone noted, 'about a hundred and ninety [pounds *per annum*]: but then he is obliged to keep a curate; and what I think yet worse is, that he cannot make it *convenient* to *live* at his new situation, which is a pretty one'.[56] In fact, Jago was soon residing at Snitterfield; and he retained it after he had obtained the rectory of Kimcote, Leicestershire, worth nearly £300 a year, in 1771.[57] This was conduct that Bishop Stillingfleet had deplored: for him, 'to heap up Preferments merely for Riches, or Luxury, or Ambition' was 'an evil thing'.[58]

By the 1780s, the pattern of non-residence in the Kineton deanery appears baneful. In 1782, there were twenty-nine incumbents and ten curates for the thirty-five parishes there. Yet no fewer than fifteen parishes (43%) had no resident minister. Sometimes, financial necessity

50 Leonard W. Cowie, 'Parr, Samuel (1747–1825)', *ODNB* 42: 849.
51 Warren Derry, *Dr Parr* (London, 1966), 271.
52 Field, *Memoirs of . . . Parr*, 1: 203–4.
53 J. H. Williams, *War the Stumbling-Block of a Christian* (London, 1795), 10.
54 *Gentleman's Magazine* 83, Part 2, 315.
55 Oxford, Merton College, Archive D.2.19, *passim*; D.2.19a, 1, 3.
56 *The Works, in Verse and Prose, of William Shenstone, Esq*, 3 vols (5th edn, London, 1777), 3: 234.
57 *Poets of Great Britain*, ed. Anderson, 11: 676.
58 Stillingfleet, *Charge*, 47.

occasioned pluralism and non-residence; but, in a significant number of cases, the evidence indicates the prime cause was greed.[59]

How did Bishop Johnson (1759–74), Bishop North (1774–81), and Bishop Hurd respond to such growing self-indulgence? Seemingly, with insufficient concern. Johnson produced a printed visitation return, bearing the words 'know of nothing presentable' and requiring just one churchwarden's signature: a plain discouragement to lay complaint.[60] Similar forms followed in 1776 and 1790.[61] During his primary visitation, Hurd, while recognizing that poor livings might necessitate pluralism,[62] deplored frivolous reasons for non-residence: 'for the convenience . . . of living in a better air or neighbourhood; of seeing a little more, or, what is called, *better*, company; or sharing in the advantages and amusements . . . of the larger and more populous towns'.[63] Yet, in 1807, Hurd admitted that he did not enforce residence strictly: to do so, he maintained, would throw 'numbers of the Clergy into . . . a state of uneasiness and discomfort'.[64]

* * *

In the early eighteenth century, Dissent had stagnated in south Warwickshire – a mark of the Established Church's well-being. At Stratford-upon-Avon, there were three hundred Presbyterians in 1715; by 1782, there was but a 'little [Dissenting] remnant'.[65] Yet, from the later eighteenth century, the Church's failings permitted renewed Nonconformist encroachment. At Kineton, after the departure of an evangelical vicar, William Talbot, one Charles Parsons began evangelical preaching, supplementary to the Church's services; and a chapel, later used by Independents and Baptists, was erected.[66] Methodist meetings were held at Shipston on Stour in the 1770s, and, by 1782, there were some Methodists at Oxhill and Stratford-upon-Avon.[67] In Victorian times, there were folk memories of the Tysoe men who, to

---

[59] Haydon, 'Kineton Deanery', 154–5, 156.
[60] Worcestershire RO, BA 2289, Ref. 807.
[61] Ibid.
[62] *The Works of Richard Hurd, D.D.*, 8 vols (London, 1811), 8: 76–7.
[63] Ibid., 8: 78.
[64] *Parliamentary Papers* 9 (1808), 253.
[65] Haydon, 'Kineton Deanery', 169; John Sibree and M. Caston, *Independency in Warwickshire* (Coventry and London, 1855), 198.
[66] *The Evangelical Magazine* 12 (1804), 386–7; Sibree and Caston, *Independency*, 272.
[67] P. Drinkwater and F. W. Mayo, *An History of Methodism in Shipston on Stour* (Shipston on Stour, 1981), 1; *Bishopric*, ed. Ransome, 177, 179.

see John Wesley, had walked a round journey of sixty miles.[68] Wesleyan chapels were established at Tysoe (1796), Oxhill (1814), and Shipston (1828).[69] Independency grew in Stratford-upon-Avon, Warwick, and Leamington in the late eighteenth and early nineteenth centuries, and the towns' pastors assisted congregations in neighbouring villages including Loxley and Newbold Pacey. In 1802, a chapel, served by nearby Baptist and Independent ministers, was built at Ettington.[70] An itinerant evangelical preacher had some success in Samuel Parr's Hatton; and, in 1825, Samuel West, a former Methodist, opened an Independent chapel at Long Compton.[71]

Was this Dissent unequivocally 'popular religion'? It was at Newbold Pacey: the grouping there originated with 'a poor but pious man' who organized a Sunday school while friends preached or read a sermon.[72] Elsewhere, the picture was more complex. The mission of Charles Parsons, formerly William Talbot's servant, was distinctively to the poor; but he and his hearers received Communion in Kineton church.[73] Though merely wanting 'to preach the gospel freely to the *poor*', Samuel West was a shopkeeper and schoolmaster, typically part of the lesser rural 'middling sort'.[74] The Ettington chapel was built by a successful businessman. It was partly a sober, middle-class rebuke to elite selfishness and insensitivity. In 1795, the Shirley family's enclosure at Lower Ettington had resulted in the ancient church's closure; and, although a new church was consecrated in 1802, it was inconveniently situated for most parishioners.[75]

* * *

This essay's findings resemble those of some other modern studies of the Church of England from the Revolution to the early nineteenth century. In south Warwickshire, the Toleration Act not only produced a crisis for the Established Church by permitting religious pluralism,

---

68 M. K. Ashby, *Joseph Ashby of Tysoe, 1859–1919* (London, 1974, repr. 1979), 84.

69 Drinkwater and Mayo, *Methodism*, 1–2; *Victoria County History, Warwick*, 8 vols (London, 1904–69), 5: 124. A Primitive Methodist chapel was also erected in Tysoe: Ashby, *Joseph Ashby*, 77.

70 Sibree and Caston, *Independency*, 136–45, 198–206, 275–8, 294–303.

71 Field, *Memoirs of . . . Parr*, 2: 335; Sibree and Caston, *Independency*, 316–17. The 1851 religious census shows later Dissenting growth in south Warwickshire: TNA, HO 129/406.

72 Sibree and Caston, *Independency*, 302–3.

73 *Evangelical Magazine* 12 (1804), 385–8.

74 Sibree and Caston, *Independency*, 317.

75 Ibid., 274–5.

and hence competition, but also gave a spur to more effective pastoral endeavour.[76] But, for the later period investigated, the essay portrays the Church's condition more gloomily than have some recent 'optimistic' scholars.[77] The essay is largely a cultural variation on the primarily economic themes explored by Eric Evans and W. R. Ward;[78] and it endorses the picture of the lower orders' cultural alienation from the Established Church produced for the diocese of Salisbury by Donald Spaeth and for Lancashire by M. F. Snape.[79] The piece also supports some older writing: Norman Sykes's view of the Church's calcification in the late eighteenth and early nineteenth centuries; even Macaulay's sketch of the country clergy's 'gentrification' between the late seventeenth century and his own times.[80] But, whereas Macaulay viewed that change favourably, and modern historians are impressed by the clergy's gradual 'professionalization',[81] the south-Warwickshire evidence emphasizes that an increasingly refined clerical caste could prove alienating to parishioners. Not that there was a straightforward patrician/plebeian, elite/popular religious polarization. There were tiers of alienation from the Established Church in the rural society examined here. Still, one is not surprised that when, about 1840, some Methodist preachers came from Wellesbourne to Barford, Joseph Arch was among those who attended their meetings, held in a barn. Nor is it surprising that he later became a Primitive Methodist lay preacher.[82]

South Warwickshire is particularly interesting because it was potentially an optimum locality for the Established Church. The Kineton deanery – some twenty miles north to south, ten miles east to west – comprised compact parishes with small populations. In 1782, it had

---

[76] Cf. Jeremy Gregory, *Restoration, Reformation, and Reform, 1660–1828* (Oxford, 2000), 234.

[77] On the debates on the Church's condition, see Jeremy Gregory, 'The Church of England', in H. T. Dickinson, ed., *A Companion to Eighteenth-Century Britain* (Malden, MA, 2002), 225–40.

[78] Eric J. Evans, 'Some Reasons for the Growth of English Rural Anti-Clericalism, *c*.1750–*c*.1830', *P&P* 66 (1975), 84–109; W. R. Ward, 'The Tithe Question in England in the Early Nineteenth Century', *JEH* 16 (1965), 67–81.

[79] Donald A. Spaeth, *The Church in an Age of Danger* (Cambridge, 2000), 254–9; M. F. Snape, *The Church of England in Industrializing Society* (Woodbridge, 2003), 193–9.

[80] Norman Sykes, *Church and State in England in the Eighteenth Century* (Cambridge, 1934), 407, 409; Lord Macaulay, *The History of England from the Accession of James the Second*, ed. Charles Harding Firth, 6 vols (London, 1913–15), I: 313–14.

[81] E.g., Rosemary O'Day, *The Professions in Early Modern England, 1450–1800* (Harlow, 2000), 110.

[82] Pamela Horn, *Joseph Arch* (Kineton, 1971), 8.

ample clergy. Yet, in that year, thirteen parishes held only one Sunday service, and just one monthly service was performed in another.

Did it matter that, in 1782, forty per cent of the deanery's parishes violated the double duty enjoined by the Church's canons? Could not villagers go the extra mile to another parish church, if there was no convenient service in their own? Is not criticism of the clergy easily dispelled by a 'counter-factual' conceit – the amalgamation of adjacent parishes into seventeen, still-manageable, units, each holding two Sunday services? Arguably: but this is hardly satisfactory, given the example of commitment and service which clergymen were expected to set. Or the challenge from Dissent. Or congregations' sentimental ties to their parish churches – buildings in which the laity took pride, the settings for weddings and baptisms, with churchyards containing parents' and ancestors' graves. And, in the early nineteenth century, it was not for the polite clerics of south Warwickshire to complain about those, like Joseph Arch, whom they had driven away.

University of Winchester

'. . . THIS CONGREGATION HERE PRESENT . . .': SEATING IN PARISH CHURCHES DURING THE LONG EIGHTEENTH CENTURY

by W. M. JACOB

PARISH churches during the 'long eighteenth century' were meeting places for the whole community, elite and popular. Accommodating the hierarchically ordered and theologically aware society of England and Wales in church was not a simple matter. How might the elite and the popular, the squire and his relations, and his groom, and boot boy and the milk maid, and aspiring farmers and attorneys and their wives and sisters and cousins and aunts, along with day labourers and paupers, be included together as the body of Christ before God? People were sensitive about their social stratification. Richard Gough, in his history of his parish of Myddle in Shropshire in 1702, writing about the families of the parish on the basis of their seats in church, cautioned thus:

> I hope no man will blame mee for not naming every person according to that which hee conceives is his right and superiority in the seats in Church, because it is a thing impossible for any man to know; and therefore I have not endeavoured to doe it, but have written the names according as they came to memory.[1]

The Church Building Act of 1818, providing for new churches to accommodate the rapidly increasing population, set out the ideal that all classes should be brought together in church to worship God.

* * *

Eighteenth-century society, like all societies, was both differentiated, culturally structured and hierarchical, and also undifferentiated and homogeneous. Individuals were able to encounter one another, disregarding their statuses and roles.[2] The parish church was the most obvious context in which this happened, and where the identity of a community, elite and popular, was achieved. A process of negotiation

---

[1] Richard Gough, *The History of Myddle*, ed. David Hey (Harmondsworth, 1981), 9.
[2] See Victor W. Turner, *The Ritual Process* (Harmondsworth, 1969), 166.

and mediation was necessary, for community does not exclude distinctions, disturbance and dissent, nor does it mean the same thing to everyone, and so tensions and conflict are likely to be a feature of the process of being a community. The parish church, usually the sole communal meeting place, was the prime arena in which the identity of a local community was worked out; the distribution of seats in the parish church expressed the construct of the community, and its identity.[3] The church was more than a place of worship; it reflected the parish's history and hierarchy.

In an ordered and hierarchical society, identity and location within the community were expressed or reinforced by the location of one's seat in church, and, as everyone was included within the compass of God's mercy, no one should be excluded from a seat in church. The whole community, in its complex social structures, was assembled, in order, before God, in the seating arrangements of the parish church. One's place in church on Sunday indicated one's status in the community. Because of the symbolic and social importance of seats in church, conflicts might arise over where people sat. Events in church encapsulated the social and personal tensions in the life of a town or village.[4] Conversely the allocation of seats might contribute towards harmony, or at least a working consensus, in a local community.[5]

Disturbance of seating arrangements was a sensitive matter. Richard Gough at Myddle noted that 'it was held a thing unseemly and indecent that a company of young boyes, and of persons that paid noe [church rates] should sitt . . . above those of the best of the parish'.[6] At Welshpool in 1728 it was alleged that a 'very common sort of people' sit in the gallery 'under the pretence of psalm singing', 'some of them spitting upon the heads of people below'.[7] Wholesale re-allocations of seats in a church may represent changing social statuses in a parish. Proximity to the pulpit, or the altar, was the defining characteristic of the most honourable pew.

---

[3] For an illuminating discussion of this in an earlier period see Christopher Marsh, ' "Common Prayer" in England 1560–1640: the View from the Pew', *P & P* 170 (2001), 66–94, and idem, 'Sacred Space in England 1560–1640: the View from the Pew', *JEH* 53 (2002), 300–5.

[4] Susan Dwyer Amussen, *An Ordered Society: Gender and Class in Early Modern England* (Oxford, 1988), 137–8.

[5] Marsh, ' "Common Prayer" in England', 93.

[6] Gough, *History of Myddle*, 20.

[7] Quoted in G. W. O. Addleshaw and Frederick Etchells, *The Architectural Setting of Anglican Worship* (London, 1948), 100.

Responsibility for managing these matters was in the hands of the lay leadership of the parish, the churchwardens, or, in a corporate borough, the mayor and common council, drawn from the parish gentry or urban elite, who were the trustees of parish society and its values and aspirations.[8] Bishops had attempted to control these matters, amid much controversy, during the 1630s, but after the Restoration they left their courts to oversee granting faculties, if they were applied for, and to resolve disputes. Otherwise churchwardens acted in virtue of an implied commission from the chancellor of the diocese. James Shaw in his *Parish Law* of 1753 stated that 'The parishioners have indeed a claim to be seated according to their rank and station', but noted that churchwardens were not to accommodate the 'higher classes' beyond their 'real wants' or 'overlook the claim of all parishioners to be seated, if sittings can be afforded them'.[9] The task of maintaining the tension between unity and hierarchy, the popular and the elite, was therefore in the hands of representatives of the local elite.

* * *

Allocation of seats was an inexact science. Only in the provision of seats for office holders – the churchwardens, and the mayor and common council men and their families – could seats totally reflect the status and honour of the occupant. Allocation of a pew indicated how a person was honoured in the community. Disputes were about defending or claiming social position and honour. Churchwardens had the unenviable task of allocating worldly and self-absorbed sinful human beings amongst the whole company of God's faithful people, to unite the elite and the popular. No verbatim accounts survive of how churchwardens made their decisions. How were they achieved?

In rural churches seats were 'appropriated' by churchwardens to individuals or families. Probably every family in a parish had, or could have had, a sitting which was free. Seats were mostly allocated according to landholdings. At Buckerell in Devon the proposed seating plan of 1773 shows the major landowner's pew next to the pulpit, commanding a view of the whole church, the vicar's pew in the

8 See Eric Carlson, 'The Origins, Functions and Status of the Office of Churchwarden, with Particular Reference to the Diocese of Ely', in Margaret Spufford, ed., *The World of Rural Dissenters 1520–1725* (Cambridge, 1995), 195–207.

9 Quoted in K. D. M. Snell, 'Free or Appropriated Sittings: the Anglican Church in Perspective', in K. D. M. Snell and Paul S. Ell, eds, *Rival Jerusalems: the Geography of Victorian Religion* (Cambridge, 2000), 321–62, at 332.

chancel, and Admiral Graves, the other prominent resident, with a seat close to the pulpit also commanding a view of the whole church. The rest were graded according to the size of their farms, down to small-holders at the rear, and at the back of the nave and the transept were seats for the poor and servants, with women and men segregated, except for the 'quality' families.[10] At South Carlton in Lincolnshire, a plan shows the major landowner's pew in the chancel, the incumbent's pew in the front of the nave, and behind, the largest farmer with 615 acres; on either side of the aisle were the other farmers, the larger towards the front, the smaller behind; sharing seats near the back were a shopkeeper, shoemaker, schoolmaster and cottagers, with a sitting reserved for 'servant maids'. There were sittings in the north aisle, from front to rear, for 'servant men' cottagers, a foreman, three labourers, two labourers, another shoemaker, two more labourers with a pauper widow, and a free sitting. Along the west wall were further free seats, and in the chancel the school children sat opposite the squire's pew.[11] It is unclear whether particular occupation groups sat in certain parts of churches. Geographical mobility in the population was presumably accommodated by the free seats.

In some rural parishes allocation of seats was related to the level of rates paid. At Overton in Hampshire the churchwardens were advised to seat their parishioners 'according to their respective degrees and qualities and according to the rates and taxes which everyone pays or ought to pay towards the repair of the church'.[12] In 1736 Winchester consistory court decided that at Hinton Admiral 'such . . . as paid most to the parish rates . . . should have the uppermost places', and the churchwardens of the then still largely rural parish of Lambeth were empowered to reallocate the seats of any who were in arrears in their rates.

There were varying ways of being close to the pulpit, and therefore demonstrating one's position at the head of the hierarchy of a parish. Even better for prominence than a seat at the junction of the nave and transepts or in the chancel was a gallery seat, which gave undisputable

[10] Arthur Warne, *Church and Society in Eighteenth-Century Devon* (Newton Abbot, 1969), 56–7.

[11] James Obelkevich, *Religion and Rural Society: South Lindsey 1825–1875* (Oxford, 1976), 109–10 [LAO South Carlton parish records].

[12] Kevin Dillow, 'The Social and Ecclesiastical Significance of Church Seating Arrangements and Pew Disputes 1500–1740', unpublished D.Phil. thesis, University of Oxford, 1990, 98.

prominence, and proximity, at the same level, to a high pulpit. At Great Cheverell in 1704 the principal landowner had the 'foremost' seat in the gallery. At Burton-by-Lincoln, rebuilt in 1795, Lord Monson sat in a small gallery at the west end over the entrance. Nearby, when Robert Cracroft rebuilt Hackthorn church in 1849, he too built a west gallery for the use of himself and his family.

A common way in towns for churchwardens to solve the problem of allocation of pews, to maintain a satisfactory tension between unity and hierarchy, was for the vestry to set the rents, so people could identify their own position in the local hierarchy by the price they paid to buy or rent a seat. At Wilton in 1759 'An Assembly of the Parishioners held in the Vestry . . .' set rents for seats, in a range from 3s to 12s, and decided how many seats there should be in each pew.[13] Sometimes this was achieved by auctioning pews. At Boston, Lincolnshire, in 1724 the seats in the new organ loft were sold to the highest bidders.[14] At King's Lynn, when the church was rebuilt in 1754, after seats had been allocated to dignitaries and officeholders,

> for the avoiding any uneasiness and discontent that may arise among the Parishioners at large or any imputation of undue preference or partiality in the Disposal of . . . Seats . . ., the Subscribers shall be divided in to four classes viz 20, 15, 10 and 5 pound subscribers. That the Subscribers shall ballot for the choice of the Seats according to their classes. The £20 to ballot first and afterwards each according to their Order and Degrees.[15]

Outright sale of pews was probably the most unsatisfactory way of dealing with pews, for they were alienated from the management of the churchwardens, and considerable power was given to pew owners, particularly when funds were required to repair the church.[16] However, ownership made pew owners serious stakeholders in a church, and might spread the burden of financing repairs among a large number of people.[17] At Trowbridge the 'Conditions of Sale and Purchase of Seats

---

[13] *Wiltshire Pew Rents*, ed. Beryl Hurley, Wiltshire Family History Society, 4 vols (Devizes, 1995–98), 3: 3 and 18.

[14] Lincolnshire Archive Office, Boston 10/1, Vestry Minute Book, 1705–1776.

[15] King's Lynn Borough Archives, unnumbered, St Margaret's Church Book, 1741.

[16] For an illustration of such difficulties see Nigel Yates, *Holy Trinity: Church, Parish and People* (Gosport [?], Gosport Society, 1980). For a detailed account of the law and practice of ownership of pews, see Dillow, 'Social and Ecclesiastical Significance of Church Seating Arrangements', ch. 2.

[17] For further examples of fundraising for church building and repairs by means of sale

in the Parish Church of Trowbridge' of 1765 attempted to moderate the effects of selling pews by requiring the churchwardens to keep a register of sales and exchanges of seats or pews, recording the number of the pew in question. Purchasers were required to be inhabitants of the parish, and a 'member of this church'; if they dissented from the church or moved from the parish they forfeited their pew. If a person nominated his own life only in the purchase, his family had to renew the purchase on his death.[18] At Calne in Wiltshire men also bought seats in pews for their sons and grandsons. Purchases were mostly for the purchaser's life, changes of ownership and exchanges, again being registered by the churchwardens. Unusually in 1754 the seats in the north gallery, formerly belonging to Sir Orlando Bridgemen were granted to the earl of Shelbourne and his successors, owners of Bowood House, forever, for 60 Guineas. People might own seats in different parts of the church, for example Jeremiah Awdry at Melksham had pews number 13, 38, 18 and 20 for his servants, and 24 for women.[19]

Application for a faculty for a pew, presumably, because of the complexity and expense of legal fees, an elite activity, took decisions out of churchwardens' hands, and may have been a way of overruling churchwardens. In forty-nine out of 110 applications for faculties for pews in the diocese of Oxford during the first half of the eighteenth century, churchwardens opposed the application.[20] There was no consistency in the terms in which faculties granting pews were drafted. Of twenty-four faculties for pews in the diocese of Gloucester between 1709 and 1716, six were given as long as the petitioner lived in a certain house, and four were restricted to residence in the parish, and fourteen had no restrictions. In London diocese between 1685 and 1730, nineteen out of seventy-six faculties for pews were granted to individuals so long as they lived in a particular house, and thirty-nine were granted as long as the individual lived in the parish, and eighteen had no limitation.[21]

Theological factors also influenced the maintenance of the tension between unity and hierarchy in allocating church seating. Joseph

---

of pews and mortgaging pew rents, see C. W. Chalklin, 'The Financing of Church Building in the Provincial Towns of Eighteenth-Century England', in Peter Clark, ed., *The Transformation of English Provincial Towns 1600–1800* (London, 1984), 292–9.

[18] *Wiltshire Pew Rents*, 2: 2.

[19] Ibid., 1: 12, 16, 18, and 45.

[20] Dillow, 'Social and Ecclesiastical Significance of Church Seating Arrangements', 76–7.

[21] Ibid., 117.

Bingham, in *Origines ecclesiasticae,* documented the ancient practices of separating men and women in church noted by Cyril of Jerusalem, Ambrose and Augustine, and cited Gregory Nazianzen and Paul the Silentiary as evidence that women sat apart from men, in galleries.[22] Two leading advocates of 'Primitive Christianity', William Cave and Sir George Wheler, stressed the importance of separating men from women 'lest . . . unchaste and irregular appetites should be kindled by a promiscuous mixing with one another'.[23] George Hickes, the nonjuror, in his Observations on John Vanbrugh's unpublished paper, 'Proposals about Building the Fifty New Churches', wished 'that in these new churches the Seats, or pews for the men should be on the one side and those of the women on the other according to ancient custom'.[24] Hawksmoor in his drawing of the plan for 'The Basilica after the Primitive Christians' notes: 'Stairs to ye Women's Gallery'.[25]

Separation of sexes in church was common. At Hambledon in Buckinghamshire in 1687 the seats were arranged so that 'men that sit in them cannot see the women in their seats'.[26] In Wiltshire at Great Cheverell in 1704, Seend in 1727, Sturton and Gasper, and Winterslow in 1768, and Collingbourne Ducis in 1770, separate seats are noted for women and men. In the towns of Melksham in 1736, when the pews and seats were renumbered, women's and men's seats were identified, at Warminster there were separate seats for women, and at Mere in 1815 men and women were listed in separate pews.[27] However at Kilmington in 1742, Compton in 1811 and Malmesbury before 1823, the pew lists give no indication of separation of men and women.[28] There seems to be no regional pattern in separation of men and women in church.

George Hickes's criticism that 'high pewes are most indecent, and the occasion of much deplorable irreverence in church', and his recom-

[22] Joseph Bingham, *Origines ecclesiasticae, or the Antiquities of the Christian Church,* 10 vols (London, 1708–22), 3: repr. in 9 vols (London, 1840), 2: 411–15.

[23] William Cave, *Primitive Christianity, or the Religion of the Ancient Christians in the First Ages of the Gospel* (6th edn, London, 1702), 89, and Sir George Wheler, *The Protestant Monastery, or the Christian Oeconomicks, Containing Directions for the Religious Conduct of a Family* (London, 1698), 100.

[24] Quoted in Pierre de la Ruffiniere du Prey, *Hawksmoor's London Churches: Architecture and Theology* (Chicago, IL, and London, 2000), 141.

[25] Ibid., 65.

[26] Quoted in Dillow, 'Social and Ecclesiastical Significance of Church Seating Arrangements', 132.

[27] *Wiltshire Pew Rents,* 1: 45; 4: 26–7 and 64.

[28] *Local Censuses in Wiltshire: Pew Lists,* ed. Beryl Hurley, Wiltshire Family History Society (Devizes, 1994), 6, 11, 15, 33, 39, and 46.

mendation that all pews should be of 'equal hight', and 'no distinction of quality be made in churches by carpets or other signes of worldly greatness, the noble and ignoble, the Rich and poor being all equal in the house and worship and solemn presence of God',[29] could be met by using galleries, as has been noted, to provide seats of honour. At Hampstead parish church in 1759, the pews in the church, re-built in 1746, were rented at between 10s 6d and 15s a sitting, but the best entire pews, in the galleries, were rented at £4 4s. However in 1834 the pattern had changed: pews in the nave were rented at £8 8s, while front gallery pews were £5 5s, and pews under the galleries were £4 4s.[30] At St Giles-in-the-Fields, the parish church of Holborn in London, in 1801 front pews in the galleries were also let at £4 4s, while those behind were merely 5s a sitting, as were the pews in the side aisles on the floor of the church.[31] At Mortlake parish church, in Surrey, in 1836, the front gallery pews were occupied by the leading parishioners, including the Marquis of Ailesbury, Viscount Sidmouth and Sir William Kaye, with their servants sitting in the pews behind.[32] At Calne in Wiltshire the 'First rank' seats in the new gallery erected in 1715 were the most expensive in the church. However at Warminster and at Mere there was no price differential between seats on the floor of the church and in the galleries.

Building a gallery might disturb the hierarchy of seating in a church, and the social ordering of the inhabitants at worship. The elite did not wish to be overlooked by the poorer sort, nor did they wish, as at Welshpool, to be the victims of what fell from the galleries. Putting up galleries for singers (as opposed to charity school children, whose elevated position illustrated the fruit of the charity of parishioners) might cause some of the poorer sort to be elevated above their betters. Subscribers to building a gallery, which had been clearly stated to be for singers, might then demand a seat in the gallery, and the vestry would be forced to a difficult arbitration.

The poor were sometimes allocated what might seem prominent seats, perhaps to demonstrate the extent to which they were cherished

[29] Du Prey, *Hawksmoor's London Churches*, 140–1.

[30] M. H. Port, *Hampstead Parish Church: the Story of a Building through 250 Years*, St John at Hampstead PCC (London, 1995), 9 and 13.

[31] London Borough of Camden Local Studies Centre, St Giles in the Fields, Vestry Minute Book, 1771–1840.

[32] Leslie Freeman, *Going to the Parish: Mortlake and the Parish Church of St Mary the Virgin*, Barnes and Mortlake History Society (Chippenham, 1993), 11.

by the elite, or perhaps to make their absence noticeable and ensure their good behaviour. George Hickes proposed to the Commission for Building Fifty New Churches that there should be

> Moveable forms for the empty spaces in the three aisles, for the poorer sort, whose modesty will not allow them to sit among their betters, as also for those who happen to come late to church, and their formes may be kept under the belfry.[33]

The 'Rules for the Fifty New Churches set down by the Commissioners and their Subcommittee' in July 1713 required that 'Moveable Forms be so contrived as to run under the seats of the Pewes and draw out into the Isles upon occasion'.[34] The Commissioners revised Gibbs's design for St Mary-le-Strand so the aisle would be ten feet wide, presumably to allow space for benches.[35] In the new churches of St Philip's, Birmingham (consecrated 1715), and St Giles-in-the-Fields in London (consecrated 1734), there were benches down the central aisle for the poor. This was not merely an urban phenomenon: at Thurning in Norfolk, where the church was reordered *c.*1830, the pews were arranged around the walls of the church for the 'better sort' and there were benches in the centre of the nave for the 'poorer sort'. The poor might also be placed in galleries, presumably for the display of charity. At Warminster a west gallery was erected in 1761 by benefactors and voluntary subscriptions for the 'sole use and benefit of the Poor'.[36] Charity school children were frequently placed in galleries. At Wilton in Wiltshire in the pew rent book for 1733–47 it was noted that 'on the left hand side of the alley are seven places which are for the people of the workhouse'.[37]

A prescriptive title to a seat (without having bought it) might be established on a variety of grounds: that their ancestors had bought it, continuous occupation and repair of it; that it belonged to a particular house; or that a faculty had been granted for it. Where seats were allocated to a particular property, to avoid disputes, the name of the property might be inscribed on the pew, as at Shermanbury and West

---

33 Du Prey, *Hawksmoor's London Churches*, 141.

34 Ibid., 143.

35 *The Commission for Building Fifty New Churches: the Minute Books 1711–1727: a Calendar*, ed. M. H. Port, London Record Society 23 (London, 1986), 60.

36 *Wiltshire Pew Rents*, 1: 5 and 13, and 4: 8; and *Local Censuses in Wiltshire*, 6.

37 *Wiltshire Pew Rents*, 3: 14.

Grimstead in West Sussex.[38] Seating plans sometimes list seats by the houses or farms to which they belong. There could be confusion, especially if owners sold a pew, and churchwardens failed to register a change.

* * *

Disputes about the allocation or 'invasion of seats' were often an aspect of social transitions in villages or towns. Kevin Dillow has suggested disputes were more likely in populous parishes, especially in market towns, and gentry were the most likely litigants;[39] Susan Amussen suggested this was because there distance between the gentry and yeomanry was closest, and the need for self-promotion was greatest.[40] However, disputes that reached the courts were relatively few. In the archdeaconries of Brecon and Carmarthen in St David's diocese, and in the diocese of Llandaff, the most cases of 'usurpation of a seat' in any decade between 1680 and 1760 was twelve, and in some decades there were no cases. In the diocese of Bangor there was only one case between 1734 and 1760.[41] However, in the dioceses of Gloucester, Winchester and the archdeaconry of Buckinghamshire, twenty-four per cent of consistory court cases between 1700 and 1740 were about pews.[42] Disputes were frequently settled out of court, or by a commission, or by a visit by the chancellor and/or registrar.

Cases also went on appeal from twenty-one diocesan consistory courts to the Canterbury provincial Court of Arches, but not in large numbers compared with other cases reflecting communal tensions, such as defamation. In the 1680s there were twenty-nine cases about pews referred to the Court of Arches, thirteen in the 1690s, seventeen in the 1700s, twenty-one in the 1710s, twenty in the 1720s, twenty-one in the 1730s and twelve in the 1740s. Thereafter, until the 1840s, numbers in any decade never reached double figures. An average of two cases a year between 1680 and 1750 does not suggest major tensions over seating arrangements. As might be expected, most cases were from town parishes.[43]

---

[38] Nigel Yates, *Buildings. Faith and Worship* (Oxford, 1991), 38.
[39] Dillow, 'Social and Ecclesiastical Significance of Church Seating Arrangements', 199–210.
[40] Amussen, *An Ordered Society*, 137–44.
[41] National Library of Wales SD/CCB(G), SD/CCCm(G), /LL/CC/G, B/CC/G.
[42] Dillow, 'Social and Ecclesiastical Significance of Church Seating Arrangements', 195.
[43] *Cases in the Court of Arches 1660–1913*, ed. Jane Houston, British Record Society 85

* * *

The general impression is that tensions inherent in bringing together elite and popular elements in the community in church were managed by the laity, in the persons of the churchwardens, and common councils in boroughs. There were relatively few disputes about seating arrangements in churches. The relative fluidity in English and Welsh society was reflected in town churches in particular by ranking seats, and allowing people to identify their own position, by offering seats for sale. Even in villages people were placed by the acreage of the land they farmed, and the level of rates paid. The ordering of communities in church reflected the socio-economic complexion of the communities themselves, even when the sexes were segregated. However, value was demonstrably placed on Christian charitable relief of the poor, by locating seats for the poor and charity children in prominent positions. The success of these arrangements for accommodating elite and popular members of society together in church is suggested by its continuance in many places until at least 1851.[44]

London

(Chichester, 1972). I am grateful to Melanie Barber of Lambeth Palace Library for this reference.

[44] Snell, 'Free or Appropriated Sittings', 34.

INDEFINITE SUCCESS:
RELIGION AND CULTURE
IN EIGHTEENTH-CENTURY GENEVA

by LINDA KIRK

THIS essay will argue that in eighteenth-century Geneva the religion of most of the lay elite followed the French pattern: learning and fashion alike steered them to a relaxed attitude to religious practice, and a mildly sceptical view of doctrine. It will be shown, however, that Geneva's clergy – not securely within the elite – often tried to resist any softening of Geneva's strict rules and social constraints even when they were keen to embrace scientific enlightenment;[1] further, no overarching account of popular religion in Geneva can convincingly be propounded. One reason for this is that Geneva's popular classes, unlike those of France, were dominated by literate, prosperous townspeople, many of whom still self-consciously lived out their protestant heritage, but some of whom found more meaning in radical, almost-secular politics.

In order to explore some of the complexity behind these assertions, I shall first sketch the layers in Genevan society. These differed from the usual European model: Geneva had no royalty and no formal aristocracy, although it was governed through a system of councils which gave secure power to a few great families. The citizen body excluded recent immigrants ('*habitants*'), and likewise most of the children and grandchildren of those who had arrived, poor, from the 1680s onwards ('*natifs*'). There were of course no bishops; Genevan clergy were (during the course of this century) increasingly marginalized and underrewarded by the city's lay rulers – in a sense squeezed out of the social elite.[2] Perhaps, even if they came of distinguished families and were

---

[1] Jacob Vernes's short-lived periodical *Choix Littéraire* wooed its readers by claiming that it would demonstrate to the Christian 'the accord there is between his reason and his religion': Jacob Vernes, ed., *Choix Littéraire* 1 (1755), ix–x.

[2] Linda Kirk, 'Godliness in a Golden Age: the Church and Wealth in Eighteenth-Century Geneva', in W. J. Sheils and Diana Wood, eds, *The Church and Wealth*, SCH 24 (Oxford, 1987), 333–46; 'A Poor Church in a Rich City: the Case of Geneva', in Marcel Pacaut and Olivier Fatio, eds, with the collaboration of Michel Grandjean, *L'Hostie et le denier: les finances ecclésiastiques du Haut Moyen Age à l'époque Moderne, Actes du Colloque . . . d'histoire*

well-educated, they may best be seen as mirroring the *bons curés* of France.[3] In 1700 all who lived in the city, including *habitants* and *natifs*, were expected to conform to the city's customs and to worship alongside their neighbours.

In earlier work I have shown how this was a century during which Geneva's Calvinist inheritance softened, eroded and split:[4] in 1706 Turrettini explained that '[t]here are not two Ways nor two Kinds of Doctrines, one for the Pastors, and another for the People that lead to Heaven',[5] nonetheless, in private, clergy held doctrinal positions sometimes more flexible than those they were keen to preach in public. They took important steps away from the *Consensus Helveticarum* of 1675. Double predestination, for instance, was quietly dropped. Vernes and Vernet, Turrettini and Pictet, their long treatises and slightly snappier sermons, have all been examined by Graham Gargett, Michael Heyd, Martin Klauber and others.[6] Doctrinal corsets were loosened, with a common-sensical approach to knottier elements in the Bible's narrative;[7] while the laymen of the Small Council, the effective government of Geneva, retained final word on ecclesiastical affairs.

* * *

Geneva's culture changed significantly in this period. In summary: illegitimacy, and pregnancy among brides, both rose (from very low bases); there were more divorces and more suicides; dancing masters and freemasons entered the city's life; more Genevans read, and fewer of them read works of theology; their wills were less likely to start by reciting their Calvinist convictions; witchcraft was no longer prose-

---

ecclésiastique comparée, Genève, août 1989, Publications de la Faculté de Théologie de l'Université de Genève 14, Labor et Fides (Geneva, 1991), 257–67. In the following notes the place of publication is Geneva unless otherwise stated.

[3] John McManners, *Church and Society in Eighteenth-Century France,* 2 vols (Oxford, 1998), I: 321–98.

[4] For instance, in 'Eighteenth-Century Geneva and a Changing Calvinism', in S. Mews, ed., *Religion and National Identity,* SCH 18 (Oxford, 1982), 367–80.

[5] J.-A. Turrettini, *Speech Previous to the Abolition of all Subscriptions at Geneva* (London, 1748), 171.

[6] Graham Gargett, *Jacob Vernet, Geneva, and the Philosophes,* Studies on Voltaire and the Eighteenth Century 321 (Oxford, 1994); Michael Heyd, *Jean-Robert Chouet and the Introduction of Cartesian Science in the Academy of Geneva* (The Hague and London, 1982); John B. Roney and Martin I. Klauber, eds, *The Identity of Geneva* (Westport, CT, 1998).

[7] What was contested, and is contested now, especially by Gargett, is how far the clergy were hypocritical in continuing to teach and preach in terms which (we know) they were themselves interpreting with growing flexibility.

cuted; the rich increasingly lived with an abundance which made honouring austerity contrived or hypocritical while lower down the social scale we can find moments where people (as individuals or groups) still clung to old-style religion, and others where modernity and its fellow-traveller secularization were clearly winning.[8] As in France, some rejoiced, and some resisted this trend: there was no single set of popular attitudes to describe.

The case of the theatre shows Genevans split over an issue which (as in Jane Austen's *Mansfield Park*) puzzles us in its moral certainties and anger. Although troupes of actors had earlier performed in Geneva, by the mid-eighteenth century the city was famous for choosing to have no theatre. When Voltaire settled, his guests could watch and take part in amateur theatricals. The Venerable Company of Pastors deplored this, reporting the problem to the Small Council, several of whom were enjoying exactly what they were being asked to condemn. The Company committed themselves to refusing any invitations from Voltaire that might reach them, and went on to denounce d'Alembert's treatment of this issue in the 1757 volume of the *Encyclopédie*. In his article 'Genève', d'Alembert applauded the city's prosperity, decency and orderly government, going on not only to allege that Geneva's pastors believed very little, but to tell his readers that the city would be greatly improved by having a theatre. This prospect aroused Rousseau's moral outrage, which he turned into a long published letter to d'Alembert.[9] The Small Council issued a ban, without much conviction, in December 1760, but in 1766 succumbed to French pressure for a theatre to be built. Tellingly, it burned down in January 1768 in doubtful circumstances: Genevan fire-drill brought out the customary responsible citizens with the usual chain of buckets, but once people became aware of precisely what was burning, they threw down their buckets and went home, substantiating Rousseau's claim to have captured ordinary Genevans' values.

In 1772 Samuel Mestrezat told the Council of Two Hundred that the threat of a new theatre's opening could be quashed if every member

---

[8] See n. 4, above.

[9] Rousseau, *Lettre à Mr. d'Alembert . . . sur le projet d'établir un théâtre de comédie en [Genève]*, (Amsterdam, 1758); J.-D. Candaux, 'D'Alembert et les Genevois: quelques documents inédits', *Musées de Genève* 77–8 (1967), 3–6. See especially John Hope Mason, 'The *Lettre à d'Alembert* and its place in Rousseau's thought', in Marian Hobson, J. T. A. Leigh and Robert Wokler, eds, *Rousseau and the Eighteenth Century: Essays in Memory of R. A. Leigh* (Oxford, 1992), 251–69.

of all the Councils and their families undertook to stay away.[10] But by the 1780s the State of Geneva had invested in the Theatre Company;[11] in 1784 a stone theatre was built outside the walls and the city gates had to be re-opened to let audiences back to their beds. When some clergy preached against theatricals in April and September 1784 the Small Council rebuked them.[12] In 1785 William Beckford, remarking the change towards decadence, saw Genevans 'of the old stamp, chewing the cud of sober sermons' waiting for younger members of their families to emerge from a performance.[13] In April 1787 the Consistory deplored theatrical performances competing with the confirmations taking place just before the Easter Communion.[14] These paying audiences must have included all but the poorest for the theatre to flourish.[15] Here is an instance where the lay elite moved first and fastest to embrace novelty, enjoying what had previously been forbidden, while in the 1760s popular reaction suggests that ordinary Genevans, like their clergy, were still conscientiously opposed to play-acting. By the 1780s, however, none but a few die-hard clergy, and their elderly parishioners, resented the change: popular and elite attitudes towards theatre and religion, newly configured, had almost fused again.

* * *

Political disputes drew Roman Catholicism into contention. France, Bern and Zurich became the Guarantors of the 1738 *Règlement* which resolved the clashes of the 1730s. France, easily the most powerful, routinely supported the smaller councils against popular demands, and reaction to this spilled over into a well-founded sense that Geneva's protestantism meant more to clergy and people than to the city's rulers. As in the case of the theatre, it was the lay elite, the Small Council, who moved fastest towards accommodation. When Isaac Prestrau, who had briefly converted to Roman Catholicism, was made regent to the fourth class at the *Collège*, men of the General Council, the body to which all

---

10 *Proposition faite en Conseil des Deux-Cent, le Lundi 1 Juin 1772.*

11 *Reconnoissance d'Action sur La Salle des Spectacles établie à Genève.*

12 Bibliothèque Publique et Universitaire de Genève (hereafter: BPU), Registre Vénérable Compagnie, 9 April, 1 October 1784.

13 William Beckford, *The Travel Diaries of William Beckford of Fonthill*, ed. G. Chapman, 2 vols (Cambridge, 1928), 1: 320.

14 Archives d'Etat de Genève (hereafter: AEG), Registre Consistoire, 5 April 1787.

15 In December 1782 safety precautions at the theatre were ordered: fire buckets should stand ready; nobody should throw leaflets about, or try to make a speech; footwarmers should be locked shut so that they could do no harm if overturned.

citizens belonged, made representations against his being appointed without formally abjuring his apostasy. Protestants, mainly from Huguenot areas of France, still made their way to Geneva, and even if some of them might today be deemed economic migrants, they honoured their new home's confessional identity.[16] Throughout the century, the French authorities, still perceiving these exiles as bad Frenchmen, used threats and interventions to affect the welcome accorded to those freed from the galleys, or escaping the Cévennes. Mass was celebrated at the *Résident*'s house, and numbers attending rose; awkwardnesses followed the rationalizing of the city-state's frontiers with Savoy and France, since territory had been ceded, but villagers still acted as if it had not: *curés* needed protecting, but some needed warning off if they handed out Roman Catholic tracts to protestant villagers, or closed in too eagerly on sick beds.

By 1788 the Consistory commented that although it was as tolerant as people in enlightened countries had to be, it was uneasy about the numbers of Roman Catholics being allowed to settle in Geneva. These people could not be disciplined like protestants, and their doctrines, even if not formally taught, would seep into the citizenry. It might, they conceded, be politically necessary to admit them, but such political judgements were for the Small Council.[17] These men and their families, who happened to enjoy many French fashions, knew that defying the French was a risk that Geneva should not run.

The near-simplicity of this dichotomy – that only the lay elite was willing to be soft on popery; clergy and people were angry – cannot reliably be discerned within Geneva's complicated attitudes at the interface between religion and internal politics. During the struggles which sometimes flared into violence between the ruling magistracy, their citizens, and (eventually) *habitants* and *natifs*, people, including clergy, wrote, published,[18] demonstrated and even fought, in ways which came to resemble modern politics.

---

[16] According to Alfred Perrenoud, *La Population de Genève du seizième au début du dix-neuvième siècle*, Mémoires et documents publiés par la Société d'histoire et d'archéologie de Genève 47 (1979), 291, around seventy men a year settled in this way through the eighteenth century; but (287) after 1750 French protestants seeking a life amidst co-religionists no longer constituted the majority.

[17] Registre Consistoire, December 1788.

[18] The vast pamphlet literature which fuelled Geneva's conflicts tended to address issues in terms of constitutional law, trust, utility and public order. A near-complete listing can be found in Emile Rivoire, 'Bibliographie historique de Genève au XVIIIe siècle', *Mémoires et*

In 1765 a majority within the General Council was successfully challenging the Small Council's authority by refusing to elect next year's officers from the short list chosen by their superiors. In November, organized insolence drowned out Jean-François Pictet's sermon; he could not be heard for coughing, nose-blowing and spitting. Pictet was trying to tell his flock to give in, and behave with proper deference – a message they refused to accept. In November 1782 crowds outside the church at St Gervais (on the commoner side of the Rhone) disrupted the service by shouting insults. Some young people even ran about irreverently inside the church. These two incidents point us in opposite directions. The likelihood is that this second rowdiness was intended to demonstrate support *for* their pastor, Essaïe Gasc, an engaging man who had got into trouble in 1773 for appearing at a festival dressed as a dragon: he had just been named as one of those ringleaders who were to be exiled for their part in the 1782 revolution.[19]

Throughout the century, magistrates liked to use the pastors as expendable auxiliaries. Like modern clergy, and French clergy before spring 1791, when the Pope condemned the Civil Constitution of the Clergy, pastors could be found on both the political right and left, while Geneva's rulers, often sitting lightly to organized religion, expected its help when they demanded it. The clergy preferred the role of seekers after compromise, although when the troubles of 1734–8 were resolved they found themselves reading aloud a prayer which made it clear that God had been on the rulers' side – who yielded little in return. Often the Venerable Company's registers have scratched-out accounts of seeking the magistracy's backing, and optimistic notes of 'consultation', while the same event in the Council's register is recorded as 'informing' or 'instructing' the pastors.[20] The Small Council did not support the Venerable Company when they sought to rebut the charge of near-Socinianism which d'Alembert levelled; they took no action against the dangerous sentimental sexuality of *Nouvelle Héloïse*.

The pastors wondered sadly whether Geneva's annual fast-day should be shifted from September to March, since gentlemen were apt

---

Documents publiés par la Societé d'Histoire et d'Archéologie de Genève 26 and 27 (1897), with additions and corrections in 35 (1935).

[19]   AEG, MS hist., Marie-Pierre Moren, 'Etude sur Modes d'insoumission du Gouvernement de Genève . . . seconde moitié de XVIIIe Siècle', Mémoire, Faculté des Lettres, 1978.

[20]   As in the Small Council's response to the *Lettres écrites de la Montagne* (1764).

to go to the country for the summer. Later in the century they lamented that it would be hard to reimpose Sunday observance: distinguished people were setting a bad example, sitting in cafés during service times.[21]

* * *

I will now show how some people, and some occasions, linked political radicalism to dwindling religious commitment, while the survival of traditional religious views amongst both political activists and other members of the lower orders confirms that there was no homogeneous popular religion.

The political struggle of 1762–8 had grown out of the authorities' banning and burning Rousseau's *Emile* and *Social Contract* in 1762, and we know that *Emile* was condemned for its deistic Profession of Faith. Rousseau could plausibly be seen as spearheading a movement which fused demands for political freedoms and religious liberalism: the men who were challenging the magistracy had his *Lettres écrites de la Montagne* bound with *Post tenebras lux* on the cover.[22] That is, they were taking the proud claim of the city's motto adopted at the Reformation to be peculiarly their own, with a new light driving away the darkness of recent political tradition. In March 1768, when this phase of discord ended, d'Ivernois wrote in exultation that the *représentants* had won; the bells were ringing; everyone was going to church to thank God.[23] Everyone? We know that this settlement was called the Edict of Pistols, and members of the governing group resented it and tried to undermine it – yet enough worshipping Genevans were delighted by the (limited) popular victory to fill the churches. Jacques-Antoine Du Roveray, who was to become a figurehead of the popular movement, expressly linked the ideas of religious freedom, and government's resting on consent. In 1769 he wrote:

> It is indifferent to the Supreme Being . . . whether you mumble certain words or eat certain crusts of bread . . . the sole means of serving him is to will good and to do it . . . [while] all human power, to be legitimate, must derive from the consent of men.[24]

---

[21] Reg. Ven. Co., 24 August 1758; 12 March 1788.

[22] Jean-Jacques Rousseau, *Correspondance complète*, ed. R. A. Leigh, 52 vols (various places, 1965–98), 23: 3833.

[23] *Correspondance*, 35: 6289.

[24] Du Roveray to Jain, *Correspondance*, 27: 6594.

On 5 June 1761 Genevan militias drilled and exercised, then feasted alongside the ruling magistrates: a living example of classical civic virtue. Mollet's account, consciously moulded to parallel what Rousseau had described in his *Lettre à d'Alembert,* included a description of sturdy citizens' dancing in their own quarter. Dancing, of course, was judged dangerous by early Calvinists; while Dupan thought Rousseau might as well have rejoiced in nude, Spartan-style, exercises.[25] Nonetheless, Théodore Tronchin (Voltaire's doctor) saw that d'Alembert was mistaken: Christianity mattered to Genevans.[26] Once Rousseau's true doctrinal position became known, many of those who shared his politics, and had called themselves his disciples, could not accept it, and wrote to him begging him to re-express or modify his beliefs about Jesus. Paul-Claude Moultou explained that 'our people are real believers, very attached to their religion, without being fanatics';[27] the watch-maker and radical leader Jacques-François Deluc, who had already seen Voltaire as a wolf loose, blaming Geneva's elite for steering decent citizens towards falsehood, display and pleasure-seeking, even published his own theological reflections.[28] A letter to Rousseau from a barely-literate young woman survives: I thought you were a great man, I now know that you mean to destroy our holy religion and you are wicked and dangerous.[29]

We have other evidence that common people still took their city's faith seriously. Excessive enthusiasm, and some Pietist housegroups, worried the authorities. More tamely, we know of treasured psalters; many, it would seem, owned by ordinary women.[30] Although there are cases where people barred from Holy Communion by Geneva's Consistory seemed to shrug off the penalty, not troubling to present themselves for readmission, these were rare.[31] For those born in Geneva,

---

25 *Correspondance*, 5: 735.

26 *Correspondance*, 5: Appendix A191.

27 *Correspondance*, 10: 1663.

28 Jacques-François de Luc, *Observations sur les savants incrédules et sur quelques-uns de leur écrits,* 1762; Douglas C. Creighton, 'A Genevan Reaction to Diderot's *Pensées philosophiques*: Jacques-François de Luc', in P. Firtz and D. Williams, eds, *City and Society in the Eighteenth Century,* Publications of the McMaster Association for Eighteenth Century Studies 3 (Toronto, 1973), 259–80. Deluc accepted what he took to be the tenets of current scientific teaching. What he could not understand was a critical reading of the Bible, and, still less, atheism.

29 *Correspondance*, 12: 2051.

30 *Le Psautier de Genève, 1582–1865: images commentées et essai de bibliographie,* ed. J.-D. Candaux (1986), 161.

31 Even rarer were the cases of criminals overtly unrepentant at execution. Michel Porret

formal admission to Holy Communion after 1736 was by way of catechism classes. We have no figures for those who evaded this process,
but the presumption throughout the records is that adult protestants
were eligible to receive communion, and that they would do so four
times a year.

* * *

This examination both of the theatre, and of Genevan politics, suggests
a distinct elite religion, but a blurred and complicated popular religion.
This essay will finally touch on elusive questions of science, sensibility
and sentiment, where we find, as in many protestant settings, little of
the angry cynicism with which some French *philosophes* attacked their
church, and little to distinguish elite from popular attitudes.

So, for instance, Jean-André Deluc, son of the watch-maker,
collected fossils and improved the barometer, always supposing his
findings consistent with orthodox Christianity; by the 1770s ordinary
Genevans could buy lessons in theoretical and experimental chemistry,
and read natural sciences and mathematics;[32] in 1785 Beckford resented
eager butterfly-hunting, fossil-collecting watch-makers high on the
Salève.[33] Amongst the elite, Charles Bonnet, the naturalist, recalled
discussions about free-will and determinism, and a hell which sounds
uncommonly like purgatory: the pains, thought Gabriel Cramer, might
well fit one for heaven.[34] Cramer saw science in the fate of Sodom:
perhaps that site had always been perched over a sulphurous pit, and
God foresaw when a pebble would strike a spark to detonate the catas-
trophe.[35] Death and misfortune prompted serious reflection at any
social level: Bonnet found comfort in his faith when his eyesight began
to fail; a poor mother abandoning her child in 1777 left a note with the

tells of one who shouted at Pastor Picot in 1784, that having lived like a dog, he would die
like one: 'La Biographie des scélérats ou les circonstances de la dangerosité criminelle durant
l'ancien régime', *Traverse* 2 (Zürich, 1995), 55–64, 62.

[32] Karl Küttner, *Briefe eines Sachsen aus Schweiz an seinem Freund in Leipzig* (Leipzig,
1785–6), in J.-D. Candeaux, ed., *Voyageurs Européens, à la Découvert de Genève 1685–1792* (1966),
118–28, 123, although Marc Neuenschwander, ' "Le Livre triomphant": le cas de Genève
dans la seconde moitié du XVIIIe siècle', in *Sociétés et cabinets de lecture entre lumières et
romantisme*. Actes du Colloque organisé par la Société de Lecture ... 1993 (1995), 69–97, 70,
challenges his view.

[33] Beckford, *Travel Diaries*, 1: 317.

[34] Charles Bonnet, *Mémoires autobiographiques de Charles Bonnet de Genève*, ed. Raymond
Savioz (Paris, 1948), 98; André Gür, 'Les Notes de lecture de Jean de Caze [*c.*1682–1751]',
Revue de Vieux Genève 14 (1984), 32–7.

[35] Bonnet, *Mémoires*, 137.

baby begging that he be baptized as Jean David, and weeping as she wrote; another in 1783 spoke of her child as a 'young Christian', whose father might one day be brought by heaven to soften his heart and recognize the child.[36] In 1769 a 22-year-old suicide, Jaques Aimé Mellaret, a watch-maker, left a fifteen-page note to explain his despair, meshing his enlightened understanding of nature with his need for the grace bought by Jesus's blood.[37] These examples challenge Moultou's conviction that Genevans were without warmth; that their virtue was bleak and left the heart untouched.[38] They also suggest a broadening Christianity, at both elite and popular levels, coming to embrace Enlightenment.

A dispute about a burial in 1774 highlights the intersections of new and old ways of thinking.[39] The Pictets had been forbidden to bury their daughter in the family plot at St Gervais. They explained to the Council that they wanted to be buried together, acknowledging that this idea was not 'bien philosophique'; it could however 'sweeten the most bitter sorrow'. The cult of sensibility was jostling with utility and reason, for the Council had to be assured that the girl's body had been embalmed and would not be offensive. Burial was now understood through a 'philosophical' filter, which required educated people to know about public health and to own up to ignorance about where we go when we die. In this formal appeal we have a layered discourse which discloses much typical of its time and place: urban, literate Genevans, both members of the elite and common people, could still believe, but could no longer believe as if they were peasants.

University of Sheffield

[36] Daniel Aquillon, 'Le Don et l'abandon d'enfants à l'Hôpital au XVIIIe siècle', in Bernard Lescaze, ed., *Sauver l'âme, nourrir le corps: de l'Hôpital Général à l'Hospice Général de Genève* (1985), esp. 217.

[37] Jeffrey Watt, 'Reformed Piety and Suicide, 1550–1800', in *The Identity of Geneva*, 119–22.

[38] Moultou to Suzanne Necker, *Correspondance*, 37: 6615.

[39] *Reqêtes présentées par la famille Pictet . . . touchant l'ensévilissement de feue Demoiselle*, 1774.

ULSTER PRESBYTERIANISM AS
A POPULAR RELIGIOUS CULTURE, 1750–1860

by ANDREW HOLMES

BOTH the study of popular religion and popular culture in the eighteenth and nineteenth centuries suffer from a number of methodological and definitional problems. Historians of religion often assume that popular religion is synonymous with superstitious beliefs that have little or no relation to confessional orthodoxy. It is further claimed that during the nineteenth century superstition was abandoned as a consequence of the modernization of society and the imposition of respectable behaviour.[1] Complementing this tendency, historians of popular culture in this period have generally ignored the religious aspects of everyday life and describe culture primarily in secular terms. This has much to do with the tendency to adopt, consciously or otherwise, a world-view that automatically assumes the subservience of religion to culture in the modern world. According to this view, once the events of the Enlightenment and the French Revolution had cast their spell, organized religion and personal religious faith were jettisoned, often in favour of the nebulous term 'culture', and a wedge driven between the sacred and secular. Given the overwhelming amount of evidence to the contrary, it is obvious that this tendency significantly hinders our understanding of the everyday lives and thoughts of our ancestors, especially in the Irish and specifically Ulster context where religion still has an importance that some fail to credit with sufficient patience, let alone understanding. As a result of these problems, the study of popular religion in the modern period lags well behind the advances made by historians of religion in sixteenth- and seventeenth-century Europe.

As our attention moves to the relationship between Reformed protestantism and popular culture, similar blind spots may be noted. Until recently, the general view was that Reformed denominations displayed an antagonistic attitude towards culture of any description, attempting

---

[1] For a revisionist view, see Bob Bushaway, '"Tacit, Unsuspected, but Still Implicit Faith": Alternative Belief in Nineteenth-Century Rural England', in Tim Harris, ed., *Popular Culture in England, c.1500–1850* (London, 1995), 189–215.

to repress popular expressions through social and religious discipline. Presbyterians in particular are often characterized as dour, phlegmatic and unadventurous. However, neither the relationship between religion and culture nor that between 'superstition' and orthodoxy is as monochrome as this suggests. Furthermore, the laity adopted a variety of possible responses to the imposition of discipline including 'resistance, indifference, acquiescence, collaboration, and active support'.[2] Compared with this variety, historians have too often separated orthodox religious faith and practice on the one hand and secular rituals and magical superstition on the other, which has failed to do justice to the complexity of lay belief and practice. A much more satisfactory approach has been modelled by Leigh Eric Schmidt, who, in his study of Scottish communion seasons, stated that he had

> tried to disclose continuities and discontinuities between elite and popular religion. It has sought to explore the dynamic relationship between ministers and congregations, between clerical expectations and lay experiences.[3]

Instead of uncovering a structuralist *mentalité*, Schmidt emphasizes the variety of lay experience and the relationships between different social groups. Rather than equating popular religion with superstition, David D. Hall suggests that it 'designates the ways in which ordinary people understood, appropriated and put to use the customary motifs of the Christian tradition'.[4]

Following their lead, this essay questions the dichotomies often made between elite and popular religion and between religion and popular culture by examining the experience of Ulster Presbyterians in the years between 1750 and 1860. The contours of a popular religious culture will be outlined and its formation and maintenance traced to cultural and theological brokerage between ministers and the laity, and the latter's adoption and adaptation of the beliefs and practices of the Presbyterian tradition. Two important themes will be emphasized: first, the indebtedness of Ulster Presbyterian popular culture to the religious ideas and practices of official Presbyterianism; second, the variety of

---

[2] R. Po-Chia Hsia, *Social Discipline in the Reformation: Central Europe, 1550–1750* (London, 1989), 143.

[3] Leigh Eric Schmidt, *Holy Fairs: Scotland and the Making of American Revivalism* (2nd edn, Grand Rapids, MI, 2001), 7.

[4] D. D. Hall, 'The Literary Practices of Dissent', in Kevin Herlihy, ed., *Propagating the Word of Irish Dissent, 1650–1800* (Dublin, 1998), 11–23, at 13.

responses to popular culture exhibited by the Presbyterian laity and clergy, and the symbiotic relationship between taught orthodoxy and lay experience. The first part of this paper outlines the contours of Presbyterianism as practised by the laity in the second half of the eighteenth century, especially emphasizing Sabbath observance, church discipline, psalmody and preaching. The second charts the development of evangelicalism within Presbyterianism and the impact it had upon the beliefs and practices of the laity. The overall aim is to outline the existence of a Presbyterian popular culture in the north of Ireland, distinct from that of Anglicans and Catholics. In that regard, much work is yet to be done upon the interaction between the three main religious groupings in Ulster at a local level. Certainly Presbyterians shared with their Catholic and Anglican neighbours the same superstitious beliefs and popular practices of 'folk Christianity', though even then, these had distinctive Presbyterian elements and were associated with unique denominational structures that framed how these were expressed.[5]

* * *

Sabbath attendance and observance are important indicators of the social importance of religion. At first glance, the figures for attendance at meeting seem to offer limited support for widespread adherence to Presbyterianism. According to figures compiled for the official 1834 education inquiry, between a fifth and a quarter of those Presbyterians who could attend meeting did so.[6] In addition, there were around 130,000 persons described as Presbyterians who had no formal attachment to the denomination. The existence of this sizeable group has significant implications for understanding Presbyterian identity. Being a Presbyterian for some did not involve attendance at public worship. For them, the label signified attachment to certain cultural and political ideals that were informed but not beholden to official standards. When talking about 'the Presbyterian laity', care must be taken to acknowledge that this group was divided along social, cultural and theological

---

[5] For an argument in favour of this shared framework see Marianne Elliott, *The Catholics of Ulster: a History* (London, 2000), 287–9. For further comments to the contrary and details about Presbyterian attitudes to superstitious beliefs see Andrew Holmes, 'Ulster Presbyterian Belief and Practice, 1770–1840', unpublished Ph.D. thesis, Queen's University Belfast, 2002, 77–88, 321–35.

[6] Ibid., 44–69.

lines that make it difficult to speak with confidence about a unified Presbyterian community.

This should not lead us to conclude either that the Sabbath was not an important part of Presbyterian popular culture or that attachment to Presbyterianism was weak. The very means by which congregations were organized often militated against attendance, particularly the pew rent system and the chronic lack of accommodation before the 1830s.[7] There is also plenty of evidence to show that Presbyterians dressed in their finest clothes to attend meeting and performed the stipulated family and personal devotions that were expected of them.[8] Others, however, saw the Sabbath in social terms, not least the practice of ''tween sermon' drinking. Generally speaking, before the onset of the temperance movement in the 1820s, the consumption of alcohol by Presbyterian ministers and the laity was remarkable and was not perceived as either a socially or religiously unacceptable activity, unless it led to wrongdoing.[9] An anonymous writer related the following example of Sabbath drinking in 1812:

> As we entered Broughshane, the people were coming out from worship, between sermons and not a few entering the public-houses; our inn was soon nearly full to the door, old and young merrily sacrificing to the 'jolly god', in a manner which fully evinced, that they were 'o'er all the ills of the life victorious'. This scene left some doubts in our minds, which our short stay did not allow us to solve; namely, what was the chief object of the people coming to Broughshane on Sundays?[10]

The simple answer was that the Sabbath had an important social function in the life of rural communities. The incidence of ''tween sermon' drinking in this and other areas of County Antrim, where settlements were dispersed and the urban network non-existent, was part of the Sabbath's function in providing 'one of the regular social meeting points in the pattern of rural life'.[11] The prevalence of vending stalls

---

7 Ibid., 48–53.

8 Ibid., 59–60; for family worship, see 275–81.

9 For an overview of Irish drinking patterns and the early temperance movement see, Elizabeth Malcolm, *'Ireland Sober, Ireland Free': Drink and Temperance in Nineteenth-Century Ireland* (Dublin, 1986), 1–100.

10 *Belfast Monthly Magazine* 8 (1812), 368.

11 Alan Gailey, 'Folk-Life Study and the Ordnance Survey Memoirs', in idem and Dáithí Ó hÓgáin, eds, *Gold Under Furze: Studies in Folk Tradition* (Dublin, 1983), 150–64, at 153.

outside the meeting-house gate selling all sorts of goods, including alcohol, emphasizes this point. In that regard, how Presbyterians marked the Sabbath fitted into a calendar of popular social customs that surrounded the high points of the agricultural year and other notable dates including Halloween and Christmas Day.[12] Even the Presbyterian Sabbath, it seems, was incorporated into popular culture.

The exercise of Kirk session discipline, often seen as one of the most disagreeable aspects of Presbyterian practice, was nevertheless embedded in the experience and moral consensus of rural communities.[13] For discipline to work effectively depended upon the interaction of the community and the willingness of individuals not only to uphold the values being enforced but also to inform on their neighbours. Given the small size of communities in Ulster, good neighbourliness was important. Church members often used the Kirk sessions to solve interpersonal conflict or to quash false rumours concerning alleged bad behaviour. Despite the lack of legal sanction, very few individuals refused to appear before the session or to submit to the sentence passed. The reasons for submitting were various and included community pressure, a desire for reconciliation with God and one's neighbours, and concern about the social and spiritual effects of not doing so. Being the subject of discipline damaged an individual's place within the local community and it was only through the formal rituals of church discipline that they could be reintegrated. Furthermore, by remaining unrepentant, individuals excluded their children from baptism, which, given the importance many attached to the spiritual and physical effects of that rite, was thought to have serious consequences for the eternal well-being of the child.

Various aspects of public worship were also given distinctive meanings by the laity and used in everyday life. Psalm singing is an obvious example.[14] An observer of rural life in Ballynure, County Antrim, in the 1830s was impressed with the singing voices possessed by Presbyterians, 'though in the meetinghouses, in which the entire congregation everywhere join, the nasal and monotonous hum of their psalm tunes would

---

[12] Holmes, 'Presbyterian Belief and Practice', 77–88.

[13] Andrew Holmes, 'Community and Discipline in Ulster Presbyterianism, *c.*1770–1840', in Kate Cooper and Jeremy Gregory, eds, *Retribution, Repentance, and Reconciliation*, SCH 40 (Woodbridge, 2004), 266–77.

[14] Holmes, 'Presbyterian Belief and Practice', 99–109.

form a contradiction to this statement'.[15] Judging by a comment made by one contemporary 'that a drawling, vulgar nasal style, is no proof of orthodoxy, either in preaching or singing',[16] the style of singing was seen by sections of the laity as constituting true Presbyterianism. Furthermore, though reformers lamented the use of twelve, or in some cases only four, tunes, this low number had great significance for churchgoers and some ministers. Some believed that 'the twelve' were the 'true Covenanter tunes' of seventeenth-century Presbyterianism, while others believed they had been composed by David himself and used in the Old Testament temple.[17] Presbyterians were therefore unwilling to discard 'the twelve' and sing anything other than the metrical psalms, as these were associated not only with their Scottish ancestors who had upheld Presbyterianism but also God's people in the Old Testament.

Psalm singing also informed the daily lives of the laity at work, during family worship, and in times of stress or joy. Psalmody was undoubtedly as much a part of popular culture as a religious exercise and one indication of this was the many singing schools that dotted Presbyterian Ulster. Along with book clubs, these schools began to proliferate in the last decades of the eighteenth century and were well attended by those wishing to learn or practice psalm tunes. Doggerel verses were composed to help pupils practise the tunes and also because some believed that it was inappropriate to sing inspired psalms outside of a religious context.[18] Often they were based upon the name of the tune and included information as to how it should be sung. Others had more of an edge to them:

> When Satan in the days of old
> The herd of swine destroy,
> He left one surly boar behind.
> McKinley you're the boy![19]

---

[15] *Ordnance Survey Memoirs of Ireland, vol. 32: Parishes of County Antrim 12, 1835–40*, ed. Angélique Day and Patrick Williams (Belfast, 1995), 37.

[16] *Orthodox Presbyterian* [hereafter *OP*] 7 (1836), 238.

[17] The names of the twelve tunes given by Millar Patrick are: Common, King's, Duke's, English, French, London, Stilt (York), Dunfermline, Dundee, Abbey, Martyrs and Elgin; Millar Patrick, *Four Centuries of Scottish Psalmody* (Oxford, 1949), 111.

[18] For examples of these verses, see John Stevenson, *Two Centuries of Life in Down, 1600–1800* (repr. Dundonald, 1990), 196–200.

[19] *Irish Presbyterian* n.s. 16 (1910), 68.

Singing schools provided an opportunity for social interaction and entertainment alongside religious or musical instruction, as poets developed their literary gifts and couples met for the first time at the dances or kissing games that sometimes rounded off the practice.[20]

Preaching was another area that both informed Presbyterian popular culture and was itself shaped by the demands of the laity.[21] Though an educated minister was a person apart, he was also called upon to embody the values and identity of the community. If a minister articulated a contradictory doctrinal view to that of his congregation in an unacceptable style, they could adopt a variety of responses including chatting or sleeping through his sermon, heckling, or reporting him to presbytery. Doctrinal content and accuracy was important for the laity, but as with psalmody, their understanding of orthodoxy extended to how the Word was preached. Extempore sermons were especially popular. One old lady boasted that her minister 'just stands up, opens his mouth, and it rins oot o' him like water'.[22] There are two reasons for this preference. First, it was the common view, considerably reinforced by the Seceders, that ministers who read sermons were unorthodox.[23] Second, some lay Presbyterians thought that ministers who read sermons were patronizing them. The lay preference for simple, biblical sermons was one of the reasons for the growth of the Secession church in Ulster as their preaching was fervent, biblical, earthy and often theatrical.

Sermons provided an important conversation topic for the week ahead. The following lines by the Seceder weaver poet, Francis Boyle, capture well the seriousness with which the laity took such discussions:

> Twa or three neebors met thegither,
> To talk a while wi' ane anither:
> The subject o' their conversation,
> Wha preach'd at Grenshaw ordination!
> A man spak' out "I dinna ken him".
> Anither said, "His name is Den__m;
> He in a lasty strain does speak,

[20] *The Select Works of David Herbison, with the Life of the Author by David McMeekin* (Belfast, 1883), 113; Stevenson, *Two Centuries*, 200.

[21] For further details see, Holmes, 'Presbyterian Belief and Practice', 110–52.

[22] Thomas Croskery and Thomas Witherow, *Life of the Rev. A. P. Goudy, D.D.* (Dublin, 1887), 9.

[23] John Gamble, *A View of Society and Manners, in the North of Ireland, in the Summer and Autumn of 1812* (London, 1813), 246–7.

Sometimes in Latin – sometimes, Greek,
And aye a sentence now and then,
That we poor sinners dinna ken".
Ane says, "That shews the able scholar".
"Forsooth I wadna gie a dollar
To hear sic preachin' seven years,
It pleases men o' itchin' ears;
I like the truth in laigher strains,
Sic as the sacred page contains." [24]

This extract confirms that the Presbyterian laity preferred and expected a certain type of sermon. It also suggests that the centrality of preaching within public worship was matched by the laity's concern to critique the delivery and content of sermons in the weeks that followed.

* * *

During the nineteenth century, reformers of various descriptions challenged aspects of the popular Presbyterianism outlined above. At the forefront of reform, Presbyterian evangelicals set their face against Sabbath breach, intemperance, dancing, animal cruelty and other aspects of popular practice. They elevated the significance of the Sabbath, revived the disciplinary powers of the church courts, sought to reform public praise and the abuses associated with singing schools, and advocated an 'evangelical' style of preaching.[25] The triumph of Victorian evangelicalism, it seems, produced the stereotypical view of the dour, hardworking Ulster Scot.[26]

Yet, there are many paradoxes associated with evangelicalism. It also was a popular religious movement that was initially condemned by the clerical and lay elite within British and Irish society for its lively itinerant preaching, hymn singing, cognisance of omens, and certain physical manifestations associated with conversion.[27] Indeed, these same criticisms were to be expressed by the evangelical Presbyterian elite at the height of their power during the 1859 revival.[28]

---

[24] Francis Boyle, *County Down Poems* (n.p., [*c.*1812]), 10–11.
[25] Holmes, 'Ulster Presbyterian Belief and Practice', *passim.*
[26] I. R. McBride, *Scripture Politics: Ulster Presbyterians and Irish Radicalism in the Late Eighteenth Century* (Oxford, 1998), 75.
[27] David Hempton, *The Religion of the People: Methodism and Popular Religion in Britain, 1750–1900* (London, 1996).
[28] David Hempton and Myrtle Hill, *Evangelical Protestantism in Ulster Society 1740–1890* (London, 1992), 145–60.

Some evangelical ministers also exhibited flexibility in their attitudes towards popular belief and culture to ensure that the essential aspects of their reform programme were achieved. The Revd Robert Magill, for example, assumed an important role in the defeat of Arianism within the Synod of Ulster in the 1820s while at the same time colluding in the marking of unofficial calendrical customs. He recorded in his diary for 31 October 1832 that he 'distributed to 130 Sunday school scholars of Millrow 4 bushels of apples and 7 quarts of nuts as gifts for Halloween – the apples cost me 2*s*. 6*d*., the nuts 3*s*.'.[29] Later in the year, and breaking from orthodox Presbyterian practice, Magill held a Christmas Day service, preaching on Luke 2:27 and examining one hundred children in their catechism. When he had finished, he gave them 'gingerbread nuts', sugar candy, lemon balls, almonds and lozenges amounting to £3. 3*s*. 6*d*.[30] Both examples show the flexible attitude of Magill towards customary practice and his use of the occasion for religious ends.

Another example of this flexible approach is provided by Henry Cooke, the figurehead of evangelical Presbyterianism, who in the late 1820s outlined his views on the reform of wakes to a young minister. Cooke believed that any attempt to root out drunkenness and impropriety ought to begin with the personal conduct of the minister and thereafter be carried out with caution and sensitivity. He recommended:

> Introduce no violent departure from old custom, except where it is sinful; but introduce improvement gently and rationally, and God will bless your labours. Substitute for the late hours of wakes something better as soon as you can; but even that do with caution, lest your good be evil spoken of.[31]

The reaction of the laity to reform embodied a range of religious and social concerns. At one extreme, there was a dogmatic refusal to accept changes in popular religious practice, including the consumption of alcohol at wakes.[32] The following anecdotes published in 1836 give an indication of lay reaction to the imposition of new practices, in this case psalm tunes not popularly associated with 'the twelve':

---

29 Belfast, Presbyterian Historical Society, 'Diary of Rev. Robert Magill', 31 Oct. 1832.
30 Ibid., 25 Dec. 1832.
31 J. L. Porter, *The Life and Times of Henry Cooke* (People's edn, Belfast, 1875), 120–1.
32 Holmes, 'Ulster Presbyterian Belief and Practice', 233–4.

In one [congregation], for example, so soon as an unstereotyped tune was raised, a number of the people snatched up their hats, and were off, one of them exclaiming, 'It is time to be out when the Devil is in'; in another, the clerk having resigned because an elder had threatened, before the assembled congregation, to collar him like a dog; when on the next Sabbath there was a long dead silence on the giving out of the line, another elder rose, and said very sarcastically, 'I think we had better never mind praising God for a while, till we agree about how we are to do it'; while in many other congregations one party with an old stereotyped tune strove, by dint of loud shouting, to sing down the new fangled party with their unstereotyped tune. One venerable old man told me, a short time since, that he sung down the whole congregation of——; and on my looking into his face somewhat incredulously, as he supposed, he assured me solemnly that he did, and could do it again.[33]

On the other hand, there was a high degree of lay approval for other changes, especially amongst the upper-working and middle classes. Increasing support for Sabbath observance and the spread of prayer meetings, temperance societies, Sunday schools and missionary societies attests to the popularity of evangelicalism's moral seriousness.[34] Evidence for this may be gleaned from the 1861 census. It recorded that few Presbyterians provided amusement when compared with the 465 Anglicans and 2,279 Catholics who did so. The *Evangelical Witness* commented favourably that of 'the 204 "actors and actresses", for example, [Presbyterians] have only 4; of the 27 "ballad singers", 14 "billiard room keepers", . . . 62 "markers", 147 "brothel keepers", and 5 "quacks", they have not one!'[35]

Why did the laity support these reforms? Nineteenth-century evangelicalism built upon the pre-existing evangelical impulses of the Seceders and others who on account of their popular preaching, strict discipline and strong sense of community, became the growth sector of Ulster Presbyterianism between 1740 and 1800.[36] In addition, the

---

[33] *Christian Freeman* 4 (1836), 97; also, *OP* 1 (1829), 99.
[34] Holmes, 'Ulster Presbyterian Belief and Practice', *passim*.
[35] *Evangelical Witness* 3 (1864), 101.
[36] Andrew Holmes, 'Tradition and Enlightenment: Conversion and Assurance of Salvation in Ulster Presbyterianism, 1700–1859', in Michael Brown, C. I. McGrath and T. P. Power, eds, *Converts and Conversions in Ireland, 1650–1850* (Dublin, 2005), 129–56.

success of evangelicalism in gaining numerical support is equally due to its resonance with the prevailing mood of nineteenth-century Ulster.[37] This mood of self-improvement and respectability was the product of a variety factors. The influence of the Enlightenment, the failure of the 1798 rebellion, the industrialization of Belfast, and the difficulties experienced in domestic linen manufacture, all reduced the attractiveness of morally and economically questionable activities.[38] The contribution of religious opinion in this process should not be underestimated as the crusading zeal and organizational capacities of evangelicals were instrumental in channelling the mood of the times into areas perceived to be in need of reform. A symbiotic process was at work as evangelicalism promoted changes within Ulster society and was itself shaped by those same changes. The *Orthodox Presbyterian* in 1830 noted that

> Whether from an increasing depression in their worldly circumstances, or from an increasing elevation in their religious feelings, or rather from both causes conjointly, they [northern Presbyterians] are every year evincing less inclination to engage in those wild and licentious festivities which they formerly pursued with so much eagerness.[39]

More 'rational amusements' it seems had replaced oaths, gambling, intemperance, 'disorder and impurity'.[40]

It is clear from this brief overview of lay Presbyterianism that religious beliefs and practices informed many aspects of popular culture in Ulster and were themselves shaped by the needs and attitudes of the laity. It is also obvious that clerical and lay attitudes to popular belief and culture depended upon a complex mixture of religious principle, reformist pragmatism and social utility. Truly popular religious cultures developed in both the eighteenth and nineteenth centuries from a similar mixture of reasons in addition to the 'canny sense of priorities' exhibited by some Presbyterian ministers.[41] Even in the

---

37 D. N. Hempton and Myrtle Hill, 'Godliness and Good Citizenship: Evangelical Protestantism and Social Control in Ulster, 1790–1850', *Soathar* 13 (1988), 68–80.

38 S. J. Connolly, '"Ag Déanmah *commanding*": Elite Responses to Popular Culture, 1660–1850', in J. S. Donnelly and K. A. Miller, eds, *Irish Popular Culture 1650–1850* (Dublin, 1998), 1–29, at 23–4.

39 *OP* 1 (1830), 110.

40 Ibid.

41 The phrase is taken from Ronald Hutton, 'The English Reformation and the Evidence of Folklore', *P&P* 148 (1995), 89–116.

rapidly changing and modernizing society of nineteenth-century Ulster, religious faith and principle played a central role in the lives of countless individuals. In that regard, religion ought to be reintegrated into our histories of popular culture in the 'modern' world and our definition of popular religion should be expanded to include the beliefs and practices of the laity in all their variety.

Queen's University Belfast

ELITIST LEADERSHIP AND CONGREGATIONAL PARTICIPATION AMONG EARLY PLYMOUTH BRETHREN

by TIMOTHY C. F. STUNT

W HEN identifying the 'catalyst for disaffection' and the 'trigger for individual secessions' from the Establishment in the early nineteenth century, Grayson Carter recently concluded that 'theological "extremism" was probably a more significant irritant than pastoral exasperation'.[1] It is nevertheless evident that episcopal restraints on any ecclesiastical 'irregularities' and the dubious spiritual credentials of some of those controlling the appointment of both higher and lower clergy were also significant factors in the discontent of many who seceded in the 1830s. A quest for freedom from such constraints therefore often accompanied the special doctrinal emphases of those who would sooner or later quit the establishment. This was particularly true of the seceders known as the Plymouth Brethren whose congregations proliferated in the 1830s and '40s.[2] With clerical ordination abandoned as unscriptural, their meetings came to be noted for spontaneous prayer and exhortation by any member of the congregation, but such an 'institutionalizing' of unprogrammed participation was liable to attract 'free spirits' whose orthodoxy and 'manners' could be questionable. This paper considers the way in which the precise doctrinal convictions and conservative social assumptions of such seceders could come into conflict with, and sometimes, at least for a while, keep at bay some of the elements unleashed by their professed desire for ecclesiastical freedom. Of particular interest is the interplay of social and doctrinal motivation.

---

[1] Grayson Carter, *Anglican Evangelicals: Protestant Secessions from the Via Media, c.1800–1850* (Oxford, 2001), 45.

[2] For accounts of the early Brethren, see W. Blair Neatby, *History of the Plymouth Brethren* (2nd edn, London, 1902); Harold H. Rowdon, *Origins of the Brethren 1825–50* (London, 1967); F. Roy Coad, *History of the Brethren Movement* (Exeter, 1968); Timothy C. F. Stunt, *From Awakening to Secession: Radical Evangelicals in Switzerland and Britain 1815–35* (Edinburgh, 2000).

* * *

The social parameters of the early Brethren were interestingly described by one of their former associates. After his secession in 1835, Joseph Philpot's ministry was exercised among the predominantly working-class Strict Baptists and he was keenly aware of how different life was among the Brethren. Writing in 1842 he observed three social features of the movement. First, it had

> *an aristocratic atmosphere*, a kind of Madeira climate which suits the tender lungs of gentility. Gentlemen and ladies dissatisfied with the carnal forms of the establishment can join the Plymouth Brethren without being jostled by 'vulgar Dissenters'. Baronets and honourables throw a shield of protection over the meaner refugees.[3]

Philpot suggested that parental opposition would be much less if a young lady attended a conventicle where the ministry was given by a titled layman rather than 'a poor cobbler or a Calvinistic stocking weaver in a cottage'.[4] Secondly he noted the effect of the Brethren's 'ascetic tendencies': 'Mahogany chairs and tables, as well as carpets, are discarded from their houses; their dress is plain even to the point of shabbiness.'[5] A third observation was that

> *The great liberality shown to poor members* is a strong attraction to that numerous class of professors, who love that religion best which does most to pay their rent, clothe their backs and feed their bellies. Some of them are men of considerable property, and most liberal in the distribution of it. We need not wonder if many of the poorer classes are drawn by such motives.[6]

There was some truth in Philpot's description. Although a generation later the situation would be changed, in the earliest days of the movement there was a significant sprinkling of sons and grandsons of baronets such as John Parnell,[7] George Wigram,[8] Charles Brenton[9] and

---

[3] J. C. Philpot, 'The Christian Witness', *The Gospel Standard* 8 (1842), 83.

[4] Ibid.

[5] Ibid.

[6] Ibid.

[7] The Parnell baronetcy dated from 1761, but Sir Henry Brooke Parnell was only raised to the peerage in 1841. John Vesey Parnell succeeded as the second Baron Congleton in 1842.

[8] George Vicesimus Wigram was the twentieth child of Sir Robert Wigram of Walthamstowe. His brother, Robert, succeeded as the second baronet, changing his name to Fitz-Wigram in 1832.

[9] Lancelot Charles Lee Brenton succeeded his father, Rear-Admiral Sir Jahleel Brenton, in 1844.

Sir Alexander Cockburn-Campbell.[10] Although the titles of these men's families were almost all of a very recent creation, other Brethren were from a slightly older vintage of nobility. Captain William Wellesley, a cousin of the duke of Wellington, was a grandson of the earl of Mornington, while Captain Percy Hall's maternal grandfather was the fifth Viscount Torrington. The social standing provided by aristocratic connections of this sort was firmly under-buttressed by a solid phalanx of gentry which unmistakably identified the early Brethren leaders as predominantly members of the wealthy landed classes.

Some of the early Brethren leaders were neither aristocratic nor particularly affluent, but they were all well educated and could at least be identified with the professional classes. Thus Benjamin Newton, whose widowed mother was probably dependent upon some financial help from fellow Quakers, could still stipulate, when planning the vacation with his mother, 'that the servants should be read to by me morning and evening'.[11] Such a paternalistic attitude to the working-classes was reflected in Brethren evangelism and in the establishment of their early meetings. The family of Major-General Edward Baynes of Woolbrook Glen, Sidmouth, provides a good example. Shortly after Baynes's death, his widow and daughter, Harriet, were influenced by the teaching of Anthony Norris Groves[12] to engage an evangelist, Christopher Passmore, to preach in his garden in the nearby parish of Colaton Raleigh. The recollections of Passmore's daughter suggest something of the social divide between the circle from whom the Brethren leaders would be drawn and their audience:

> We removed to a village, about four miles from Sidmouth, among a very uncultivated people, and under the influence of a Church minister and his son (who associated with the lower class). There was great persecution.[13]

[10] When Alexander Cockburn succeeded to his maternal grandfather's title in 1824, he was required to add on his grandfather's name, Campbell.

[11] B[enjamin] W[ills] Newton to Mrs [Anna] Newton, 23 May 1829, Manchester, John Rylands University Library, Christian Brethren Archive [hereafter: JRULM, CBA] 7179 (7). When he resigned his Oxford Fellowship in 1832, Newton had to take pupils for a living, but in later years he was financially comfortable either as a result of a delayed inheritance from his grandfather or following his second marriage.

[12] Groves left for Baghdad in 1829, the year of Baynes's death. On his return to England in 1835 he married Harriet Baynes: see Stunt, *Awakening to Secession*, 122 and 287.

[13] For Harriet Passmore's account and for Passmore's association with Wigram and the earliest Brethren at Plymouth I am indebted to the genealogical researches of Mr Gordon Faulkner; see www.faulkner-history.fsnet.co.uk/Passmore_frame.htm (consulted August 2005).

To avoid the threat of eviction arising from local opposition, Passmore relocated his evangelistic venture to other premises that were owned by Mrs Baynes. In such ways landed patrons made the spread of the movement more feasible. On the other hand, when such an evangelistic outreach was successful the working-class element in the congregation was bound to increase.

* * *

The early evolution of the Brethren assembly at Plymouth was a curiously *ad hoc* process by which a chapel that George Wigram had bought to provide a place for expository Bible lectures gradually assumed an ecclesiastical identity with meetings for the Lord's Supper.[14] Divergent teachings and sacramental positions appear to have co-existed and, for a time at least, fraternal love and tolerance seem to have covered a multitude of doctrinal and social differences. With what seems to have been a remarkable degree of social integration, the wealthier members – albeit somewhat paternalistically – made accommodations for the poorer. William Kelly wrote of how one of the early teachers, John Darby, went to work in a humbler Plymouth brother's barbershop when the barber was taken ill.[15] A Swiss observer in 1836 was struck by the fact that 'the rich meet with the poor without the latter overreaching themselves', adding that 'only the Spirit of God can maintain such a rare balance'.[16] The social integration of the community is underlined in a later recollection of Benjamin Newton:

> The Brethren lived a great deal in each other's houses and company. There was no such thing as domestic privacy among the very early Brethren. I always had seven or eight to dinner besides my own household.[17]

It is wrong to suggest that in their quest to recover the primitive life-style of the apostles the early Brethren practised the community of goods described in Acts 2: 44–5. Nevertheless the myth of 'communism' was sufficiently established in popular perceptions of the early

---

[14] For this process see Stunt, *Awakening to Secession*, 291–5.

[15] Kelly's account of Darby, written in 1900, is quoted in W. G. Turner, *John Nelson Darby* (2nd edn, London, 1944), 77.

[16] For a fuller extract of Charles de Rodt's letter, including his account of the 'restraint and simplicity' of Sir Alexander Campbell's home, see Stunt, *Awakening to Secession*, 302.

[17] Fry transcript of B. W. Newton, 'Recollections', see Manchester, JRULM, CBA 7049, p. 306.

Brethren for C. M. Davies, an observer in the mid-nineteenth century, to feel the need to deny it.[18]

Participation by the poorer and less well educated in Brethren worship was not unusual – indeed in some assemblies their contributions were liable to predominate. Edward Nangle had been familiar with several well-educated brethren in Dublin during the very early days of the movement, but when he visited the assembly there he was unimpressed:

> The speakers were all uneducated men of the artisan class; and without a single exception their effort at display in the use of big words, and abortive attempts at oratory, left no room for any feeling but that of thorough disgust.[19]

Another observer commented on how often the manner of such contributions tended to be derived from the example of a more advantaged brother. When Dr John Epps, a Scotch Baptist, visited the London Brethren, meeting near Cavendish Square in the early 1840s, he noted that

> Mr Wigram appeared to be the only one of any striking talent ... his mode of speech was slow and languid, specialities interesting in him as belonging to him; but when these specialities were assumed by others they became absurd. We could not but notice how, most probably unconsciously, the speakers imitated Mr Wigram.[20]

At Plymouth however, although there was a lack of uniformity in some of the assembly's teaching, exception could be taken to contributions from the less 'gifted'. Newton's recollection of the man in question may be exaggerated but the overall situation is credible:

> There was a rag-gatherer, a curious figure, blind of one eye and only one-legged. ... He rose in the middle of the chapel, and said he couldn't read – would the man next him [*sic*] read that chapter about Christ washing the disciples' feet? The man did so and then the rag-gatherer said we ought to do so literally. That, he said, was

---

[18] C. M. Davies, *Unorthodox London: or Phases of Religious Life in the Metropolis* (London, 1873), 176. The idea lingered on, as in *Notes and Queries* ser. 6, 12 (5 Sept. 1885), 188.

[19] E. Nangle, *Recollections of Separatists, a Plea for the Reformed Church of England* (Dublin, 1867), 29; for Nangle's earlier contacts with Brethren, see H. Seddall, *Edward Nangle, Apostle of Achill* (London, 1884), 44.

[20] John Epps, *Diary of the late John Epps, MD*, ed. Mrs [E.] Epps (London, [1875]), 209.

our duty now. . . . [Newton intervened, saying:] 'It appears to me that what you are saying is not to edification, and I beg you to stop' and happily he did.[21]

That this incident was no isolated case is evident from an independent source. A. N. Harris's parents had Quaker relatives but were members of the Plymouth assembly during the 1840s and '50s and in his reminiscences he described a similar episode. 'Peter, a fisherman whose contributions were liked by the poor, but embarrassed the educated' was asked to stop and he acquiesced, but some left the assembly because of it.[22] Harris also indicated that another brother, William Morris, was excluded not only from ministering but also from the fellowship for his belief in annihilation rather than eternal punishment. Newton, who was responsible for the excommunication, described Morris as 'a better preacher than any of us and a most acceptable preacher'.[23] Morris established another congregation in Princess Street and 'quite a lot of people followed him thither'.[24]

* * *

Having rejected as unscriptural the traditional practice of ordination, which had resulted in what they pejoratively referred to as 'one-man-ministry', the early Brethren laid emphasis on the variety of gifts with which the risen Christ had endowed his Church (see Eph. 4: 11; 1 Cor. 12: 7–12). In later years this meant that Brethren meetings for worship were noted for a somewhat heterogeneous series of contributions but there can be little doubt that in the early days at Plymouth this was not typical.[25] Although ministry was by no means confined to one or two people, there was a presiding elder (at first Benjamin Newton and later James Lampen Harris) and it was accepted that he could intervene if he thought the congregation was being subjected to

---

[21] Newton, 'Recollections', p. 261.

[22] A. N. Harris, 'The Plymouth Brethren, Reminiscences of over Fifty Years Ago, November 1911'. The MS was formerly, but apparently is no longer, in Plymouth and West Devon Record Office, Acc. 499, pp. 17–18 [xerox copy in Manchester, JRULM, CBA Box 13 Item 29].

[23] Newton, 'Recollections', 268.

[24] Harris, 'Reminiscences', 21–2. For his heterodox views see W. Morris, *The Question of Ages: What is Man? Outlines of Testimony in Relation to Life, Death and Immortality* (3rd edn, Plymouth, 1887). The first (unlocated) edition was published in or before 1849.

[25] See Timothy C. F. Stunt, *Early Brethren and the Society of Friends* (Pinner, 1970), 23–6, where I suggested that the influx of Quakers to the Brethren in the 1830s following the Beaconite controversy significantly contributed to a less structured congregational worship.

unprofitable ministry. An important witness to this state of affairs was the biblical scholar Samuel Tregelles, who was Newton's cousin by marriage and who from 1835 was regularly associated with the Plymouth Assembly. In a pamphlet written in 1849, when critical opposition to Newton had come to a head, Tregelles insisted (and none of his critics ever contradicted his statement) that intervention by the elders had been the accepted practice. At least once, he claimed, Newton had intervened 'to stop ministry which was manifestly improper' in the presence and with the full concurrence of his later critics, J. N. Darby and G. V. Wigram.[26] In describing the principles of the early Brethren with regard to ministry, both Wigram (in 1844) and Tregelles (in 1849) cited in print the principle that ministry among the Brethren was 'stated but not exclusive'.[27] In a letter[28] to Newton in 1846 Tregelles gave a fuller explanation of this principle and the letter reveals with whom it originated:

> Edward Foley <u>used</u> to call the true thought in connection with ministry '<u>Stated</u> ministry but not <u>exclusive</u> ministry'; meaning by <u>stated ministry</u> the distinct recognition that such and such are <u>the persons</u> who at such a place minister, and in fact whose ministry may be expected; while at the same time there was no shut door [*sc.* giving rise to an undesirable situation] so that any whom the Lord might fit for ministry should be prevented from exercising gifts so given.[29]

26 S. P. Tregelles, *Three Letters to the Author of 'A Retrospect of Events that have taken place amongst the Brethren'* (2nd edn, London, 1894 [1849]), 8.

27 G. V. Wigram, *On Ministry in the Word* (London, [1844]), 2–3. An extract from Wigram's tract was cited with approval and the principle was enlarged upon in Tregelles, *Three Letters*, 8–15.

28 S. P. Tregelles (Florence, 13 April 1846) to B. W. Newton (Plymouth). The letter was formerly in the Fry Collection but is now apparently missing from the collection as presently held in the JRULM, CBA. The text here is taken from the author's transcription made in 1962. For the vicissitudes of this ravaged source of primary materials see Stunt, *Awakening to Secession*, 313–14.

29 Tregelles's underlining of the word 'used' suggests a change of heart on Foley's part and his subsequent support of Darby and Wigram against Newton. Foley is not mentioned in any Brethren histories but we may identify him as Captain Edward Foley (1807–94) whose eighth and last child was Frank Wigram Foley (1865–1949). Born in Rochester, Edward Foley presumably left Plymouth in the 1840s and married (?1850) a younger woman; he lived in or near Cheltenham (1852–62), in Switzerland (1864–5), in Bath (1879), and by the time of the 1881 census had settled in Tonbridge; see Debrett's *Peerage, Baronetage, Knightage and Companionage* (London, 1902), 929; Joseph Foster, *Alumni Oxonienses 1715–1886*, 4 vols (Oxford, 1888), 1: 472 (*s.v.* Foley, Arthur Paul); www.thepeerage.com/p1609.htm; and www.familysearch.org/ (consulted August 2005).

Ironically, although Wigram was later a severe critic of Newton, his earlier opinions on ministry (according to Tregelles) were 'not at all in accordance with the feelings of those who wished to leave everything without restraint'.[30] As a leader of the Brethren assembly at Rawstorne Street in London he had written his tract on ministry, using Foley's phrase – to oppose these 'democratic views of ministry'.[31]

There can be little doubt that there were times when Newton somewhat autocratically imposed his will (in the form of approval or disapproval) on the Plymouth congregation and silenced those whom he considered to be lacking in gift or having views at variance with his own. As his views on prophetic subjects did not coincide with those of John Darby we need not be surprised to find the latter taking Newton to task for his authoritarianism in the Plymouth assembly. His account of the situation may well be overstated but Darby evidently found it easy to pose as the champion of the poorer and less educated elements whose participation appeared to have been muzzled somewhat high-handedly by Newton and his supporters. In a characteristically carelessly written letter of early 1846 Darby criticized Newton's 'clericalism':

> Each Sunday was as regularly N.[ewton] and H.[arris] as in the establishment, and everybody knew it: there was no arrangement written – nothing to be proved. A poor man gave out a hymn, no-one would raise it. . . .[32] It had been openly taught by N[ewton] and B[orlase?][33] that the Lord did not now use poor uneducated men, as those he chose before his resurrection, but after that such as Paul, Luther and Calvin, Wesley and Whitfield, and myself now. It came to such a point, preventing people speaking in the room, that S[?oltau] called it jockeyship.[34]

---

[30] Tregelles, *Three Letters*, 12.

[31] Ibid. On one occasion in the 1830s Newton substituted for Wigram in the newly established London assembly and, following his practice in Plymouth, refused to allow an open discussion proposed by Friedrich Bialloblotzky, who left the meeting in high dudgeon; see Newton, 'Recollections', 262, 301, 304. The episode was unknown to Bialloblotzky's recent biographer, N. M. Railton, *Transnational Evangelicalism: the Case of Friedrich Bialloblotzky (1799–1869)* (Göttingen, 2002).

[32] I.e. no-one would lead in the singing. Brethren considered musical accompaniment as unscriptural.

[33] Henry Borlase (1806–35) had been a leading teacher with Newton in the early movement.

[34] 20 Jan, 1846 to William Kelly, [J. N. Darby] *Letters of J.N.D.*, 3 vols (London, n.d.), 1: 89.

When criticized on this point Newton's supporters had apparently replied that, even if the intervention to silence the uneducated participant had been hasty, it had enjoyed widespread support from the congregation. Darby's scornful portrayal of the scene suggests a further dimension of gender in the conflict, with Newton's authority bolstered by support from the women who were not permitted to take part vocally, but nevertheless appear to have been a force to be reckoned with. Darby continues:

> But what could be proved here? Someone got up too quick, that was all – and perhaps did it in a case where the majority would go with him as to the effect, keeping down some speaker they did not like; and in the particular case the sisters had already tried to silence him by making a noise with their feet.[35]

It is an open question whether Darby was really as concerned for the voice of the poor and the uneducated to be heard in the assembly as he claimed or whether the issue was a convenient stick with which to beat Newton whom he clearly saw as a rival. When, a little later, he was able to pin the charge of heresy on Newton rather less was heard of Newton's clericalism and autocratic government. Darby often claimed to love the poor, but his compassion was very paternalistic. He was vocal on such issues as the desirability of keeping the pedestrian (rather than the carriage) gates of the parks open on Sundays, to enable the poor man to enjoy 'the one day he has with his family', rather than being concerned with poverty itself.[36]

With the full development (after 1840) of Darby's ecclesiology by which the church was considered to be irretrievably in ruins, there would be no elders in the assemblies of Exclusive Brethren. In contrast, some of the Open Brethren, tracing their ecclesiastical lineage back to Groves and George Müller, sought to re-create the primitive pattern of the New Testament and elders were often a feature of their assemblies. Yet Open Brethren would soon be perceived as a working-class movement associated with gospel halls and a less sophisticated style of ministry. Fifty years later, the Brethren had lost most of their aristo-

---

[35] Ibid. Two months earlier (12 Nov. 1845) Darby had similarly accused Newton of neglecting the poor saying that, of the two ministers, Harris was 'the only one who visited, and whom the poor really knew and loved. All the poor, I think I may say, have felt the evil' (ibid., 1: 85).

[36] J. N. Darby, 'The Sabbath or, Is the Law Dead, or Am I?', in *Collected Writings*, ed. William Kelly, 34 vols (London, n.d.), 10: 278.

cratic identity and their assemblies had become a happy hunting-ground for socially confident gentlemen with academic inclinations. Self-educated retired officers from the armed services had often replaced the earlier university educated teachers.[37]

* * *

Curiously enough when the Brethren movement found its way to Italy, one of its leaders was the aristocratic Count Piero Guicciardini who, as an exile in England, had associated with the Open Brethren.[38] The tensions that developed between this Florentine nobleman and his fellow Brethren in Italy call to mind some of those we have considered at Plymouth, but Guicciardini was very much an exception. At least one British observer of the development of Protestantism in Italy in the 1850s found that 'the strong republican character and tendencies of large masses of the Italian people' were dangerously responsive to 'the spiritual socialism of the Plymouthian system'.[39] It was a far cry from the 'Madeira climate' observed by Philpot in the 1830s. In the long run the popular element appears to have triumphed.

Wooster School, Danbury, CT

---

[37] As Edward Groves observed, 'A forlorn Brethren's meeting was exactly suited for the development of gift in a retired military officer or civilian. Requiring no support of a material kind from those who formed the assembly, he was free to expound Scripture as he pleased, especially if he undertook to make up the deficiency that constantly happened in the matter of rent and expenses': E. K. Groves, *George Müller and his Successors* (London, 1906), 375.

[38] For the Brethren in Italy, see Domenico Maselli, *Tra Risveglio e Millennio, Storia delle Chiese Cristiane dei Fratelli 1836–1886* (Turin, 1974); Timothy C. F. Stunt, 'The *Via Media* of Guicciardini's Closest Collaborator, Teodorico Pietrocola Rossetti', in Lorenza Giorgi and Massimo Rubboli, eds, *Piero Guicciardini, 1808–1886. Un riformatore religioso nell'Europa dell' Ottocento*, Atti del Convegno di Studi, Firenze, 11–12 aprile 1986 (Florence, 1988), 137–58.

[39] Anon., *Religious Liberty in Tuscany in 1851: Documents relative to the Trial and Incarceration of Count Guicciardini and Others Exiled from Tuscany by Decree 17 May 1851* (London, [1852]), 4. Cf. J. W. Brown, *An Italian Campaign or the Evangelical Movement in Italy, 1845–87, from the Letters of R. W. Stewart of Leghorn* (London, 1890), 103.

POPULAR AND ELITE RELIGION: THE CHURCH AND DEVOTIONAL CONTROL*

by SHERIDAN GILLEY

OPULAR and elite are imprecise terms, but it may be possible to give them a closer definition by relating them to categories in the work of John Henry Newman. In 1877, Newman was growing old. He was republishing his Anglican writings, both to preserve what they contained of value and to draw what poison remained. A particular difficulty attached to his *Lectures on the Prophetical Office of the Church*, published forty years before, in 1837, which classically defined the peculiar merit of the Church of England as occupying a middle way or *via media* between Romanism and popular Protestantism. The work contained some sharp attacks on Rome, which Newman had retracted even before his Roman conversion.[1] There remained, however, a particular matter which had long been an obstacle to his submission to Rome, his conviction that the honours which Roman Catholics paid to the Virgin and saints derogated from the unique worship due to Christ, which Newman combined with a fastidious distaste for the more 'unmanly' and sentimental or sugary aspects of modern Catholic devotion.[2]

This feeling abated during Newman's first decade as a Roman Catholic, when he took the name of Mary in confirmation and built a church in her honour; but his mistrust of Mariolatry revived in the 1850s as he fell out with his co-Oratorian disciple Frederick William Faber, who called the Virgin 'Mama' and propagated new Marian devotions among Catholics in England. In 1866, Newman replied to the Anglican Pusey's listing of such Marian excesses of doctrine as well as of devotion[3] that they were typical neither of the sober piety of Rome

* I am grateful to Dr Mary Heimann for reading a draft of this essay, which I would like to dedicate to the memory of John Fuggles.

[1] See John Henry Newman, 'Retraction of Anti-Catholic Statements' (1845), *The Via Media of the Anglican Church*, 2 vols (London, 1891), 2: 425–33, esp. 428–33, quoting his retractions of February 1843. The quotations come from this edition.

[2] See, for example, John Henry Newman, 'The Catholicity of the Anglican Church', *Essays Critical and Historical*, 2 vols (London, 1871), 2: 1–73, esp. 71–2. Originally published as 'Catholicity of the English Church', for the *British Critic* 27 (January, 1840), 40–88.

[3] E. B. Pusey, *The Church of England a Portion of Christ's One Holy Catholic Church, and a*

itself nor of the tradition of devotional reserve among English Roman Catholics.[4] This criticism was reinforced by Newman's estrangement from the second object of Pusey's criticism, the neo-Ultramontane movement to exalt the pope's authority over the entire Catholic Church,[5] which was to bear fruit in the definitions of papal infallibility and jurisdiction at the First Vatican Council of 1869–70.

Indeed the pope, Pius IX, Pio Nono, the longest reigning pope in history, himself set the seal on the Marian revival in 1854 by defining the dogma of the Immaculate Conception of the Virgin, that she had been born, though in a perfectly natural manner, free of the stain of Original Sin; the pope's action being an exercise of infallibility *avant la lettre*. Pius believed that Mary had cured him of youthful epilepsy, and Catholic devotion to the Virgin went with what Fr Faber himself described as devotion to the pope,[6] in a seeming perfect synchrony between elite and popular religion. The great acts of authority of Pio Nono's pontificate were all bound together, the Immaculate Conception with his condemnation of liberalism, and with the doctrine of papal infallibility itself. For Pius, the dogma of the perfect woman was the answer to the social and political upheavals of the age. His Virgin Mary was not just a symbol of purity, but, as in the Song of Songs, as terrible as an army with banners. The pope's two favourite texts were Genesis 3:15, in which the woman crushes the serpent of sin,[7] and the seventh antiphon of the third nocturn of matins of the common of feasts of the Virgin, 'Rejoice, O Virgin Mary, for you have put down heresies throughout the world',[8] made familiar in England from the 1840s as appearing on the title page of every one of the Oratorian saints' lives.[9] Pius decided to define the Immaculate Conception while in exile

---

Means of Restoring Visible Unity. An Eirenicon, in a Letter to the Author of 'The Christian Year' (London, 1865), 101–90, esp. 116–20 on Fr Faber.

[4] *A letter to the Rev. E.B. Pusey, D.D., on his recent Eirenicon* (London, 1866).

[5] Pusey, *Eirenicon*, 287–8.

[6] Frederick William Faber, *Devotion to the Pope and Devotion to the Church* (London, 1867).

[7] Quoted as '. . . she most decisively triumphed over him by crushing his head with her immaculate heel'. See *Ineffabilis Deus*, the bull of 1854 defining the dogma of the Immaculate Conception, in Roberto De Mattei, *Blessed Pius IX*, transl. John Laughland (Leominster, 2004), 168, and also 170.

[8] '*Gaude Maria Virgo, cunctas haereses sola interemisti in universo mundo*': *Brevarium Romanum . . . Pars hiemalis* (London, 1946), 178. Partly quoted in *Ineffabilis Deus*: see De Mattei, *Pius IX*, 176. The text is also cited on p. 123 from *Quanta Cura*, the encyclical accompanying the Syllabus of Errors.

[9] Frederick William Faber, ed., *The Saints and Servants of God*, 42 vols (London, 1847–56).

from the Roman republic at Gaeta, and originally intended to promulgate it in 1854 with a condemnation of nineteenth-century liberalism, which became the Syllabus of Errors, issued exactly ten years later to the day, on the feast of the Immaculate Conception in 1864. In the Syllabus of Errors, Pius denounced the sinning men of the Risorgimento and the whole modern French revolutionary tradition which threatened his throne, by condemning eighty major errors of the age, concluding with the notion of reconciling the Church to 'progress, liberalism and modern civilisation'. The Vatican Council which defined papal infallibility was opened on the same feast day, again exactly five years later. Pius declared Mary Immaculate, and the Church declared him infallible. Indeed some neo-Ultramontanes thought that the pope's attack on liberalism in the Syllabus was infallible as well.[10]

Newman himself was suspect at headquarters as a theologian unconvinced of the value of the Syllabus or of the need to defend the pope's temporal power as an Italian prince against the Italian liberals, and as an Inopportunist opposed to defining papal infallibility in 1870. Indeed, the Roman Congregation of Propaganda Fide wanted at first to censure the critical and measured terms of Newman's defence of infallibility, in 1875, in his *Letter to the Duke of Norfolk*, and though Cardinal Manning stepped in to protect him, and a new pope, Leo XIII, conferred a cardinal's hat upon him four years later, to many neo-Ultramontanes, Newman remained a liberal Catholic, that is a bad one, with misgivings about the two dominant trends in the Church in his time, towards a more fervent Marian piety and a doctrine of infallible authority in Rome.

With these considerations, Newman wrote a new preface to the *Lectures on the Prophetical Office*[11] both to defuse their anti-Romanism and to explain why 'It is so ordered on high that in our day Holy Church should present just that aspect to my countrymen which is most consonant with their ingrained prejudices against her', in 'the difference which at first sight presents itself between its formal teaching and its popular and political manifestations',[12] or, to be more explicit than Newman was, as a Marian superstition and a papal tyranny.

---

[10] Thus W. G. Ward. See Wilfrid Ward, *William George Ward and the Catholic Revival* (London, 1893), 248.

[11] For a critical commentary, see H. D. Weidner, 'The Preface of 1877', in idem, ed., *The Via Media of the Anglican Church by John Henry Newman* (Oxford, 1990), xxxviii–lxxv.

[12] Newman, 'Preface to the Third Edition', *The Via Media* (1891), 1: xxxvii.

Newman argued that Christianity is, like any religion worth the name, at once a philosophy, a body of worship and devotion, and an institution, and that these three things, the philosophy, the worship and the institution, correspond to the three offices which the Church discharges under Christ who is Prophet, Priest and King.[13] The Prophetical Office is exercised by the theologian; its instrument is reason, its end is truth, its mark is Apostolicity, that is, fidelity to the truth taught by the apostles, and its danger, none more so than in the present age, is rationalism or liberalism. This was peculiarly Newman's own office as a theologian. The Priestly or Sacerdotal Office is exercised by the clergy and people. Its instrument is the affections, its end is love, its mark is Holiness, and its abuse or danger is superstition and enthusiasm; see Newman's reservations about some Marian devotions. The Regal Office is generally exercised by the Papacy and Curia; its instrument is obedience, its marks are Oneness and Catholicity and its abuse or danger is ambition and tyranny. Newman was personally fond of the pope, but privately thought that he had lived too long and become a tyrant, so it is not difficult to see his target here. ' "Who" ', he wrote, 'in St Paul's words, "is sufficient for these things"? . . . What line of conduct, except on the long, the very long run, is at once edifying, expedient, and true?'[14] All three offices have their functions and dangers, as they should cooperate but may clash as they crowd one another for a place in the ecclesiastical sun.

The tone of the essay is, therefore, a judicious one, an exercise on the difficulty of reconciling love, truth, and order, when love and order are both so often hostile to truth, which can be both disorderly and unloving. Newman concluded that the Church may wisely prefer love and order to truth, as in permitting a spurious relic which arouses the people's love or in suppressing an unseasonable truth which would cause doubt and unbelief until the time was ripe for it, as in the case of Galileo. Yet though none can bear the whole truth, there are times when truth must be told despite the consequences. Newman himself thought that the French Revolution's suppression of so many Catholic

---

[13] These categories were fully enunciated by Calvin from Scripture, and so were known by Newman from the English Protestant tradition, as from Pearson and Bishop Butler. See Weidner, *The Via Media*, l–lviii. Newman's ideas are greatly expanded in the Baron Friedrich von Hügel's 'The Three Elements of Religion', Chapter II, *The Mystical Element of Religion as Studied in Saint Catherine of Genoa and her Friends*, 2 vols (2nd edn, London, 1923), I: 50–82.

[14] 'Preface', *The Via Media* (1891), I: xliii.

universities and faculties had gravely weakened the Prophetical or theological office in the Church, to the aggrandizement of the other two: indeed that this was one of the worst evils in modern Catholicism. Hence the arousing of the prejudices of ordinary Englishmen, who saw a church which had gone to a tyrannical and superstitious extreme, overvaluing order and piety against the necessary work of critical theologians.

Yet Newman's own ecclesiology is strikingly Ultramontane, in locating the Regal Office in the papacy and curia, and not in that warfare of competing jurisdictions, of pope and emperor, king and bishop, and secular and regular clergy characteristic of the later Middle Ages and the Counter Reformation, let alone in that odd modern construction, the people of God.[15] Newman thought of the exercise of theological reason and of authority as belonging to elites, while it was worship which was of the people, in a distinction of formal theology from the religious experience which provides theology with its materials. Yet Newman had also argued elsewhere that, in the fourth century, the ordinary faithful had kept the faith in their devotion when the Church's hierarchy had betrayed it.[16] He thought that the only *real* religion was a popular one, and he complained in the *Lectures on the Prophetical Office* that unlike popular Protestantism and Roman Catholicism, Anglicanism or Anglo-Catholicism – he changed the word from the first edition of the work to the second[17] – lacked reality, having merely been the theory of theologians. Again, in his novel *Loss and Gain*, his hero Charles Reding reflects with satisfaction in a London Catholic chapel belonging to the Passionist order, 'This *is* a popular religion'.[18] Revelation itself was originally imprinted on the mind in experience before it was rationalized by the theologians and regulated by authority, and 'a poor Neapolitan crone, who chatters to the crucifix'[19] had the element of true devotion in her.

It is, however, impossible to consign Newman's third category of the

---

[15] I say odd because it is unclear how the 'people of God' should exercise authority except through representatives, who invariably take authority to themselves.

[16] John Henry Newman, 'On Consulting the Faithful in Matters of Doctrine', *The Rambler* n.s. 1 (July, 1859), 189–230.

[17] See p. 21 of the *Lectures on the Prophetical Office of the Church Viewed Relatively to Romanism and Popular Protestantism* (Oxford, 1837) and the same work (Oxford, 1838). The clause '. . . it still remains to be tried whether what is called Anglicanism . . .' in 1837 becomes 'Anglo-Catholicism' in 1838.

[18] *Loss and Gain: the Story of a Convert* (London, 1891), 426.

[19] 'Preface', *The Via Media* (1891), lxviii.

devotional simply to the realm of the popular, endorsed as we have seen in the matter of the Immaculate Conception of the Virgin by the highest authority in the Church. Liturgical worship was closely regulated by the missal and breviary, and, in the nineteenth century, was increasingly Romanized by the Congregation of Rites, as in the papal suppression of the so-called Gallican variants in the Mass in France,[20] even if this was by no means initially at the pope's wish and occurred at the insistence of the neo-Ultramontane party in the French Church.[21] The canonization of the saints was reserved to the Holy See and was governed by Benedict XIV's famous treatise on the subject,[22] and even extra-liturgical devotion could be enriched with indulgences or simply left to wither or be condemned. Thus in an ever more clerical Church the local traditions of German pilgrimages and confraternities were reorganized as an instrument of militant demonstration under the authority of priests, on the pattern established by the exposition of the Holy Coat at Trier in 1844.[23] The effectiveness of this strategy appeared after 1870 in the massive German Catholic resistance to the *Kulturkampf*, when the State failed in its persecution of the Church in the face of public protest. The home and pattern or pilgrimage-based character of Irish Catholicism, set in a local sacred landscape of holy wells, islands and mountains, was transformed by new, clerically-inspired devotions in new, brilliantly decorated chapels, both in Ireland and necessarily across the Irish diaspora abroad.[24] The spread of popular education formalized inchoately held folk belief into formally held doctrine. The new popular English vernacular hymnody was largely the work of priests. There were limits to actual Roman influence, as Mary Heimann has shown: thus the Roman book of indulgenced devotions, the *Raccolta*, though admirably translated by Newman's bosom friend

[20] The Roman rite was adopted in France under Charlemagne. The so-called Gallican variants from this rite in the nineteenth century were mostly modern, dating from the seventeenth and eighteenth centuries.

[21] Austin Gough, *Paris and Rome: the Gallican Church and the Ultramontane Campaign, 1848–1853* (Oxford, 1986), 119–30, 171–80; see also 126 on the lack of papal interest in making the liturgy uniform.

[22] *De Servorum Dei beatificatione et beatorum canonizatione*, 4 vols (Bologna, 1734–8). Partly translated into English as *Heroic Virtue: a Portion of the Treatise of Benedict XIV on the Beatification and Canonization of the Servants of God*, 3 vols (London, 1850–3).

[23] Jonathan Sperber, *Popular Catholicism in Nineteenth-Century Germany* (Princeton, NJ, 1984), 70–1.

[24] See Emmet Larkin, 'The Devotional Revolution in Ireland, 1850–75', *American Historical Review* 77 (1972), 625–52, and for a discussion, see Sean Connolly, *Religion and Society in Nineteenth-Century Ireland* (Dundalk, 1985), 47–60.

Ambrose St John, never became popular in England and Ireland.[25] Lay-led bodies in the Portuguese local pilgrimages or *'romarias'* largely escaped such regulation, in spite of the vast officially sponsored pilgrimage to Fatima,[26] and many Parisian working-class Catholics worshipped at their favourite saints' shrines while not attending Mass.[27] Lay-led religion in the nineteenth century, however, became more of an exception to the rule.

There is another problem with the word popular. In high elite culture, the Romantic current of the early nineteenth century, even in Protestant lands, was favourable to Marian themes, partly out of its fascination with popular belief and behaviour. Sir Walter Scott wrote the 'Hymn to the Virgin' in *The Lady of the Lake*[28] later set to music by Schubert, while Wordsworth penned a sonnet on the Immaculate Conception, describing the Virgin as 'Our tainted nature's solitary boast/ Purer than foam on central ocean tost. . .'.[29] To modify Wordsworth's meaning elsewhere, Our Lady was the era's 'perfect Woman, nobly planned/ To warm, to comfort, and command'.[30] The English Catholic historian John Lingard dared to criticize the poetic phraseology of the Litany of Loreto, invoking the Virgin as Mystic rose, Tower of David, Tower of ivory, House of gold, Ark of the covenant, Gate of heaven, and Morning star, as not 'suited to the taste of the present age'.[31] He earned the justified rebuke of Nicholas Wiseman, later first archbishop of Westminster, that he 'knew but little' of what that taste was.[32]

The popular dimension of nineteenth-century Marian devotion partly arose through a feminization of religion, arising from the

---

[25] Mary Heimann, *Catholic Devotion in Victorian England* (Oxford, 1995), 73.

[26] See Pierre Sanchis, 'The Portuguese *romarias*', in Stephen Wilson, ed., *Saints and their Cults: Studies in Religious Sociology, Folklore and History* (Cambridge, 1983), 261–89.

[27] Stephen Wilson, 'Cults of Saints in the Churches of Central Paris', in idem, ed., *Saints and their Cults*, 233–60.

[28] *The Lady of the Lake* (6th edn, Edinburgh, 1810), Canto III, 136–7.

[29] 'The Virgin', XXV, *Ecclesiastical Sonnets*, in *The Poetical Works of William Wordsworth*, ed. Thomas Hutchinson and Ernest de Selincourt (London, 1956), 341. See Orby Shipley, *Carmina Mariana: an English Anthology in Verse in Honour of or in Relation to the Blessed Virgin Mary* (London, 1893), for other examples.

[30] 'She was a Phantom of delight', *The Poetical Works*, ed. Hutchinson and de Selincourt, 148.

[31] John Lingard, 'Proselytos on the Litany of Loretto (*sic*)', *The Catholic Magazine and Review* 4 (September, 1833), 111–13.

[32] Paul Alexander Richardson, 'Serial Struggles: English Catholics and their Periodicals, 1648–1844', unpublished Ph.D. thesis, University of Durham, 2003, 188.

different male and female experiences of the anti-religious French Revolution, which for a time had closed the churches and massacred the clergy. Men joined the Jacobin clubs and were conscripted into the revolutionary armies, to be the warriors of the new order across Europe. On the other hand, Richard Cobb suggests that the Revolution was misogynist and did nothing for women,[33] while Olwen Hufton has shown that as early as 1795, resentment of conscription and guilt over involvement in the sacrilege of the Revolution and the starvation caused by bad harvests at home in France helped to produce a counter-revolutionary female religious revival. 'A bas putain', cried the women of Bayeux, shattering a bust of Rousseau. 'Quand le bon Dieu était là, nous avions du pain',[34] as 'Citoyenne Defarge, ex-*tricoteuse*, put down her needles and reached for a pair of rosary beads'.[35] The fishmonger's wife of Saint-Patrice in the Calvados turned the fishmarket back into a church in the teeth of her husband's unavailing protests,[36] while the women of the clerical diocese of Le Puy bared their bottoms to the celebrant of the new cultus of the Supreme Being[37] and clawed to death or tore to pieces the Jacobin officials and triumphantly raised up the altars.[38]

This religious mentality, born out of suffering of the horrors of the anticlerical Revolution, identified itself strongly with Christ's humanity, and stressed the meaning of suffering in reparation for sin, in a church crucified like Christ and purified by its sufferings with him. This also led into new devotions to the Passion, as we will see. This feeling was strongest in the foundresses of the new religious orders of women: the young Sophie Barat, foundress of the Sacré Coeur, submitting to the penitential disciplines imposed by her young cleric brother who had just emerged from Saint-Lazare where, before the fall of Robespierre, he had daily awaited his execution;[39] Julie Billiart, foundress of the Sisters of Notre Dame, who hid in a haycart as a mob sacked

---

33   See for example his 'Masculine Violence', in *Reactions to the French Revolution* (London, 1972), 142–8.

34   Olwen H. Hufton, *Bayeux in the Late Eighteenth Century: a Social Study* (Oxford, 1967), 232.

35   Olwen Hufton, 'Women in Revolution, 1789–1796', *P&P* 53 (1971), 90–108, 107.

36   Ibid.

37   Olwen Hufton, 'Counter-Revolutionary Women', in Peter Jones, ed., *The French Revolution in Social and Political Perspective* (London, 1996), 285–307, 299.

38   Hufton, 'Women in Revolution', 108.

39   M. L'Abbé Baunard, *The Life of the Very Reverend Mother Madeleine Louise Sophie Barat,*

her patroness's chateau, willing to offer her life as a sacrifice to God.[40] The resulting population explosion in nuns was at its greatest in nineteenth-century France, where by 1878 there were 135,000 *religieuses*,[41] the number of these orders, in an old Catholic witticism, being one of the things that even God does not know. Again, post-revolutionary France experienced the most numerous and celebrated appearances of the Virgin: to a novice Sister of Charity, St Catherine Labouré, in the heart of Paris in the midst of the July Revolution in 1830; to children at La Salette in the Pyrenees;[42] and to St Bernadette at Lourdes. One of St Catherine Labouré's visions inspired the creation of the Miraculous Medal with the inscription 'O Mary conceived without sin, Pray for us who have recourse to thee', and included pictorial reference to Genesis 3:15 in the woman bruising the snake with her heel, as in the subsequent papal definition of the Immaculate Conception. Millions of these medals were cast and distributed from 1832, by permission of the Archbishop of Paris, remaking popular piety. The Virgin of Lourdes said to Bernadette, in Pyrenean patois, 'I am the Immaculate Conception', confirming the dogma defined by Rome only four years before, winning the local clergy to her cause and giving the subsequent shrine its global significance to Catholicism.[43] Major cases of apparitions of the Virgin in France peaked at nine in the 1870s,[44] when other officially approved apparitions occurred at Pontmain in Brittany[45] and Knock in Ireland, which attracted educated and wealthy as well as peasant supporters,[46] and there has been an attempt to relate some of them to purely local agrarian anxieties, as to potato blight at La Salette and to the phylloxera which destroyed the French vineyards.[47] Tech-

Foundress of the Society of the Sacred Heart of Jesus, transl. by Lady Georgiana Fullerton, 2 vols (Roehampton, 1876), 1: 13–21.

[40] James Clare, S.J., ed., *The Life of Blessed Julie Billiart: Foundress of the Institute of Sisters of Notre Dame by a Member of the Same Society* (London, 1909), 31.

[41] Ralph Gibson, 'Female Religious Orders in Nineteenth-Century France', in Frank Tallett and Nicholas Atkin, eds, *Catholicism in Britain and France since 1789* (London, 1996), 105–14, 105.

[42] Hilda Graef, *Mary: a History of Doctrine and Devotion*, 2 vols (London and New York, 1965), 2: 99–103.

[43] See Ruth Harris, *Lourdes: Body and Spirit in the Secular Age* (London, 1999).

[44] Ralph Gibson, *A Social History of French Catholicism, 1789–1914* (London, 1989), 146.

[45] Graef, *Mary*, 2: 103–6.

[46] See John White, 'The Cusack Papers: New Evidence on the Knock Apparition', *History Ireland* 4 (1996), 39–43; James S. Donnelly, 'The Marian Shrine of Knock: the First Decade', *Eire-Ireland* 28 (1993), 54–99.

[47] Gibson, *Social History*, 147.

nology also played a part, as in multiplying the Miraculous Medal, as well as portraits of the pope, and bringing the railway to Lourdes, which downgraded the nearby Marian shrines and spas with a purely local reputation. But the subsequent cultus of Thérèse of Lisieux, from a wealthy middle class family, whose *History of a Soul*, published posthumously, sold in the millions, went far beyond France, testifying to the power of female sanctity within the Church, which in reaction to revolutionary impiety looked to the visionary powers of the innocent and helpless, to young women and children, to save it in its hour of need.

This is not, however, quite a distinction between the elite and the popular, and as in the person of St Thérèse, the Virgin did not restrict her favour to the poor. St Bernadette was, notoriously, from a pauper family, but St Catherine Labouré came from wealthy farming stock. In 1842, a sceptical Jewish lawyer-banker, Alphonse Ratisbonne, given a Miraculous Medal by his convert brother, was himself converted by an apparition of the Virgin of the Immaculate Conception on the medal in the church of Sant'Andrea delle Fratte in Rome. Ratisbonne went on to become a Jesuit and then enter his brother's new order of Our Lady of Sion.[48]

Nor can nineteenth-century neo-Ultramontanism be simply dismissed as superstition in the service of tyranny, as described in a recent appalling and entertaining book by Nicholas Perry and Loreto Echeverría, *Under the Heel of Mary*:[49] it fed revolution in Ireland, in the close association between nationalism and Catholicism, and in Poland, which saw itself as the crucified Christ of the nations, while it also sustained Catholic resistance to Protestant governments in Prussia, Holland, and Switzerland, and to Protestant establishments in the British Empire and the United States. Even in Latin countries, Catholic conservatism could be populist, the resistance of peasantries like the traditionalist Bretons and the Navarrese supporters of the Carlist pretenders to the Godless cities, above all to the great sin-city of Paris, whose archbishops died in the revolutions of 1848 and 1871. In Poland, the Mariavite movement made the Virgin a messianic figure, based upon the revelations to a woman tertiary, Felicia Kozlowska, who was

---

[48] M. J. Egan, *Christ's Conquest: the Coming of Grace to Theodore Ratisbonne, the Jew* (Dublin, 1948).

[49] Nicholas Perry and Loreto Echeverría, *Under the Heel of Mary* (London and New York, 1988).

excommunicated by Rome in 1906 and at the height of her influence had a following of two hundred thousand people.[50]

Yet in both its popular and elite dimensions, and in its conservative and radical ones, nineteenth-century Catholicism was newly affective or emotional to a degree which was rarer in the Church of the *ancien régime* before 1789. Elite mysticism of the sort pioneered by St Catherine of Siena and St Catherine of Genoa had been in decline, indeed had been suspect for a very long time. Under the decrees of Trent, visionaries bore the heavy weight of formal canonical enquiries. Any historian of religious experience might be depressed by the persecution experienced by some of the great religious figures of the Counter-Reformation, which is not a matter that Newman addresses. Ignatius Loyola, accused of Illuminism, John of the Cross, imprisoned by his fellow Carmelites, Teresa of Avila herself, were raised to the altars of the Church, while Luis de León, imprisoned by the Inquisition, was acquitted and released, but from the golden volumes of Henri Bremond it seems that the condemnation of the Quietism of Miguel de Molinos by Innocent XI in 1687 and then of Fénelon in 1699 and of his intimate Madame Guyon concluded the golden age of Catholic mysticism.[51] The late eighteenth century, when elements of the Church reacted against Baroque pietism to embrace the Enlightenment, was a black time for the visionary. Of course, there were always failures in mysticism, like the humbly born Magdalena de la Cruz[52] and the aristocratic Maria de la Visitación[53] who were said to have faked the stigmata, though the latter's main sin seems to have been to have supported Portuguese independence from Spain. Yet some of the Spanish *beatas*, holy women outside the cloister, survived episcopal attempts at their regulation, while the mystic could be too powerful for papal authority. The Holy Office in 1681 and Pope Innocent XI, then Bishop Bossuet, and in 1696, a hundred and two doctors of the Sorbonne condemned the posthumously published revelations of Maria de Agreda in her *The Mystical City of God*, a divine history of the Mother of God, which taught that the Virgin had been present at creation, was conceived by

---

[50] Jerzy Peterkiewicz, *The Third Adam* (London, 1975).

[51] Henri Bremond, *Histoire littéraire du sentiment religieux en France, depuis la fin des guerres de religion jusqu'à nos jours*, 12 vols (Paris, 1916–36).

[52] See Herbert Thurston, S.J., *Surprising Mystics* (London, 1955), 83; *Enciclopedia universal ilustrada europeo-americana*, 70 vols (Madrid, 1958–69), 16: 645–6.

[53] Thurston, *Surprising Mystics*, 83–92; *Enciclopedia universal ilustrada europeo-americana*, 19: 460–1.

processes unique in gynaecological history, was born in ecstasy, and was quasi-omniscient, universal mediator and coredemptor. Maria's letters show her closeness to King Philip IV, who was, like her and most of Spain, a vigorous champion of the doctrine of the Immaculate Conception. Her work was attacked for teaching Scotist doctrine as of divine Revelation, but it was approved by the Spanish Inquisition in 1686, and the pope seems to have lifted his condemnation after it was imposed; it did not operate in Spain. The work was also approved by the universities of Salamanca, Alcala, Toulouse and Louvain, described as 'curious' by Benedict XIV, attacked by the polymath Bavarian Eusebius Amort and enjoyed a wide readership through the eighteenth century.[54]

This elite, indeed, royal religion, may suggest that the distinction between elite and popular was the polemical product of the Enlightenment and its attempt to distinguish superstition and enthusiasm from the views of the enlightened, as in Edward Gibbon's famous sneering reference to the pagan cults which were 'all considered by the people as equally true; by the philosopher as equally false; and by the magistrate as equally useful'.[55] The cult of the Virgin, and visions of the Virgin, and the miracles wrought by her, were to nineteenth-century liberals like Rudolf Virchow, who christened the Prussian battle with the Church the *Kulturkampf*, a sign of hysteria in women and of the backwardness of Catholicism, and so liberal historiography has treated them, as marginal to the great progressive movements of the time, just as it has treated as marginal such Protestant phenomena as the 1859 revival.

But the distinction between elite and popular makes little sense in Catholicism itself, outside so-called 'enlightenment Catholicism'[56] and the adoption of liberal Protestant attitudes by some Catholics in the twentieth century. Neither Newman nor any contemporary mainstream Catholic doubted the possibility of miracle. Thus John Talbot, sixteenth Earl of Shrewsbury, a great church builder and patron of Augustus Pugin, undertook a pious pilgrimage to Maria Mörl, the Estatica of Caldaro, near Botzen, and Domenica Lazzari, the Addolorata of Capriana. These two interesting mystical females, who both bore the

[54] 'Maria Coronel de Agreda', in Thurston, *Surprising Mystics*, 122–32.

[55] Edward Gibbon, [abridged by D. M. Low], *The Decline and Fall of the Roman Empire* (London, 1961), Ch. 2, 11.

[56] I am thinking especially of some of the 'reforms' of the Emperor Joseph II. See Owen Chadwick, *The Popes and European Revolution* (Oxford, 1981), 416–17.

stigmata or wounds of Christ first borne by Francis of Assisi, formed the subject of Shrewsbury's first public letter in 1841[57] to Ambrose Lisle Phillipps, a Leicestershire squire converted to Catholicism when young after a private revelation that Mohammed and not the pope was the Antichrist.[58] Shrewsbury was no populist himself, but a moderate Whig, and subsequent letters from Shrewsbury to Phillipps denounced the priesthood's connivance in the political propensities of the Irish Catholic peasantry.[59] Yet Phillipps did not regard his piety as elite, in spite of his importation of Cistercian monks vowed to silence to convert his tenants and labourers. Again, the distinction was unimportant to the uppercrust converts to Victorian Catholicism, who included nearly sixty peers and peeresses[60] and Gladstone's sister Helen, a lady who was cured of a nervous illness by Bishop Wiseman wielding a relic, and who made subsequent use of works in her library by Protestant divines as lavatory paper.[61] The writings of Anna Katherina Emmerich, an uneducated Westphalian ex-novice who also suffered the stigmata, and has been recently beatified in the best of company with the last Austrian Emperor, Karl, were taken down in excellent German by the distinguished Romantic poet Clement Brentano, as *The Dolorous Passion of Our Lord Jesus Christ*.[62] The collaboration of the brilliant intellectual, Brentano, and the ignorant peasant sister suggests not a gulf between the popular and the elite but a subtle interaction between the two, which I attempted to express more generally a quarter of a century ago, in arguing that the 'vulgar piety' of the Victorian Catholic Church was classless.[63]

If Marian devotion was one aspect of Catholic piety, the other great concurrent nineteenth-century devotion, as suggested by the stigmata, was based upon Christ's Passion, connected to Marianism in the

[57] *Letter . . . to A.L. Phillipps Esq. descriptive of the Estatica of Caldaro and the Addolorata of Capriana* (London, 1841).

[58] Margaret Pawley, *Faith and Family: the Life and Circle of Ambrose Phillipps de Lisle* (Norwich, 1993), 15.

[59] *A second letter to A. L. Phillipps* (London, 1841); *A third letter to A. L. Phillipps* (London, 1842).

[60] See Hon. Vicary Gibbs, ed., Appendix G, 'Peers and Peeresses converted to the Roman Catholic Faith since 1850', *The Complete Peerage of England Scotland Ireland Great Britain . . . by G.E.C.*, 13 vols (London, 1910–40), 3: 639–41.

[61] Philip Magnus, *Gladstone: a Biography* (London, 1954), 83–4.

[62] 'Anne Catherine Emmerich', in Thurston, *Surprising Mystics*, 38–99.

[63] Sheridan Gilley, 'Vulgar Piety and the Brompton Oratory, 1850–1860', *Durham University Journal* 74 (1981), 15–21, repr. in Roger Swift and Sheridan Gilley, eds, *The Irish in the Victorian City* (London, 1985), 255–66.

Gospels in the sword which St Luke declared would pierce Mary's heart also, and in St John's depiction of the Virgin at the foot of the Cross. The mother's sorrow in her dying son, the son's sorrow in the mother's suffering as the type of redeemed humanity, were formalized in Catholic tradition in the sorrowful mysteries of the Rosary, in Our Lady of Sorrows, in the Pietà, in the Stations of the Cross and in the most famous of medieval sequences, the *Stabat Mater*, set to music by Palestrina, Pergolesi, Haydn, Rossini and Dvorak.[64] Most stigmatists have been women, like the twentieth-century Theresa Neumann,[65] though the most famous in our day is Padre Pio. One outgrowth of such Passion devotion, that to the Heart of Jesus, originating in the visions of the thirteenth-century St Gertrude and St Mechtild, and linked to the wounds of Christ in the Middle Ages, was revived through the visions of the Visitandine sister St Margaret-Mary Alacoque in the seventeenth century.[66] It was promoted by her Jesuit confessor St Claude de la Colombière, sometime chaplain to Mary of Modena, now the patron saint of toy makers and turners, and by the Jesuits after him, and acquired a counter-revolutionary meaning among the peasants of The Vendée in the 1790s in their armed rebellion against the French Revolution. Its popularity burgeoned in the nineteenth century, especially among conservatives, as here, as elsewhere in French Catholicism, Christ's sufferings were identified with the collapse of true and right political order, whose recovery could only be achieved by penitential suffering with him. After the defeat of France in the Franco-Prussian War of 1870 and the violence of the revolutionary Commune in 1871, the shocked French Assembly voted millions to build the huge white Byzantine basilica of the Sacré Coeur to dominate the great revolutionary sin-city of Paris. Innumerable new societies, orders and institutes received the dedication, again with encouragement from Rome, which authorized a universal office for the feast in 1856, and dedicated the whole of humanity to the Sacred Heart in 1899. St Margaret-Mary was only beatified in 1856 and canonized in 1920, and her shrine at Paray-le-Monial became from 1873 a centre of

---

[64] See Jaroslav Pelikan, *Mary through the Centuries: Her Place in the History of Culture* (New Haven and London, 1996), 125–36.

[65] See *New Catholic Encyclopedia*, 17 vols (Washington, D.C., 1966–78), 10: 365–6. Also the numerous references to Neumann in Herbert Thurston, S.J., *The Physical Phenomena of Mysticism* (London, 1952).

[66] See 'Paray-le-Monial', 'Sacred Heart', in Michael Walsh, *A Dictionary of Devotions* (London, 1993), 190 and 226–8.

nineteenth-century monarchist and aristocratic pilgrimage.[67] It was the nineteenth century rather than any earlier era which wore its Sacred Heart on its sleeve.

The cultus of the Sacred Heart was sometimes, in a form pioneered by the seventeenth-century St John Eudes, who composed the first public mass and office for the feast, bound up with devotion to the Heart of Mary, a cult which only received a Mass from Rome for use in some congregations in 1855.[68] St Catherine Labouré's vision of the Miraculous Medal included the hearts of Jesus and Mary, the first crowned with thorns, as in some medieval imagery, the second pierced with a sword, as in Luke. The confraternity of the Immaculate Heart of Mary established in 1836 at Notre Dame des Victoires in Paris and combining the Virgin's Heart with her Immaculate Conception claimed twenty-five million affiliated members. Its popularity was confirmed by the Fatima apparitions of 1917, and Pius XII dedicated the world to Mary's Heart in 1942 and established a universal feast on 22 August in 1944.

Devotion to the Immaculate Virgin and to the Sacred Heart went closely together. The missionaries of the Sacred Heart of Jesus, founded in the diocese of Bourges by Abbé Jules Chevalier, under the inspiration of the definition of the dogma of the Immaculate Conception, established a devotion to Our Lady of the Sacred Heart centred at Issoudun on a cult statue of the Virgin standing with the Christ child standing between her knees. Its archconfraternity claimed twenty million associate members. There was a cultus extended to the heart of St Joseph, as in one of Faber's hymns, 'Where Jesus lovingly imparts/To Mary's and to Joseph's hearts/ The light with which His Own is glowing!',[69] in the earthy Trinity of the Holy Family of Jesus, Mary and Joseph, which is bound into the heavenly Trinity by Christ Himself.

The Protestant emphasis on the doctrine of the Atonement, of salvation through the blood of Christ, the great simplifier of all the late-medieval indulgences into one great indulgence, produced Protestant parallels to blood-and-wounds Catholicism in Passion-based revivalism. The blood-soaked Passion, as Mel Gibson's recent film on the subject has shown, arouses both an automatic response in Evangelical

---

[67] Gibson, *Social History*, 148.

[68] 'Heart of Mary', in Walsh, *Dictionary of Devotions*, 123–4.

[69] 'The Banner of the Holy Family [for the Confraternity of St Anne's, Spitalfields]', Frederick William Faber, *Hymns* (London, 1861), 181.

Protestants as well as a horrified incomprehension among the irreligious. In spite of their superior visual aids of bloody crucifixes and Holy Week processions and feasts of the Holy Cross and Precious Blood, some of what Catholics have done in this area can be paralleled among pietists, Moravians, and Methodists, from the sublime Charles Wesley's reflection upon the wounds of the Lord of the Second Coming, in an echo of a wonderful passage in the Revelations of Mother Julian of Norwich:[70]

> Those dear tokens of his Passion
> Still his dazzling body bears,
> Cause of endless exultation
> To his ransomed worshippers:
> With what rapture
> Gaze we on those glorious scars![71]

to the bathetic Moravian

> O precious Side-hole's cavity
> I want to spend my life in thee ...
> Yes, yes, I will for ever sit
> There, where thy Side was split.[72]

The eighteenth-century William Cowper's 'There is a fountain filled with blood', and Augustus Toplady's 'Let the water and the blood/ From Thy riven side which flowed' had something in common with contemporary Italian Catholicism, with its revival missions conducted to parishes by new orders like the Passionists founded by St Paul of the Cross and St Alphonsus Liguori's Redemptorists. The Italian mission hymn, 'Viva! Viva! Gesù', translated by Newman's Oratorian disciple Edward Caswall, found an easy entry into Protestant hymnals:

> Lift ye then your voices;
> Swell the mighty flood;
> Louder still and louder
> Praise the precious Blood.[73]

---

[70] Julian of Norwich, 'The tenth revelation . . .', *Revelations of Divine Love*, transl. by Clifton Wolters (London, 1972), 100.

[71] *Hymns Ancient & Modern Revised* (London, 1972), nos 51, 56.

[72] Quoted and ridiculed with sub-Freudian commentary on 'the perverted eroticism of Methodist imagery', in E. P. Thompson, *The Making of the English Working Class* (London, 1963), 370–1.

[73] *Hymns Ancient and Modern*, no 107, 131.

Revivalism was as much at home in Italy as in England in the eighteenth century, when the most learned and 'enlightened' of the popes of the era, Benedict XIV, consecrated the Colosseum as a shrine for Christian martyrs, and spread the ancient Franciscan devotion of the Stations of the Cross, following Our Lord's passage through Jerusalem, to churches other than Franciscan ones, and most spectacularly, presided at the pre-Lenten preparations in 1749 for the Roman Jubilee of 1750 in the Piazza Navona, as St Leonard of Port Maurice, wearing a crown of thorns and chains, scourged himself before a congregation of a hundred thousand people.[74]

Another great early eighteenth-century evangelist, the apostle of western France, St Louis-Marie Grignion de Montfort, founder of the Company of Mary, encouraged his converts to wear chains to declare their 'Holy slavery of Love' to her. The devotion was medieval in origin and had passed to de Montfort via the Cardinal Pierre de Bérulle, founder of the French Oratory, but its popularity came in the nineteenth century with the publication in 1842 of *The True Devotion to the Virgin Mary*. Relics of the Passion continued to arouse traditional devotion, as in the wake of the imprisonment of the Archbishop of Cologne by the Protestant Prussians, the Holy Coat of Our Lord at Trier, already mentioned, attracted a million people who processed in continuous file past the relic between 2 am and 11 pm, every day between 18 August and 6 October 1844, effecting eighteen recorded miraculous cures, including a tumour on the knee of the grand-niece of the Archbishop of Cologne. A sceptical observer noted that sixteen of the cures were of women.[75] A second exposition, in 1891, doubled the number of pilgrims. After the Napoleonic wars, Catholic Germany showed a particular appetite for the miraculous, and one of Anna Katerina Emmerich's contemporaries, Alexander-Leopold Hohenlohe-Waldenburg-Schillingsfürst, a canon of Bamberg and later titular bishop of Sardicia, from one of the best Würtemberg Catholic families, set out on his career of miraculous cures, having himself been made well by the prayers of a peasant, Martin Michel, with whom he cured the Princess Mathilda von Schwarzenberg of paralysis. Hohenlohe caused a sensation, and much Protestant ridicule, so that Rome decided that his cures should henceforward take

---

[74] See Chadwick, *Popes and European Revolution*, 163–4.

[75] Wayne Detzler, 'Protest and Schism in Nineteenth-Century German Catholicism: the Ronge-Czerski Movement, 1844–5', in Derek Baker, ed., *Schism, Heresy and Religious Protest*, SCH 9 (London, 1972), 341–50, at 341–2.

place in private, but his prayers for cures remained effective in Europe and America, including of one Mrs Ann Mattingly of Washington D.C.[76] Roman Catholic forms of enthusiasm may have been better controlled by the relevant authorities than their Protestant counterparts – Passionist and Redemptorist missions needed the approval of parish priests and bishops – but they found difficulty in containing the wilder reaches of enthusiasm, as when the Anglican Bishop Butler told John Wesley that 'the pretending to extraordinary revelations and gifts of the Holy Ghost is a horrid thing, a very horrid thing'.[77]

Indeed faced with such manifestations, authority was often incredulous. The great authoritative treatise on beatification and canonization by Pope Benedict XIV defines sanctity in terms of heroic virtue, in the theological and cardinal virtues. These are in some tension with the charismata of the spirit in healing and miracles, and with all the strange physical phenomena of mysticism, which are to be judged by whether they bear fruit in a holy life. Such phenomena include, as well as the stigmata and revelations, 'locutions' or interior illuminations; the reading of the hearts of others; 'hierognosis' or the ability to recognize a holy person or object; 'flames of love' or sensations of burning; tears of blood, or a bloody sweat like Our Lord's in Gethsemane; the exchange of the mystic's heart for Christ's symbolic heart; a wedding ring of flesh to Christ; agility, or the immediate passage from one place to another; bilocation; levitation; compenetration, or passing through other bodies, like Christ after the Resurrection; incombustibility in fire; bodily elongation or shrinking; inedia, or abstention from food for long periods (a variety of this consists in living solely on the Sacrament, a surprisingly common phenomenon);[78] transfigurations with aureoles or halos; sweet odours as in the proverbial odour of sanctity, in the living or the dead; and after death, bodily incorruption.[79] All such occurrences required official testing, and in the end, even if at local prodding, various levels of authority decided who was to be a saint, and that implied much else.

There were ecclesiastical attempts to control Marian and Passion-

---

[76] *The Catholic Encyclopedia*, 17 vols (New York, 1910–12), 7: 384–5; also *DSp* 7: 586–7.

[77] Henry D. Rack, *Reasonable Enthusiast: John Wesley and the Rise of Methodism* (London, 1989), 209.

[78] See the extraordinary list of such prodigies in Frederick William Faber, *The Blessed Sacrament or, the Works and Ways of God* (London, 1861 edn), 483–6. Faber dedicated the work to Newman, who claimed not to have read it.

[79] See 'Mystical Phenomena', *New Catholic Encyclopedia*, 10: 173–4; Thurston, *Physical Phenomena*, for these and others.

based piety, especially in France after 1870.[80] In 1879, Rome censured a devotion to Our Lord's Sacred Shoulder, on which, according to a spurious revelation to St Bernard, he had received the worst of his wounds: a religious exercise being propagated in the diocese of Nantes. Rome suppressed first, in 1892, a form of devotion to the Holy Face, practised by a priests' association in Tours, though a distinction was made between this and the ancient devotion to the image, as of Veronica's veil; and second, in 1896, a devotion to the Sacred Hands, also the place of the Passion wounds, revealed to a French Jesuit, Pierre Campagne. The Holy Face devotion was known to a late-Victorian Lancashire school teacher, Teresa Helena Higginson, 'the Spouse of the Crucified', who propagated devotion to the Sacred Head as the human seat of the Divine Wisdom, drawing on St John's gospel. Again, this was in accordance with the French cultus of reparation for sin through suffering with Christ's wounded head. Teresa was a teacher with a mixed reputation: she underwent the mystical marriage, suffered the buffets of the devil and experienced bilocation to Africa. She was venerated by some priests and opposed by others, her bishop maintained a judicious reserve, she enjoyed a considerable celebrity among Lancashire Catholics, and she was given posthumous publicity in a biography by the aristocratic Lady Cecil Kerr, with a note of approval by the Dominican Fr Bertram Wilberforce, of the family of the Evangelical emancipator of the slaves.[81] Her fame suffered eclipse when Rome condemned the cultus of the Sacred Head in 1938. On the other hand, Pope Pius XI authorized indulgences for the revival of devotion to the Sacred Wounds through a rosary of Mercy based on prayers revealed to Marie-Marthe Chambon of Chambéry, but this was discouraged by the Holy Office in 1939, perhaps because there was already a devotion to the wounds encouraged by the Passionists. Prayers

---

[80] Much of the following comes from Alfred de Bonhome, 'Dévotions prohibées', *DSp* 3: 778–95.

[81] Cecil Kerr, *Teresa Helena Higginson: Servant of God 'The Spouse of the Crucified' 1844–1905* (London, 1927). There is an extensive body of literature on the subject including A. M. Sullivan, *Teresa Helena Higginson, the Servant of God, Schoolteacher* (London, 1924); Frederick William Kershaw, *Teresa Helena Higginson. A Short Account of her Life and Letters* (London, 1934); *Letters of Teresa Higginson. Selected and Discussed by a Monk of St. Augustine's Abbey, Ramsgate* (London, 1937); and *Life of Teresa Helena Higginson, the Teacher Mystic* (Rochdale, 1937). See also John Davies, 'Traditional Religion, Popular Piety, or Base Superstition? The Cause for the Beatification of Teresa Higginson', *Recusant History* 24 (1998), 123–44. While Mr Davies rightly makes this a matter of debate between 'traditional' and 'modern' Catholics, the distinction was not obviously one of either education or social class.

to the heart of St Joseph were suppressed in 1873, as in 1892 was a prayer to St Joseph as a friend of the Sacred Heart disseminated by the Fathers of the Sacred Heart, though this had been approved by the pope, and in 1876 a prayer to St Joseph was condemned, based upon the Ave, 'Je vous salue Joseph, plein de grâce'.

Some of the elements in this devotional cocktail appeared in the condemnation by the Holy Office in 1893 of the revelations to a royalist lady, Mathilde Marchat, who had been divinely instructed to found an order dedicated to the Sacred Heart of Jesus the Penitent. Rome argued that as Jesus was sinless he could not be penitent, and had reason to suspect Marchat's subordinate agenda of restoring an alleged grandson of Louis XVII to the French throne as 'king of the Sacred Heart'. Marian devotion also received regulation, as in 1875, when the Holy Office condemned two books on the most pure or sacred blood of Mary. Also suppressed in 1894 was a statue of the sorrowing virgin with a crucifix. Here the objection was that the image was not a traditional one, as required by the relevant canon of Trent, which was also the basis for suppressing the new cross of the Immaculate Conception, comprising images of the Virgin, the Sacred Hearts of Jesus and Mary and the Virgin's monogramme. Rome decided that the cult statue of the standing Virgin with the Christ Child standing between her knees at Issoudun should be suffered to remain, but should not be reproduced, as derogating from Christ's authority, and in 1895 condemned two books of prayers issued by the shrine giving Mary an empire over her son. The Congregation of Rites discouraged statues of Our Lady of Lourdes or La Salette or the Immaculate Conception emitting rays of light from their hands as not in strict accord with Trent, though this image appeared on the Miraculous Medal.

The cult of Mary as priest was also rooted in the reparationist mentality of French Catholicism, among the Daughters of the Sacred Heart of Jesus founded by Marie Deluil-Martiny in 1872, who saw themselves as victim souls united with Mary in her suffering with Christ. A Belgian cleric who was closely connected with the order, Monsignor O. Van den Berghe, extended this notion to Mary's priesthood in a work praised by Pius IX called *Marie et le Sacerdoce*, and prayers to the *Virgo sacerdos* were drawn up on papal instruction by two cardinals and approved in 1906. A picture of the Virgin in vaguely neo-sacerdotal vestments was disseminated to the chapels of the Daughters of the Sacred Heart of Jesus, but was condemned by the Holy Office in 1913, in a document published in 1916, as was the actual devotion in 1927, on the obvious ground that Mary was not a priest, though the 'metaphorical' title *Virgo-sacerdos* for Mary apparently remains licit, it is unclear in what sense.

Most of the many nineteenth-century apparitions of the Virgin were not encouraged or were suppressed by the Church. The history of the shrine at Marpingen in the Saar is the theme of the best book on modern German Catholicism in English, by David Blackbourn.[82] Here the three eight-year-old girls who saw the Virgin of the Immaculate Conception in 1876, in the midst of the *Kulturkampf*, admitted at one stage or another to have lied, but had converted their priest and fellow villagers and brought down upon them the heavy-handed persecution of the liberal anti-Catholic German press and of the Prussian state. Despite the support of the Princess von Thurn und Taxis, Prince Edmund Radziwill, and the Centre Party, the Church's refusal to endorse the apparitions lost the village the chance of becoming the Lourdes of Germany. In this respect, Newman's model has a partial truth for his era. The theologians were under the thumb of authority, but so were the people. Yet in the case of Marpingen, the decisions were not taken in Rome, but in the local diocese, and in a wider sense, Rome itself was arguably riding the wave of popular devotion, and not simply controlling it.

Yet Rome encouraged the most historically doubtful of nineteenth-century cults of the *femme forte*, that of St Philomena, whose very existence was inferred from some tiles on a tomb in the Roman catacomb reading 'Lumena pax tecum fi', reinterpreted as 'Pax tecum Filumena'.[83] An artisan, a priest, and a Neapolitan nun then received revelations of the life of the saint, who had been spectacularly executed by the emperor Diocletian, whose advances she had refused. A canon of Mugnano near Naples, where the relics and inscription had been taken, wrote a fictitious life, Gregory XVI ordered a mass for her, Pius IX added her to the calendar, and the thaumaturge Curé d'Ars, St Jean-Baptiste Vianney, patron saint of French parish priests, attributed his

---

[82] David Blackbourn, *Marpingen: Apparitions of the Virgin Mary in Bismarckian Germany* (Oxford, 1993).

[83] See Caroline Ford, 'Female Martyrdom and the Politics of Sainthood in Nineteenth-Century France: the Cult of Sainte Philomène', in Tallett and Atkin, eds, *Catholicism in Britain and France*, 115–34. Cf. also Vincent Viaene, 'Gladiators of Expiation: the Cult of the Martyrs in the Catholic Revival of the Nineteenth Century', in Kate Cooper and Jeremy Gregory, eds, *Retribution, Repentance, and Reconciliation*, SCH 40 (Woodbridge, 2004), 301–29, at 301–3.

miracles to her. Pauline Jaricot, foundress of the Association for the Propagation of the Faith, was cured at her shrine, and though her cultus was criticized in the 1911 *Catholic Encyclopedia*, as not belonging to the grave of a martyr,[84] it flourished and was brusquely closed down by Rome only in 1961. A good number of semi-legendary figures in the calendar, some venerated for centuries, like St George and St Christopher, went the same way in 1969.

The last scene in this story need only be briefly told. The small elite cabal of so-called liturgical experts who destroyed the traditional riches of Catholic prayer and worship in the 1960s represented a sort of revolt of the Prophetical Office against the Priestly one, in an onslaught upon what was ignorantly ridiculed as extra-liturgical devotion, and was then hunted from the sanctuary. In a period of sudden secularization in which the Church needed above all to be counter-cultural, it mistakenly tried to embrace the culture, and even Benediction, the quintessentially traditional English Catholic service of adoration of the Blessed Sacrament, became rare to vanishing. This so-called 'reform', which in Anglophone societies limited worship to a barebones Mass in lacklustre English, was only effective, however, because it was heavily imposed in a sort of *trahison des clercs* by the Regal Office in Rome, in a last hurrah for a clericalism which now brooked no opposition in the Church. Catholicism only remains vigorous where there are plenty of poor or awkwardly reactionary Catholics who remain true to an older tradition in resistance to the liberal parts of both the theological and regal offices; who worship the Sacred Heart and say their rosaries.

Ronald Knox, the wittiest of twentieth-century scholars, planned his great work *Enthusiasm* as a refutation of all the heresies. He concluded otherwise:

> How nearly we thought we could do without St. Francis, without St. Ignatius! Men will not live without vision; that moral we would do well to carry away with us from contemplating, in so many strange forms, the records of the visionaries.[85]

Visionaries encourage belief, and may compel it by their transparent kindness and purity of life, but leave reason and authority with the problem of whether to believe them. I see no reason why this problem

---

[84] *Catholic Encyclopedia*, 12: 25.
[85] R. A. Knox, *Enthusiasm: a Chapter in the History of Religion with Special Reference to the XVII and XVIII Centuries* (Oxford, 1950), 591.

should disappear. The great utilitarian apologist for progress through education and growing material wealth, Lord Macaulay, wisely thought that religion lay outside this realm of improvement. In his famous essay on von Ranke's history of the popes, he predicted the future prosperity of the Catholic Church when a New Zealander would 'take his stand on a broken arch of London Bridge to sketch the ruins of St Paul's'.[86] The dogma of transubstantiation is absurd, reflected Macaulay, but if 'one of the choice specimens of human wisdom and virtue' such as Sir Thomas More could believe in it, then anyone could.[87] Macaulay may have been also thinking of the extremes of the Evangelical Revival led by his father Zachary; the Evangelical apostles of the doctrine of the impending premillennial advent, such as Edward Irving and Henry Drummond, constituted an educated elite if ever there was one. Premillennial adventism is now devoutly accepted by uncounted Americans, including many a Texan millionaire who derives his millions from the very geological ages whose existence he denies. The modern fascination with the Holy Blood and the Holy Grail and the Da Vinci code suggests that modern credulity is endless. As Newman himself reflected elsewhere, the

> heart is commonly reached, not through the reason, but through the imagination . . . Persons influence us, voices melt us, looks subdue us, deeds inflame us. Many a man will live and die upon a dogma; no man will be a martyr for a conclusion.[88]

Nor is the problem confined to believers. Chesterton famously said – no one knows where – that 'When men stop believing in God they don't believe in nothing, they believe in anything';[89] and in the end, the difficulty of distinguishing the popular from the elite by any rational criteria may be that anyone, elitist or populist, can believe in anything.

University of Durham

---

[86] T. B. Macaulay, 'Von Ranke', in his *Critical and Historical Essays*, 2 vols (London, 1946), 2: 39.

[87] Ibid., 42.

[88] 'The Tamworth Reading Room', in *Discussions and Arguments on Various Subjects* (London, 1911), 293.

[89] Elizabeth Knowles, ed., *The Oxford Dictionary of Modern Quotations* (Oxford, 2002), 64.

ELITE AND POPULAR RELIGION IN
THE RELIGIOUS CENSUS OF 30 MARCH 1851

by JOHN WOLFFE

IN December 1853 Horace Mann, summing up his report on the census of religious worship conducted on 30 March 1851, offered some of the more famously sweeping generalizations in English religious and statistical history:

> Even in the least unfavorable aspect of the figures just presented, and assuming (as no doubt is right) that the 5,288,294 absent every Sunday are not always the same individuals, it must be apparent that a sadly formidable portion of the English people are habitual neglecters of the public ordinances of religion.[1]

Mann went on to assert that the 'labouring' classes made up the main portion of the absentees and hence that

> From whatever cause, in them or in the manner of their treatment by religious bodies, it is sadly certain that this vast, intelligent, and growingly important section of our countrymen is thoroughly estranged from our religious institutions in their present aspect.[2]

Such estrangement was more a matter of 'negative, inert indifference' than of articulate infidelity, but it still meant, according to Mann, that they were 'never or but seldom seen in our religious congregations'.[3]

The 1851 religious census established a lasting perception of English working-class estrangement from organized Christianity. The picture has been qualified in various ways, notably by the acknowledgement that overall attendances on census Sunday were sufficiently high to indicate a substantial working class presence, even if one presumes universal middle and upper class attendance.[4] There has also been recognition of significant denominational exceptions, notably Primitive Methodism and Roman Catholicism, and of enormously variegated

---

[1] *Census of Great Britain, 1851: Religious Worship, England and Wales – Report and Tables,* House of Commons Sessional Papers 1852–3, 89 (London, 1853), clviii.
[2] Ibid.
[3] Ibid.
[4] D. W. Bebbington, *Evangelicalism in Modern Britain* (London, 1989), 111.

regional and local situations.[5] The underlying implicit assumption, however, has been that the attendance figures reported on 30 March 1851 provide a statistical basis for drawing a distinction between churchgoers and non-churchgoers in the population, and indicating their relative proportions as well as the relative strengths of different religious groups. This presumption was established by the detailed tables in the original census report, and has continued to underlie much recent research.[6]

The 1851 religious census, however was a snapshot taken on one particular Sunday, which was not necessarily a typical one. Moreover, as Mann himself acknowledged, it should not be assumed that the congregations present on the following and subsequent Sundays consisted entirely of the same individuals. It would indeed be consistent with the figures to argue that the entire English population attended church regularly, but usually only once every two or three weeks. Such an argument is of course implausible, but it is stated here in order to indicate an opposite pole from the debateable assumption that the 30 March 1851 figures identified a sharply defined body of worshippers, amounting to only between a third and half of the overall population, who all regularly attended every Sunday. The main object of the present paper is thus to offer an exploration of some of the evidence, both in the census itself and in other near contemporary sources, for irregular and occasional attendance, which provides essential but neglected context for interpreting the figures. Individual patterns of attendance at public worship are also highly relevant to wider analysis of the interface between elite and popular religion and to the assessment of working-class religiosity.

Material for this research derives primarily from the author's work on the Yorkshire returns.[7] The publication on a county basis, during

---

[5] For an overview of the literature on the census, see Clive D. Field, 'The 1851 Religious Census of Great Britain: a Bibliographical Guide for Local and Regional Historians', *The Local Historian* 27 (1997), 194–217.

[6] K. S. Inglis's influential article, 'Patterns of Religious Worship in 1851', *JEH* 11 (1960), 74–86, was founded on Mann's figures and assumptions. W. S. F. Pickering, 'The 1851 Religious Census – a Useless Experiment?', *British Journal of Sociology* 18 (1967), 382–407 and D. M. Thompson, 'The 1851 Census: Problems and Possibilities', *Victorian Studies* 11 (1967), 87–97, developed more critical approaches. However the most recent substantial work on the Census, K. D. M. Snell and Paul Ell, *Rival Jerusalems: the Geography of Victorian Religion* (Cambridge, 2000), continues to treat statistics of attendance as an index of religiosity, although computerization facilitates a sophistication of analysis impossible for Mann.

[7] *Yorkshire Returns of the 1851 Census of Religious Worship*, ed. John Wolffe, 4 vols,

the last twenty years or so, of numerous editions of the actual returns for individual places of worship provides the scope easily to extend the enquiry to a national basis.[8] Yorkshire, however, with returns from over three thousand places of worship, covering remote rural areas as well as heavily industrialized urban districts, is itself sufficiently large and internally diverse to provide a very substantial and useful sample. Qualitative indications in the 'Remarks' sections of the returns provide patchy but cumulatively significant evidence regarding patterns of attendance.

Three main conclusions emerge. First it seems very probable that overall the attendance on 30 March 1851 was somewhat lower than the average, and that attendances could fluctuate widely from Sunday to Sunday, especially in rural areas. This impression is supported by numerous remarks – not only from Yorkshire, but also from counties as far away as Buckinghamshire, Devon, Norfolk and Sussex – of the adverse effect of bad weather, and sometimes also epidemic disease.[9] There has been a tendency among scholars to make light of complaints about the weather,[10] but this was not a trivial factor, particularly in dispersed districts where many might need to walk substantial distances on unmade roads in order to attend a place of worship. A further factor in rural areas was the widespread alternation of Anglican services between the morning and the afternoon in successive weeks, with attendances generally higher when they were in the afternoon.[11] It was also widely observed in Yorkshire that attendances were higher in summer than in winter, with 30 March perceived as closer to the latter.[12]

Second, some respondents specifically referred to the intermittent attendance of individuals. Where there was more than one service on a

---

Borthwick Texts and Calendars 25, 31, 32 and forthcoming (York, 2000, 2005 and forthcoming) [hereafter: *YR*].

[8] For a list, see *YR*, 1.ii, n. 4.

[9] *YR*, 3.1781, 4.2684 (these citations give the volume number and the number of the individual return); *Buckinghamshire Returns of the Census of Religious Worship 1851*, ed. Edward Legg, Buckinghamshire Record Society 27 (Oxford, 1991) 109, 118; Michael J. L. Wickes, *Devon in the Religious Census of 1851* (n.p., 1990), 30, 125; Janet Ede and Norma Virgoe, eds, *Religious Worship in Norfolk*, Norfolk Record Society 52 (Norwich, 1998), 43, 83; *The Religious Census of Sussex 1851*, ed. John A. Vickers, Sussex Record Society 75 (Lewes, 1989), *passim*.

[10] For example Snell and Ell, *Rival Jerusalems*, 45.

[11] *YR*, 2.1052, 4.2726; Ede and Virgoe, eds, *Norfolk*, 220.

[12] *YR*, 2.1393, 2.1404, 3.1651, 3.2655. A few southern returns, however, reported the converse: see *The Religious Census of Hampshire 1851*, ed. John A. Vickers, Hampshire Record Series 12 (Winchester, 1993), 59, 201.

Sunday it was often affirmed that the congregations were different, and there was also variation from one Sunday to another. The Anglican incumbent of Kenninghall in Norfolk wrote: 'To call the No. attending at any one time the congregation is not a correct mode of reckoning, for if all that do attend ... the Church attended at one time, it would be doubled and more.'[13] At Ripon the Independent minister noted 'The whole congregation never present at one time' and at Salendine Nook Baptist Chapel, near Huddersfield, the minister similarly remarked 'We very seldom have the whole of our Members and Congregation together at one service.'[14] Conversely at Eastbrook Wesleyan Chapel in Bradford the remark that the congregation was 'particularly uniform and invariable' implied a consciousness that the situation was different in other nearby places of worship.[15] A few respondents endeavoured to quantify the overall numbers who identified with their places of worship, albeit not always attending. Thus at Ilkley, the Wesleyan chapel steward reported attendances on 30 March of 60 in the morning and 78 in the evening, and remarked that 'The average number of the resident population that attends the Chapel in the winter months may be estimated at 150'.[16] In a licensed Anglican school room at the Farnley Iron Works near Leeds, the officiating curate reported attendances of 30 adults and 55 Sunday scholars in the morning and 50 adults and 90 Sunday scholars in the afternoon. He then commented that 'many who attend this Place of Worship attend *frequently* but not regularly' and estimated 'the entire number of persons attached to this place of worship' at 250. It is unfortunately unclear whether or not he included the Sunday scholars in this calculation.[17] At St Mary's Quarry Hill, Leeds, the attendance on 30 March was estimated at 300 adults and 300 Sunday scholars in the morning, and 300 in the evening, but the incumbent reported the 'professed' membership of the congregation at '1500 or upwards', noting that 'the neighbourhood being entirely poor, the people offer many excuses for staying at home'.[18] Identification could extend even to those who never attended, as a correspondent in the parish of Sandal, near Wakefield, wrote to Bishop Longley of Ripon in 1845: 'The inhabitants of that village boast that they are good

13   Ede and Virgoe, *Norfolk*, 220.
14   *YR*, 2.933, 3.1790.
15   *YR*, 2.1335.
16   *YR*, 2.1104. Summer visitors to the resort doubled this figure.
17   *YR*, 2.1458.
18   *YR*, 2.1597.

churchmen though in years and years though within a few yards of the Church – by far the most part never entered the building'.[19] Such an assessment appears pessimistic, however, in the light of the average figure of 550 adults in the morning, 400 in the afternoon, and 160 Sunday scholars reported in 1851. These represented more than half the population (2009) of the townships of Sandal Magna and Walton served by the church.[20]

Especially in Anglican churches, pew rents and appropriations were a factor in limiting attendance but not identification. On the one hand there were evidently many who felt a sufficient connection with a church to wish to retain a pew even though they did not attend regularly, and on the other hand there was demand from those who wanted to attend, but for whom there was no place to sit even though the church was by no means full on Sundays. At Wath upon Dearne near Rotherham, where the adult attendance on census Sunday was 163 in the morning and 237 in the afternoon, 460 out of 520 seats for adults were appropriated.[21] In his visitation return in 1865 the vicar complained that 'Most of the pews are unoccupied until new attendants use them and the appropriators come and claim their rights, or write insulting letters to the persons who have sat in their seats.'[22]

Third, many individual churchgoers lacked a sustained exclusive denominational identification, and changes of personnel or of styles of worship could have a dramatic effect. At Knaresborough, the Independent minister noted that in recent years his congregation had declined due to competition from an Evangelical Anglican vicar as well as from other Dissenting chapels.[23] The impact of personality was evident in the open admission of the incumbent of Farnley in 1858 that 'During the time when the late curate officiated the congregation was much larger.'[24] At East Witton in Wensleydale, the churchwarden reported in 1851 that average attendance had dropped from 100 to 35

[19]   University of Leeds Library [hereafter: ULL], MS Holden Dep2/2, letter dated 7 Feb. 1845.

[20]   *YR*, 3.1918.

[21]   *YR*, 3.2368.

[22]   University of York, Borthwick Institute [hereafter: BI], Primary Visitation Returns to Archbishop Thomson, V.1865/Ret.1, 9. Among surviving visitation returns for the diocese of York these are the closest in date to the census.

[23]   *YR*, 2.1029.

[24]   West Yorkshire Archives, Leeds [hereafter: WYL], CB/1, Primary Visitation Returns to Bishop Bickersteth.

over the previous year 'through the services being alter'd'.[25] Conversely, at Seacroft, near Leeds, attendances of 91 in the morning and 122 in the afternoon in 1851 increased to 250 and 400 respectively in 1856, after a new incumbent had taken over in 1854.[26] In the very week of the census, the incumbent of Woodhouse, near Huddersfield, who had just reported attendances of 400 in the morning and 491 in the afternoon, warned a prospective successor: 'They are a strongly attached people, but I cannot disguise from myself that they are so independent and so soon offended, that they would quickly scatter from the Church if they were not pleased'.[27]

If such cases are indicative of a denominational serial monogamy, or of a frame of mind in which any kind of churchgoing was conditional on a congenial environment, there is also evidence for what might be termed denominational polygamy. At Bishop Burton, near Beverley, the vicar reported that 'many of the inhabitants' attended services at both the Baptist and Wesleyan chapels as well as at the parish church.[28] Similarly, at Long Preston, near Settle, which also had Wesleyan and Baptist chapels, the vicar remarked 'that many of the people go in-differently, at one time to the Parish Church, and at another to the Dissenting Chapels'.[29] There was widespread reporting in rural Yorkshire, both in the census itself and in subsequent visitation returns, of individuals attending both the Anglican church and a Methodist chapel – either Primitive or more usually Wesleyan – on the same day. Indeed service times appear to have been negotiated in order to facilitate such practice. At Armthorpe, near Doncaster, the rector wrote in his 1865 visitation return that the Primitive Methodist chapel in the village was not opened at the times of church service and that 'some of the principal supporters of, and attendants at the Chapel are in the constant habit of attending the Morning, and, less frequently, the afternoon Service at the Parish Church'.[30] On 30 March 1851, 118 adults had attended morning service at the parish church, when there was no chapel service; in the afternoon attendance was divided with 76 at the church and 27 at the chapel; in the evening there was no Anglican service and 57 attended

25   *YR*, 4.3294.
26   *YR*, 2.1516; ULL, MS Holden Dep 2/2, fol. 37v.
27   ULL, MS Holden Dep. 2/2, letter from J. W. Grane to Mr Attwood, 2 April 1851.
28   *YR*, 1.317.
29   *YR*, 2.782.
30   BI, V1865/Ret.1, 22.

the chapel.[31] Elsewhere, dual Anglican and Wesleyan attendance was reported as 'all but universal' in north Lincolnshire and several instances were recorded much further afield, in Devon.[32] In the 1865 York visitation returns, a number of Anglican incumbents drew a distinction between a numerous body of worshippers who moved readily between church and chapel, and a small hard core of Dissenters who did not ever attend church. For example, from Askham Bryan, near York, it was reported that 'The number of those who entirely dissent from the Church of England is very small, not more than 10 or 12'.[33] Such a situation was characteristic of agricultural villages: in industrial and urbanized areas it was not a matter for remark in the same way, and one can infer that congregations were likely to be more distinct. In the city of Lincoln, however, it was reported that people 'go from church to church, from chapel to church, and from church to chapel'.[34]

Taken together, these three conclusions indicate the need to qualify what might be termed an elite religious perception of the census, whether from contemporaries or from subsequent historians, as delineating defined bodies of regular worshippers with consistent denominational allegiances. Rather, there was a spectrum of commitment, from regular Sunday attendance, often at more than one service, through occasional attendance, if favourable weather or personal inclination allowed, to an identification that was seldom if ever expressed in actual participation, other than for the rites of passage. Also intriguing is the recognition that some of those most committed to organized Christianity, in general terms, by attending twice or more on a Sunday, also lacked the strong denominational identifications which, at a political level, appeared characteristic of the period. The overall implication is that the body of regular worshippers was probably rather smaller and less denominationally conscious than has generally been supposed, but that diffuse religious influence and identification extended much more broadly.

* * *

In order to give greater specificity to the argument, the remainder of this paper consists of a case study of the parish of Selby. The choice of

---

[31]   *YR*, 2.2478, 2.2479.

[32]   *Lincolnshire Returns of the Census of Religious Worship 1851*, ed. R. W. Ambler, Lincoln Record Society 72 (Fakenham, 1979), 934; Wickes, *Devon*, 288, 1252, 1307.

[33]   BI, V1865/Ret.1, 24.

[34]   Ambler, *Lincolnshire*, 584.

Selby has been determined particularly by the survival from 1854 of a *Speculum gregis*, or partial parish survey,[35] which provides valuable complementary information to that in the census itself. It can, however, also be seen as more broadly representative. Selby was a market town with a population of 5340 in 1851, with a mixed economic base and occupational structure. It was a developing railway centre and declining inland port located in the midst of a low-lying agricultural district.[36] Its overall index of attendance (that is the sum of all attendances as a percentage of total population) on census Sunday was 59.92, which is very close to the overall index of attendance for England and Wales, which was 60.8.[37] Its peculiarity, clear from Table 1, was the apparent relative weakness of the Church of England, despite possession of the magnificent, if decayed, medieval Abbey church, and the considerable strength of the Wesleyans. There was also a significant Roman Catholic presence.[38] The recently arrived Anglican incumbent in 1851 was Francis Whaley Harper, who was to acquire notoriety in the 1870s for his blunt advocacy of cooperation rather than confrontation between parsons and publicans, indicative perhaps of a pastoral outlook more accommodating to popular culture than that of many clergy.[39]

The Anglican figure in Table 1 can unfortunately be no more than an educated guess, as Harper merely wrote on the form where the attendance of the general congregation was requested 'I cannot undertake to say.' He did though note the attendances of 127 Sunday scholars at both morning and afternoon services.[40] In the 1865 visitation return, however, the average Sunday attendance was given as 550. At this date there were three services, at 10.30, 2.30 and 6.30.[41] In 1868 attendance was reported at 300 in the morning and 500 in the evening.[42] In 1865 attendance was described as increasing 'as fast as the churchwardens can

---

[35] BI, PR/SEL/270.

[36] David Hey, *Yorkshire from AD 1000* (Harlow, 1986), 215; Patricia Scott, *The History of Selby and District Part Two* (Leeds, 1987), 21–32.

[37] This figure is the 'corrected' one (that is making allowance for defective returns) as given by B. I. Coleman, *The Church of England in the Mid-Nineteenth Century: a Social Geography*, Historical Association Pamphlets, General Series 98 (London, 1980), 40.

[38] Cf. John Gillingham, *Worship North and East of Leeds* (Leeds, 1998), 200–6.

[39] F. Boase, *Modern English Biography*, 6 vols (Truro, 1892–1921), 5: 580–1; F. W. Harper, *The Parson and the Publican* (London, 1877); *The Official Report of the Eighteenth Annual Meeting of the Church Congress, Held at Sheffield, 1878* (Sheffield, 1879), 199–200.

[40] YR, 3.2583.

[41] BI, V1865/Ret.2, 461.

[42] BI, V1868/Ret.2, 470.

Table 1[43]
Religious Attendance in Selby on 30 March 1851

	Total Attendance	Largest Service	Index of Attendance
Church of England	450 (estimate)		8.43
Roman Catholic	408	214 (morning)	7.64
Wesleyan Methodist	1516	600 (evening)	28.39
Primitive Methodist	166	90 (evening)	3.11
Independents	468	197 (morning)	8.76
Friends	45	25 (morning)	0.47
Unitarians	146	105 (evening)	2.73
TOTAL	3200	1681	59.92

supply additional seating', so it seems probable that the figure in 1851 would have been significantly lower. 450 (including the 127 Sunday scholars) is therefore suggested as a plausible estimate.

Selby well illustrates the difficulty of moving from the raw attendance figures to any confident judgement on how many individuals actually attended church on census Sunday. There would certainly have been some double and sometimes even triple attendance by individuals, especially among the Wesleyans who had three large services, but its extent is impossible to ascertain from the census returns. Even the figures for the largest service may count some individuals twice, because of the likelihood that some went to the Abbey in the morning and the Wesleyan chapel in the evening. On the other hand, few Roman Catholics are likely to have gone to mass twice, so the 194 present in the evening were almost certainly largely different individuals from the 214 who had attended in the morning. We can only conclude that while the 1681 present at the largest services (31.47% of the population of the parish) is also certainly something of an underestimate, the figure would have been substantially less than 3200.

To gain more insight into the popular attitudes and religious practice that lay behind the census figures, we turn to the 1854 *Speculum gregis*. This was a systematic survey, based on parish visiting, by Harper or his curates, of a number of streets on the eastern side of the town,

[43] Calculated from *YR*, 3.2583–9.

Table 2
Reported Religious Practice of 399 Selby Residents in 1854

	Male	Female
Church	48	66
Church 'sometimes'	14	19
Church 'seldom' 'very seldom'	1	2
Church 'if anywhere'	12	0
Independent	8	10
Primitive Methodist	3	4
'Christian Believers' (secession from PMs)	3	3
Wesleyan Methodist	41	44
Roman Catholic	9	10
Unitarian	4	2
Chapel (unspecified)	0	1
'Goes nowhere'	4	0
No practice reported	47	44
TOTAL	194	205

close to the canal and the tidal river Ouse. The population was artisan and labouring, with a predominance of occupations related to river and maritime activity, including sailors, watermen and rope weavers. The survey records the year of birth, state of health, occupation, and professed religious practice of those visited.

Table 2 summarizes the reported religious practice of 399 individuals, excluding long-term absentees, young children born from 1848 onwards, those obviously physically unable to attend religious worship, and those for whom the information given is too scanty to allow categorization.

When considered alongside the attendance at the Abbey in 1865, the much higher proportion of Church of England allegiance reported here suggests some wishful thinking by the Anglican compilers and anxiety to please by respondents. However it was recorded that of the 152 individuals who professed some kind of church identification, 26 also attended the Wesleyan chapel and 2 the Primitive chapel. If these 28 are redistributed then the proportions look somewhat closer to those reported in the census and visitation returns. The continuing relative strength of the Church of England when assessed by this measure of professed rather than actual attendance suggests a wider circle of occasional practice than for Nonconformity. It is indeed evident from the document that some of those identified as 'Church' were not at present attending regularly. There was also the possibility that between 1851 and 1854, Harper, who had apparently introduced an evening service, had gained some ground relative to Methodism.

The most striking conclusion is the low reported level of total non-association with organized religion even in this predominantly working-class district. Of the 91 individuals for whom no practice was reported, nearly half (20 males and 23 females) were children and teenagers born between 1840 and 1847. Given that some of these were reported as attending day or Sunday school, and others had reportedly churchgoing parents, it seems unlikely that they were all in reality without church links. Discounting these 43, but including the four men who avowedly went nowhere, there were only 31 males and 21 females in the sample for whom no religious associations were recorded. These included 12 married couples, some evidently constrained by the care of young children. The remaining men were predominantly single and under thirty, and the women generally older widows. Among this last group particularly there were indications of the extent to which economic and social pressures could preclude organized religious activity. Sarah Pearson (b. 1792), a washerwoman, said that she lacked suitable clothes and in any case felt 'tired and badly on Sundays: lies rather too long to get to Ch in the morning'.[44] Hannah Nappy, a single woman, was 'rather lightheaded and much troubled by her brother's drinking'.[45] Most poignant of all was the case of Hannah Goodwith (b. 1776) and her widowed daughter Sarah Lund (b. 1804), who had recently taken in four of Hannah's orphaned grandchildren (b. 1842, 1847, 1851 and 1852) rendering the old woman 'much distressed "in mind body and estate"'.[46] Even men, for whom non-attendance was a matter of choice rather than pressure of circumstance, could have ambivalent personal and family histories. Thomas Robinson, a mast and block maker (b. 1819), went nowhere now, but in the past had been a Church singer, and subsequently attended the Independent Chapel.[47]

---

[44] BI, PR/SEL/270, 8.
[45] Ibid., 11.
[46] Ibid.
[47] Ibid., 6.

John Brumyard, landlord of the Nelson Inn, was hostile to his clerical visitor, and seemed to go nowhere himself, but three of his children attended the Wesleyan school and his daughters subsequently sought confirmation.[48]

Material of the kind available for Selby is unfortunately rare. Nevertheless the Selby evidence has a much wider than local significance in pointing to a complex variety of religious practice lying behind the crude headcounts and estimates of those physically present at worship on a single rainy early spring Sunday. Statistical work on matters such as patterns of relative denominational strength needs to be complemented by focused study of particular localities, using the census alongside other sources, in order better to understand the numerous permutations of churchgoing and non-churchgoing, and of elite and popular religion, in mid-nineteenth-century England.

The Open University

---

[48] Ibid, 10. This family was not counted in the sample used for table 2, because of the ambiguous and incomplete nature of the information recorded.

ELITE AND POPULAR RELIGION:
THE CASE OF NEWMAN*

by DERMOT FENLON

MONG the signal insights of twentieth-century scholarship
was the recognition that early Christianity accorded personal
importance to the plebs. First, Eric Auerbach analysed the
humble speech forms of early Christianity, contrasting them with the
literature of learned pagans.[1] The point was developed by Ramsay
MacMullen in an important essay entitled 'Sermo humilis'.[2] Arnaldo
Momigliano applied these insights to the theologians, historians and
hagiographers of the fourth and fifth centuries. He showed how Augustine, Jerome, Socrates, Sozomen, and Theodoret of Cyr succeeded, as
pagan intellectuals had not succeeded, in 'abolishing the internal frontiers between the learned and the vulgar'.[3] Finally, Peter Brown, in a
series of brilliant works from *The Cult of the Saints* to his revised biography of Augustine, supplied a means of discerning in the practice of
universal baptism the 'antidote' to the exaggerations of fourth-century
ascetical elitism. Augustine imparted to the Western Middle Ages a
confidence in the power of sacramental grace as efficacious not only for
the ascetic few, but as communicating to the many a capacity for
growth in charity, purity, and prayer.[4] Such a perspective on the religion of the many bids adieu to Gibbon's story of 'philosophy' collapsing
into 'barbarism and religion'; to Hume's account of the superstitious
and the credulous; and to Henry Hart Milman's Romantic brand of
Liberal Anglicanism as marked by 'condescension' towards 'popular
religion' occluding 'the thought processes of the average man';[5] a habit

* My thanks are due to Lewis Berry, Philip Cleevely and Sheridan Gilley for helpful criticism. My thanks are also due to Peter Brown for his deeply generous response to this paper.

  1 Erich Auerbach, *Mimesis: the Representation of Reality in Western Literature* (Princeton,
NJ, 1953).
  2 Ramsey MacMullen, 'A Note on Sermo humilis', *JTS* n.s. 17 (1966), 108–12.
  3 Arnaldo Momigliano, 'Popular Religious Beliefs and the Late Roman Historians', in
G. J. Cuming and Derek Baker, eds, *Popular Belief and Practice*, SCH 8 (Cambridge, 1972),
1–29, 8, quotation at 17.
  4 Peter Brown, *Augustine of Hippo* (2nd edn, London, 2000).
  5 Henry Hart Milman's *History of the Jews* was published in 1829; in 1840 his *History of*

of mind to which Peter Brown surprisingly appended the name of Newman.[6]

Newman, in fact, rejected Milman's account of religious development, regarding it as the reduction of religion to a form of collective self-reference. In reality, Newman's critique of Gibbon, Hume and Milman emerges with fresh authority precisely to the extent that it relocates the phenomena of Christian history within the explanatory framework of the sources. Newman's account of the 'rise of the holy man', of monks and of the miracles of early Christian history, when linked with his designation of 'the Benedictine Centuries', actually anticipates the curriculum, and much of the agenda, of twentieth-century historians. This is a fact that merits a measure of attention.

Newman, like Gibbon, had read 'the good Tillemont'. He too had studied the great patristic collections of St Maur, together with the ecclesiastical historians of the fourth and fifth centuries; but he learned to read them, after a series of false starts, from within. His point of departure in 1825–6 was shaped by a concern to meet Hume's objection to miracles.

Newman's first 'Essay on Miracles' accepted Hume's requisite of consistency in God's works, but reversed its application: the miracles of Scripture did not falsify but answered the criterion of antecedent probability. Where Voltaire and Bentham had supposed miracles to argue the 'mutability of God', and Religion to derive from 'popular superstition' and 'mere weakness or eccentricity of the intellect', Newman turned the question from the mechanistic to 'the moral character of the Miracle'. The miracles of Scripture, on this view, confirmed the faith of the faithful. Scripture miracles were authentic. The miracles of Christian history, however, were 'corruptions' introduced by Romanism. In this Newman followed the Anglican apologists of the eighteenth century, Conyers Middleton and Bishop Douglas.[7]

As the Tractarian Movement got underway, Newman's attention turned to the historical development of the Church's liturgies, and to the place of Rome in that development. Newman's use of the Breviary from 1836 increasingly impressed on him a style of holiness reflected in

---

Christianity to the Abolition of Paganism in the Roman Empire appeared; in 1849 he was made Dean of St Paul's; in 1855 he published his *History of Latin Christianity*.

[6] Peter Brown, 'Religion and Imagination', in *Society and the Holy in Late Antiquity* (London, 1982), 10–13, and idem, *The Cult of the Saints* (Chicago, IL, and London, 1981), 16.

[7] *Two Essays on Biblical and Christian Miracles* (Westminster, MD, 1969), 1–94.

the lives of the saints. He found them attractively 'unexciting, grave and simple'.[8]

In 1840 he communicated to his diary the cryptic reflection that, in its 'refusal of economies', Protestantism was corrupting into rationalism, and society into Pantheism: an ethos, on its religious side, sentimental, and self-serving. The cultural expression of this process was summed up for Newman in Henry Hart Milman's account of historical Christianity which appeared that year. Urged on by Pusey, Newman undertook to review it for *The British Critic*.[9]

Milman's presentation of Christianity as answering historically to social needs made it, as Newman remarked, subservient to temporal purposes. When these needs and purposes changed, the product itself became dispensable. Studied according to criteria which were alien to its sources Christianity was emptied of its religious meaning. Such an account of a doctrineless Christianity, however palatable to the nineteenth-century mind, was simply a production of and for that mind. As Newman went on to express it in his second 'Essay on Miracles' in 1842–3, 'the Fathers wrote for contemporaries, not for the eighteenth or nineteenth century'.[10]

* * *

Henceforward, Newman's understanding of Christian history was defined by what he called 'the sacramental principle' drawn especially from Origen, and reinforced by Origen's seventeenth-century editor, the Catholic apologist Daniel Huet.[11] Newman's proposal that 'the visible world is the instrument, yet the veil, of the world invisible' subserving 'a system of persons, facts, and events beyond itself' became henceforward an explanatory principle capable of interpreting the supernatural phenomena not only of early and medieval history, but also of post-Reformation Catholic development in terms adequate to the faith of the participants.[12] Milman had celebrated the 'primeval

8   *Letters and Diaries of John Henry Newman*, ed. C. S. Dessain *et al.*, 28 vols (Oxford and London, 1961–) [hereafter: *LD*], 6: ed. Gerard Tracey, 47.

9   *LD* 7: 283, 487.

10   *Two Essays*, 226–7.

11   Newman to T. W. Allies, 30 September 1842, in *Correspondence of John Henry Newman with John Keble and Others* (London, 1917), 196–7. The place of Huet calls for investigation.

12   'Milman's view of Christianity' in *Essays Critical and Historical* II (2nd edn, London, 1871), 192. For Newman's application of the principle to the natural sciences, see his *University Sermons*, no. 15, (originally 14, in the 1843 edn); and for the relation between natural religion and the rise of Christianity, his critique of Gibbon in the *Grammar of Assent*, especially

poetic element' in the religion of Abbot Samson. Carlyle had retorted that for Abbot Samson '[i]t was Reality'.[13] Newman articulated the retort into a principle. He called it 'the sacramental principle'.

Newman's second Essay on Miracles of 1842 revised his earlier refusal of ecclesiastical miracles, as conceding too much to the scepticism not only of Hume and Gibbon, but to the critics of the later Roman world. Celsus, the target of Origen's theology, had considered the miraculous claims of Christians as illustrating the lamentable decline of noble minds into the superstition and credulity of the crowds. In place of an intellectual polarity between the educated and the vulgar, Newman now posited the presence of Christ manifested to the hearts of a people schooled in the obedience of faith, and sacramentally active in a continuum across the centuries. Newman's originality lay in his ability from this time forward fully to allow for the corruptions of Christianity (into sacerdotal tyranny, into theological rationalism, into superstition) without surrendering the supernatural character of its activity. Thus, in the case of ecclesiastical miracles, Newman made few concessions to credulity:

> Fiction and pretence, follow truth as its shadows; the Church is at all times in the midst of corruption, because she is in the world and is framed out of human hearts; and as the elect are fewer than the reprobate, and are hard to find amid the chaff, so false miracles at once exceed and conceal and prejudice those which are genuine.[14]

What must strike us in this passage is Newman's doctrine of the few and the reprobate. It was his subsequent reformulation of this question, beginning in a letter to Keble of 1843 with the observation that the 'Roman additions to the Primitive Creed' were perhaps best understood as 'developments', which left him increasingly open to the charge that as an Anglican he had deceitfully economized his meaning, and that, as a priest of the Church of Rome, he had succumbed to the instincts and superstitions of the crowds.[15]

If the charge against Newman of corrupting the Church of England was repeatedly advanced against him in the wake of Tract 90, the

---

chs 9 and 10. Newman's insistence (against Milman) on the significance of the doctrines of Christianity in the world of Late Antiquity is illuminated in the works of Peter Brown.
[13]   D. Forbes, *The Liberal Anglican Philosophy of History* (Cambridge, 1952), 81.
[14]   *Two Essays*, 239.
[15]   Newman to Keble, 4 May 1843 (*Correspondence*, 219).

charge of corrupting the realm as a Catholic priest was framed at its most memorable by Kingsley in 1864, and, more subtly, a year later by Pusey. Kingsley accused Newman of exchanging the standards of 'honest gentlemen and noble ladies' for those of 'the majority of the Romish priesthood' and 'those hapless Irish Celts over whom they rule'.[16] Newman had crossed the Irish sea and 'gawn native'. The process had covertly begun in Oxford. In this at least, Kingsley was not mistaken.

* * *

I owe to Sheridan Gilley the suggestion that Newman's sense of mission to the poor has its roots in his Evangelical conversion. As an Evangelical, Newman had prayed to be delivered from condescension towards 'those I meet in the streets'. As a Tractarian, he insisted on the Church as a popular power, served by those sent by God. His attention to the religion of the illiterate began with his adherence after 1843 to the belief that the honours accorded to the Blessed Virgin and the Saints, as to miracles and relics, rightfully occupied a central place in Christianity. We can see this conviction growing in Newman's diary entries which served as a prelude prompting him to begin his *Essay on Development*, and to embrace in 1845 what he described in his novel, *Loss and Gain*, as 'a popular religion'.[17]

The crux of this development was found in Newman's changing understanding of 'superstition'. From a simple 'corruption' of Christianity, it became increasingly for him a fact of human nature, whereby the Saviour accommodated His self-revelation to the poor.

There is an arresting passage in Newman's *Essay on Development* which encapsulates the nature of the change. It concerns the pastoral methods employed by St Gregory Thaumaturgos as related in the *Life* by Gregory of Nyssa. Gregory, perceiving 'the need of holydays for the multitude' as recommended by Origen, turned the pagan festivals into a Christian instrument 'to reclaim the people' from their 'gross habits'.[18] This is not the language of the later twentieth century. But it is

---

[16] Kingsley's text repr. in the Fontana edition of Newman's *Apologia* (London, 1959), 29–65, quotation at 65.

[17] *Autobiographical Writings*, ed. H. Tristram (London, 1957), 175; *Loss and Gain*, ed. Alan G. Hill (London, 1986), 294. Frank McGrath draws attention to the theme of the saints in Newman's diary for 1843, in his impending edition of Newman's *LD* 9. I am grateful to him for permission to read the text in advance of publication.

[18] *An Essay on the Development of Christian Doctrine* (6th edn, Notre Dame, IN, 1989), 372–3.

the language of the sources, and it illuminates for us the critical question of educated Christians and uneducated pagans.

In the *Essay on Development*, Newman further directed his attention to the 'antagonistic principle' which he considered had entered Christianity with Locke: the proposition that doctrines are to be considered 'true as they are logically demonstrated'. 'Such a philosophy', wrote Newman, would 'cut off from the possibility and the privilege of faith all but the educated few'.[19] That was what Newman deemed to have happened to the Christianity of the past two centuries. He now set himself to redress the imbalance.

He began, at Littlemore, from 1843–4, by studying the Catholic spirituality of the centuries following the Protestant Reformation, in particular, the *Spiritual Exercises* of St Ignatius of Loyola. After ordination to the Catholic priesthood in 1847 Newman, inspired by the Roman Oratory of St Philip Neri, gradually incorporated into his pastoral ideal the eucharistic and Marian theology of St Alphonsus Liguori. At Maryvale, in Birmingham, the first home of the English Oratorians, he and his companions prayed in 'the small chapel' where Bishop Milner 'set himself to soften and melt the frost which stiffened the Catholicism of his day, and to rear up, safe from our northern blasts, the tender and fervent aspirations of Continental piety', establishing 'the first altar dedicated in England to the Sacred Heart of our Lord'.[20] By 1852 the mission of the Birmingham Oratorians, drawing on these traditions of piety, began to extend its scope from the wealthy suburb of Edgbaston, with its orphanage and prison, to the outlying industrial wastelands of Smethwick.

* * *

As a writer, Newman found a new voice.[21] From now on he spoke as the apologist of a popular religion: in *The Present Position of Catholics*; in the *Difficulties of Anglicans*; in the *Apologia pro vita sua*.

In his reply to Pusey's *Eirenicon* in 1865 Newman found himself obliged explain a devotional rhetoric taken for granted by Catholics, but reprehensible to Anglicans. Newman remarks upon language which 'formalized into meditations or exercises' might appear 'as repulsive as love letters in a police report', yet which 'even holy minds'

---

[19] Ibid., 327–8.
[20] *Sermons Preached on Various Occasions* (Westminster, MD, 1968), 261.
[21] Ian Ker, *The Catholic Revival in English Literature: Newman, Hopkins, Belloc, Chesterton, Greene, Waugh* (Notre Dame, IN, and Leominster, 2003), 13–33.

adopted as their own when recommended by custom. He then reflected on the phenomenon of 'trickle-down' distortion:

> what has power to stir holy and refined souls is potent also with the multitude; and the religion of the multitude is ever vulgar and abnormal; it will ever be tinctured with fanaticism and superstition, while men are what they are. A people's religion is ever a corrupt religion.

These are words very shocking to contemporary minds. But Newman intended to refer to something actually shocking. In the text, the 'multitude' he speaks of is the 'mixed multitude' described in the Mosaic Exodus; a people whose potentiality for corruption was a Biblical 'given'. In the manuscript for the second edition Newman crossed out the words 'if you have a Catholic Church you must put up with', and then his thought changes again; 'in spite of the provisions of the Holy Church', he writes, so that his thought runs: 'a people's religion is ever a corrupt religion in spite of the provisions of the Holy Church. If she is to be Catholic, you must admit within her net fish of every kind'; thus arriving at the kind of Church which so unfavourably impressed English travellers abroad: 'a high grand faith and worship which compels their admiration, and puerile absurdities among the people which excite their contempt'.[22]

The *Tablet* of 3 March, and the *Dublin Review* of April 1866 called upon Newman to explain himself. Publicly, Newman replied by simply reiterating his concern to deny the Protestant misreading of 'such strong passages about the Saints as occur among Catholic authors from St Athanasius downwards'.[23] In addition, he privately explained his reference to popular corruptions of religion as extending from the early African practice of 'administering the Holy Sacrament to the dead', to the contemporary belief of the Irish poor 'that a suspended Priest has the gift of healing'.[24] The point illustrates Newman's capacity to learn from the Irish poor the potentiality of a high sanctity coexisting with a measure of actual superstition, the latter left to achieve its own level by the good sense of a pastoral elite.

Newman had earlier touched on the Italian case: 'the strange stories

---

[22] *The Mother of God*, ed. Stanley Jaki (Pinckney, MI, 2003), 74. The advantage of this edition is that it supplies Newman's emendations.

[23] *LD* 22: 173–4.

[24] Ibid., 196–7.

of highwaymen and brigands devout to the Madonna' who told how the Blessed Virgin was apt to deliver the reprobate from hell, and to transfer them to purgatory; 'and absolutely to secure from perdition all who are devout to her, repentance not being contemplated as the means'.[25] He had multiplied the examples most calculated to shock Protestant feelings, only to urge that it is 'the necessary consequence of its being Catholic . . . of mixed multitudes all having faith'.[26] Such faith must needs be regulated by 'holy and refined minds' – by theologians such as Gregory of Nyssa; by bishops such as Gregory Thaumaturgos.

In the 1873 edition of *The Church of the Fathers* Newman published his essay on Theodoret of Cyr. Momigliano, citing it, remarked that 'Cardinal Newman was naturally puzzled by "the stupid credulity of so well-read, so intellectual an author"'. But 'Theodoretus lived', Momigliano observed, 'in the world of the miracles he described'.[27] Remarking on 'the Christian abolition of the internal frontier between the learned and the vulgar' Momigliano further drew attention to the consequence: for 'cultured people', the 'acceptance of . . . miracles, relics, and apparitions'; and for 'the vulgar', an appreciation 'to the point of fanaticism' of doctrinal controversies which could and frequently did erupt into 'mob theology'. Momigliano gave as his example the two banishments of John Chrysostom.[28] In this, his thought, in point of fact, was identical with Newman's. Momigliano, surprisingly, had missed the fact.

As an historian of the fourth century and a student of Chrysostom, Newman shared with Momigliano an appreciation of the 'tincture of fanaticism' available to the Court for titration against a troublesome bishop. But as between elite and people, the historical problem in the Christian sources remained, for Newman, the question of credulity. Thus in Theodoret's account of the Solitaries of Syria, Newman took up the question of his 'easy credence' in miracles which 'seems to moderns wonderful . . . especially considering the circumstances of his education'. 'Was it', Newman asks,

> that at least some miracles were brought home so absolutely to his
> sensible experience that he had no reason for doubting the others

---

[25] *Certain Difficulties Felt by Anglicans in Catholic Teaching Considered* I (Westminster, MD, 1969), 279.

[26] Ibid., 288–9.

[27] Momigliano, 'Popular Religious Beliefs', 16.

[28] Ibid., 17–18.

which came to him at second hand? This certainly will explain what to most of us is sure to seem the stupid credulity of so well-read, so intellectual an author.[29]

Newman is here accommodating his argument to his readers. He is attempting seriously to advance an understanding of the *manner* in which Theodoret inhabited a world of miracle. Theodoret himself, he declares, was 'aware that he should try the faith of his readers'. But Newman identifies the critical fact that 'the strange penances of these hermits, as St. Simeon's continuance upon his pillar' were 'protected' for Theodoret by 'various observances, divinely commanded in the Old Testament' such as Ezekiel's departure at night 'through a hole broken in his house-wall'; acts 'intended to teach by their very strangeness'.[30]

In his account of the desert solitaries, Newman thus identified both the biblical matrix of symbolic action, and the historical form of 'the sacramental principle' as accommodated to a fifth-century audience:

> nothing was more adapted to convert Orientals in that day than excesses of asceticism and anomalous displays of power, – manifestations, in short, which would shock and revolt an educated European of the nineteenth century. The Solitaries were *de facto* missionaries.[31]

St Simeon Stylites converted the crowds by means which made him to later ages 'the laughing stock of unbelievers and a subject of profound astonishment, nay perplexity, to believing minds. And he was likely to convert them in no other way'.[32] For this was God's doing, God's economy with His people, God's condescension.

Actions 'intended to teach by their very strangeness', addressed to 'unbelievers and believing minds': Newman's long dialogue with Hume and Gibbon is here resolved in the encounter between the many and the few in the Biblical perspectives of fifth-century Asia Minor. He did not disallow the feelings of perplexity such experiences aroused in the educated minds of the fifth century itself. Newman's conclusion is not unlike Momigliano's:

> my inquest into popular religious beliefs in the late Roman historians ends in reporting that there were no such beliefs. In the

---

[29] *Historical Sketches* 2 (Westminster, MD, 1970), 315.
[30] Ibid., 315–16.
[31] Ibid., 317.
[32] Ibid.

fourth and fifth centuries there were of course plenty of beliefs which we historians of the twentieth century would gladly call popular, but the historians of the fourth and fifth centuries never treated any belief as characteristic of the masses and consequently discredited among the elite. Lectures on popular religious beliefs and the late Roman historians should be severely discouraged.[33]

To this Newman would only have added that the constant practice of the Church was to discern between true and false 'miracles, relics, apparitions'; the inescapable responsibility of an elite.

* * *

I have tried to show that Newman's habit of mind was not insensitive to 'the thought processes of the average man'. In this I do not think that he was always followed by the Catholic exponents of a twentieth-century 'nouvelle théologie'. Among these we can, I think, identify a Catholic development corresponding to Peter Brown's concept of 'condescension'. The proponents of the 'new theology' explicitly categorized the devotional traditions of four centuries as mere 'compensation' for popular 'exclusion' from an ancient liturgy. In this they offered an assessment alien to Newman's mind. Its devastating consequences have been compellingly reassessed by Eamon Duffy.[34]

From his discovery of the Roman Breviary in 1837, to his posthumously published *Meditations and Devotions*, Newman's life of prayer was continuous with the liturgy which he celebrated with solemnity and inner conviction. For Newman, the emotional piety of the Catholic populations of the modern world was something to learn from and to encourage within the forms of an artistically sensitive eucharistic and Marian theology. Perhaps the supreme expression in his Catholic writings is the sermon 'Omnipotence in Bonds', described by Horton Davies as 'the finest sermon Newman ever wrote'.[35]

It was not the 'corruptions' of religious life which impressed the mature Newman. It was the potentiality of the faithful to preserve the faith. As a young man, in writing the *Arian Crisis of the Fourth Century* he

---

[33] Momigliano, 'Popular Religious Beliefs', 18.

[34] *Faith of our Fathers* (London and New York, 2004), 25–7. I cannot, however, concur with the description of Newman as a 'romantic individualist' whose 'vision of purgatory' was 'an all but absolute loneliness' (ibid., 132). Newman's doctrine of purgatory was taken from St Catherine of Genoa and St Francis de Sales.

[35] *Worship and Theology in England IV: From Newman to Martineau, 1850–1900* (London and Princeton, NJ, 1962), 302–3.

had come to recognize the historical failure of large areas of the theological and episcopal leadership of the fourth century. At the end of his life it remained for him 'the great evangelical truth' that in the Church it is 'not the wise and powerful, but the obscure, the unlearned and the weak who constitute her real strength'. This was the 'moral' to which he drew attention in his third, 1871 edition of this book.[36] It was, I think, intended as a testimony for posterity.

The Oratory, Birmingham

---

[36] Appendix V to the third edition (1871) of *The Arian Crisis of the Fourth Century*, at 454–5. This, it seems to me, supplies the perspective requisite to a reading of his Preface to the final edition (1877) of the *Via Media*.

THE BOLTON PRELUDE TO PORT SUNLIGHT:
W. H. LEVER (1851–1925) AS PATRON
AND PATERNALIST

by CLYDE BINFIELD

CHRIST Church United Reformed Church (formerly Congregational), Port Sunlight, and St George's United Reformed Church (formerly Congregational), Thornton Hough, do not spring to mind as Free Church buildings. There is scarcely one architectural respect in which either announces a Dissenting presence. Each conforms to nationally established tradition. Their quality, however, is as incontestable as it is incontestably derivative. Their role in their respective village-scapes is important, even dominant. As buildings, therefore, they are significant and perhaps suggestive, but do they say anything about ecclesiastical polity? The answer to that question illustrates the interaction between elite and popular religion in Edwardian English Protestant Nonconformity, for the polity to which these two churches give space is in fact successively congregational, Congregational, and Reformed. It is representative throughout but never democratic. Yet can any shade of congregationalism truly develop in either a squire's village or a manufacturer's? And what might be deduced of the man who provided these buildings, created their villages, shaped their communities, and regarded himself lifelong as a Congregationalist even if a masonic lodge were the only fellowship to which he could stately commit himself? These questions prompt this paper.

Before the Garden Suburb and the Garden City, those disconcertingly authoritarian harbingers of liberal community, there was the Model Industrial Village, that prototype of paternalism. The pace was set in the 1850s by Saltaire, the creation of Sir Titus Salt, Congregationalist, Liberal, autocrat, and pioneer of worsted, mohair, and alpaca. The consummation came forty years on with Port Sunlight (and its truly rural companion, Thornton Hough), the creation of W. H. Lever, Congregationalist, Liberal, autocrat, and maker and marketer of soap. Both men were model paternalists, enlightened despots in Congregational clothing. How could such extremes be representative, let alone communitarian, even congregational? Since, however, there can be no community that does not in some way explore what it means to be family and since paternalism implies at least some of the dimensions of family life, the Model Industrial Village should demonstrate the possibilities as well as the limits of the elite-and-popular.

The tensions and dynamics of such places and what they said about their creators fascinated social, literary, and religious commentators. Thus Edward Thompson, E. P. Thompson's once Methodist father, went wickedly to town with both limits and possibilities when, in *Introducing the Arnisons*, he enjoyed a safari – or pilgrimage from grace – to a Nonconformist paradise, Oakenshaw, the Manchester dormitory suburb built by Noah Burgess J.P., speculator, jerrybuilder, and Baptist.[1] Burgess was omnipresent – the Burgess Higher Grade School, the Burgess Women's Institute, the Burgess Temperance Society, the Burgess Women's Temperance Society, the Burgess Tiny Tots' Temperance Association – everything, it seems, save a Burgess Memorial Baptist Church. Perhaps that reflected the softening influence of Mrs Burgess, to whom there was a statue in the market place, presented as a Grecian muse, 'lifting skywards a lyre and a book', above the inscription (for the sculptor was also a Baptist): 'Of such is the Kingdom of Heaven'.

It was Felicity Burgess who had persuaded her husband to name Oakenshaw's streets Linden, Hawthorn, Birch, and Maple, and its houses 'Orpheus', 'Shelley', 'Keats'. Her true memorial, however, 'the last sight that will remind you, even faintly, of anything but muck and money, until you have overpassed Manchester by at least another dozen miles on the other side', was 'The Jolly Shepherdess'. Once a coaching inn, then upgraded to 'The Burgess Arms', it became 'The Jolly Shepherdess' as better suited to 'Ye Olde Inne of Ye Oakenne Shawe'. Above its bar hung a floral-bordered, gilt-lettered, six-stanzaed lyric, its verse wholly worthy of the authoress of Chants to Pan 'by a Gentlewoman of Feeling', which is how Mrs Burgess thought of herself.[2] Though the lyric deserves full quotation, its first and last stanzas suffice to convey the wicked accuracy of true caricature:

> The Shepherdess Calls to You, Traveller
> O Pilgrim, thridding your dusty road,
> I prithee, pause and tarry!
> Ah, lay aside your weary head,

[1] Edward Thompson, *Introducing the Arnisons* (London, 1935), 53. The best introduction to the model industrial village remains Walter L. Creese, *The Search for Environment. The Garden City: Before and After* (New Haven, CT, 1966).
[2] Thompson, *Introducing the Arnisons*, 53–9.

For here there is sanctuary
[...]
The shepherdess bids thee dance and sing,
  With her face like a bright sweet cherry.
The time is dawn and the season is Spring
  Pilgrim! dear Pilgrim! be merry![3]

Who were these Baptists so effortlessly on the downgrade? Novels are not histories as historians say they understand History. Oakenshaw has to be a composite. It is impossibly popular and perversely elite (on the assumption that Noah Burgess was, like most Baptists, a Particular Baptist, it was by definition elite). So what and whom had Thompson in mind? We might at once think of the Quaker Cadburys at Bournville or Rowntrees at New Earswick, of the Primitive Methodist Hartleys at Aintree, the Unitarian Kenricks at Harborne, the Congregational Crossleys in Halifax and Salts of Saltaire, the New Connexion Methodist turned Anglican Akroyds of Akroyden, the Congregational turned Anglican Crittalls of Silver End. We might indeed think of the Moravians of Fulneck and Ockbrook and especially of the Mancunian Moravians of Fairfield hard by Audenshaw. None of these are fictional, all exemplify elite-and-popular living. Of them all the most representative, and yet the most extreme in scale, concept, and appearance, are the Congregational Levers of Port Sunlight and Thornton Hough.

The extremities were admirably caught by the press coverage ('A Victorian workers' paradise goes on sale to modern executives') which greeted the repackaging of Port Sunlight in 1990 'to attract a more successful sort of person to the Liverpool area'. Port Sunlight was for sale. It had indeed been so for some years. Thornton Hough was to follow a decade later. Their creator, W. H. Lever, 'purveyor of soap, oil and dreams, believed that contented workers would be loyal workers – in the classic synergy of profit and nonconformist religion which characterized industrialists then'. That synergy had been liberated in both villages in the English Vernacular Revival, 'a sort of Inglenook and Exposed Beams special, which brought Tudor nostalgia to the poor, but with plenty of plumbing with which to use the firm's best-selling Sunlight soap'. At Sunlight all was set in a gardened landscape of lawns (forty acres), flower beds (an acre and a half), rose bushes (17,000), hanging baskets (ninety of them), trees (2,000), art gallery, hotel (suspi-

---

[3] Ibid., 59.

ciously like Oakenshaw's 'Jolly Shepherdess') and, although no church was mentioned, 'the developers say that Cub and Brownie packs flourish'.[4]

Sunlight's paradise had a long innings. In 1926 the William Wedgwood Benns had tasted it while travelling from Odessa to Moscow. They met an

> old lady who had visited England twenty-five years before . . . She had stayed near Port Sunlight, a model community designed to improve the conditions of working people, and thought that its founder, the soap manufacturer William Lever was a saint: 'There would have been no revolution had there been people like him in Russia'.[5]

The encounter was aptly timed. Lever had died the year before and although by 1925 William Hesketh Lever and William Wedgwood Benn belonged to rapidly diverging strands of Liberalism as well as to different generations, they were both Congregationalists of a sort and they had overlapped as Liberal MPs.[6] Benn's elder brother Ernest, whose politics were much closer to Lever's, publicized Lever's creation in the trade journals which were the staple of his publishing empire.[7]

* * *

What might explain this Congregational Wirral-and-Mersey industrial icon for despairing Russians? What made it, as is the way with icons, representative? The answer is threefold: sociological context, the power of personality, and the combination of context and personality as refracted through ecclesiology. The first is Bolton, the second is William Hesketh Lever, the third has to pass as Congregationalism. My emphasis, in considering the three, is on the first.

In 1855 a remarkable but remarkably bruised young Congregational minister found himself in Manchester poor and without a pastorate. That circumstance was largely of his own making. Nonetheless he had

---

[4] R. North, 'Workers' Paradise Put Up For Sale', *The Independent*, 4 May 1990; see also T. Hodgkinson, 'Soap Owners Stir New Discord in Arcadia', *The Independent on Sunday*, 7 March 1993, 6.

[5] Margaret Stansgate, *My Exit Visa* (London, 1992), 103.

[6] Lever, later 1st Viscount Leverhulme of the Western Isles, was Liberal MP Wirral 1906–10; Wedgwood Benn, later 1st Viscount Stansgate, was Liberal MP Tower Hamlets 1906–18, Leith 1918–27; Labour MP Aberdeen North 1928–31, Gorton 1937–42.

[7] Lever and Ernest Benn may best be compared in David J. Jeremy and Christine Shaw, eds, *Dictionary of Business Biography*, 5 vols (London, 1985), 1: 280–4 and 3: 745–52.

the entrée, thanks to a Congregationally well-connected wife and the promptings of a Congregationally ambitious brother, to that city's highest Dissenting circles. Those were days – or so that minister's son recalled years later from the social security of the Surrey hills – 'when the second generation of mushroom cotton-lords were asserting their right to a sunny place in Society'.

> My mother would tell us of bizarre entertainments, mostly of an afternoon. The display of expensive costumes with wide sweeping crinolines and waspish waists was astonishing, not to mention the bare arms and bosoms, exhibiting as much ruddy area as the comparative modesty of that day would allow, and adorned with outrageous costly jewellery – and this by daylight![8]

There was, however, another side, and Manchester's racy vulgarians showed a kindness which 'was never patronizing like that so often of the better-born'. Indeed up in Bolton 'a company of 70 seat-holders' had invited the young minister to preach to them for a year in the first instance:

> They say: 'Speak out; tell us what you think; no one will interfere with you; that desk is yours'. And all that the chapel raises, which will not probably exceed £100 and may be less, will be mine. . . . Indeed they give one all the liberty I could wish; nor have I ever seen such promise of generous faith in a spiritual teacher before.

He wrote about it to his father in Scotland:

> Sunday ministrations to a congregation largely composed of spinners, weavers, and mechanics, all with terribly long hours and insufficient wages, with Chartist passions still surging in their bosoms and the Peterloo massacre keeping alive their indignation against mill-owners grown suddenly rich and powerful.[9]

Seventy years later another young Congregational minister was in Bolton. He too wrote about his people:

> The membership consisted mainly of upright, decent minded artisans (I learned a great respect of the Lancashire working man; for his home life, his reliability and warmth). There were also a collec-

---

[8] Greville MacDonald, *George MacDonald and His Wife* (London, 1924), 210.
[9] Ibid., 250–2.

tion of people of a little greater education; clerks, tradespeople and a few folk in the professions. A few younger people were pupils at the Bolton School and so on. But there was only one 'class' of people in Bolton then; some had a little more money, some a little more education but there was a splendid sense of community and mutual respect. There was a strong moral sense but the bond which united church communities all over the town, and certainly at Blackburn Rd, was basically social.[10]

These two young ministers, George MacDonald and H. A. Hamilton, differed no doubt by more than seventy years. MacDonald was at the end of a short and troubled ministry. Ill health terminated any thought of a future in Bolton, and temperament and evolving views ensured that there would be no pastorate elsewhere. Hamilton was at the beginning of a long and fulfilling ministry.[11] MacDonald, however, powerfully accented the mental climate in which Hamilton grew. They were both communicators concerned to educate. What links them here is the social continuity of some of those with whom they communicated. What should alert us are some possibly discordant aspects of that continuity: there is an independency in creative tension with Congregationalism, a culture shaped by individuals who come to dominate a community on which they never cease to depend. MacDonald's people in Albert Place's Hope Chapel, so similar in key respects to Hamilton's people in Blackburn Road Congregational Church, were of recent growth (although a statedly Congregational Church had been formed), and they were soon to rest contentedly in Free Methodism. One of their chapel's first trustees was an already prospering grocer, a pillar of Bolton's Duke's Alley Chapel, who had found his spiritual as well as his commercial feet in one of Manchester's grander chapels. This was James Lever (1809–97).[12] He plays little further part in the Albert Place story, although one of Albert Place's Methodist families, the Greenhalghs, were to produce one of the Lever family's staunchest commercial lieutenants, but Lever and his family

---

[10] Rev. H. A. Hamilton to author, 25 February 1977.

[11] For Herbert Alfred Hamilton (1897–1977), minister at Blackburn Road Congregational Church, Bolton 1924–9, Principal Westhill College, Selly Oak, Birmingham 1945–54, see *The United Reformed Church Year Book 1979* (London, 1979), 259.

[12] For James Lever, see F. W. Peaples, *History of the St George's Road Congregational Church and its Connections* (Bolton, 1913), 107–12; for Hope Chapel, Albert Place, see ibid., 191–206, esp. 191–4. See also Benjamin Nightingale, *Lancashire Nonconformity: the Churches of Bolton, Bury, Rochdale, etc.* (Manchester, 1892), 36.

were to envelope Hamilton's first pastorate. The magnificently spired, apsed, and windowed building in which Hamilton conducted worship, and the lavishly equipped institute across Bolton's Blackburn Road in which he explored the possibilities of Lancashire's Sunday-school culture, had been provided in 1897 by William Lever and his brother in memory of their parents, James and Eliza Lever, while Colin Cooper, the man whose personality stamped itself on schools and congregation alike, was another of the Levers' prime commercial lieutenants.[13] Hamilton remembered Cooper, Lever, church, schools, and contradictions, as well as he remembered their people. First Cooper and Lever:

> The building of this community at Blackburn Road was largely the work of Mr. Colin Cooper, a dedicated wealthy but childless man who gathered his own family in this way. He was a chartered accountant who had developed his own business. He used the facilities of his office to train some of the liveliest young men and encouraged them to help him in his educational project. He was a benevolent despot, unsparing in his generosity and largely unconscious of his need to dominate. He had no conception of Congregationalism and feared any form of democratic control. He held back nothing that would further his aim. He bought and equipped playing fields, billiard tables, furnished a choice small library and saw the Church as the centre of the life of the people. It was a good vision and had he tried to draw men and women into accepting the responsibility of realizing it instead of doing everything for them, it would have been a better one!
>
> Very much in the background was the figure of Lord Leverhulme (still Bill Lever to Boltonians). He was not a member of the Church or I think of any Church in Bolton; but he financed the formation of a group of Congregational Churches for their mutual sustenance and efficiency... I only met him twice. On the first occasion we talked of his experiment at Port Sunlight and he confessed to me something of the great disappointment it had brought him. On the other occasion when he was to be Chairman of our Anniversary Meeting, he turned to me unexpectedly to say – 'You know, I am mentioned in the Te Deum and churches sing about me each

---

13 For Blackburn Road Congregational Church, see *Congregational Year Book 1900* (London, 1900), 144; Inez Abbott, *Blackburn Road Congregational Church, Bolton, 1871–1967* (Bolton, 1967); [C. A. Catherall], *The 'Iron' Church, 100 Years, 1872–1972. Blackburn Road Congregational Church* (Bolton, 1972); Peaples, *History of the St George's Road*, 275–308.

week: 'He has opened the Kingdom of Heaven to all "Bill Levers" '!!
A jolly, simple man, who like Colin Cooper found the sharing of
control difficult.[14]

Thus a young minister, recalling the personalities of 'five of the most
instructive years' of his life. The buildings echoed their creators. The
great church 'certainly helped the people, as it did me, to give dignity to
worship. The centre aisle was an added boon'; so was the surprising but
effective fact that the floor was raked,

> but neither the rear font nor the communion altar were used in
> services. The carved symbols over the peaks of the arches gave me
> the chance for processional use and for exposition but I think the
> congregation missed the intimacy of contact and freedom of
> encounter of a normal Free Church Building.[15]

The tensions in this account are instructive. 'Processional use',
however much in the service of exposition, suggests a liturgical adven-
turousness not immediately associated with cotton-town Congregationalism in the 1920s. It is a tribute to the power of a credible
minister's personality. Hamilton found what George MacDonald had
found. Perhaps it also says something about the spirit which the
building had liberated as well as constrained. That building was still
new, since it was barely thirty years old. Hamilton soon recognized that
the 'sociological climate of even such a stable community as Bolton was
changing and swiftly', but plenty of his congregation remembered what
had gone before. They 'had nostalgic feelings about the warmth and
intimacy . . . the heartiness and the "fug on the windows" ', of the old
iron chapel.

> This led many of them to have an ambivalent attitude to the new
> building. They were truly proud of it but it was not an expression
> either of their life-style or of their tradition of worship. It was,
> besides, a very heavy financial burden to carry for there was no
> endowment! The heating of the large space, the maintenance of the
> fabric of a 'soft' stone building and of the 'Father Willis' organ all
> pressed heavily. None of the building was used other than on
> Sundays. Meanwhile, the vigorous educational and social life of the

---

[14] H. A. Hamilton to author, 25 February 1977; for the Cooper family see Peaples,
History of the St George's Road, passim, esp. 171–5, 290–6, 302–8. The Bill Lever story was
clearly often told; a version appears in Edward Thompson, *John Arnison* (London 1939), 38.
[15] H. A. Hamilton to author, 25 February 1977.

community continued every day and evening in the buildings of the Sunday School and Institute across the road. The forty yards or so of that divide was very hard to cross in spirit. The School – with its membership of over seven hundred 'pupils' of all ages – was the living heart of the community; it suited the mental and social associations of their essentially practical attitude to the Christian faith. The Congregational Church was composed almost entirely of the over two hundred members who could be persuaded to cross that road to discover what the Church offered![16]

That reference to the lack of endowment reveals a raw nerve. Endowments, although by no means unknown, ran counter to the best Congregational ecclesiology. They struck at the heart of Independency. Blackburn Road was the first of five Congregational churches built solely at W. H. Lever's expense and it was the only one not to have some form of endowment. There is the suggestion that while the new church's deacons could tolerate Lever's insistence on the architectural style and accoutrements, they drew the line at a Prayer Book service, at Common Prayer indeed, and lost out accordingly on any endowment.[17]

* * *

These tensions illustrate the rhythm rather than the incompatibility of elite-and-popular in Congregational cotton Lancashire. Blackburn Road and Albert Place were not the only chapels in Victorian Bolton. The Congregationalists alone had Mawdsley Street, St George's Road (formerly Duke's Alley), Chorley Old Road, and more besides. Their congregations criss-crossed as well as competed; each knew everything about the others, and all knew that even the tallest poppies were rooted in the same soil. There resulted a confederacy of clear-eyed mutual help. W. H. Lever played on that confederacy for most of his life. On the whole it worked quite as well for him as the Westminster Whigs' Venetian oligarchy of aristocrats had worked for them, since what seemed nepotism was in fact founded on a shrewd shared knowledge of ability. The most suggestive section of the jubilee history of Bolton's St George's Road Congregational Church is a closely printed five-page appendix listing nearly twenty-years' worth of seatholders at its predecessor, Duke's Alley, covering the period 1837–54, during which James Lever returned to Bolton from Manchester and his son William was

16 Ibid.
17 Rev. W. J. Else to author, 27 February 1977.

born. The list incorporates every aspect of what made Bolton and of what was making Lancashire: industry, education, local and national politics, the press, shop-keeping, the professions, butchers, bakers, bleachers, shoemakers, managers, farmers too. This was not exclusive, it was inclusive. It was at once self-selected, divinely elected, mutually recognized. It was elite-and-popular. Neither was it purely local. In 1913, the year of the jubilee publication, when 'Sir W.H. Lever . . . and . . . Lady Lever are amongst our most respected adherents and supporters',[18] the history also noted that R. J. Campbell, protagonist of the 'New Theology' and minister of London's City Temple, was the son of John Campbell who had ministered at the then Methodist Albert Place.[19] We might note that H. A. Hamilton went on to minister at the Brighton Church where Campbell too had once notably ministered, and that W. H. Lever's 'official' London memorial service was at the City Temple, conducted by Sidney Berry, Secretary of the Congregational Union of England and Wales (and therefore its best-positioned wheeler dealer) and son of Charles Berry who had been the most formative ministerial influence on the young Lever.[20] Such links are inevitable with small denominations but in days when Congregationalism punched well above its weight few Congregational laymen packed a more powerful punch – however many punches he also pulled – than W. H. Lever. However questionable to purists, his Congregationalism and the Congregationalism which he fostered becomes significant to historians; no aspect of it can be taken for granted.

* * *

My final illustration, which incorporates all these Congregational, familial, and sociological points, takes us from Bolton to Port Sunlight and by inference to Thornton Hough.

The Athertons were a Blackburn Road family. James Atherton was a surveyor, his son was a mining engineer. The younger Atherton married a Tillotson. Her family were the St George's Road family who turned the Bolton Evening News into the provincial newspaper at the hub of a significant newspaper group. She herself was W. H. Lever's niece, married in style at the famous Dr. Horton's Lyndhurst Road

---

[18] Peaples, *History of the St George's Road*, 323–7.

[19] Ibid., 326 and 200–1.

[20] Hamilton ministered in Brighton 1954–66; for Charles Berry (1852–99), minister St George's Road, Bolton, 1875–84, see J. S. Drummond, *Charles A. Berry DD: a Memoir* (London, 1899).

Congregational Church, Hampstead, from The Hill, her uncle's mega-suburban home on Hampstead Heath.[21] H. A. Hamilton recalled Mary Atherton, as she now was, as 'a rare person – she had quality of spirit and of character – a rare kind of flower in a rough garden'.[22]

Her son William had his future mapped out for him. He entered Lever Brothers and never looked back. As his mother had married at Hampstead's leading Congregational church from the mansion land-scaped for Lever by T. H. Mawson, the landscape architect, so when he eventually settled at Hest Bank, on the acceptable side of Morecambe, he worshipped at the small Congregational church both tended and attended by the Mawson family. In the intervening years Atherton's wandering work for Lever Brothers and Unilever had brought him into membership of eight Congregational churches. Christ Church, Port Sunlight, however, was not one of them. In Atherton's view it was not properly Congregational. It could not possibly be. I believe he was wrong about that, although I can quite see why he thought as he did.

William Atherton's non-attendance at Christ Church brings us full face to Port Sunlight and its creator William Hesketh Lever. Christ Church and Port Sunlight remind us that appearances count. Atherton and Lever remind us that personalities matter. Fiction, journalism, correspondence, reminiscence, the chronicle and the minute book anchor and interpret the appearance, the personality, and the motiva-tion. They illuminate the far-reaching significance and complexity of what might seem parochial. They illustrate the evolution of a denomi-nation. They explain why it was both important and necessary to begin in Bolton to get to the Wirral.

University of Sheffield

---

21   W. Atherton to author, 24 March 1977; interview 10 April 1977; for T. H. Mawson, see his *The Life and Work of an English Landscape Architect: an Autobiography* [n.d., *c*.1927]; for the Tillotson family, see F. Singleton, *Tillotsons 1850–1950: Centenary of a Family Business* (London, 1950).

22   H. A. Hamilton to author, March 1977.

THE ROMANCE OF THE SLUM:
GENDER AND CROSS-CLASS COMMUNICATION OF RELIGIOUS BELIEF, 1880–1920[*]

by M. C. H. MARTIN

D ESPITE relatively low working-class church attendance over the nineteenth century,[1] evidence of religious practice in working-class households[2] and a more diffuse religious mentality[3] have been identified by historians, even until the mid[4] or late twentieth century.[5] Yet little analysis has been undertaken into how such a mentality was created. While Cox noted of late nineteenth- century Lambeth that the most successful churches were those which contained vast philanthropic networks, elsewhere he claimed that 'philanthropy . . . did little to promote definite Christian belief'.[6] Indeed, both he and Williams regarded schools as the primary agency for conveying religious teaching: Cox claiming that Board schools were more effective than Sunday schools,[7] Williams, that Sunday schools provided not only a means of instilling religious belief in children but a form of 'religion by deputy' for their parents.[8]

This essay will analyse the work of selected philanthropic women as religious teachers in slum areas in the context of welfare or political structures they had created, with a close focus on the nature of the phil-

[*] Previous versions of this paper were presented at the Women's History Network Tenth Annual Conference, The Women's Library, London Guildhall University, September 2001, and to the WHN Midlands Region Annual Conference, November 2001. I am grateful to the organizers and participants for their comments and questions, and to Angela John for subsequent comments on the text.

[1] Hugh McLeod, *Religion and Society in England, 1850–1914* (Basingstoke, 1996), 59–70, 223.

[2] S. C. Williams, *Religious Belief and Popular Culture in Southwark, c.1880–1939* (Oxford, 1999), 126–62.

[3] Jeffrey Cox, *The English Churches in a Secular Society* (Oxford, 1982), 93–128.

[4] Callum Brown, *The Death of Christian Britain: Understanding Secularisation, 1800–2000* (London and New York, 2001), 170–5; Hugh McLeod, *Secularisation in Western Europe, 1848–1914* (Basingstoke, 2000), 7–8.

[5] Grace Davie, *Religion in Britain since 1945: Believing without Belonging* (Oxford, 1994), 199.

[6] Cox, *English Churches*, 178, 101.

[7] Ibid., 187–90.

[8] Williams, *Religious Belief*, 134, 126–62.

anthropic relationship, between 1880 and 1920. In this period, fears about 'outcast London' were at their height,[9] and many historians have commented on the appeal of 'slumming'[10] and the deluge of visitors which invaded the working-class home.[11] I will argue that my subjects constructed new forms of outreach, which in turn modified the structures of the institutional churches (whether Anglican or Roman Catholic) to which they belonged. They then worked through such ancillary structures to communicate Christian belief and practice to other social classes, and to bring their 'target groups' closer to the institutional church. In theological terms, they perceived no difference between elite and popular religion. While the slum might have had a romantic appeal,[12] it was also exhausting and could be demoralizing. Whereas the precise impact of their work is impossible to estimate, especially as regards numbers of souls, it is clear that they were respected and regarded as effective by contemporaries. This essay also highlights the significance of a neglected group of lay women, those with High Church Anglican or Roman Catholic sympathies.[13]

The Women

Isabella Gilmore (1842–1923), sister to William Morris, daughter of a bill-broker, married Lieutenant Gilmore, aged eighteen, but was widowed, aged forty, and then decided to train as a nurse, a move opposed by most of her family. She founded a deaconess order in 1886, at the suggestion of Bishop Thorold of Rochester.[14] Brought up in an

---

[9] The seminal text being Andrew Mearns's *The Bitter Cry of Outcast London* (London, 1883).
[10] Most recently, Seth Koven, *Slumming* (London, 2004).
[11] George K. Behlmer, *Friends of the Family: the English Home and its Guardians 1850–1940* (Stanford, CA, 1998), 31–72; F. Prochaska, *Women and Philanthropy in Nineteenth-Century England* (Oxford, 1980), 97–137; J. Walkowitz, *City of Dreadful Delight: Narratives of Sexual Danger in Late-Victorian London* (London, 1992), 52–9.
[12] Koven, *Slumming*, 183; Ellen Ross, *Love and Toil: Motherhood in Outcast London, 1830–1910* (Oxford, 1999), 15–16.
[13] For example, in Nigel Yates, *Anglican Ritualism in Victorian Britain, 1830–1910* (Oxford, 1999); Ross, *Love and Toil*, 12. For sisterhoods and deaconess orders, see Sean Gill, *Women in the Church of England From the Eighteenth Century to the Present* (London, 1994), 146–69. But see also Sue Morgan, 'The Power of Womanhood: Religion and Sexual Politics in the Writings of Ellice Hopkins', in Anne Hogan and Andrew Bradstock, eds, *Women of Faith in Victorian Culture* (Basingstoke, 1998), 209–25; Prochaska, *Women and Philanthropy*, 11, 39, 106, 139, 191.
[14] Mary Clare Martin, 'Isabella Gilmore, 1843–1923', in *ODNB* 22: 307. Church of

Evangelical household, she allegedly came 'to value the full sacramental life of the church which belongs to the Catholic tradition'.[15] Flora Lucy Freeman (1869–1960), a single woman, lived with her parents, her father being a surgeon, first in St George's Square, London, SW1, then in Hove, Sussex, from about 1898.[16] She started work with clubs for working girls at the age of twenty-one.[17] By 1916, Freeman had moved from Anglo-Catholicism to Roman Catholicism and to Catholic organizations with a national focus.[18] By 1925, she was a member of the Third Order of St Francis, a lay religious order.[19]

Sarah Louise Donaldson (1861–1950), from a family of well-to-do Oxford ironmongers and aldermen, married the Rev. Frederic Lewis Donaldson, formerly an Oxford undergraduate, and a future leader of the Christian Socialist movement, in 1885.[20] She was involved, not only in parish work, but in a range of religious, socialist and feminist national and regional organizations.[21] Elise, Geraldine and initially also Josephine Dolling, b.1841–51, the elder sisters of the radical ritualist slum priest, the Rev. R. R. Dolling (1851–1902), from an Irish gentry family, came to live in and help with their brother's parishes in Stepney, Portsea and Poplar, 1883–1902.[22]

Ancillary Structures to the Established Church

These women created a range of structures, ancillary to the established church, which enabled them to make personal contact with the poor, despite the differences in social class. Unlike sisterhoods, deaconesses lived, not in religious communities, but alone, subject only to the local clergy. The deaconess house run by Gilmore was a training institution. She and the 'probationers' (deaconesses in training) used to go into poor

England Record Centre (hereafter CERC), 'Reminiscences of Isabella Gilmore from 1886', CWMC/19/4, 24–6, 48–9, 51–2.

[15] Janet Grierson, *Isabella Gilmore: Sister to William Morris* (London, 1962), 9. CERC, CWMC/16/5, 16 March 1924. Talk on Isabella Gilmore's Life, Southwark and Rochester Deaconess Institution, 2.

[16] *Census of Great Britain*, 1881 RG 12/75, p. 23; 1891 RG 13/89, p. 25, fol. 16.

[17] F. L. Freeman, *Religious and Social Work Amongst Girls* (London, 1901), 138.

[18] Mary Clare Martin, 'Flora Lucy Freeman, 1869–1960', *ODNB* 20: 925.

[19] F. L. Freeman, *Thoughts on St Francis of Assisi: Selected and Arranged for Every Day of the Year* (London, 1925).

[20] Personal information, with thanks, from the Rt Rev. G. H. Thompson.

[21] *Peterborough Citizen*, 23 Nov. 1920. *Annual Reports of the National Council for the Abolition of the Death Penalty*, 1925–47.

[22] Charles E. Osborne, *The Life of Father Dolling* (London, 1903); R. R. Dolling, *Ten Years in a Portsmouth Slum* (London, 1898), 74.

districts, wearing a uniform, a blue 'lady's dress', and offer help to the sick, cleaning the house, nursing, and caring for the children.[23] Indeed, deaconesses had to show they were capable of undertaking the most menial forms of housework in order to complete their training. Collecting for subscriptions to the subsidized parochial clubs (initially for clothing) was an important means of gaining access to poor homes.[24] Deaconesses had to liaise with representatives of different agencies, such as the Relieving Officer, and the school attendance officer, the local hospital, doctor and charities.[25]

Gilmore wrote that 'People say the poor are so difficult to talk to. I can't say any of my sisters in Christ find this. Tongues go fast enough and merrily enough in cottage and mission room and even on a tram.'[26] Both Gilmore and Freeman were clear about the need to respect the privacy of the homes of the poor. Their writings indicate compassion and respect for the way poor people coped with their difficulties, with no tolerance for condescension.[27]

While the extent of the association of working-girls' clubs with the Anglican parochial structure varied, Freeman made effective use of Anglican clergy and other ministers to build up her organization. In 1908, she noted how association with the parish would reinforce the primary, religious purpose of the club, the disadvantage being that the club worker's position was dependent on the co-operation and approval of the incumbent.[28] By 1909 Freeman had visited all the ministers in Brighton, including the local rabbi, to attract interest in the formation of the interdenominational Brighton Girls' Club Union, formed to enable girls' clubs to come together for competitions and social activities.[29] By 1917, with eleven other regional unions, this was affiliated to the Federation for Working-Girls' Clubs.[30]

Freeman's clubs provided a range of activities, intended to attract and educate working-class girls, including games and dancing. She was

[23] Martin, 'Gilmore', 307–8.

[24] *Deaconess Gilmore: Some Memories Collected by Deaconess Elizabeth Robinson* (London, 1924), 31 and 34.

[25] Lambeth Palace Library (hereafter LPL), G4423 R6, Deaconess Institution for the Diocese of Rochester, *Annual Report of the Head Deaconess*, 27 Jan. 1893, 5.

[26] LPL, *Annual Report*, 27 Jan. 1893, 6.

[27] CERC, Gilmore, 'Reminiscences', 27; Freeman, *Religious and Social Work*, 29, 77.

[28] F. L. Freeman, *Our Working Girls and How to Help Them* (London, 1908), 10–24.

[29] F. L. Freeman, 'How to Start a Local Club Union', *Girls' Club Journal* 1.3 (October 1909), 60–1. The London Girls' Club Union was founded in 1880.

[30] *Federation of Working Girls' Clubs Handbook*, No. 1, 12.

clearly skilled at arranging theatricals and folk-dancing displays, and as a Guider promoted outdoor activities such as camping.[31] Pastoral care of club members, notably visiting in their own homes, particularly in times of sickness, was recommended.[32] However, she warned club leaders of the danger of attracting excessive numbers, as at a dance at St Barnabas' Hove in 1900, held in the club-room which, significantly, was also the church parish room.[33]

Although she appears to have known many of the Roman Catholic clergy in Brighton, her activities were recorded in association with the Catholic Women's League rather than local parishes. She was credited with founding Catholic Girl Guides in Brighton in 1916,[34] was Captain of the 6th Hove Girl Guide Company in 1923–4,[35] and ran the Catholic Women's League girls' club from 1919 until 1924.[36]

Donaldson's philanthropic and political activities followed her husband's work. During his London curacies, 1885–95, she lectured in the schools of the London School Board and attended meetings of the Women's Liberal Federation.[37] She was involved in parish work in Nailstone, Leicestershire (1895–6), the slum parish of St Mark's Leicester (1896–1918), where she managed provision of 'Maternity Bags',[38] and Paston, near Peterborough (1918–24). Her political activities included the Women's Labour League, appointment to the magistracy in 1924, and membership of the National Council for the Abolition of the Death Penalty, of which she was Vice-Chairman, 1931–7.[39] While her writing is full of sympathy for the poor, it could have a didactic tone. In the magazine *Goodwill*, she was critical of the way many homes were organized and emphasized the need for houses to be clean and have plenty of fresh air.[40]

[31] Martin, 'Freeman', 924–5.

[32] Freeman, *Religious and Social Work*, 120–34.

[33] Ibid., 76–7.

[34] *Catholic Women's League Magazine: the Organ of the Catholic Women's League* (hereafter *CWL Magazine*), April 1924, No. 150, 9.

[35] Guide Association, archive dept., Warrant returned by Miss F. L. Freeman, captain of 6th Hove C.W.L., 12 March 1923, WR, 12.6.1924.

[36] *CWL Magazine*, April 1919, No. 90, 7; ibid., April 1924, No. 150, 9.

[37] Westminster Abbey Muniments (hereafter WAM), Donaldson Papers, 10, Diary of the Rev. F. L. Donaldson (personal), 8 May 1888; F. G. Bettany, *Stewart Headlam: a Biography* (London, 1926), 83.

[38] WAM, Donaldson Papers, 5, *St Mark's Parish Magazine*, 1905.

[39] Christine Collette, *For Labour and For Women: the Women's Labour League, 1906–1918* (Manchester, 1989), 54, 137, 196; *Peterborough Citizen*, 23 November 1920; *Annual Reports of the National Council for the Abolition of the Death Penalty* (1925–47).

[40] WAM, Donaldson Papers, 5, *Goodwill*, 3 May 1903, 43.

The organizational skills and personal sympathy of Robert Dolling's sisters facilitated the setting up of a welfare infrastructure which supported their brother's work. Between 1883 and 1885, at St Martin's Mission, Maidman Street, Mile End, meals were provided three times a week for the children of the neighbourhood, and the 'Miss Dollings gave shelter to the poor girls of the street'.[41] The 'open house' kept at St Agatha's Parsonage, Portsea, provided free meals daily and large numbers stayed there. Dolling cited his sisters as saying 'We want to go into every house in Landport, to know every man, woman and child'.[42] Miss Dolling suggested and presided over dances as a way for young people to meet, and Miss Geraldine Dolling over mothers' meetings.[43] When, at St Saviour's Poplar (1898–1901), Miss Dolling, who allegedly 'gained a wonderful hold over the factory girls', organized a summer camp for sixty girls at Hayling Island (her brother managing the boys' camp),[44] she also managed the funds of this vast charitable endeavour, which in March 1901 amounted to about £800.[45] Their sympathy with the condition of the poor is illustrated by Dolling's statement: 'My sisters . . . tell me . . . it is impossible to imagine much of what they go through'.[46]

Religious Teaching

Whereas my subjects engaged in effective philanthropic activity, often through the openings afforded to make contact with women and children, communicating religious belief was regarded as of central importance. While recognizing the social barriers to fully participating in the religious life of the institutional church, these women aimed to overcome these rather than present a diluted version of Christian belief. The evidence indicates that they did have some success.

Gilmore made it clear that religion was not to be forced upon the poor, but deaconesses were rigorously trained in theology so they could answer any kind of religious question.[47] Some of the poor already had some religious knowledge, as in the case of a dying old lady to whom

41 J. Clayton, *Father Dolling: a Memoir* (2nd edn, London, 1902),11, 15.
42 Dolling, *Ten Years*, 24.
43 Ibid., 43.
44 Osborne, *Dolling*, 267–8.
45 Clayton, *Dolling*, 22, 116–17.
46 Ibid., 123.
47 Grierson, *Gilmore*, 150–2.

Gilmore read the Bible.[48] Gilmore set up cottage meetings in people's houses, where they could discuss religious issues, which led to an increase in communicants.[49] Arranging for services to be held at different times also facilitated participation. Gilmore persuaded the clergyman to set up weekday baptisms, and on the first occasion, ninety-four were baptized.[50] One woman came to the 5.30 communion in her husband's boots because she had none of her own.[51] When Gilmore took 'my rough school' to St Mary's Old Battersea, Canon Erskine Clarke 'held the children like magic',[52] and by 1900 there were 200 in the Ragged School.[53] The matron in the Girls' Preventive Home set up in 1892 had, according to Gilmore, the ability to make the girls 'fear and love God'.[54] In 1889, Gilmore reported that church attendance at St John's, Battersea, had improved.[55] That some of the poor did become communicant members of the church, and also active as, say, Sunday school teachers, was recalled as a great joy.[56]

Freeman believed the primary purpose of clubs was religious, and took pains to recruit 'rough girls' whom she felt were neglected by the church. Despite her shyness, she adopted active forms of outreach, as on one Good Friday, in Brighton, the first day of the 'skipping season', when she approached a group of 'rough' young men and women on the street, invited them to a Lantern service, and gave them picture cards.[57] She insisted that clubs should have family prayers, and gave examples of how the girls had come to enjoy these, for example, by encouraging them to pray for people who were sick. Writing essays constituted an early form of adult education, and she recorded how one girl was scolded for staying up late on Saturday nights for doing this.[58] She also arranged special services, for example at 9 p.m. on weekdays, at St Barnabas' Hove, for her 'Perseverance League for Laundry Girls'. While noting that the first experience of church could make a deep impres-

[48] Ibid., 114–16.
[49] Ibid., 125.
[50] CERC, Gilmore, 'Reminiscences', 35–7.
[51] Ibid., 33.
[52] Ibid., 41.
[53] Grierson, *Gilmore*, 123.
[54] LPL, *Annual Report*, 27 Jan. 1893, 8.
[55] LPL, *Annual Report*, Jan. 1889, 3.
[56] Grierson, *Gilmore*, 113.
[57] Freeman, *Religious and Social Work*, 70.
[58] Ibid., 2–12.

sion, and making weekly attendance a rule, she warned workers not to expect too much of 'rough girls'.[59]

Polly, a Study of Girl Life (1904), a 'rags to riches' story based on Freeman's own experiences of 'rescue', clearly advocates the Anglo-Catholic style of worship and theology. Pictures and other visual imagery make far more impact on Polly, a working-class girl, than sermons.[60] Confession is represented as providing huge relief, and the support and guidance of the priest as invaluable.[61] Symbolically, on starting her second and better job in service, she is confirmed and makes her first communion.[62]

Freeman clearly regarded 'ladies' as the most effective religious instructors, initially, since she claimed that

> The ordinary inexperienced ... curate will look in with the benevolent intention of helping you, will give them a sermon on the Holy Eucharist, not one syllable of which do they understand, and remark on leaving 'He hopes all present will present themselves next month to be prepared for confirmation'.[63]

She warned club workers not to succumb to pressure from the clergy to bring large numbers to confirmation before they were ready, though citing the story of a factory girl from 'an indifferent home' who had been trained since her confirmation 'by one of the most experienced priests in the Church of England'.[64]

In 1921, Freeman advised Roman Catholic Girl Guides to attend Mass and confession regularly, but that they should not attend services with non-Catholic Guides, thus emphasizing the importance of Catholic identity.[65] Reviewers of *Religious and Social Work* (written while she was an Anglo-Catholic) and *On the Right Trail*, while recognizing their respective religious and denominational specificity, recommended both books as of interest to all concerned, whether club leaders or Guides.[66]

Donaldson's writing, which contained references such as 'the Social

---

[59] Ibid., 74, 94.
[60] F. L. Freeman, *Polly: a Study of Girl Life* (London, 1904), 78, 154–5.
[61] Ibid., 96, 100, 104.
[62] Ibid., 99.
[63] Freeman, *Religious and Social Work*, 75.
[64] Ibid., 77–8, 101.
[65] F. L. Freeman, *On the Right Trail: Friendly Counsel for Catholic Girl Guides* (London, 1921), 31–3, 80, 102.
[66] *GCJ*, Jan. 1909, Vol 1, No. 1, 21; *CWL Magazine*, Feb. 1922, No. 124, 3.

Gospel' and 'The Cause' indicates the inter-relatedness of religion and socialism in her thinking, and also suggests she was an effective teacher.[67] In 1913, she noted how she had taught the facts of life to children in schools in London and Leicester and had never had any trouble in communicating with them about such matters.[68] Donaldson's parish work as a vicar's wife included instructing the surpliced choir at Nailstone, Leicestershire, 1895–6, and later at Paston, Peterborough, 1918–24, as well as giving confirmation classes.[69] At St Mark's Leicester, where her husband was vicar from 1896 to 1918, she gave 'Classes of Religion' to 'Youths' in St Mark's Schools on Sunday afternoons, and on Tuesdays at 8 p.m. to 'senior girls'.[70] She recalled using Headlam's 'Laws of Eternal Life', his interpretation of the Church catechism, at Leicester with countless classes of girls and young men.[71] Her daughter Eanswythe repeatedly described her as 'very good with young men'.[72] Between 1910–20 she was lecturer for the Mothers' Union of the Peterborough diocese.[73]

Like her husband, she believed in making church worship and the sacraments attractive and accessible.[74] Thus, in the *Church Times* of 1903, responding to Lady Wimborne's attack on ritualism, she argued that Anglo-Catholic worship provided the poor with light and colour in their lives, which the aristocracy took for granted.[75] Her leaflet *The Spiritual Welfare of the Child* for National Baby Week, about 1930, emphasized the importance of teaching very young children about God and Jesus, and bringing them to church to a service which would be short and interesting. The difficult stage of adolescence could be helped by bringing the young to 'the wonderful gift of confirmation'.[76] Within the Women's Labour League and other socialist organizations which

---

[67] Letter Sarah Louise Donaldson to Euan Donaldson, 12 March 1924. Possession of the Rt Rev. G. H. Thompson.

[68] *The League Leaflets*, 1913.

[69] B. J. Butler, 'Frederic Lewis Donaldson and the Christian Socialist Movement', unpublished M.Phil. thesis, University of Leeds, 1970, 148–9. Letters SLD to ED, 12 March, 8 April 1924.

[70] WAM, Donaldson Papers, 5, *St Mark's Parish Magazine*, 1905.

[71] Bettany, *Headlam*, 96.

[72] Personal information, December 1990, from Eanswythe Thompson (1897–1993).

[73] *Peterborough Citizen*, 23 Nov. 1920.

[74] WAM, Donaldson Papers, 5, *St Mark's Parish Magazine*, 1906.

[75] Sarah Louise Donaldson, 'Lady Wimborne and Ceremonialism', *Church Times* (1903, repr., author's possession).

[76] WAM, Donaldson Papers, 4d (Mrs Donaldson's Papers), *The Spiritual Welfare of the Child*, National Baby Week Council, No. 62.

contained both middle- and working-class women,[77] she forefronted religious issues. Her address, as President, in 1917, *Women's Place in the Nation*, ended by emphasizing the need for spiritual, moral and religious reform.[78] In 1924, she was addressing the Peterborough Labour Party Women's Section, of which she was President, on 'Labour and Religion'.[79]

Religion, and particularly attendance at Holy Communion, were regarded as of primary importance, including for children, in the Dollings's ministry. The children's celebration in church at Landport was at 10 o'clock, and allegedly attracted five to six hundred children by 1896.[80] Charles Osborne, Robert Dolling's friend and former curate, stated that

> the art . . . of making religion lovable, and, in a true sense, human, [has] been granted to these ladies to a very marked degree. . . . It is especially to Miss Dolling's influence that is due the development among the younger women of a spirit at once religious and naturally wholesome.[81]

Dolling recorded how the dancing class (at Portsmouth) 'has for the past five years been one of the most valuable parish institutions . . . nearly all the members are communicants'.[82] In his 1894 *Annual Report* he noted how his sisters' 'girls' 'very often came to confirmation', more so than the boys' club members, as women were less shy about talking on these subjects.[83]

Conclusion

Assessing 'success' in transmitting religious belief is always fraught with difficulty, and my subjects were less concerned with reaching large numbers, than with bringing relief and comfort. Much of the evidence of 'success' comes from the anecdotal evidence of middle-class

---

[77] Collette, *For Labour and for Women*, 58–92.

[78] Sarah Louise Donaldson, *Women's Place in the Nation* (author's possession).

[79] Letter SLD to ED, 1924. Possession of the Rt Rev. G. H. Thompson.

[80] Dolling, *Ten Years*, 50; W. N. Yates, *The Anglican Revival in Victorian Portsmouth* (Portsmouth, 1983), Portsmouth Papers, No. 37, 12, citing *Hampshire Telegraph*, 15 Feb. 1896.

[81] Osborne, *Dolling*, 49 and 85.

[82] Dolling, *Ten Years*, 45.

[83] Portsmouth City Record Office, CHU 10/3A, Winchester College Mission (St Agatha's), *Annual Reports 1883–1894, No. 8, Annual Report by Rev R.R.Dolling, 1894, Vicar Designate*, 6.

observers, but nevertheless contrasts with the more negative comments on popular religion from others.

This essay has suggested that through social action, doctrinal religious teaching, and their published work, these women drew others closer to participation in the full sacramental life of the Anglican, and in Freeman's case, the Roman Catholic, Church than might be supposed from Cox's model of 'diffusive Christianity' or Williams's of 'religious sentiment'. Gender played a crucial role in the process which began with initial outreach and extended to discussion of religion, to facilitating contact with the institutional Church.

Gilmore and her deaconesses offered the unique combination of immediate, practical assistance and a sound theological education, and deaconess orders were regarded as a particularly important form of evangelism.[84] While working-girls' clubs within an Anglo-Catholic context have been little documented compared to those for men and boys,[85] Freeman was frequently praised by her contemporaries for her 'wonderful work' amongst girls,[86] and regarded 'ladies' as more effective religious teachers than most clergy. She also wrote the first handbook for Catholic Girl Guides, who by 1920 Cardinal Bourne, archbishop of Westminster, believed were an important means of evangelizing young people.[87] The importance of the Catholic Women's League in supporting such organizations (possibly in the absence of Catholic clergy families) underlines the significance of gender.

Donaldson's activities occupied a much wider stage than the traditional role of a vicar's wife, including local and national organizations in health, suffrage, the labour movement and socialism. Arguably, she was an important and neglected influence in forefronting religious issues within women's labour and suffrage organizations. Bettany claimed that 'few women can have done more than she has done to carry on Headlam's teaching and perpetuate his influence in the Church'.[88] Robert Dolling's sisters organized the infrastructure of his 'welfare state in miniature', which arguably drew huge numbers to the orbit of the established Church.[89] He and others argued that his pastoral

---

[84] G. K. A. Bell, *Randall Davidson, Archbishop of Canterbury* (Oxford, 1935), 211–12.

[85] Hugh McLeod, *Piety and Poverty: Working-Class Religion in Berlin, London and New York, 1870–1914* (London and New York, 1996), 155–6.

[86] Martin, 'Freeman', 924–5.

[87] *CWL Magazine*, Sept. 1920, No. 107, 2–3.

[88] Bettany, *Headlam*, 224.

[89] See Alan Hascombe, *Robert Dolling, Mission Priest: a Biographical Sketch* (London, 1907), 22–3.

work would not have been possible without them.[90] Dolling regarded women workers as essential for reaching poor women and working-class families, and considered they were more effective in bringing members of girls' clubs to church than the organizers of boys' clubs.[91]

Cox has argued that churches which produced huge networks of welfare organizations in the period 1880–1920 were the victims of their own success, since when the state took over these welfare functions, the churches became redundant.[92] There are a number of problems with this argument. Firstly, the welfare reforms of the early 1900s did not address many of the material and medical needs of women and children, for which churches continued to make provision. Secondly, material provision by the state could not replace the 'philanthropic relationship' which many women workers made a central plank of their work.[93] Thirdly, as this essay has demonstrated, these women considered bringing the poor to Christian belief as a vital part of their endeavours, and the provision of welfare was not a substitute for this. Although, by the 1920s, my subjects had died, retired or moved on, the Rochester Diocesan Deaconess Institution, girls' clubs, and Catholic Girl Guides continued and flourished, as did a similar ministry to Dolling's in Portsmouth, and to Donaldson's in Leicester.[94] Accounts of these women's work were widely publicized, and may have inspired others.

University of Greenwich

---

90 See dedication to Osborne, *Dolling*.
91 Ibid., 84.
92 Cox, *English Churches*, 270–4.
93 See also Williams, *Religious Belief*, 134–6.
94 Grierson, *Gilmore*, 204–27; Yates, *Anglican Ritualism*, 283; Marcus Collins, *Modern Love: an Intimate History of Men and Women in Twentieth-Century Britain* (London, 2003), 63–8. *CWL Magazine*, Jan 1929, No. 207, 5. *Leicester Evening Mail*, Sat April 23, 1932.

SEEING PROTESTANT ICONS:
THE POPULAR RECEPTION OF VISUAL MEDIA IN
NINETEENTH- AND TWENTIETH-CENTURY AMERICA

by DAVID MORGAN

ALTHOUGH it is commonly asserted that Protestantism bears an intrinsic antagonism toward images, this claim is manifestly contradicted by a long history of the production and use of images among Protestants the world over.[1] At the end of the eighteenth century and the beginning of the nineteenth, British organizations such as Hannah More's Cheap Repository and the Religious Tract Society, and a host of tract and Sunday school societies formed in the United States, all made zealous use of illustrated tracts, handbills, broadsides, newspapers, magazines and books in order to address the disparity between the small number of evangelists and the vast number of those requiring evangelization. Founded in 1825, the American Tract Society invested unprecedented sums in materials and technology to illustrate its tracts and children's literature and attracted the best wood engraver in the United States to do so. British and American tract producers explicitly felt that illustrations were a strong form of appeal to children and the semi-literate, such as immigrants and the poor. And they happily relied on images in urban settings to compete with secular advertisements and the rival trade of books and pamphlet sellers.

The membership of the American Tract Society drew largely from two wings of Reformed Protestantism: Presbyterians and Congregationalists. But the by-laws of the Tract Society stipulated that no tract would be issued that offended or promoted the sectarian views of any Protestant denomination. So when we see the illustration of Tract No. 30 (fig. 1), 'The Benevolence of God', which shows the centurion plunging his spear into the side of the crucified Jesus, it is safe to assume that the portrayal of the event did not find objection among America's conservative Protestants. A caption to the image urges readers to be

[1] For a good introduction to this problem in the history of American Protestantism, see Sally M. Promey, 'Pictorial Ambivalence and American Protestantism', in Alberta Arthurs and Glenn Wallach, eds, *Crossroads: Art and Religion in American Life* (New York, 2001), 189–229.

No. 30.

THE

BENEVOLENCE OF GOD.

Go to Calvary! What a wonderful scene strikes our senses! The heavens grow black—the rocks burst asunder—the thunder of the Lord waxeth louder and louder—the vail of the magnificent temple is rent asunder by an invisible hand—the dead arise, and appear in the holy city! What event do these prodigies attest?—*Page* 5.

PUBLISHED BY THE

AMERICAN TRACT SOCIETY,

150 NASSAU-STREET, NEW-YORK.

D. Fanshaw, Printer.

Fig. 1. 'Benevolence of God', No. 30.
New York: American Tract Society, 1825. Photo by author.

407

viewers: 'Go to Calvary! What a wonderful scene strikes our senses!' The small vignette evokes such a scene, responding to the imperative by envisioning the death of Jesus. The image emerges from the biblical text's description of the crucifixion, fashioning a continuity between word and image for American Protestants. This coupling of word and image to promote the Protestant cause was nothing new. Luther had opposed the destruction of images in churches by zealous iconoclasts by proclaiming in a sermon that he could not think of the Passion of Jesus without seeing an image in his mind of Jesus on the cross.[2] But even if some Calvinists might object to Luther's epistemology, and Calvin himself might have found the illustration of Tract No. 30 a violation of the second commandment, few nineteenth-century American Protestants expressed opposition to illustrated tracts and other texts, even the Bible. By the nineteenth century, of course, any misgiving about published images was long gone. This is clearly signaled by the massive Bible edition issued in 1846 by the Methodist Harper Brothers, a Bible which featured no less than 1,600 illustrations.[3]

The home is often pictured in tracts as the location for receiving and reading the tract as well as putting it to use. With the rise of the Protestant theology of nurture in the nineteenth century, championed by Congregationalist minister and theologian, Horace Bushnell, the formation of faith in young children was considered a priority of Christian homes, particularly of mothers: the home took front and centre as the most sacred space in American Protestantism, resulting in images showing a mother hard at work in her home, rearing Christian children.[4] By mid-century, advice books, tracts, illustrated children's books, gift books, and photo albums were standard features of the Christian home, describing and visualizing the practices of Christian nurture as well as providing emotional support for parents who

---

[2] Martin Luther, *Against the Heavenly Prophets in the Matter of Images and Sacraments* (1525), in *Luther's Works*, 55 vols (Philadelphia, PA, 1958), 40: 99.

[3] On the visual culture of the American Tract Society, see David Morgan, *Protestants and Pictures: Religion, Visual Culture, and the Age of American Mass Production* (New York and Oxford, 1999), 43–120, with a discussion of the Harper Bible at 61–4; and Paul Gutjahr, *An American Bible: a History of the Good Book in the United States, 1777–1880* (Stanford, CA, 1998), 70–6.

[4] I have examined at length the iconography of mothers and absent fathers in Evangelical devotional materials in nineteenth-century America in *The Sacred Gaze: Religious Visual Culture in Theory and Practice* (Berkeley, CA, 2005), 191–210. An instructive study of the domestic culture of nineteenth-century American Christianity is Colleen McDannell, *The Christian Home in Victorian America, 1840–1900* (Bloomington, IN, 1986).

suffered the loss of children. The rapid spread of daguerreotypes and other forms of early photography offered American parents the visual means of remembering their departed children. In a poem entitled 'The Little Daguerreotype', published in a religious gift book in 1855, a clergyman wrote of the picture of his departed daughter as a kind of icon. It is difficult not to read it and recall a pair of daguerreotypes from the 1850s, one showing a little girl while she was alive and the other after she had died, a common use of photography in the mid-nineteenth century:

> Thus gaze I often daily,
>   On that little face and fair;
> In weary hours of night-time,
>   Come the cheering light-beams there,
> Of a presence more than earthly,
>   Of a realm where angels dwell
> Of a higher life and glory
>   Than those silent lips can tell.[5]

Nineteenth-Century Popular Reception

Already my remarks will have signaled that popular Protestant visual practice over the last two centuries was not grounded in the church sanctuary or in formal liturgy, but in the home, in devotional practices, in what might be called the liturgy of everyday life. To these general observations I'd like to add several more as the burden of this paper. I want to draw attention to several recurrent features in the Protestant reception of visual media from the 1880s to the present. First, there has been a distinct tendency among Protestants to regard images as more than arbitrary symbols or signs, indeed, to see them as presences, thereby according visuality a higher estimation as a medium of revelation. Second, a significant aspect of the likeness of Jesus in Protestant experience since the late nineteenth century has been his masculinity: the likeness of Christ is deeply gendered. Third, the Protestant experience of imagery has relied on commerce and mass-culture for its vitality, its appeal, and its widespread success. Rather than scorn

5 Rev. J. G. Adams, 'The Little Daguerreotype', in *The Rose of Sharon: a Religious Souvenir for 1855*, ed. Mrs C. M. Sawyer (Boston, MA, 1855), 254. For the daguerreotypes I have in mind, see Heinz K. Henisch and Bridget A. Henisch, *The Photographic Experience 1839–1914: Images and Attitudes* (University Park, 1994), 179–82.

modernity's technological, industrial, capitalist features, American (no less than Dissenting British groups) Protestants in the mainstream have often nurtured a visual piety that thrives by virtue of modern economy. Finally, the proper modality of Protestant experience, expressing the mass-produced and commercial character of Protestant visual piety, joins entertainment to edification in a combination that suits the prevailing practices of nurturing children and the opportunity of enjoying an unprecedented amount of leisure, which capitalism affords the middle class. Each of these features has contributed to the formation of a visual field, or what may be fashionably called a 'Protestant gaze', in which the practice of seeing images structures a sense of community, a discretely Christian public in which believers take their place, in which they are visually constituted as part of a locally and even nationally imagined body of viewer-consumers who share a communal identity by virtue of this shared imagining. This gaze was challenged by the emergence of film around 1900, as we shall see, which ushered in new visual practices that formed a rival gaze. But the conflict was negotiated by a variety of means. Never entirely resolved, the tension has allowed two forms of seeing to persist, if unequally and often in contention with one another. There are, however, moments when they are deftly integrated, as in Mel Gibson's much-discussed film, *The Passion of the Christ*. More on that later.

Compelled by the desire to refine American taste for the sake of elevating national sensibility as well as refitting Christianity to appeal to a more cosmopolitan life-style than the older order of Calvinism had allowed, many Protestant clergy traveled to England and Europe in the middle decades of the century to acquire the necessary veneer of culture for their mission.[6] The clergymen enjoyed visiting British and Continental art cities in order to frequent galleries and museums. Many wrote memoirs of their travels and described their experiences in art galleries and cathedrals. One of these art-pilgrims was the Rev. Henry Ward Beecher, who was quite moved by the architecture and paintings that he saw on a trip to England in 1850. His description of the experience suggests a response to images as something more than mere representations, as capable of evoking a real presence and engaging the viewer in a direct relationship. While visiting galleries in Oxford,

---

[6] Neil Harris, *The Artist in American Society: the Formative Years, 1790–1860* (Chicago, IL, 1982), 28–53, has provided an authoritative study of mid-century Protestant clergy and art treks to Europe.

Beecher wrote that paintings 'cease to be pictures. They are realities. The canvas is glass, and you look through it upon the scene represented as if you stood at a window. Nay, you enter into the action'.[7]

The sort of art that Beecher and his brethren saw abroad varied greatly. Sometimes it was art of leading painters of the Renaissance such as Fra Angelico, Leonardo, or Raphael. But it was also quite often the more familiar art of European contemporaries – narrative tableaux and historical pictures by celebrated artists such as William Holman Hunt and Paul Delaroche, the latter serving as one of Beecher's favorites. Other European painters whose Christian subject-matter appealed to American viewers included the German artists Heinrich Hofmann and Bernhard Plockhorst, whose images of the life of Jesus, particularly as portrayed in pastoral and devotional subjects such as The Good Shepherd or Prayer in Gethsemane or Christ Blessing the Children, became the most frequently reproduced and emulated religious subjects in late nineteenth- and early twentieth-century America. Artistic quality was far less important than the appeal of such imagery to devotional sentiment and narrative clarity, particularly as both liberal and Evangelical Christianity in the United States developed a piety of personal relationship with Jesus that rose in intensity in tandem with the scholarly assault on the historicity of the Bible in the second half of the nineteenth century. If the European art lauded by American clergy was often not great art itself, its intended effect on the refinement of American taste may likely have relied more on its appeal to American piety.

The manifold endorsement of the history of Christian art in European galleries by eminent American clergy contributed to the preparation of American audiences for contemporary religious art brought to the United States from Europe. One of the most popularly celebrated of these events took place in the 1880s, when a very large canvas, *Christ before Pilate* (1881; fig. 2), by the Hungarian painter Mihály Munkácsy (1844–1909), was exhibited in New York and purchased by the Philadelphia department store owner and devout Methodist, John Wanamaker. The painting was viewed by scores of Protestant ministers in New York, and in London and Paris before it had crossed the Atlantic. Clergy registered their praise for the work in many newspapers and sermons. Charles Kurtz, member of the National Academy of Design, gathered and published dozens of their notices, commentaries, sermon extracts

---

[7] Henry Ward Beecher, *Star Papers; or, Experience of Art and Nature* (New York, 1855), 53.

Fig. 2. Mihály Munkácsy, *Christ Before Pilate*, 1881, oil on canvas.
Photograph courtesy Library of Congress.

and editorial letters, and added an essay of his own in order to promote the reception of the painting in New York, where it was publicly exhibited in the Twenty-third Street Tabernacle from November 1886 to March 1887. In his introductory essay to this volume, Kurtz noted that

> the first glance at the picture usually gives the spectator the impression that the scene is real, and that the figures before him are living persons; this feeling is one which it sometimes seems to require an effort to shake off.[8]

This signals a leitmotif in the Protestant reception of visual media in the late nineteenth century, as will become clear in following examples; pictures were no problem for Protestants when they were not viewed as pictures, but as real people, that is, as metamorphoses of pictures into reality. An image was an idol only if it did the opposite: when it morphed the living deity into a dead representation. But images that acted like *tableaux vivants*, real people posing like a picture, were widely experienced by Protestants as arresting and compelling presences.

Another form of presence celebrated in the response to Munkácsy's painting was the transport of viewers to another age. A Boston clergyman was also struck by the scene of the picture's exhibition:

> the effect, after one enters [the Tabernacle], is unique and startling; there seems a subdued and reverent atmosphere pervading the place. You feel as if suddenly carried back eighteen hundred years, and standing in the very presence of the dread reality which is there portrayed before you.[9]

The clergyman recalled the touching effect of watching mothers bring their children before the image in order to explain it to them. 'The little ones', he reported, 'would look up and become awestruck. How real and how much the picture seemed to them, especially as they gazed so earnestly at the Redeemer, of whom they had so often heard!'[10] The exhibition of the painting was a spectacle for children as well as adults. Many viewers observed that 'the utmost stillness prevailed in the Tabernacle all afternoon'.[11] To be sure, not everyone was taken by the

---

[8] Charles M. Kurtz, *Christ Before Pilate: the Painting by Munkácsy* (New York, 1887), 9.
[9] Rev. William Butler, from *Zion's Herald*, Boston (March 30, 1887), excerpted in Kurtz, *Christ Before Pilate*, 42.
[10] Ibid., 42–3.
[11] *The New York Tribune* (18 November 1886), in Kurtz, *Christ Before Pilate*, 49.

picture or its theatrical presentation. Some critics objected to the exhibition in the Tabernacle as comparable to methods 'used in the ordinary "show" of a prodigy'. Most observations culled by Kurtz, however, mirrored that of a Philadelphia writer who proclaimed that 'you feel as if you had really entered the Judgment Hall of Pilate, and were an actual spectator of the more than tragic event, which the artist has delineated'.[12]

Second point: the issue of Jesus' likeness arose often in response to the painting, as it had regarding other images of Jesus. A new market in images emerged with the halftone engraving, which allowed for the inexpensive, yet good or even high quality mass-production of fine art imagery and photography in the 1890s. Other admirers of Munkácsy's picture pointed to the painter's rejection of less than masculine portrayals of Jesus as unequal to the character they found limned in the New Testament. Kurtz, for example, asserted that Munkácsy sought to correct the misrepresentation common in 'old Italian painters'. To the artist of *Christ Before Pilate*, Kurtz wrote, the images of Jesus found in churches repeated the mistakes of older art:

> they seem effeminate – personifications of too much humility and too little inspiration and strength of purpose. The faces seemed rather to portray the character of a weak, submissive man than that of a man of strong will but great forbearance.[13]

Another commentator remarked that Munkácsy's Jesus was not 'one of those vapidly mild and enervated Christs' but 'the Christ of the Gospel'.[14] This is all quite ironic since Munkácsy himself was indisputably Roman Catholic. Kurtz noted this in passing, but stressed the historical accuracy, the realistic drama of the painting, and the manly character of Jesus, as if that were all that was necessary to cleanse the artist and his work of any papist tinge. He never cited the response of Catholic priests to the picture since he wanted to preserve the putative masculinity of *Christ Before Pilate* as a distinctively Protestant characteristic.

In addition to a way of differentiating Protestant from Catholic and cordoning off the unacceptable aspects of Catholic immigrant piety

12 From *Beck's Journal of Decorative Art*, Boston (30 March 1887), in Kurtz, *Christ Before Pilate*, 54; *Philadelphia North American* (2 March 1887), in Kurtz, *Christ Before Pilate*, 55.
13 Kurtz, *Christ Before Pilate*, 6.
14 Dr A. Guéneau de Mussy, 'Study', excerpted in Kurtz, *Christ Before Pilate*, 19.

that would need to be eliminated in Americanist socialization (i.e., the sort of Protestantizing undertaken by Evangelical groups such as the tract and Bible societies), the preoccupation with the masculinity of Jesus corresponded to a late nineteenth-century American concern to counter the threat posed by the so-called feminization of Christianity. This arose from a decline of masculinity due to urban life, over-refinement, and the loss of appropriately masculine male heroes. Christian art reflected this alleged waning of machismo in representations of Jesus, which were lamented by theologians, clergy, and educators across the political and Protestant theological spectrum. If previous sacred *Catholic* art had emasculated Jesus, nineteenth-century American Protestants were prepared to believe that the right kind of image could reverse this trend and rescue the masculinity of the Messiah, as well as safeguard Protestant America beset by massive Catholic immigration.[15]

The third point I wish to make is the importance of commerce in Protestant visual piety in the nineteenth century. Viewers of Munkácsy's painting at its New York venue deposited fifty cents in order to see the picture and were happy to do so by all accounts. One report indicates a long line on the street outside of the Tabernacle, requiring a thirty-minute wait to gain entrance. The commerce involved did not detract from the opportunity for piety that it procured. American Christians were used to spending money for religious edification. Panoramas of sacred subjects such as Jerusalem, the Holy Land, and portions of the Bible were quite common in American cities and commonly charged admission. As one of the most popular forms of visual entertainment, panoramas enjoyed a period of wide attention from mid-century until the 1890s, when film eclipsed their appeal for the sense of verity and presence. Until then, however, as popular response to Arthur Butt's 1880 panorama of the Book of Revelation (fig. 3) and his 1885 panorama of Great Bible Stories shows, the medium captured great attention for the realism comparable to what viewers experienced gazing at Munkácsy's *Christ Before Pilate*. In addition to indulging popular scopophilia, the panorama worked out the rudimentary commercial apparatus that greeted the rise of film in the late 1890s and remains very much in place today. It is important to understand that commerce and pious entertainment were not regarded as antithetical in principle by most nineteenth-century Americans, who had at least as much P. T. Barnum in their souls as they had Emerson or Thoreau.

---

[15] For further discussion, see Morgan, *Protestants and Pictures*, 326–30.

Fig. 3. Arthur Butt, *Whore of Babylon and Dragon*, panorama, 1880, painting on canvas. Courtesy North Carolina Museum of History.

Scholars such as Laurence Moore have demonstrated how mass print and such later media as radio were part and parcel of the American religious landscape.[16] The very same can be demonstrated regarding visual imagery. In fact, mass-produced print and imagery were first produced on a larger scale by antebellum Protestant organizations such as the American Tract Society than by secular publishers in the nineteenth century.

Beginning in the 1840s, the moving panorama commanded an enthusiastic popularity. Consisting of hundreds of yards of scenically painted canvas gathered on two rollers, these panoramas were gigantic scrolls (from 10 to 15 feet high, and reportedly even larger) that were slowly rolled from one spool to the other as a speaker narrated a journey, often accompanied by a pianist or other musicians.[17] The Book of Revelation was the subject of a traveling panorama, created in the late 1870s by the entrepreneurial Arthur Butt, a Methodist native of Charlotte, North Carolina. In 1880, Butt toured his panorama through the South to enjoy excited reviews and large crowds in Charlotte, Atlanta, Raleigh, Knoxville, Nashville, and Chattanooga, as well as a host of smaller cities and towns in the upper South, eventually going as far as west and north as Louisville and New Harmony, Indiana, and as far east as Annapolis, Maryland.

Arthur Butt was an enterprising fellow. He sent his brother off to towns before he arrived in order to work out logistics, but also to begin advertising for the appearance. In addition to posting placards and large lithographs and placing show cards in windows, the 'advance man' was able to work with local clergy, newspapers and journalists, and operators of such facilities as opera houses, schools, churches, or theatres, where the panorama show would be staged. Butt himself spoke to his audience, narrating the complex Book of Revelation. But the enterprise quickly became a family business. He employed his father, who was a Methodist clergyman, as speaker, and his wife provided musical accompaniment. Admission varied from 25 to 50 cents for adults and 10 to 25 cents for children. Newspaper accounts indicate that Butt frequently filled the house and that long lines formed awaiting entrance. Churches were happy to sponsor the event since they took a cut of proceeds. The

[16] R. Laurence Moore, *Selling God: American Religion in the Marketplace of Culture* (New York, 1994).

[17] For a general history of the panorama in Europe and the United States, see Stephan Oettermann, *The Panorama: History of a Mass Medium*, trans. Deborah Lucas Schneider (New York, 1997).

Whore of Babylon and the Pearly Gates of the New Jerusalem (for which he used a large number of real pearls, sewn to the canvas) 'were greeted with hearty cheers', as a Charlotte newspaper put it. 'So enraptured were a portion of the audience at the last scene of The New Jerusalem, that some of them lingered after the close of the entertainment to gaze upon it'. Others proclaimed that the show was better than any concert, play, or lecture they'd witnessed in town. Religious entertainment, at least among Southern Protestants, could rival all forms of public entertainment.[18]

No doubt much of this tone was part of the rhetoric of public hyperbole and advertisement. But what seems quite significant in the published reception of Butt's panorama is the willingness of conservative American Protestants to allow images of Scripture a commanding stature, even to become the *visual equivalent* of Holy Writ. One clergyman assured readers that Butt's images were 'faithful delineations' of their biblical texts, and even suggested that the authority directing the artist's work was spiritual in nature:

> If the one was inspired to write, the other must have been inspired to paint these visions. The chaste, sweet, refined and enraptured spirit of John glows on the living canvas as if he were present pointing the way from the deformities and discords of earth to the beauties and symphonies of Heaven.[19]

Observers often noted that words failed to convey the effect of the panorama. 'It must be seen to be appreciated', claimed the clergyman just cited. Visual spectacle in the form of the panorama's popular version of the sublime rivaled, even surpassed words, making access to the events portrayed in biblical text immediate and riveting. As one fan put it after seeing the panorama: 'a person can learn more of the Book of Revelation in one evening than he would from reading it in a life-time'.[20] Another viewer, recalling Bunyan's recognition of 'eye-gate' but pushing well beyond it, asserted that the panorama 'ministers to the eye, and to the heart as no language can'.[21] Though John Calvin

---

18 'The Apocalyptic Vision', *Chattanooga Daily Times* (2 August 1880), excerpted in *Comments on Arthur L. Butt's Panorama* (Charlotte, NC, c. 1898), 30.

19 J. J. Renn, Pastor, Methodist Episcopal Church, Salisbury, North Carolina, no date; excerpted in *Comments*, 12.

20 *Brookhaven Ledger*, 1881, repr. in *Comments*, 35.

21 'Exhibition', *Economist*, Elizabeth City, North Carolina (14 June 1881), repr. in *Comments*, 41.

must have been spinning in his grave, it seems clear that for many Protestant viewers of such sacred spectacles as Butt's panorama, *seeing* paintings of biblical subjects had joined *hearing* the biblical word as a celebrated (and even favoured) channel of revelation. It is noteworthy that the power of images to entertain did not compromise their capacity to reveal Evangelical truths, but even enhanced their ability to do so. And so my fourth point – the allegiance of visual entertainment and revealed truth among American Protestants in the late nineteenth century.

Twentieth-Century Visual Piety and the Protestant Gaze

The four features apparent in the Protestant experience of visual media in the nineteenth century – image as presence, the masculinity of Christ, the commercial packaging of religious imagery, and the fusion of entertainment and edification – collectively raised Protestant estimation of images. The easy manner in which devotional imagery was linked to entertainment and mass media helped launch the voluminous career of mass-produced religious imagery in twentieth-century American Protestantism. Yet Protestants in the century that followed the days of panoramas and parlour devices like stereoscopes faced very different circumstances in which images were presented to viewers. Film changed matters irrevocably. The way in which Protestants saw paintings like Munkácsy's, panoramas like Butt's, and Passion plays like the one at Oberammergau, that is, as a gathered company of believers, was no longer how most Americans experienced film. The difference and how it has been negotiated by some Christian image makers in the twentieth century occupies the remainder of this essay.

Wending its way through a variety of visual media in the late nineteenth and early twentieth centuries was the Passion play, recreated during Lent in local Catholic and Protestant congregations or on stage in major cities as well as presented at various sites in Europe, the most famous of which was the version produced every ten years by the members of the village of Oberammergau in the south of Germany.[22] By the end of the century, more than half a dozen versions of the

[22] On the Passion play at Oberammergau, which was paradigmatic for many Americans since it received the most attention in travel literature from 1880 to the present, see James Shapiro, *Oberammergau: the Troubling Story of the World's Most Famous Passion Play* (New York, 2001).

Passion play were commercially available on film.[23] It is difficult to overemphasize the importance of this genre of popular devotional theatre since it endorsed and circulated what I consider the linchpin of Protestant experience of presence in visual media in nineteenth- and twentieth-century America: the *tableau vivant*. Passion plays were an ongoing intertextual reinforcement of the *tableau vivant*, infusing the still image with a direct tie to public presence before the real thing, the original event transmitted by Scripture. Moreover, the Passion play assembled the devout as a community of believers before the sacred story enacted *by believers for believers*.

The Protestant penchant for seeing together, for experiencing a common scene as a gathered body of the faithful, is found imprinted in a new organization of Protestant worship space in the nineteenth-century United States. The auditorium style seating, presaged in the tabernacles and theatres used for public entertainment such as concerts and theatrical productions, became popular by mid-century among many Protestants, in part, perhaps, because it reminded some of the revival meetings in tents, camp grounds, theatres, and public arenas. In these kinds of spaces, people gazed at one another as much as they did at the speaker's platform. Seating was hemispheric or circular and sight lines were trained virtually in the round. The same manner of seating is evident in the mega-churches of our own day, the modern heirs of Evangelical space in the nineteenth century.[24] In these instances, then as now, seeing one another meant being together as a united body.

A similar experience characterized the Protestant reception of the Passion play. The discrete episodes of the Passion story were struck on stage, anchoring the image to text, animating text as image, making pictures real bodies, and affirming the audience as a Christian public, a sacred assembly gathered before the enacted Word of God. The *tableau vivant* bridged word and image and endorsed photography as a medium of visual revelation: a frozen trace of its subject rather than an arbitrary fabrication of it. Passion plays theatricalized paintings and photographs, urging Christians to imagine that each still depiction of the passion or

[23] A fine study of the relationship between the Passion play and early film is Charles Musser, 'Passions and the Passion Play: Theatre, Film, and Religion in America, 1800–1900', *Film History* 5 (1993), 419–56.

[24] These sorts of spaces have been examined in Jeanne Kilde, *When Church Became Theatre: the Transformation of Evangelical Architecture and Worship in Nineteenth-Century America* (New York and Oxford, 2002); and Anne C. Loveland and Otis B. Wheeler, *From Meetinghouse to Megachurch: a Material and Cultural History* (Columbia, MO, and London, 2003).

suffering of Jesus is a frozen scene from an ideal translation of scriptural narrative onto an ideal stage before which the Christian public sits and observes it. By imagining that the images struck were not images but the real thing, Protestants could accept images as a powerful means of achieving and relishing sacred presence. Visual media of the concerted gaze constructed a visual field in which the image represented the Gospel events to an audience that was self-conscious, aware of the public event of *spectation*. The visual field consisted of a mode of viewing that presupposed and reinforced one's membership in a shared practice of looking. It was not simply that Protestants were placed before the real thing, but that they shared with fellow believers a common presence in the theatre of sacred presence. The *tableau vivant* presumed a live audience, a group of people self-consciously sharing a space and a temporal experience, a common presence before the sacred presentation of the Story.

The *tableau vivant* was the operative visual sign in all of the Protestant visual media considered thus far, corresponding to a visual field or gaze whose primary purpose was to gather together the public of believers into a providentially sanctioned body, for which the sacred subject of re-presentation constituted a binding communal cause. The emergence of film both affirmed and challenged this gaze. The earliest films commercially available, from 1897 to 1900, were reels of the Passion play, and consisted largely of the pageantry of *tableaux vivants*, visual episodes of the moments of the Passion narrative. The *tableau* construction of scenes is evident in 'The Messiah's Entry into Jerusalem', for instance, a cinematic representation of the Passion play executed as a series of *tableaux vivants*. The arrangement of figures is unmistakable and quite typical of such scenes in early film and photographs of scenes from Oberammergau: all the heads occupy the same level. Figures are lined up across the composition, pulled into the foreground, displayed in a full pageantry of dress, and capturing in sumptuous array a single narrative unit. All action is parallel to the picture plane and unfurls from or is directed toward the centre, where the eye is led by all elements of the composition. Architectural setting is conceived as a backdrop, tinted with aerial perspective such that it recedes promptly from importance once it has signaled only the location of the event that is to command the viewer's attention. Setting is merely atmosphere focusing our consciousness on the central, singular event.[25]

---

[25] For the image in question, see Musser, 'Passions and the Passion Play', 441; for related

In fact, virtually every film portrayal of the life of Jesus from the early twentieth century to Mel Gibson's cinematic phenomenon *The Passion of the Christ* (2004) assembled familiar iconographical tableaux drawn from the history of art, illustration, and film itself.[26] One writer noted already in 1924 of the film industry in the United States that 'there is no such thing as an original script'.[27] Indeed, film makers adapted, mixed and borrowed as artists have always done. For instance, consider the *tableau vivant* at the foot of the cross in *The Passion of the Christ*, when Mary, John, and the body of Jesus quote any one of dozens of pietas. In doing so, Gibson joined the pre-cinematic medium of the *tableau vivant* with film narrative to couple the modern cinematic gaze with the traditional visual piety of the devotional painting. Combined with the manner in which Protestants organized complete buy-outs of theatre screenings, filling the house with pious viewers, the experience of the film was powerful for many because it affirmed the community of the faithful while presenting the Passion of Jesus as a gripping narrative.

Religious art of a devotional nature invites re-cycling because of the appeal of familiarity among the devout. Perhaps the most widely repro-duced and familiar devotional imagery of the twentieth century, the art of Warner Sallman, thrived on recycling.[28] Compare, for example, Sallman's *Christ at Heart's Door* (1942) with William Holman Hunt's well-known *Light of the World* (1851; Keble College, Oxford); or Sallman's *Christ in Gethsemane* (1941) with Heinrich Hofmann's picture of the same subject (1890; Riverside Church, New York City); or his *The Lord is My Shepherd* (1943) with the same theme by the nineteenth-century German painter, Bernhard Plockhorst. Virtually every image this illustrator produced was an appropriation of an existing image. Sallman's most familiar image, *The Head of Christ* (fig. 4), was lifted from

imagery in the Oberammergau Passion play, see Burton Holmes, *Travelogues*, 12 vols (New York, 1910), 7: 176–208.

26 Herbert Reynolds, 'From Palette to Screen: the Tissot Bible as Sourcebook for *From Manger to the Cross*', in Roland Cosandey, André Gaudreault and Tom Gunning, eds, *Un Invention du Diable? Cinéma des Premiers Temps et Religion* (Sainte-Foy, Switzerland, 1992), 275–310, has noted that the 1912 film, *From Manger to the Cross*, constructed its scenes from individual illustrations of the Bible by the painter James Tissot.

27 Pauline M. Floyd, 'Motion Picture Technique: a Few Pointers on the Art of Turning out Classics While You Wait', *Public Affairs* (August 1924), excerpted in W. Brooke Graves, ed., *Readings in Public Opinion: its Formation and Control* (New York, 1928), 351–6, at 352.

28 David Morgan, ed., *Icons of American Protestantism: the Art of Warner Sallman* (New Haven, CT, 1996), 38–44.

Fig. 4. Warner Sallman, *Head of Christ*, 1940, oil on canvas.
Courtesy Warner Press, Anderson, Indiana.

a late nineteenth-century French portrayal of Jesus, Léon Lhermitte's *Friend of the Lowly* (1892; fig. 5), but transformed to conform to the early twentieth-century formulae of commercial portrait photography. The result was an image that capitalized on many of the features noted in the Protestant reception of images since the nineteenth century: authentic likeness, historical accuracy, moving expression, and manly portrayal of the Saviour. One may pause at each of these claims, but the

Fig. 5. Léon Lhermitte, *Friend of the Lowly*, 1892, oil on canvas.
Courtesy Boston Museum of Fine Art.

response is a matter of historical record: pious Protestants in the mid-twentieth century saw the image of their Saviour in Sallman's picture. Sallman himself indicated that the image came to him in a dream. The picture was a Protestant icon, not made by human hands.

For others, of course, this image is no such thing, but an example of effeminate Protestant piety. One wonders if Mel Gibson didn't have the image in mind when he told *The New Yorker* that his film was intended to correct the long history of portraying Jesus as namby-pamby: 'I didn't want to see Jesus looking really pretty', he said. 'I wanted to mess up one of his eyes, destroy it'.[29] He referred explicitly to the history of costume pageantry in biblical films, but Sallman's images cannot be separated from the iconography of Hollywood religious film. The vignetting and solemn gaze of his *Head of Christ* clearly resembles film star publicity stills from the 1930s and 1940s.

Familiarity or recognizability of images, so evident in the incessant recycling of popular as well as elite culture, recalls the inherent conservatism of Christian iconography of any age in East or West, driven as it so often is by the need for clear communication, but also by the power of the familiar to offer a secure and reliable focal point for communal gathering and corporate worship. Moreover, *tableaux vivants* are not a modern invention. Making pictures morph into real bodies is an ancient liturgical practice. From the gestures of priests performing mass to mystery plays and many other examples, the power of images has been to embody word, story, person, and community in informal no less than formal liturgics.

The reliance of familiar motifs to dominate the devotional image distinguishes popular visual piety from elite art and taste. A central task of popular religious imagery is to secure the viewer from change, offering a pastoral anchoring of self and community by the use of well-recognized visual formulae that link the viewer without ambiguity to tradition and the original object of tradition – the Saviour. Originality is far less important than an engaging manipulation of traditional visual forms. It is helpful to distinguish popular art and taste from two forms of elite artistic sensibility – fine and avant-garde art and taste. Fine art is the art of the intelligentsia, that is, the broadly defined class that premises the recognition and enjoyment of artistic value on the possession of discerning taste, which is typically the

---

[29] Peter J. Boyer, 'The Jesus War: Mel Gibson's Obsession', *The New Yorker* 79 (15 Sept. 2003), 60.

cultural domain of those who possess the distinctions of wealth, education, or leisure necessary to acquire, display and refine such taste.
Avant-garde art is the art of another, sometimes closely related elite,
namely, the art of those who understand themselves as cultural
producers rather than consumers or guardians. This art prizes innovation in order to distinguish itself and its experience from other art and
its admirers. Rather than security or comfort, adherents of avant-garde
art seek to challenge and re-define the normative templates of moral
and imaginative values. Revolution, transformation, and novelty are its
principal concerns.

The popular reception of visual media among American Christians
in the nineteenth and twentieth centuries has little to do with
avant-garde artistic sensibilities and not much more to do with the
sensibilities of fine art, though popular piety commonly appropriated
and recycled fine art. If people like Henry Ward Beecher fancied that
the religious art of Europe could elevate American taste, the art that
Americans embraced for the purpose of piety was always a mixed bag
and only intermittently engaged in the operation of refining taste.
Consequently, the class structuration of taste is not particularly helpful
for understanding the dynamics of popular visual piety. More helpful, it
seems, is the parsing of gazes that organize the visual fields in which
believers were engaged as viewers.

I conclude, therefore, with a consideration of the operation of rival
gazes in film. Not long after the advent of cinema, producers and direc-
tors developed an alternative visual field, one in which viewers became
members of an anonymous crowd, a paying audience, the film-going
public whose collective opinion did not cultivate their relationship with
one another, nor even with the story portrayed in the film as much as
with the film's stars. The new gaze shifted allegiance to the focal object
of the human being portraying a hero, a victim, a villain, a monster. In
this gaze, the *tableau vivant* was largely set aside because it got in the way
of the viewer's devotion to the persona of the star. Such a *tableau* inter-
posed a narrative pictorial apparatus between star and fan when all the
fan wanted was a devotional icon upon which to fix his or her loving
gaze. So the visual regime moves from history painting to portrait icon.
The cult of the star was not about communal identity, but about a
private, fantasized relation between fan and film idol.[30]

---

[30] The most cited discussion of this notion of the gaze is Laura Mulvey's 'Visual Pleasure
and Narrative Cinema', *Screen* 16 (1975), 6–18. For a helpful overview of the complex and

But this gaze, clearly iconic in a new, mass-culture sense, is not necessarily irreligious. It is, however, non-narrative in essence. Perhaps the best example of a still version of this manner of image and visual piety among American Protestants is Warner Sallman's *Head of Christ*. Extracted from its narrative context in Lhermitte's painting (a contemporary *tableau vivant* of the traditional Supper at Emmaus, set within a humble French peasant kitchen), Sallman's picture presents Jesus in a portrait format, thereby recalling both traditional Byzantine icons and Hollywood publicity shots.

Mel Gibson's film succeeded at engaging both visual sensibilities – the iconic and the narrative. He achieved a synthesis of sorts by casting beautiful stars such as Monica Bellucci as Mary Magdalene, who is memorably shown in one scene mopping up the sacramental blood with Mary following the dreadful and protracted scourging of Jesus. To this indelible image Gibson coupled countless other *tableaux* throughout the film in what amounts to a grisly version of the Stations of the Cross. Of course, it does not matter that most Evangelical viewers were unaware of the reactionary Catholic visual piety of the film's maker (Protestants have a long history of overlooking the Catholic identity of images and spectacles that fascinate them).[31] What they saw picked up where panoramas, passion plays, and early film left off. Evangelical Protestants experienced the film in a way that comported with the visual field of the *tableau vivant*, the manner of seeing that was part of their Victorian gaze. They filled theatres and saw the film together, not as a secular public, but as church. What they saw as a body in theatres and followed up with altar calls, Bible studies, and discussion groups (many of which were carefully programmed by Evangelical study guides produced by Christian churches and publishers) was the body of Christ as they understand the Church to be: as a community galvanized by a political stance in a world that Evangelicals (rightly) believe does not share their view. They found *The Passion of the Christ* a powerful vehicle for recalling a visual sensibility that, while by no means exclusively Protestant, may be distinctively Evangelical.

extensive discussion of 'the gaze', see Daniel Chandler, 'Notes on "The Gaze"', at www. aber.ac.uk/media/Documents/gaze/gaze.html (consulted 25 July 2005).

31 I have examined the Catholic aspects of Gibson's film in 'Catholic Visual Piety and *The Passion of the Christ*', in S. Brent Plate, ed., *Re-Viewing* The Passion: *Mel Gibson's Film and its Critics* (New York, 2004), 85–96. For discussion of Protestant fascination with Catholic visual culture in nineteenth-century America, see John Davis, 'Protestant Envy', in David Morgan and Sally M. Promey, eds, *The Visual Culture of American Religions* (Berkeley, CA, 2001), 105–28.

Moreover, conservative Protestants may have rediscovered in this film the dynamic manner in which Protestant visual piety has long thrived on a fluid exchange between high and low, elite and popular. It is not that this distinction, beloved of a previous generation of scholarship, is now meaningless, but that it is not hard and fast. Religious visual piety – whether among Protestants or Catholics or Buddhists or Hindus – relies on effectiveness in communication, which often means currency. Protestant image makers, therefore, no doubt like those in many other religious traditions over time, have shamelessly borrowed, mixed, and matched as suits their needs in the face of religious commerce and effective communication. Hence Warner Sallman's exploitation of precedents in his popular iconography, some of which came from accomplished artists, some from artists no more skilled than he. It is not that his admirers are tasteless. Indeed, they possess a distinct taste: for clarity, intimacy, gentleness, reassurance, and for touching devotion. The means are fitted to the end if we understand the purpose of the images to cultivate a devotional sensibility that stresses comfort and stability. And this underscores the novelty of the Protestant response to Gibson's film: its shocking violence passes most Evangelicals by. In fact, they report seeing no gratuitous violence whatsoever. Many reported to me in person and posted on websites the remarkable sentiment that the bloody violation of Jesus' body in the film proved just how much God loves them.[32] The graphic detail of the beatings and scourging served as a dramatic 'you-are-there' device for them in a way that nineteenth-century imagery had accomplished for its viewers: the image came alive and touched them personally in a way that had nothing to do with art and everything to do with divine presence.

Valparaiso University

---

[32] Interview with the author, 1 July 2004. At one Evangelical website, www.thelife.com/experience/two.html, the claim is unabashed: 'In The Passion of the Christ you saw love at it best . . . The picture of pure, passionate love is caught in the frame of Jesus loving you while hanging on the cross . . . Imagine asking Jesus, "How much do you love me?" He would stretch out His arms, with His nail-pierced hands, and say, "This much"' . . . Jesus was brutally beaten and killed because that is what it took for us to be forgiven of our sins. It was an enormous cost that He was willing to pay for you' (consulted 20 August 2004). For similar commentary, see the Campus Crusade for Christ website and links at www.passionofchrist.com (consulted 20 August 2004).

ANGLICAN 'ESTABLISHMENT' REACTIONS TO 'POP' CHURCH MUSIC IN ENGLAND, 1956–C.1990

by IAN JONES and PETER WEBSTER

THE use of popular styles of music in the Church has often proved contentious,[1] and perhaps particularly so in the later twentieth century. Anecdotal evidence abounds of the debate provoked in churches by the introduction of new 'happy-clappy' pop-influenced styles, and the supposed wholesale discarding of a glorious heritage of hymnody. In addition, a great deal of literature has appeared elaborating on the inappropriateness of such music. Welcoming a historical study of hymnody in 1996, John Habgood lamented the displacement of traditional hymn singing by 'trivial and repetitive choruses'.[2] Lionel Dakers, retired Director of the Royal School of Church Music, also saw choruses and worship songs as 'in many instances little more than trite phrases repeated *ad nauseam*, often with accompanying body movements'.[3] This paper investigates the reactions of the musical and ecclesiastical establishments to the use of popular music in public worship in the Church of England from 1956 to c.1990. The period began with a new wave of experimentation epitomized by Geoffrey Beaumont's *Folk Mass* and the controversy surrounding it, and ended in the early 1990s, by which time the pop-influenced worship music of the renewal movement had become firmly established in some sections of the Church, with its own figure-heads and momentum.[4] This paper argues against the assumption, common to many social historians,[5] that the religious establishment unreservedly hated popular music, or, as some recent general

---

[1] For other examples from the English context, see Jim Obelkevich, 'Music and Religion in the Nineteenth Century', in Jim Obelkevich, Lyndal Roper and Raphael Samuel, eds, *Disciplines of Faith: Studies in Religion, Politics and Patriarchy* (London, 1987), 550–65.

[2] Foreword to Bertram L. Barnby, *In Concert Sing – Concerning Hymns and their Usage* (Norwich, 1996), vii.

[3] Lionel Dakers, 'Church Music in the Twentieth Century – A Rise and Fall?', in P. R. Hale, ed., *IAO [Incorporated Association of Organists] Millennium Book* (2000), 149–64, 153.

[4] For a brief history, see: Pete Ward, *Growing Up Evangelical: Youth Work and the Making of a Sub-Culture* (London, 1996), 80–140.

[5] See John Street, 'Shock Waves: the Authoritative Response to Popular Music', in Dominic Strinati and Stephen Wagg, eds, *Come on Down? Popular Media Culture in Post-War*

commentaries on the Church have assumed, that there was a simple bi-polar division 'for' or 'against' it.[6] Instead, the history of the debate reveals a wide and complex range of 'establishment' reactions, particularly in the early part of the period.

* * *

The 'establishment' in question may loosely be defined as that nexus of individuals and institutions that in the 1950s were dominant in the music of the Church of England: the Royal School of Church Music; cathedral and other salaried organists; concerned clergy; and the musical critics and academics who treated new church music with the same seriousness as they did concert and chamber works. This 'establishment' is clearly visible in the list of contributors to the journal *English Church Music*, published by the Royal School of Church Music. Between 1955 and 1970 the journal carried articles from clergy such as Joseph Poole, Precentor of Coventry, academic musicologists such as Peter Le Huray and Watkins Shaw, professional musicians such as Christopher Dearnley, organist of St Paul's, and also from those not directly employed by the Church, such as Sir Thomas Armstrong, Principal of the Royal Academy of Music. Indeed, in the first half of the century the conjunction between the 'sacred' and 'secular' musical professions was arguably at its closest for a hundred years, following the involvement of 'professionals' such as Charles Villiers Stanford in a previously marginal cathedral world.[7] This establishment is also given coherence by external forces, as the (more or less willing) guardians of tradition in the face of a newly emerging mass culture of popular music, disseminated by easily-available recordings to increasingly affluent listeners.[8] Of course, throughout history, popular music had often been deployed in the services of the Church, but in the early twentieth century much of it was either heavily refined into a more classical idiom[9] or confined to the margins, for use in mission services

---

Britain (London and New York, 1992), 302–24; Martin Cloonan, *Banned! Censorship of Popular Music in Britain: 1967–92* (Aldershot, 1996).

[6] See, for example: Ysenda Maxtone Graham, *The Church Hesitant: a Portrait of the Church of England Today* (London, 1993), 213–39.

[7] Erik Routley, *Twentieth-Century Church Music* (London, 1964), 13–19; Horton Davies, *Worship and Theology in England,* Book III: *The Ecumenical Century, 1900 to the Present* (Cambridge, 1996 edn), 102–7.

[8] Arthur Marwick, *The Sixties: Cultural Revolution in Britain, France, Italy and the United States, c.1958–c.1974* (Oxford, 1998), 55–80.

[9] Such as Vaughan Williams's treatment of folk songs in *The English Hymnal* (1906).

or Sunday Schools. By the late 1950s however, the Anglican musical establishment were faced with renewed attempts to write music in a popular style specifically for Sunday worship, striking at the heart of the English hymn and choral tradition.

Defining the 'pop' church music in question here requires similar care, just as musicologists and music historians more generally have struggled to delineate so diverse a phenomenon as 'popular music' in the later twentieth century as a whole. Some have used 'pop music' and 'popular music' interchangeably, whilst others have identified 'pop' as a distinctive sub-category with particular characteristics; for example that it is guitar-driven and reliant on technological advances such as amplification,[10] or that 'pop' is any music which is mass-produced for a mass-market.[11] Still others have found the terminology so problematic as to eschew any such neat definition.[12] To this extent, debates about the nature of 'pop' amongst musicologists mirror the problems faced by historians of religion in defining 'popular' belief. In this paper, 'pop' church music is used in a broad sense, encompassing several different strands of popular music written for a church context. In the 1950s and 1960s, this largely meant light music, light swing or folk, as found in Geoffrey Beaumont's *Folk Mass* (in the Anglo-Catholic tradition) and the compositions of the Twentieth Century Church Light Music Group (TCCLMG). At roughly the same time, Anglican evangelicals were experimenting with similar styles, out of which came the collection *Youth Praise* (1966).[13] From the late 1960s to the early 1990s, as folk hymns (such as those by Sydney Carter) became more generally accepted, establishment critiques turned towards the more youth-orientated, verse-chorus format guitar song, whose introduction to English church life owed much to the charismatic renewal; first in the folk-pop style of *Sound of Living Waters* (1974) and *Fresh Sounds* (1976), then in the soft rock/rock ballad feel of the *Songs of Fellowship* books, which reflected the additional influence of the Restoration Move-

---

[10] See for example Iain Chambers, *Urban Rhythms: Pop Music and Popular Culture* (Basingstoke, 1985), 9–15.

[11] Roy Shuker, *Understanding Popular Music* (2nd edn, London, 2001), x. See also Theodor W. Adorno's influential (though contentious) work 'On Popular Music' (first published in 1941), repr. in Simon Frith and Andrew Godwin, eds, *On Record: Rock, Pop and the Written Word* (London and New York, 1990), 301–14.

[12] See for example John Connell and Chris Gibson, *Sound Tracks: Popular Music, Identity and Place* (London, 2003), 4–5.

[13] Nicholas Temperley, *The Music of the English Parish Church*, 2 vols (Cambridge, 1979), 1: 341–2.

ment.[14] Whilst a diversity of musical styles is represented here and the difficulties of precise definition are recognized, this broad definition of 'pop' church music is appropriate, since the Anglican musical 'establishment' under discussion here tended to lump together a range of different styles under the general heading of 'pop'. Moreover, just as 'popular music' had by the 1940s come to denote not just 'the music of the people' but music with specific styles and characteristics,[15] so by the same period the Church of England's musical commentators discussed a variety of different genres under the heading of 'church pop' and assumed some common qualities between them.

The authors recognize that applying notions of 'popular' and in particular 'elite' to this period is problematic. As the paper will argue, there was no uniform view on popular music in church amongst this loosely-defined establishment. Many of the early advocates of 'church pop' were themselves part of it; often clergy (sometimes high-ranking) who justified the new music on the grounds that it was something to which the man in the pew could relate. At the same time many laity as well as clergy opposed the changes. Nor were the attitudes of this loosely-defined 'elite' either wholly accepting or rejecting; anthropologists such as Mary Douglas have alerted us to a much wider range of responses to the 'anomalous', from studied indifference, to outright attempts to repel it, to attempts to incorporate or domesticate it within existing structures.[16] All of these responses are found towards the new music in this period. The paper also identifies key polarities in debates about the nature of church music (many of them scarcely defined or worked out): order versus spontaneity, reverence versus relevance, expertise versus participation, the beautiful versus the vulgar.

* * *

The initial experimentation with 'light music' by Geoffrey Beaumont and the Twentieth Century Church Light Music Group began with the publication of Beaumont's *Folk Mass* in 1956, subsequently televised in 1957. Several collections of hymn tunes in a similar style followed. The *Folk Mass* attracted a range of responses, many of which were hostile

---

[14] The first of several major collections was published as: *Songs of Fellowship Book 1* (1st edn, Eastbourne, 1981). For hymns and songs in the evangelical tradition from *Youth Praise* to *Songs of Fellowship*, see Ward, *Growing Up Evangelical*, 80–140.

[15] Shuker, *Understanding Popular Music*, 5.

[16] Mary Douglas, *Purity and Danger: an Analysis of the Concepts of Pollution and Taboo* (London, 1966), 37–40.

and gave it no quarter. The response of W. Greenhouse Allt in 1957 is a good example of the tone, blending exalted purpose with withering criticism. The bishop of Leicester, R. R. Williams, had welcomed the piece and called for a reconsideration of music 'until the musical medium is found which is natural to our modern folk', which then might become a weapon to combat the indifference of present-day youth, and 'draw them in thousands into the Church's fold'.[17] In reply, Allt countered that

> We should tell the Right Reverend the Bishop that the cultivated mind of a skilled musician understands too well that sensuous appeal, and revolts against the use of such a sensuous appeal to replace Church Music, the finest of which is hallowed by tradition, inspired by spiritual experience and capable of satisfying our deepest spiritual needs when there is an understanding and sympathetic mind ready to receive it.[18]

For Allt, this deplorable trend was to be countered in musical education, and it was for the Incorporated Association of Organists (IAO) 'so to strive and fit yourselves that you may worthily uphold the dignity of your contribution to the worship of Almighty God and keep inviolate the integrity of the Art of Music'.[19] Here we see illustrated several of the key themes: a juxtaposition of the cultivated musical taste of the tradition against the supposedly vulgar and crude sensuality of the popular, and the assertion of the establishment's role as gatekeeper and guardian. However, we also see an important difference of opinion *within* the establishment; between those who saw high standards of music and musicianship as essential to true worship, and those (including high-ranking clergy) whose pastoral sensibilities suggested greater latitude over permissible styles of music, a point explored further below.

Amongst those who saw popular music as simply inadequate for worship, several key strands of criticism recur: firstly, 'pop' could be portrayed as primitive or primal. Allt contrasted music which had 'passed through the discipline of intellectual effort and brought delight to a higher pitch by masterly design' with skiffle, 'a manifestation of the primitive folk-habits of the unskilled-in-music', invoking Carl Jung on

17 Quoted in W. Greenhouse Allt, 'The Presidential Address', *Quarterly Record of the Incorporated Association of Organists* 43 (1957), 3–6, 5.
18 Ibid., 3–6, 5.
19 Ibid.

the ease of re-animating 'archaic patterns of behaviour'.[20] Concerns over 'primal' music could sometimes take on racial or national dimensions: church musician and writer Charles Cleall could even quote approvingly from Aldous Huxley that 'Barbarism has entered popular music from two sources: from the music of barbarous people . . . and from serious music which has drawn on barbarism for its inspiration'.[21] Even those who adopted more measured tones could suggest that since jazz-influenced music was non-indigenous to British culture, it was therefore undesirable. For Erik Routley, a Congregationalist minister who was nevertheless widely read and admired by Anglican audiences, 'the cultures from which Western European music and "jazz" spring are profoundly different in all their ways, and there is nothing to be gained by minimising or pretending to ignore these differences'.[22] To import this music directly into services could only ever be 'a cult of the exotic. It would be tourism saying aren't those Polynesians fascinating?'.[23]

A second key theme is that even in the majority of cases where racial or national characteristics were not invoked, some commentators clearly saw popular music as part of a wider cultural crisis. 'How easy it is', argued Cleall,

> for an old civilisation like ours to fail to hand on to the next generation the rich and complex culture which is the Englishman's birthright. Such a culture is painfully achieved, over centuries: it is shockingly easily lost, by men who are more concerned to be 'with-it' than to know the Good, the True and the Beautiful.[24]

Sir Thomas Armstrong saw the 'JAZZ-MASS' as part of a 'rebellion of the inarticulate, uninformed and illiterate – a deliberate deification of bad taste' arising from a despair about modern life. These were dangerous times, he believed, but the situation could be saved by people of talent and good will.[25] Such views reflect a much wider sense of anxiety in the late 1950s and early 1960s amongst the guardians of 'respectable' values that post-war hopes for a Reithian elevation of national taste were failing.[26]

[20] Ibid., 6, 3 and 5.
[21] Charles Cleall, *Music and Holiness* (London, 1964), 44–5.
[22] Erik Routley, *Is Jazz Music Christian?* (London, 1964), 3.
[23] Ibid., 10.
[24] Letter of Charles Cleall to *Church News*, January 1963.
[25] Thomas Armstrong, 'Presidential Address', *Quarterly Record of the IAO* 44 (1958), 3–5, 4 and 5.
[26] Robert Hewison, *In Anger: Culture in the Cold War, 1945–60* (London, 1981), 177–81.

Thirdly, as Armstrong's criticisms imply, it was commonly asserted that church music could never legitimately be of the same everyday kind that advocates of the Beaumont *Mass* had argued for. In 1960, light music hymn-writer Patrick Appleford had argued that, just as common prayer was in the common tongue, so it was natural that 'the musical idiom of what is sung in worship should as far as possible be common to everyone'.[27] This would be neither Bach nor the very latest jazz, but 'the kind of music that is the background of all our lives – light music of various kinds'.[28] This was in direct response to the suggestion from *Musical Opinion* that

> by its very nature this music cannot bring any association of thought and idea other than that with which it is commonly connected, the dance hall, the radio band, the TV show. It can never become 'church music' merely because of an association of time and place.[29]

The insistence that only the best music was admissible in worship had a long pedigree and pervaded much of the discussion, as exemplified in the 1951 report of the Archbishops' Commission on *Music in Church*, which asserted simply, as the second of the four key principles, that church music should be 'good, as music'.[30] Little consideration was given to the criteria by which goodness was to be defined, and the report reflected the prevailing pre-pop understanding of taste. The report was subsequently and frequently invoked as authoritative; at the 1959 congress of the IAO, a plain assertion of the report's principle was deemed sufficient to close a debate on the worth of Beaumont's *Folk Mass*.[31]

For a minority of commentators, the charge that popular music was simply inadmissible *per se* was overlain with a second accusation: that the works of Beaumont and others were not even good examples of the style in which they were written. Despite Patrick Appleford's insistence that church music should be of the common tongue rather than cutting

---

[27] Patrick Appleford, 'Music in Worship and Mission Services', *Theology* 63 (1960), 329–33, 330.

[28] Ibid.

[29] Leader 'From Minerva House', *Musical Opinion* 963 (1957), 149–51.

[30] *Music in Church: a Report of the Committee Appointed in 1948 by the Archbishops of Canterbury and York* (1st edn, London, 1957; revised edn, 1960), 6.

[31] On the IAO conference at Newcastle, see the IAO *Quarterly Record* 45 (1959), 5.

edge (to enable more than just devotees of the style to use it),[32] the charge of 'bad jazz' became a constant refrain amongst opponents, occasionally lapsing into an audible sneer. 'It is really rather pitiful', said Ivor Keys in 1974, to introduce tunes with

> the type of syncopations . . . that Bertie Wooster might have danced to. . . . A staid Stanfordian feels a fool in lending himself to it, and the young find the situation just as embarrassing as if he had turned up in purple trousers.[33]

Even amongst commentators better-disposed to popular music in church, a more moderate version of the same argument was found, though here relating more to the commonly-expressed need to offer only the best to God. If, argued Allan Wicks of Canterbury Cathedral, the church was to have pop, then let it be the real thing, and not 'a sort of sentimentalized and watered-down concept of pop. The idea of the Church as something which continually takes the edge off things, spoils the fun of things, makes mediocre, is still very strong'.[34] It is here that the common stress on the idea of the best of all things being the only suitable offering to God can be seen across the spectrum of opinion, but with the resulting practical implications being contested.

Not all commentators from within the 'establishment' denied positive value, or at least some utility, in this new style. It is among these writers that principles held in common with the more hostile can be observed being shaped and transmuted by other, wider pressures within a volatile church. Some, while still emphasizing the need for musical quality, nevertheless saw some place for the new. Stephen Rhys and King Palmer argued that while the glories of the tradition were something in which to rejoice, church music was not an end in itself, and must stand or fall by the degree to which it enabled Christians to worship. It may well have been the case that those embracing the *Folk Mass* were more influenced by 'the evangelical [sic] possibilities than by the fitness and quality of the music'.[35] However, before condemning,

[32] Patrick Appleford, 'Music in Worship and Mission Services', *Theology* 63 (1960), 329–33, 330.
[33] Ivor Keys, 'Church Music – Change or Decay', *English Church Music* (1974), 7–10, 8. See also Allt, 'Presidential Address', 6.
[34] Allan Wicks, 'Towards the Relevant – in Church Music', *Modern Churchman* 8 (1964–5), 80–3, 83. This paper was part of a conference of the same year on 'Symbols for the Sixties', which included papers on church architecture, liturgy and the new Coventry Cathedral.
[35] Stephen Rhys and King Palmer, *The ABC of Church Music* (London, 1967), 63. Rhys

'perhaps we should reflect that we, the children of God, are "all sorts and conditions of men"; and that, for all we know, the music which is so easy to despise may sometimes lead a doubting Thomas to the feet of the Master'.[36] Lancelot Hankey, head of Clifton College Preparatory School, asked: 'Are we to suppose that full Christian worship is to be limited to those with a taste for classical or traditional music? Music is merely a means to worship . . . the acid test of this new approach is whether it is aiding worship.'[37] Paul Chappell, chaplain and vicar choral at Hereford Cathedral, condemned the 'musical philistinism' that saw the cathedral choral service as an expensive luxury, but refused to rule out the use of 'pops' in church. Responding to Charles Cleall he wrote:

> As our Lord Himself used the common things in life to express divine truth, so the Church of our present age must use the medium of folk-song[38] in order to communicate the Gospel message to those in desperate need of God's forgiveness. . . . Sacred music requires to be related to modern culture and life, or else it will become as fossilized as the dance music of the 1920s.[39]

We have thus far identified a number of trajectories of response from among the church music establishment to experimentation with pop, and have argued that the more rigidly bi-polar debate between old and new of the 1990s is unreflective of the early years of the period. Why, then, does the range of responses narrow during the 1970s and 1980s, to the point that the 1991 debate over the inclusion of popular worship songs in George Carey's enthronement service was widely constructed as a two-way fight between 'traditionalists' and the 'happy-clappy'?[40] Further research remains to be done on charting the adoption of the new music in practice. However, that this narrowing does occur in theory can be seen in the pages of *English Church Music*. For a period from 1957 until the early 1970s the journal teemed with comment on experiments both with pop and with modernist classical music, and on the future of the whole of church music in England. After this point,

was a Professor at the Royal Academy and sometime assistant chorusmaster to the Philharmonia Chorus. Palmer was a composer, writer and conductor, who had previously worked with the BBC Light Orchestra.

[36] Ibid., 29.

[37] *Church News*, October 1964.

[38] Apparently meaning here any music used by 'folk'.

[39] Paul Chappell, *Music and Worship in the Anglican Church* (London, 1968), 111, 118–19.

[40] Robin L. D. Rees, *Weary and Ill-at-Ease: a Survey of Clergy and Organists* (Leominster, 1993), 13.

the journal increasingly concerns itself with the traditional and cathedral scenes only, and with the history of that tradition. It is at this point that some thinkers appear to shift from an aggressive posture, seeking to repel the new style, to an attitude of indifference towards it, working instead to preserve the old style in the places where it was still employed. This shift was related partly to the general pluralization of worship styles in the Church of England[41] and the comparative ease with which each sub-culture could maintain its own 'niche' style; it was also partly due to the emerging identification at this time between the new music and the evangelical and charismatic parts of the Church, with a corresponding loss of experimental impetus among other groups.[42]

* * *

That such a change should have taken place at this time arguably corresponds with wider changes of mood in the churches over the post-war period. If the turmoil of the 1960s shook the near-complacency of the church and caused a level of confusion, it also led to a radical questioning of the role of the church and the languages it used. Nothing less than a 'New Reformation' was needed, forging a church which was modern, up-to-date, relevant.[43] However, the optimism and openness to experimentation which characterized the later part of the decade had given way by the early 1970s to exhaustion, and a feeling amongst some that these experiments had not worked.[44] Those with little time for the new music for its own sake perhaps increasingly felt that the time had come to revert to old patterns, for the good of the church's own, and to reassert the church's distinctiveness in unapologetic fashion. As one contributor to *The Sign* put it in 1971, 'a time of appeasement is over and a time for fighting has come'.[45]

[41] Geoffrey Cuming, 'Liturgical Change in the Church of England and the Roman Catholic Church', in Rupert Davies, ed., *The Testing of the Churches, 1932–1982* (London, 1982), 119–31.

[42] Peter Webster and Ian Jones, 'New Music and the "Evangelical Style" in the Church of England, c.1958–1991', in Steve Holmes and Mark Smith, eds, *British Evangelical Identities* (forthcoming, Paternoster Press, Carlisle, 2006).

[43] For this, see Adrian Hastings, *A History of English Christianity, 1920–1990* (3rd edn, London, 1991), 580–1; Grace Davie, *Religion in Britain since 1945* (Oxford, 1994), 33.

[44] Adrian Hastings, 'All Change: the Presence of the Past in British Christianity', in Haddon Wilmer, ed., *20/20 Visions: the Futures of Christianity in Britain* (London, 1992), 13–29, 20; Davie, *Religion in Britain*, 36.

[45] *The Sign*, 'Signet' column, January 1971.

The career of Lionel Dakers provides an excellent case study in this change of tone. Dakers is perhaps the quintessential example of an establishment figure. After spells on the musical staff of St George's Chapel, Windsor and Ripon and Exeter Cathedrals, he became Director of the RSCM in 1973 and was made CBE in 1983. A prolific writer on church music in both theory and practice, his reactions to pop in the church shift over the years from a balanced caution to a gloomy pessimism and sense of decay. Dakers' 1995 memoir reflects a deep sense of failure on his part to maintain an appropriate balance between proven tradition and a legitimate use of the contemporary.[46] Never enthusiastic about pop in church, Dakers was nonetheless able in his earlier writing to reserve judgement to the winnowing effects of time, and also to accept it if it was at least well prepared and performed. In 1970, whilst condemning the ' "pop" element', he welcomed the exciting 'New Look' of Sydney Carter and Malcolm Williamson, and stressed the need for the church periodically to be jolted from its 'complacent ecclesiastical museum'.[47]

By his retirement in 1988, however, a clear sense of failure in this had set in. In the theological colleges he had lost his fight to moderate the 'angry young men' who were guilty of

> playing to the gallery, being gimmicky, drawing in the crowds through *ad hoc* free for all unstructured services, with music at its lowest common denominator of quality and performance.[48]

Worst, this had been done 'in defiance of the established and proven traditions and values'.[49] He and they clearly spoke different languages and no meeting of minds had been possible, despite Dakers's perception of his own openness to debate.[50] By 1988, a decline in 'traditional' music, at least in the parishes, had left him feeling that ideas of accommodation and synthesis of twenty years previously were misplaced. Dakers's reflections are at least in part conditioned by a broader sense of cultural and religious decay: 'the rejection of awe and reverence, the wholesale matiness, the clatter and chatter of so much contemporary worship' sent him reaching for the warden of Barchester and Jeremy

---

[46] Lionel Dakers, *Places where they Sing. Memoirs of a Church Musician* (Norwich, 1995).
[47] Lionel Dakers, *Church Music at the Crossroads* (London, 1970), 129–33.
[48] Dakers, *Places where they Sing*, 207.
[49] Ibid.
[50] Ibid., 206–7.

Taylor, Bunyan and T. S. Eliot as representative of a simpler, more noble past now seemingly irrevocably lost to a cult of the shoddy and unworthy.[51]

* * *

Whilst Dakers's pessimism was emblematic of a common trend amongst members of the Anglican musical 'establishment', his negativity towards popular music in church was not universally shared. A paper concerning the attitudes of the musical 'elite' inevitably neglects the widespread adoption of the new music in practice: one 1991 survey estimated that two of the most popular new songbooks of the 1980s – *Mission Praise* and *Songs of Fellowship* – had sold one and three quarter million copies between them in their first six years, many to Anglicans.[52] Even within the Anglican musical 'establishment', attitudes towards popular music for church were complex and varied. Whilst this loose nexus of individuals and organizations shared a strong sense of responsibility as guardians of the Anglican musical tradition, opinions differed considerably on how far the new music posed a threat or an opportunity. Whilst the criteria for 'good' church music were all too rarely articulated in depth, this paper has highlighted several important polarities in the discussion: the preservation of 'beauty' and rejection of 'vulgarity'; the merits of 'reserve' as distinct from 'impulsiveness' and 'spontaneity'; a search for the 'indigenous' in preference to the 'foreign'; and a juxtaposition of 'reverence' for tradition and excellence with the need for 'relevance' to society.

This last axis cut particularly deep across the Anglican musical establishment, between those who insisted that true worship demanded above all the highest standards (with only certain types of music making the grade) and those who saw music as ultimately subordinate to the needs of the parishioner, and could pragmatically accommodate the new music if it seemed to touch hearts and attract new folk to worship. In this respect the debates on pop music for church from the 1950s to the 1990s appear as yet another chapter in a much longer history of the struggle for power between religious and musical expert, clergy and organist.[53] However, even here the lines of debate did not

---

[51] Ibid., 224–9.

[52] Tony Collins, 'Blockbuster Tales and Gospel Songs', *Church Times*, 1 March 1991, 8.

[53] On this relationship, see Lionel Dakers, *A Handbook of Parish Music* (Oxford, 1982), 46–87.

neatly fall between ordained minister and professional musician; this should not surprise us, given the extent to which the religious ferment of the post-war period radically re-shaped the ecclesiastical landscape, confounding the expectations of some historians that the Anglican musical establishment's view of 'pop' in church would be uniformly dismissive.

University of Manchester and
Institute of Historical Research, University of London